ART
HISTORY
101

. . .

Without the Exams

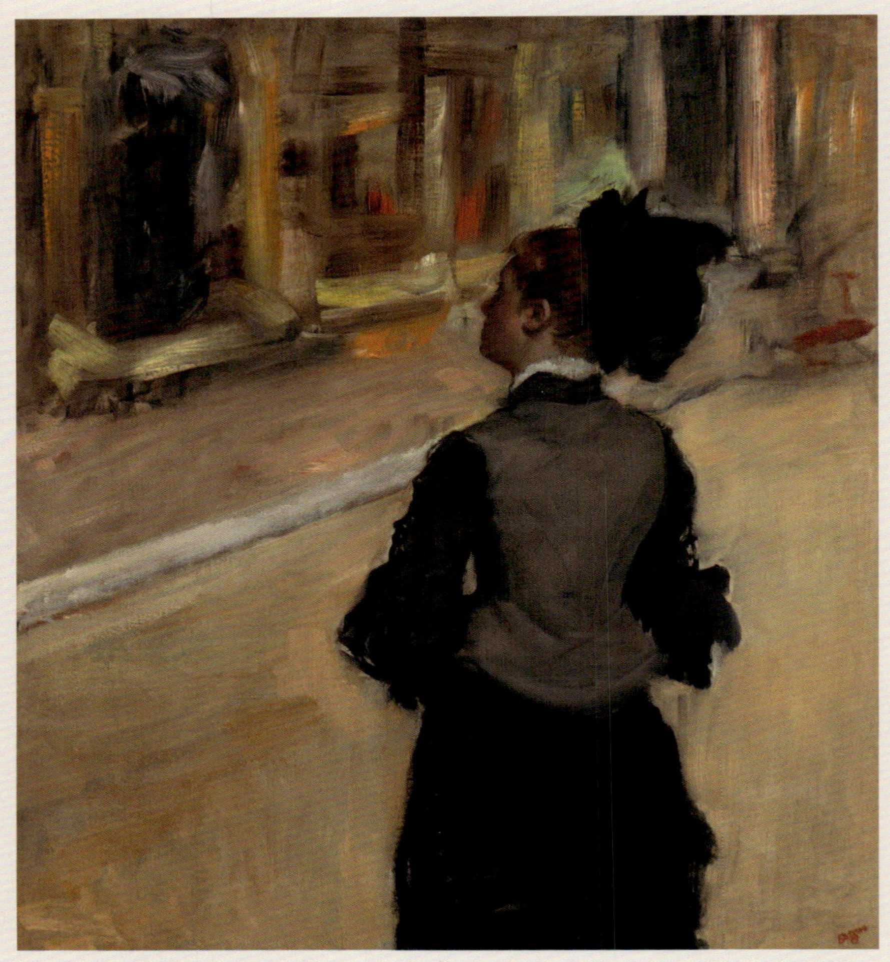

Edgar Degas, *Woman Viewed from Behind (Visit to a Museum)*, ca. 1879–1885. National Gallery, Washington D.C. 81.3 × 75.6 cm.

ART HISTORY 101

. . . WITHOUT THE EXAMS

Looking Closely at Objects from the History of Art

Annie Montgomery Labatt

TRINITY UNIVERSITY PRESS

San Antonio

Published by Trinity University Press
San Antonio, Texas 78212

Book design by BookMatters
Cover design by Notch Design
Author photo by Andrew Kranis

Printed in Canada

ISBN 978-1-59534-878-4 paperback
ISBN 978-1-59534-879-1 ebook

Trinity University Press strives to produce its books
using methods and materials in an environmentally
sensitive manner. We favor working with manu-
facturers that practice sustainable management of all
natural resources, produce paper using recycled stock,
and manage forests with the best possible practices
for people, biodiversity, and sustainability. The press
is a member of the Green Press Initiative, a nonprofit
program dedicated to supporting publishers in their
efforts to reduce their impacts on endangered forests,
climate change, and forest-dependent communities.

The paper used in this publication meets the
minimum requirements of the American National
Standard for Information Sciences—Permanence of
Paper for Printed Library Materials, ANSI 39.48-1992.

CIP data on file at the Library of Congress

28 27 26 25 | 5 4 3 2

For my parents

CONTENTS

INTRODUCTION

Going to a museum, standing in front of the *Birth of Venus* in the Uffizi or the Nike of Samothrace in the Louvre, is an exhilarating experience. But it can also be confusing and frustrating. Perhaps we have been told that this is an important work of art, one that we should know and admire. But we may not be sure exactly why. It is in the canon and therefore "essential"—but that tautological logic really does not help.

What is the piece about? How did the original owner look at this piece? Where was it originally placed? Why is it in this museum now? The flurry of other visitors and the desire to see as many pieces as possible keep us from being able to spend time with the object, to observe the details of the work of art, and to let those questions simmer, let alone find answers. Our more probing questions are often left for a later time, if we can find time.

Being an art historian means taking time to think about what to say about works of art. In graduate school we are surrounded by people who think about art history all day long; as teachers, we have to justify to our students why they are not wasting their time by taking our courses. But art history is important outside of the academy too. When I have answered the question "What do you do?" with "I am an art historian," I have met responses of various forms of surprise and curiosity. Some people reminisce about loving their university art history classes, about missing that subject and that kind of discourse. Others wish they had taken classes in art history and are disappointed that they will never have the chance to do so. These conversations inspired me to want to take art history beyond the university walls, to an audience made up of individuals who are curious to know more about the pieces they might travel to see or even have seen with some of those lingering questions remaining.

This was the idea behind "Art History 101…Without the Exams." Between

September 2013 and December 2015, I offered three series of monthly lectures at the San Antonio Museum of Art, for a total of twenty. The talks took place on Friday nights, which was important because the experience was supposed to show that scholarly learning is rewarding, enriching, and, most importantly, fun. The grocery chain H-E-B provided food that reflected the art—freshly pulled mozzarella for Botticelli, a whole (and quickly devoured) roasted pig for Velázquez, a mock-up peacock pie (really chicken) for Rembrandt. The museum provided wine. All in all, the experience met the expectation that the lecture series would be like "happy hour meets book club."

Before the series started I was advised to keep the content simple, at a low and easy level. That is something I would not do. I wanted the lectures to be scholarly but with a sprinkle of humor and pop culture. I believe we naturally crave information and challenges. We only consume the "low" because it is easy to access. The low surrounds us at every turn; we need no more of it. The success of the series spoke volumes. There were lines to get into the auditorium, which was full long before the lectures started. The museum added outside seating in the foyer with a monitor to show the images. Often that outside seating would also be full.

The work of art history begins with the art of seeing. The great Joseph Conrad once wrote in a famous preface, "My task which I am trying to achieve is, by the power of the written word, to make you hear, to make you feel—it is, before all, to make you see. That—and no more, and it is everything." Conrad's words could stand as the goal of art, and of talking about art. In fact, visual art begins by making us see literally. We begin with the literal eye, then move to the kind of mind's eye appealed to by the novelist, making inferences, interpreting patterns, perhaps deducing narrative. Then, if we keep going, we can begin to ask questions about context, patrons, even museology.

Actually, Conrad goes further, saying, "If I succeed, you shall find there according to your deserts...and, perhaps, also that glimpse of truth for which you have forgotten to ask." I too believe that it is by looking carefully, by developing our skills of perception and observation, that we have a better chance of experiencing the sensations Conrad mentions, a fuller and richer gamut of human emotions and humanity. Surely that qualifies as what Conrad calls a "glimpse of truth."

This is the sequence I have tried to build into my method. In each lecture I focused intensively on one work of art. I would start with a consideration of what exactly we could see, what exactly the artist was trying to make us see. Then I worked outward, discussing the context of the work of art. I discussed inspirations and influences related to the piece while considering the social and historical contexts to which it belonged: Who were these artists, patrons, viewers? What were they trying to say? What moved them? This was the way that I had first learned to practice art history, when I was a college student taking Art Humanities classes, part of the Core Curriculum at Columbia University. The concept behind "Art Hum," as it is called, is to provide a sense of the entire art historical canon in just one semester. Each lecture focused on one masterpiece that epitomized the period.

Similarly, for the "Art History 101" series, I chose pieces that are part of the canon, grand masterpieces. I chose works that I myself wanted to know better, works of art that I longed to understand in a deeper way. They were works that appear in the art history textbook I use in my own classroom. I hoped, in these lectures, to provide a sense of the shape of art history, of its grand narrative over time. I wanted the flow from one period to the next to expose connections and ties, but without any sense that later is better. Each moment, each monument, has a specific and remarkable story to tell, one that may have informed later artists, consciously or not.

I approached these focal pieces like jewel boxes, as though I was holding up a magnifying lens, looking at often minuscule details. I used a zooming presenter, Prezi, in order to home in on special details without losing any resolution in the image. I also utilized the incredible high-resolution imagery provided by the Google Cultural Institute, which allowed us to interact with the image and see aspects that are not easily visible to the naked eye. For instance, I had never before noticed the dome-shaped building through the window or the incredible details on floor tiles in the Van Eyck *Annunciation*. Even in the clearest printing of the image, those details are hard to find. But these elements are absolutely part of the artist's message.

In addition to pulling up the Google Cultural Institute as I spoke, I also drew on other teaching tools. The wonderful game provided by PBS showing the effects of pointed versus rounded arches helped explain the physics of those forms. I also played clips of videos. The gasps were audible when I showed a video clip of the height of the jumps of a caracal—a feat that has to be seen to be believed. I also showed a video that had been produced by the Rijksmuseum to publicize its reopening, in which a group of actors re-create *The Night Watch* in the middle of a shopping mall. It had the audience in stitches. The links for these and other resources appear in the footnotes of the text.

These are monuments and moments that can inform us, that can enliven and invigorate that which we see on a daily basis—in our travels, in our readings, in our jaunts about whatever town we live in. After my first college course in art history everything around me, my surroundings, started to look different. I came home to San Antonio during the winter break, and of all the places that I had known growing up had undergone a complete change. Columns on houses were just like the Roman columns I had been studying in class. There were pediments and dentils and corbels from Greek architecture. The Alamo was like the Arch of Constantine; it had Solomonic columns, just like St. Peter's Basilica. Everything was more meaningful, richer. My present could reach into a deep sense of the past. These kinds of connections also shaped the lectures at the San Antonio Museum of Art.

I intentionally have left in place those elements of the lectures in which I made reference to current echoes of the masterpieces of art—a reproduction of the Nike of Samothrace in a former sculpture garden, a modern mosaic on the façade of a theater, Works Progress Administration frescoes in lost post offices, the baroque costumes of a prominent marching men's organization like the one in *The Night Watch*. If looking at art helps us to learn to see, one of the things we should see is the presence of art in the communities we live in. These references are not meant to be narrowly provincial but to assure us that the discussion of art masterpieces has a "local habitation"—in this case, San Antonio, Texas. Our challenge is to continue to seek these kinds of resonances and references wherever we visit, to connect our deep, historical past with our deepening sense of the present.

In the lectures I discussed a great number of images, some of which do not appear in this publication. Some of those images can be found in high resolution through the Google Arts & Culture website.* For those that are not, high-resolution images are easily available on the internet.

The series would not have happened without the help of many individuals and institutions. I would like to thank the former director Katie Luber and the Board of Directors of the San Antonio Museum of Art for enthusiastically promoting the lecture series throughout its run. Greg Elliott, Dan Gelo, and John Frederick of the University of Texas at San Antonio affirmed my dual role of professor and museum lecturer. President Meredith Woo of Sweet Briar College made special efforts for the progress of the book, giving me every means of support, including tenure. Finally, the H-E-B grocery company was an invaluable champion of the lectures. Dya Campos of H-E-B was the first person to say, without hesitation, "Let's do it!" when I brought up the idea of the series.

I am grateful to Tom Payton and Barbara Ras for making it possible to turn the lectures into a book, and to Marguerite Avery for helping me along the way. Daniel Simon was a thoughtful editor for the manuscript. All in all, it was an honor to work with the Trinity University Press team.

Friends and supporters like Lynda Bailey and Christina Rutherford were a constant help with the book and book-related concerns. Anne Slaughter and her team (Jeshua Mauldin, Philip Rush, Sarah Cooper) were ever-willing to help with photography, videography, and all manner of documentation. Lindsay Wade made a big contribution in the collection of the image permissions.

There are many individuals who have influenced and inspired my thoughts about how to engage with art history and how to communicate about those studies: Maryan Ainsworth, Rich Aste, Heather Badamo, Leonard Barkan, Tim Barringer, Eric Bianchi, Barbara Boehm, Corey Brennan, Shira Brisman, Martin Brody, Sarah Brooks, Gudrun Buehl, Caroline Walker Bynum, Jon Calame, Jonathan Conant, Anne Dunlop, Teresa Eckmann, Bernie Frischer, Carmella Franklin, Sarah Graff, Stephen Greenblatt, Erik Gustafson, Melanie Holcomb, John N. Hopkins, David Humphrey, Jennifer Josten, Ray Keck, Beatrice

---

* Google Arts & Culture, https://artsandculture.google.com.

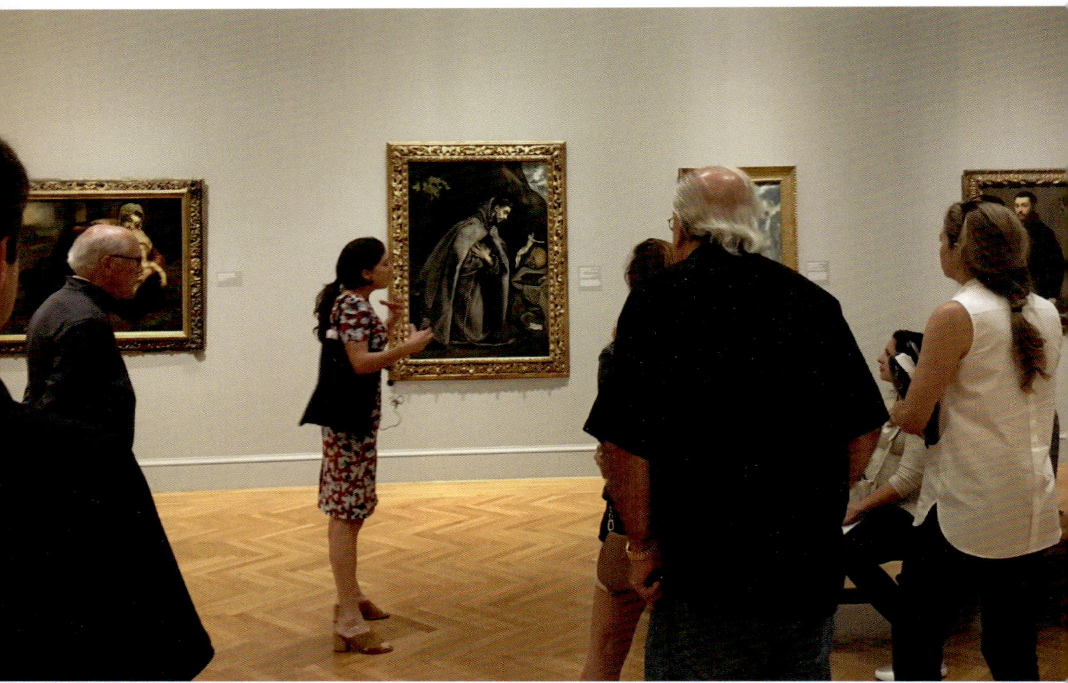

FIG. 1.1 Author giving a tour at the Legion of Honor, San Francisco.

Kitzinger, Holger Klein, Andrew Kranis, Maryann Kranis, Teresa Lai, Griffith Mann, John Marciari, Russell Marret, Katherine McAllen, Margaret Mullet, Alexander Nemerov, John Parker, Kurt Rhode, Nina Rowe, Eileen Ryan, Simon Schama, Annie Schlechter, Nancy Sevcenko, Betsy Dospel Williams, and Frank Wiswall. I owe the deepest gratitude to my academic mentors—Helen Evans, Mary Miller, Robert Nelson, Christopher Wood, Marcus Burke, and Meredith Woo.

I also have many thanks to give to my San Antonians. Dya Campos, Rachel Hollon James, Liz Tullis, Becky Pietch McNeel, Laura Dixon, Sara Huerta, Andy Russ, Albert Carrizales, Suhail Arastu, Sara McCamish, Mary Moorman, and former teachers Sharon Moe and Ruth Frederick—all came to listen and provide encouragement when I was at the podium. Some of the people I admire most also came to hear the lectures, like John L. Santikos, Linda Seeligson, and Charles Butt. My family—my parents, Blair, and Grace—made everything possible. They were at every lecture and supported me in every conceivable way. I cannot thank them enough for teaching me how to look, how to see.

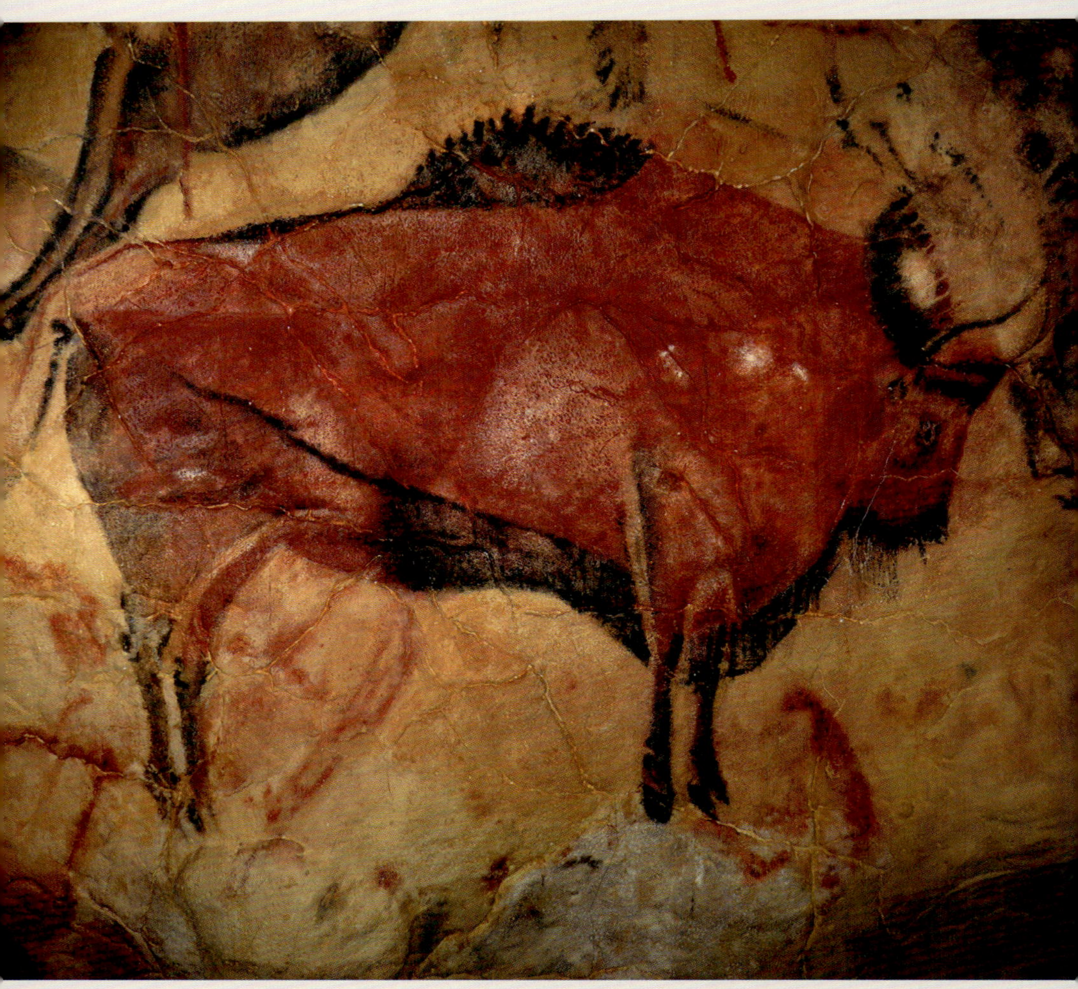

FIG. 1.1 Bison. National Museum and Research Center of Altamira, Spain.
Replica dated 2001, based on original paintings from ca. 12,500 BCE. Paint on limestone.

Altamira

CA. 12,500 BCE

PREHISTORIC ART

Each chapter in the story of the paintings at Altamira, Spain, is one of surprise and discovery—from the first uncovering of the paintings in 1879 to the modern twenty-first-century scientists currently redating the paintings based on calcium carbonate formations. Surprise and discovery. And so it was when I went to see the paintings at Altamira. I didn't intend to see the cave paintings at all. Instead, like a good medievalist, I went to Santillana del Mar solely to see the medieval cloisters. The church with the cloisters, called the Colegiata, is splendid—filled with wonderful carved capitals from the twelfth century. The capitals are decorated with a wide array of vignettes, many of which involve animals—violent lions; a knight killing a tiger; strange, mythological, hybrid animals; Daniel surviving the lion's den. The city of Santillana del Mar is similarly delightful. It is known as the city of the Three Lies: there is no Saint (*sant*), it is not flat (*llana*), and it has no sea (*mar*). Deceptive name aside, it is completely charming, with winding medieval streets and buildings from the fourteenth, fifteenth, sixteenth centuries. Just outside of Santillana del Mar is the place called Altamira, a massive cave running about nine hundred feet long filled with paintings from 12,500 BCE. In one portion of the cave, twenty-seven deep-red bison, outlined in black charcoal and ranging from 110 to 170 centimeters, huddle and bow, charge, bellow, gallop, and pause in an unorganized constellation on the ceiling of the Paleolithic cave. (Figs. 1.1 and 1.2)

The bison are not alone. Four does, one stag, and two horses join the fray. This

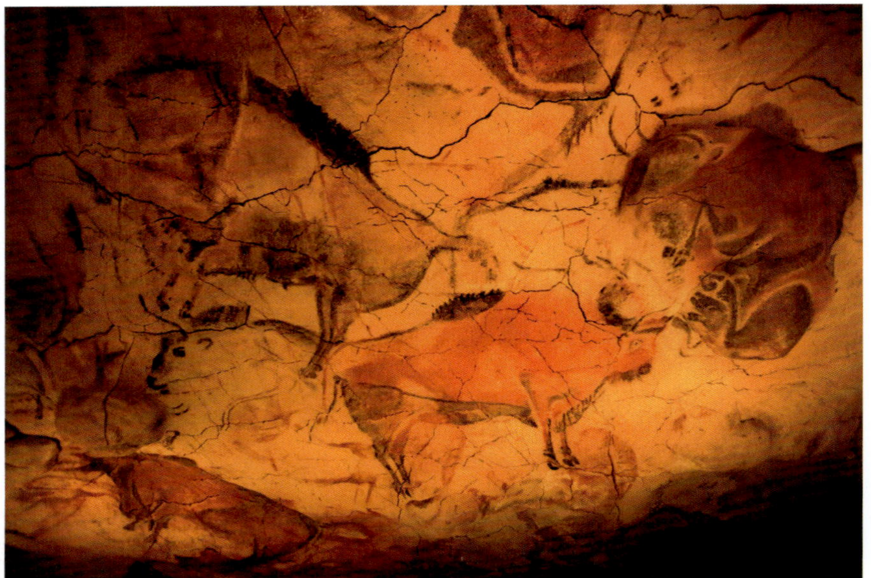

FIG. 1.2 Group of painted bison. National Museum and Research Center of Altamira, Spain. Replica dated 2001, based on original paintings from ca. 12,500 BCE. Paint on limestone.

unchoreographed mass of animals creates a sense of activity, energy, and vitality. What your traditional art historical textbook cannot convey, however, is that the walls are not flat. There is energy in the accumulation of images, but also in the fact that the paintings are positioned so as to bring the walls to life. Bumps on the walls become bison on the walls. The effect is that the animals have dimension to them because they have been placed on natural protuberances on the ceiling of the cave. Reliefs and cracks act as outlines. Thus the wall is more than a flat, blank canvas. It's almost as though the wall makes these animals look alive. For a backward-looking bison, the head is placed on a prominent outcrop of rock and the hindquarters on a rounded natural boss. A bellowing bison appears on a more uniform and flat part of the ceiling, and is thereby distinguished from the herd. Most striking are the bison who curl inward, creating outlines for the large knots or stalactites that emerge from the ceiling.

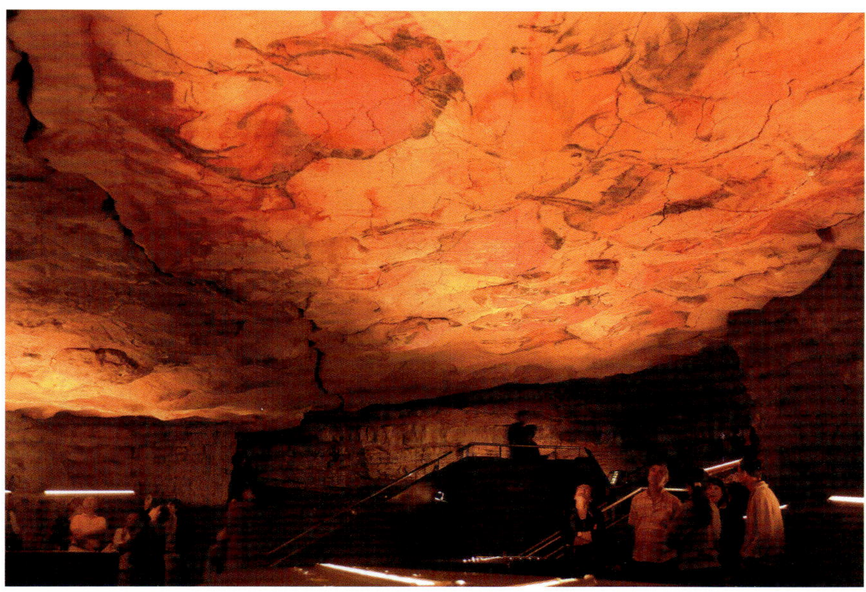

FIG. 1.3   Altamira cave ceiling. National Museum and Research Center of Altamira, Spain. Replica dated 2001, based on original paintings from ca. 12,000 BCE. Paint on limestone.

Imagine, therefore, entering this space, with the paintings above your head starting at about six and a half feet high and slowly encroaching downward onto you, into your space, finishing at about half that height by the end of the cave. Imagine the effect of lights and torches. Little natural light would have penetrated this gallery. So the only way to properly see the bison would be with a lamp with animal fat for fuel, a flickering, changeable light source that would have made the images seem to move and come to life as the light bounced about the walls, bison appearing and disappearing as the vagaries of the flame determined. The colors too would have been variable. The burning animal fat would have created a yellowish-orangish light, which would have affected the tonalities of the pigments on the wall. In this light the red ocher pigments would have transmogrified seamlessly from pale red to brown, mirroring the variations in the coat of the moving animal. Even the rock itself, even the walls, are mutable. The humidity in the cave changes with the seasons such that when the rock surface becomes more damp, the colors become more intense—redder, brighter, more vibrant, more alive.

I'll admit it—I did not get to see the caves in this kind of lighting (Fig. 1.3). In fact, I didn't actually see the Great Hall, if I am being completely factual. What I saw were replicas of the caves. This might make my introduction appear to be a little less than honest, or perhaps just naïve. Who wants to see a fake version of a site? Isn't that like saying you have seen the Doge's Palace at San Marco in Venice by going to San Marcos, Texas, to the outlet mall? I can promise that it is not, although I was suspicious myself. In the reproduced space, somehow the lighting, the process of entering the narrowing spaces, the mood, and the growing anticipation all combine to express the majesty, the mystery, and the emotion of the bison at Altamira.

The fake version of the caves had to be made because the paintings were being destroyed by our breath, human breath. The environment of the caves, where there is little water, no light, and very little air, reacts with carbon dioxide in such a way that bacterial and fungal growth is inevitable. The paintings were fading. Adding the other things humans bring—body heat, debris from outside, electrical lighting—puts Altamira's paintings at great risk. Even the movements and motions of visitors added to the disruption of the environment by stirring the air and encouraging the release and spread of usually dormant bacterial and fungal spores. Not to mention the fact that the walls were terribly unstable. In 1925 Hugo Obermaier, one of the earliest scholars to record and publish on the caves, was nearly killed by falling rocks from upper vaults. In fact the cave itself remained hidden until 1868 because of a collapse of the roof, which obstructed the view of the entry chamber.

Authorities were aware from the outset that the environmental conditions were fragile. For example, as early as the 1950s only ten people were allowed in the caves at a time. However, these measures were not going to counter the high numbers of visitors to the site. In the 1950s there were 50,000 coming to the caves yearly. By 1973 there were 177,000 entering the caves a year. Thus, although the alarm had already been raised by the 1950s that there were dangerous calcite concretions in the Great Hall, it wasn't until 1976, with the political regime change in Spain and the creation of the Ministry of Culture, that steps were taken to close the caves. Without the threat of human air, the color of the paintings improved and the faded color returned—in just five years. The locals, as you might imagine, were very much against the idea of closing Altamira. It was the source of local pride and a great deal of tourism, and still is. So the scientists, curators, museologists looked to the project of Lascaux II, a successful facsimile of the original caves of Lascaux. Without the intervention of scientists and the creation of the replica Lascaux, which also has a cave covered in bulls accompanied by equines and stags, the original paintings would have been lost to a pernicious black mold.

Still, they are fake. So how much of it are you really experiencing? Well, more than you would think. First, this is not a simple process. The contours and topography of the Great Hall were documented with a system that recorded one data point for every five millimeters. At the entrance area 500,000 points were recorded, one for every ten centimeters. With this data in hand, the scientists used a milling machine that could, through a computerized procedure, accurately reproduce the natural reliefs and all of the cracks in the rocks over which the Paleolithic artists painted. The physics and the shape of the caves, down to the tiniest fissures, have been accurately replicated. Even many of the original painting techniques were employed. Thus, even though the paintings are not the originals, even though the cave is not precisely where our long-lost ancestors convened, the experience of these fake caves deny Walter Benjamin's criticisms about the creation of the copy. In his essay "The Work of Art in the Age of Mechanical Reproduction" of 1936, Benjamin asserted,

> That which withers in the age of mechanical reproduction is the aura of the work of art. This is a symptomatic process whose significance points beyond the realm of art. One might generalize by saying: the technique of reproduction detaches the reproduced object from the domain of tradition. By making many reproductions it substitutes a plurality of copies for a unique existence. And in permitting the reproduction to meet the beholder or listener in his own particular situation, it reactivates the object reproduced. These two processes lead to a tremendous shattering of tradition which is the obverse of the contemporary crisis and renewal of mankind.

But these caves produce quite the opposite effect. They do provide the "aura," the emotion of the original. In addition, the replicas help explain the originals in a way that might have been impossible if the caves were more stable. For example, the necessity of studying the scientific makeup of the caves for their preservation provided stimulus for understanding the techniques of the artists and the ways in which prehistoric man used these spaces.

The way that the caves relate to the originals in such a positive and explicative way makes me think of another cave, Plato's cave. In *The Republic*, the late fifth-century Greek philosopher Plato records how his mentor Socrates describes a group of people who have lived chained to the wall of a cave for all their lives, facing a blank wall. As forms pass in front of a fire, the people in the cave ascribe meaning to the shadows. Socrates goes on to explain that the philosopher is like a prisoner who escapes from the cave and understands the true form of reality rather than just the shadows. The notion that objects and materials are mere reflections of higher knowledge relates to the copies of Altamira. What we see is a reference, an index, of the truth that lies beyond our perception. The walls we see make us understand the walls we cannot, just as the bison the prehistoric man painted helped him understand the bison beyond the walls, the bison he feared and revered.

Discovery, surprise, admiration are, as I said at the outset, integral to the story of Altamira; but so is skepticism. The incipience of the study of the caves was far from smooth. One might think that discovery would equal acclaim. But this is not what happened at all. The cave was first found in 1868 by a hunter allegedly in pursuit of a lost dog. Whatever may have happened to the dog, the hunter did uncover the mouth of the cave. A few years later, in 1879, he showed the entry to Marcelino Sanz de Sautuola, who owned a manor in a neighboring village. Sautuola had a law degree and a great interest in local history, natural sciences, antiques, insects, fossils, and minerals. So although he wasn't trained in the scholarly academy, he was a scholarly type of fellow. The story is that he went into the cave on an exploratory excavation with his daughter María. She wandered farther into the caves and exclaimed: "Look, Papa, look at the bison!" (*Mira, papá, los bueyes!*), which makes for a number of goofy reproductions.

And just so that this is not confusing, when I say bison, these are not North

American bison or what we call buffalo, but European bison, which were slighter and lighter than the American buffalo, with shorter hair but a longer tail and horns.

Sautuola shared his discovery with a scholar in Madrid, Juan Vilanova. Vilanova excavated the cave, classifying the skeletons and fossils from the site as being from the prehistoric period, thereby confirming Sautuola's theory that the paintings were prehistoric. Sautuola's story—his jubilant discovery, his excitement about the paintings and the site—becomes a bit grim from this point on. In 1880 he published his findings, and they were completely rejected. Based on the belief that Stone Age people did not have the intelligence to produce such work, the scholarly community determined that Sautuola's bison were fakes and Sautuola was a joke. One scholar argued that the cave had been created by Spanish Jesuits attempting to make a laughingstock of the emerging sciences of paleontology and prehistory. Elaborate! Another scholar, Émile Cartailhac, suggested that they were the work of conservative Spanish clerics hoping to defend belief in divine creation. Both arguments had greater traction than Sautuola's ideas about the paintings. They also expose an anti-Spanish sentiment rife among the French academy. Thus Sautuola's paintings were left to scholarly oblivion.

It was not until 1895, when other caves started being discovered, caves like La Mouthe, Pair-non-Pair, Les Combarelles and Font-de-Gaume (both of which are about thirty miles southwest of Lascaux), and Marsoulas, that Altamira was given a second look. Cartailhac published an article, "Mea Culpa of a Skeptic," in 1902. In it he admitted to "an error, committed for twenty years, an injustice that must be acknowledged and made reparation for publicly.... For my part I must bow to reality, and render justice to M. de Sautuola." But for Sautuola this vindication came too late, as he had died in 1888. Cartailhac did visit María the daughter after publishing the article, and I hope that she was really awful to him.

It is strange for us to consider such skepticism, such vituperative scholarship, and such bizarre suggestions for the existence of the cave paintings. But no one had ever seen anything like it. Without other precedents it would be hard to conceive of such a space, of such a painting program. Who were the authors of these paintings? How were these paintings done? And why? These are questions that would have easily drawn scholars toward the conclusion that they were a modern joke. And it must be said that even though we now know that they are prehistoric images, these same questions plague modern scholars today.

For example, nineteenth-century historians had a particularly difficult time understanding the capacities of the prehistoric artists because they assumed that these "primitive" peoples could not produce images of this sort. What little Paleolithic art was known was limited to engraved bones found at sites like Chaffaud and La Madeleine, in southwestern France. Evolutionists saw in Altamira's magnificence a clear threat to their concept of evolution as a path toward greater evidence of civilization and perfection. That perfection was clearly already present at Altamira. Classicists, in their Eurocentric view of art history, could not admit similarities of ancient Greece, Rome, and Phoenicia with engravings from a prehistoric moment.

But consider the recent discoveries at El Castillo, like Altamira in northeastern Spain. In 2012 scientists reported that advances in testing techniques—replacing radiocarbon testing with uranium-thorium—completely redated the paintings on the walls. With uranium-thorium, researchers take the calcium carbonate deposits from the water that seeps into the caves and dissolve the sample to extract the traces of uranium and thorium atoms. Uranium decays into thorium. A measure of the ratio of uranium to thorium can tell the minimum age of the art beneath the calcium crust. A recent dating of the hands at El Castillo has indicated that they were produced around 40,000 BCE. This new information allowed NPR's clever and cheeky title, "Famous Cave Paintings Might Not Be from Humans." Human hands not made by human hands? Aliens? Well, that's the joke. But no. Rather, the idea is that modern humans were not in Spain at this time. Neanderthals, understood as a different species from modern humans, would have been producing the images at this early date. *They* were *Homo sapiens. We* are a special subgroup—*Homo sapiens sapiens.* One of the distinguishing features is that Neanderthals could not create artistic works beyond simple abstract markings. They are not considered to have had an aptitude for higher cognitive thinking like symbolism and allegory. Yet Neanderthals were performing ritual burials, making beads, producing tools. It seems only natural that they would have put images on walls too. These new dating techniques have provided enough evidence to suggest that the Neanderthals are closer to modern humans than once thought. This has shaken the academic community significantly. A major art history textbook published in 2014 makes the distinction as clear as can be: "Indeed, it is the cognitive capability to create and recognize symbols and imagery that sets us as modern humans apart from all our predecessors and from all our contemporary animal relatives. We are defined as a species by our abilities to make and understand art." The El Castillo story suggests that maybe we aren't so far superior to our predecessors. Maybe we aren't all that much less prejudiced and Eurocentric than the nineteenth-century scholars. Certainly with all of the questions that we still have about these cave paintings, it is pretty clear we don't understand art as well as we think we do.

The discoveries at El Castillo are directly relevant to Altamira. One symbol found on the wall with the bison has been dated to earlier than 35,600 years ago, making it 20,000 years older than the bison paintings. Thus, the Great Hall is a massive palimpsest of prehistoric paintings, and records thousands of years of art historical traditions. The Great Hall is not alone. In fact, it is one of many painting programs in the caves. The Great Hall is about 20 × 10 meters (65 × 32 feet). But the entire cave winds a total of 300 meters or about 900 feet—about three times the length of a football field. In a sense, the caves create a number of interconnected galleries, like a modern museum. And, like a museum or a modern art gallery, there is a thematic unity or "single concept" linking the separate spaces—they all take advantage of natural formations, they are produced with similar techniques and materials, and there are always bison and does and horses leading us through the spaces, looking out at us from these variously painted walls.

But each gallery is different. Each space is unique (Fig. 1.4). After leaving the Great Hall, there is a chamber with figures drawn with fingers in soft clay, the so-called macaroni chamber. A short, narrow gallery beyond the "macaroni" chamber has ladder-form signs in red paint that the viewer must lie on his back to see fully. In the room known as the Pit, the viewer confronts a figure of a bison drawn in black and a panel with the head of a doe surrounded by goats also drawn in black. Beyond the entrance to the Pit is the narrow gallery called the

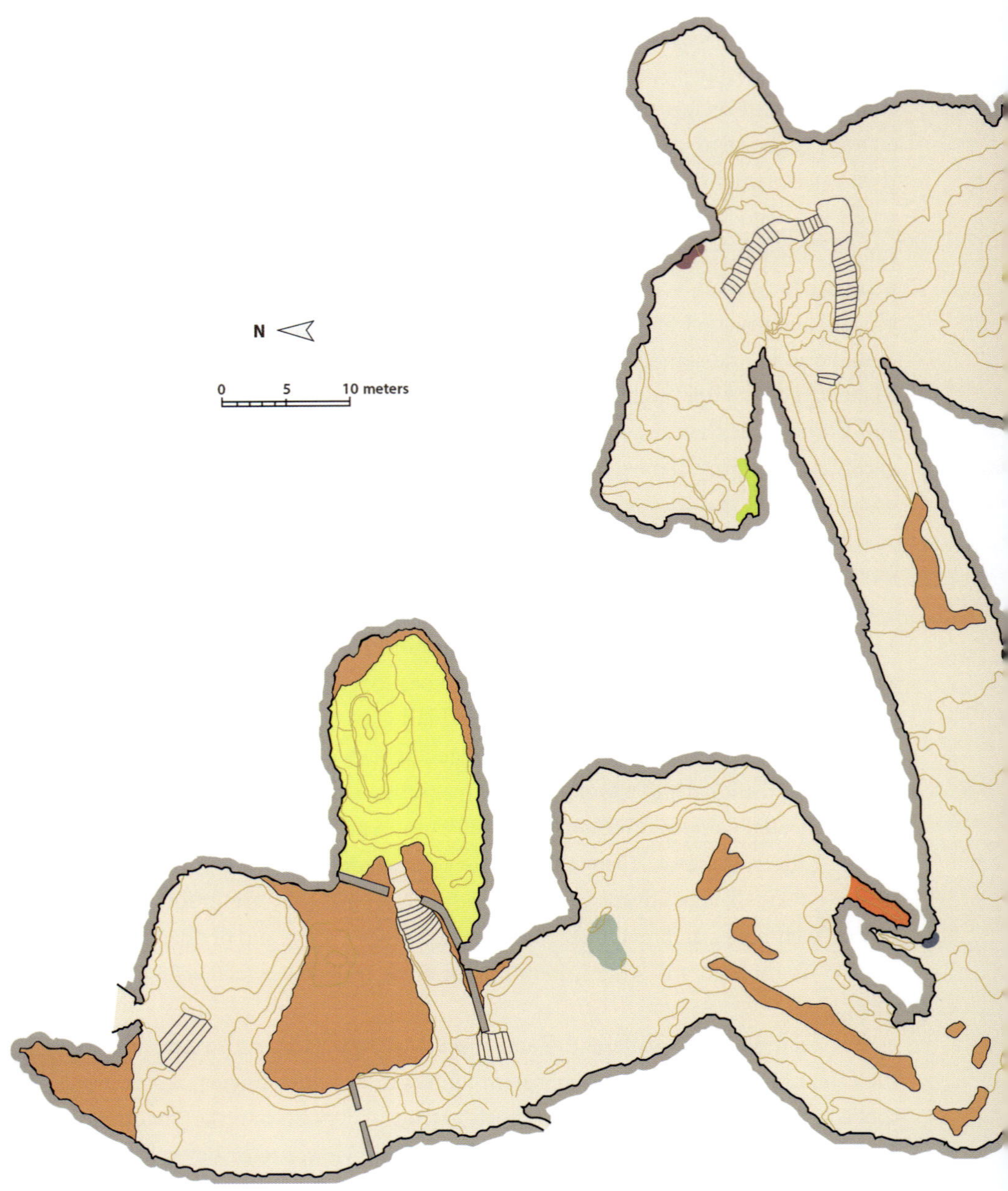

FIG. 1.4 Drawing of Altamira cave.

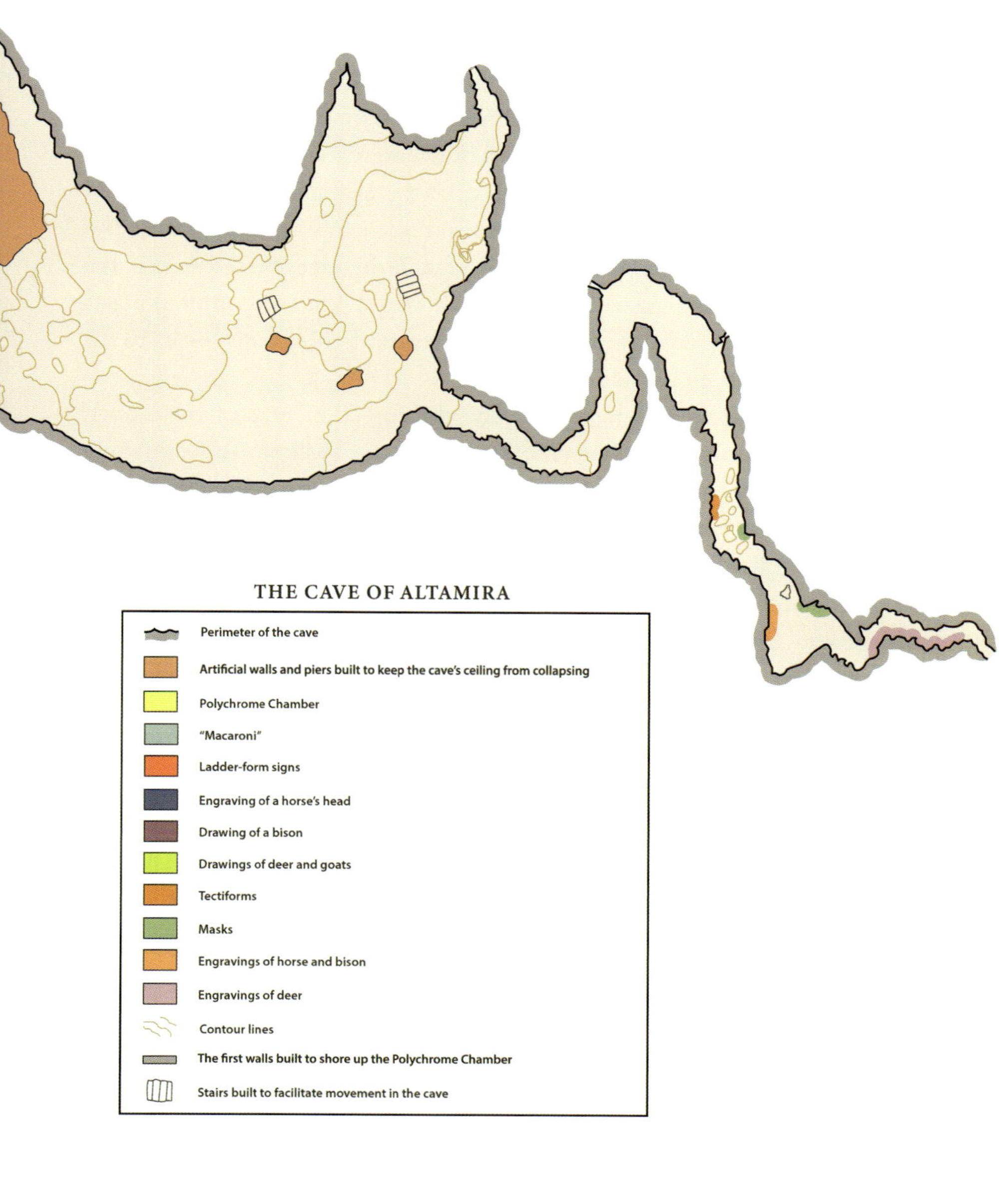

THE CAVE OF ALTAMIRA

Perimeter of the cave
Artificial walls and piers built to keep the cave's ceiling from collapsing
Polychrome Chamber
"Macaroni"
Ladder-form signs
Engraving of a horse's head
Drawing of a bison
Drawings of deer and goats
Tectiforms
Masks
Engravings of horse and bison
Engravings of deer
Contour lines
The first walls built to shore up the Polychrome Chamber
Stairs built to facilitate movement in the cave

Horse's Tail. After a series of engraved figures of bison and deer, the cave opens into a corridor with tectiforms, that is, black squares or quadrangles filled with oblique lines. On the opposite side of this corridor are several masklike faces. According to the scholars who have visited these interior spaces, the masks only become visible as the visitor leaves the space of the chamber. The effect is that once the visitor comes to the farthest reaches of the caves and turns around so as to begin the journey back, he is guided through the caves by the masks. The rock faces turn into faces. And, depending on how and when the visitor interacts with that particular space, they come into existence, they become guides to the pilgrim returning to the outside world.

These swirling images, surrounding and defining the space of the viewer, have been called the "Sistine Chapel" of prehistoric art. Perhaps. To see Michelangelo's chapel, you do have to bother with interminable lines and small, dark corridors. Yet, leaving aside the irritating fact that Michelangelo is always the measuring stick for art (why can't the Sistine Chapel be the Altamira of painted spaces?), these visitors would have been far more intrepid than their Renaissance progeny. These caves were dark—pitch-black. Even with a torch, going in, walking those winding 300 meters would have been insane. Also, it was freezing cold. The temperatures in the Cantabrian hills during the Magdalenian period were closer to Scotland's meadows. Perhaps the cave was a safe retreat from the bison, reindeer, aurochs, deer, rhinoceroses, elephants that roamed the prairies of northern Spain. But still.

So again: Who were these people? Who painted these images? How did they do it? And why?

Something of the artist's (or artists') creative process has been reconstructed by the scholars at Altamira. For instance, scholars speculate that the artist of the bison in the Great Hall would have produced the paintings standing toward the north, with the slight natural light entering over his shoulder. Since the light from the outside would have been slim (the entire north and east walls would have been in darkness), artificial light (torches) would have been essential to the process. There is a myth that Michelangelo was on his back as he painted the Sistine Chapel. But in fact, he painted standing. The Altamira artist would also have stood to paint his bison, perhaps kneeling to complete the bison at the

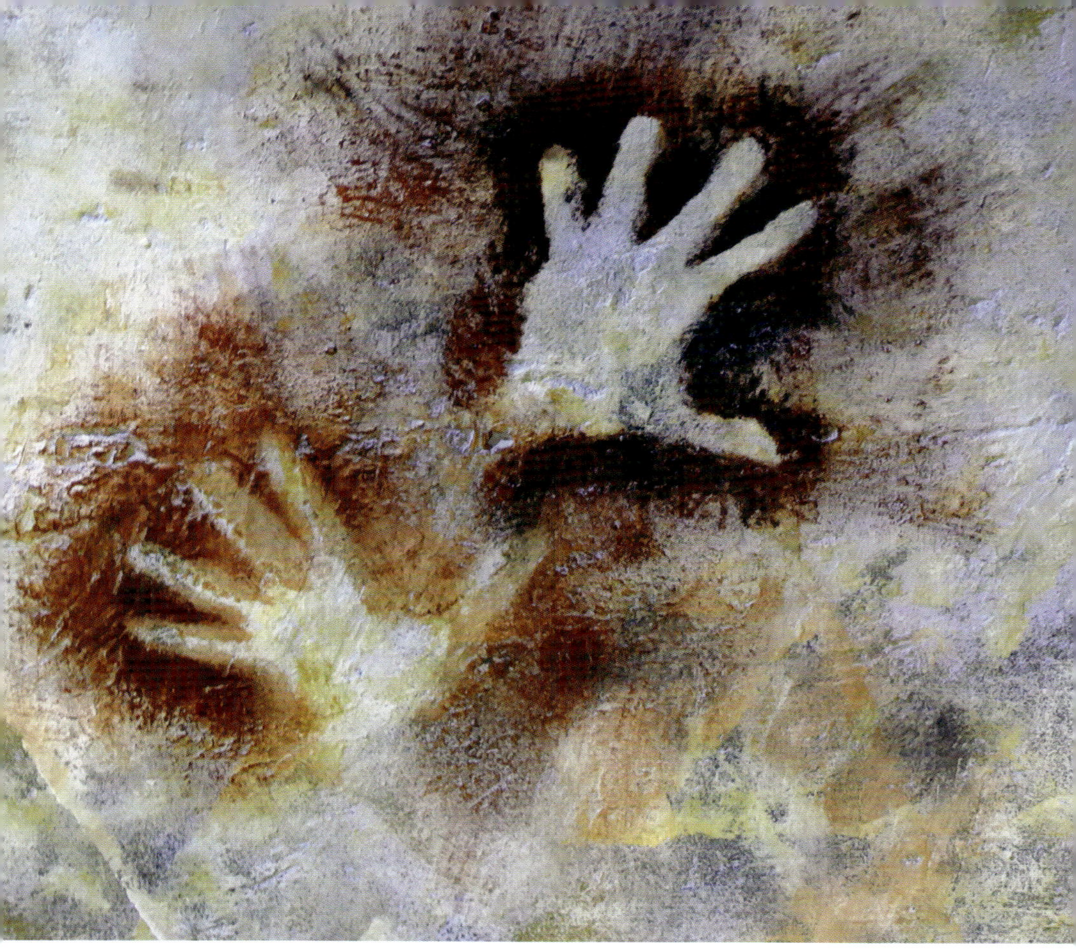

far end of the chamber where the ceiling is lower. The artist would have first engraved the wall with stone tools, lavishing most attention on the heads of the bison—the horns, the eyes, the ears, the muzzles, the beards. Next the artist drew black outlines with charcoal. Finally, the artist painted the red of the bison with iron oxides and ochers that used water for a binder. The artist would have used a long stick to draw and paint the ceiling. Remnants of shells from the caves would have acted as the prehistoric artist's palette. They would have been used to hold the crushed charcoal or pigments. The canvas, or wet limestone, was also an integral part of the painting campaign. The wet limestone of the walls would have facilitated the engraving. And the characteristics of the limestone would have reacted with the iron oxide and ocher paint in a way that the color bonded to the wall. This chemical process is akin to the bonding that occurs in Renaissance frescoes.

The unity to the style of the bison and the shape of the charcoal strokes indicate that the artist of the bison may have even been one individual. Although one person may have done the bison, it is hard to imagine that the painted hands are all singular. Amid the bison are a series of positive and negative handprints (Fig. 1.5). The positives are made by coating the hand in pigment. The negatives would have been made by a spraying technique whereby the artist put the charcoal in his mouth and sprayed or spit out the colored pigments onto the wall. The effect is a ghostly mist. And from that mist the image emerges, the image that is a nonimage, the absence of paint, but the distinct mark of the maker—his mouth, his saliva, his hand, his eye, his imagination. To my mind, such hands, which are found at many different prehistoric sites, would have been marks by a group of people as a sign of unity or community. As a sign of communion with the animals. As a sign of witnessing and experiencing this space.

We do know that the prehistoric communities would have been living in close connection with these hidden caves. The entry to the caves was open to the elements. These spaces would have been centers of shelter for these people. As the visitor, as the prehistoric man, moved farther into the cave, there would have been progressively less and less light. Thus what it meant when they entered into the caves—when they left behind their safe dwellings with access to the outer world and natural sunlight—and what they believed that they were seeing as they entered the caves—this is all still a mystery.

Since the discovery of the caves, scholars have had numerous interpretations of the images on the walls of Altamira. The first scholars assumed that the paintings were simply idle doodlings, graffiti, playful and mindless decorations. Twentieth-century scholars interpreted the images as evidence of a magical-religious purport. For example, the French scholar Henri Breuil read all of the bison as evidence of a ritual killing—the artists were painting the bison in order to subjugate them, to symbolically kill off the threat of these beasts. Other scholarship suggested that the animals were supposed to be "spirit animals," not imitations of bison but hallucinatory images representing the insights of shamans during trance performances. Another reading is that the artists were depicting the bison in the hope that they would reproduce and flourish, thereby providing food for their communities. This interpretation supposed that the animals were mating in the images—that they were males advancing on females. Bison curled up in balls were, according to this theory, rolling in urine-impregnated dirt in order to mark their territory, or perhaps a female bison giving birth. But it is not possible to tell whether the bison in either case are male or female. The lack of any indication of gender weakens this argument, although the importance of reproduction cannot be entirely dismissed. More recently, scholars have likened the caves to computers, as a great database or storehouse of information about experiencing the world. The dangers of traveling into the cave in order to see the images may have been intended as a part of understanding the dangers of the world beyond the cave, and might have been particularly instrumental in educating young members of the community who would soon be hunting these very animals.

Is this why, when the visitor progresses deeper into the cave, the techniques become progressively simpler—from the bison to simpler engravings? Is this stylistic change about the experience of the visitor? Is it a means of representing the dangers present in the world beyond the cave, dangers that are inexplicable, mysterious, abstract? Or is it purely practical, because there is less light? Because it is harder to carry the materials needed to execute the work? Or are these techniques related to ritual practices that took place closer to the heart of the cave? One scholar suggested that symbolic forms, like the tectiforms, were placed in the parts of the caves with the best acoustics and meant to tell shamans where to stand. What about the paintings that are hidden from view, like the red ladder shapes that you must lie on your back to see? Were they meant to be discovered? Or are they too part of a lost religious meaning, meant to be present,

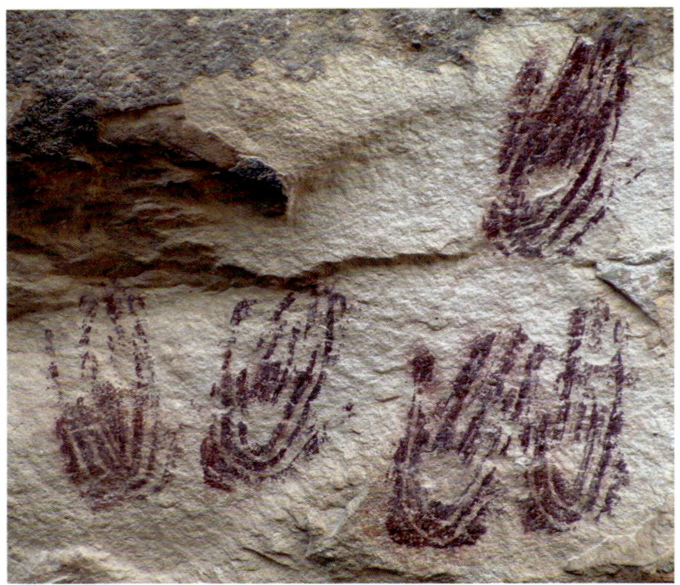

FIG. 1.6 Hand paintings at Seminole Canyon, ca. 5,000 BCE.
Seminole Canyon State Park and Historic Site, Comstock, Texas.
Paint on limestone.

not consumed? Are the bison to be feared or loved? One scholar has written that the direction of the brushstrokes intentionally mirrors the way that one might stroke an animal. It sounds silly, but all the brushstrokes are in one direction. Did the artist, in creating the animal in paint, consider himself to be controlling the bison, respecting the bison, creating a "real" bison?

There is still no conclusive understanding as to why the bison were painted. But perhaps part of the not-knowing is the point of art. Perhaps good art makes you think and rethink, question and pursue and change. Werner Herzog's movie *Cave of Forgotten Dreams* is such an incredible portal into the caves of Chauvet because he shows images of the paintings that we will never get to see. Still, Herzog, in his inimitable way, also gets us "into" the caves because he asks questions—the craziest kinds of questions. Like when he interviews the scientist about his work on the cave and focuses predominantly on the man's past as a

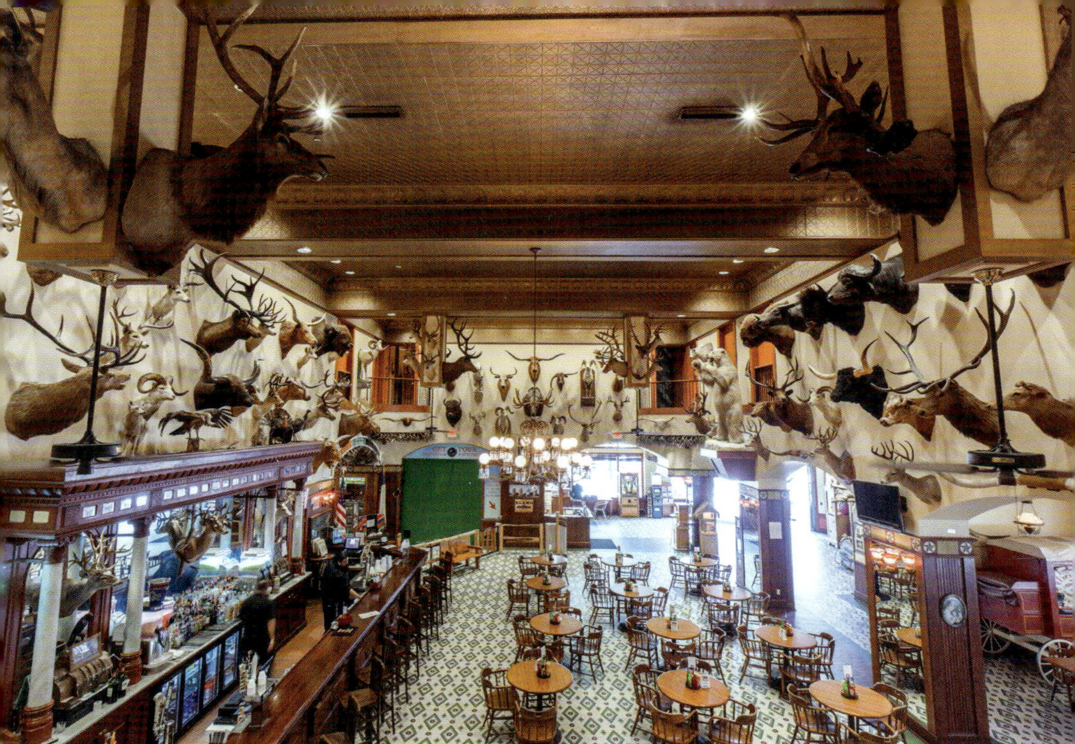

FIG. 1.7 Buckhorn Hall of Horns, founded ca. 1890. San Antonio, Texas.

circus performer—as though that kind of life, that dreamlike existence, is truer to the experience of the caves than any collection of data points or scientific studies could reveal. As Herzog says after one particularly beautiful scene in which he demands utter silence, "These images are memories of long forgotten dreams. Is this their heartbeat [that we hear] or ours?" And Herzog ends the movie with an allegory of some radioactive albino crocodiles from a nuclear plant twenty miles away from the caves, suggesting again that the caves defy science, just like the bizarro, mutant crocodiles. He wonders, in his Herzogian way, what the crocodiles will make of the paintings of the bison, not if but when they go there. These abstract and off-the-wall queries force you to think in the realm of the absurd, to think abstractly about these impenetrable meanings of the images on these walls. And that's as powerful and perhaps as true as it gets.

In 1902 a twenty-five-year-old Pablo Picasso made the trip to Altamira.

Following a second visit after World War II he allegedly proclaimed, "After Altamira, all art is decadence." In other words, we know nothing. We have learned nothing since Altamira. There is some doubt that Picasso actually said just this. But what he may not have said with words he certainly said in his art. In his lithograph called *Bull* from 1945, the monumental, naturalistic bison becomes progressively abstracted and lost to simple lines (Figs 20.2, 20.3, 20.4, 20.5). We are left with a ghost of a bull, almost insectlike. The bulls at Altamira also reflect different degrees of fullness and completeness. Yet Picasso's drawing provides a sense of linear progression. It is a plotted and organized statement about naturalism and how it does and does not hold up; the final bull is as much of a bull as the first bull, as much an image as the first image. In Altamira, images are more than what they represent. They are more than images of bulls. They represent the lifeblood and livelihood of the viewer. They represent danger and hunger and fear. They are overwhelming, hovering above our heads. And, in their poses of curling and resting and standing, they are somehow comforting. They are the world beyond the walls and within the walls. And, for that matter, they are the walls.

Art that surprises us, that constantly defies a precise definition, that shakes up a comfortable sense of self, that's what makes Altamira spectacular. Perhaps you might reflect on the ways in which Altamira's images are part of *your* reality. How is a constellation not of stars or sky scenes but of large, terrific animals meant to affect us, the viewer? Do the images inspire fear? A sense of control? Feelings of harmony and peace? What do these images say about man and the constant need to communicate through art? How does light and space and the movement of the viewer define and shape how the bison appear? Consider how it is possible to drive three hours from downtown San Antonio, Texas, to look at the paintings from 4,500 years ago in the caves at Seminole Canyon. How amazing is it that the same techniques and traditions connect northeastern Spain and West Texas at Seminole Canyon—red painted hands, red painted bison (Fig. 1.6)? Finally, consider how striking it is that we, modern men and women, with our millions of fancy iPads, so far from 12,500 BCE, are still putting images on walls—even hanging the same kinds of images on walls, heads of deer and bison. At the Buckhorn Saloon and Museum, in my home city of San Antonio, antlers and horns from all variety of animals line the walls (Fig. 1.7). These were amassed by the original owner, Albert Friedrich (1864–1928), from his own hunting trips, and that he purchased through a curious bartering system that involved his swapping a drink for each set of horns brought to the saloon. Today there are approximately 1,200 "trophy mounts." Friedrich's aesthetic may be unusual. But many a living room is decorated with antlers and horns. Symbols of conquest? Of the majesty of nature? Or of humanity and our relationship to our remote past selves?

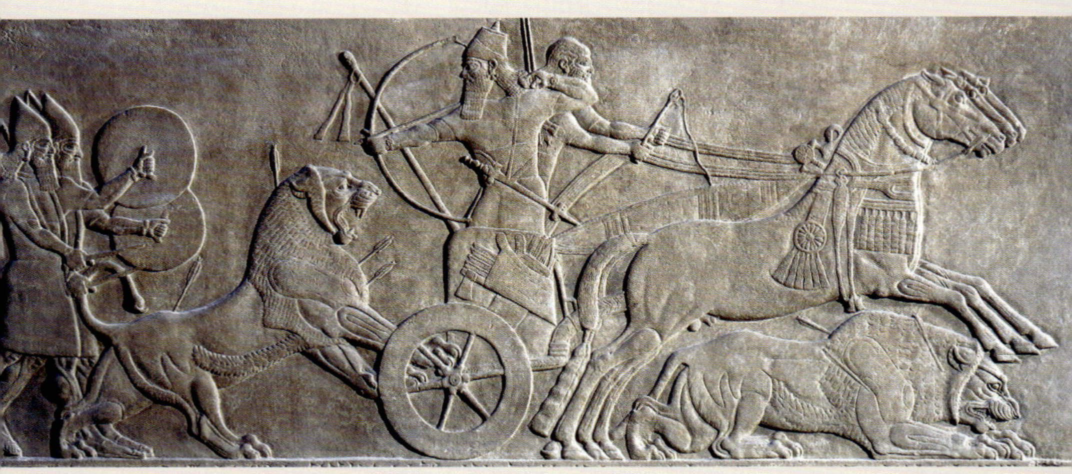

FIG. 2.1 Ashurnasirpal II Killing Lions, ca. 883–859 BCE. From the palace of Ashurnasirpal II, Nimrud (Iraq). British Museum, London. Gypsum alabaster, 99.1 × 88.65 cm.

Ashurnasirpal II Killing Lions

CA. 883–859 BCE

ASSYRIAN ART

The British Museum in London has a spectacular collection of treasures—tremendous Egyptian statuary, the Rosetta Stone, the Parthenon sculptures, and the Sutton Hoo horde. Yet there is one room that is typically quieter than those other galleries, where a series of massive reliefs in a cool, creamy stone line the walls. Because of the monotony of the color palette, the scenes might not immediately grab your attention or jump out at you. The carvings are very thin, in a bas or low relief, and almost flush with the walls. But as you walk through this long hall, the images draw you in, you become part of a story or history that pulls you through a series of conquests and rituals, which all speak to the powerful rule of Ashurnasirpal II, the king of the Assyrians who reigned from 883 to 859 BCE.

Ashurnasirpal's assumption of power was cause for celebration. The years preceding his reign were characterized by a 300-year period of decline and isolation. Under Ashurnasirpal the Assyrians started to pull together and assert their power. He oversaw an intense and complete expansion, annexing large regions of land throughout the Mesopotamian region, consuming Aram (modern Syria), much of Asia Minor, and the Zagros Mountains in modern Iran. About five years into his reign, he moved the capital from Ashur to Kalhu, the city called Calah in the tenth book of Genesis and now known as Nimrud. The site sits only twenty miles south of Nineveh or modern Mosul. In order to commemorate the move the king ordered a banquet that fed 69,574 men and women from Calah, including 5,000 delegates from distant regions and inhabitants of the wider

Assyrian realm. For ten days the party raged on. An extensive menu and the enumeration of the large guest list appears written in cuneiform on the face of a stone block that sat in the great king's newly constructed palace. A big party in a big, brand-new city. The fortified section of the city covered fifty acres. It encompassed nine temples and a massive palace in the northwestern section of the complex, which sat on the Tigris River.

Ashurnasirpal was generous and protective, concerned about the well-being of the entire empire, and artistically inclined. Yet in addition to memorializing his ability to throw the party of the century, Ashurnasirpal makes certain to set in stone the impermeable fact that he is a terrific force: "[This is] the palace of Ashurnasirpal, the high priest of Ashur…the legitimate king, the king of the world, the king of Assyria…the heroic warrior…the shepherd of all mortals, not afraid of battle [but] an onrushing flood which brooks no resistance; the king who subdues the unsubmissive [and] rules over all mankind…has personally conquered all countries…takes hostages, [and] triumphs over all the countries from beyond the Tigris to the Lebanon and the Great Sea. Ashurnasirpal is the king whose fame is power!"

What the inscriptions on the sandstone asserted in words was reified in sculpted imagery, in a carved white gypsum from northern Iraq known as Mosul marble. This is especially the case in the scenes in the king's throne room, which was covered in large eight-foot-tall reliefs, including the scene of Ashurnasirpal hunting the lions—the top half of one of these tall panels (Fig. 2.1). This scene is an example of how the imagery in Ashurnasirpal's palace speaks a language of power, from the subject matter to style. Just look at the way the king's face is carved. The forceful and strict outline of his profile exudes solidity and imperme-ability, authority and might. His eyes are wide, alert, determined. The intensity of his eyes is heightened by his thick, arching eyebrows, which continue to the bridge of his nose. This piercing vision is all the more heightened by the fact that his hair creates a frame, a mask almost, that exposes only his eyes and his regal nose. That hair is remarkable. His beard cascades in a bevy of tightly wound curls and undulating, vertical locks. The beard is almost a metaphor for the gaze of the king—tightly wound, concentrated, unforgiving, orderly, austere.

That intense and unremitting gaze is to be expected as Ashurnasirpal is on a major campaign to conquer his enemies, which, in this panel, means the lion. And what a lion he is. Fury and rage emanates from this profile—his ears pulled back, his gum-lined maw baring rows of teeth and a pair of knifelike fangs, his muzzle snarling with savage ferocity. The lion does not have a long mane, as one might expect. These particular lions, known as Asiatic lions or Persian lions, were native to Mesopotamia, although they were eradicated from that region in the tenth century CE. A small community still exists in northwestern India, although they are on a list of endangered animals. The characteristics of these lions include a closely cropped mane and an angular muzzle. They also have a feature rarely seen in African lions, a fold of skin running along the abdomen. The artist of this piece knew these animals well. The short S-shaped tufts of hair in the mane of the lion also appear along the curve of the band of fur along the belly of the beast. Another sinuous line of hair draws along the weighty, muscular back haunch of the lion and spirals elegantly in the hook of his tail. The undulant back of the lion responds to these curving forms and heightens the sense of strength and power of the animal. So does his emphatic musculature. His leg muscles are thick and bulging and sharply defined through deep incisions in the stone. That weight pressing down on his back paws is massive and palpable. But his weight is not awkward or burdensome. Blended with those curving outlines and shapes, his muscular body is alluring, noble, and leonine.

This representation of the lion might bring to mind the moment in the twentieth book of the *Iliad*, when Achilles is likened to a lion: "Achilles charged toward Aeneas like a lion. . . . The lion passes by, indifferent at first, but when a youth agile in a fight strikes it with a spear it roars and gathers itself, jaws foaming, its powerful spirit groaning within, lashing its ribs and flanks with its tail, rousing itself to fight, then rushing with glaring eyes to the attack, plunging in fury among the foremost, either to kill or be killed." The *Iliad* was written down some two hundred years after the date of the palace of Ashurnasirpal. But Homer's words almost read the image for us. You might also think of the peculiar riddle that Samson proffers to the Philistines in Judges 14: "Out of the eater came something to eat." The riddle is curious because the answer is a question: "What is stronger than a lion?" Here, in these panels, the answer is singular—Ashurnasirpal.

The lion tries his mightiest to stop the chariot. He sticks his front paws into the spokes of the wheel and throws his weight against its movement. But it is to no avail. He might be able to ignore the arrows in his rear, his neck, his breast, but the king is going to be the victor. One obvious indication of that fact is the fate of the lion ahead of the chariot. This lion with downcast eyes seems to be slowly closing its mouth, having emitted its final roar. Instead of a powerful, elegant arched back, this lion is hunched over, conquered and in pain. He drags his left leg as though trying to continue his once powerful gait. But the energy still left in his back paws is spent and exhausted by the time it reaches the front of the animal—from a lifeless tail to a sinking gaze. Above, three elegant horses move swiftly over the body of the lion. The quickness of their stride, the completeness with which they hurdle the dead lion in one mindless swoop, is a striking contrast. The horses are just a series of repetitious and indistinguishable bodies, no life in their eyes, ignorant of the noble, dying animal below. Not that they are in any way inferior in terms of artistic skill. These bodies too are done with utmost precision. Delicate, elegant rosettes and flaring tassels embellish their stout bodies. In a sense, however, that is all they are—modes of display for the imperial regalia. They wear those decorative elements and pull the chariot. Their entire bodies are not even really that important. We see enough heads to assess that there are three horses, even though there are only two discernible tails, maybe the outline of a second torso, a lot of missing legs and only one set of genitalia. The attention to the lions, the weight and entirety of their bodies, shows that these are the animals that matter, these are the worthy enemies of the king.

Consider, by contrast, the panel that precedes our lion hunt (Fig 2.2). There are a number of rather obvious similarities. The king rides in the chariot—same coiffeur, same hat. There are also two animals, two bulls, that fall victim to Ashurnasirpal. One bull, who is encompassed by the group of insouciant horses on parade, is quite done for—his weight sits squarely and motionlessly on his hind haunches, his tail is tucked under his body, and his head lies weightily on his front hoof, mouth closed. There is still power in the bull that is alive. But there is something less noble about the bull when compared with the lion. The wheel cuts across the bull's body, interrupting and undermining whatever power that torso might have designated. He is waving his tail energetically, frantically, sticking out his tongue haplessly, and even hanging in the spokes of the wheel.

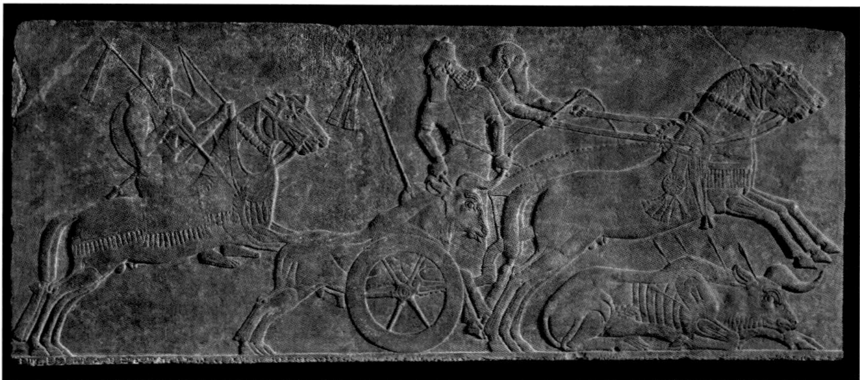

FIG. 2.2 Ashurnasirpal II Killing Bulls, ca. 883–859 BCE. From the palace of
Ashurnasirpal II, Nimrud (Iraq). British Museum, London. Gypsum alabaster,
99.1 × 88.65 cm.

The lion pushes down on the wheel and pulls at it with his mighty paws. The bull
is an easy target; four shots hit in quick succession. The dying lion has been shot
in different angles, suggesting that he was twisting and turning in his attempt
to escape. The king, without even looking, grabs the horns of the bull with his
left hand and stabs the animal with his right. Admittedly, Ashurnasirpal does
not look directly at the lion either. But it would seem as though his lofty gaze
extends a certain respect that is missing in the exchange with the bull. In the lion
hunt, the king is ready and primed—pulling the bow taut, readying his arrow,
two extra in hand. The sword secured over his shoulder and the two crisscrossed
bags of quivers (and one axe) hanging from the chariot suggest that he has made
every consideration, every last preparation for this hunt. Thus, the bull hunt is
about showing Ashurnasirpal's brute strength. The lion hunt is about showing
the king's skill, his agility, his poise in the face of a terrific beast, and his ability
to protect the people of his realm.

Two soldiers follow the action with their shields held aloft in their left hands
and unsheathed swords in their right. They are strong and muscular, but they
march along, much like the horses, with little inspiration and as a series of repetitive, interchangeable bodies. They are drones, men in the service of Ashurnasirpal,

stepping in line and in order. They share many features of the king's guise. They wear heavy earrings, tightly curled beards and tight tunics that expose their strong arms. But it is clear that Ashurnasirpal is a different breed. There are specific details that enhance a sense of difference between the king and his soldiers. The iconography of his headgear, for example, is distinctive. Ashurnasirpal wears a royal miter composed of three parts—a fez, a cone-shaped point that emerges from the fez, and a fillet. Only the king could wear the fez. The cone emerging from the fez is the top of the helmet like that worn by the two soldiers, thus emphasizing that the king was also a warrior. Wrapped around the fez is a fillet, a crescent-shaped band of cloth, the ends of which appear just under his shoulder, flying in the wind. The fillet meant that Ashurnasirpal had been carefully chosen by the gods as their representative. The difference between the soldiers and the king is also established in their movements. The soldiers are flatfooted and static. Their muscles are weighty and grounding. Ashurnasirpal's body is elegant and agile. He balances in that swiftly speeding chariot with grace, turning to the lion with a twist.

This twist is actually rather surprising because we are looking at the back of the king. That is radical. I cannot find any other example of the back of a king in Assyrian art nor in any images from traditions that were dominant at the time, such as the Egyptians. The Assyrians and the Egyptians were always in close contact, even before Ashurnasirpal's time. We can see that in the art. If we look at the Palette of Narmer we can make a number of connections that heighten the sense that the Egyptians were extremely influential in the way that the Assyrians chose to produce images (Fig. 2.3).

Palettes were used for grinding cosmetics, but this one is so large that it was most likely used as a ritual or votive object. The scenes are composed in rectilinear registers and carved in low relief. Two lionlike creatures (technically known as serpopards) are powerful, unruly, and must be controlled. Bulls represent brute strength and stare out at us with savage directness. Like Ashurnasirpal, the pharaoh, Narmer, wears implementations of his power and godlikeness. Narmer appears on both the front of the palette and the back, which also depicts the mythical serpopard. The tail of the bull (which Narmer wears around his waist) was a traditional symbol of royal power reserved for the pharaoh. He also wears special crowns to show his omnipotence—on the front of the crown is

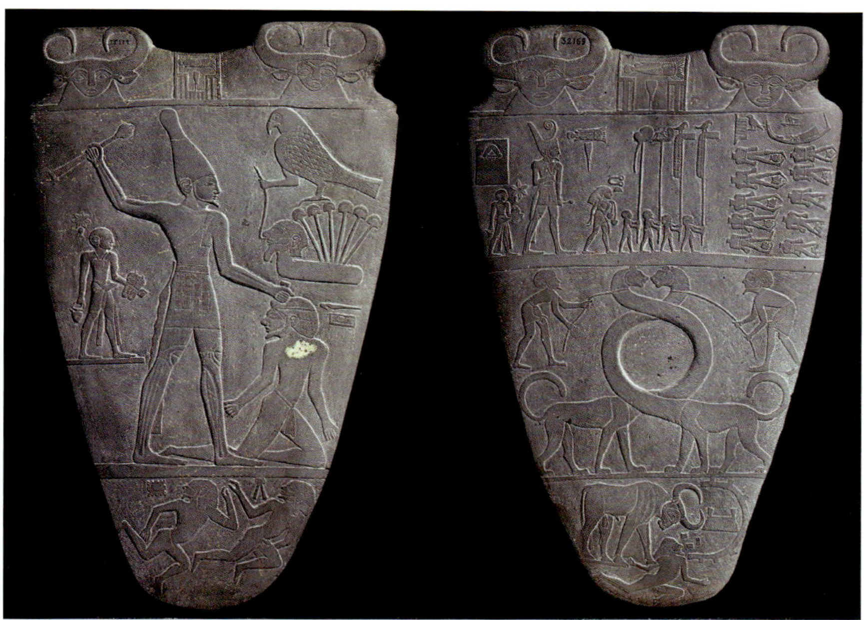

FIG. 2.3 Palette of Narmer, ca. 2950 BCE. Front (on left) and back (on right). From Hierakonopolis, Egypt. Egyptian Museum, Cairo. Green schist, 64 × 42 cm.

representative of Upper Egypt and on the back, the serpopard side, the crown is representative of Lower Egypt. On both sides the pharaoh's body is untouchable and expansive. The artist shows all of Narmer's body, a view facilitated by the dramatic diagonal that leads our eye from the mace he holds high in his right hand down to the hapless victim, held by a tuft of hair. Only the conquered enemies have contorted, twisted, broken bodies. Only they are seen from behind. The way Ashurnasirpal shows his back truly works against the tradition of how kings were shown.

The twisting king brings us back to the lion. Unlike the comparison with the drones that clomp along mindlessly behind the chariot, with whom Ashurnasirpal has little in common, the lion is a true reflection of the king. Both lion and king are powerful, muscular, and hyperalert—eyes activated, bodies in motion. The lion's body, the diagonal in which he moves, is akin to the angle of the sweep

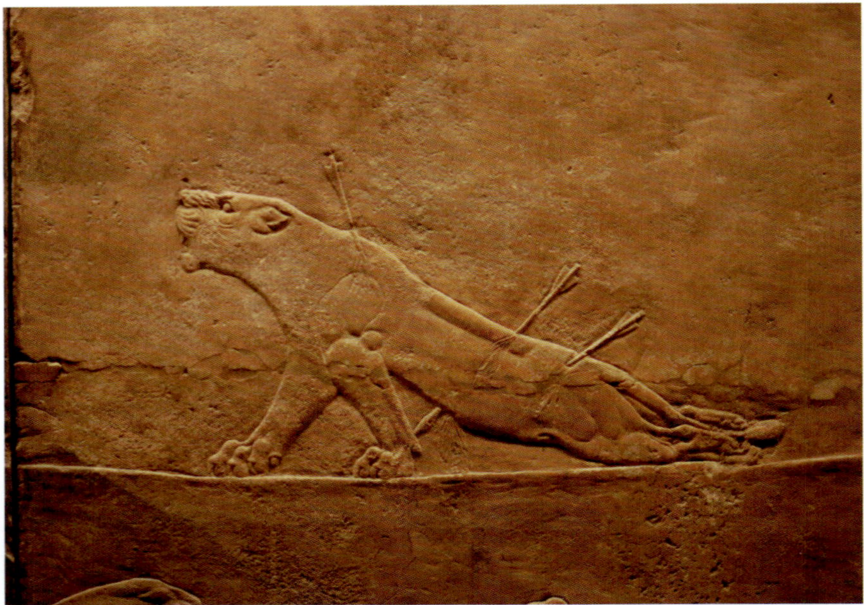

FIG. 2.4 Detail of Lioness Dying, ca. 645–640 BCE. From the palace of Ashurbanipal, Nineveh (present-day Kuyunjik, Iraq). British Museum, London. Gypsum alabaster.

of the king's arms, which draw from lower left to upper right. This connection between the king and the lion is something Ashurnasirpal makes very clear in one of his inscriptions: "I am king, I am lord, I am praiseworthy, I am exalted, I am important, I am magnificent…and I am a lion."

Ashurnasirpal's art was extremely influential for later generations of Assyrian rulers. Ashurbanipal, who ruled from 668 to 627 BCE, was not actually Ashurnasirpal's descendant by blood. Yet he certainly wanted to affiliate himself with Ashurnasirpal's reign, doing so through the selection of imagery and decorative motifs, most specifically the lion hunt. The king (wearing the same tripartite hat as Ashurnasirpal and sporting the same tightly woven beard) rides in his chariot. His bow is pulled tight, as is his focused gaze as he chases after the lions. Yet the scene does not quite sit right. Ashurbanipal knocks off a few rounds of arrows

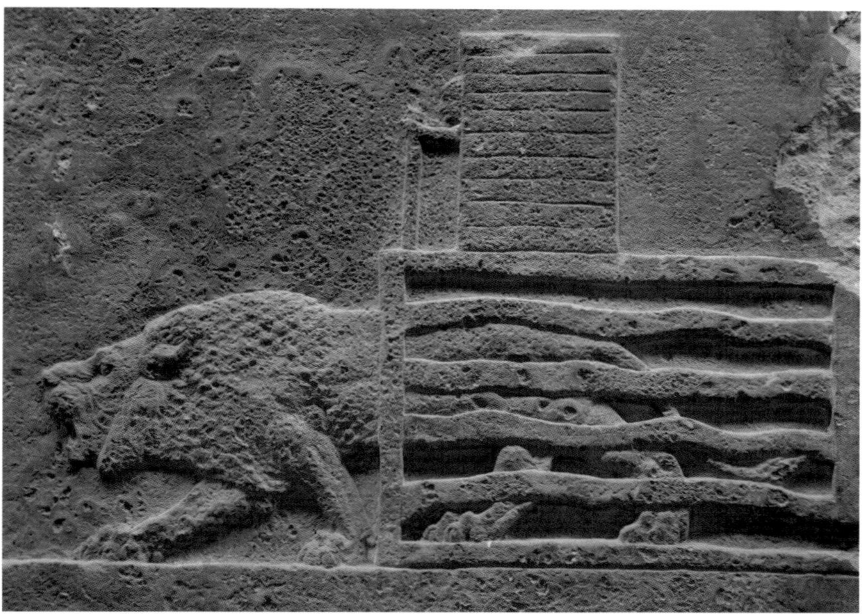

FIG. 2.5 Detail of lion being released from a cage, ca. 645–640 BCE. From the palace of Ashurbanipal, Nineveh (present-day Kuyunjik, Iraq). British Museum, London. Gypsum alabaster.

and then leaves the final killing to his minions. Lions lie in brutal slaughter in the chariot's wake, left to die, writhing in agony, twisting and tucking their heads in woeful and desperate pain. Majestic animals are shown in various modes of humiliation—vomiting, bleeding, limping, licking their wounds.

Then there is the lioness who wrinkles her nose as she cries out in pain (Fig 2.4). The deep, dramatic angle of her body heightens the sense of her misery. Our eye moves from her head along her muscular back to her hind legs, which she drags with great effort, and feet and legs that are impossible to distinguish because they have been so badly mangled, broken, battered. The arrows cut through her body utterly and entirely. Ashurbanipal admits that he cares not, describing the hunt in an inscription as "great sport." The lions were actually held in cages and let out for the king to catch within the confines of his playground (Fig. 2.5). Some scholars even believe that the lions were poisoned or drugged before the hunt during Ashurbanipal's reign. The cages are incompatible with the idea that the lion represents the nobility and ferocity of nature. This is sport. This is hubris and decay. When we see Ashurbanipal after the hunt, depicted in another one of the panels in the British Museum, he is relaxing, drinking, and gruesomely enjoying the view of the head of one of his enemies, which hangs upside-down from the branches of the tree like a big perverse jewel dangling on a necklace.

Ashurnasirpal's hunt retains the sense of the sacred. He repeatedly asserts that the hunt of the lions has been approved by the gods, and he shows himself pouring libations over the bodies of the lions just below the hunt. The Standard Inscription also stresses the fact that the lion hunt is divinely sanctioned. This cuneiform text is so called because it appears in almost the same form on every stone slab, repeated over and over. The inscription varies slightly, running from eighteen to twenty-six lines, but the focus is always on Ashurnasirpal's power, his titles, and his major achievements. It also emphasizes his connection with the gods, calling the king the "vice-regent of Ashur." It is no longer possible to see the inscription on the lion hunt panel because when these pieces were transferred to London, the texts were cut off and discarded. (You can just make out the cuneiform at the bottom of the panel.) This shaving may have facilitated transport of these pieces, but it certainly hinders a complete study of the original context of these texts. Indeed, some of the minor variations within the Standard Inscription include city names and regions. Without the accompanying texts it is impossible to identify the cities where the events depicted on the walls may have occurred. Not only were the panels sawed down to make them smaller, they were also shaved so that they would be thinner. This is quite something because there were also texts on the backs of the panels—more of the same inscriptions. Scholars have counted about four hundred or so incidents of the same Standard Inscription. Imagine how many more would have existed. The number may have even reached the thousands. Thus, Ashurnasirpal, through seemingly infinite af-firmations, was asserting that he was the representative of Ashur. Ashurnasirpal was also, in these many repeated inscriptions, establishing that all he did was protected and justified by Ashur himself, as his name means "Ashur [is] guardian of the heir."

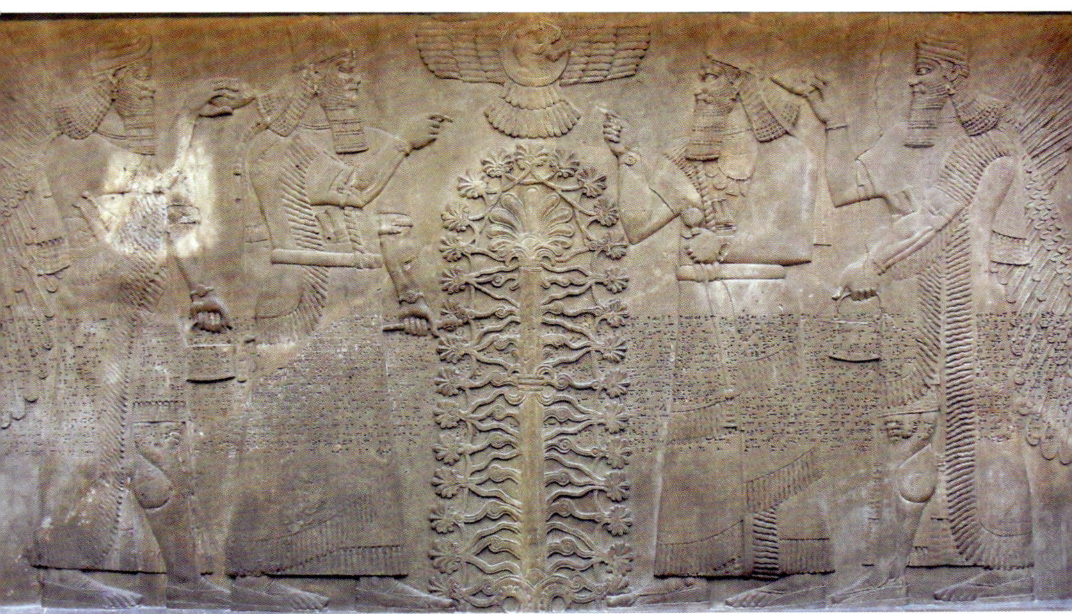

FIG. 2.6 Ashurnasirpal II at the Sacred Tree with the god Ashur above, ca. 883–859 BCE. From the palace of Ashurnasirpal II, Nimrud (Iraq). Room B, panel 23. British Museum, London. Gypsum alabaster, 195 × 432.8 cm.

He also asserted this connection artistically. If we move from the lion hunt panel, which appeared to the right of the throne, and look at the panel behind the throne, we again have the Standard Inscription (Fig. 2.6). In this instance, rather than dividing two registers, as in the lion hunt, the words cut across the bodies of the four large figures, literally inscribing them with the message of the king. This procession includes the king, whom we can identify by the tripartite hat and elegantly braided beard. But he appears not once but twice, shown from both sides. This might be a bit confusing, especially since the two versions of the same king show him doing different things. On the left side his right hand crosses over his breast, but on the right his hand stretches away from his body, showing a number of divine symbols. The left king's right hand points down to the floriated tree, known as the Sacred Tree. The right king's right hand points to a representation of

Ashur, who hovers in a round disk surrounded by fluttering wings. The mirroring of the king emphasizes his omnipresence and omnipotence. The two figures that follow Ashurnasirpal in the procession are genii—winged protective spirits that bless and purify the king with cone-shaped objects by which they sprinkle liquid from ritual buckets. These figures are fully divine, and yet they look like the king or rather the king looks like them. The message is that the king is everywhere. If he were sitting in his throne, directly in front of this particular panel, that mirroring effect would have come to life even more dramatically. Four figures would have been pointing toward him, while his body would have been encompassed by the Sacred Tree. Those radiating branches, shivering in coruscating divinity, would have seemed to surround him in a halolike glow.

The final crowning element is the figure above the Sacred Tree, where the winged wheel holds the god Ashur. It is natural to make connections between the standing figure of the king in the lion hunt and this depiction of the god. Because of the chariot, we see only the torso of Ashurnasirpal's body, just as we see only the head of Ashur. The king's bow has a round shape to it, just like the circle around the god. Neither the king nor the god fit entirely within the circumscribed space. Their heads protrude from the top of the sphere. The connection is most emphatic in the versions of Ashur that appear in other panels from the palace, in which the god holds a bow. The lion also participates in this sharing of visual forms or divine iconography. It is possible to see a spinning wheel etched into the upper region of the lion's right leg. This might just be a decorative rosette. However, after so many images of haloes and circumscribing forms with shivering rays, it is not unlikely that this might also be the mark of Ashur.

Those spinning wheels and halolike forms permeate the lion frieze in a way that encourages a sense of movement. We can read the frieze from the center, from the eye of Ashurnasirpal, as we have done. But we can also read from left to right. Starting with the shields held aloft by those dullards in the back, we can move through a series of rounded forms that includes the shape of the bow, rosettes, empty eyes. All those rounded forms, combined with the swiftness of the leaping horses, gives the reader the sense of an inexorable push forward, of the inevitability of the king's command over the lion and everyone else with whom he comes into contact. This is a visual manifestation of the way he describes himself in the first inscription we discussed—as a flood that consumes all in its wake.

That flood imagery comes to the fore in a passage showing the Assyrians crossing the Euphrates in another panel in the British Museum. Ashurnasirpal, the third man in from the left, stands on solid ground, waving the men forward into the sea. Blowing into animal skins, the soldiers create inner tubes upon which they float toward the citadel of Cardemish. If the representation on the walls has anything to do with what the men of Cardemish saw as they looked out into the sea, it is not too surprising that they had no interest in opposing the Assyrian ruler and instead offered many tributes. The movement and progression of these floating men is spectacular—the way their bodies lean on the curving, inflated animal skins and simultaneously arch backward for balance, the way their taut leg muscles kick at the water in the push forward, the way the men blow into the skins as they pull at the water with their right arms, their cupped hands. The spindly contours of the water move in variable ways—pushing and pulling, curling and wiggling. There is a lot of activity. Horses and boats and a couple of plucky-looking fish are all intertwined, blended in the sea. But the men are unified in their movement—strict in body and direction, left to right, shore to shore. Both aft and fore, and always at the helm, is the figure of the king. He stands at the beginning of the campaign, calling his men to action, and then he appears again, above the watery mass of men, elevated not only by the boat but also by the chariot in which he stands tall and above it all.

Ashurnasirpal is also above these watery scenes in the panels that accompany the crossing of the Euphrates. Here he is the king that kills. In this series his hunt is not relegated to large, vicious animals, although the outlines for this slaughter are quite similar. Like the bull and the lion, these men appear face-down under the arc of the leaping horses. These men are making the very pose of prostration and utter humility that they should have been making in the king's presence while they were alive. Deny Ashurnasirpal his due if you like, but ultimately you will do as he says, you will bow to his rule. You might think that your city walls will protect you. But that is foolhardy too. In a vehicle that looks not unlike a modern tank, Ashurnasirpal and his army move forward to lay siege to an unknown city. The extended arm of this seemingly anachronistic machine might not shoot cannon balls, but it quickly and efficiently decomposes the wall, smashing the towers that hold the fighting men aloft.

The repetition of the king, the anointing genii, the god Ashur, the cuneiform of that Standard Inscription draw the reader into and around the room. The visitor witnesses the events. Yet the closer we read, the more of the story that we follow, the more we become part of the story. This is not a passive experience. The connections we make go beyond the symbolic and formal. They become personal. We respect and mourn the bull, the lion. We are drawn into the frenzy of the battles. We are astounded at the men swimming on the skins. Like those dying men in the friezes, we become subjugated, literally turned into a subject of Ashurnasirpal. We can experience this sense of the images taking on a life of their own, of the immersion felt by the original audience through a video produced by Learning Sites.* The video draws us into the palace and shows how moving through these spaces was engaging and all-consuming, transformative. In order to see these panels you must walk around the space of the palace. In so doing you are enacting the stories, bringing them to life. And, whether you originally intended to or not, at the end of your journey through the panels you will have acknowledged and submitted to the king's vision of history and his own authority.

Magnificent hybrid beasts, known as lamassu, flanked every door, every moment of transition from one room to the next (Fig. 2.7). Despite a human head, which welcomes you with a slight smile, the bulk of the creature is animalistic, made up of a body that looks like a bull or (in this case) a lion with massive, expansive, multilayered wings. This colossus not only engages with the viewer frontally, acting as a massive totem, but when you walk along the side of the animal you realize that he too is walking. Human and animal, static and moving, watching and looking beyond you. The beast is divine too, as indicated by the horned cap that wraps around his head and those expansive flightless wings. Multiplicity, then, defines this beast. When the visitor first walks past the lamassu, he is many different, disparate beings and shapes and forms. The effect is

---

* "Digital Reconstruction of the Northwest Palace, Nimrud, Assyria," www.metmuseum.org/metmedia/video/collections/ancient-near-eastern-art/northwest-palace-nimrud.

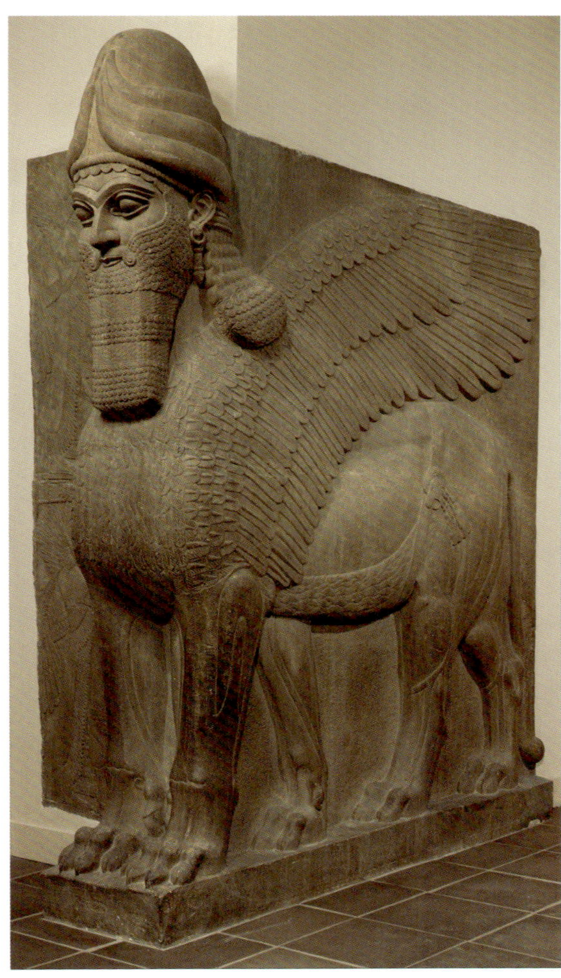

FIG. 2.7 Lamassu, ca. 883–859 BCE. From the palace of Ashurnasirpal II, Nimrud (Iraq). Metropolitan Museum of Art, New York City. Gypsum alabaster, 311.2 × 62.2 cm.

overwhelming. What is this beast? What is he communicating? When the visitor leaves the rooms, these incompatible parts actually do come together. Specific features that appear inside the room are repeated and synthesized in the body of the lamassu—the elegant beard of the king, the wings of the genii, the bodies of lions, and the panoramic view of the king's body as he hunts and walks and prays.

Thus the visitor undergoes a metamorphosis, a change from individual to Assyrian, from passive viewer to full participant in the sculpted drama. The lamassu also changes, transmogrifying into an entity that encapsulates or summarizes the experience of the throne room and all of its participants. Walking out the door, the visitor is now in step with the five-legged beast, continuing in that inexorable push forward promoted in the friezes.

Dante Rossetti, the Romantic artist, seems to have felt the same push. In his poem "The Burden of Nineveh," he describes a visit to the British Museum and what he termed a "winged beast from Nineveh": "A human face the creature wore, / And hoofs behind and hoofs before, / And flanks with dark runes fretted o'er. / 'Twas bull, 'twas mitred Minotaur, / A dead disbowelled mystery; / The mummy of a buried faith / Stark from the charnel without scathe, / Its wings stood for the light to bathe,— / Such fossil cerements as might swathe / The very corpse of Nineveh. . . . Its crown a brow-contracting load: / Its planted feet which trust the sod / (So grew the images as I trod); / O Nineveh, was this thy God?" Rossetti literally describes the images as growing.

This movement through the space of the palace also acts as a metaphor for the power of Ashurnasirpal that spread across the empire. In fact, the room is a microcosm of the entire state run by Ashurnasirpal. Carved representations of campaigns and conquest serve to act as a visual synthesis of the extent of the empire. When entering the room, the first carved panels that the viewer would have seen were images of men from subjugated regions bringing tribute to the king. In addition to the hunts and battles, there are men on parade, bringing status symbols and luxury goods representative of their territories. In one panel, a man enters the palace with two monkeys—one standing on his shoulders and one walking ahead on a leash. These animals suggest a close relationship with Egypt. Another man walking in the same panel has a soft, conical hat and shoes with tips that curl upwards, both of which are asssociated with Phoenician dress.

But even though these walls speak the age-old language of conquest and promote the absorption of powerful empires both culturally and politically, it is essential to establish that the decorative scheme—its form, its content, its expansiveness—was unprecedented. We have seen hints of Egypt in the styles and forms. But when Ashurnasirpal razed the old city of Nimrud to construct his palace—or, as he puts it, "removed the old hill of rubble"—he was making a monument that would visualize the new regime he was building. He was making something new, something surprising, and something otherworldly, marked by the divine.

The friezes in Ashurnasirpal's palace were all-consuming, innovative, and wildly colorful. Those carvings were painted. In fact, when writing about his palace, he does not once mention that stone of which we have become so fond. Ashurnasirpal mentions every other possible material—brick, at least forty types of wood, bronze. Yet the only stones he mentions are "red gold and shining," in other words precious or semiprecious jewels. He speaks of painting the walls with vivid blue paint and setting the walls with lapis lazuli–colored glazed bricks. Now imagine the Sacred Tree shimmering in golden hues, the blues of the waves of the Euphrates, the red of the wounds of the lion. A painted tile from the British Museum showing Ashurnasirpal in a procession gives evidence of the polychromy of the walls, though here too we must supplement the visual material. The yellows would probably have been far more golden, and the green would most likely have been a shade of red, an instability caused by the copper in the pigment. It's not easy to adjust your eye to that vision of the completely painted space. It might feel a bit garish. The producers of the Learning Sites video actually chose not to show the reliefs fully painted until the one panel at the end.

Ashurnasirpal's painted palace, his assertion of power and empire in the friezes, has a complicated epilogue. The video pulls together reliefs from a number of museums—Williams College Museum of Art, the Hood Museum of Dartmouth, and the Oriental Institute in Chicago. Two truncated deities are in the Kimbell Art Museum in Ft. Worth. Many panels are in the Metropolitan Museum of Art and the British Museum. Bits and pieces of Ashurnasirpal's empire have been disseminated throughout the world. We probably don't even know where all the relics of his empire are. In 1992 the scholar John Malcolm Russell visited the tiny school of Canford in England to see a series of plaster casts of Assyrian reliefs that were lining the walls of the cafeteria. Something did not seem right, and so he returned with the stone conservator from the British

Museum. After removing several layers of paint, it was revealed that the cast was the original stone. These pieces were sold at Christie's for $11.9 million in 1994 to the Miho Museum in Japan.

How does an Assyrian relief end up in the cafeteria of a tiny private school? This has much to do with Henry Layard, a twenty-eight-year-old adventurer, who started unearthing the treasures of Nimrud in 1845. (Layard also painted a series of imaginative re-creations of the complex at Nimrud.) His friend Stratford Canning, the British ambassador to the Ottoman Empire, gave him a grant of one hundred pounds and told Layard to "excavate and export to your heart's content." Layard did just that until 1847, when he returned to London to see his treasures in the British Museum. But he did not send all his booty to that one institution. He also shared some with his cousin, Lady Charlotte Guest, who happened to own the mansion at Canford before it became a school. Her delight in the monuments was both aesthetic and religious. In her extensive diaries she records parallels with the Bible, and she invited clergymen to her home to study ways that her cousin's remarkable discoveries could corroborate the Holy Scriptures.

Proof of the Bible, Victorian imperialism, interest in possible predecessors of Greek art, perspicacious collecting—many motivations underpin the interest in and the spread of Layard's loot. There was also a deepening scholarly fascination with these lost empires. The excavations of Nimrud did not end in 1847. They continued again in 1949 under the British School of Archaeology. This second phase was supervised by Sir Max Mallowan, who was known for his scholarship, the discovery of numerous Assyrian ivories, and his marriage to Agatha Christie, who took a number of documentary photos of their research and excavation. A third phase, undertaken by Iraqi scholars between 1988 and 1990, revealed tombs of Assyrian queens that held astonishing quantities of gold objects and jewelry. One tomb alone held 450 items of gold and silver that weighed at least fifty pounds each. With the outbreak of the First Gulf War in 1991, excavations, at least regulated ones, stopped. Those were terrible times. Sadly, they continue apace. The invasion of Iraq in 2003 unleashed a frightening illegal trade in antiquities, much facilitated by the destruction and looting of the Iraq Museum. In his book *The Thieves of Baghdad*, Matthew Bogdanos recounts the difficult quest to quell this pernicious market, which involved not just criminals and smugglers but dealers, brokers, and even professors and museum staff. Bogdanos, now the assistant district attorney in Manhattan, was a colonel in the Marine Corps Reserves at the time of the invasion and subsequent looting. In addition to tracking the pieces lost in looting, Bogdanos explains how he worked to create a dialogue between law enforcement and the academy, police and professors. In other words, an important part of saving the treasures was awareness, open dialogue, and mutual respect.

The image on the cover of Bogdanos's book is a majestic ivory plaque of Phoenician origin (Fig. 2.8). The piece was discovered at the bottom of a muddy well in the palace at Nimrud. In fact, this is one of the ivories that Sir Max Mallowan uncovered in his excavations. Perhaps the ivory was one of the gifts brought by Phoenician dignitaries, as represented in the tribute figures carved in the gypsum walls. A less well-preserved twin is housed at the British Museum. Considering the emphasis Ashurnasirpal placed on the colorful blues and reds of the walls of his palace, it is not difficult to imagine his deep appreciation of the gold leaf, lapis lazuli, and red carnelian stones that illuminate the ivory plaques. And Ashurnasirpal's great respect for the power of lions means these pieces would certainly have fit the aesthetic of his paradisiacal painted palace. The piece from the British Museum is safe. Sadly, the ivory from the Iraq Museum has not been recovered. Bogdanos was looking for it in 2003. Hopefully, somewhere, someone is looking for it now.

When Saddam Hussein was deposed in 2003, his palace, bizarrely enough, was covered in genii, kings, and paintings showing reconstructed life in ancient Assyria. Hussein's claim was that he was like the Assyrian kings. What we must remember, however, is not how these images were appropriated and interpreted by terrible regimes. Rather, we must focus on what they record about the Assyrians, what they tell us about lost civilizations, and what they mean for us today. These are vestiges of our collective human history.

The Metropolitan Museum of Art hosted an exhibition in 2014 called *Assyria to Iberia at the Dawn of the Classical Age*. The catalogue is incredible. The reviews are filled with praise. The show amasses a tremendous collection of pieces from Ashurnasirpal's world, pieces that in their country of origin were being attacked and destroyed. The Tomb of Jonah in Mosul (again, only twenty miles from

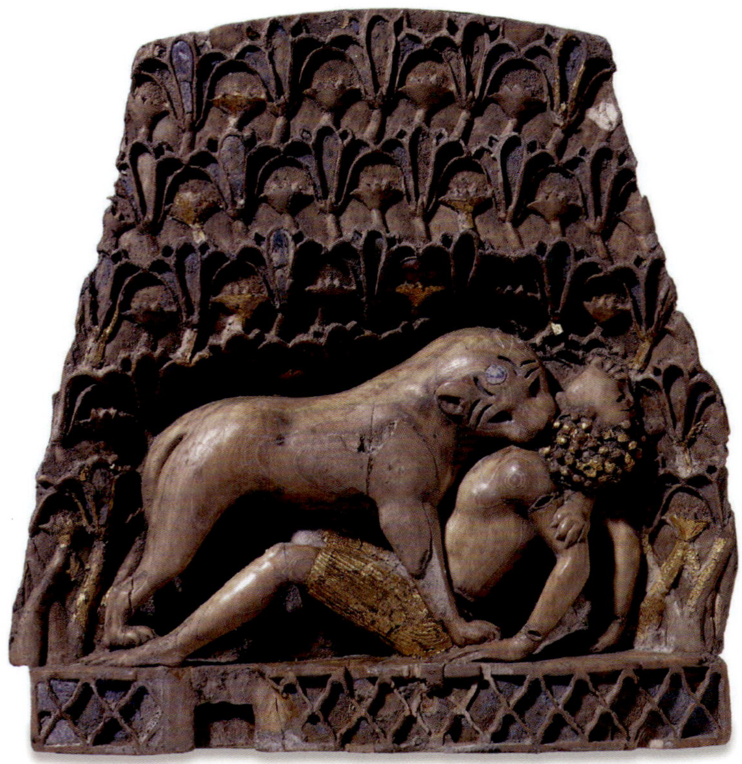

FIG. 2.8 Ivory plaque of a lioness devouring a boy, ca. 900–700 BCE. British Museum, London. Ivory, gold, cornelian, lapis lazuli, 10.35 × 10.20 cm.

Ashurnasirpal's palace) was blown up in July 2014. It was a sacred place for Jews, Christians, and Muslims. We have the lions of Ashurnasirpal; but the lions of Raqqa, two eighth-century BCE statues that once guarded the city of Hadatu, are lost forever. It is diabolical. It is criminal. It is terrorism. So what can we do? Maybe we aren't in Iraq or Syria, but we are part of these events. We are losers in this. We are losing our human heritage. One answer, and it is obviously not completely satisfying, is to be aware and to understand. Those people with guns and hammers are brutes. They lack all respect for religion, art, and life itself. By studying these stories and cultures, by talking about them, we can participate in spreading respect and a sense of the majesty and history of these pieces. At the very least, we can appreciate what we have in safe-keeping. Museums allow objects like the friezes of Nimrud to thrive and tell their histories. Museums can save us. Ashurnasirpal can speak to us from the distant past through the carvings of the gypsum walls, telling us about powerful rulers, sacred bodies, lost lands. He gives us that gift. And in return, we must spread that treasure, those stories and histories. It is incumbent upon us to do as those Assyrians did. We must walk the walls, we must undergo that transformation brought about by knowledge and visual stimulation, and we must leave ready to spread the word. Because that is how cultures are saved.

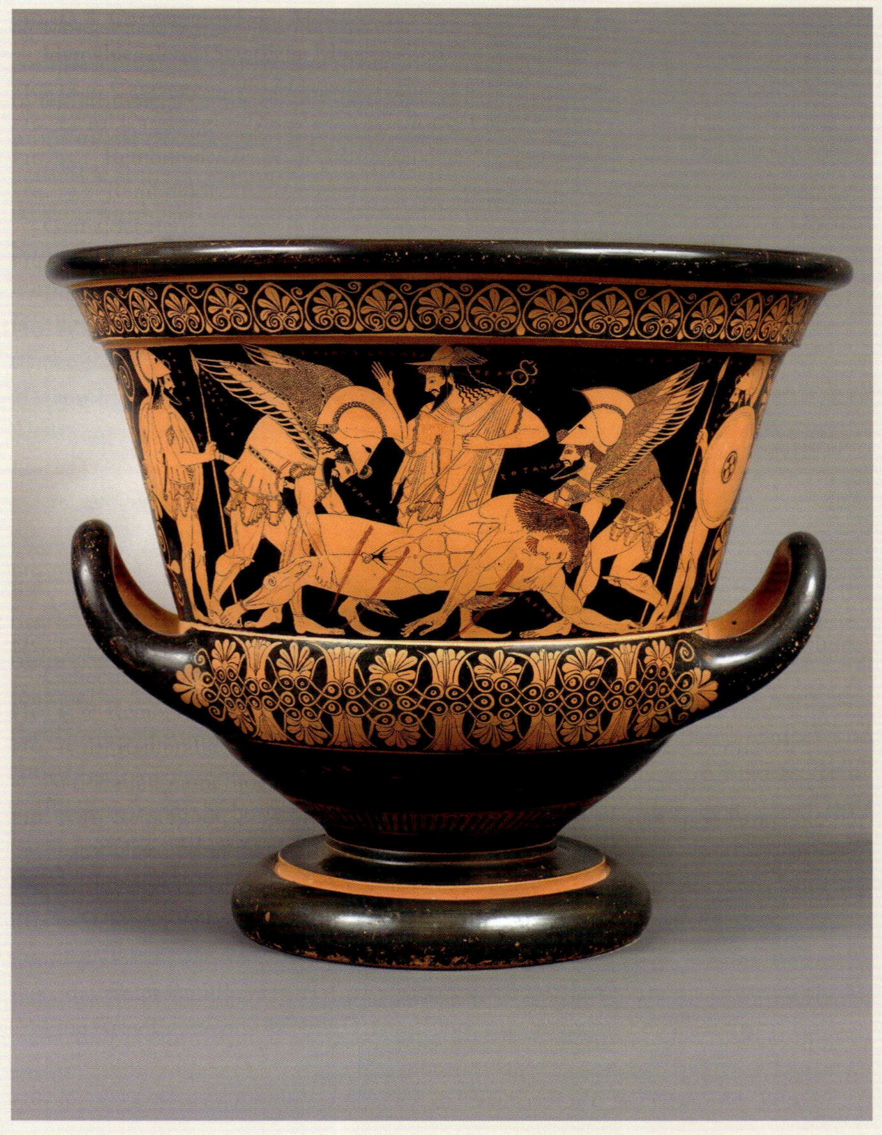

FIG. 3.1 Euphronios krater, front, ca. 515 BCE. National Museum Cerite, Cerveteri, Italy. Red-figure decoration on a ceramic calyx krater, 45.7 × 55.1 cm.

GREEK ART

Sarpedon is dying and being dragged across the body of a large ceramic vessel called a krater, dated to the sixth century BCE (Fig. 3.1). As he moves from life to death, from left to right, Sarpedon's body loses its breath, its spirit, its soul. Swiftly Hermes, whose name appears to the right of his winged helmet, moves behind the body of the hero, guiding the grim work of the two winged figures who seem to speak their names. On the left is Sleep or Hupnos. On the right is Death or Thanatos, whose words come out in retrograde or from right to left, mirroring the direction of his speech, of his breath. Sarpedon's name also appears, running along his lifeless left arm. Those red letters flow along his arm in a manner not unlike the diagonal streams of red blood coming from his body. Sarpedon's identity, his name, is now inextricably linked with his death.

Sarpedon appears in the *Iliad*, where he fights nobly for the Trojans against the Greeks. In the epic poem he is repeatedly likened to a lion. He is "strong as a lion raiding crook-horned cattle" and later "like a mountain lion starved for meat too long." Thus we have another noble, dying lion, just as we did in the Assyrian friezes. Sarpedon is brave, noble, unstoppable—until he comes up against Patroclus, that is, in book 16. Patroclus is on a rampage, brutally killing Sarpedon's Trojan comrades. Usually a sure shot, Sarpedon hurls a lance at Patroclus. But he misses. Twice. The poet tells us: "Again Sarpedon missed—over Patroclus' left shoulder his spearhead streaked, it never touched his body. Patroclus hurled next, the bronze launched from his hand—no miss, a mortal hit. He struck him right where the midriff packs the pounding heart and down Sarpedon fell as an oak or white poplar falls or towering pine that shipwrights up on a mountain hew down with whetted axes for sturdy ship timber—so he stretched in front of his team and chariot, sprawled and roaring, clawing the bloody dust. As the bull a marauding lion cuts from the herd, tawny and greathearted among the shambling cattle dies bellowing under the lion's killing jaws—so now Sarpedon, captain of Lycia's shieldsmen, died at Patroclus' hands and died raging still.... Death cut him short."

It is not fair. Sarpedon was the lion. Now he is the lion's prey? It is cruel and unexpected. Yet inversions of this sort, reversals and retractions, lead to the death of the noble, fallen oak of a man. Sarpedon was actually one of Zeus's offspring with a mortal woman. As the son of Zeus, one might suppose that Sarpedon would have had an advantage in this battle, unlike Patroclus whose parents were both mortal. Zeus does save Sarpedon from death in book 5. After being struck by a spear, Sarpedon's comrades lay the warrior under a large oak tree. The men push the spear shaft out through his wound and Sarpedon dies: "his spirit left him—a mist poured down his eyes…but he caught his breath again. A gust of North Wind blowing round him carried back the life breath he had gasped away in pain."

But in book 16 Zeus does not stop the death of Sarpedon. He considers it, crying out to Hera, his sister and his wife, "My cruel fate…my Sarpedon, the man I love the most, my own son.…My heart is torn in two as I try to weigh all this. Shall I pluck him up, now, while he's still alive and set him down in the rich green land of Lycia, far from the war at Troy and all its tears?" But Hera, in no uncertain terms, tells Zeus that it is a huge mistake to save his son. If he saves Sarpedon, she argues, then all of the other gods will save their own sons. Furthermore, the other gods would think less of Zeus, and disrespect would lead to disorder. Zeus acquiesces, but not before he bemoans the loss of his son, showering "tears of blood that drenched the earth." Zeus is undone, as is his capacity for protecting his son. Reversals define and frame these painful moments. When Sarpedon dies, the reader is reminded of that earlier instance when the hero comes back to life. In book 5, the removal of the spear strangely brings Sarpedon back to life—that's when his breath returns. In book 16, however, it is this action, the removal of the spear, that kills Sarpedon: "Patroclus…wrenched the spear from his wound and the midriff came out with it—so he dragged out both the man's life breath and the weapon's point together."

The painting on the pot is a beautiful exposition of the tale told in the *Iliad*. It is clear that the painter, Euphronios, knew his *Iliad*. (He signs his name under the upper row of palmette motifs—*Euphronios egrap*[*sen*].) Sarpedon's large, muscular body has fallen across the body of the pot in a way that is easily likened to a fallen oak or a white poplar. He is weighty and trunklike. Sleep and Death appear to be safely carrying the body back to Lycia, just as Hera promises they will in her conversation with Zeus. Euphronios gives the viewer enough of the story to know where we are in the *Iliad*, enough to know who is dying and why the gods are present. He uses text, these floating identifying inscriptions, to keep us grounded, to make us feel like we can read the pot and know what is happening.

But the painter, like the Homeric poet, inverts and subverts expectations. The scene does not stick to the script of the *Iliad*. In the epic poem, the god Apollo appears to stop the bleeding wounds of Sarpedon and sweeps Sarpedon off the battlefield. Hermes has no part in these activities. Yet here he is as a great master of ceremonies, orchestrating the move of this large man, like a conductor of a grand and tragic opera. High in the air, Hermes holds his baton, which is known as the caduceus, a staff reserved for heralds and messengers. The upheld caduceus and extended right hand made a V-shaped frame for Hermes's strict profile. From the torso up, Hermes looks like he is turned to face the left—he looks toward Hupnos/Sleep, and his shoulders seem angled in that same direction. Yet by the time we move down to his hips, it is clear that he is really darting to the right. The way the wings above his special shoes mimic the shape of those shoes heightens the sense of Hermes as a god on the move, moving quickly, with feet that can fly. The emphatic sense of speed and movement, that quick switch in direction, heightens the moment as a transitional one. Sarpedon is in the process of dying, and the selection of Hermes over Apollo highlights that point, draws attention to the fact that this is a moment of the in-between, the liminal. Hermes is, after all, the god of transitions, the protector of travelers, the conductor of souls after death.

Hermes quite resembles Thanatos/Death. His profile is almost an exact match in terms of the shape of the outline, the angle at which his head is placed, and the detailing. A delicate, single line marks both of their eyebrows, and the angular black beards jut outward, ending in a fine point, creating a shape that looks remarkably like the wings that decorate Hermes's shoes. Feathery beards and boots and hats create a circle around the body of Sarpedon, like a halo, creating a sense of weightlessness and airiness even while the body of Sarpedon is so heavy. The extended wings on the backs of the grim brothers participate in this circular dialogue of feathery forms. Like the wings on Hermes's hat, the wings of the brothers have the tiny, knotted forms, like miniature mosaics, tightly tessellated, and are finished with longer, sweeping plumes. The wings on the backs of Thanatos and Hupnos are dramatically expansive and ready to rise, which adds to this sense that Sarpedon is suspended amid a circular halo of wings.

The repetition of profiles and faces adds to this circular, centripetal motion. While the placement and profile of Thanatos's head is like that of Hermes, Hupnos and Sarpedon have the same connection, the same angle in their profiles. Sarpedon is most like Hupnos, more in a state of sleep than in a state of death. For now. But the dip in his head is lower than that of Hupnos. This deepening droop shows Sarpedon passing from sleep, with whom he is temporarily aligned, that of death. The feathery lashes that encompass the eyes of Thanatos are unlike those of his brother, but much like those of Sarpedon. We can just make out the iris of our hero as his heavy lid closes. His mouth, which is shaped much like his eye, also seems to be slowly closing. Teeth exposed, he grits out his final breath. Hupnos has jet-black hair. Sarpedon and Thanatos have blond hair, indicated by the lighter shading to their flowing locks. One final detail suggests a deeper tie between Sarpedon and Thanatos—the decorative feature at the base of the shin guard worn by both figures. This little anklet ties together with a little bow. Thanatos has it. Sarpedon has it. But Hupnos does not. Our reading of Sarpedon's dying takes us around this foursome in circles. We can start with Hermes who looks at Hupnos, who looks like Sarpedon, who subtly and slowly becomes more like Thanatos as he is dying. Thanatos's profile is positioned to look like Hermes. Thus a circular composition, facilitated by mirroring and repeated forms (wings, beards, and faces), shapes the scene. The circles on Hermes's caduceus, which looks like a hovering tuning fork, almost seem to set the tone for the circular composition below.

The encompassing combination of Hupnos, Thanatos, and Hermes also indicates a different destination than that described in the poem. In the *Iliad*, Hupnos and Thanatos take Sarpedon back to his home, to "the broad green land of Lycia," so that his brothers and countrymen can bury him with full royal rights. The pot seems to be skipping that step, however, and instead describes Sarpedon's entry into the Underworld. The dark, black background of the Greek krater might make us think of that space of the murky unknown, which is characterized by a darkness. Things are upended in this world of death. Men and women lack all strength and purpose, wit and agency. It's a grim fate for all, but especially for Sarpedon who, in life, is the antithesis of these characteristics—he is noble, clever, and active, and speaks beautifully when he encourages his men on the battlefield.

The loss and tragedy of the youthful warrior cut down in the prime of his life inspired a prominent form of statuary in the Greek archaic world. The modern name for these statues is *kouros* (or *kouroi* in the plural), which translates to young male. *Kouroi* statues were used to mark the graves of the young men. These massive carvings, which could stand as much as ten feet tall, celebrated the nobility and virility of these young men, while also memorializing or grieving the loss of those same characteristics.

The Anavysos Kouros (so named because of the city in Greece from which the piece came) is a perfect and idealized version of Attic manhood (Fig. 3.2). He has beautifully symmetrical features, his shoulders are broad, and his muscles are defined and powerful. He walks authoritatively into our space with a slight smile, the so-called archaic smile, which brightens and enlivens his marble face. There is a space between his body and his arms. This denies the weight of the stone, suggesting movement and vitality, as does the fact that the arms angle backward, making it look as though the body is pitched forward. The same vivacity appears in the face of a young man from Cyprus dated to the first half of the fifth century BCE, now at the Metropolitan Museum of Art. Before the loss of this youth's legs, he too would have stepped forward with his left leg, with confidence. He too has those high cheekbones, the prominent nose, that perky smile.

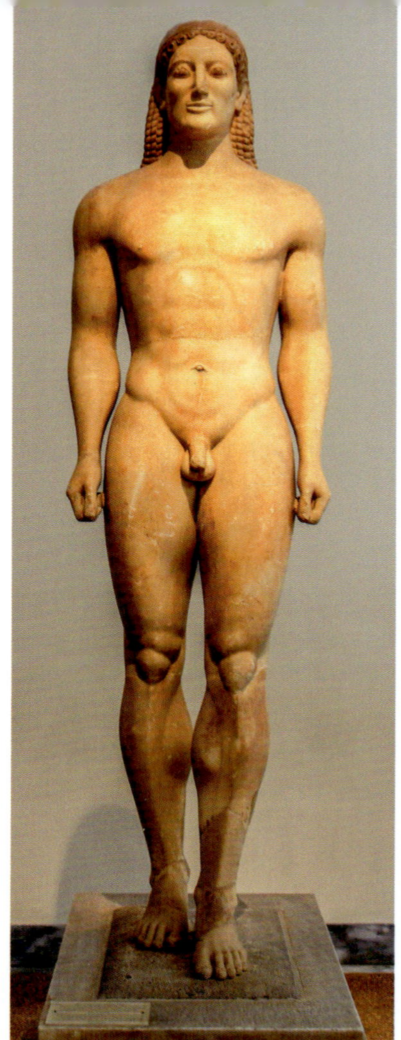

FIG. 3.2 Anavysos Kouros, ca. 530 BCE. National Archaeological Museum, Athens. Marble, 193 cm.

But the Cypriot was meant for a sanctuary, as a worshipper or guardian of that space. The Anavysos *kouros* speaks the language of death. An inscription at the base of the statue mourns a death and gives the name: "Stay and mourn at dead Kroisos' tomb / Whom in the first ranks raging Ares did destroy." Thus Kroisos, this handsome youth, died at the hands of the cruel and raging god of war, Ares. Kroisos and Sarpedon have a lot in common—they are both tall, weighty, and emphatically muscular. Their hair falls in tight, regularized curls, held down with a thin diadem. Even their feet are placed similarly—left in front of right. If we were to imagine Hupnos and Thanatos, after washing Sarpedon of his blood-ied wounds, setting him upright, he would look quite like Kroisos. And there is something quite striking about the idea that the *kouros* statue is on Kroisos's tomb. The image, the statue, is his shrine. Similarly, the image of Sarpedon is like a shrine. We look at his image on the pot and remember the fallen hero. In fact, the depiction of his body looks like a long marble altar or shrine.

Was Kroisos quite so young when he died? Did he look anything like this statue? Well, probably not. His statue is the embodiment of youth and strength and vigor. These ideals trump realism. Sarpedon was theoretically not so young either. The artist has given him a clean-shaven face, with hints of youthful down on the upper part of his jaw. In the epic poem Sarpedon is married and has a child, and he is also the commander of all Trojan allies, not a job for a sapling. Yet the painter is not interested in the exact version of Sarpedon provided by the poem. He wants to draw attention to the tragedy, to focus our attention on suffering and on the loss of youth. The painter also takes artistic license in the way he represents the wounds—the gaping holes with those unstoppable streams of blood. It is only once that Patroclus hits our hero in the poem, but the painter stabs him three times, again heightening the drama, gore, and pathos.

Those effusive wounds might remind us of another feature at funereal sites, ceramic vessels that were also used to mark the tombs of dead men. The funerary krater from the Dipylon Cemetery belongs to one of the earliest Attic pottery styles, the Geometric period (Fig. 3.3). Scholars have a specific periodization for these styles. The "geometric" aspects of this piece are easy to recognize. Bodies are composed of shapes and forms. Arms become rectangles that frame simple circular faces with single dots for eyes. Upside-down triangles are torsos. Thick, almond shapes make thighs and also form the massive posts on the bier that support the dead warrior. The faces of the mourning men—circles with dots for eyes—seem to reappear behind the funereal bier, this time as disembodied heads. However, it is hard to know for certain that these are faces of mourning men, because when those shapes appear under the funeral bier, where sacrificial animals gallivant, they seem to be something else entirely—abstract, inscrutable forms. Checkerboards and chevrons frame the scene of mourning, where bodies

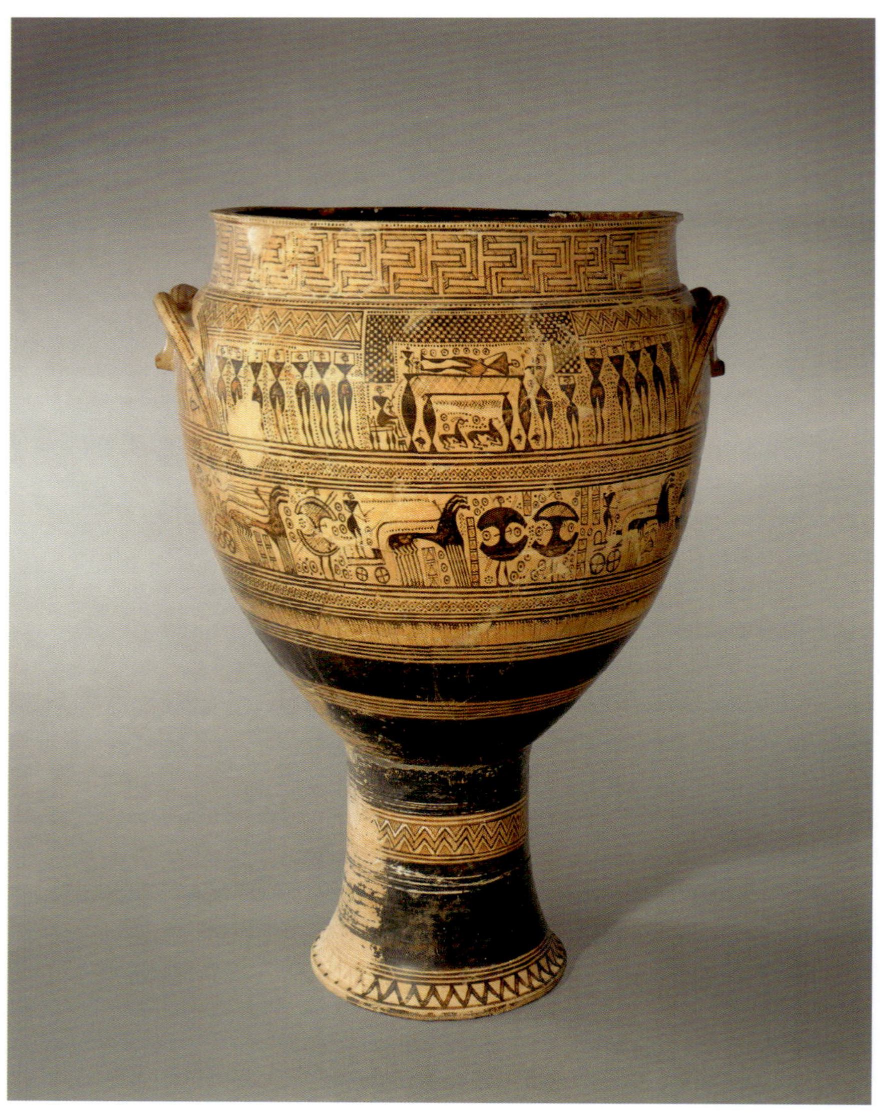

FIG. 3.3 Terracotta krater, from the Dipylon Cemetery. Attributed to the Hirshfeld Workshop, Athens, ca. 750–735 BCE. Metropolitan Museum of Art, New York. Ceramic, 108.3 × 73.4 cm.

are reduced to their most essential. Soldiers below *are* their weapons. Their bodies, their essence, cannot be extracted from what they do, which is to wield weapons. The bodies of the figures above are similarly defined by their sorrow. They are abstracted versions of themselves, repetitious representations of woe. They are not individuals. They are not the graceful bodies we see in the scene of Sarpedon.

These two vessels are perhaps not so far from each other as we imagine, however. Both vessels show scenes of sorrowful deaths. In fact, it is most likely that the unnamed man on the Dipylon krater is a soldier because of the militaristic activities shown below. Thus both men were fighters, and both appear to have had a wife and young children. We know this of Sarpedon from the poem and of the unnamed warrior on the Dipylon krater by the female figure to the left of the funereal bier, the small child on her lap, and the children standing at their father's feet. Both vessels are kraters, a word that comes from the Greek verb "to mix," most often referring to the mixture of water and wine. (Drinking wine neat was something only barbarians did, and it was a sure way to become completely insane, as the Greek writer Herodotus tells us in his *Histories*.) In the early Greek tradition, with pottery from the Geometric period, these vessels were used as grave markers, like the statuary of the *kouroi*.

Yet in this case the krater was not only a marker of the dead young warrior; it was also a means of communicating with or providing for the lost family member. A hole in the bottom of the krater allowed the mixture of wine and water produced by the family in this world to seep into the grave of their lost son, into the subterranean world below. Thus the family could connect with him one last time and provide him with sustenance for his journey to the Underworld. The Sarpedon krater would not have been used as a funerary marker in this manner. It seems this tradition did not continue much later than the Geometric period. However, there are ways in which the original purpose of the krater, as a conduit to the underworld, was retained in the later red-figure pottery, even though those earlier traditions were no longer alive. That theme of transitioning from life to death is retained in the narrative of Sarpedon on the pot. And it is hard not to see the wounds of Sarpedon, the way in which the wine-red blood pours from his body, which is simultaneously the body of the vessel, as being like the holes in the earlier Greek pottery, like the holes in the krater from which wine flowed into the graves below. The depiction of Sarpedon—the form of the pot and the form of the painted funeral—points to the historical past, to the earlier and lost traditions of uses for the krater. It is a tool of memorialization on many levels, reminding us of its original purpose, just as it honors and memorializes youths lost to wars.

Unlike the grave markers, our later krater was made for a symposium, which is what is depicted in this painted tomb found in Paestum, what was at the time a major Greek site and is now in the Italian region of Campania (Fig. 3.4). "Symposium" literally means drinking together, and it was in essence a big boozy party for wealthy upper-class men. The participants would gather together after a meal, mix wine in a large krater, say a few prayers, recline on couches, and then drink all hours of the night while listening to music. If it sounds like a frat party, that is basically the idea. Men would band together and solidify their friendships in small social groups called *hetaireiai* or companionships. They even played drinking games. Not Beirut or flipcup, something a bit more languid, though still requiring "skill," like *kottabos*, the game depicted on the back of the tomb. Here the participant throws or flings the last dregs of his wine from his drinking cup at a particular target, like a statuette or a lampstand. The most hits meant the most points, and that determined the winner.

Wine and their painted containers were central to the symposia—both in the sense that these were the key to all of the fun, but also because they were physically, literally, in the center of these rooms. You, the symposiast, have to walk up to the vessel. You have to lean over it to get more wine. You have to walk around it to see your friends. Thus we must think of the pot as a three-dimensional object. These are not images that are to be seen as framed paintings on a wall. Nor are the two sides supposed to be discrete, separated scenes. They are meant to be read together. Take, for example, an amphora from the Museum of Fine Arts, Boston, in which two athletes practice their jumping skills. On one side we see the men airborne with their arms bent at their elbows, parallel to their shoulders, with their fists clenched. When the pot is turned around the bodies of the boys are jumping, but now we see their sinuous backs, and they have extended their arms. They are shapely and handsome, all vim and vigor. Their suspension in midair makes us almost suspend our breath—in admiration, in adoration.

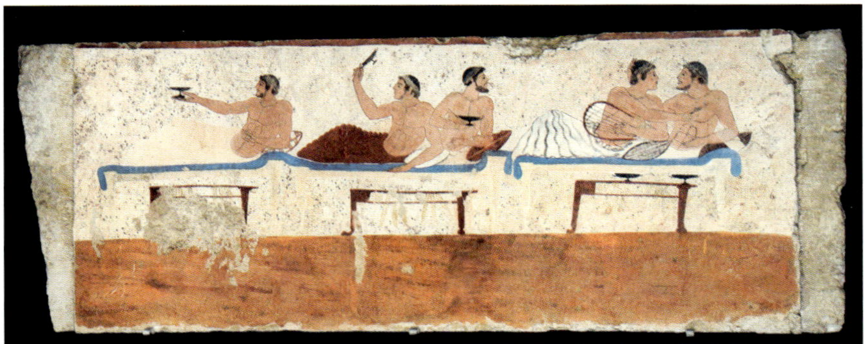

FIG. 3.4 Interior of the Tomb of the Diver, north panel. ca. 470 BCE. National Archeological Museum of Paestum, Paestum, Italy. Painted limestone, 78 × 212 cm.

In fact, that is literally what the amphora asks us to do, to admire the athletes. On one side the inscription tells us the names of the boy on the right (Aineas) and the piper (Kallipides). Below, it says, "Leagros is handsome" (*Leagros kalos*). On the opposite side we get the name of the second boy in retrograde (Smikythion) and again in retrograde, flowing along their bodies, "Leagros is handsome, yes indeed!" Leagros is nowhere to be found on the pot. In fact, he is probably not a particular individual at all but an idealized notion of a man. The *Leagros kalos* trope appears in thousands of forms, on pottery, on walls as graffiti, and, according to textual sources, was even carved on trees. Other names are associated with *kalos* on ceramic vessels from the period, but Leagros seems to have gotten a great deal of play. He is even mentioned on the Sarpedon vessel. In retrograde, moving away from the helmet of Hermes, the inscription tells us the same, *Leagros kalos*. When we turn the vessel around, Leagros's name reappears, hovering above the head of a soldier who bends over to fix the armor for his left shin. (Fig. 3.5)

The dialogue between two sides of these vessels provides a sense of that lightness of being—jumps are joyous, as are the compliments that are completed by reading from one side to the next. But there is something simultaneously weighty, a gravitas that pervades, especially in the case of the Sarpedon krater. That compliment to Leagros is accompanied by men preparing for battle: Hypeirochos,

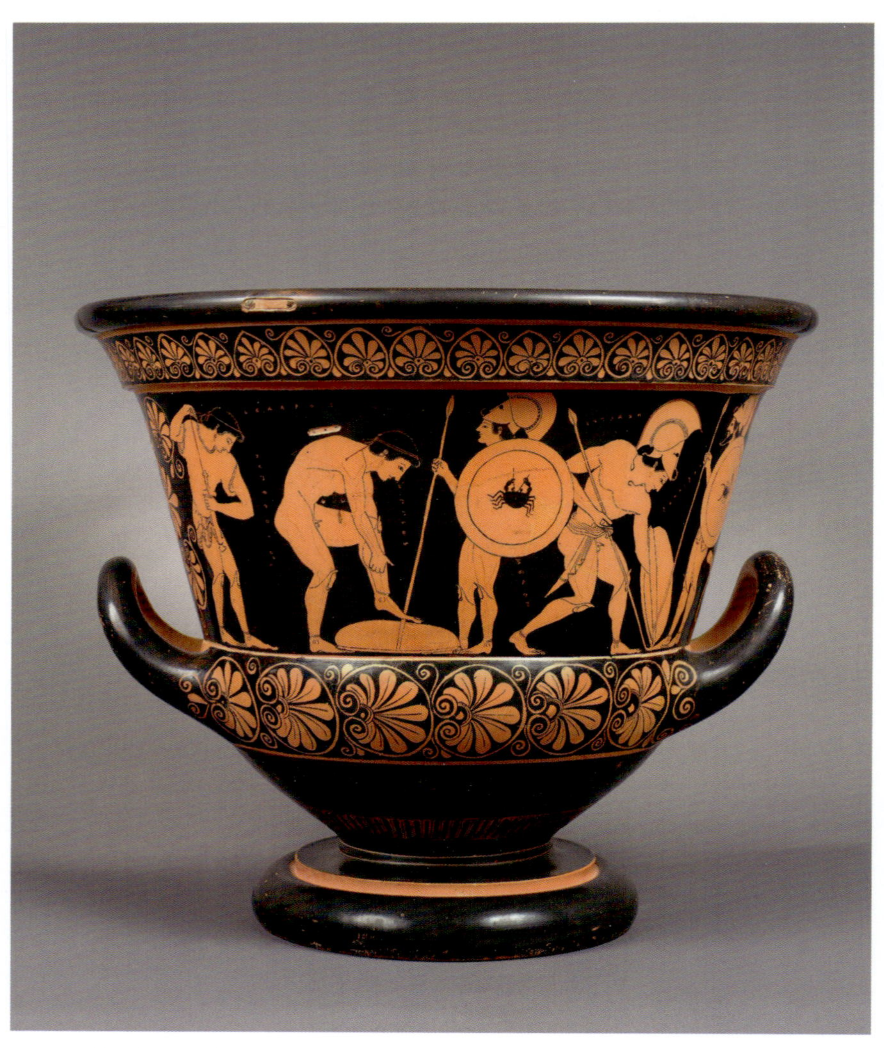

FIG. 3.5 Euphronios krater, back, ca. 515 BCE.

Hippasos, Medon, Akastos, Axippos. It is almost as though we are hearing the roll being called as these men gear up for war. These are specific names, but they are not attached to any historical figures. Rather, these are examples of the kind of men that bravely fought during the wars described in the *Iliad*, and ideally the kind of men prepared to fight in future wars. Their actions and poses add further pathos and weight to the scene of Sarpedon. Medon's head turns in the same direction as that of Hermes, while Akastos's legs are positioned to look like Hermes's legs. The sense of Hermes being in two places at the same time, moving from this world to the next, is thus heightened by the combination of figures on the second side of the vessel. The way Hippasos leans over makes us think of Hupnos. In fact, Hippasos's pose is just like that of Hupnos—head down, back hunched, arms extended. Will these men become like Hupnos? Will they too travel into the Underworld, the world of eternal sleep?

Finally, the fanning fingers of Akastos are accordion-like and exactly like those of the dying hero. Those cascading fingertips further the sense of Sarpedon's elegance at the time of death—how he can be graceful even when the scene is gruesome, how he was once like the men readying for battle, and how death cut him short. Thus, when the two sides of the vessel are brought together, as scenes of young men going to war on one side lead us to a young man dying because of war on the other, the message of the painted vessel becomes all the more profound and weighty.

Even small details toggle between serious and light. Take the crab on Medon's shield. It is supposed to be threatening, like the scorpion that appears on the shield to the far right, held by Axippos. These are dangerous animals with hard, protective exoskeletal shells. The selection of a crab is significant. The Greek word for crab means "hard shell." Of course the shield itself is a hard shell. By carrying the shield aloft, the soldier becomes like a crab, wearing his own hard shell. But this particular crab is kind of fooling around. He seems to be playing with his antennae. Perhaps he is preparing for battle, like the soldiers. Or perhaps he is playing music, as one scholar has suggested, using his pincers to play his antennae, making them sing, which might mean that his legs are splayed because he is actually dancing. The message is complicated. Like the crab, the tone is

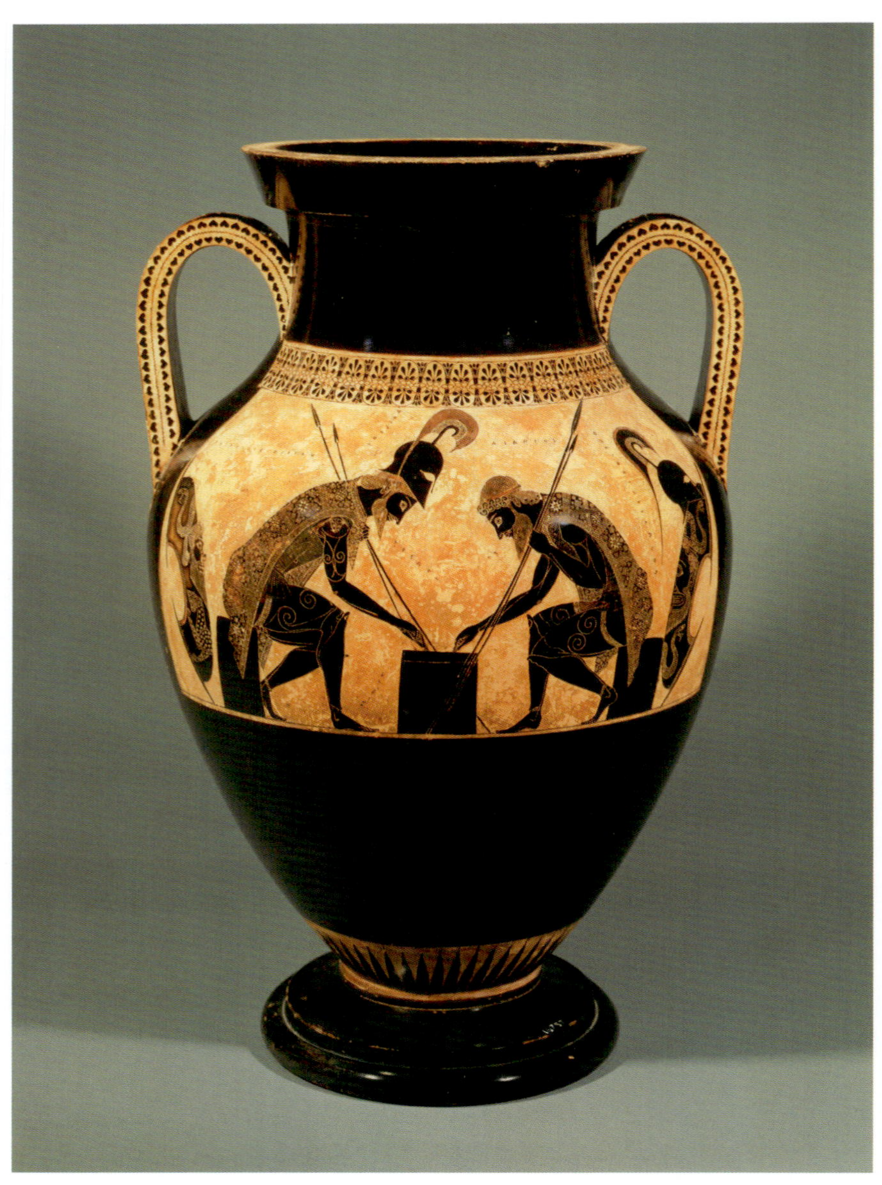

FIG. 3.6 Ajax and Achilles Playing a Game, ca. 540–530 BCE. Vatican Museums, Vatican City. Black-figure decoration on a ceramic amphora, 61 cm.

both intimidating and engaging, threatening and welcoming—and these kinds of complexities add a depth and weight to the first side, to the depiction of Sarpedon.

This blending of two seemingly incongruous tones—light and serious—also appears on an amphora signed by Exekias (Fig. 3.6). Dated to ca. 540–530 BCE, this vessel shows two of the most famous heroes from the *Iliad*, Ajax and Achilles. Not unlike Thanatos and Hupnos, the two men bend over, weighted down by their elaborate armor and by the tension of the game upon which they are so intently focused. It is just a simple board game. Yet the die that they cast is a rather more serious affair and has implications beyond the board. In retrograde Ajax calls out three (*tria*). Achilles calls out four (*tesara*). Achilles is the clear winner both in the number and his position, which is elevated. He sits on a higher stool than Ajax, and his powerful helmet glowers over the unprotected crown of Ajax. Achilles is grander, stronger, and better prepared for the battle or for the game. He is the central hero in the *Iliad*, the leader of the Greeks, noble and beloved by the gods. In many ways he is one of the gods. Like Sarpedon, Achilles is part man and part god. Although not described in the *Iliad* specifically, the tradition recorded by later writers held that Achilles' mother, Thetis, dipped her son into the river Styx in order to make him immortal.

But she held him by his heel and in so doing left him vulnerable in just that one area—the Achilles' heel. It is precisely this body part that the artist hides from view, perhaps as a means of intimating Achilles' mortal weakness. The artist hides his weak spot and showcases his glorious, godlike nobility. But we know he is going to die. That death happens outside of the *Iliad*, although his death is expressly predicted throughout. Just as death is foreshadowed and predicted, there is a certain sense that these men will be called back into battle at any minute. The immediacy of war surrounds and frames the two men. Ominous shields watch over the backs of the two soldiers with wide, gorgonlike eyes and wickedly elongated smiles. Achilles keeps his helmet on, and both men grasp their spears with tightly clenched hands. These same spears create an important set of diagonals that draw the eye of the viewer to the table upon which the men play the game. Again, war and play are strangely intertwined. There is a sense that the risk and chance taken in battle can be equated with rolling the dice, with the luck of the draw. Perhaps this is why their names are written in the genitive, which is the possessive case. Aiantos means *of* Ajax. Achileos is *of* Achilles. The men, their identities, their names, their portraits—are defined by the throw they make, the lot they draw in life. Achilles is defined by the throw *of* Achilles. Thus winning and losing is not just specific to the game, it has grander, more serious implications.

While the complex blending of light and serious links the Sarpedon krater and the Achilles amphora, there is a clear break in terms of technique, the shift from black-figure to red-figure painting. This term refers to the color of the figures. In the case of the Ajax and Achilles amphora the figures are painted in black. In the case of the figures in the Sarpedon krater, the painting is only in the background, leaving the figures in reserve, thus as red figures. This latter style did not become prominent until around 530 BCE. Until this point black-figure painting dominated, and had done so since as early as 700 BCE.

So why the change? Some scholars have argued that the shift happened because artists were hoping to show more accurate representations of space and anatomy. But it is just as likely, as the scholar Richard T. Neer has suggested, that the opposite was true, that it was the invention of red figure or the experimentation with this technical inversion itself, which encouraged an exploration into naturalistic forms, foreshortening, and the like. This might just be a chicken-and-egg situation, another reversal, this time a scholarly one. Yet I think Neer's argument is compelling. The switch from black on red to red on black was a novelty, and artists were keen to show new ways of being virtuosos, of being on the cutting edge. There are a number of bilingual pots from the period where neither side is superior. The artist is saying he can do both types of painting styles. And it might have ended there. However, this reversal seems to have opened up a new way of thinking, a new way of approaching these rounded vessels. It was not until about fifteen years after the development of red-figure painting that Greek pottery shows evidence of an interest in developed pictorial space and anatomical foreshortening. Yet this technical inversion allowed artists to play with depth, to manipulate the picture plane in a way that was not possible with the black-figure forms.

Black-figure painting still conveys a sense of drama, as in the case of the Ajax and Achilles amphora. Yet Ajax and Achilles seem to be floating on top of the body of the vessel. Sarpedon seems to be emerging from those surroundings, emerging out of that black background. The incisions used to create the musculature of Ajax and Achilles are clearly the work of a stylus, which gives their anatomy a static quality, a more geometrical and stylized form. Sarpedon's body seems to exist despite outlines. Those lines are suggestive, not definitive, and this gives his form a sense of fluidity, of a more organic presence. There is a particularly masterful moment in the foreshortening of his lower left leg. The knee enters into our space; the foot falls behind. Sarpedon's body drags through space and rounds the body of the vessel with weight and conviction. Thus the body of the vessel and the body of the hero are all the more in sync. And ultimately the body of Sarpedon *is* the body of the pot. The colors and forms of the bodies on the red-figure vessel are composed of the terracotta (or cooked earth) that defines the vessel, that *is* the vessel. We may never know whether the transition from black figure to red figure inspired an interest in anatomy or the interest preceded the technological shift. What we can say with certainty is that these artists were pushing the parameters of pot and paint.

The purpose of this enterprise would seem to be a new means of catching the attention of the viewer. More robust and fleshed-out anatomy, curving bodies, foreshortened forms—these were ways of drawing in the viewer, of suggesting deeper and more clever capacities of representation, of image production.

Another insistent feature of the vase is the presence of eyes, an ambiguity wherein the pot appears to look back at the viewer. Leodamas and Hippolytos, two soldiers at the far ends of the composition, watch intently as Hermes guides the body away. So do Hupnos and Thanatos. Twice over, in fact, as their helmets repeat their eyes—contrasting black, dead eyes with their bright, enlivened eyes below. Even Sarpedon is fighting to keep his eyes open. And these eyes are emphatically forward-looking. The eyes are set to be frontal, as though the men are looking straight at us, even though the profile of their heads says that they are technically not. The patterned palmettes participate in this riddle of looking. In the lower register the looping fronds are filled with forms that remind us of the shapes on the Dipylon krater, those round forms with centrally placed dots. They might be decoration, further stylization. Or maybe they are heads. Maybe they are eyes. Maybe the forms in the loops are eyes too, like those on the shields of Achilles and Ajax, watching us watching them. This might seem a bit far-fetched, but eyes were painted on many kalyx pots from the period, cups called eye-cups. As the drinker pulled the cup to his mouth, he would be showing his symposiast friends a pair of wild eyes. The vessels energetically point to the act of looking—in a manner that is, again, both amusing because of the eyes and not a little aggressive.

The artists are an integral part of this experience—they are also telling us to look carefully. As we know, Euphronios places his name to the right of Hermes's hat, just above the name of the god, and tells us that he is the painter. Euxitheos, known as the potter, signs his name in a diagonal. He writes *Euxitheos Epoiese* or "Euxitheos created this." How striking it is that he places his name next to the spear of the standing soldier. Perhaps this is a way of asserting his role as a crafts-man, as a man that works with tools to shape the pot or mark incisions in the forms. Clearly there is a great pride taken in the production of this masterful pot. Because of the remarkable skill of the red-vessel artists, scholars have placed Eu-xitheos and Euphronios in what they call the Pioneer Group. It has been argued that the pieces produced by these men exploited the shift from black figure to red to its fullest capacity. Still, it is important to be careful with terminology like the Pioneer Group. The idea of an individual artist who joins similarly minded craftsmen in order to challenge the status quo is perhaps a bit anachronistic. This is not a school of rebels like the Impressionists. These artists were exploring new forms, not trying to break with tradition. It is also important to establish that the artists, Euphronios and Euxitheos, cannot be approached in the way we think of artists like Rembrandt, Raphael, or Caravaggio. We will never know where Euphronios trained or what his philosophies were. We will never be able to con-struct a biography of him. In fact, a number of vessels have his signature but are nothing alike. The signature signifies something more than just the identity of an individual. The name Euphronios is suspiciously close to the Greek word for well-meaning (*eu* = well and *phronios* = intended). The artist may have chosen to sign his name with a play on words, as a way of telling the viewer to enjoy the experience of the pot, a big "you're welcome." The name may be a benign joke, as slippery as the pseudonym used by Odysseus—Outis, "no one."

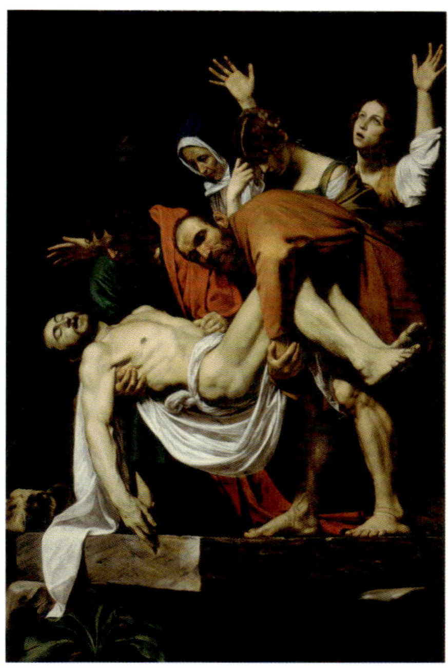

FIG. 3.7 Caravaggio, *Deposition of Christ,* ca. 1600–1604. Pinacoteca Vaticana, Vatican Museums, Vatican City. Oil on canvas, 300 × 203 cm.

We cannot superimpose our modern connotations of "The Artist" on the names painted on the pots. But strangely there is an anachronistic spin that we can take, strangely, even though it is unsettling to do so. Glibly, the scholar Karl Schefold wrote in 1972 of the Euphronios krater, "Thus begins the history of one of the fundamental images of western art, which will culminate in scenes of the deposition of Christ." When you look at the *Deposition* by Caravaggio, you have to admit there is something to it (Fig 3.7). Christ's blanched body drags across the canvas not unlike the drawn body of Sarpedon. Just as the body of Sarpedon is all terracotta, all the body of the vessel, the whiteness of Christ's form might make us think about the canvas underneath. Christ's fingers roll over the slab of stone with delicacy, in a way that might remind us of the dragging, fanning fingers of Sarpedon. The bleeding wounds of Sarpedon seem to reappear in the shock of red produced by the robe of John the Evangelist hanging diagonally. What were streams of painted clay are now deeply cut folds in the heavy painted garment. John and Nicodemus hunch over, like Hupnos and Thanatos, as they lower the weighty and muscular body of Christ into the tomb below. Darkness pervades and surrounds the figures, like the blackness of the Attic pot. Mary Magdalene holds hands in a gesture that reminds us of Hermes's upheld hand, she who was a similarly transitional figure—from sinner to saint. The comparison is truly seductive. But it is false. Greek ceramic ware was probably known in Italy in the sixteenth century, but it was not starting to be collected until the mid-1600s. And a real interest in this pottery belongs to a much later period, predominantly in the eighteenth century.

It is possible that Caravaggio saw a few pieces of Attic pottery. But it is entirely impossible that he would have seen the Euphronios krater, because this object was not unearthed until 1971. The moment of the piece's discovery is quite precise and very scandalous. The piece was purchased by the Metropolitan Museum of Art, under the auspices of the director at the time, Thomas Hoving. Hoving purchased the krater from Robert E. Hecht in 1972 for $1.2 million. Hecht claimed to have acquired the piece from a family who had had the vessel since 1920. But Hoving was troubled by the pedigree of the piece as soon as it was purchased. Ever dramatic, Hoving called the piece a "hot pot" in his memoirs, called *Making the Mummies Dance*, published in 1993. It was not until 2006 that his suspicions were confirmed by the discovery that it had indeed been looted from an Etruscan tomb near Cerveteri in December 1971.

After much deliberation, the Met agreed to return the Euphronios krater and other pieces of art to Italy. (An Italian judge issued a warrant for Hecht's arrest, which was subsequently revoked.) In 2008 the pot was in Rome and the centerpiece of an exhibition entitled *Nostoi: Recovered Masterpieces*. *Nostoi* is the ancient Greek word for homecoming. But just how "Greek" is this homecoming? As Michael Kimmelman of the *New York Times* put it: "A Greek pot (originally) sold to an Etruscan buyer and stolen from an Italian site and ending up in New York, it has become a Greek pot in a Roman museum dedicated to Etruscan art." Kudos to Kimmelman for pointing this out. At the same time, his article interviews one of the tomb robbers from 1971 who, while laughing, asserts that he is "honored to be associated with something so great."

What is so great? Robbery, looting, swindling a major museum? Quoting a criminal who is making light of his looting seems more than a little questionable. Yet there he is, with his wife, drinking a coffee and laughing about how the krater might just be stolen again if it were in Cerveteri and not Rome. The whole story, from Hecht to the *tombarolo*, is disturbing. This krater is now safe. Ironically enough, ultimately the krater was in fact moved to Cerveteri, to the archaeological museum there. The Anavysos Kouros was saved too, just before it left Greece, although the statue had to be sutured together because his legs and arms had been sawn off for export. However, another vessel painted by Euphronios with the scene of Sarpedon's death was dropped and shattered during a raid on antiquities smugglers in Geneva. How many other pieces are in similar peril?

Our study of this Grecian vessel might make us think about that poem by John Keats, his "Ode on a Grecian Urn." In his art historical analysis he tells us, "Beauty is truth, truth beauty,—that is all / Ye know on earth, and all ye need to know." He tells us that the urn calls for an aesthetic reaction of pure perception—that the vessel "teases us out of thought." Is Keats saying that we don't need to ask so many questions about the workings of our vase, about the nature of the figures, about the two sides and that complex combination of life and death? I don't think so. Keats himself asks questions as he tries to understand his vessel: "What men or gods are these? What maidens loth? / What mad pursuit? What struggle to escape?" Keats really wants to understand what he is seeing, wants to know what is going on and who these people are. He tries to absorb every detail and asks one question after another—just like us. Because that is what works of art call out for us to do.

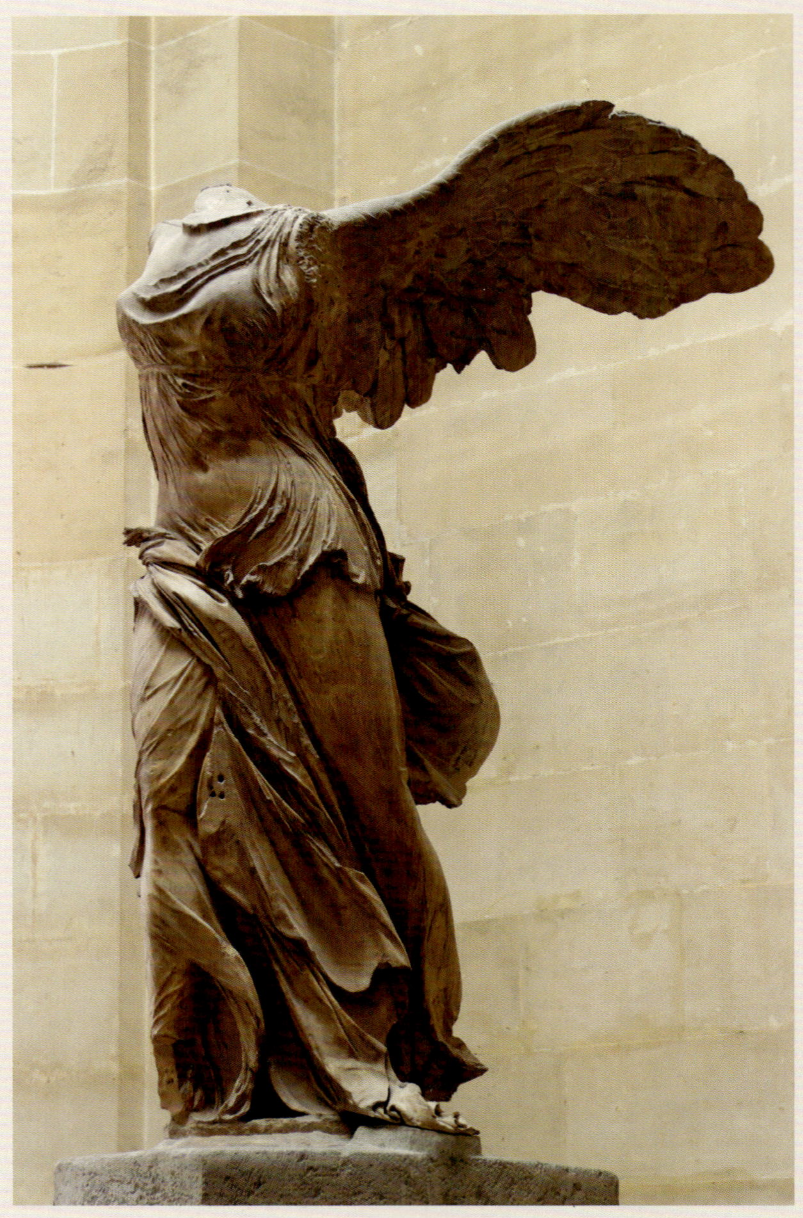

FIG. 4.1 Nike of Samothrace, from the Sanctuary of the Great Gods, Samothrace, ca. 190 BCE. Musée du Louvre, Paris. Parian marble, 244 cm.

Nike of Samothrace

CA. 190 BCE

GREEK ART

There is a rather large gap between the painted bison of Altamira and the sculpture of Hellenistic Greece—from 12,500 BCE to perhaps the third century BCE. Yet there are features of the Spanish cave paintings that align with the impact and meaning of the Nike of Samothrace, an eight-foot-tall marble statue currently housed at the Louvre (Figs. 4.1 and 4.2). In a most basic way, both are evidence of man taking stone and shaping its natural properties (through paint or chisels) in order to create images of power. The great bison charge and bellow and gallop; even when they are standing still they convey a sense of energy and authority, as though they are about to bound away. The statue of the Nike of Samothrace embodies the same kind of energy—her descent from on high, her frantic drapery, her dramatic setting (both ancient and modern) all speak to a potent, taut, suggestive, and even emotional message of power.

Much of the power exuded by this statue comes across through a beautiful interplay of contrasts. For example, take her striking pose. She appears to have just landed on the prow of the ship below, descending with grace and authority from above. Her outstretched wings are actively helping her landing, still hugging the air so as to aid in her divine descent. But her movement works on multiple axes. She moves down *and* forward, vertically and horizontally, jetting at great speed into our space. Nike leans onto her right leg with command, stepping toward us with authority. Yet as she steps forward, something also pulls her back. The wind? The movement of the ship? She depends on her left leg as a ballast. The

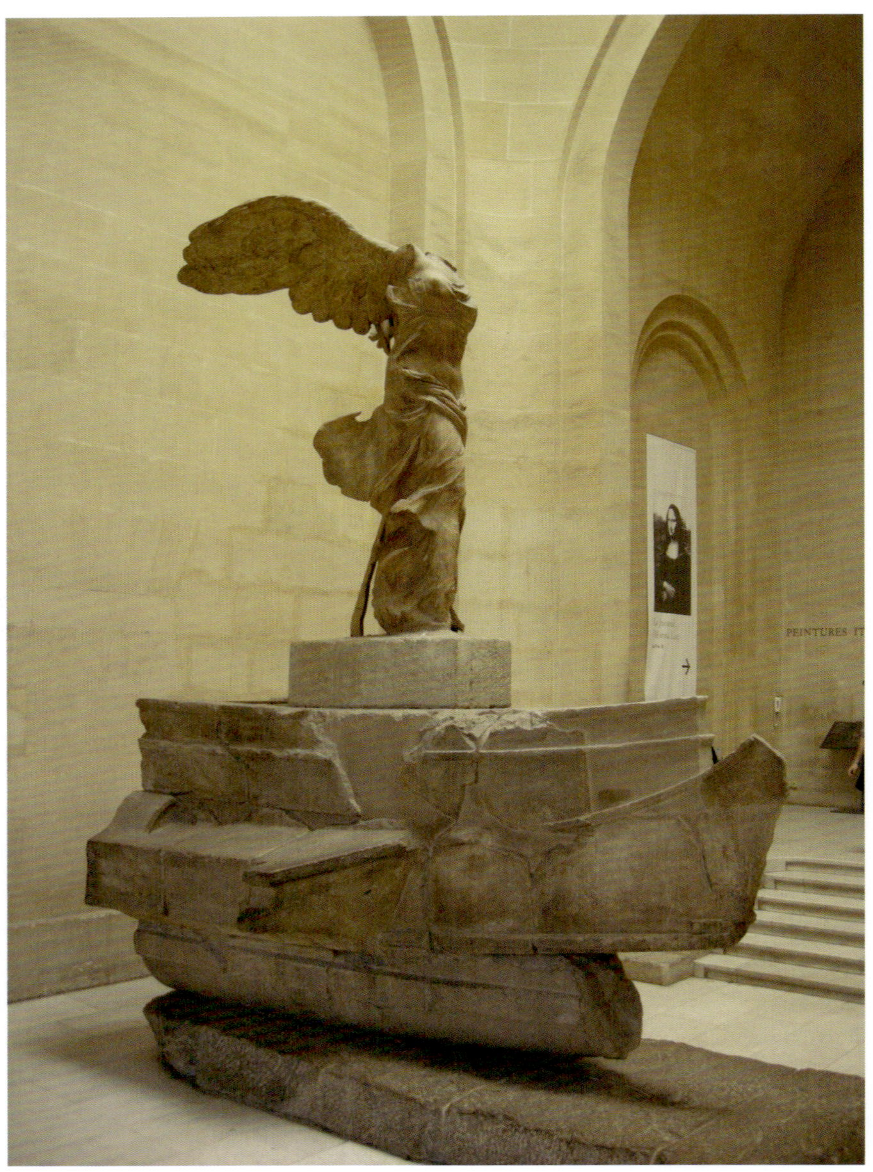

FIG. 4.2 Nike of Samothrace on a boat of Rhodian marble. Musée du Louvre, Paris.

twist of her hips responds to the placement of her feet, creating a perceptible crease in her abdomen, just at her navel. This imbalance also affects her torso such that her left shoulder pulls toward her backstretched left leg.

It is almost as though she is trying to pull her shoulders into alignment, but for the moment she is still being pulled in two different directions—forward and backward. We have spotted her while she is in the middle of catching her balance, while sticking the landing. Nothing is quite settled. The torsion created by her twisting pose—the way she appears to draw her left shoulder forward to balance the placement of her right foot—also produces the sense that she is in a state of preparedness should she decide to return to Mount Olympus, to the home of the gods. Like a great big marble whirligig. Down, left, right, up. She twists and turns in a complex series of directions—moving toward us, pulled away from us, arriving and perhaps just as easily taking off.

Now, for those of you who enjoy doing yoga, you might say that this position is reminiscent of a certain Warrior Pose. That wouldn't be too far off the mark. *Nike* means "victory" in Greek, after all, so the general context surrounding her and her creation is one of war and conquest. There has been a good deal of scholarly debate surrounding the precise historical event that she was meant to commemorate. Dates range from Demetrios I of Macedon (who was known as Poliorketes or the Besieger) and his annihilation of the Ptolemaic fleet in 306 BCE off Salamis in Cyprus, all the way to the Emperor Augustus's triumph at the Battle of Actium in 31 BCE. The general consensus among scholars is that the Nike of Samothrace belongs to the period between 200 and 180 BCE and celebrates naval victories of the Rhodians over Antiochos III of Syria. The Rhodians turned the tide of a long Syrian war, which led to the defeat of Antiochos III on land at Magnesia in 189 BCE. The resultant Peace of Apameia led to thirty years of power and prosperity for Rhodes. Still, not all scholars are entirely convinced that the Nike belongs to this particular historical moment. The evidence by which scholars support this dating is problematic. This includes a batch of pottery and a fragmentary inscription reading "[…]s Rhodios […]" that was found near the statue—not much to go on. And this is doubly so when one considers the history of the site from which the Nike heralds.

The Sanctuary of the Great Gods on the island of Samothrace was one of the most visited Pan-Hellenic religious sanctuaries in the Greek world. It was best known for its unique mystery cults that were dedicated to a number of gods and goddesses. Inhabitants and visitors were coming to celebrate the mysteries starting as early as the seventh century BCE. Much of what we know about these mysteries, interestingly enough, comes from travel logs kept by one of Samothrace's most famous pilgrims, the fifth-century writer/traveler Herodotus, who tells us about the oddities of the religions in book 2 of *The Histories*. The site continued to draw visitors as late as the fourth century CE and only was completely abandoned in the sixth century CE after a massive earthquake. In order to accommodate the wide number of visitors, the site changed and grew over time, as a groundplan of the sanctuary shows.* Thus, archaeological remains such as the pottery from the second century BCE definitely speak to the *popularity* of the site, but they don't necessarily date the statue.

What the archaeological records do provide is a sense of how the Nike of Samothrace sat within the large complex and how she would have been positioned to welcome her many visitors. The space dedicated to the Nike was at the southern end of the complex. She was positioned just south of the main theater. If you were watching a performance, the backdrop was the Great Altar and the Hieron, the "holy place" or shrine where the newly initiated were cleansed and welcomed into the cult of mysteries. If you were walking toward the theater, or standing up to stretch your legs during the show, you would look up to see Nike, hovering above the last row of seating. She is eight feet tall, and the ship is six feet, seven inches tall. So the statue is already over life-size and overwhelming. Set into the hill, above the amphitheater, she would have appeared even bigger and more authoritative. The direct physical and psychological connection between the theater and the statue was no accident. She dominated the entry to the theater and she presided over its offerings. Even if you were not turning in her direction, once you saw her I think it would have been hard to get her out of your mind.

Another means of approaching the statue was through a long portico running along the western framework of the site. Emerging from this dark, covered 300-foot colonnade to see the Nike astride the prow of the ship would have

* ttps://commons.wikimedia.org/wiki/File:Plan_Samothrace_sanctuary-en.svg

been intense, theatrical, surprising. She would have been visible from afar as the colonnade was open to the elements. Walking along the portico, seeing her getting closer and closer, would have been like a film from the 1920s with its frame-by-frame flipbook construction. The columns intermittently interrupting the view—revealing, concealing, revealing and concealing—would have enhanced and intensified the anticipation, the majesty of her power.*

That intense theatricality was also enhanced by the presence of water. The bright blue expanse of the Aegean Sea would have provided a distant and dramatic backdrop. Water also provided an outline of the sanctuary. The oldest parts of the complex were actually situated between two streams. Later additions to the sanctuary, including the Nike terrace, extended beyond the rivulets. Nevertheless, these streams remained an integral part of the complex, defining and dividing the various hallowed halls and temples. And those streams were probably what fed the fountains framing the Nike statue.

In the excavations of the 1950s, archaeologists discovered that the Nike was set slightly at a diagonal in a small precinct with a low retaining wall at the sides and the back. The floor was paved with rippled marble (to imitate water), and there were dowel holes embedded in the floor by which to attach bronze objects, like dolphins or other sea creatures. Archaeologists also found traces of pipes that were believed to have been for a fountain that poured water from an upper basin into a lower one. Water, water everywhere.

And it is this effect, the dramatization of the sea upon this watery stage set, that explains the way her draperies twist and turn and tangle, defining and complicating her counterbalanced pose and movement. Nike wears two garments. One is the long chiton, or tunic, of a thin and fine cloth. The fluttering garments struggle against the constraints of two belts, one hidden under the folds hanging over her hips, and a second beneath her breasts. The fabric is so light that it flutters uncontrollably and exposes Nike's feminine form—her strong, round thighs, her upright bosom, and the contours of her soft abdomen. But the drapery also clings to her because she is supposed to be in the water,

* A series of videos produced by Emory University digitally reenvision the situation of the statue within the complex: https://samothrace.emory.edu/visualizing-the-sanctuary.

soaked through by the spray of the Aegean Sea suggested by the fountains. That wet, clinging, diaphanous tunic is dramatic and erotic, as is the himation or cloak, which slips between the figure's legs, gathering there, and exposing her left hip and left leg.

Like the chiton, the heavier himation flips and twists in the sea-soaked wind. The way the himation struggles in the wind is best shown in the color-coded representation from the Louvre's website.* The outside is blue, the inside is red. Ironically, the wind both challenges the integrity of the cloak and seems to keep it in place. The himation, unlike the chiton, is carved with thick, deep grooves. The contrasting carving techniques add to the tension of the uncontrolled drapery and to the drama of her movement and presence. And all of those contrasts—tight, loose, inside, outside—take on an even greater significance when set against the solid and staid ship below. Her flustered drapery, juxtaposed with the bulk of the utterly symmetrical ship, further heightens the tension of her body, her clothing, of her arrival. The keel is even, although she is not.

To what end? It should be a joyous moment. One of victory. Success! Right? So why is it so tense and fraught? Why is there so much drama when this is supposed to say that peace has been achieved?

If we were to look for help from the world of art historical scholarship, the answer would be that this particular period, the so-called Hellenistic period, is defined by excessive drama, even artistic decay. Early art historians considered the final years of the Greek Empire as having produced art that was over the top, histrionic, "baroque." Johann Joachim Winckelmann spearheaded this interpretation. His book *History of the Art of Antiquity*, first published in German in 1764, set up the paradigm for understanding Greek art, one that had a cyclical underpinning. Artistic periods could be read as having stages of growth, maturity, and decline. The Hellenistic period was the last. Winckelmann privileged repose and calm because he believed that it would best "portray the true character of the soul." Violent or extreme forces were incompatible with that state of tranquility, and so he hated Hellenistic and Baroque art.

---

* "A Closer Look at the Victory of Samothrace," http://musee.louvre.fr/oal/victoiredesamothrace/victoiredesamothrace_acc_en.html.

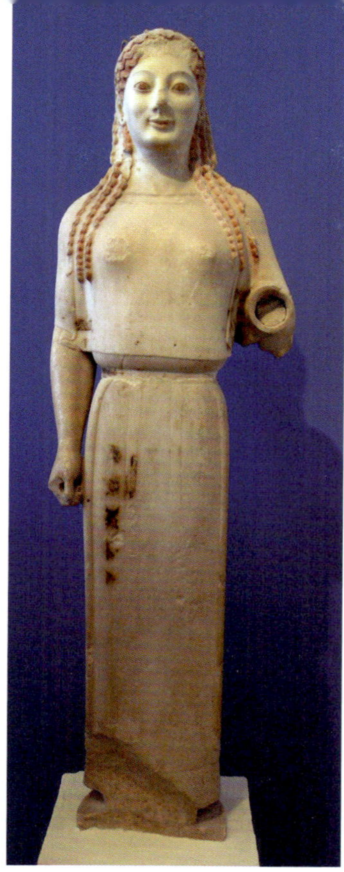

FIG. 4.3 The "Peplos Kore," ca. 530 BCE. Akropolis Museum, Athens. Marble, 118 cm.

Bernini was his nemesis, *der Kunstverderber* ("art ruiner"). What, you might ask, does our Nike have to do with a statue produced in the seventeenth century? Can you really explain something happening in the second century BCE by a statue produced over a thousand years later? Hard to back that up, but the philosophy outlined by Winckelmann had a lot of staying power. One of the most well-respected scholars of the Classical world, J. J. Pollitt, wrote in 1986 in support of this analogy, saying that both Bernini and Hellenistic art emphasized "dramatic crisis," "agonized facial expressions," and "extreme contrasts of texture." Pollitt's language is charged and not a little critical. But my favorite is the way the prudish Victorian critic John Ruskin described the Hellenistic period as "corrupt."

At this point it is worth taking a step back to look at the freestanding statuary

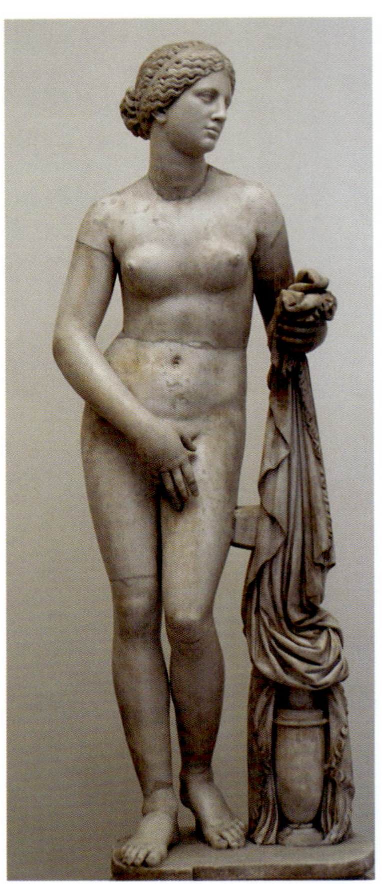

FIG. 4.4 Aphrodite of Knidos, composite of two similar Roman copies after the original marble by Praxiteles in ca. 350 BCE. Vatican Museums, Vatican City. Marble, 203 cm.

of the earlier centuries, to see whether this progression of growth, maturity, and decay promoted by art historians holds up. The first period, the so-called Archaic period (ca. 600–480 BCE), is generally comprised of white marble figures called *korai* (for females, meaning young women) and *kouroi* (for young male statues). *Korai* were always clothed and shown holding different accoutrements, like flowers or pomegranates. The "Peplos Kore" gets her name from her drapery (Fig. 4.3). Early scholars thought that the young woman was wearing a mantle pinned at the shoulders called a *peplos*. Ironically, the "Peplos Kore" is not actually wearing a *peplos*. She wears a long robe and a cape. The effect of the drapery is quite rectilinear and makes the *kore* rather columnar. The drapery does not move, and neither does she. Her feet, which barely show from under the garment, are solidly affixed to the ground. She gestures with her left hand, but not in any particularly activated manner. Her regularized and ornamental hair, her symmetrical and immobile smile, her constrained stance, could not be more different from the fervor of the Nike statue.

The next period is that of the Classical period, considered to be the highest form of Greek art and Winckelmann's favorite. This is the moment of the construction of the famous Parthenon frieze and the lovely Aphrodite of Knidos (Fig. 4.4). A composite of two Roman copies, the Aphrodite of Knidos is understood as an example of the perfection of Greek sculptors. Attributed to the sculptor Praxiteles, she was one of the most renowned and most often mentioned statues in literary sources. She was a tourist attraction and an inspiration for a multitude of copies over the Mediterranean. This period introduced an interest in ideal proportions, idealized forms, and naturalistic poses. It is during this period—roughly 480–323 BCE—that we see the appearance of the contrapposto, the pose wherein the figure rests its weight on one leg and relaxes the other. This choreographed imbalance allowed a gentle curve of the spine that countered the slight shifting of hips and also produced a subtle drop in one shoulder. Aphrodite expresses this contrapposto to perfection. She shifts her hips just so. The graceful and gentle S-curve of her figure is inviting, although she covers herself in a gesture of modesty.

Certainly we can see an evolution in the definition of the body through drapery and movement—from the columnar and static *kore*, to the soft modeling and naturalistic contrapposto of the Aphrodite, to the frenzied imbalance of the Nike. We can also see the same changes happening in male freestanding statuary—from static and immobile, to the contrapposto shift in the stance of the Kritios Boy (ca. 480–475 BCE), to the frenzied and emotional forms of Laocoön and his doomed sons (early first century CE).

But there are definitely problems with this clean periodization. For example, the Aphrodite of Knidos is perhaps not quite so tranquil and staid as Winckelmann and his followers proposed. One thing to consider is the suggestiveness

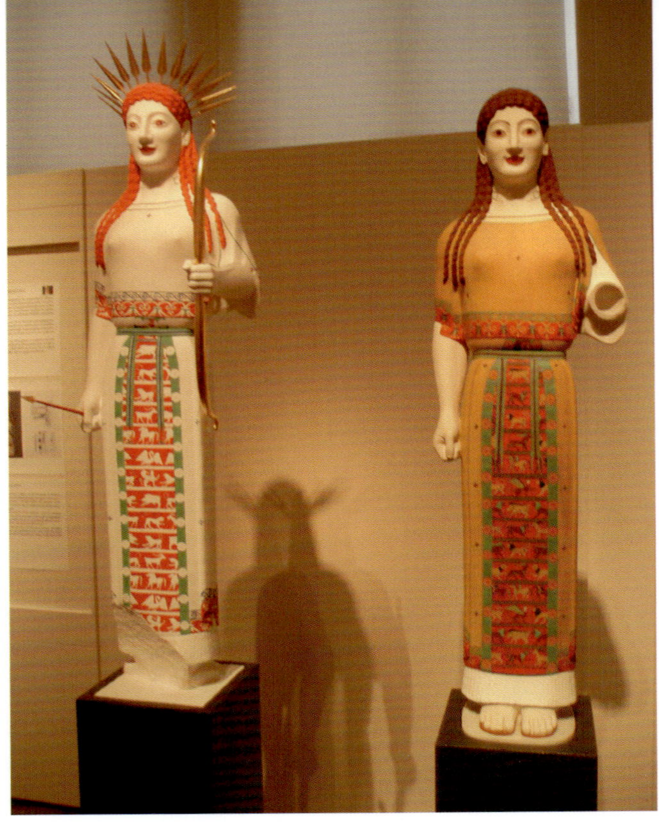

FIG. 4.5 Reconstructions of the "Peplos Kore" as Artemis (left) and Athena (right) for the *Gods in Color* exhibition, Athens, Greece, in 2007.

of her pose. Yes, she is covering herself from the preying eyes of the viewer. But how well? Doesn't that pose, like the lone bracelet on her left arm, actually draw more attention to her nudity than conceal it? She turns her head, but is it out of surprise? She does not appear to be too shocked or scandalized. Maybe she expects to be watched. Like the Nike of Samothrace, the Aphrodite was set in a shrine open only from the front, placed on display for the visitor to enjoy. One particular account of the enjoyment of the statue recorded by Pliny the Elder in the first century CE suggests that, pure or not, she could inspire impure thoughts and behaviors.

And then there is the fact that she was painted, something that Winckelmann probably would not have been able to handle. In 2003 the Munich Glyptothek put on an exhibition called *Gods in Color* that shook the academic world. (The catalogue was translated into English in 2007.) Through the use of refined methods of analysis and documentation, which allowed the detection of even the smallest traces of lost color on ancient statues and reliefs, the scientists and art historians re-created a number of shockingly colorful images, such as two versions of the "Peplos Kore" produced by Vinzenz Brinkmann (Fig. 4.5). So much for the pure and calm and tranquil. With the advances in technology, scientists found rich blues, greens, and reds on many statues. The "Peplos Kore" was particularly surprising because it revealed a band of wild animals and riders on the central part of her skirt, and because it now became apparent that the famous "Peplos Kore" was not wearing a *peplos* at all.

The Aphrodite would have been colored as well, although in the case of later marble statuary the sculptures were rarely *completely* covered in paint. An example of this selective painting is the Augustus of Prima Porta from the first century CE (Fig. 4.6). Artists added paint to highlight details—hair, the iris of the eye, lips, and embroidered ornaments on the drapery. The flesh was most likely left exposed and polished so as to reveal and even highlight the natural beauty of the marble. Aphrodite of Knidos's bracelet as well as her hair would probably have been gilded since most sources from the period call her "golden." And her eyes, cheeks, and lips would have been painted too. What better way to entice someone coming to pay a visit?

Although there has not been a study of painting traces on the Nike statue that I know of, it is impossible that she was left unpainted. I would think that she wasn't completely covered in paint because the type of marble seems to have been an important consideration on the part of the artist or artists. The ship upon which she stands was carved out of a dark gray and white veined marble known as Rhodian marble. If the monument was meant to celebrate Rhodes, the use of marble from that particular region would have been a strong way of reasserting exactly who was the victor, proclaiming their success by promoting and privileging their own marble. Nike was carved out of a whiter, purer marble, called Paros marble. The selection of different marbles was not accidental. This juxtaposition would have added to the many contrasting aspects of the statue. Painted details

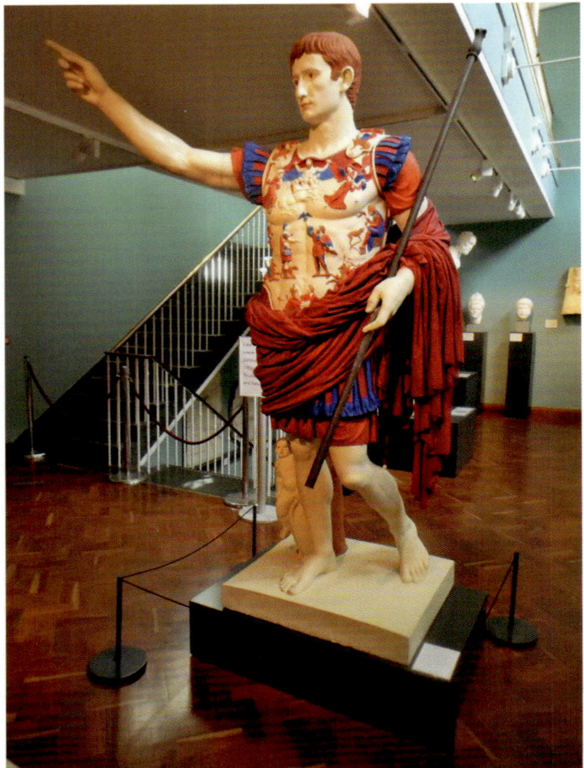

FIG. 4.6 Reconstruction of Augustus of Prima Porta. Ashmolean Museum of Art and Archaeology, University of Oxford, Oxford, England. Painted plaster cast made in 2004 based on original statue of marble from early first century CE, height 203 cm.

in the drapery would have enhanced these contrasts without undermining the distinctions between the marbles. For example, perhaps the different sides of the himation (something that is difficult to see) were defined through color. Imagine the effect of painted eyes, hair, and wings.

Not to mention that there are plenty of examples of Nike from the Classical period that are quite analogous to the Nike of Samothrace. One example would be the relief decoration from a parapet that once surrounded the Temple of Athena Nike on the Acropolis, dated to the last quarter of the fifth century. The difficult stance as she reaches to fix her sandal while simultaneously turning, as though someone has called to her from her left; the large wings that beautifully shape and mirror the movement of her arms; the drapery that folds and bunches and slips with her movements, provocatively exposing her right shoulder—these seem "Hellenistic" even though they don't fit within that art historical timeline. A second grand example from the Classical period of a Nike statue is from Paionios and was discovered in Olympia, Greece. The way the drapery clings to the body of the Nike of Paionios, defining her legs and feminine form as she powers through the sky, is far from Winckelmann's definition of the calm, peaceful, tranquil Classical phase.

Understanding the Nike and her Hellenistic brethren as evidence of excess, decay, and overwrought drama denies the power and significance of the statue. Rather than understanding the irony, theatricality, and drama of the statue as an example of the end of an era, as art historians have done, we should think about the Nike of Samothrace as evidence of the way all Greek statuary was meant to challenge and shock the viewer. Her drama is psychological, not gratuitous.

As her name suggests, it is a moment of exuberance. Victory. This is evident in the way that she has been reconstructed. Those who excavated the site at Samothrace in the 1950s came across what might have been the right hand of Nike, sitting in the basin. This fragment fit with a series of smaller fragments that had been found by the original Austrian excavators of the nineteenth century and kept in the Kunsthistorisches Museum in Vienna. Thus with her right hand she might have been blowing a fanfare on a trumpet just like the Nike on the coinage of Demetrios Poliorketes, the Macedonian king that we talked about earlier. That Nike also stands, as our Nike does, on the prow of the ship, leaning forward with her right hip ahead of her left and wearing a diaphanous and fluttering garment. The Nike on the coin has massive wings that balance the forward thrust of her pose and the long, extended trumpet from which she proclaims that which she represents, victory.

Scholars are still uncertain as to the left hand. Perhaps Nike held the standard of the enemy's navy, which is what appears on Demetrios's coins. This is also how she was reconstructed by the scholars Benndorf and von Zumbusch from Berlin University in 1875—once with the standard upright, and again with the standard upside-down. Maybe she held a palm branch in her left hand. A trophy is another option. Other scholars (like Cordonnier) replaced the trumpet altogether and gave her a victory wreath. Or perhaps, as Karl Lehmann suggested, her hands were empty and she was making a "great gesture of command."

Joy and triumph are a major part of the monument, but, as the classicist Andrew Stewart points out, that is not the entire message. Nike is not a "figure of command." She does not crown the victor, nor does she determine who is going to win. Zeus does that. She is simply his messenger. That relationship is beautifully illustrated in a watercolor by Antoine Chrysostome Quatremère de Quincy, the first scholar to challenge Winckelmann's assumption that Classical statuary was all white. Nike sits on the right hand of Zeus, at *his* command. This changes the nature of our Nike statue. It destabilizes her meaning. She goes from representing a sure thing, a certain victory, to representing the decisions made by her boss, Zeus, who is not on the scene at all, with whom we as the viewer have no direct relationship.

Second, the prow of the ship of the Nike statue (and on the coin) is broken. That makes sense since it is an enemy ship that has been conquered, subjugated. But wouldn't the constant reminder of the enemy be discomforting? Is the combination of victory and the vessel of the defeated meant to suggest that victory is fleeting and cannot be taken for granted? And who is steering this boat? Who is in control of its movement? Is she, even though it looks as though she just landed and is struggling to keep her balance? What kind of victory is this? What kind of Victory is she? The consistent combination of formal contrasts—her pose and her drapery—plays straight into this deepening labyrinth of psychological possibilities.

The expanse and drama of Nike's wings draw upon a rich trove of poetical references that further these intellectual challenges. In the Greek tradition, wings are often associated directly with Eros, the Greek god of love. Sappho, Anakreon, and other poets describe love as the sensation of being winged: the heart flies "like a wing" in the lover's chest. Wings appear on gods and goddesses that are shown chasing objects of desire, not always in the loftiest of ways. Thus

Nike's wings carry a series of meanings that are not necessarily all that satisfying. The wings also suggest a sense of fickleness, that she might shift her favors or take off just as quickly as she appeared. The more we want it, the more we hope for Victory to come, the more it hurts when it does not or it disappears.

Wings also might make us think about Daedalus and the story of his tragic flight. Daedalus translates to mean "clever worker" in Greek. By tradition Daedalus was such a masterful sculptor that he made his statues appear to come to life. The stories about Daedalus show a tradition that linked deceptiveness with creation, danger with art. Take the story of Daedalus and his son Icarus, most famously told in Ovid's *Metamorphoses*. Daedalus and Icarus have been locked in a tower by a distrustful King Minos. Daedalus makes wings for himself and his son out of wax and string so that they can fly out. Before leaving, Daedalus warns his son: "Now, Icarus, listen carefully! Keep to the middle way. If you fly too low, the water will clog your wings; if you fly too high, they'll be scorched by fire. Fly between sea and sun." As we know, Icarus cannot obey because, Ovid tells us, he falls in love with the sky. The sun softens the wax and he drowns in the blue-green Icarian Sea. Here too, wings are associated with flawed and painful love—Daedalus for his lost son, Icarus for the distant sun. The Daedalus story also resonates with the Nike statue because she appears in an in-between space—above the waves of the blue-green water but no longer flying in the sky. She is also representing a longed-for, hoped-for salvation.

The message seems to be that one must be constantly vigilant and aware, must question everything. The wings seem to be the key to total salvation, but when Icarus loses focus and gets distracted, the wings lose their power. Nike appears to bring the best of news, but she may also bring a message of warning that the enemy is ever-present and that victories cannot be taken for granted.

These warning signs apply to art and how to interact with it, and relate to an important topic in early Greek writings. You might remember my discussion of Plato in the chapter on Altamira. In the *Republic*, in his allegory of the cave, Plato described how the shadows created by the fire were illusions. Forms and ideas are true. Objects and materials are a mere reflection of this higher knowledge. The corollary is that mimetic or imitative art is false.

But there is one instance in which Plato gives us a pass, and that is with the idea of Beauty. We can, Plato says, see the image of Beauty in the face of our beloved. In the lover's gaze, a beautiful body can be both *mimesis* (a material imitation) and *eidolon* (image). Plato extends this to statuary. Just as a beautiful figure is the place where the Idea of Beauty can shine through into the phenomenal world, the statue is a place where the godhead can permeate wood, bronze, or stone. But this only works if the viewer is filled with *pothos*. This is a word that means desire, but in a delicate way—it means desire based on something that is not there. Desire that feeds on absence. Another element to viewing emphasized by Greek writers was the use of *phantasia* or imagination. Philostratus the Elder (writing in the second century CE) explained that without *phantasia*, art was just a mechanical copy. *Phantasia* infuses art with inspiration, wisdom, and ultimately truth.

Thus understanding the visit of Nike and her presence is not about passive consumption. Without *pothos* and *phantasia* we won't be able to understand what she truly means. We won't understand or even be able to take up her challenge. And she is challenging us. She is a message of joy and its fleetingness. She is in control and trying to find her equilibrium. She is strong and fragile. She is lofty, divine Victory and, at the same time, its earthly or human material reflection. She represents the fickleness of nature, of triumph, and of man. This idea of the viewer being responsible for completing her story, the idea that it is incumbent upon us to perceive the Idea for which she is the material relic, is even more of a challenge for the modern viewer. We are missing so much—her arms, her head (which was never found), her original setting. The inscription that was found near her original home is more fragment than artifact. Yet grappling with the complexities beyond the actual statue is part of the discourse, part of the enterprise—I would say that it is what the Greek statues and Greek authors want us to do. In a sense, the fullest meaning of Nike is created by the viewer.

You might even say that she has entered into our imagination so thoroughly that we can see her in lots of places. Take her reappearance in Delacroix's *Liberty Leading the People: July 28, 1830*. Delacroix takes the great statue and fills in the fragments. Her wings disappear into a burst of wispy clouds and gunpowder. The enemy boat becomes a mass of intertwined dead bodies in various states of distress and undress. Her victorious outstretched arm holds the pristine, albeit fragmentary flag of France (since its top is cut off in the composition).

Actually in making this comparison I am taking liberties. The Nike of Samothrace was not discovered until thirty-three years after the painting by Delacroix. Yet if we can have an anachronistic moment together, it is pretty amazing to think about the relationship between the Romantic painting and the Greek statue. To think about the fact that Delacroix's symbol of liberty and victory belongs to the same museum that was constructed under the French Revolution, the very regime that the painting praises, and then to think that thirty-three years later Nike was discovered and twenty years after that was installed in that same museum, at the top of a stairway built to replace a staircase that had been built under the Napoleonic regime.

The placement of the Nike at the top of the stairway in the Louvre also beautifully unites past and present in another uncanny way. The visual connection between the steps of the amphitheater in the complex on the island of Samothrace and the long line of steps in the Louvre is striking. Here too is a fortuitous and anachronistic nod to her past. The archaeologists did not actually understand and reconstruct the original terrace and the amphitheater until the 1950s, eighty years after the Nike of Samothrace was placed at the top of the stairs.

The Delacroix demonstrates how powerfully the Nike responds to or accords with images of liberty and the victory of the people. The current role of the people is actually quite instrumental in keeping her in place. The Louvre recently underwent a massive campaign to raise funds to restore the Nike statue. And the director, Jean-Luc Martinez, did it by crowdsourcing. As the *Wall Street Journal* pointed out, this approach would have once been anathema in France and certainly diverges from the previous director, Henri Loyrette, who courted only private funding for the museum's projects.

This campaign's success meant that Nike was not in her traditional spot, at the top of the stairs, for almost a year. Restoration of the statue lasted from September 2013 through the summer of 2014. Even the stairwell got a cleaning. This was probably only the second time since her installation in 1884 that the Nike left her lofty perch. The other instance was during the outbreak of World War II. In the fall of 1939 the director of the Louvre undertook the difficult and delicate task of bringing Nike down the stairs for safekeeping. The pathos and drama of this particular moment is told with peerless poignancy in the movie

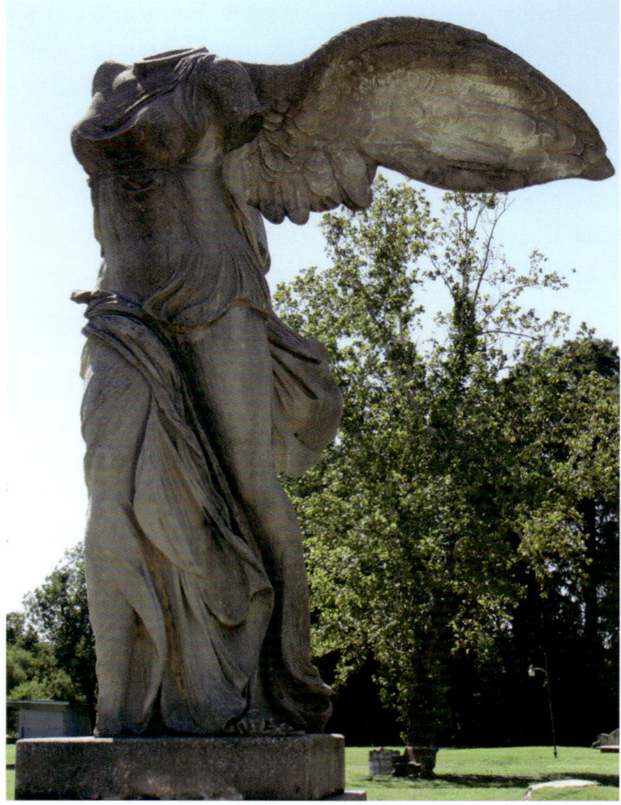

FIG. 4.7   Nike of Samothrace, from the Urrutia estate
(Miraflores), ca. 1918. San Antonio, Texas. Concrete.

The Rape of Europa, based on Lynn Nicholas's 1994 book of the same name. One
witness recalled, "The statue rocked onto an inclined wooden ramp. We were all
terrified and the silence was total as the *Victory* rolled slowly forward, her stone
wings trembling slightly. The curator of sculpture sank down on the stone steps
murmuring, 'I will not see her return.'"

All of those formal contrasts—in her pose, her drapery, her message—come
to the fore in this piece. She is an image of victory and power, yet she is so utterly
fragile, composed of so many fragments, that she might shatter into thousands

of pieces. The statue of Nike could be a metaphor for the fragility of art. It is the responsibility of the viewer to understand but also to preserve. And even though *we* may not have paid for the restoration of the Louvre statue, the imperative that we understand and preserve remains our challenge.

The art of Greece may appear when you least expect it. In San Antonio, for example, if you happen to be driving down a street called Hildebrand, just when you begin to despair about the traffic…look to the side. What might salvage your journey is the chance to see the splendid copy of the Nike of Samothrace, which once belonged to Dr. Aureliano Urrutia (1872–1975) (Fig. 4.7). Dr. Urrutia immigrated to San Antonio in 1914, fleeing the Mexican Revolution. Within four years he had reestablished his medical practice, built a grand garden known as Miraflores, and constructed a mansion called Quinta Urrutia. The mansion was home to a large collection of works of art, many of which were replicas of famous masterpieces, as in the case of the Nike statue, which originally sat above the doorway of the mansion. Currently she is surrounded by machines and piles of dirt and a pretty lame fence that some people have jumped over. Powerful and confident, she appears to disdain the chaos around her. Another famous Greek figure appears in San Antonio, on the proscenium art of the Majestic Theater, what was once a classic movie theater. This is a replica of the Aphrodite of Knidos.

Aphrodite, in her coy nudity, would probably be consumed by the din and mess on Hildebrand. Aphrodite belongs in the theater where she turns suggestively away, expecting the viewer but telling him to look away, perhaps at the stage below. She is playful and false. A consummate actress. At the top of the stage, Nike would dominate and distract from the performances below. Nike belongs on a street whose name means sword battle (Hildebrand). She belongs around scenes of chaos and destruction and battle. She is triumphant amidst all that. Or is she? Like the original Nike, she represents a series of complex contradictions—in her pose, in her drapery, and in what she is announcing… that victory doesn't come easily; it often comes at a price. So perhaps when you do not jump the fence around Dr. Urrutia's lost garden, remember that mimesis can be a trick, that images of power and authority are not always what they seem. It is incumbent upon us to make certain that the statue in the Urrutia garden does not turn out to be an example of loss rather than victory.

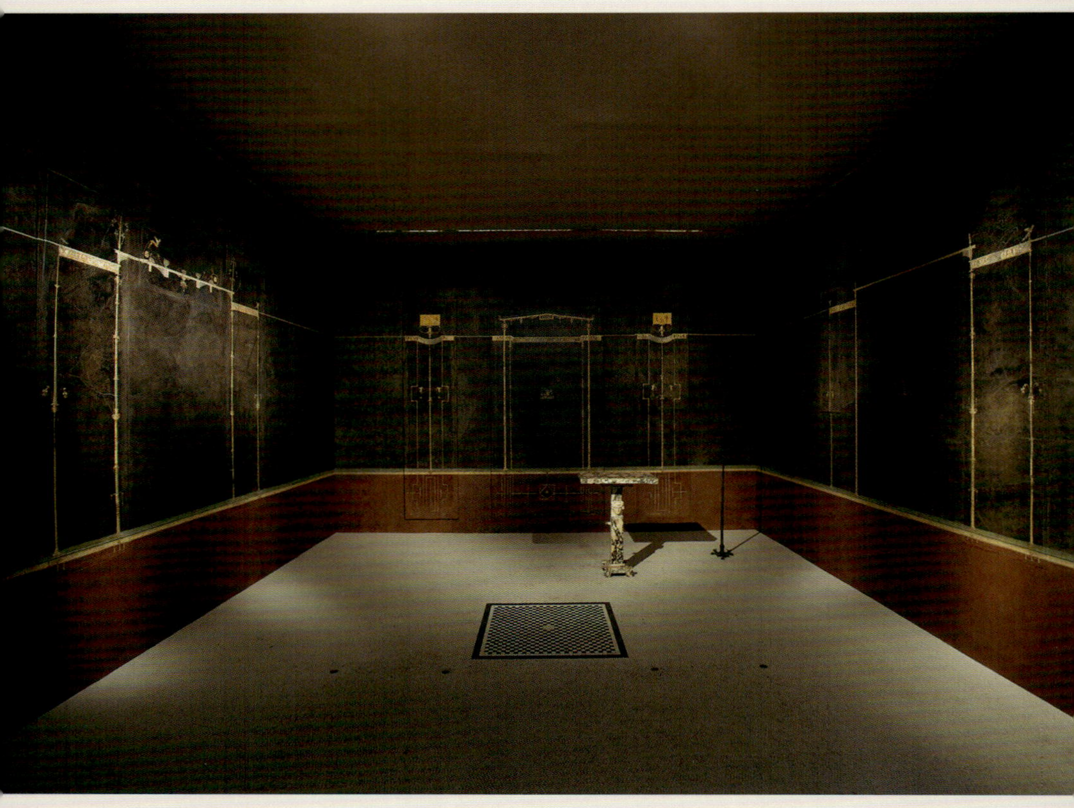

FIG. 5.1 The Black Room. From the imperial villa at Boscotrecase, Italy, last decade of first century BCE. Metropolitan Museum of Art, New York. Fresco.

Villa at Boscotrecase

ROMAN ART

Excavations of the ruins in southern Campania, between Naples and Sorrento, have been happening in fits and starts since 1709, when the construction of a well shaft accidentally tapped into the remains of the theater of Herculaneum, a city destroyed by the eruption of Mount Vesuvius in 79 CE. The nearby city of Pompeii, also a victim to the ash and pumice of Vesuvius, was discovered soon thereafter. The excavations of that site started in earnest in 1738, sparking what we might call Pompeii-o-mania. The unearthing of the city inspired all kinds of romance and drama, evident in the archaeological "documents" from the period—from watercolors in the eighteenth century showing aristocrats surveying the emerging city to massive mid-nineteenth-century oil paintings showing very attractive peasant girls at work (originally for Napoleon III's private eyes only).

Sir Edward Bulwer-Lytton's *The Last Days of Pompeii* of 1834 inspired the stage drama *Nydia: A Tragic Play* and the sculpture *Nydia, the Blind Slave Girl of Pompeii*, which was reproduced about a hundred times to satisfy demand. Scholars have connected this particular fascination with the burning of Pompeii to the fate of many American cities during the Civil War. Yet even when the threat of real cities burning was no longer a concern, Pompeii-o-mania raged on—such as in the show *Last Days of Pompeii,* which had the tagline "Pompeii! The Ancient City Will Be Destroyed Again Tonight." On almost any night of the week, spectators could go to Coney Island and witness gladiatorial fights, chariot and foot races, swimming feats, acrobatic routines, dancing Pompeiian girls, and, across an artificial lake meant to represent the Bay of Naples, a massive display of fireworks. And Pompeii-o-mania is still going strong today. If you think the nineteenth-century spectacle sounds silly or over the top and that their tastes were unsophisticated, just watch the trailer to the movie *Pompeii* that came out in 2015.

Three hundred years after the discovery of the accidental well shaft, archaeologists are still finding painted rooms and ancient artifacts at Herculaneum and Pompeii. However, as you may have read, the walls of the latter are not being protected properly. In 2011 Silvio Berlusconi, who for the longest time was somehow simultaneously the most loathed *and* most popular figure in the Italian government, was blamed for the collapse of a wall in Pompeii. This occurred a few months after a wall from the House of the Gladiators fell and the ex-prime minister swore to provide better funding and manpower for the UNESCO World Heritage Site. Unfortunately, blaming and even incarcerating that delightful little tax evader Berlusconi does not solve the problems of Pompeii. In 2013 the painted plaster of the House of the Small Fountain collapsed because of rains and wind. Nature keeps winning.

Take the story of the Villa at Boscotrecase and its paintings from about 11 BCE (Fig. 5.1). This villa was essentially a wealthy suburb of Pompeii. It was located just three miles from Pompeii and right at the base of Mount Vesuvius. So as quickly as the people of Pompeii were suffocated by the heat and ash on August 24 in the year 79 CE—which took about a day—Boscotrecase was hit even more quickly. If the recent *Pompeii* film were happening at Boscotrecase, it would be over as soon as it started, which, judging from the trailer, might be a huge relief. The site of Boscotrecase was only discovered in 1903, during the construction of the Circumvesuviana, the railway line that runs from Naples and all around the mountain. The owner of the land, Cavaliere Ernesto Santini, excavated much of the great villa before it was covered once again by a second eruption of Vesuvius in 1906. The Metropolitan Museum of Art and the Naples Archaeological Museum purchased a number of the paintings and removed them from the site during those three years, which was fortunate for had they not, these too, along with the rest of the villa, would have been lost forever.

What both the Met and the Naples Museum have done beautifully is to place

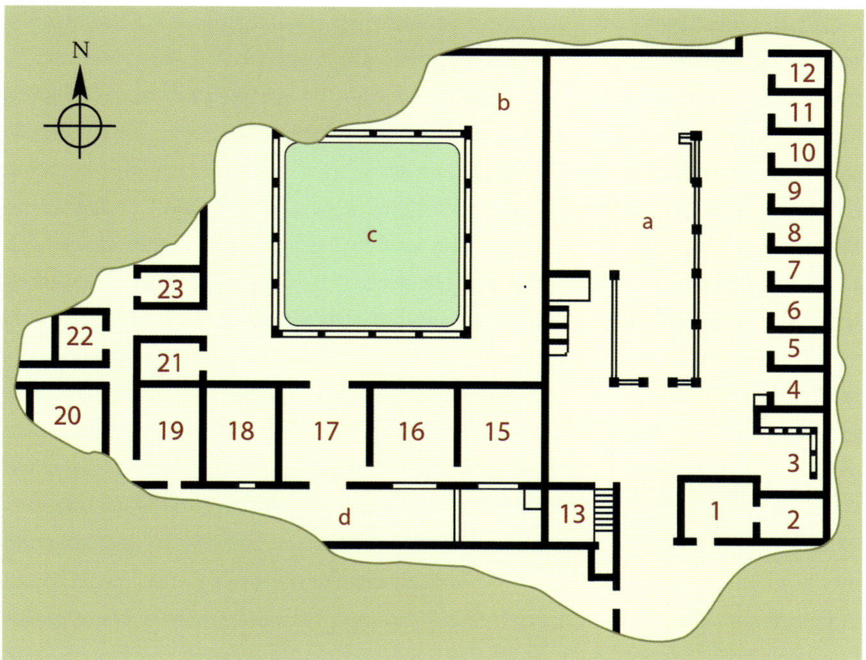

FIG. 5.2 Ground plan of the imperial villa at Boscotrecase.

the paintings as they originally were, in rooms. In this figure we are looking at the ground plan of what was briefly excavated of the large villa (Fig. 5.2). (What was excavated covered about 165 feet, or 30,000 square feet, but this was only a part of the complex.) The painted rooms that survived the twentieth-century volcanic eruption were originally set on the southern side of the western wing of the villa, set around a peristyle or columned porch. The Naples Museum got the paintings from the Red Room (room 16). The Met got a few fragments from room 20 and a number of frescoes from the Mythological Room (room 19). The Met also has paintings from the ominously named Black Room (room 15). The Met's reconstruction of the Black Room allows the visitor to enter the space just as the ancient Roman visitor would have done.

The rooms of this wing at Boscotrecase were private rooms (including bedrooms) in private homes owned by prominent people—Marcus Agrippa and Julia, daughter to Emperor Augustus. So unlike the Nike of Samothrace, which was out in the open and meant for public display, these rooms were designed and decorated for enjoyment on a smaller scale, for a limited number of viewers. Nevertheless, we can make some important connections between the two monuments, between these two major fragments. Like her complex pose and draperies, the meaning of Nike the statue had surprising twists and turns. Similarly, the frescoes from Boscotrecase are not straightforward. The images are suggestive and tricky. They seem to appear and disappear, resemble and dissemble, all in one sweep.

And, although there is a sense of exclusion in the fact that these painted walls were not out in the open, on a hilltop like the Nike, these paintings still had a significant communal importance. The late first-century writer Vitruvius wrote that people of high rank (such as the owners of the Villa at Boscotrecase) needed stately rooms because it was there that important political and business dealings would occur, not to mention where guests were entertained. These spaces were a means of showing off the wealth and intelligence of the owner. They were spaces of personal pride and shared storytelling. In these rooms, in front of these paintings, viewers were provoked into conversations about looking at art. Explaining, describing, and understanding these walls encouraged conversations and shared responses. Even in the rooms that were most private, such as the bedrooms, there is still a sense that the viewers, husband and wife perhaps, were studying, enjoying, and explaining the content of the painted walls.

When I imagine the experience of visiting these Roman homes, room after room of painted stories and landscapes and tiny vignettes, I can't help but turn to a book called the *Imagines* written by the third-century writer Philostratus the Elder. In this book, a narrator takes a group of people through a building covered in painted walls. In one of my favorite "rooms," called "Looms," our narrator takes us into a room that appears to have been abandoned, where the columns no longer support the roof, much like these abandoned ancient cities. He begins by telling the group of listeners about a painted scene of Penelope who is sitting and weaving (or unweaving, as you might remember from the *Odyssey*) and crying hot tears. Almost as soon as he mentions her, he turns to a painting of a colony of different weavers, a colony of spiders—a creature that "loves to weave

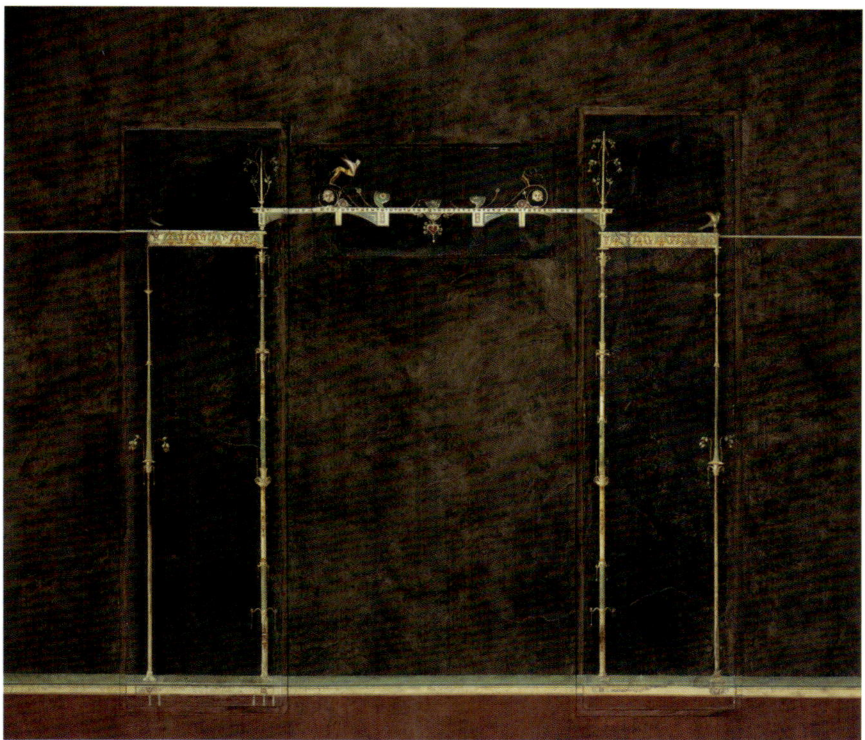

FIG. 5.3 Painting with a griffin, masks, and a bird from the west wall of the Black Room, Boscotrecase. Fresco, 213.36 × 114.3 cm.

its web in quiet." The spinning of the spiders makes the room, well, spin: "Look," Philostratus tells us, "at the threads also, for as the spiders spew out their yarn they let it down to the pavement—and the painter shows them descending on it and scrambling up and 'soaring aloft,' as Hesiod says, and trying to fly—and in the angles they weave their nests, some spread out flat, some hollow; the flat ones are good to summer in, and the hollow sort they weave is useful in winter."

The spiders seem to be doing the crafting, the creating. They are tiny, fuzzy artists. And as the room that was all columns and walls dissolves, the little creatures make a new room, a new home out of their tiny threads: "For look!

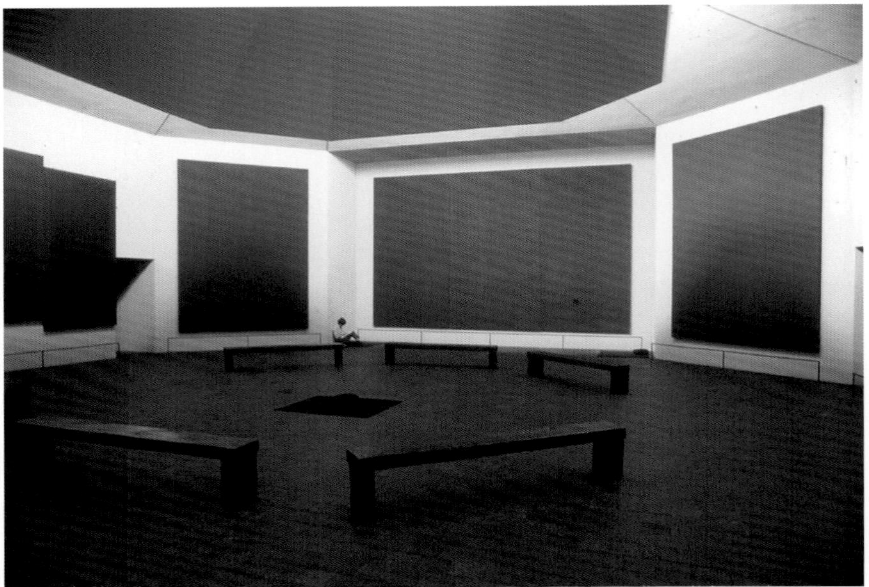

FIG. 5.4 Mark Rothko, Rothko Chapel, 1971. Houston, Texas.

here is a cord forming a square that has been thrown about the corners to be as it were a cable to hold the web, and to this cord is attached a delicate web of many concentric circles, and tight lines, making meshes, running from the outside circle to the smallest one, are interwoven at intervals corresponding to the distance between the circles. And the weavers travel across them, drawing tight such of the threads as have become loose." The gossamer threads that make up these paintings are, as Philostratus describes, moving and changing and fixing themselves in front of our eyes.

There is something poetically resonant between this room of spinning spiders and the Black Room from Boscotrecase housed at the Met. When we first walk into the room, the darkness of the walls is the most striking effect. Pitch-black walls, with very thin, light, imperceptible details—white bits and little dabs of yellow (Fig. 5.3). Fans of modern art are familiar with sanctuary-like spaces composed of black walls.

At first blush, the painted panels in the Rothko Chapel in Houston make a striking comparison to the walls of Boscotrecase (Fig. 5.4). The Rothko Chapel was the inspiration of John and Dominique de Menil, who commissioned the artist Mark Rothko and a series of well-known architects, the first of whom was Philip Johnson. At the opening of the chapel in 1971, Dominique de Menil spoke lovingly about the indescribable quality of Rothko's paintings, about "the enigmatic, gripping presence of his paintings, the ineffable beyond-everything sensation...[and] the disembodied absolute, of an image of the not-seen." The varying depths of saturation in the dark blacks, reds, blues, purples of the panels and the almost imperceptible change in the artist's brushstroke—sometimes horizontal, sometimes vertical—relate in a superficial way to the paintings at the Met. And I don't mean superficial in a pejorative way. I mean to say that the effects on the surface are similar. At both sites the paintings also hover above the ground—Rothko's panels hang above the benches, and the Boscotrecase black is set on a band of deep red. Both are calming and meditative spaces.

But Rothko's purpose is to bring the viewer deeper and deeper into that meditative state. The perception of blackness gives the viewer more blackness, more interiority. In contrast, when we look more closely at the walls in the rooms from Boscotrecase, as in the room with Philostratus, they give back something different, something more complicated and intricate. As in Philostratus, the paintings almost look like tiny, gossamer threads, hovering and delicate. These slight painted lines link the room and tie it together, but in a way that plays with the very notion of walls and architecture. These delicate and spindly forms almost seem to laugh at the idea of the very walls upon which they appear—structures seemingly so solid, so strong. These fragile and poetic structures are eerily prescient considering the fact that Mount Vesuvius was soon to prove that, indeed, walls and architecture, those impervious structures created by man, are utterly ephemeral.

If we trace the columns on the panel of the west wall upward, the artist tricks us over and over again (Fig.5.3). The column farthest to the right becomes thinner and thinner as it gets taller, almost to a thin filigree. There is nothing about this form that would support the painted entablature above or the bird that rests upon it. The second column is similarly thin and delicate. The pinnacle comes to the tiniest pinprick at the top. This inner column appears to be a composite of differ-ent kinds of marbles and mini-colonnettes—some are decorated with crisscrossed green shapes, others have ornamental forms, some are painted yellow, others are purple, perhaps mimicking porphyry. At each juncture of these unrelated bits and pieces, there are elegant forms that look somewhat like flowers, which in turn drip thin, threadlike shapes. Perhaps they are filigrees of gold? Or perhaps they are stem stalks, as on the right-hand column, where the strands flower and then droop. But this is confusing too because some of these florid forms have strands that drip upward. The paintings are fantastic in more ways than one.

They were not always considered to be so. Until the latter part of the twenti-eth century, the most standard truism about Roman art was that it was wholly indebted to the Greek culture. That is somewhat inevitable, since the Romans knew Greek art thoroughly through trade, travel, conquest. Yet I think we can all agree that these paintings are not slavish, mechanical copies. They are thor-oughly original. In fact, Vitruvius lamented this painting style in his book *De Architectura* because it was *too* imaginative: "Imitations based upon reality are now disdained by the improper taste of the present.... Instead of columns there rise up stalks; instead of gables, striped panels with curled leaves and volutes. Candelabra uphold pictured shrines and above the summits of these, clusters of thin stalks rise from their roots in tendrils with little figures seated upon them at random.... Slender stalks with heads of men and of animals [are] attached to half the body. Such things neither are, nor can be, nor have been."

This ethereal and hypothetical architecture is traditionally labeled as being of the Third Style, a categorization determined by August Mau in 1882. It sounds like a plodding and pedantic term, but the category is still used in scholarship and museum studies, and I think it does help to see that there are distinctions between the different periods in Roman wall paintings.

There are four different periods. The First Style runs from ca. 200 to 90 BCE and is mostly paintings of simulated marble of various types. The walls were generally divided into three horizontal painted zones and crowned by a stucco cornice. For the most part the mosaic floors took precedence over the walls. The mosaic floor showing Alexander the Great combatting Darius III of Persia from the House of the Faun in Pompeii is a perfect example. Yes, those are tiny cubes

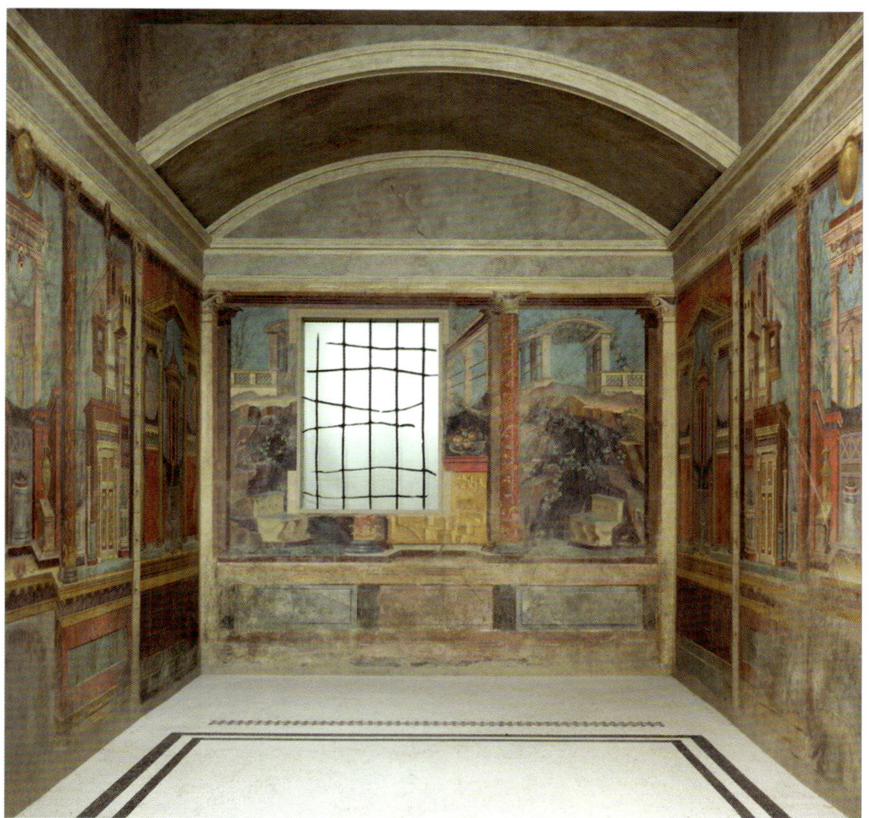

FIG. 5.5 Cubiculum (bedroom) from the villa of P. Fannius Synistor at Boscoreale, Italy, ca. 50–40 BCE. Metropolitan Museum of Art, New York. Fresco.

of stone. Stone also characterizes the fourth and final style, which lasted from 40 CE to the eruption of the volcano in 79. Marble sculptures were placed into the painted walls as "ornaments."

The Second Style, which lasted from about 90 BCE until 25 BCE, is characterized by fantastic panoramas and architectural confections. A second painted room at the Met, from another Pompeian suburb, Boscoreale, provides a phenomenal example of this period (Fig. 5.5). Receding colonnades, grand archways and arches,

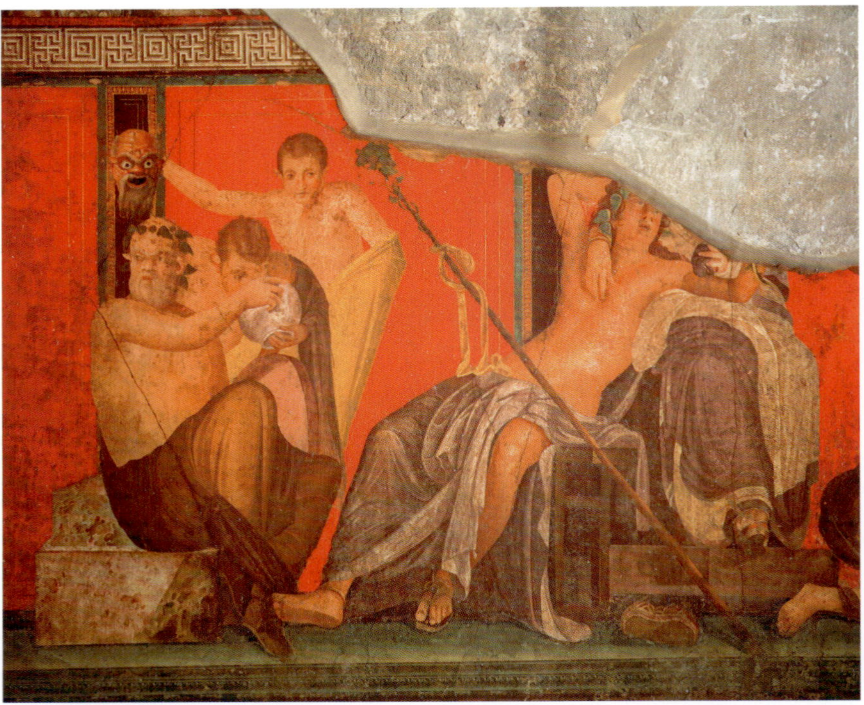

FIG. 5.6 Detail of Bacchus and Ariadne from the House of the Mysteries, Pompeii, Italy, ca. 60–50 BCE. Fresco.

projecting bases, and rectilinear entablatures metabolize the walls. It is all so weighty and grand and seemingly functional. These kaleidoscopic structures are highlighted and shaded so that they look naturalistic, thereby creating a sense of a receding perspective. But here is where this all breaks down. The perspective is not one-point perspective that becomes de rigueur in the Renaissance. Rather, the perspective is circular—nothing leads anywhere in particular, and ultimately this labyrinthine quality leaves you with a world of spinning, structureless forms and shapes.

A room from the Pompeian House of the Mysteries reveals a second characteristic of this second style—large, weighty figures (Fig. 5.6). Although it might seem like figural images would be easier to comprehend than the abstract architectural ones, they are just as baffling, and it is from this room that the villa gets its name. Mysteries. The scene is most likely related to a ceremony in honor of the wine god Bacchus, who reclines drunkenly across a bench and onto the lap of a woman identified as Ariadne because of the ball of deep-purple yarn that she holds in her left hand. Ariadne helps Theseus out of the labyrinth inhabited by the Minotaur by giving him a ball of thread. Not soon thereafter, Theseus abandons her and, in many accounts of the tale, Bacchus marries her. These myths aren't entirely stable, but that flexibility is important in these rooms, in these paintings. We cannot pin down the exact meaning of this particular room. We cannot say that she is or is not Ariadne. Still, in thinking about her, in imagining her story, in placing it in this strange context, we are spinning our own stories, like she does with her thread, like the spiders do with theirs. It is no surprise that the word Philostratus uses for thread is *mythos.*

Philostratus is the most masterful wordsmith. To use one of his favorite words in the imperative form, *Hora!* (Look!). As we get closer to the spindly forms back in our Third Style rooms of Boscotrecase, images start to emerge from the walls—birds and faces, masks and bucolic vignettes. At the top of the thin white entablature in the center of the western wall, our thin dripping filigrees spin in looping circles supporting what was once a pair of yellow griffins with wild tattoos and wings of white, pink, and purple. The curlicue of their tails mirrors the finishing touch of the delicate tightropes upon which they stand and which terminate in a pair of ridiculous faces—funny little men with pert, round faces and thick, arched eyebrows that mirror the shape of their yellow-tinged diadems. Who are these little men? Are they just masks? But they seem so intent, so keen. What they doing there? What do they want? Some scholars have determined that these are Gorgon or Medusa faces. You may recall that this mythological creature turns anyone that looks in her face into stone. There is definitely a gotcha feeling to these images—snap a thread and it will all come tumbling down, look too close and you'll get caught, don't look at all and you'll be surrounded by dark, black walls.

These are not the only faces that emerge from the walls. The first wall that the visitor would see, even before entering the room from the terrace, was the north wall. Again, two sets of thin column-shapes frame a central canopy-shape. These three panels sit in front of a frieze that becomes temporarily concave in order to accommodate the two flanking columns and recedes slightly underneath the canopy. Atop the two central columns, those that appear to support the canopy shape, are two medallions surrounded by thin off-white lines and with dark purple backgrounds. Unlike the masklike men, these two figures do not look back at us. They are austere, in profile, and isolated from all the folderol. The composition of these round portraits is much like an ancient Roman coin, showing the image of an imperial figure. However, the tenderness implicit in a cameo seems more appropriate to these images than an impersonal, mercantile coin. Here the two figures look across the void into each other's eyes. Stylistically they are also different from the images one might see on a coin. These figures are unique, unlike coins, which are produced in large quantities and depend on mechanical, reliable replicas. Also, metal is solid, immobile, constant.

Until the 1980s, the medallions were both understood to represent the same, unidentified male sitter. This was until scholars unearthed a photograph taken in 1929, before the wall paintings underwent a major conservation campaign. The photograph revealed that the zealous restorer accidentally transformed an image of a woman into that of a man. From these black-and-white photographs the scholar Maxwell Anderson identified the female sitter on the left as Julia, the daughter of Emperor Augustus and the mistress of the villa. The companion medallion, he argued, was that of her stepmother, Livia. Scholars have shown evidence of Augustus trying to link Julia and Livia in official art on multiple occasions—both in coinage and on the Roman monument called the Ara Pacis. Thus, the closer we look, the more time we spend in this room, these images become more than playful and contradictory forms. Historical figures and political realities are constantly alluded to and, as in this case, are participants in this swirling economy of images. They are acting as part of the structure, holding it together as much as they can, linking one spindly form to another.

Two other framed images allude to Augustus and his success at the Battle of Actium in 31 BCE. These frames appear at the top of the panels that framed the larger, central canopy. These framed images balance on the pinnacle of two shoots that emerge from a calyx upon which rests a lidded vase, which also

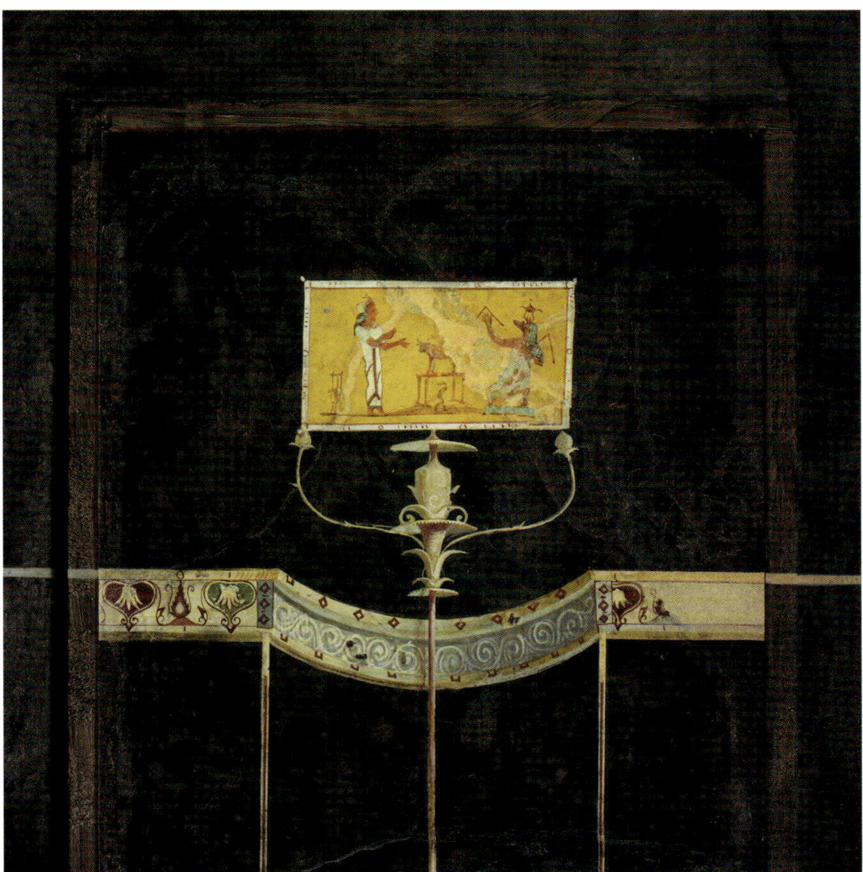

FIG. 5.7 Detail of Egyptianizing scene from the north wall of the Black Room, Boscotrecase.

participates in "supporting" the images. The yellow background of the framed images is meant to suggest papyrus, the most common material upon which Egyptians wrote. The image on the left shows two figures flanking a table upon which stands a horned animal, possibly referring to the Apis bull, a symbol of fertility, renewal, and, during this period, the afterlife (Fig. 5.7). Under the table there is a *uraeus*, the cobra-shaped protector of kings, who rears his hooded head.

A female votary of Isis stands to the left of the table wearing feathers and a queenly headdress. On the right is a kneeling male who appears in the guise of the crocodile god Sobek with a sun disk and cowlike horns of the goddess Hathor atop his head. The idea is that these two are a princely couple in the act of worshiping at a specific and sacred site.

Similarly, the second painting shows a kneeling ruler wearing the ceremonial beard and the *nemes* (regal headcloth). He offers an olive branch to an image of Anubis, the jackal-headed god associated with the afterlife. A female figure officiates with a container of holy water as a priestess of Isis. Egyptologists have taken issue with the accuracy of Egyptian motifs in Roman art. But as the scholar Elfriede Knauer points out, the same argument could be made about monuments in Egypt themselves that were produced during this period, since the confluence of different cultures was already corrupting or modifying those cultic images. In other words, the Egyptian hieroglyphs were, by the Roman period, no longer entirely stable as a result of the influx of peoples from different areas with different cultures. The point is not that the Roman artists may have mixed up a few details. The point is that Egypt is on their mind. Knauer suggests that the presence of these images reveals a huge sense of relief about the victory at Actium after decades of brutal civil war. She argues that these framed paintings might have been meant as representations of Julia and Agrippa, dressed as Egyptianizing figures, extending symbols of peace to the central images of the Egyptian gods affiliated with death. In the context of this particular room, swirling with fantastical imagery and eerie black walls, we cannot ignore the fact that there might be some element of admiration, of evoking mysterious and foreign religions with their animal-faced gods and cultic sacrifices.

Other animals emerge from the walls—specifically birds. The delicate pair of swans below the papyri paintings gracefully arc their necks and extend their wings while holding aloft a string that appears to be composed of tiny pearls or dewdrops (Fig. 5.8). The swans are also an allusion to Augustus. Swans were affiliated specifically with Apollo and were alleged to have heralded his birth as the beginning of the Golden Age, the first of five stages in the Ages of Man, a legend from Greek mythology. Augustus considered himself to be under the special protection of Apollo and certainly understood himself as the initiator of

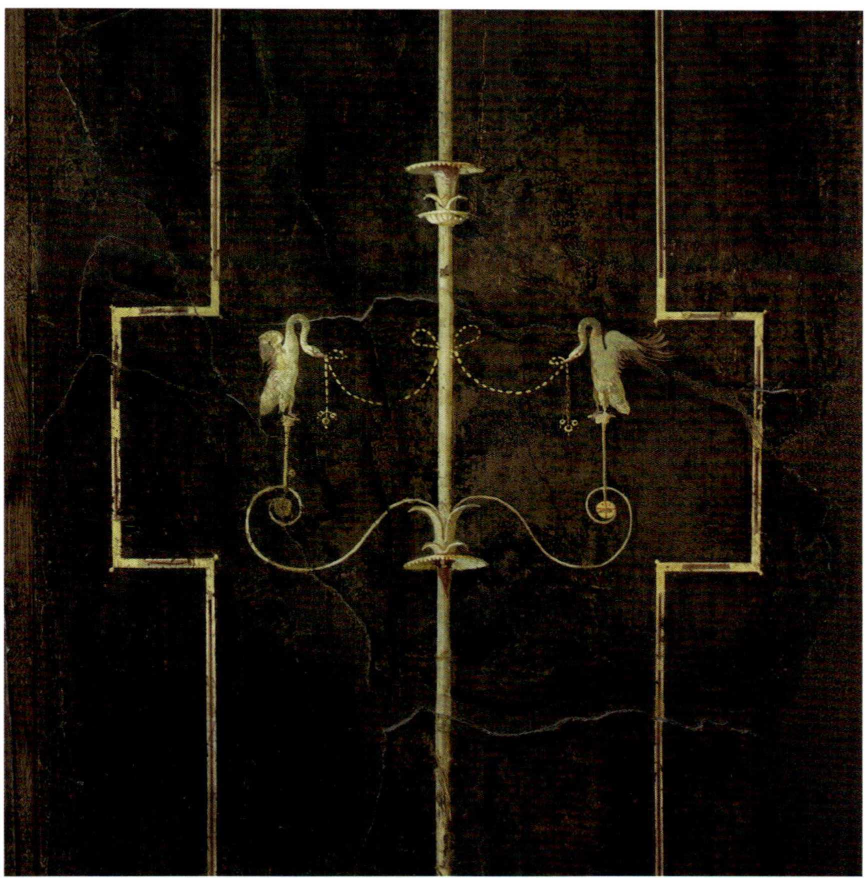

FIG. 5.8 Detail of a pair of swans from the north wall of the Black Room, Boscotrecase.

a new Golden Age—one of prosperity, harmony, stability, and peace. Augustus also had asked for Apollo's help in the Battle of Actium. Thus references to the struggles in Egypt and the divinely sanctioned victory of the Romans color the walls in the Black Room.

In many ways the paintings in the villa are about peace and prosperity. In this way we might think of similarities to another monument celebrating peace during the time of Augustus, the Ara Pacis in Rome. The monument was started in 13 BCE, in honor of Augustus's successful return to Rome after three years in Hispania and Gaul, and consecrated in 9 BCE. The north and south friezes represent a procession of important figures in Augustus's world. Bodyguards (*lictors*), priests, women and children, and attendants compose the solemn groups. Marcus Agrippa appears on the south frieze, with his head covered, as though he is a priest. He carries a scroll, indicating his significant role as Augustus's advisor. Behind him stands Julia (although some say Livia) and, between them, their young son, Gaius Caesar.

The lead figure, who is missing most of his body, has been identified as Augustus. But Augustus is clearly the tie that binds. Here too his special symbolic swans adorn the monument—holding out their wings as an invitation to the monument, arching their necks in a way that flows rhythmically in step with the swirling, curving acanthus vines. The visitor walks around the monument identifying important figures, counting swans, following the flow of the vines, and participating in the procession leading toward the door of the internally placed altar. Remembering peace and prosperity was physical and visual.

The Black Room was also a physical experience. Like the Ara Pacis, you cannot understand the images without moving around the monument, from panel to panel, and, in the case of the Boscotrecase villa as a whole, from room to room. The room originally next to the Black Room, the so-called Red Room (room 16), is now housed in the National Archaeological Museum of Naples. Both rooms use a number of the same motifs—suggestive and playful architectural shapes, delicate flora, and isolated minipaintings. The painting schemes also seem to correspond with each other—the prominent black from the Met room retreats to the lower panel in Naples, while the rich red of main panel in Naples makes up the lower zone at the Met. Thus the rooms of the villa are playful inversions of each other.

The zones within the paintings also seem to converse with each other. Panels from the White Room (room 20) have white backgrounds in the upper part and a black lower zone. Very little from this room remains, and what does is housed at the Met. In one of these fragments, a small bird, perching in the lower, black zone appears to be surveying the scene, making sure he won't get caught, before eating two little red fruits. In the lower black zone of the Red Room there is a

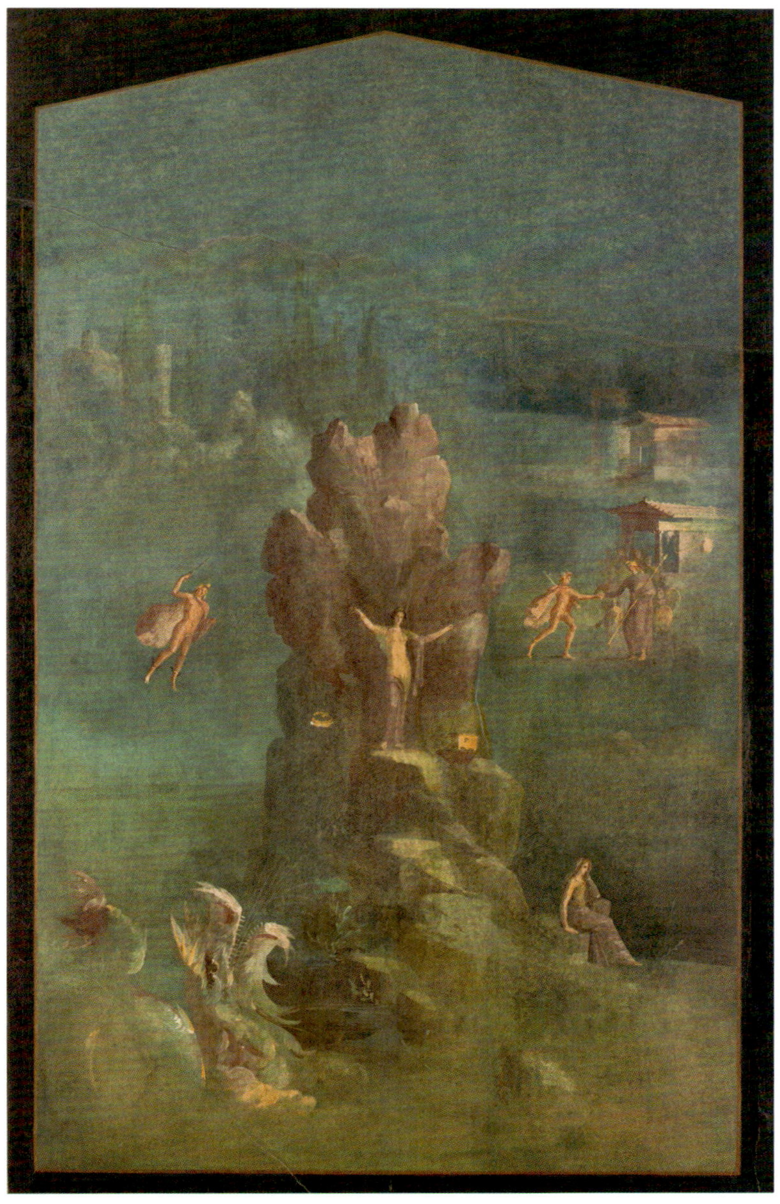

FIG. 5.9 Perseus and Andromeda in a landscape. East wall of the Mythological Room from the imperial villa at Boscotrecase. Fresco, 159.39 × 118.75 cm.

small pile of eight green figs. The black zones in the White Room and the Red Room seem to correspond, seem to suggest a continuity across the hall of rooms, as though this little green-tailed bird might finish the cherries and then continue along that black band to discover the figs waiting in a pile nearby.

The immediacy of the inviting figs in the Red Room contrasts with the framed image above. This scene appears to be, like the pile of fruit, easy to grasp. Ah yes, a simple pastoral scene. But in fact the painting as a whole is less tangible than the fruit. It is as though the artist gives us just enough, teases us into feeling like we "get it," and then gives us a scene with no story, no setting, no sense of time, no characters.

Why is there a column with a large amphora on it? What city is that in the background? Why is this scene hovering in the middle of a white "canvas"? Who are those figures? There are scenes of this sort in the Black Room too—one that was originally in the museum in Naples (now lost) and another one at the Met.* As we zoom in closer and closer, the light, fluffy brushstrokes become more and more meaningless. They are hints of an image that becomes more elusive the closer we get, the more we pry. The way these paintings dissolve is suggestive of that state of *hypnagogia* (sleep + leading), that weird moment just before we fall asleep, when we are still conscious but slipping into our dreams, which is appropriate since the Black Room was a bedroom.

Not all of the images from the villa are abstract. There are some paintings in the villa that actually do tell stories. But even these seemingly straightforward stories leave room for imaginative slippage, which might also speak to that state of slipping consciousness. Bedtime stories, perhaps, but serious ones. Two of the framed panels from the Mythological Room (room 19) represent mythological tales that were popular in the ancient world. The panel on the east wall of the room shows the scene of Perseus and Andromeda, the daughter of the king and queen of Ethiopia (Fig. 5.9). Andromeda's mother, Cassiopeia, boasts that her own daughter is more beautiful than the Nereids, the nymph daughters of the sea god Nereus. Cassiopeia is punished by Poseidon, the god of the sea, who calls

* "Wall painting on black ground: Aedicula with small landscape, from the imperial villa at Boscotrecase," www.metmuseum.org/toah/works-of-art/20.192.1-.8,.10,.11.

upon a sea monster to ravage the coast of Ethiopia. Andromeda's father discovers that his kingdom will be saved only if he sacrifices his daughter to the monster. It is at this point that the artist throws us into the painting—with the sight of Andromeda chained haplessly to the craggy rock.

At first glance, one might not think she is chained because her arms seem to hang so softly and elegantly in the air. But the artist clues the viewer into the relationship between the rock and the lady by a number of clever details—the himation hanging over her right leg is the same color as her rocky cage, a deep purple, and the formation of the craggy outcrop itself is shaped specifically as an expression or mirror of her pose. That resonance with the rocks behind her, her contrapposto stance with the forward-placed right leg, the slipping himation, extended arms that look like outstretched wings—these all might make us think back to our Nike of Samothrace. According to Ovid, Perseus has a similar reaction: "When Perseus noticed the maiden tied by the arms to a jagged rock face (but for the light breeze stirring her hair and the warm tears coursing over her cheeks, he would have supposed she was merely a marble statue), unconscious desire was kindled within him."

As we broaden our gaze outward from the centrally placed victim, the artist also gives us more clues about how the painting is meant to be read or how to follow the narrative flow, which is principally through gestures and repeated poses. The figure of Perseus appears to the left of the torturous rock with his right arm held aloft. He wears the special winged sandals and carries the hooked sword described in Ovid's account of the story. It is the hook of his arm that draws the eye of the viewer through the outstretched arms of Andromeda and across to his own extended arms as he shakes the hand of Andromeda's father. The repetition of Perseus provides a visual continuity that leads us through the painting, from the beginning of the story at the left to the conclusion at the right, where Perseus shakes the hand of the father who started the whole mess. The pose of the father, who faces toward the center of the composition, adds to this visualized dénouement. His curved back and lowered head create the shape of a closed parenthesis. Thus, his pose and the meaningful handshake signal an end to the drama.

The mother, also responsible for these troubles with the sea monster, sits below, at the base of the mountain—either feeling shame about her actions or *maybe* concern for her daughter, since she is looking away and does not see the appearance of the savior Perseus. The handshake above is also possibly the finalization of Perseus's betrothal to Andromeda, a match negotiated when everything (including Perseus) is up in the air, after Perseus has seen Andromeda but before slaying the monster. Poor Andromeda. Her name translates to "ruler of men," but the truth is nothing close. She has no agency. She is either chained to a rock by her father or claimed by a flying man with fancy shoes and a hooked staff.

And then there is the monster—the third claimant for our pathetic heroine. Like a brilliantly colored salamander, purple and green and pink, with yellow and white highlights, he curls delicately in the left-hand corner. His fuzzy muzzle, the tiny row of lightly jagged teeth, the tiny strands of white mist he spits at Andromeda—he is almost too lovely and tantalizing to be the source of angst. In Ovid's account, the beast is a true threat. He comes after Andromeda by "parting the waves with the thrust of his huge breast, just as a war-galley, strongly propelled by its sweating oarsmen" and "spewing forth seawater mingled with crimson blood, drenching Perseus' sandals in spray and weighing them down." But in our painting, there is something else at play. Our response is less repulsion and fear of the beast, and more an appreciation and admiration of his kaleidoscopic beauty.

The painting on the other side of this Mythological Room is also an inversion of our expectations and replaces repulsion with star-crossed longing (Fig. 5.10). When we think of Polyphemus, it is usually as the one-eyed, savage man-eating giant in the ninth book of the *Odyssey*. Odysseus, after watching Polyphemus eat four of his men, gets the large giant drunk and blinds him in that one eye with a wooden stake. The next morning Odysseus and his men tie themselves to the undersides of Polyphemus's flocks and escape from the cave. Polyphemus shouts for help from his father Poseidon, demanding that Odysseus find "great trouble in his house," while throwing bigger and bigger rocks at the escaping ship. This scene does appear in the painting. We see Polyphemus off-center holding a boulder that he is ready to throw at the swiftly departing ship. Standing against a rocky cliff that is much like Andromeda's—purple-hued and craggy—Polyphemus prepares to throw the boulder, holding it just about at the place of his now blinded eye.

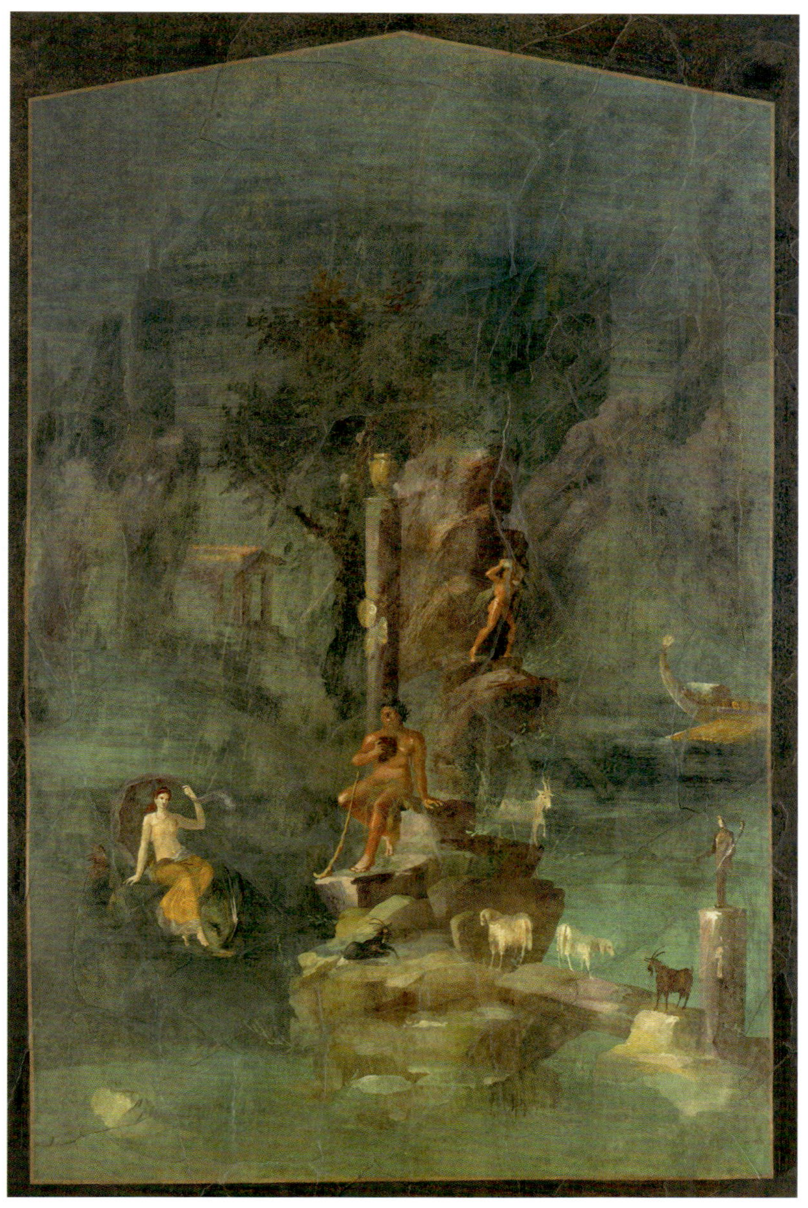

FIG. 5.10 Polyphemus and Galatea in a landscape. West wall of the Mythological Room from the imperial villa at Boscotrecase. Fresco, 187.33 × 119.38 cm.

But the main image of Polyphemus is in the center, a moment before Odysseus and the blinding. Polyphemus sits at the base of a column topped with a large acanthus shape that is not unlike the centrally placed columns in the Black and Red rooms. That reference to those bucolic scenes, to those idyllic moments of pleasure and peace and love, are more fitting for this primary representation of Polyphemus. Thus the goats might refer to Odysseus's escape, but they also play an even more important role as participants in this pastoral. Polyphemus leans against the column, playing the panpipe, and looking with longing and wistfulness at Galatea, the woman who blithely enters the scene riding the back of a turquoise dolphin with purple fins. Her yellow dress, which only covers her lower body, responds to the painting of the beautiful Andromeda on the opposite-facing wall. The purple himation Andromeda wears on her lower body now hovers above and around Galatea's upper body—puffed up with air as she flies across the deep-green sea.

Alas, Galatea does not return Polyphemus's love. Galatea is in love with someone else, Acis, who does not appear in this painting. When you read her description of her love triangle in Ovid, you can't help but feel for the giant. She ridicules his attempts to impress her, scorning the way he trims his beard with a pruning hook and combs his hair with a pickaxe. According to the myth, she and Acis are caught by Polyphemus canoodling, and the giant kills the boy with (no surprise here) a large boulder. What does appear in the painting is a sense of longing and imminent despair. She looks away, out of the picture plane, into our space. All of a sudden we are part of the love triangle. We are seeing the moment before everything falls apart—just before he is rejected, just before she is caught with Acis, just before Acis dies from Polyphemus's stone, a foreshadowing of which is just in the upper corner. Polyphemus misses Odysseus, but he doesn't miss Galatea's lover. These paintings aren't really about illustrating stories, although they show aspects and bits of those stories. They are really more about seeing and looking. The paintings really seem to point toward concerns about sight and desire, toward that singular and pathetic monogaze of Polyphemus set in opposition to Galatea's distracted and disdainful gaze beyond the framed painting.

The Boscotrecase Galatea makes me think of another Galatea, the one painted by Raphael in 1514 for the Villa Farnesina in Rome. This scene shows

Galatea mostly clothed in a fluttering purple cloak as she darts across the sea in a large conch pulled by two dolphins. Galatea is encircled by all manner of love and lust—notoriously salacious satyrs, a merman vigorously grabbing a lady with a yellow fluttering scarf (in much the same pose as the Galatea at Boscotrecase), and three cupids (a fourth if you count that fellow hiding in the cloud) that flutter ominously above, ready to pierce her from all angles with their primed bows and arrows. Polyphemus appears in the panel to the left of the Galatea scene. Painted in 1512 by Sebastiano del Piombo, Polyphemus sits alone, rejected, completely separated from his beloved by water, by the thick frame that distinguishes the two scenes, by their emotional dissonance. As in the ancient fresco, here too Polyphemus holds his panpipe (a symbol of his rejected love songs) and rests against the mountainside, watching her quickly disappear. He looks like he might try to get up and follow her, but then again, he seems to sigh, "Why bother? She is too quick, too distant…literally out of my league."

One ineresting coincidence about the Villa Farnesina is that the first building on that site, underneath the Renaissance villa, belonged to Agrippa and was painted in 21 BCE in commemoration of his marriage to Julia. The paintings from these rooms were all transferred to the incredible collection at the Palazzo Massimo in Rome. If you have been to Rome and haven't seen this museum, that is a grave and hideous tragedy that must be rectified. This museum is extraordinary. It is filled with masterful paintings from these early Roman domiciles, like the deep-blue garden scenes from Livia's private home originally in a Roman suburb, and nine rooms from the original Villa Farnesina. And, wouldn't you know, one of the rooms, Triclinium C, is black with Egyptianizing motifs that refer to the pharaoh Bocchoris (from the eighth century BCE) and tiny, spindly, weblike scenes that slowly emerge from the darkness. Those forms and scenes are impossible to see in any published image. Just more reason that you should make sure to get to this museum.

Swirling associations, emerging images, scenes we can't see but very much want to…before we know it we have been enmeshed in this world of paintings. It is almost as though we are caught in a tangled web of paint, a web of little, curious lies or fictions. This is precisely what happens in the passage by Philostratus. Throughout the narrator's description he confuses the spiders with the painters, real webs with painted webs. He dances back and forth between reality and fiction. One moment he is praising the truthfulness of the artist's representations of the spiders, detailing their "repulsive fuzzy surface" and "savage nature." The next moment the narrator is describing the room as though the spiders are in our midst, fixing and spinning and weaving.

Who is actually making these paintings? What is happening in this room? By the end of the poetic passage, we have all become completely entangled in these painted webs: "But they [the spiders] win a reward for their weaving and feed on the flies whenever any become enmeshed in the webs. Hence the painter has not omitted their prey either; for one fly is caught by the feet, another by the tip of its wing, the head of another is being eaten, and they squirm in their effort to escape, yet they do not disarrange or break the web." The viewer is also the prey. Art has tricked us into looking closer and closer. It has caught us and we like it. We are consumed by that art, by that web, and we might squirm but we don't really want to escape or break the spell. We are complicit in the story of Andromeda because we too stare at her, we too claim her with our eyes. We watch Galatea hurt and leave Polyphemus, knowing what is about to happen and thereby becoming part of their tragedy. And as we become part of these stories, we are trapped. We are literally stopped and stunned by the images. We become like the birds in the paintings, flightless and trapped—caught in a beautiful gilded cage. Like the Romans, we are actually living inside their art.

I like juxtaposing Philostratus's tiny black spiders wiggling and working on the walls, weaving their webs, with the Black Room from the Met. As if black walls were actually the backs of tiny, spinning, black spiders. We are seeing their intricate works, things we couldn't see at first, come to life. Just like Philostratus. And like Philostratus, our eyes are darting in totally nonlinear ways from black forms to paintings and back, from reality to fiction.

Philostratus is, in fact, pure fiction. Those paintings in the *Imagines* by Philostratus do not exist. They never did. There are no spiders. There are no painters. There are no paintings of spiders. There are just words. Early nineteenth-century German scholars tried to reconstruct the rooms that Philostratus describes. But those scholars missed the point. The idea is not to think about physical painting

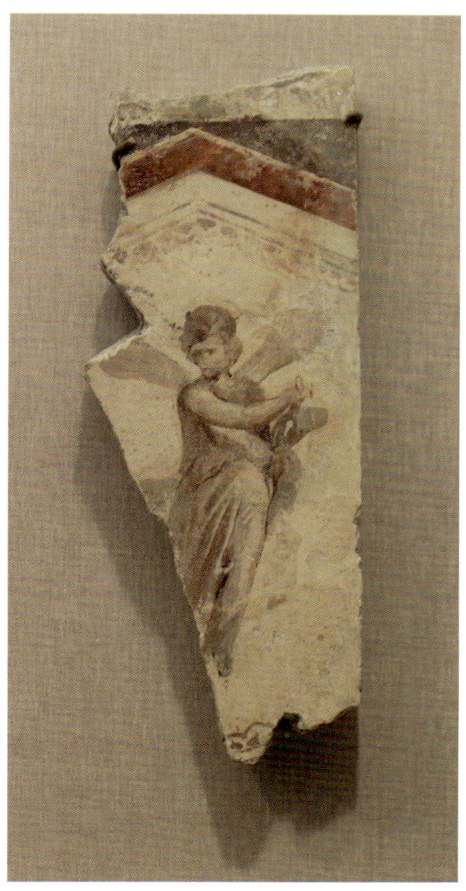

FIG. 5.11 Psyche, ca. first century CE. San Antonio Museum of Art, San Antonio, Texas. Fresco.

but to consider what the paintings mean in a deeper, more intellectual way, a more abstract way. An important part of seeing art involves an element of fantasy. *Phantasia* is actually the exact word used by early writers like Philostratus to explain the creative act of the artist, to define what separates a mechanical copy from an inspirational work of art. In this sense *phantasia* also translates as "imagination." Visual images are not real or even trying to be real. They are a means of connecting the viewer with more abstract and more sophisticated ways of understanding those images or objects. *Phantasia* allows those images, those external and tangible objects, to impress themselves upon your memory and soul. Just the other day I saw a man who tried to stick his entire hand through the banderole on a sarcophagus. Yes, the images and the objects make you want to touch them, but with your mind, with your imagination or *phantasia*, not with your hands.

Also in the galleries at the San Antonio Museum of Art, safe from that overly tactile man, is a beautiful and rather haunting image in a glass vitrine, a Roman fresco fragment that, I think, visualizes the concept of *phantasia* and mirrors the way we visited the rooms at Villa Boscotrecase—a villa that, one might argue, exists more in our imaginations than in reality, just as in the case of Philostratus's rooms (Fig. 5.11). This fragmentary wall painting shows a delicate, winged figure hovering against a white background. She appears to be pulling a sword from a sheath that sits on her left hip. Her right arm sweeps across her upper body, and she looks with concern or disdain toward her lower right. Is there someone there? Where is there? Where is she? She appears in the center of a chevron or a pediment-like form. But this is the same kind of "architecture" that we had in the Black Room, not structural but imaginative. In a sense, she is too. She looks like she is made out of the delicate fibers spun by the spiders in the poem—light and airy and ethereal. She is almost transparent. The thin paint that we see and almost see through reveals the white paint beneath, which might even be the same color as the plaster beneath the painting. She almost dissolves into the wall. We think of other winged figures with manifold meanings—Nike of Samothrace, the perfectly poised swans in the Black Room. As this winged figure seems to retreat from our eyes—both literally and through an ever-widening series of associations—we realize that we are enveloped in this world of images and imaginations and *phantasia*. Associations and connections draw the viewer more deeply into a world of looking and imagination. A conversation about the delicate columns and floating figures in the Black Room drew us into a dialogue with the images of other painted rooms situated down the hall, and into an even broader discourse that moved beyond the walls of that villa altogether, into the world of Augustan and Roman politics. And if *phantasia* allows us to impress images upon our soul, it is delightful to note that the label for this winged woman calls her Psyche, the word for soul. The image is impressed upon our soul, and now perhaps the idea is that we are looking at our own soul in that painted image.

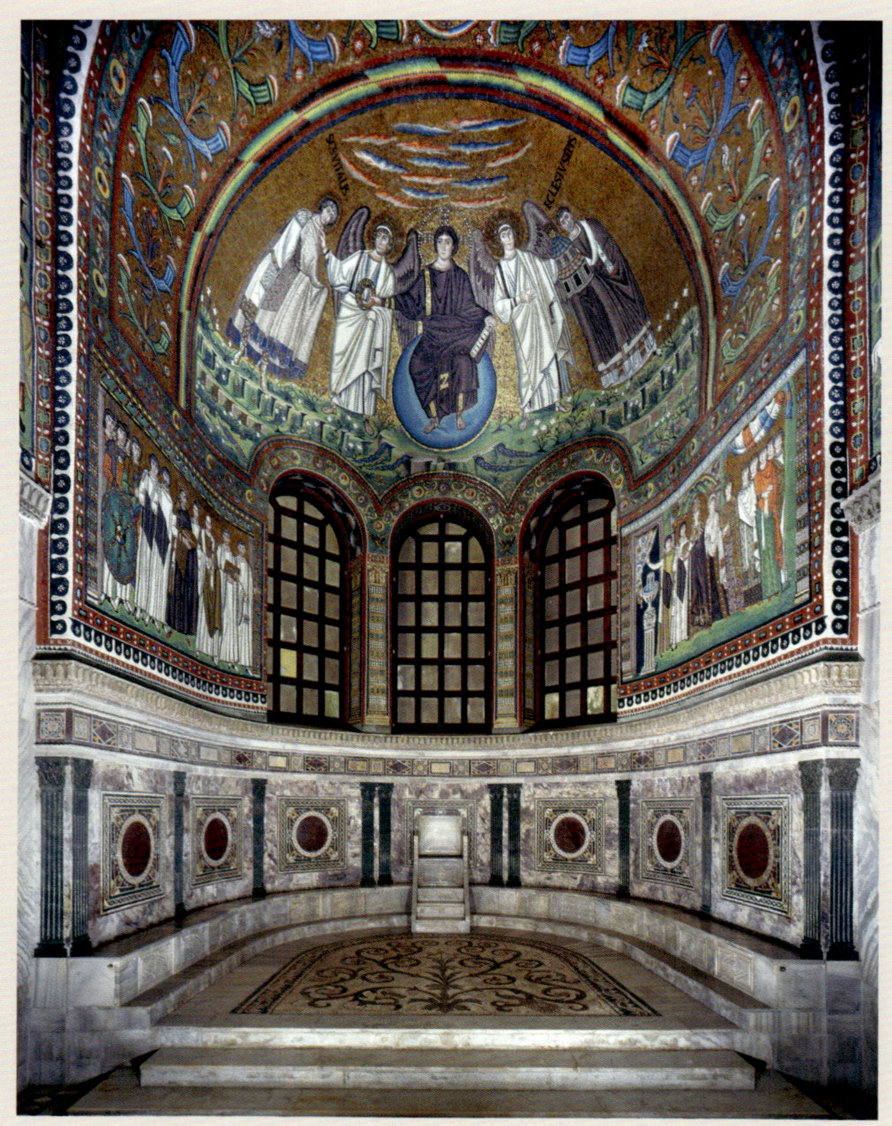

FIG. 6.1 Apse of San Vitale, ca. 547. Ravenna, Italy.

EARLY BYZANTINE ART

So far we have studied two noble historical and fictional figures, Ashurnasirpal and Sarpedon, killing and being killed, neither of whom have looked us in the eye. In the sixth-century mosaics of San Vitale in Ravenna, the Emperor Justinian (in the center) confronts us with a striking directness—frontal, formidable, and frank—exuding strength and power (Figs. 6.1 and 6.2).

By the time of his death in 565 CE, Justinian had conquered the majority of the Mediterranean. Thus Justinian brought Constantinople (in the East) and Ravenna (in northern Italy) back under the same rule, his rule. Representatives of Justinian's pan-Mediterranean power appear in the San Vitale mosaic. Soldiers and dignitaries and major ecclesiastical figures surround the emperor, confronting the viewer with an intense, direct gaze. But Justinian's eyes are slightly off-center; he does not exactly look us in the eye. In fact, the base of the panel is about thirteen feet high. Thus he actually looks across the apse, past the space where the altar would have sat and toward the panel of his bejeweled wife, the Empress Theodora, who also appears with a retinue of frontally facing ladies and two male attendants (Fig. 6.3).

These panels are an exuberant expression of imperial authority cloaked in the most exquisite finery—elaborate patterned silks, spectacular dripping pearls, settings that convey abundance and luxury, and lots of gold. Yet these expressions of power are surrounded by resplendent evidences of piety. The ultimate ruler is Christ, who hovers above the apse enthroned on a brilliant blue globe. Christ

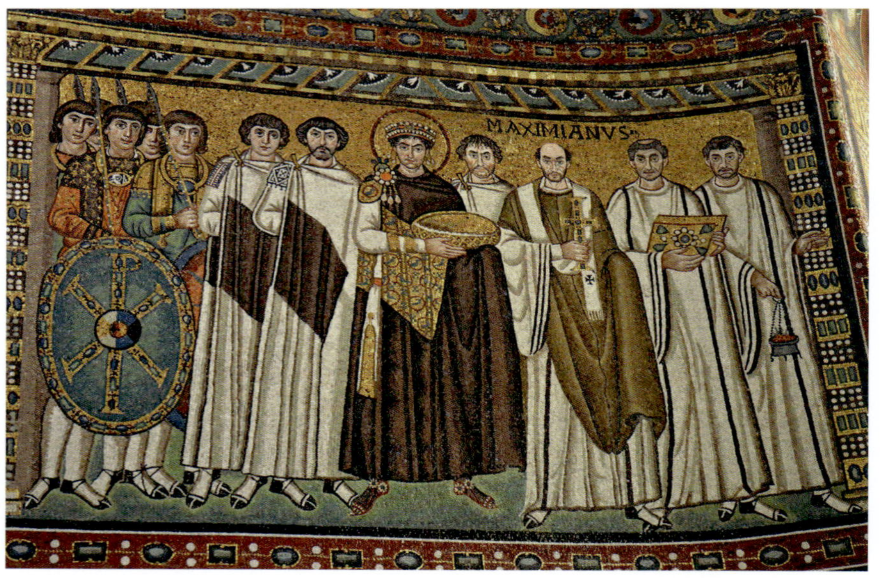

FIG. 6.2 Emperor Justinian and his attendants. North sanctuary wall of San Vitale. Mosaic, 264 × 365.7 cm.

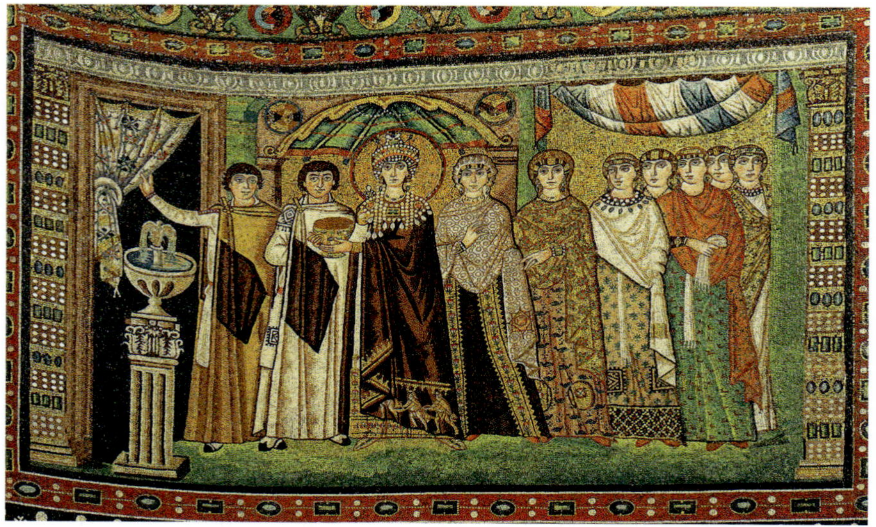

FIG. 6.3 Empress Theodora and her attendants. South sanctuary wall of San Vitale. Mosaic, 264 × 365.7 cm.

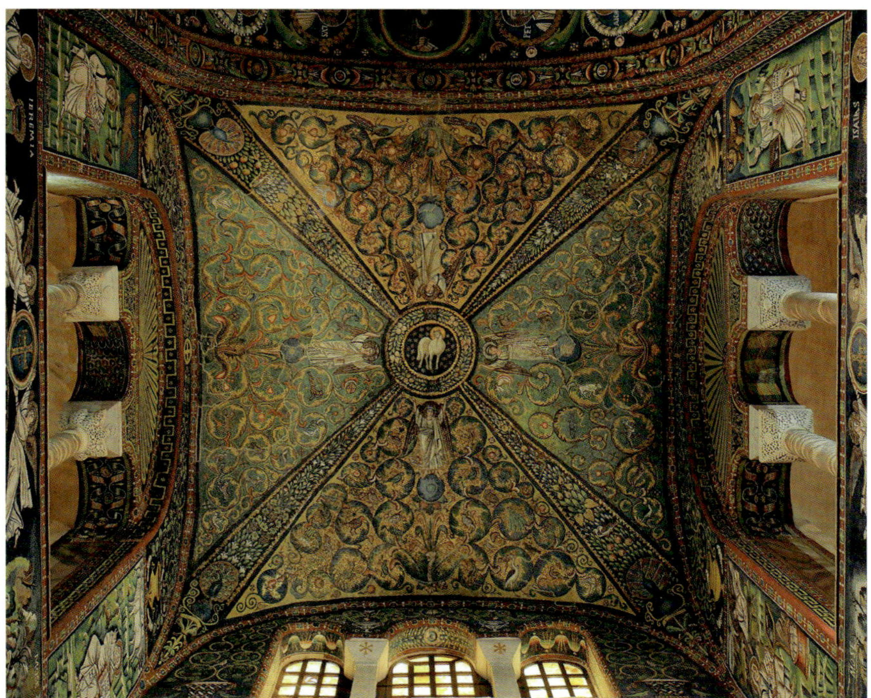

FIG. 6.4 View of the mosaic canopy above the presbytery in San Vitale.

holds a scroll closed with the seven seals of the Apocalypse in his left hand and extends a crown toward the martyr San Vitale with his right. Two angels with massive purple wings flank Christ, and at the far right a bishop labeled *Eclesius Epis* holds out a model of San Vitale, of the very church in which these paradisiacal mosaics appear. Paradise is defined by color and brilliance. The famed Four Rivers of Paradise flow out of the rocks below Christ's blue globe into a verdant landscape punctuated by tiny, bright, white flowers and beautifully variegated peacocks. Within the rich golden background hover wispy red, white, and blue clouds. But Paradise expands beyond these borders, swirling all around the area above the altar, surrounding us, enveloping us, in a seemingly endless expansion of tendrils and gold (Fig. 6.4).

The mosaics of San Vitale are not the first example wherein Justinian asserted his authority through a massive artistic campaign. Justinian moved to Constantinople from the countryside when still young, following his uncle Justin. Through a series of underhanded maneuverings, Justin paid his way into becoming the emperor in 518. When Justin died in 527, Justinian was named emperor. Justin was a bit of a brute, but Justinian was educated and literate. He oversaw a complete revision of all Roman law, organizing and publishing what had become a disorganized mess, and doing it so beautifully that his laws were still being used in twelfth-century Europe. Also, unlike his uncle, Justinian made strong appointments, selecting individuals that were much like himself, from humble origins and extremely ambitious. One such figure was Justinian's famed general Belisarius, who appears to the right of the emperor in the mosaic. Belisarius commanded the Roman army in suppressing threats from the Sassanid Empire and in the effort to expand the holdings of the Byzantine realm. More than anything else, it was his participation in suppressing the Nika Riots that proved how truly invaluable he was going to be for Justinian. These were riots that were predicated on sports, on really intense affiliations with teams of chariot racers.

We are familiar with passionate sports fans. But this was a little different. The two most prominent teams, the Blues and the Greens, went on a weeklong murdering spree—thirty-five thousand people were killed, and much of the city was burned to the ground, including the main basilica, Hagia Sophia. According to the court historian, Procopius, Justinian was beside himself with despair and considered fleeing the city. His wife Theodora, however, insisted that they stay, allegedly proclaiming: "The royal color purple makes a fine burial shroud." Theodora stood her ground. Belisarius suppressed the riots. And Justinian rebuilt the Hagia Sophia, undoubtedly the most majestic and breathtaking way of saying that the city would never see riots like that again. It never did.

Hagia Sophia, or Holy Wisdom, is an architectural marvel. Five years after the riots, in 537, the building was finished and consecrated. But only twenty years later an earthquake caused the dome of the church to fall. Undeterred, Justinian hired a new architect to build a dome that was even higher than the first, by 22 feet. Thus the building as we see it today is 182 feet tall. Light streams into Hagia Sophia by means of a series of forty arched windows that surround the

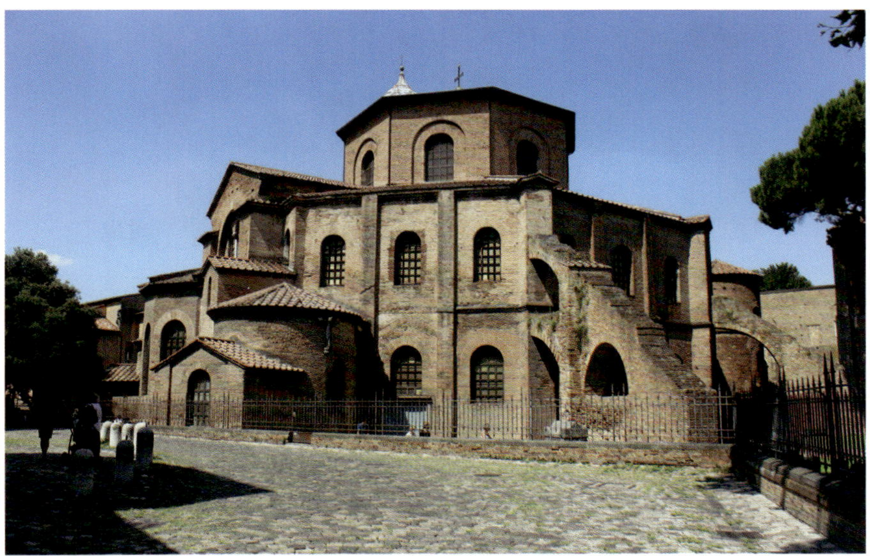

FIG. 6.5 Exterior of San Vitale.

102-foot-diameter dome. Domes appear to beget domes, and the effect is one of mystifying and breathtaking confusion. Procopius thought so too, calling the church a "bewildering sight" in which one does not know where to look or how to focus. The light flashing from the gold-covered ceilings and colonnades and galleries, he says, is beyond description. The variegated marble seems to glow in shades of purple, green, and crimson and reminds the historian of "a meadow in full bloom." The church "seems not to rest upon solid masonry, but to cover the space with its golden dome suspended from Heaven."

Interlocking systems of domes, streaming light, and a paradisiacal color scheme—these also characterize the experience at San Vitale. Of course there are some fundamental differences between the two churches. San Vitale is octagonal, unlike the square setting of Hagia Sophia (Figs. 6.5 and 6.6). Nor is San Vitale as large as Hagia Sophia. The entire complex is about half the size of Hagia Sophia, as is its central dome. But San Vitale creates a similar sense of mystery and majesty.

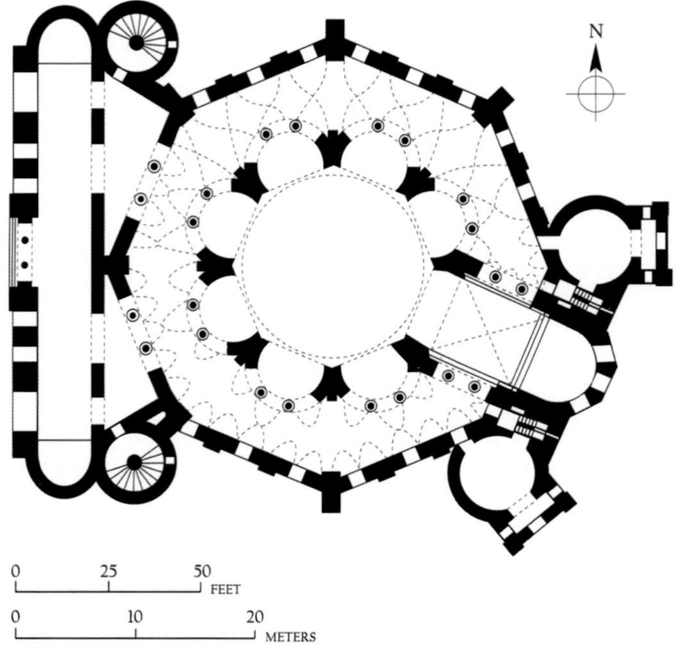

FIG. 6.6 San Vitale ground plan.

The central area of the church has a domed octagonal core, indicated by the rounded shapes in the center, like a daisy with seven petals. The eighth, longer "petal" that extends to the southeast is the apse, where the altar sits, and where the mosaics of Justinian and Theodora appear. Between the rounded central area and the exterior walls is an ambulatory, or a space to allow movement throughout the church. Although they are now closed, seven of the exterior walls originally had doors that allowed entry into the church.

It might not be too surprising that these external, side doors would have provided an oblique and disorienting sense of the interior of the building. But the view was (and is) no clearer from the so-called main entrance. The main entry into the church faces northwest. From this door the visitor enters a narthex, basically the antechamber into the church, which we can see running along the

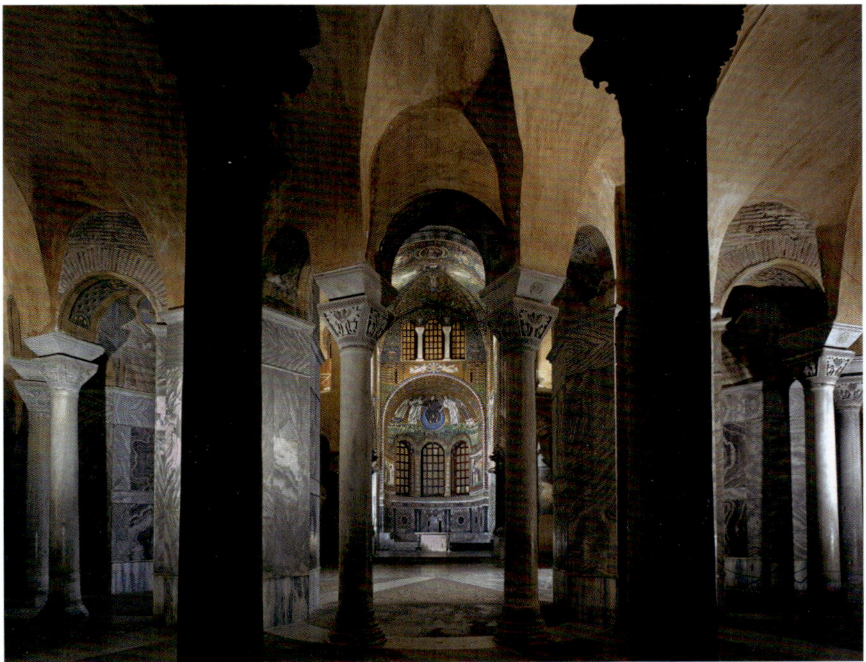

FIG. 6.7 View toward the apse of San Vitale from the narthex.

left or northwest corner of the octagon in the ground plan. Two doors lead into the church from the narthex. The one on the right provides a view of a forest of columns, arcades, and domes, but not the mosaics. The door on the left does give a view of the apse. Yet even when you take this door, which might seem to be the main entrance, the mosaics are distant and difficult to see, and almost engulfed by a seemingly infinite series of arches—arcades and domes that seem to multiply into deeper and deeper cavelike spaces, almost as though the octagon is undulating (Fig. 6.7).

Variations in darkness and streaming light add to the mysterious and ethereal sense of the building. Light enters the windows of the exterior walls and eight large windows at the base of the dome. During different times of the day, however, light enters different windows. The rays of sun act like a movable spotlight,

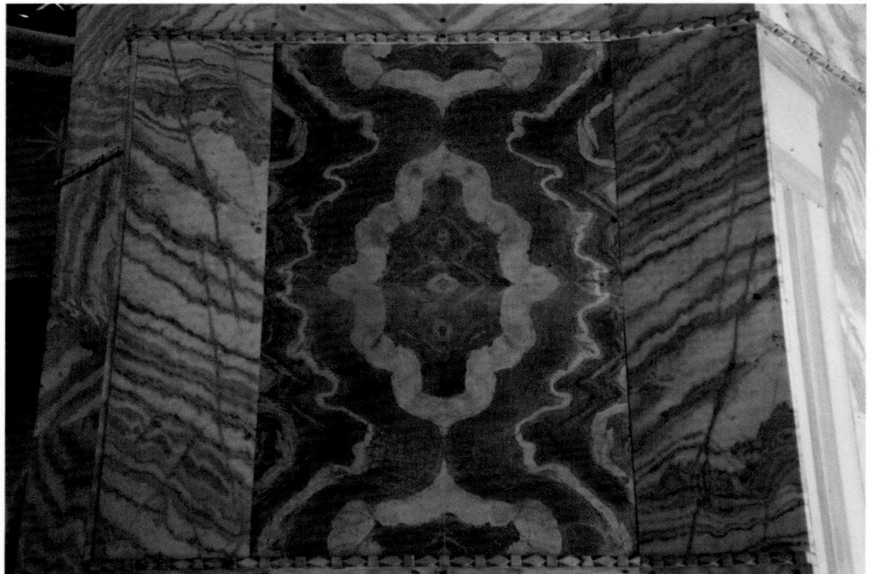

FIG. 6.8 Marble revetment from San Vitale.

variably highlighting the monument. Nuances and delicate details in the architecture and design call for this theatrical, cinematic lighting. The load-bearing piers are not flat. They are both fluted (at the top) and curved (on the bottom)—shapes that are designed to produce shadows and play with light. The marble is similarly variegated (Fig. 6.8). Sliced veined marbles splay beautifully into patterns of waving and weaving diamonds, chevrons, and elegant amoebalike forms. As in Hagia Sophia, San Vitale mystifies the viewer as a marble monument that moves.

Movement also appears in the mosaics. I know what you are thinking. The standard understanding of Byzantine art is that it is formal, frontal, flat, fixed. And when juxtaposed with images from the Roman classical past, the later mosaic does have a static quality, a lack of the fluid naturalism of the more ancient forms. The Augustus of Prima Porta statue depicts the emperor striding confidently toward the viewer as though speaking to a crowd, perhaps proclaiming a victory to his people, perhaps the very victory represented on his elaborate

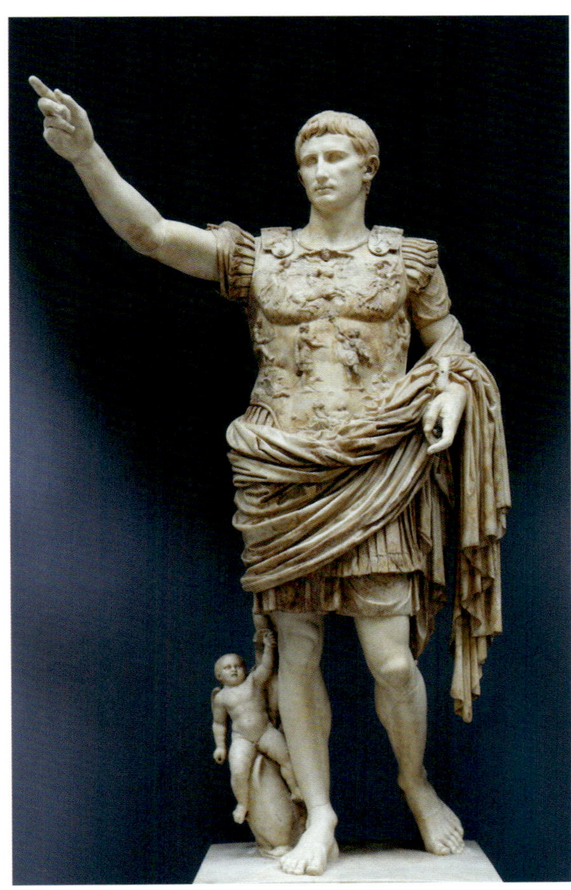

FIG. 6.9 Augustus of Prima Porta, early first century CE. Vatican Museums, Vatican City. Marble, 203 cm.

breastplate (Fig. 6.9). From his pointing finger, along that elegant extended arm, down to his half-raised left foot, his form is swooping and graceful, which is much facilitated by the contrapposto stance, the pose where the figure places his weight on one leg. The entirety of the sculpture is about Augustus's body. A beautiful body is equated with a strong ruler.

Justinian lacks the idealism and naturalism of Augustus. As the famous art historian E. H. Gombrich explained, the San Vitale mosaics show "pronounced geometry, order and abstractness." Unlike Augustus's tilt toward his right foot,

Justinian stands with both feet firmly planted. And yet that sense of physicality is missing. He seems to hover on the green strip of ground. The green of the mosaic shifts as it moves away from the body of the man—from a brighter, lime green to a deeper, more emerald shade. The hue of the mosaic cubes or tesserae tells us precisely where he is standing. But it does not suggest bodily weight. Nor does the drapery. The garment on Augustus's arm embraces and enhances the sense of the emperor's form, wrapping around his hips and hanging over his left arm in deep, heavy, bunched-up folds. It participates in asserting the emperor's swaying pose, his confident stride. The pull of the robe also highlights the fact that his left arm is apart from his body, a further expression of his physicality and the sense that Augustus is moving into our space.

Justinian's drapery is formal and linear. Darker purple cubes distinguish the folds in the garment. It is not a plain flat wall of purple, but it is not as malleable as the robe cradled by Augustus. It does not suggest any sense of his body. We do not have strong, defined muscles here. We do not know precisely where Justinian's legs are or how his knees bend. His right arm bends. We know that. Yet unlike Augustus's crooked elbow, Justinian's is held close to his body—lacking any sense of the swinging swagger suggested in the statue. In fact, Justinian's arm does not really hold the large golden bowl or paten with any true conviction. Rather, his hand seems to be gesturing more than holding the paten.

Bodily weight is not a priority. But political or imperial weight is emphatically clear. The Byzantine artists focused on the external expressions of power instead of anatomical ones. Justinian's crown is embellished with pearls, rubies, emeralds, sapphires, all of which continue dripping and fluorescing all over his regalia. A massive *fibula* or brooch at Justinian's right shoulder holds up the emperor's heavy, purple cloak. Smaller, lesser versions are worn by vassals. Lesser individuals also wear *tablia*, the rectangular band of cloth decorating the outside of the cloaks. But of course, while theirs is solid and simple, Justinian's is far more elegant—golden with small blue birds. Some aspects of the dress were not shared, however. The special embellished *fibula*, the crown, and the full-length purple cloak were only to be worn by the emperor. In fact, Justinian issued a law on this very point. For example, only the emperor could decorate the bridles and saddles of his horses and wear belts with pearls, emeralds, and hyacinths. The fine for disobedience was one hundred pounds of gold and capital punishment.

A similar law was applied to the donning of purple garments. Obtaining purple dye was extremely labor-intensive and not a little bizarre. To make the color required thousands of tiny sea snails. The snails would be soaked until their tiny snail glands could be removed. The liquid from the glands would then be placed in the sun, where it would slowly transform into a progressively darker violet hue. Mountains of shells have been found by archaeologists, indicating the popularity of this particular dye. The same color, that deep reddish purple, was coveted in porphyry stone. This stone was also extremely expensive, rare, and reserved for imperial tombs. The unique association between emperor and purple held fast. In fact, the phrase "born to the purple," or *Porphyrogenitus*, was an essential title for Byzantine emperors until the fall of the empire.

Justinian is swathed in purple. Even his shoes are purple. These shoes are most likely made out of leather, like a pair of gold-painted shoes housed at the Walters Art Museum, also from the sixth century, which even seem to have the same little finials that appear at the end of Justinian's boots. The difference is that Justinian's shoes have rows of emeralds and pearls and more medallions of the same—emeralds surrounded by pearls. The emperor, through his dress, from crown to toe indicates that he is of a different status from the men around him and from the viewer standing below. Augustus is untouchable in his bodily perfection. Justinian's dress says that he too is untouchable.

And yet he seems to be standing right on top of someone's foot. That is because this is not just a static lineup of important figures in Justinian's circle. This is an important liturgical procession, and the placement of the feet shows us the order of the men. At the helm is the one identified individual, Bishop Maximianus, who was responsible for overseeing the completion of San Vitale. There are two main processions in the Orthodox service—the little and the great. The Great Entrance happens in the second half of the liturgy, when the bread and wine are carried by the deacon to the altar. This is a representation of the Little Entrance, and we know this for two reasons. First, the emperor had a bigger part in the Little Entrance. He would proceed with the bishop down the nave of the church and offer elegant gifts, like the large golden paten. Second, because it involved the introduction of the liturgy, the Little Entrance was understood as Christ's coming as Logos or the Word. The mosaic places an emphasis on the Word in the golden, bejeweled Book of the Gospels.

Maximianus himself holds a golden, bejeweled crucifix and leads the procession. His feet are at the forefront of the picture plane and in front of the other priests. He is thus in front of the man with the gospel book, who is in turn in front of the man swinging the censer. Justinian follows these three men, with the two dignitaries and tightly packed soldiers in a bit of a jumble at the rear.

We can read this mosaic in terms of the religious procession, which is oriented by a compositional flow that draws the eye of the viewer from left to right, from the actual entrance of the church in the northwest toward the altar in the southeast. Our eye moves through a row of heads that are almost on the same level. We can read across in the same manner by looking at the comparably crooked elbows and the flow of the hems at the base of the coats. The diagonal position of the gold-colored spear shafts, which is repeated in the smaller golden *fibulae* of the three men around Justinian, also creates tick marks that help indicate the left-to-right movement, which leads us to the final figure, who is almost out of the picture plane, his left hand cutting across the bejeweled column. The placement of his hand is also indicative of the fact that the men are moving from back to front. He is in front of the bejeweled column. The soldiers are still hovering behind the porphyry-shaded column, which is behind the jeweled column. Movement underpins the mosaic—from left to right, back to front.

There does seem to be a bit of a conflicting message. The bishop's feet precede the emperor's. Yet Justinian seems to be holding his paten in front of Maximianus's elbow. It might be a small detail, but inconsistencies of this sort are rather curious, especially considering how precise the mosaic is in terms of representing the liturgy and imperial garb. The mosaicists were making two points. One was about the liturgy, about the religious procession, which would have actually occurred in the space above which the mosaic hangs. The second reading is abstract and ideological, one that proclaims the centrality of the emperor. Justinian stops everything, makes everyone pause. Those white coats that surround him seem to create a halo or a white frame for his purple-shrouded body. The golden *tablion* and paten arrest the eye of the viewer, as does the bright-red gem of the *fibula* and the thick red halo. Thus, although he is technically in the middle of the procession, he is untouchable, preeminent, protected, and on a different vertical plane altogether—both part of the procession and not.

The idea that the mosaic must be read in two ways at the same time was central to medieval modes of viewing and reading, and to the pictures at San Vitale. As early as the second century, medieval scholars used allegorical interpretations in order to explain relationships between the Old and New Testaments. When things were unclear or even irrational in the Old Testament, they needed to be understood as having an allegorical message. The deeper, fuller meanings were found in the New Testament. These cross-testament associations are called typological readings.

Typological imagery appears in lunettes in the presbytery, the space preceding the apse. In two slightly recessed lunettes, vibrant mosaics depict a series of moments from the Old Testament: on the northeast wall there are scenes from the life of Abraham and, on the southwest wall, Abel (on the left side of the apse) and the king and priest Melchizedek (on the right). The Old Testament figures are important in their own right, but there is a second, typological reading at hand as well, one that emphasizes divinely sanctioned sacrifices and the importance of the functions of the priests. For example, the image of Abraham about to slay his only son, Isaac, was understood as a prefiguration of Christ's acceptance of death on the cross and his ultimate triumph over death. The story of Isaac's sacrifice was included in a prayer read during the liturgy of the Eucharist. Thus the Old Testament scene is simultaneously about Abraham and Isaac, God and Christ, and the sacrament happening in the space below, at the altar, which probably looked somewhat like the object upon which Isaac kneels and probably exactly like the altar between Abel and Melchizedek. These two men are further examples of proper sacrifices. Abel's sacrifice to God was accepted when his brother Cain's was rejected. The writer of the New Testament book of Hebrews interpreted this as being because Abel sacrificed with faith. The same writer saw the rather obscure Melchizedek as a type of Christ himself, the great high priest, and also the ultimate in self-sacrifice.

The Justinian mosaic is both a liturgical procession and a visual panegyric to the emperor—but not a record of a real event because Justinian was never in

Ravenna. He never entered this particular space. He was always in Constantinople, celebrating services in Hagia Sophia. For this reason we cannot expect this to be a portrait of the emperor. Certainly his facial features are less idealized than those of Augustus. The earlier emperor's visage is smooth and elegant, all symmetry and perfection—a pertly smiling mouth, high cheekbones, gently sloping eyebrows. There is the hint of a furrowed brow, but only a very subtle one. Justinian's is far more creased, a fact that is highlighted by his thick, dark eyebrows, which arch dramatically, adding to a sense of aggression and intensity. Augustus's smooth shave is perennial. Justinian's has long since lost its edge, suggesting the end of a long day of hard work. Augustus's hair is tousled in a manner befitting a J. Crew catalogue. Justinian's jet-black hair juts in all kinds of directions, just barely tamed by the elegant crown.

When comparing Justinian's face to Maximianus and the man standing between them, we see a strange and striking stylistic difference. The bishop's head is significantly oversimplified, much more linear and lacking in shading. Tesserae are set in sharp, unmodulated V lines. There are somewhat random orange accents, and the flesh tones are far lighter than those of Justinian. For many years scholars were perplexed by this discrepancy in style, and the fact that Maximianus was the only person in the panel with an inscription. Why would the bishop be named and not the emperor? In 1989 a team of conservators started to untangle the much damaged mosaics, in a laborious process that took over fifteen years. Earthquakes, a rising water table that was increasing the dampness in the basilica, and flawed restoration techniques were causing the mosaic cubes to fall off the wall and whiten, as we can see in the image of Sarah from the Abraham panel. The transformation produced by their work is remarkable. Not only did this team of Italian conservators save the mosaics, but their close study of the setting of the panel revealed that the cubes used in the faces of the two men to the right of Justinian were of stone. The rest of the mosaics in the panel are glass, including the body of the bishop. This discrepancy revealed that Maximianus added his own head later. He removed the head of the original prelate, Victor, who had started the construction of the church, and put in his own face, just in time for the consecration of the church.

This maneuver was obviously a means of promoting his own power in the church and taking credit for the final product. And the specificity of the portrait makes sense because he was actually in the church, whereas Justinian never was. But there was a political necessity as well. Tensions were high in Constantinople, as the Nika revolts revealed, until Justinian put his foot down and established control. Justinian's ambitions to control Italy, reestablishing the borders of the Roman Empire as they were in Augustus's time, were much more complicated. Ravenna had always been an important part of the Roman Empire, both because it was easily defendable, since it was surrounded by swamps and marshes, but also because it was a port city, which allowed lucrative trade to the larger Mediterranean, including, of course, Constantinople.

But the beginning of the fifth century witnessed the rise of the Visigoths and Ostrogoths, nomadic tribes of Germanic peoples set on expanding into Italy. In 476 Odoacer, a barbarian, deposed the last Roman emperor in the West. Odoacer ruled Ravenna until the Eastern emperor Zeno sent Theodoric to take control of the city, which he did in 493, allegedly slaying Odoacer with his own hands. Theodoric was a strong ruler and basically independent. He kept the Romans, Goths, and external forces in a peaceful ecosystem while building tremendous monuments throughout Ravenna. But Theodoric was a barbarian, an Ostrogoth, a fact that displeased Justinian. So when Theodoric died without a clear successor to the throne, Justinian sent Belisarius into Italy in order to reconquer Ravenna and the entire Western empire. Belisarius landed in Italy in 535 and conquered Ravenna in 540. The first phase of these so-called Gothic Wars brought a huge victory. But the second phase picked up again in just one year and did not conclude until 554. Thus when Maximianus was putting his head into the mosaic, it was during a time of wars and uncertainty. Belisarius was not as successful in this second round of fighting with the Goths, and thus hopes were pinned on a new general, John the nephew of Vitalian. It is likely that it is he, John, who hovers so oddly between the emperor and the bishop. And although it left no space for feet or a proper body, this placement was ideal as it would allow the new general to balance the image of the older general Belisarius.

Reconfiguring a mosaic would seem to be a rather difficult thing to do. Undermining the plaster setting for the small pieces of glass would seemingly threaten the integrity of the entire composition. But this practice was used throughout

Ravenna when the Ostrogoths were removed from power, as a means of asserting not only the rule of Justinian but also of the Orthodox faith. Theodoric himself was a Christian; however, he was an Arian Christian. Arians believed that Christ was the creation of God the Father and therefore a subordinate being. This belief was vehemently condemned as a heresy in the Council at Nicaea in 325. Nevertheless, there were still many followers. Thus Justinian was fighting Theodoric's political authority *and* his religious beliefs. As such, when Justinian's followers wanted to assert the impact of their reconquest of Ravenna, they made their mark on Theodoric's churches, like Sant'Apollinare Nuovo (Fig. 6.10).

There was probably nothing particularly Arian about the church or its decorations. But the changes Justinian made signified a new leadership. The apse in the monument collapsed in the eighth century, but the nave walls preserve three original horizontal registers of mosaics running from the western entry to the eastern apsidal area. The lowest register, which is about ten feet tall, begins in the western end with representations of two cities. On the north wall is Classe (Civitas Classis), the ancient port of Ravenna, and, interestingly enough, a city established by Emperor Augustus. Three boats hover against a bright-blue sea awaiting entry into the harbor.

From Classe emerges a long procession of elegantly dressed virgin saints, walking against a colonnade of fruitful palm trees and extending jeweled crowns of victory. These women, all of whom are named, follow the Three Magi toward an enthroned Virgin and Child. Opposite Classe, on the southern wall, is a depiction of Ravenna. From this cityscape twenty-six male martyrs offer their own crowns to Christ, who sits on a jeweled lyre-shaped throne and holds a strange object that scholars believe to be a confused nineteenth-century restoration. A sixteenth-century account of the mosaic says that he held a book with the words "I am the king of glory," which would be more in keeping with other images of Christ from this period.

Justinian's restorations at Sant'Apollinare Nuovo are rather curious. A close look at the representation of Ravenna reveals these early restorations. Ravenna is dominated by a large arcaded building, which has the word Palatium (or palace) above its central archway (Fig. 6.11). Elegant winged victory figures hover in the spandrels above the colonnade composed of pristine, white Corinthian columns,

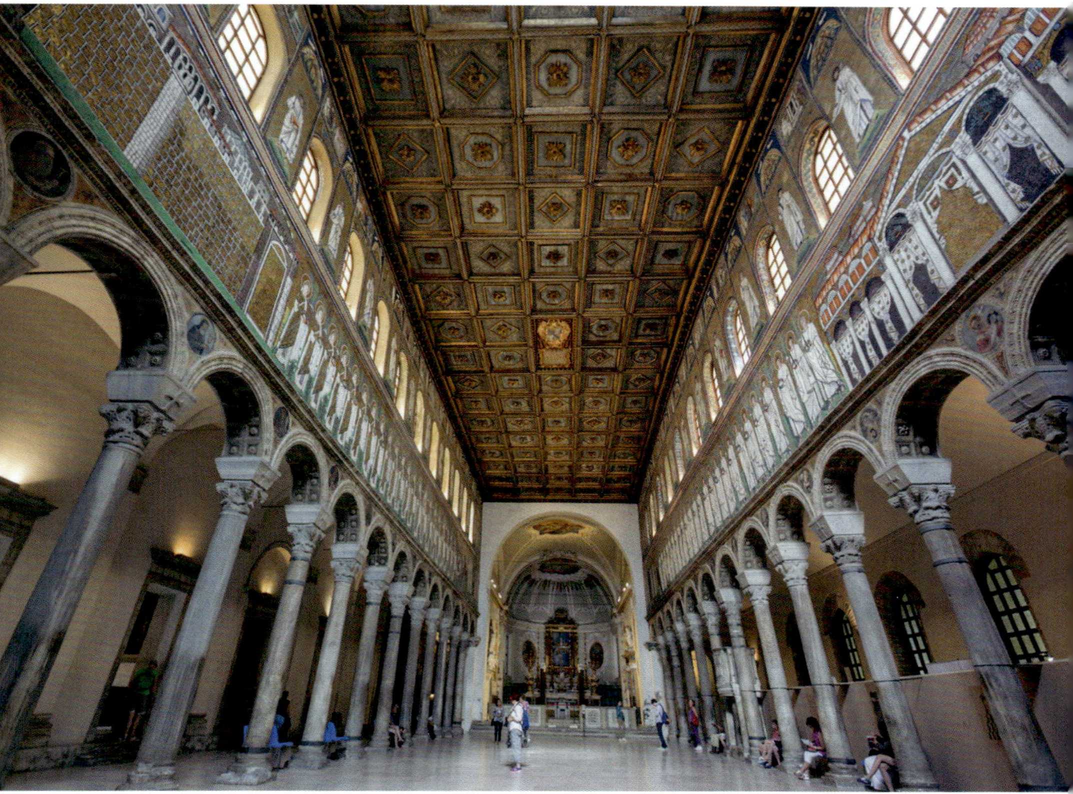

FIG. 6.10   Interior view of Sant'Apollinare Nuovo, first dedication 504, reconsecrated 561. Ravenna, Italy.

which visually proclaim the lavishness and prominence of Theodoric. So too did a series of happy men, standing with their hands raised in a gesture of welcoming and joyousness. You can see remnants of some of the hands, but for the most part the figures were carefully excised, mosaic cube by mosaic cube, from the composition and replaced by hanging curtains.

The reason for removing these figures is still a mystery. Some scholars asserted that the erased figures included Theodoric and members of his court. It is unlikely that Theodoric would have placed himself here rather than in the

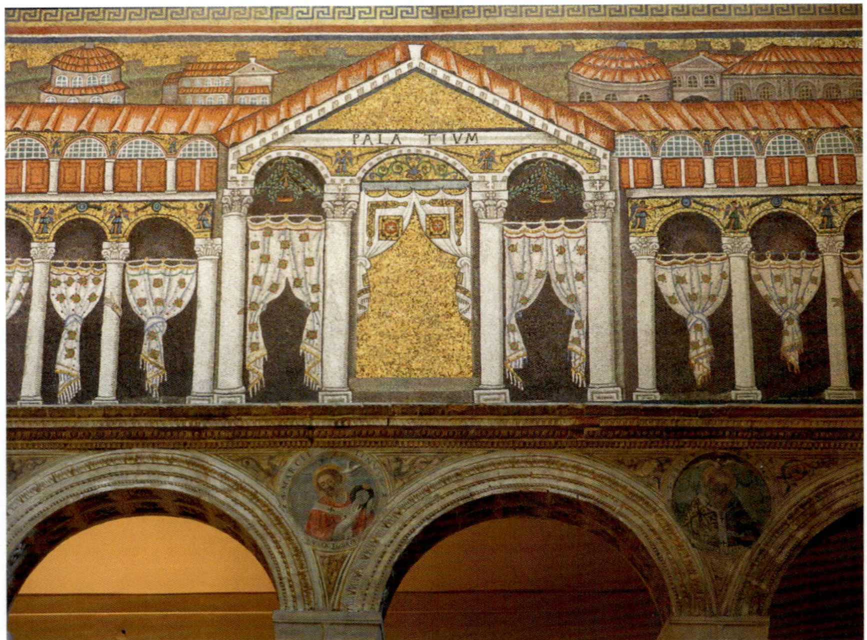

FIG. 6.11 Detail of south wall showing the Palatium (palace), Sant'Apollinare Nuovo.

lost apsidal mosaic (which is a more important position of the church). But this proves how determined the new Justinianic regime was to assert its presence. In fact, if they could remove as much as they did, why not go all the way and remove those floating hands? Perhaps leaving these disembodied hands, little waving ghosts from the past, was a way of allowing the memories of that Arian rule to peek out, to remind the viewer just how fully disgraced and small the Ostrogoths were in the wake of Justinian.

The Sant'Apollinare Nuovo restorations appear to be referred to in San Vitale, in the mosaic panel showing the Empress Theodora (Fig. 6.3). As we saw, the Ostrogothic men in Sant'Apollinare Nuovo were cut out of the darkened doors and replaced by patterned, embellished curtains. The doors in the earlier church are emptied out, removed of their scenes of jubilation and population. The doorway represented in the mosaics of San Vitale is about to be filled up, to become a place of passage. Theodora, gracefully and ceremoniously, is about to walk through that very portal, past the embellished, ornamented curtain, which is not unlike the curtain in Sant'Apollinare Nuovo. The man who holds the cloth aloft is active, present, not just a lost, floating hand. San Vitale is vibrant and alive, brimming with color. It is almost as though the jubilation that was removed from the earlier church finds its home in San Vitale.

Theodora is instrumental in this transferal. In fact, she seems to embody the walls of the nave of Sant'Apollinare Nuovo. She wears a crown like the virgin saints and carries her bejeweled chalice much like the way the saints carry the heavenly crowns. But her crown makes theirs look tired and small. She is encased in jewels and pearls. The mosaics are generally glass, but these pearls are real—she is really wearing shaved pieces of pearls. These hanging strands flow over her collar, interweaving in a flood of the bright, white spheres that terminate in a cascade of teardrops. She too wears a *fibula*, like her husband, but it is barely visible in this resplendent cascade. She also wears the purple-dyed garment, like her husband.

The deep shading in Theodora's garment creates V-shapes, indicating that she is moving toward the door, gracefully carrying the chalice just like the golden, embroidered Magi on her hem, who carry their own gifts. The zigzag of her heavy purple robe falls just like the gold-edged curtain leading into the doorway. Not only do the shapes relate in a formal sense, but both the curtain and the hem of Theodora's dress make us think of Sant'Apollinare Nuovo. The three wise men on her robe also appeared in the earlier church. Thus Theodora embraces the imagery of the earlier Arian church so fully that she literally wears it. The images that were deactivated in the Arian church are brought to their fullest expression in San Vitale.

Garments and curtains speak volumes. They even help assert the claim that there is a clear line of succession in place—that even though the empress and emperor were not physically in Italy, their representatives had their fullest support. Belisarius's wife, Antonina, appears next to Theodora, which is appropriate as she was the highest-ranking woman in Ravenna. Next to Antonina is a young woman who is most likely her daughter Joannina. The sea of colors and patterns in the garments of these women illustrate a chain of command. Red flowers along the hem of Theodora's white dress reappear in two long bands on the dress of Antonina. Those red flowers seem to explode exuberantly on Joannina's golden shawl. The dark, solid purple that Theodora wears reappears on Antonina's dress, although with slight modulations and roundels such that it is not solid imperial purple. The purple is further tempered in a light violet shade worn by Joannina. Her dress is speckled with little blue ducklike shapes that face in two directions, as the falling fabric dictates, which might remind us of the birds on Justinian's golden *tablion*. The arrangement of this mosaic—the placement of these figures—complements and balances the format of Justinian's panel. The two portraits work together to emphasize the incontrovertible authority they had given to their representatives in Italy.

Theodora is also moving toward the altar, just like her husband. But her group should be seen as the second part of the procession. Justinian's men are at the helm; she and her ladies follow. This division is evident in the fact that she is in a different space from her husband. The background in Justinian's panel is all gold, with an abstract green archway over his head and a series of porphyry columns on the sides. Theodora stands in a more complicated space—with the darkened doorway, a fountain, and a draped red, white, and blue curtain. She, like her husband, is under a green niche flanked by porphyry columns; however, this one is far more embellished, with hanging pearls and dripping emeralds. If they are in different spaces, however, where exactly are they? Scholars have tried to determine where Justinian and Theodora were standing in relation to the actual church, suggesting that he might be in the nave, and she might be waiting in the colonnaded atrium outside the church. But Justinian and Theodora are not supposed to be standing exactly in the same space as the visitor. They are above the viewer, simultaneously in spaces like those of the church and in an elevated space. They are mediating, in a sense, between our space and that which is sacred, that which hovers above in the glorious representation of Christ in the apse.

There are important visual connections between the imperial panels and the imagery of paradise in the apse, suggesting a more spiritually elevated role for the emperor and empress. The shape and color of the green niche surrounding Theodora reappears upside-down in the form of two intertwining green acanthus-like shapes, U-shapes that lead our eye along the thick frame toward the seated

Christ. We might connect the red, white, and blue clouds that hover above Christ to the red, white, and blue hanging curtain. A variegated rainbowlike arch connects Theodora to Christ, leading from just about the top of her head all along the curve of the apse and finishing directly over the head of Justinian. All three—Justinian, Christ, and Theodora—wear that imperial purple. All three extend circular, golden forms (Christ's is a wreath) and are set against golden backgrounds.

Theodora participates in a grand economy of religious and political achievements and assertions. In the mosaic she is spectacular, powerful, and pious. But this is not precisely how she appears in the accounts written by Procopius. In the chapter "How Theodora, Most Depraved of All Courtesans, Won [Justinian's] Love," she engages in all kinds of immodest and oversexed behavior, none of which I can quote here. Suffice to say, Procopius makes it clear that she has absolutely no morals and beguiles Justinian with her wild dancing so fully that he cannot see straight. In fact, according to the historian, she is generally gallivanting without clothes on. In one episode, geese eat barley off of her nude body and she does not even blush. Ironically, Theodora in the mosaic is all clothes and little body, and she blushes ever so subtly.

It is hard, with these two contradictory accounts, to know exactly what Theodora was like. But we can certainly say that she was no milquetoast—this woman elicited strong responses wherever and however she appeared. And this was not limited to the sixth century. Her legacy is rather remarkable. One of the medieval images that becomes extremely popular is that of the Maria Regina, a representation of the Virgin Mary as an imperial queen. Theodora's hanging pearls and placid face reappear clearly in a twelfth-century Roman mosaic at Santa Maria in Trastevere. More modern appearances of Theodora focus less on her piety and more on her theatricality. The play *Theodora* made Sarah Bernhardt's career. A later reference to that play appears in *Gaslight*, the 1944 film with Ingrid Bergman and Charles Boyer. One of the most dramatic and suspenseful moments in the movie is the moment when the young heroine reveals the painting of her brutally murdered aunt. The aunt is dressed as Theodora, hanging pearls and all, in the role she was best known for on the stage. *Theodora, Slave Empress*, a movie from 1954, looks terrible and ridiculous but is further evidence of the titillation that she

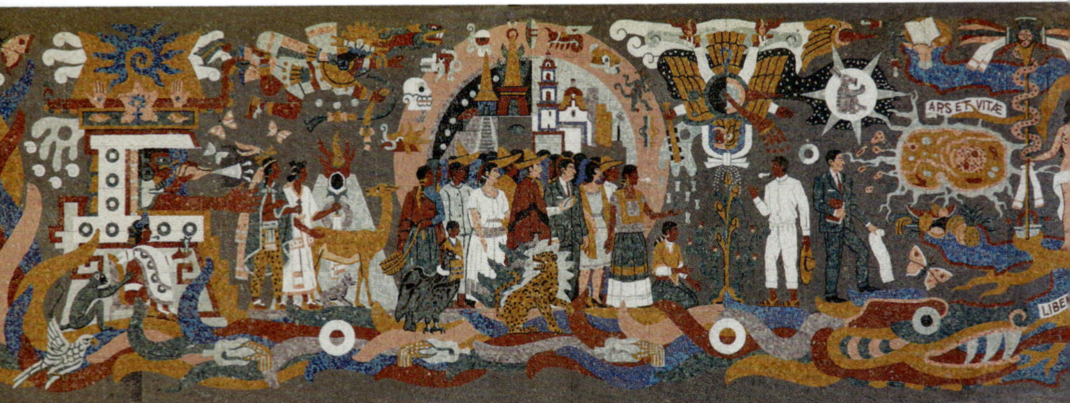

FIG. 6.12 Juan O'Gorman, *Confluence of Civilizations in the Americas*, 1968. San Antonio, Texas. Mosaic, 670.56 × 3962.4 cm.

inspired 1,400 years after her rule. In 2013 Dolce & Gabbana turned Theodora's procession at San Vitale into a catwalk, dressing his models in garments covered in gold and pearls and even images of Byzantine-inspired imperial figures. These modern iterations of Theodora and Justinian draw out more obvious or hyper-sexed aspects of their supposed characters, especially in the Dolce & Gabbana advertisements for their dresses.

But it is also possible to find common features between our earlier mosaics and modern art. I am not going to argue that Juan O'Gorman's mosaic at Hemisfair Plaza in San Antonio is trying to replicate the mosaics of San Vitale, but there are ways in which, when we look at this massive mosaic, we can see echoes of the sixth-century monument (Fig. 6.12). Both are mosaics, composed of stones and glass, 1.2 million pieces of stone and glass in the case of the San Antonio mosaic. The central focus of the scene is a male and a female, perhaps Adam and Eve, who proclaim their protective role, as the banderole below reads *Libertatis Cunabula* or Abode of Liberty. Processing toward this central, seminal pair are evidences of the past, both the Indigenous American past (on the left) and that of Western Europe (on the right). Representations of Christian stigmata imagery

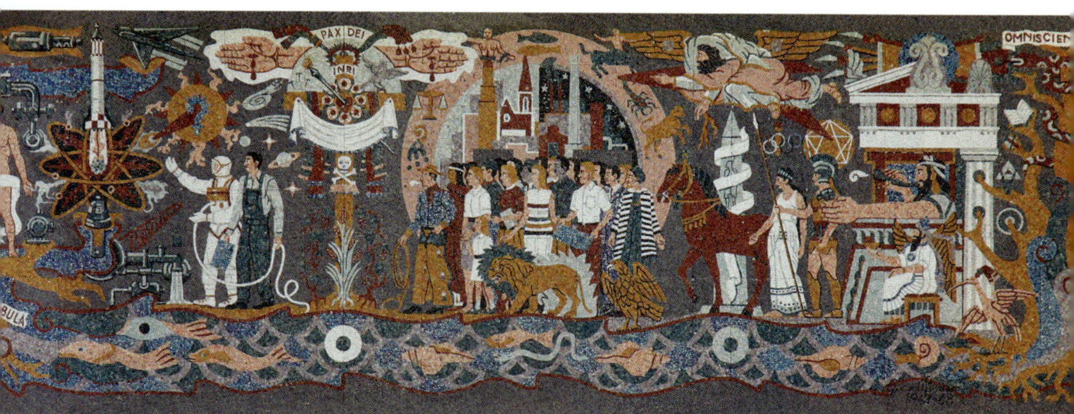

mirror Aztec zoomorphic forms. Women in traditional Mexican dress meet a Texan cowboy. In the San Antonio mosaic, the focal point is an ideological altar, one dedicated to liberty and the conciliation of two cultures. This masterpiece was a perfect call to San Antonians to embrace their rich cultural heritage in light of the event for which it was created, the Hemisfair Exposition, which was the World's Fair in San Antonio in 1968. But its celebratory and assertive tone is not solely specific to '68. It reflects a tone and style that has a parallel with the sixth-century mosaic. The mosaics at Ravenna also assert the importance of two cultures—Latin West and Greek East—coming together as a unified political and cultural entity. It didn't work entirely for Justinian and Theodora. The Roman West and the Roman East soon split politically, theologically, and culturally. The Eastern Empire held fast until the fifteenth century, another nine hundred years, but it was distinctive from the West, and their interactions were generally antagonistic. A confluence of cultures is essential to San Antonio. Thinking about what motivated the sixth-century mosaicists helps us think about what motivated Juan O'Gorman, and how important those impulses are to a modern, multicultural city.

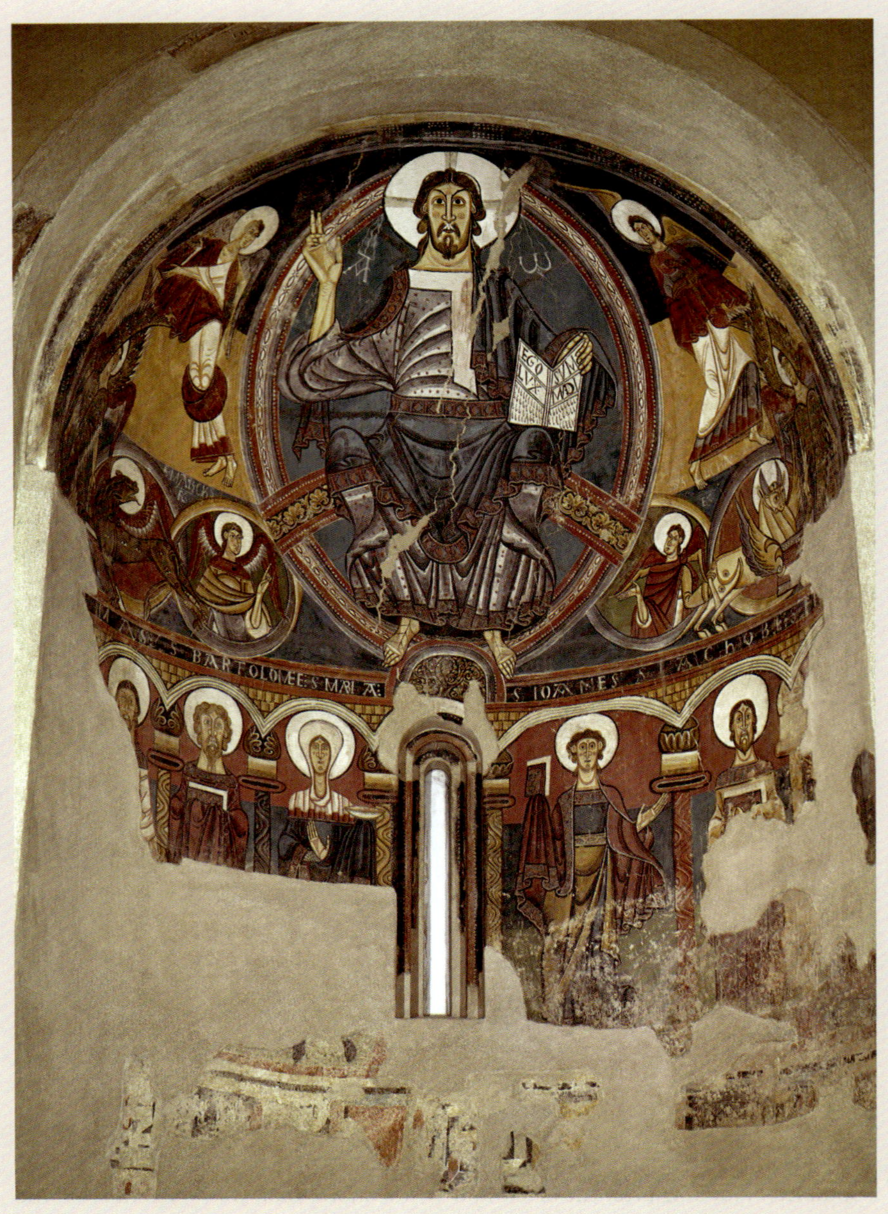

FIG. 7.1 Apse showing Christ in Majesty from Sant Climent, Taüll, Spain, ca. 1123. Museu Nacional d'Art de Catalunya, Barcelona. Fresco.

Sant Climent de Taüll

CA. 1123

ROMANESQUE ART

Considering how widespread and important the Romanesque style was, it is frustrating that this period, spanning the eleventh through thirteenth centuries, is one of our more problematic inheritances from the nineteenth-century art historians. Of course, we know that the term is simply meant to help classify a period in art. We know that terms like these are just constructs, made up by a batch of scholars, and that they would have been bizarre and meaningless to the artists, viewers, patrons of the time. Yet even as a label, this term is particularly aggravating and off-putting. Dark spaces, tiny windows, weighty walls, rounded Roman-style arches (hence the term *Roman*-esque)—these are the supposed characteristics of the period.

If you are looking at an older image of the apse of Sant Climent in Taüll next to Sainte-Chapelle, you will probably think that, yes, the Romanesque is grim (Fig. 7.2). But wait. Later additions to this church covered a brilliant fresco showing Christ in Majesty, which is just barely visible below the arch of the vault. This painting is an extraordinary visualization of the Second Coming with strange beasts and multi-eyed seraphim, in rich, vibrant colors that almost pulsate with everything that the pejorative term fails to express—movement, brightness and light (Fig. 7.1).

Despite its unflattering associations, Romanesque art has had its moments of popularity. Not long after the black-and-white photograph was taken in 1904, the world started to take notice of Romanesque paintings like that in the apse at Sant

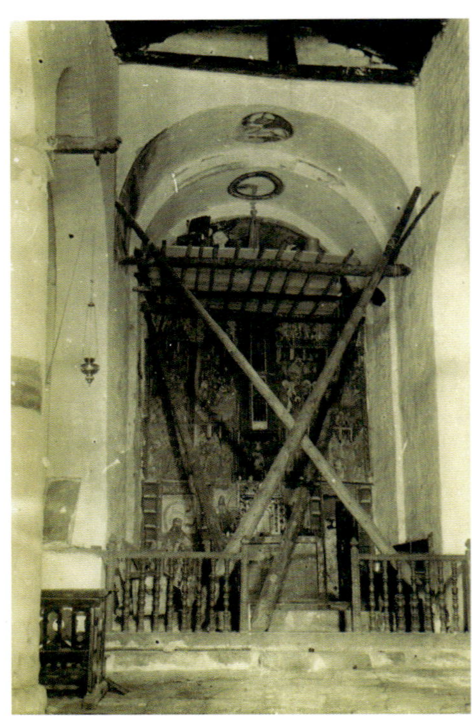

FIG. 7.2 Interior of
Sant Climent before its
restoration, ca. 1920.

Climent. One such appreciator was George Grey Barnard, who actively collected medieval works of art in the early years of the twentieth century. In 1925 John D. Rockefeller Jr. bought Barnard's collection and placed it in the newly built castlelike museum called the Cloisters, set on the Hudson in Fort Tryon Park at about 190th Street, and named after the four complete sets of Romanesque cloisters that Barnard brought wholesale from Spain and France. The central cloister of the museum comes from the Benedictine abbey of San Michel de Cuxa in Catalonia, in the northeastern region of France. Or at least, I should say, what little Barnard left is in Catalonia, and that is not much. Although Barnard's activities gave us great access to majestic examples of Romanesque art and architecture, it is kind of hard not to sympathize with the Spaniards and Frenchmen alike who still bemoan the piracy of the "Yanks."

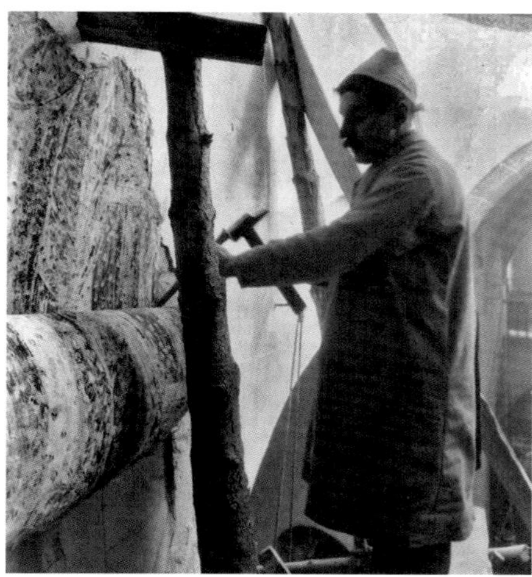

FIG. 7.3 Removing the frescoes, ca. 1920.

During the medieval period, cities located in Catalonia were extremely vibrant and wealthy. These cities were a natural stopping point for those travelers going from France to Santiago de Compostela, the famous pilgrimage site in Spain. Wealth and trade followed and bolstered these travelers. Catalonia is also on the sea, and this position facilitated trade throughout the Mediterranean, bringing greater wealth to the region. These early seeds of Catalonia as an autonomous and wealthier region of Spain are relevant to this day, as Catalonians battle for the right to secede from Spain, arguing that their wealth is used to bolster the greatly poverty-stricken country. Their medieval prosperity is evident in the explosion of church building and decoration that enlivened the mountainous border between Spain and France. But by the beginning of the twentieth century these churches were in a poor state. It is not surprising that the owners of these sites, often deconsecrated and in the hands of local politicians, were happy to sell pieces of their churches to willing foreigners like Barnard.

It wasn't until 1919 that the Spanish government called a halt to this exchange. From 1919 until 1923 a group of scholars and conservators traveled throughout the mountains of the Pyrenees looking for Romanesque churches with imperiled frescoes. This was not a small task for a number of reasons.

The infrastructure of these churches was one concern. Contemporary photographs indicate long wooden poles being used as supports. Another concern was the technique by which these paintings were created, the fresco technique. In order to create a fresco the artist would paint pigments onto a layer of thin, wet, fresh plaster. After a number of hours the plaster would dry such that the pigment particles were permanently fixed into the wall, through a process of carbonation. This meant that the bands of scholars traveling to save the paintings had to essentially scalp them off the walls through a procedure called *strappo*, meaning stripping or tearing (Fig. 7.3). The workers would first cover the painting in cotton cloths soaked in glue. Once the glue was dried, the cloth would be pulled away from the wall with a palette knife, although in this photograph the worker seems to be using a significantly sized hammer. We have photographs of the men peeling and rolling the frescoes off the walls. The frescoes would later be unrolled and the cloths painstakingly removed.

Getting the frescoes to these conservation studios was still a huge task. The scholars would take these rolled-up masterpieces, strap them to the backs of donkeys, probably the only animals that could handle the rough and ragged terrain of the Pyrenees, and head to Barcelona. This landscape and mode of travel would have been another legitimate cause for concern. Precious works of art bouncing around on the backs of stubborn animals, across rivers, over mountains with uneven surfaces, through forests with unpaved roads—it just was not ideal, but they did it. In four years, from 1919 to 1923, these traveling scholars removed 345 square meters of paintings, 3,700 square feet of paint. These frescoes found their home in Barcelona in the Palau National, a grand palace built between 1926 and 1929 for the International Exhibition and situated on the hill known as Montjuic. The collection is known as Museu Nacional d'Art de Catalunya or MNAC. In talking about Boscotrecase I mentioned the museum in Rome, the Palazzo Massimo, that everyone must see. Now you must put MNAC on your list. Just like in the Palazzo Massimo, you wander from painted room to painted room. This time, of course, the paintings are religious, describing biblical heroes and exploits rather than mythological ones; envisioning scenes of future paradise rather than immediate moments of revelry or triumph. But the experience in both is magical and almost eerie in its evocation of times past.

Eerieness or the uncanny is inherent to the content of the painting because it

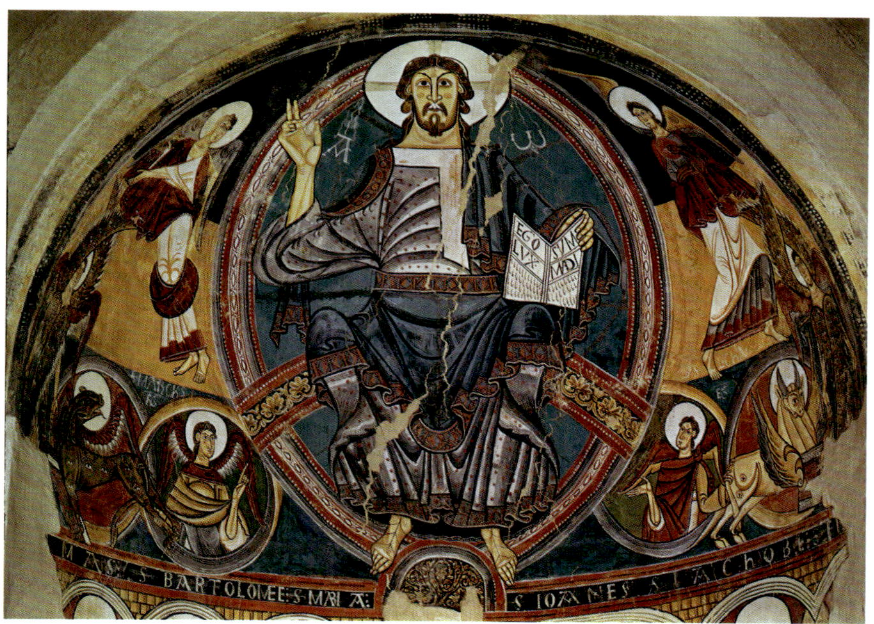

FIG. 7.4 Detail of Christ in Majesty from Sant Climent.

illustrates the events from the final book of the Bible. Well, as much as one can. I say this because there are a number of bizarre moments that occur in Revelation—numerous plagues and wars, hordes of demonic horsemen, a seven-headed dragon, a satanic beast marked with 666, and a harlot drunk on the blood of saints and martyrs. These mysterious and inexplicable moments seem to relate to that state of precarious and undefined consciousness we discussed once before—*hypnagogia*, that eerie moment when one is awake yet somewhere close to the realm of sleep. The combination of the mysterious and mystical biblical text with the painted images on the walls of churches, such as those at Sant Climent, inspires a similar sort of state—one that speaks to a present moment, to an alertness and awareness, while also speaking to a moment in the beyond, to a time outside of time, where we will wait in an eternal sleep until we are awakened for a triumphant, resplendent moment known as the Second Coming.

This return of Christ at the end of days is promised at the end of Revelation, and it is this which appears with such grandeur in the church of Sant Climent, in what is called the apse. In the traditional basilica, the apse is at the end of a long corridor called a nave. It is the focal point architecturally and liturgically, as it is where the altar sits, the place where Christian communities celebrate the most important liturgical ceremonies, such as the Eucharist. It thus makes sense that an illustration of Christ's promised return was selected for this focal point of the church. The painting shows the moment when Christ asserts: "And, behold, I come quickly; and my reward is with me, to give every man according as his work shall be. I am Alpha and Omega, the beginning and the end, the first and the last." He is immediate *and* imminent; ever present *and* from the future; judging *and* ready to judge; the beginning *and* the end. It is an awesome assertion, and that powerful confidence is precisely what Christ exudes in the painting. His words have come to life.

The letters that he uses to verbalize his own entirety, the Alpha and Omega, have come to life too. The Alpha and Omega frame the formidable figure, hanging from quivering white threads (Fig. 7.4). Is that an expression of the intensity of the moment? Are they responding to heavenly reverberations, shuddering sound waves emitted in the aftershock of his explosive appearance? Perhaps they respond to the blasting trumpets that appear in chapters 8 through 11? Or maybe the white threads are reacting to movement rather than sound, to the winds at the four corners of the earth, which are held at bay by four angels in chapter 7: "And after these things I saw four angels standing on the four corners of the earth, holding the four winds of the earth."

Beyond the jeweled frame or mandorla (meaning almond) that surrounds Christ are angels that appear in the four corners of the composition. But instead of winds, the angels (excluding the angel in the upper left) are holding onto animals, representing the episode in chapter 4 of Revelation when four living creatures appear around Christ's throne: "The first living creature like a lion, the second living creature like an ox, the third living creature with the face of a man, and the fourth living creature like a flying eagle. And the four living creatures, each of them with six wings, are full of eyes all round and within, and day and night they never cease to sing." The four living creatures also appear in the Old Testament in the Book of Ezekiel. In the first chapter Yahweh approaches

Ezekiel in a chariot drawn by four living creatures, each with four faces, those of a lion, ox, eagle, and man.

Yet the biblical resonances are only the beginning. These four beasts became important in writings by the Church Fathers. Jerome, who famously translated the Bible into Latin, was one of the earliest theologians to interpret the animals as representing the four authors of the gospels or evangelists, which combines the words for "good" (*eu*) plus "I bring a message" (*angelo*), the origin of the word angel. These are Mark, Luke, John, and Matthew.

Mark appears in the lower left of the composition. Mark was understood to be the lion because the opening verses of his gospel have a voice crying in the wilderness. The lion's angelic chaperone grabs him by the left hind leg and appears to restrain the beast from darting off to the left. The lion's flaring, curlicue nostrils; his unfurling, pointed tongue; those exuberant curls; exposed teeth, exposed claws—elegant and holy though he may be, this lion seems to want to return to the wilderness alluded to in the gospel. The ox also has a chaperone, although his work seems less energetic—this angel only rests his left hand on the rump of the beast. The ox was a common animal of sacrifice, and he was affiliated with Luke because this gospel opened with the sacrifice offered by Zacharias. The ox of Luke is stronger and weightier than the lion. His neck is muscle bound, which keeps him from turning toward Christ, which is perhaps the cause of what appears to be an expression of great consternation. His hind legs are straight and strong, with hooves that are firmly planted on the band at the base of the apse. The evangelist John was depicted as the eagle. According to bestiaries, popular books that affiliated animals with morals and lessons, the eagle was understood to gaze straight into the light of the sun, which was appropriate for the penetrating prose of John's Gospel.

The final evangelist, Matthew, appears in the upper left of the composition. According to Jerome, Matthew is represented as having the "face of a man" because his gospel begins with the genealogical table of the ancestors of Christ, in other words the human side of Christ. In medieval art Matthew is often shown as an angel, or at least a man with wings, which is how we see him at Sant Climent. Matthew's body bends slightly backward in a way that repeats the shape of Christ's jeweled mandorla. He holds his gospel securely with both hands and turns to face the source of his inspiration. In a unique detail, one that does not appear in other representations of this evangelist, his legs are tied in a thick knot in the same red that colors his cloak, hem, and book. Why is he so oddly bound? And why is there no companion angel here, as with the other evangelists? These are questions that might lead to further discussions and future investigations.

We must make the loop around the painted apse again because the medieval writers also understood these beasts as representative of the nature of Christ and the virtues required for Christian salvation. The link between lion and Christ relied heavily on the descriptions in the bestiaries. The tradition recounted therein stated that lions slept with their eyes open and were thus symbolic of the Resurrection. Christ seemed to sink into a sleep of death, yet he was always alive and watching—he was physically dead (or asleep) after the Crucifixion but spiritually alive in his divine nature. Bestiaries also asserted that lion cubs were born dead and it was only after three days that their parents would breathe life into them. This points to Christ's death, his three days in the tomb, and then his Resurrection through a parent, through the Father. The ox, the sacrificial victim of the Old Law, referred to the Passion and sacrifice of Christ. And the eagle is the figure of Ascension. Christ rose to Heaven just as the eagle rises into the clouds. Matthew the man recalled the Incarnation, emphasizing the fact that the Son of God became a man.

There are many layers of meaning from just that one brief passage in Revelation that alludes to the four beasts. That one verse harks back to the textual antecedents found in the Old Testament and simultaneously draws us into contemporary (meaning medieval) exegesis. Those dangling letters—the Alpha and Omega—are more than simple representations of Christ's announcement in Revelation. They are a metaphor for the way that texts were read in the medieval period, with one eye to the past and one on the future.

Like the Alpha and Omega, the inscriptions in the painting are much more than simple labels. Take the inscriptions identifying Luke and Mark. One thing of note is that they are strangely unbalanced (Mark's is in the lower register and Luke's is above). We might expect some sort of standardization in a labeling system that is, by its nature, supposed to categorize and organize. Labels are supposed to be grounding, not floating. Stranger still are the two letters EG.

The little tilde means that the letters stand for a word that has been compressed. The most obvious would be EG for *evangelium* or *evangelli*, meaning evangelists, which of course they are. But if you turn to your copy of Latin abbreviations, like the 1912 *Lexicon abbreviaturarum* by Adriano Cappelli, you will see a number of other words for which EG is the contraction. One is *aegrer*, meaning troublesome. This is not far from the mark as these beasts require their angelic chaperones. Another possibility is *edgreditur*, meaning to step out or to surpass. This final possibility for the two letters is intriguing since Mark and Luke do just that, moving beyond their prescribed wheel-like frames.

There is a sense of variety and multiplicity throughout the fresco—in both words and image. For example, Christ's cloak and garments flutter and fan in unpredictable ways, as though responding to winds that are cosmically generated. They bundle and crease in waves and hooks and loops. Shading and highlights create a sense of depth and movement in the garments but not in a naturalistic, unified way. This is not realism. The aim is to show variation, variegation, volume, and vigor. One detail that adds to this drama is at the hem of Christ's white garment. We can see the interior of the back part of his garment, the pitch-black of the lining of his dress. That detail is evocative, as though he has just arrived, as though he has just descended from above and his garments are still trembling in response, like those quivering letters Alpha and Omega above.

Even with all of these visual twists and turns, all those hooks and dots and swirls, underpinning this apparent chaos is complete stability and order. Behind the spinning wheels, recalcitrant animals, and wide-eyed wings are bands of systematic, solid color. And the pinnacle of Christ's shuddering garments—so bright and colorful, punctuated by the little red dots and whirling hemlines—is the totally formidable, serious, and terrific face of Christ. Binaries interrupt and disassemble each other. There is chaos *and* calm, disorder *and* order.

In addition to his face, there is another element in the depiction of Christ that is orderly and immovable. This is the thick white band that goes across the top of his chest, just below his neck, and down the left side of his body. The purity and solidity of the shape contrast strikingly with the vibrant colors and movements of Christ's garments. But in a strange way it unifies the entirety of the composition. That whiteness speaks to the whiteness of the halos of the evangelists. The shape also points us in the direction of the lower band of figures, saints and apostles that stand beneath an arcade of rounded arches (Fig. 7.1). Their white halos echo the thick white band on Christ's chest, but so do the books that they hold. Bartholomew, John, and Jacob hold versions of the Bible that have the same white shape at the edges, indicating the pages of the closed text. All three apostles hold the holy book with their hands covered, a gesture indicating absolute respect for the word of God. This manner of holding the Bible would have mirrored the behavior of the priests below, in the space of the church. The emphasis is on the text as a source of untouchable and eternal knowledge, a reverence that is emphatically expressed in book 20 of Revelation: "And I saw the dead, small and great, stand before God; and the books were opened: and another book was opened, which is the book of life: and the dead were judged out of those things which were written in the books, according to their works."

Mary, with her bulbous head covering, does not hold a book; rather, she is shown with a shallow white bowl exuding thin strands of fire. This curious shape has been understood by some scholars as an image of the Holy Grail, which held the glowing blood of Christ. However the tradition of the grail of the Arthurian romances does not really appear until fifty years later, as the scholar Joseph Goering emphasized. His theory was that the reddish-orange contents of the bowl represented the pure oil known as the chrism, used for anointing. The exact meaning of the bowl is still uncertain, another mystery. Perhaps it alludes to the Eucharist. Perhaps it refers to Pentecost and the "tongues like fire" that descend upon the apostles and prompt them to speak in other languages. Or maybe the Virgin is holding one of the seven bowls from Revelation, although she seems to be too placid for that to be the case since those bowls each cause untold amounts of grief and destruction.

Unknowable though it may be, the mystery of the meaning of that bowl ties nicely with the mystery of the white shape on Christ's chest. The two figures are connected—not just as mother and son but also visually, through those peculiar and unique shapes. They also both assert the important tenet of Christ as the light of the world. The text that Christ holds proclaims, "I am the light of the world." That assertion is visualized in a literal way just below Christ's feet, in the presence of the thin window that would have let in the actual light. This literal light ties into the bright light that comes from Mary's mysterious bowl, which is right by that window. Thus there is a vertical axis of meaning whereby the lights below reify the light above.

But there is a horizontal axis at work as well, thereby creating a cross shape of meaning. The appearance of the Alpha, the way the top line descends along the right, communicates directly with the strange band on Christ's chest, which also guides the eye to the shape of the opened book. Words and letters unify the composition. In fact, one might even comment on the compositional similarities between the Alpha and the way the cloak hangs below, which looks very Alphalike. With these connections in mind, we can understand the fact that Christ *is* the Word, his body is literally inscribed by the peculiar shape that draws attention to the books and letters that surround him.

There are a number of ties between the celestial realm above and the more earthly world below, that which is inhabited by the standing apostles. The connections are both thematic (like notions of light and the importance of the book) and stylistic—repeated color schemes, decorative hemlines, facial peculiarities such as the emphatic dots at the four corners of the face and the barbed-wire eyebrows. Yet the distinction between upper and lower realms is significant. Structure and architecture creates order in the lower, earthly realm. Arcades, columns, bricks, capitals—these earthly forms characterize the spaces on the part of the wall closest to us, closest to the viewer. The visitor would have also been standing in a similar type of space because, as we said before, Romanesque buildings were ordered by such architecture—arcades created by low-lying, regular, repetitive arches resting on rounded columns.

That characterization may sound lackluster. But there is great drama to this architecture. The walk down the aisle, with those repeating arches, is meditative and calming. That walk simultaneously creates a sense of suspense, through that repetition, which explodes in the apse with a riot of color, with figures that are unusual and slightly bizarre (like the living creatures), and with the shocking appearance of a man who was killed, then came back to life, then ascended to heaven to sit at the right hand of God the Father Almighty, and then comes back *again* to judge the quick and the dead. Low levels of light would have added to that drama. Candles and lighting devices, perhaps like the strange lamp that

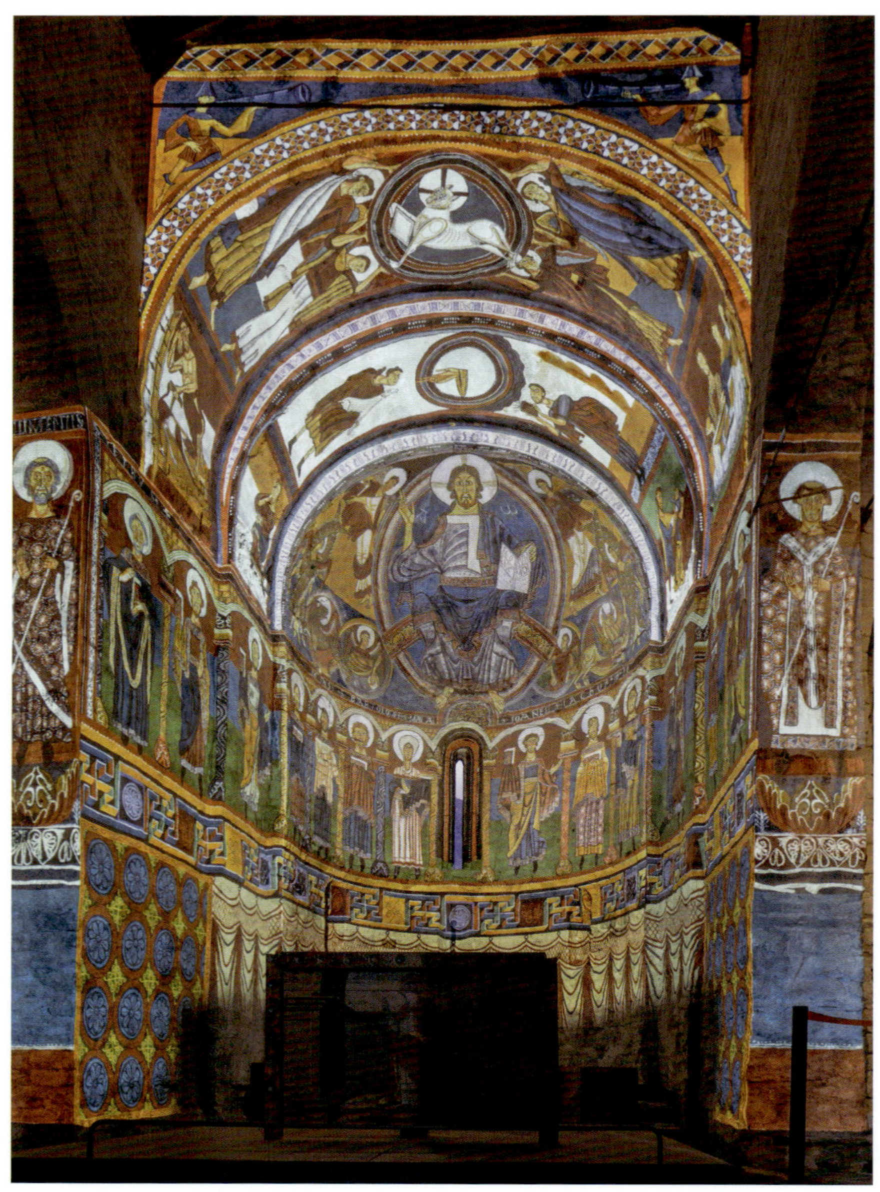

FIG. 7.5 Recreation of the frescoes in projected light, based on original setting in Sant Climent in Taüll.

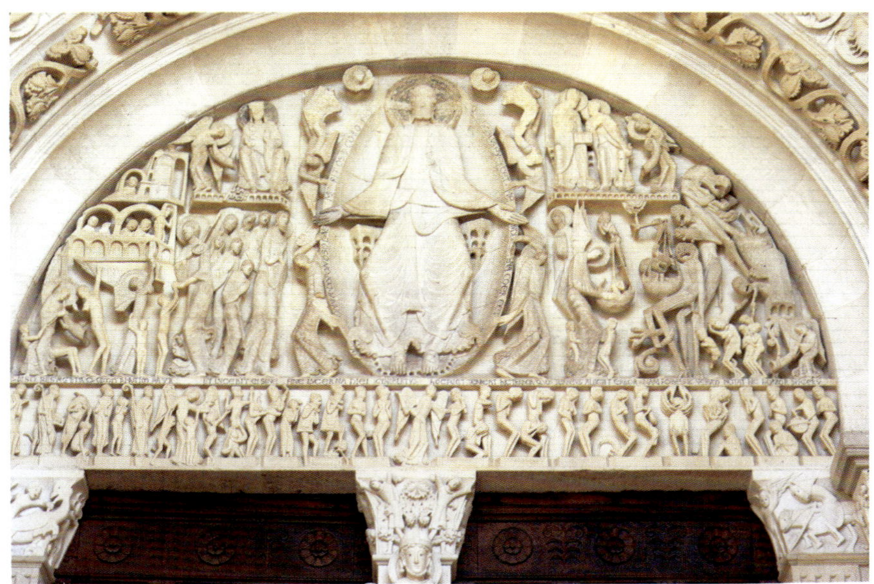

FIG. 7.6 Last Judgment tympanum from the west portal, Cathedral of Saint-Lazare, ca. 1120–1130 or 1130–1145. Autun, France. Stone.

the Virgin holds, would have been placed throughout the church. Flickering lights would have illuminated the images at different intervals, bringing those dramatically painted faces in and out of the light as though they were appearing and disappearing, variously emerging from the walls.

How can Romanesque art be synonymous with gloom and darkness when there are color schemes of this sort—wild and surprising and explosive? And these paintings were not just in the apse, they were all throughout the church. A computer-generated program produced by Burzon Comenge shows how expansive the colors and imagery of the apse were (Fig. 7.5).* There were images and paintings everywhere that required the viewer to turn and twist to see them all. The paintings were basically everywhere.

* "Mapping Sant Climent de Taüll," www.burzoncomenge.com/en/works/videomapping-1123-sant-climent-de-taull.

The columns in Romanesque churches were painted too, just like the motley-colored columns in the lower register at Sant Climent. Durham Cathedral in England is known for its powerful and majestic columns decorated with deep grooves of chevrons and striations and bands. Columns that you cannot even wrap your arms around. Now imagine them colored and painted. The same goes for the tympana—the large lunettes over the doorways—on the outside of our Romanesque buildings. Take the tympanum of St. Lazare in Autun, France. Again there is a powerful Christ in Majesty, centrally placed in the confines of a rounded mandorla (Fig. 7.6). He seems rather placid—both arms open, mirrored by his splayed legs. But the severe judgment he brings plays out all around him. On his right (the traditional place of honor) the saved souls huddle in happiest anticipation. Angels help lift childlike souls into the gates of heaven. One little naked soul gets pushed right up through the rounded arches above. Peter holds his famous keys, those which allow entry into heaven, over his left shoulder in his right hand, and with his left hand clasps the praying hands of another soul destined for paradise.

The opposite is much more grim. Here too angels blow their horns, waking the dead. But these figures are facing the horrors of hell. Michael, the winged angel, weighs souls that are (literally) in the balance. He gingerly places one soul on his side of the scale while other souls shudder and clasp at his garments. But the opposition is serious. The devils do not play nice. Here the long-legged opponent pulls against the scale with his right hand. A little minion-fiend jumps onto the scale to weigh it down further.

A second long-legged devil (holding a frog, a medieval symbol for lust) laughs at the whole thing, cackling so fiercely that the muscles in his neck strain and pull at the effort. His wide, toothy mouth almost consumes his whole face. You can almost start to hear the sounds of this mayhem—the clattering nails on the feet of these beasts, their screams of demonic glee and (in the case of these descending souls) horror and fear. Belching dragons, choking miscreants, the patter of little shoeless feet, and blasting trumpets that are loud enough to wake the dead. As these dead emerge fearfully from their tombs, still in their wrappings, the consequences of their failings are immediate and perverse—shame, pain, helplessness, bizarre resignation. The Latin inscription at the bottom of the

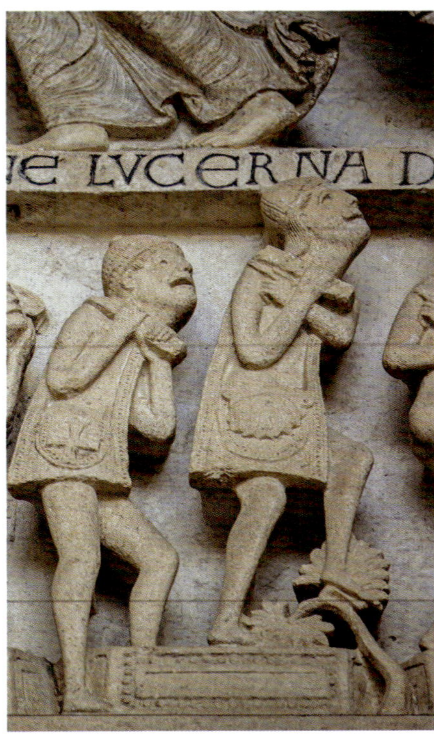

FIG. 7.7 Detail of tympanum at Autun showing pilgrims.

tympanum reads: "May this terror terrify those whom earthly error binds for the horror of the images here in this manner truly depicts what will be." Words like "terror" and "error" appear above the heads of the frightened souls on the right side of the composition, those on the side of the damned. But if we return to the side of the composition on Christ's right, there is hope. Figures emerging from these tombs look upward with expectation, awe, and uncontained joy as they move toward the center, toward the feet of Christ.

Two figures on Christ's right move with greater strides than the other figures, which is appropriate as they are representations of individuals known for their movements, because these are two pilgrims (Fig. 7.7). It is possible to identify the men as pilgrims because of their tight skullcaps and, over their right shoulders, walking sticks to which they may have tied their few earthly possessions, the

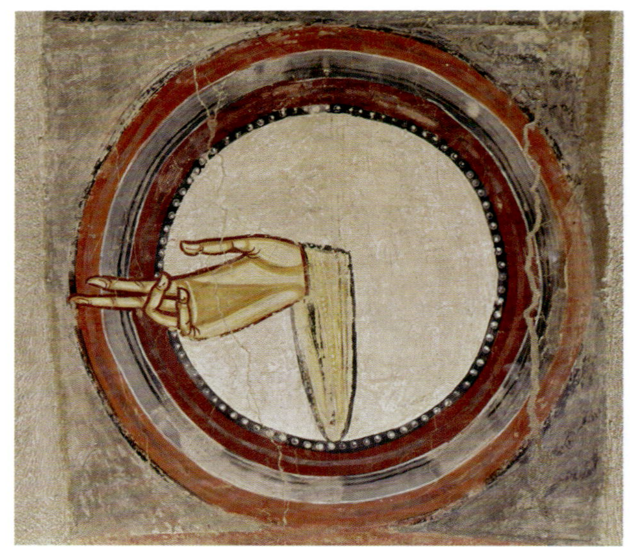

FIG. 7.8 Detail showing the Hand of God, center of arch before the apse, Sant Climent.

ends of which have broken off. Most important are the satchels and the images upon them. These centrally placed images—the cross on the left and the shell on the right—are meant to evoke pilgrim badges. As pilgrims arrived at their destination, they would receive a badge to represent their journey, which was both physical and spiritual. The way that the upturned conch shell is a mirror image of the shrubs below, through which the pilgrim must walk, is a means of illustrating this spiritual exchange. He must go through difficult passageways, forests, and the like before he arrives at the holy site, before he gets his badge, before he hopes to attain access to paradise. The shell is also special because it is indicative of Santiago de Compostela, the pilgrimage site that visitors still travel to in droves. Autun was one of the starting points for this famous walk to northwestern Spain.

Medieval frescoes must be understood through the eyes of the pilgrim. The experience of the church, the way that the images were approached, has every-thing to do with the way the viewer moved through or into these spaces. The building anticipation as the viewer walked down the nave was like a miniversion of the travails of the pilgrim. Those repeating columns might have been evocative

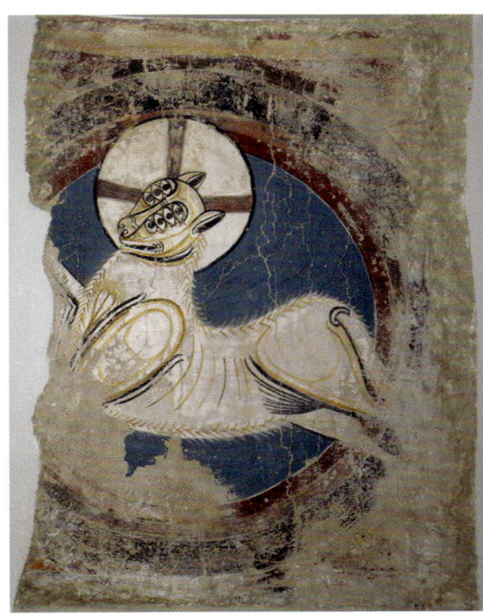

FIG. 7.9 Detail showing the apocalyptic lamb, center of arch before the apse, Sant Climent.

of actual forests. A forest of columns. Memories of trials and tribulations both physical and spiritual. Even if the visitor wasn't a proper pilgrim, even if he hadn't walked for hundreds of miles, everyone entering the church was, in a sense, a pilgrim. Everyone shared the experience of walking through the weighty (both physically and theologically) doors; they shared the sense of leaving behind the profane world and entering a sacred one; and they shared the hopes of shedding the sin and error and darkness in the space of the light created by Christ.

One might suggest that our run-of-the-mill pilgrim or even medieval viewer would not have picked up on the exegetical or theological meanings behind the painting. A common understanding of the medieval period is that there were lots of uneducated or illiterate people and a few smart theologians. The idea is that images primarily served these uneducated masses, and as such the images were the "Poor Man's Bible." But I think we should be wary about understanding images as solely for the illiterate or uneducated. As we have seen, the images go far beyond simple identification of scenes or figures. Yes, we can identify Christ in Majesty and the fact that this is his Second Coming. But that takes us only so far. Looking at images goes beyond those identifications and into a whole world

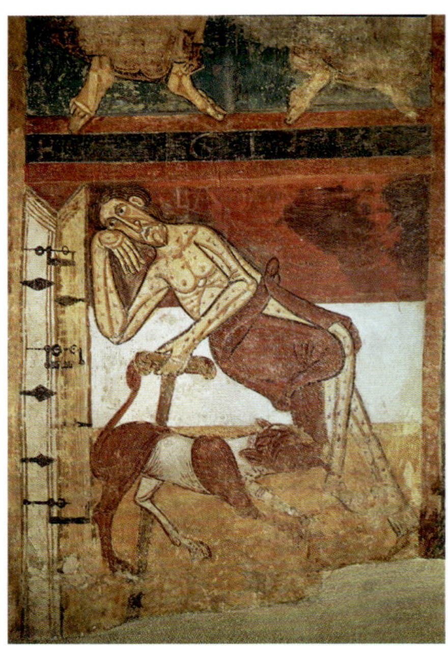

FIG. 7.10 Lazarus the beggar, lower left side of arch leading to the apse, Sant Climent.

of meaning. Images are more than labels. Even labels are more than just labels, as we have seen.

Letters like Alpha and Omega, or *E* and *G*, create a whole series of meanings. I think that is why the book held by Christ looks the way it does. The letters start clearly and powerfully, but then they descend into a series of hooks and scribbles. Words are ultimately just marks. They take on meaning because we illustrate them and explain them and study them. These holy scrawls are also perhaps a way of illustrating that there is something about the written word that is beyond comprehension even for those who can read. The viewer turns to texts in order to fully understand the images; the reader turns to images to fully understand the text. Images and texts work in a complementary way. Together they promote, complicate, and explain the mysteries of the stories of Christianity.

That process of visualizing the text and reading the images would have likely been facilitated by a resident priest who would have helped explain certain scenes to the visitor, congregant, or pilgrim. The importance of teaching and explaining

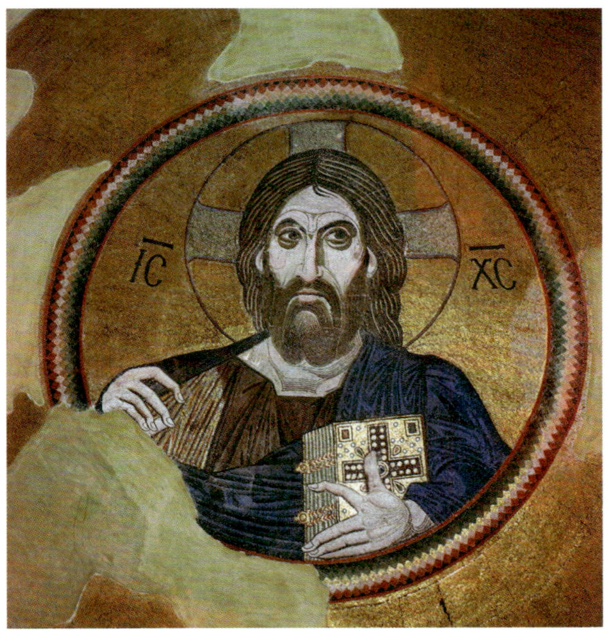

FIG. 7.11 Christ Pantocrator, central image in the dome of Daphni Monastery, ca. 1100. Athens, Greece. Mosaic.

is perhaps one reason that there is such a beautiful emphasis on gestures. Pointing and signaling is prominent in the fresco. Some angels present Christ. Others point, with fingers that are elongated and thin, almost like feathers. Mary's outstretched hand below mirrors the angle of Christ's, which points upward to another hand, God's, which appears disembodied in the center of a banded mandorla, just below the apocalyptic Lamb of God with seven eyes (Figs. 7.8 and 7.9). As we can see in the recreation of the frescoes in the light projection, the hand of God offered a benediction directed at an image of Abel who was proffering the sacrifice of the lamb, while on the opposite side of the apse Cain was shown offering wheat. However, these paintings were in such a bad state that they did not travel to join the MNAC collection.

The gesture of God also leads the eye to other parts of the painting composition, such as the framed panel showing Lazarus (Fig. 7.10). This is not Lazarus whom Christ resurrects from his tomb, but Lazarus who begs at the door of the rich man. By tradition we call that rich man Dives because that is the Latin word for rich man. Lazarus translates as "God is my help." In the biblical passage, found in Luke 16, Lazarus the beggar comes to the door of the rich man, but the rich man does not aid Lazarus. The two men see each other again after their deaths, but this time the rich man is on the outside, so to speak. He is in torment while Lazarus resides in the bosom of Abraham in paradise. The rich man begs: "Father Abraham, have pity on me and send Lazarus to dip the tip of his finger in water and cool my tongue, because I am in agony in this fire." But Abraham responds to say, "Son, remember that in your lifetime you received your good things, while Lazarus received bad things, but now he is comforted here and you are in agony. And besides all this, between us and you a great chasm has been set in place, so that those who want to go from here to you cannot, nor can anyone cross over from there to us."

Lazarus is utterly hapless—sores consume and speckle his skin; his ribs are prominent; his muscles pulled taut. He is, as the painting suggests, on the level of the dog that licks his wounds. The animal has a coat made of the same red color as the wounds on Lazarus's chest and his ragged and piecemeal wrapping. The white bands on the dog's body are of a similar shade to the pale flesh of Lazarus's skin. His twisting, contorted pose emphasizes his despair and lack of power as he gazes mournfully toward the door, which is slightly ajar but held fast with a series of nonnegotiable locks. We can see the same telling of the story in an illuminated manuscript from the eleventh-century Codex Aureus of Echternach. Dives is having a great time while Lazarus is out in the cold with the dogs. In the next register down Lazarus dies and is happily received in the bosom of Abraham. At the bottom comes the suffering of Dives who calls up to Lazarus, but it is much too late. In the manuscript, the "great chasm" mentioned in the biblical story is created by pink bands of paint surrounded by gold borders. In Sant Climent that chasm is architectural. The event on the inside of that door, from which Lazarus is shunned, the fabulous life of the rich man, would have appeared on the other side of the arch, another image that no longer exists. Thus a whole body of space, the entire central area of the church, divides Lazarus and the rich man.

Reading the story of Lazarus is physically demanding. We must twist and turn, much like Lazarus does, to see both sides of the story. And we should realize he is on Christ's right, Dives is on Christ's left. That realization draws us

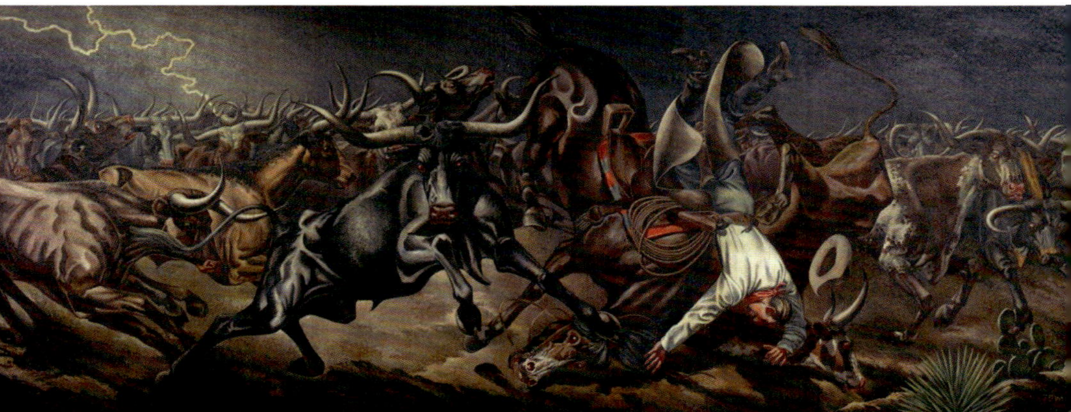

FIG. 7.12 Tom Lea, *Stampede,* 1940. Originally in the U.S. Post Office of Odessa, Texas. Currently in the Ellen Nöel Art Museum, Odessa, Texas. Oil on canvas, 213.36 × 518.16 cm.

back to the central image, to the eternal judgment of Christ. And as we glance back and forth, to the right and back to the left, we find ourselves as part of this moment, this judgment. We are like the pilgrims marching upward toward the feet of Christ in the center of the tympanum at Autun, standing in this space as though this is a rehearsal for what is to come, hoping to be like Lazarus, on the right side of Christ.

The image of Lazarus is interesting because it is, in a sense, standardized. Even though Lazarus appears in different media or spaces—in fresco, in a manuscript, in sculpture—his shape is and was identifiable. Images or forms, called iconography in art historical circles, could behave like language. Another example would be the representations of Christ in a mandorla that appear throughout the Mediterranean, in places like Autun, and even as far as Athens in the church known as the Monastery of Daphni in Athens (Fig. 7.11). Forms of art were their own language. Like words in a sentence, these scenes or forms could be shifted around, put in different places. In this way they would accrue additional meanings and contribute to their surrounds in new ways. This is what makes a trip to MNAC so spectacular. Not only do we experience the painting of Sant

Climent like a would-be pilgrim, but we also have the chance to compare other frescoed apses, just like those men and women traveling from site to site looking for spiritual support and physical respite.

Scholars dislike the term "Romanesque" because there is no one word that can combine Durham Cathedral with its colossal columns, the imaginative sculpture at Autun Cathedral, and the paintings at Sant Climent. But maybe the term works better than they think. Maybe one simple, throwaway word is the only way to show how interconnected all these regions were, the only way to overcome the nationalistic divisions that far postdated the medieval period. It is so fascinating that we of the twenty-first century have taken to such an extreme that tendency to label and name and divide first developed by those nineteenth-century scholars. We have Generation X, Generation Y, the Me Generation. Things are so eighties or so nineties. Medieval frescoes are about a completely different sense of time, one that transcends decades and styles and looks toward an eternal beyond.

I want to play with that idea of porous notions of time just one more degree in a mini-epilogue. While the Spanish scholars and conservators were traveling through the forests and mountains of the Pyrenees, their country was suffering through a series of wars. Trauma from World War I was still fresh, and a brutal civil war was soon to erupt. On the other side of the Atlantic, Americans were suffering through the Great Depression. Supported by the Works Progress Administration, men and women created tremendous paintings for post offices across the country. It is stunning that there was an entire campaign to save the country and restore patriotism through paint, and that this was precisely what was happening in Spain. On both sides of the ocean art was a means of bolstering patriotism, of fighting against the overwhelming trauma that was tearing at the infrastructure of both countries. It was a means of articulating fear and of fighting to overcome it, a notion that pulls us closer and closer to the medieval period and the ways that they addressed fear and death and uncertainty.

Tom Lea's painting *Stampede*, in Odessa, Texas, is perfectly apocalyptic—natural disasters, frightfully demonic longhorns, a world where humanity is turned upside down (Fig. 7.12). The paintings in Brownfield, Texas, show another apocalyptic scene, sweeping fires being fought by men gruesomely dragging a sacrificial animal, a skinned steer, through the wheat. As post offices move (or become obsolete), these paintings are being forgotten, or they fall off the walls altogether and are lost forever. There are many examples of paintings that have been completely destroyed. We may need a new band of traveling conservators.

Paintings tell our story, not just in Texas or in America, not just in the twentieth or twenty-first century, but across space and across time. It's not quite the same notion of collapsed time that we read about in Revelation and that we see in the medieval frescoes. There is a special collapsing of time at the Museu Nacional d'Art de Catalunya. There, the rescued medieval frescoes are a lens into a world view that is composed of layers of time—past, present, and the apocalyptic future.

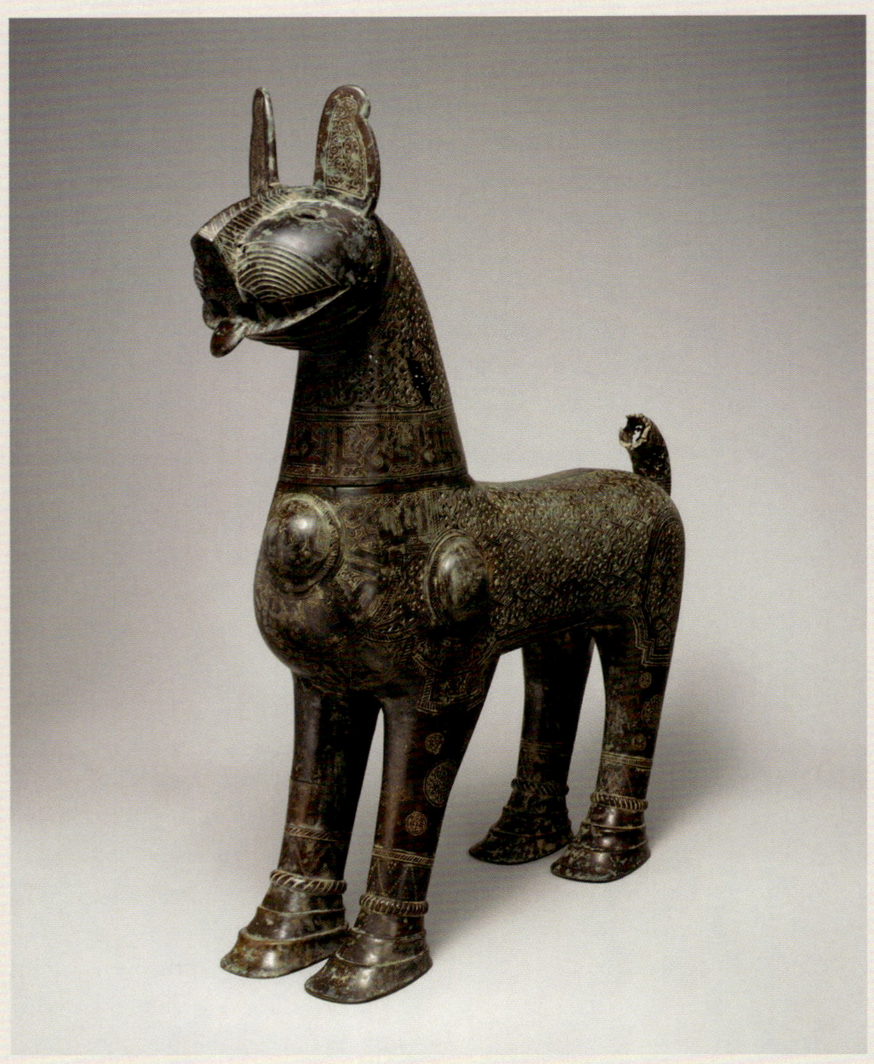

FIG. 8.1 Incense Burner of Amir Saif al-Dunya wa'l-Din ibn Muhammad al-Mawardi, ca. 1118–1182 (AH 577). Metropolitan Museum of Art, New York. Bronze, 85.1 × 82.6 × 22.9 cm.

Incense Burner of Amir Saif al-Dunya wa'l-Din ibn Muhammad al-Mawardi

CA. 1181–82 (AH 577)

ISLAMIC ART

When you think of Islamic art, it is quite possible that the first image that comes to mind is *not* a large twelfth-century bronze censer in the shape of a plucky, smiling cat (Fig. 8.1). And you would be justified in being a bit surprised. Technically, the piece cannot be Islamic because it is not a religious object. It was presumably owned by pious Muslims, but it would have had no place in a mosque, where calligraphic and abstract images dominate. And yet the cat eagerly awaits your entry into the glorious Islamic galleries at the Metropolitan Museum of Art, which were reopened in 2011. You almost get the sense that, if he still had his tail, it would be wagging vigorously, welcoming you into his abode. In his excitement the cat pulls back, as though he is getting his momentum, about to rush forward to greet you or, more likely, jump. This particular cat is called a caracal, coming from the Turkish word *karakulak* meaning black ear. His black ears and the elegant long tufts of hair that extend from them are distinctive. The rest of his body is a tawny red.

These animals were particularly prized by Islamic princes in the twelfth century, both for their beauty and grace, but also because they were fabulous hunting animals. The caracal can jump up to twelve feet.* Because of this incredible lever-

* "Caracal Explosive Jump," www.youtube.com/watch?v=4dCXK6KhkTw.

age, they were trained to catch birds on the wing. Most engaging and welcoming of all is the caracal's hilariously happy face. His wide-open eyes are elegantly outlined with stylized curlicues and arabesque shapes. Those flourishes seem to give the cat a twinkle in his eye. And originally he would have, as his eyes were most likely filled with bright turquoise stones. The way the chevrons on the bridge of his nose point upward in a series of peaks gives a joviality to the center of his face. The row of little pitched roofs terminates in a broad, angular nose and branches out in a series of cascading, thin, rounded arches that run across the caracal's cheeks—his whiskers. Inverting the arching shape of the whiskers is the crescent shape of that gleeful, toothy grin. He is smiling with such intensity that there are rows of folds of skin under his chin—ripples and reverberations that, when read along the neck upward, terminate in the caracal's protruding tongue. His ears sit at a slight angle, thus mirroring the way the caracal's ears move in nature, rotating and twitching as he susses out the movement of his prey. The paisley shape of his ears creates an ornamental lobe which alludes to the elegant tuft of black hair that tops the actual caracal's ears. From those perky ears to that beaming grin and wagging tongue, the caracal incense burner is contagiously lively and engaging, and perfect for princely parties.

The Met's way around the fact that pieces like this one would have been used in secular contexts, stately palaces, was to name the newly reinstated Islamic wing the following: The New Galleries for the Art of the Arab Lands, Turkey, Iran, Central Asia, and Later South Asia. It is not easy to ask the guards for directions when you need to remember eighteen words first. Yet the point is that the galleries present a series of objects that are not all religious pieces; they are not all Islamic in a religious sense. The lengthy title also asserts the diversity of the areas that are known as the Islamic lands. The term Islamic art suggests that there is a singular aesthetic, a monolithic look. To consider all artistic production from Spain to northwestern India as being essentially all the same is ridiculous, risible.

The smiling feline figure also fails to conform to the widespread notion that Islamic culture is hostile to or even prohibits representations of people and animals. We witnessed the result of these polemics taken to radical and perverse extremes in the demolition of Nimrud in spring 2015 and Palmyra in summer

2015. The footage from those sites is grotesque. That destruction is the result of a modern Muslim extremism. Not all Muslims feel the same way about art. And historically Islamic culture was not hostile to anthropomorphic art. There were periods when relationships with images were more complicated and figuration was less welcome. But we are talking about a huge period of time—one that spans from 610, the date of the Prophet Muhammad's first revelation, to 1600 and beyond. The fact that attitudes toward imagery shifted over a period of a thousand years is not surprising. (And don't forget, Christians too had periods of terrible iconoclasm—in ninth-century Byzantium, during the Protestant Reformation of the sixteenth century, and throughout the French Revolution in the eighteenth century.)

On the whole, images, and more specifically images with bodies and shapes, were very much a part of the Islamic culture. In fact, the opposition to figuration in Islam does not appear in the Qur'an, the central religious text of Islam that contains the words of God or Allah that were brought to the Prophet by the Angel Gabriel (Jibril) over a period of twenty-three years. The holy revelations, represented in these manuscripts, started in 610 and concluded in 632, the date of the death of Muhammad. Objections to figuration appear in the Hadith, a later series of reports recording the words of Muhammad. Some were written down right after his death, but the text continued to expand as late as the ninth century. The Hadith promotes depictions of trees as alternatives to images of living beings. It recommends removing the heads of figurative images to render them treelike so that there is a clear incapacity for breath or spirit (*ruh*).

The texts of the Hadith seem to account for the peculiarly repixilated mosaics that scholars had been uncovering in Jordan and Palestine until recent events in those regions put a permanent hold on further archaeological research. The upper portion of the mosaic from Madaba shows the city of Nikopolis, identified in Greek along the top (Fig. 8.2). In the lower register, in what appears to be a flurry of acanthus leaves, with arching multicolored mosaics terminating in cornucopia, is actually a muddled representation of a hunt. A red and orange spear on the left stabs the breast of what was once a cat with a spotted coat, as we can see on his legs and head. He sticks out his bright-red tongue and runs toward his now-lost aggressor. Originally the cat was probably mean and agile, a worthy opponent,

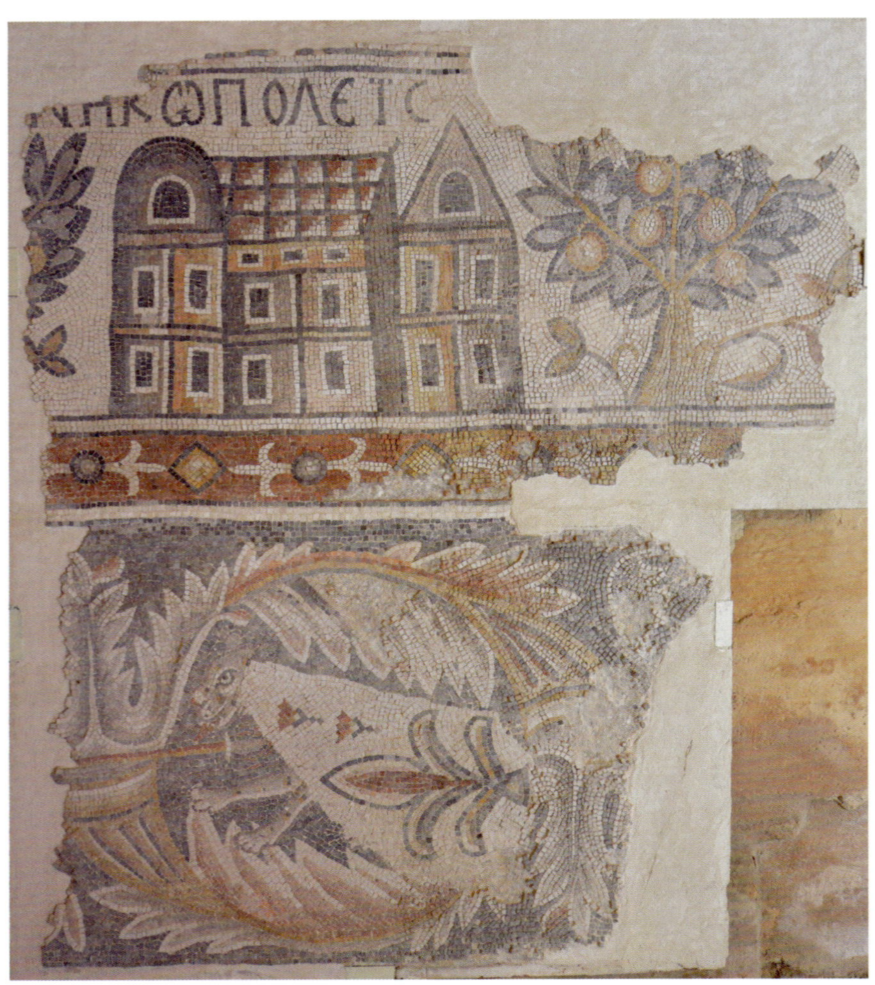

FIG. 8.2 Mosaic depicting Nikopolis set over an altered animal, ca. 719–720. Excavated from the Church on the Acropolis at Ma'in, Jordan. Madaba Archaeological Park, Jordan. Stone tesserae, 203.5 × 184.5 cm.

but in his reconfigured state he drags a triangular white sack of a body. At some point in the early eighth century, white mosaic cubes were used to replace his torso from the neck down, leaving his legs. Only two little red flowers, and a tree in a shape that might remind us of the French coat of arms, the fleur-de-lis, fill in the void. The very place that the cat would have breathed was denatured or, I suppose it is more accurate to say, natured, since it was made to look like a strange garden with random flowers.

These changes, of which there are many examples, seem to accord with the guidance of the Hadith, with its preference for vegetation over figuration. However, scholars are suspicious of the argument that cruel iconoclasts, sent from the caliph, came to cut the mosaics out of loyalty to the proscriptions of the Hadith. In fact, scholars now believe that the changes may have been done by Christian artists. Christians, like their Muslim neighbors, were also nervous during this period about the role of images and the danger of images being overvenerated or, worse, worshipped. The period of iconoclasm in Byzantium lasted from the eighth to ninth centuries. Image production was low, and many mosaics with figures like the Madonna and Child were turned into large, aniconic crosses, as at Hagia Irene in Istanbul. Taking out mosaics and replacing them is actually quite difficult to do. Artists—Christian and Muslim—may have worked together to change (and control) the subjects of the mosaics.

What is so interesting is that these mosaic images were redone, not destroyed. They were not blown up like the Buddha statues at Bamiyan or the lions of Raqqa in Syria. A line might be drawn through a neck or torso in a manuscript or a face rubbed out. Mosaic cubes were plucked out and reconfigured. It would have been far easier to put a huge slab over the mosaics than to pull out the cubes and re-lay them. Instead, the artists intentionally left enough of the original mosaic so that its past could coexist with its present, deactivated body. The redone mosaics both correct and respect the memory of the mistake of potentially having made a too-lifelike animal. In one sense, the metamorphosis of the cat in the mosaic points to the hand of the artists and their control over the image.

Artists in this culture were respected and far more frequently involved in enhancing rather than suppressing the life of figural forms. If the source of breath in the mosaic was ceremoniously suppressed and suffocated with white mosaic cubes and slightly random flower formations, the opposite occurs in the caracal. His breath is actuated and accentuated. The caracal entertains us, both with his lively facial features and with the purpose of his pierced body. He is an incense burner. The happy head would have been removed to allow a shallow bowl with incense to be placed in the interior of the hollow body. Once the incense started to burn, sweet scents and wafting, soft smoke would have emanated from the caracal. This transformation of a bronze statue into a caracal that breathes fire, delicious sweet-smelling fragrant fire, would have been a source of absolute delight. The best party trick in the palace.

There are no documents to describe the way the incense burners of the twelfth century were received or appreciated in these princely palaces. However, the mania for automata is well documented. When two Byzantine ambassadors visited the Abbasidian court in Baghdad in the tenth century, they were thrilled and amazed at the sight of a lavish artificial tree with singing birds placed in a pond. The palace engineers had rigged fountains to make the birds whistle and sing and move. The Arabic treatise the *Book of the Knowledge of Ingenious Mechanical Devices* by al-Jazari, written in 1206, is a compendium of automated devices and machinery. Its great popularity is evidenced in the fact that it was copied and illuminated at least eleven times. A delightful elephant clock shows how to tell time with the help of a bird, two humans, and a dragon (Fig. 8.3). The elephant itself is a weight-powered water clock. There is a bucket hidden inside the elephant that is filled with water, and then there is a series of complex relationships between bells and balls and dragons and seesaws, which all lead to the chiming of the time.

Evidently the elephant clock works well enough to have inspired replicas around the world. The effects of the smoke emerging from the body of the caracal is far less complicated than al-Jazari's device. However, the general fascination with animals that can do remarkable things, that are doing activities that make them seem alive even when they are mechanical or man-made, suggests that the incense emerging from the body of the caracal would have been seen with sheer excitement, surprise, wonder, and great admiration.

Most certainly, the presence and use of incense itself was evidence of the wealth and worldliness of the caracal's owner. The act of enjoying and using incense was also the purview of the learned and the elite. Writings about medieval

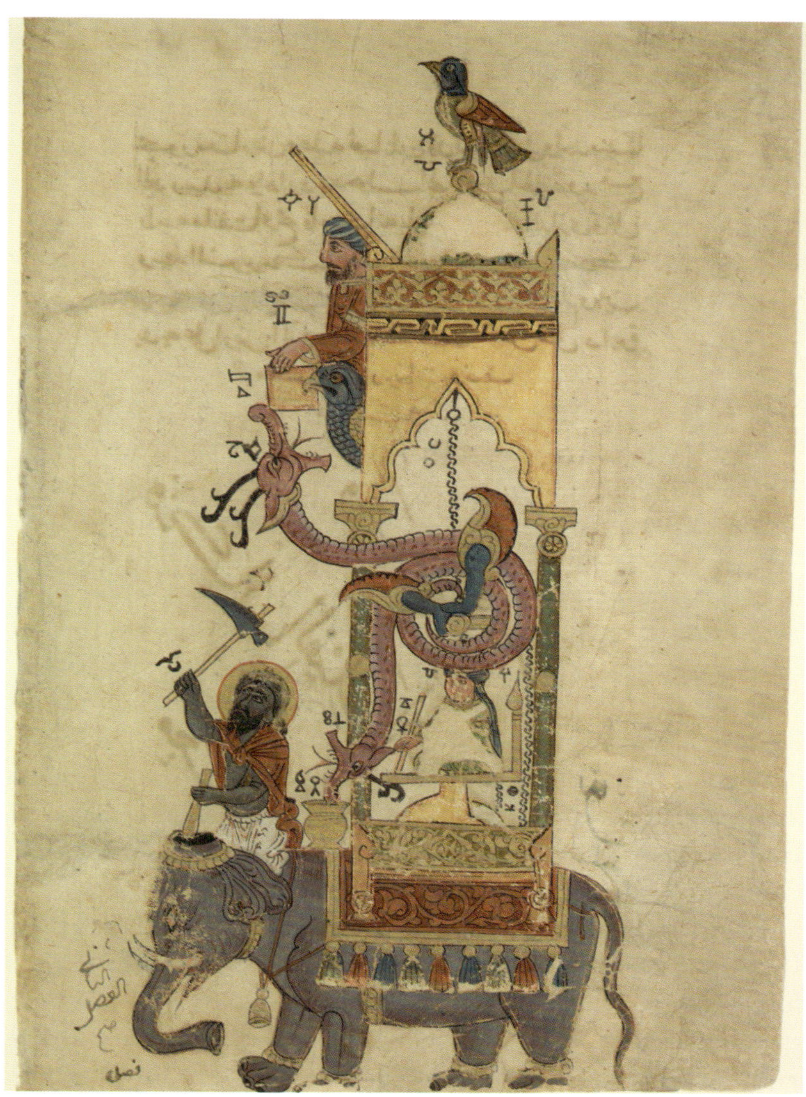

FIG. 8.3 "The Elephant Clock," folio from *Book of the Knowledge of Ingenious Mechanical Devices*, by Badi` al-Zaman ibn al-Razzaz al-Jazari (1136–1206), 1315 (A.H. 715). Calligrapher Farrukh ibn 'Abd al-Latif. Metropolitan Museum of Art, New York. Ink, opaque watercolor, and gold on paper, 30 × 19.7 cm.

Islamic courts discuss perfume as a gift fit for royalty, and, in wills from the period, gold and silver vessels are listed alongside perfumes. A ninth-century account by al-Mas'udi describes the Abbasid caliph al-Ma'mun's meetings with his most learned and valued advisers. When his advisers arrived at the palace, they were first brought into a chamber and given a meal. After this, incense burners were brought into the room so that the guests could perfume themselves before entering the caliph's presence. (We can see incense burners in the presence of princely courts in the center of an illuminated manuscript page from the fourteenth century.)

Not only did the caracal owner have the means by which to purchase the incense and shower it upon his friends, but he also seems to have been involved in the production and selling of perfumes himself. Around the neck of the caracal and continuing onto his breast is an elegant inscription that identifies the owner. The term "ibn al-Mawardi," which appears at the end of the patron's name, means "son of rosewater seller." Thus, the prince's family was also invested in the selling of perfumes, which was presumably a lucrative endeavor. In essence, the owner is proclaiming that he is intimately connected with the prestigious trade and that he has a hand in it from start to finish—from the purchasing of the raw materials, possibly from as far away as China, to the production of those goods into perfumes, which he then had a hand in selling and enjoying, burning them for his own personal pleasure. This inscription does more than just state the name of the owner and tell us he is wise and just. It *shows* us how great he is when the incense is burning in the beautiful bronze caracal that he has commissioned and paid for, perhaps by selling the rosewater perfumes.

The same message of the prince's power and prestige takes shape in the inscription naming the artist, which continues along the breast of the caracal: "Work of Ja'far son of Muhammad son of 'Ali in the year AH 577." (The year 577 refers to the Islamic calendar that begins in 622, when Muhammad emigrated from Mecca to Medina. This pilgrimage is called the *hijra*. AH is *Anno Hegirae*, Latin for in the year of the *hijra*. The dates according to the Gregorian calendar, our calendar, are 1181–82.) Most works of art from these earlier centuries are left unsigned. But it would seem that the prince wanted to make certain that the guests who saw his caracal were well aware of his ability to afford and contract pieces by this particular artist. The listing of Ja'far's father enforces the sense that this is an important artist who comes from a longer line of well-known metalworkers.

The fact that Saif al-Dunya had his name and the artist he commissioned so prominently placed is actually quite a departure from other incense burners of the period. One feature that distinguishes our caracal from other feline incense burners is his size. The caracal is 85 centimeters high and 83 centimeters long. Other feline burners are much smaller, none higher than 35 centimeters or longer than 26. The piece at the Museum of Fine Arts in Houston is 30 centimeters long and 30 centimeters high. The burner in the Khalili Collections in London is 27 centimeters high and 27 in length. In addition to being much smaller in size, none of these other examples has the name of the patron and his artist. Most inscriptions on the examples are religious, quoting passages of the Qur'an. The Cleveland Museum of Art has a bronze burner that has two passages from the Qur'an, both of which command the faithful to attend Friday services in the mosque. The caracal by Ja'far does not acknowledge the Qur'an or Friday services at all. Three bosses on the left, front, and side of the caracal read "happiness, prosperity, well-being," words that one can find in the Qur'an, but there is nothing to specifically link these three states of being to religious texts or activities.

Nasser Khalili, the director of the Khalili Collection, deemed the caracal at the Met the "Metropolitan Monster." Although that is a little unfair, it is true that the patron wanted his to be the biggest, most intricate, toothiest incense burner around. Of course the patron's point could only be made by comparison, by having his work stand out in contrast when compared to similar pieces. To be the culmination of a trend you have to work with or look like other, earlier, comparable models. Pierced incense burners were popular in twelfth-century Khurasan, the northeastern region of Persia. Khurasan was home to cities with major artistic output such as Herat, Nishapur, and Merv (written in ancient Persian or Farsi as Marw). The caracal came from Tayabad, which is currently located on the border of Iran and Afghanistan, and just between Nishapur and Herat. During the twelfth century, Khurasan was under the control of the Seljuk Sultanate, a Turkish dynasty of central Asian nomadic origins that had, by 1055, taken over Baghdad and assumed control over Iran, Iraq, and much of Anatolia.

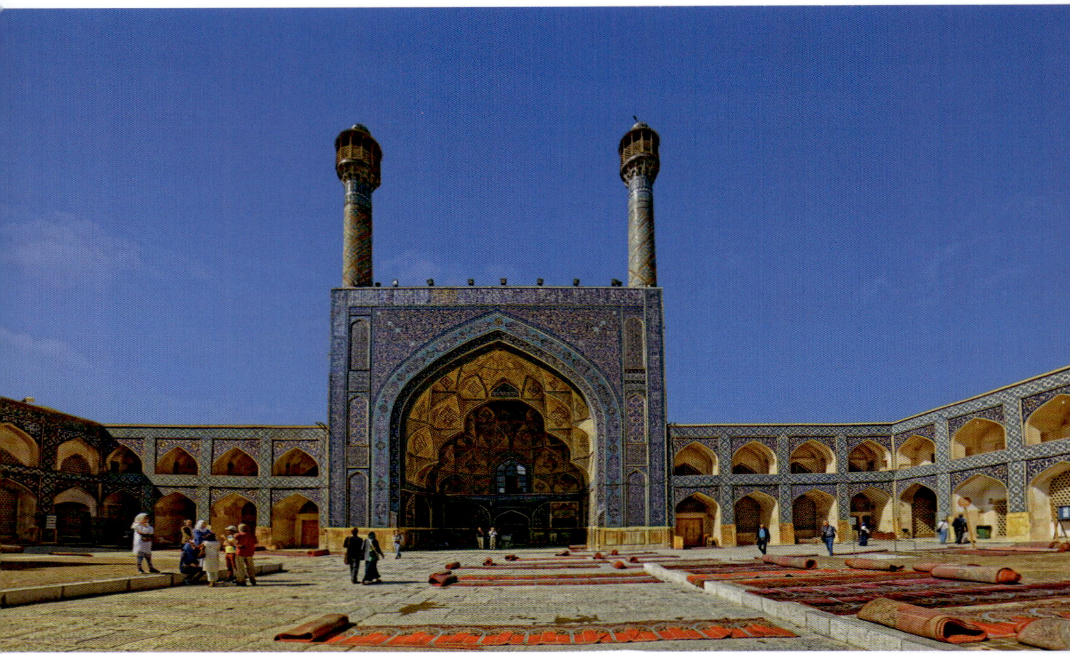

FIG. 8.4 *Qibla iwan* of the Masjid-e Jameh (the Great Mosque) of Isfahan, Iran. View to the south. Complex started in eleventh century; muquarnas added in fourteenth century; blue tiles and minaret added in seventeenth century. Glazed and cut ceramic tiles.

They retained power over these lands until the invasion in 1218 of the Mongols, who were led by the formidable conqueror Genghis Khan.

The Seljuks were tremendous patrons of architecture. One example is in Isfahan, a city in central Iran that, in 1043, the prince Malik Shah I named as the capital of the Seljuk Empire. What better way to establish the authority and power of one's new reign than to initiate the building of a tremendously large and beautiful mosque? The mosque has a large rectangular courtyard, with four large vaulted halls called *iwans* facing the interior, the center of which has a multilobed fountain (Fig. 8.4). The balance and structural clarity of the form was so admired that this became the prevalent mosque type throughout the Islamic world. Symmetry and repetition and order define the organization and experience of the mosque. As the viewer enters the space, the sense of order and balance is further emphasized through the proliferation of similar nichelike spaces, like mini-*iwans*. Shapes seem to beget shapes, arches beget arches. This process of proliferating forms continues as the viewer moves closer. Bright-blue tiles—turquoises, sapphires, cobalt, navy—lead the eye into the heart of the arch, where golden tiles coalesce into pointed forms called *muqarnas*, vaulting shapes that look like stalactites. These too are mini-niches.

The larger niche draws us inward, and as it does we see smaller and smaller niches, which hover above us, in the heavens, beautifully evoked in the many blues of the surrounding tiles. The sensation is akin to the way that fractals work in physics, wherein a never-ending repetition of patterns occurs at various scales. In a sense, the act of looking is a metaphor or illustration for the process of prayer. The way that the shapes lead the viewer deeper and deeper into the space of the arch through those repeating and increasingly smaller and more delicate forms is similar to the meditative and thoughtful act of praying, of elevating one's thoughts beyond the earthly, weighty concerns of the world and letting them move in more mysterious, abstract, and lofty ways.

The south *iwan* is special because it is the *qibla*, the direction toward Mecca that Muslims face when praying. This is identifiable by the two tall, rather imposing blue minarets. The word minaret means lighthouse, and these act in just that way, as bright, obvious signposts that help you find your way to a sacred space, a place of sanctuary and prayer. Another important shape that identifies the *qibla* wall is the niche shape called a *mihrab*, a beautiful example of which is in the Metropolitan Museum of Art (Fig. 8.5). The artists and patrons in Isfahan embraced similar spiraling shapes and scintillating ceruleans. This *mihrab* comes from a *madrasa imami*, a school for advanced study by imams who are the leaders of worship in mosques.

Again, the process of viewing becomes a metaphor for prayer. The words that orient and organize the *mihrab* are religious in nature. The first inscription, a passage from the Qur'an, appears on the outer, rectangular border in an elegant and serpentine script called *thuluth*, meaning consummate or clear. The precise and elegant script communicates words from the holy text specific to the maintenance of mosques and the practice of proper prayer. The second inscription

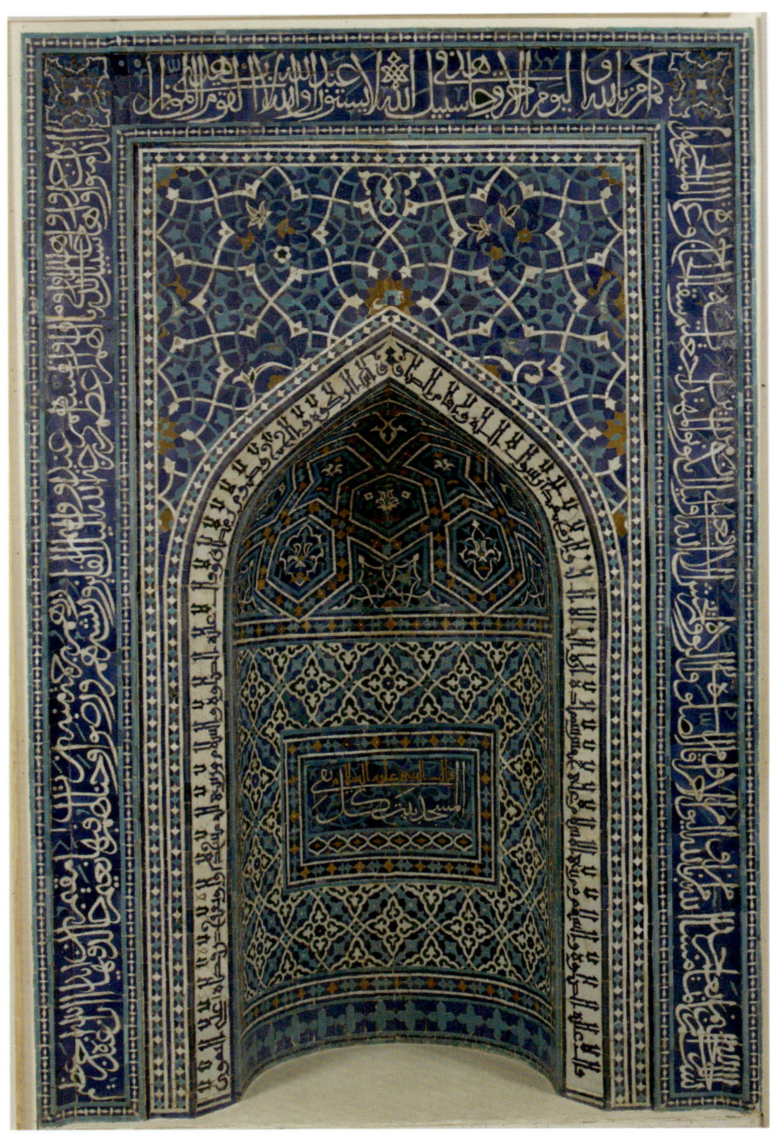

FIG. 8.5 *Mihrab* (prayer niche), ca. 1354–1355 (AH 755). Originally from Isfahan, Iran. Metropolitan Museum of Art, New York. Glazed and cut ceramic tiles, 343 × 289 cm.

inverts the color scheme of white letters on a blue background seen in the first arch into blue letters on a white background. These color shifts are subtle, like slowly moving white clouds against a blue sky—one minute the clouds dominate, the next the sky. This inner arch has writings in a shorter, blunter script known as *kufic*. Those blockier, more angular letter shapes quote the words of the Prophet Muhammad as recorded in the Hadith regarding the five pillars of Islamic faith, the rules followed by the devout Muslim, and the essential Muslim message that "there is no god but God and Muhammad is the Messenger of God."

Finally, in the central rectangular cartouche are ocher-yellow inscriptions, a blending of the *thuluth* and *kufic* scripts, which assert the role of the mosque in the words of the Prophet: "The mosque is the abode of the pious." Like the great *iwan* at the mosque in Isfahan, the devout are led toward an inner, spiritual devotion in a way that mirrors the process of reading these spiritual words on this special wall. The shapes and styles of the inscriptions also participate in that meditative and religious experience. The letters wrap around the niche, guiding your eye from right to left, articulating and emphasizing the significance of the shape of this particular wall and what its function is as a pointer toward Mecca.

The words are important, but so is the act of unlocking those intertwining forms. The cursive demands attentive, alert reading. Those forms also twist and turn in ways that relate to shapes that are not textual, to the white, flowerlike, six-pointed star shapes, which contain blossoming flowers in white and bronze. These white forms link up with other smaller versions of themselves that contain light-blue interlocking six-pointed shapes. Text and image are so beautifully intertwined that it is easy to get lost in the movements of the lines and forms of the purely ornamental, geometrical shapes. There is something spiritual and mystical about reading the inscriptions apart from and also amid the flurry of geometrical shapes, of finding the meaning in the proliferation of forms, and of seeing the interrelated beauty in all of God's creations—flowers, patterns, words.

That blurring between text and image has less spiritual, more humorous applications as well. The bronze Bobrinsky Bucket, which also was produced during the Seljuk reign, would have been used to carry water around a public bath or a *hammam* (Fig. 8.6). At first blush it might seem that the entire bucket is surrounded in letters and inscriptions. The top register does have a row of text.

But the letters terminate in the heads of open-mouthed snakes and the bodies of birds. The figures above, a row of men who are only shown from the torso up, are speaking and gesturing with great animation. It soon becomes clear that the shapes that were once letters, and then turned into snakes and birds, are also supposed to act as the long legs of the gesticulating men. More men below drink and play backgammon, and fight with staves. When juxtaposed with the hybrid bodies above, their abstract and angular poses make one think of *kufic* lettering, even though they are not letters at all.

The next register, the band on the belly of the bucket, is all textual, but reading these letters would have been a tremendous chore. The forms are more like braided Gordian knots than clear, legible words, and oddly enough look like Anglo-Saxon objects, like a well-known seventh-century belt buckle from the Sutton Hoo Ship Burial, which turns out to be a series of intertwined animals. The playfulness and imaginative quality of this work would have been a great source of pride for the wealthy merchant Rashid ad-Din Azizi, who is named in the inscriptions on the Bobrinsky Bucket. While steaming and bathing, he and his guests would have read and enjoyed the infinitely shifting images and letters, reminding themselves that they were living the high life.

The protean inscriptions on the copper bucket are similar to the inscriptions on the body of the caracal. Here too the inscriptions seamlessly shift from word to image. The letters on the neck of the caracal are stately and austere. The thick bands terminate in precise points and angular finishes. The shapes coalesce to form the collar of the cat, which cleverly associates the name of the owner with the accoutrement that indicates possession and control. (A place where cat owners still put their names and numbers.) But those letters twist and turn in the same space of spinning acanthus leaves, vine scrolls that loop and curl in ways that mirror, enhance, and complicate the original text. Floriated forms continue all over the body of the cat. They swoop and curl in the caracal's ears, blossoming into large, palmlike leaves, and similarly enliven his upturned nose. They interlock and interlope, punctuated by piercings for the perfume.

There is a sensitive awareness to the ways that the forms of letters are artistic, to the fact that they look like the vine scrolls and to the fact that they sometimes become vine scrolls. Thus words and ornament both speak to the same point.

The words define the caracal—they tell us who made it and who paid for it. The scrolling vines also define the body of the caracal—they give the vessel a shape and an aesthetic. There is a natural way in which those two, text and image, have the same instability or flexibility as on the copper bucket—with shapes and forms looking like letters and letters looking like designs. These swirling words and images would have beautifully echoes the swirling waves of smoke seeping from the piercings in the body of the caracal.

We can also see a slippage between function and ornament in the body of the cat. The piercings allow the smoke of the incense to escape the caracal's body. But those pierced parts of his body seem to be distinct from his legs and face, almost as though he is wearing an outfit, a caracal chainmail. The parts of his body that are meant to serve the incense that is burning are also the space reserved for special designs or decorations.

Simple earthenware from the Seljuk period also played with the limitless possibilities unlocked by the dialogue between ornament and function and word (Fig. 8.7). Black painted lettering runs around the rim with stark precision. Like the caracal, where the viewer has to walk around the object in order to see all of its intricate ins and outs, piercings and inscriptions, the plate must be read in the round. The writings on these plates are pithy aphorisms such as "He who speaks, his speech is silver, but silence is a ruby," or, as on this example, "Planning before work protects you from regret; prosperity and peace." If this were coming out of a fortune cookie, you might roll your eyes. But here the advice seems haunting. As the viewer walked around the piece or even turned it in his or her hands, the words might seem to come to life, to hover above the white background. A centripetal energy would also be at play—with the long letters leading you toward that strange central black dot. It is meaningless. And yet at the same time it is a shape, a sign, and even an image. Those letters point inward and, when seen from an angle, might appear to tumble toward that central speck. It is banal in its purpose (it's just a bowl) but pristine in its beauty, in its clarity, and in its point.

The Seljuks were a powerhouse, both politically and artistically—innovative and daring in architecture, metalwork, ceramic tiles, and painted earthenware. Yet it is important to recognize the ways in which these objects and images were rooted in a much deeper tradition, one that reaches back to the beginnings of

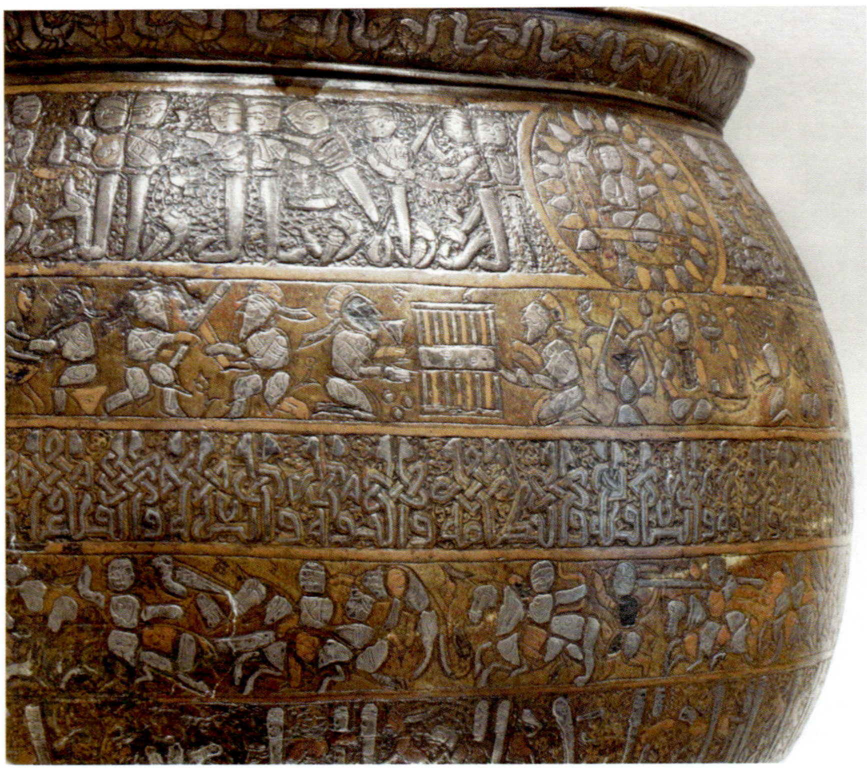

FIG. 8.6 Detail of Bobrinsky Bucket, twelfth century. Originally from Iran. Hermitage Museum, St. Petersburg. Bronze (brass), silver, and copper, 18.5 × 22 cm.

Islam. The interior of the Dome of the Rock, completed in 691, is filled with continuous acanthus scrolls, punctuated by pearls (Fig. 8.8). The eighth-century mosque in Damascus is also covered in those scrolling vegetal vines (Fig. 8.9). They grow and swirl all throughout the large mosaic on the entryway to the mosque and the freestanding building that once acted as the treasury. Although suggestive of paradise, the fronds also allude to the message that the Muslim world has a strong and united identity—that although there are many diverse cities and regions, their religious beliefs unite and connect them all, just as the

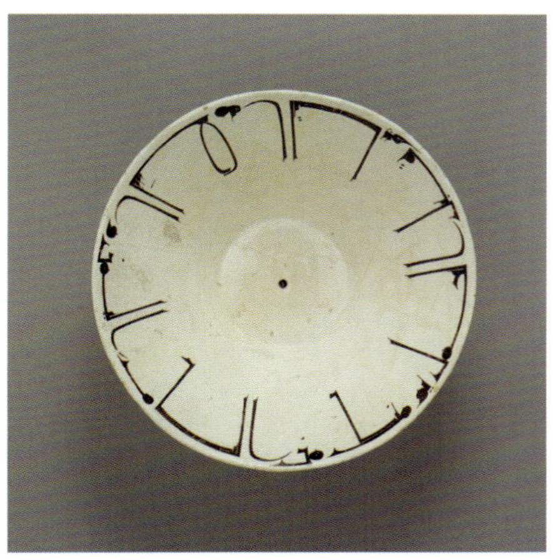

FIG. 8.7 Bowl with Arabic inscription, tenth century. Nishapur, Iran. Metropolitan Museum of Art, New York. Earthenware with white and black slip and lead glaze, 17.8 × 45.7 cm.

acanthus scrolls connect all of the discrete parts of the mosaics. Sadly, that mosaicked message of unity is being gravely undermined by the Syrian wars.

Those scrolling vines also reach past geographical and religious borders. To us, Iran and Afghanistan may seem distant, culturally and geographically. But they were not during the Middle Ages. What might represent the good life and visualize the notion of prosperity on the body of the caracal or the Dome of the Rock was similarly meaningful in religious iconography in the Christian Church. Leafy, curling vines at San Clemente, a twelfth-century church in Rome, emphasize and visualize the belief that the Crucifixion of Christ is a bridge that links the earthly and spiritual realms. The vines refer to the parable in John 15:5: "I am the vine; you are the branches. If you remain in me and I in you, you will bear much fruit." Stags, symbols of Christ's triumph over death, bracket the large leafy acanthus plant at the base of the cross. From this source the vines grow wildly. Mundane activities—men tending their sheep, next to a lovely peacock, women feeding their chickens—are connected through these vines to Church Fathers hard at work, through the Crucifixion, all the way to the pinnacle of the apse, where a multicolored cloud of heaven unfolds. The animated, swirling, verdant forms proliferate throughout the apse as a way of expressing the life and the bounty and history of the Christian church and are symbolic of the promise of eternal life to those who enter the church.

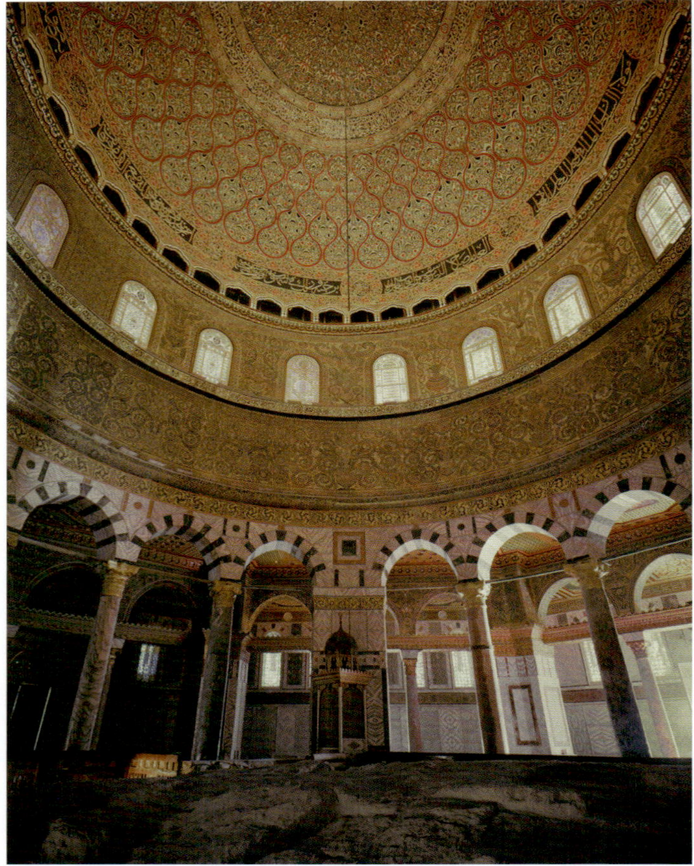

FIG. 8.8 Interior of the Dome of the Rock, begun ca. 691. Jerusalem, Israel.

The conversation between Christian and Islamic art was profound and fluid. Forms and shapes could transfer across cultures, across religious divisions, taking on new meanings and different purposes. They come from shared origins and visual cultures, like a language from common roots, like Spanish and French. The meanings shift based on where they appear and how they are appreciated, but they are from intersecting traditions.

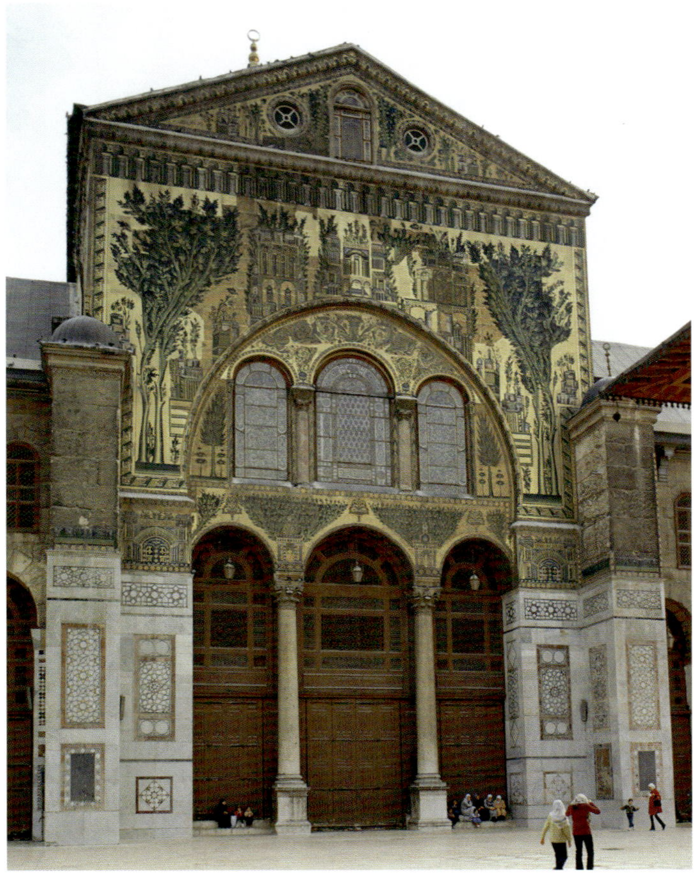

FIG. 8.9   Prayer hall façade, Umayyad Mosque of Damascus,
ca. eighth century. Damascus, Syria. Mosaic.

The conversation between Islamic East and Christian West continued throughout the Middle Ages. An illustration from the *Compendium of Chronicles* depicts the birth of the Prophet Muhammad (Fig. 8.10). Muhammad's mother, Amina, lies wearily on a makeshift bed and points toward the newly born boy. Muhammad, in the same reclining pose and position as his mother, is wrapped in swaddling clothes and held by one of two attendant angels. The second angel

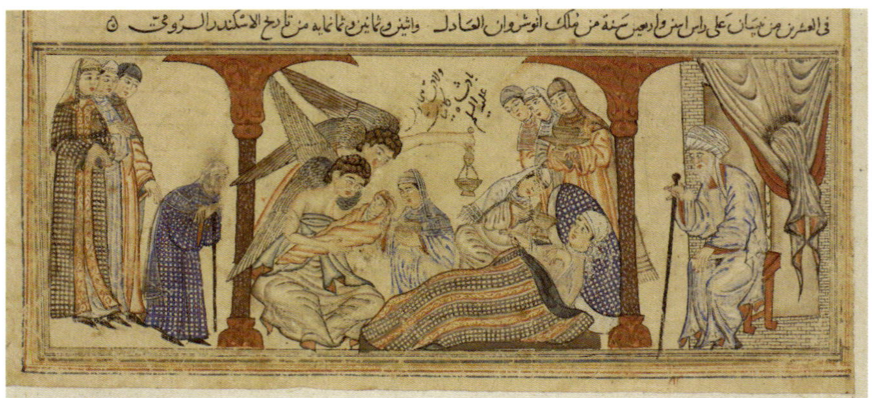

FIG. 8.10 Birth of the Prophet, illustration from *Jami' al-tawarikh* (Compendium of Chronicles), ca. 1314–1315 (AH 714). Copied and illustrated in Tabriz, Iran. Edinburgh University Library, MS Arab 20, folio 42r. Ink, colors, silver, and gold on paper, 43.5 × 30 cm.

swings a censer or incense burner, which appears to have inscriptions around the basin, not unlike the Bobrinsky Bucket. The same shape of the bowl of the censer appears in the hands of a woman tending to Amina. The woman seems to be lifting a soaking washcloth with tongs that she will put on Amina's head. The old man that witnesses the miraculous birth from beyond the column on the right is Muhammad's paternal grandfather.

Although the precise identification of some of the other peripheral individuals has challenged scholars, there is no doubt that this configuration is based on Christian images of the Nativity in which the Madonna reclines on a bier, lying in a pose similar to her swaddled son, while ladies attend to her, angels proclaim the glorious moment, and old Joseph watches from the side. This phenomenon of Christian configurations being used in Islamic contexts is not unique. It appears in painted glass and metalwork, such as on a thirteenth-century canteen at the Freer Gallery in Washington, DC, upon which there is another nativity scene. The meaning is shifted. It is not Christian. It is Muslim and tells the story of Muhammad. But the shared cultural underpinnings are clear and reveal a deep commonality between these seemingly divergent cultures.

This artistic sharing went both ways. The massive bronze griffin known as the Pisa Griffin is a perfect example of the ways in which Islamic images could be appropriated in Christian contexts (Fig. 8.11). Like the caracal, the griffin has Arabic inscriptions of wishes for complete well-being, perfect joy, eternal peace, perfect health, and happiness. Not only were the Arabic inscriptions illegible to the Italian viewer because of the foreign language, but the inscriptions would also have been quite invisible because the griffin was placed on the roof of the cathedral in Pisa, on a tall pole right above the apse. It was placed so that it would be visible to visitors coming to the city. The glimmering metal against the blue Pisan sky would have been striking from afar. It might have seemed like a strange magical beast with wings protecting the cathedral from on high, like a Gothic gargoyle. But most shocking and surprising of all would have been the sounds of the bronze beast. Recent studies have found that the vessel would have acted like a bizarre whistle. When wind moved through its open belly, the griffin would emit eerie sounds that were amplified by an internal resonating vessel. The griffin would come to life when air wafted through its body, not unlike the caracal, who came to life when the perfumed air started to be emitted from the piercings in its body. Bronze bodies were brought to life through breathlike air and wind and smoke.

The West also had an appreciation for lynxes, a broader category of felines to which caracals belong. Lynxes appear prominently in medieval bestiaries, compendia that described animals in spiritual and mystical terms. The understanding was that God had created the animals with specific roles and purposes so as to serve as examples for proper conduct and to reinforce stories from the Bible. The bestiaries were essential in promoting certain traditions, such as the belief that the flesh of the peacock did not decay, and they drew upon early writers—Pliny, Ovid, Theophrastus. These writers describe the lynx as having keen eyesight and a strange ability to create flame-colored stones. By urinating. These they hide because they are jealous and do not want humans to find the stones. The appreciation for large, agile cats like lynxes and caracals connects the East and the West.

In many ways, it is possible to read the history of the artistic production of these lands, of the whole Mediterranean, in the body of the caracal. It is also possible to reevaluate certain preconceptions that plague the study of the objects

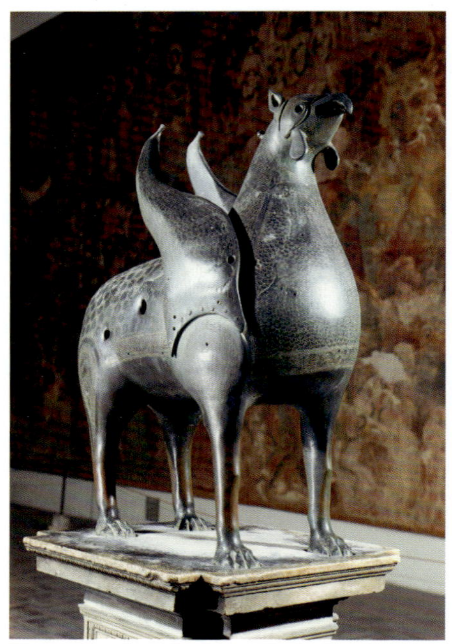

FIG. 8.11 Pisa Griffin, ca. eleventh century. Museo dell'Opera del Duomo, Pisa, Italy. Bronze, 107 × 87 × 43 cm.

from this period—such as the assumption that all artistic products are religious or that figural representation is strictly forbidden. For certain more extreme groups, that may be so. But those beliefs do not define this culture. This is why trips to the Metropolitan Museum of Art are so important. The riches in its galleries tell a story of a culture completely engaged in the world of art and artistic production. The recently opened Islamic galleries at the Louvre do the same. Covering the spaces of their collections with a huge golden billowing veil, the Louvre visualized the point that this culture is saturated, united, and defined by a rich artistic tradition. The veil is bright and golden and flutters as though responding to the movement of winds, despite the fact that it weighs 150 tons and is made up of 9,000 steel tubes.

Museums all around the world are acknowledging the importance of explaining pieces that are infelicitously lumped under the category of Islamic art. It is not an easy task. Much of the art from these kinds of galleries was meant to be used, and it is hard to show that. We will never actually see incense burning in the body of the caracal. But it is exciting to watch museums that take on the challenge. As the golden veil at the Louvre implies, Islamic art ties many different artistic cultures and trends together. Not only does the veil cover and shield the Islamic galleries, but it also is situated in a courtyard between large Neoclassical buildings that house masterpieces from the Renaissance, seventeenth-century Dutch paintings, and eighteenth-century French statuary.

A marvelous gate in the courtyard of the San Antonio Museum of Art also ties together many different cultures while drawing upon Islamic images and an Islamic past (Fig. 8.12). This arch led into Miraflores, a garden owned by Dr. Aureliano Urrutia. The bright blues of the parading peacocks along the top of the gate are naturally comparable to the blues of the *mihrab* from Isfahan. The Urrutia gate, like the *mihrab*, is also composed of inset painted tiles. Iconographically, too, there are special connections between the decorations of the gate and earlier Islamic art. Peacocks have an important place in Islamic culture. They are, in popular Islamic tradition, residents of the Garden of Eden and thus witness the expulsion of Adam and Eve. In a seventeenth-century painting from an illustrated manuscript of the Hadiqat al-Su'ada (Garden of the Blessed) Adam and Eve exit the garden. Holding hands, they march toward the left, away from the verdant landscape of Paradise. Watching this ignominious exit are the snake, a peacock, and an angel. The Urrutia gate also has peacocks watching and guarding a gate—both on high and on the pillars below. The peacocks above the entryway of the Urrutia gate are far more elegant than those below, which look wild and angry as they jump atop the sinuous branches of the centrally placed tree. These birds have spiky crowns and are composed of thicker, more abstract bands of color. At the base of the tree are two large leopardlike cats that seem to be pawing at the birds above. The cats look backward toward their tails and stick out little white tongues. Peacocks and elegant cats were also prominent in the Palatine Chapel of Roger II in Palermo, Sicily, specifically in the rooms reserved for Roger's imperial retinue. During the twelfth century, Sicily was controlled by Normans. But Sicily had been under Muslim rule from 831 until the Norman Conquest in 1072, and that Islamic tradition was very much alive. Roger spoke Arabic, and many of the monuments that he patronized are adorned with Arabic

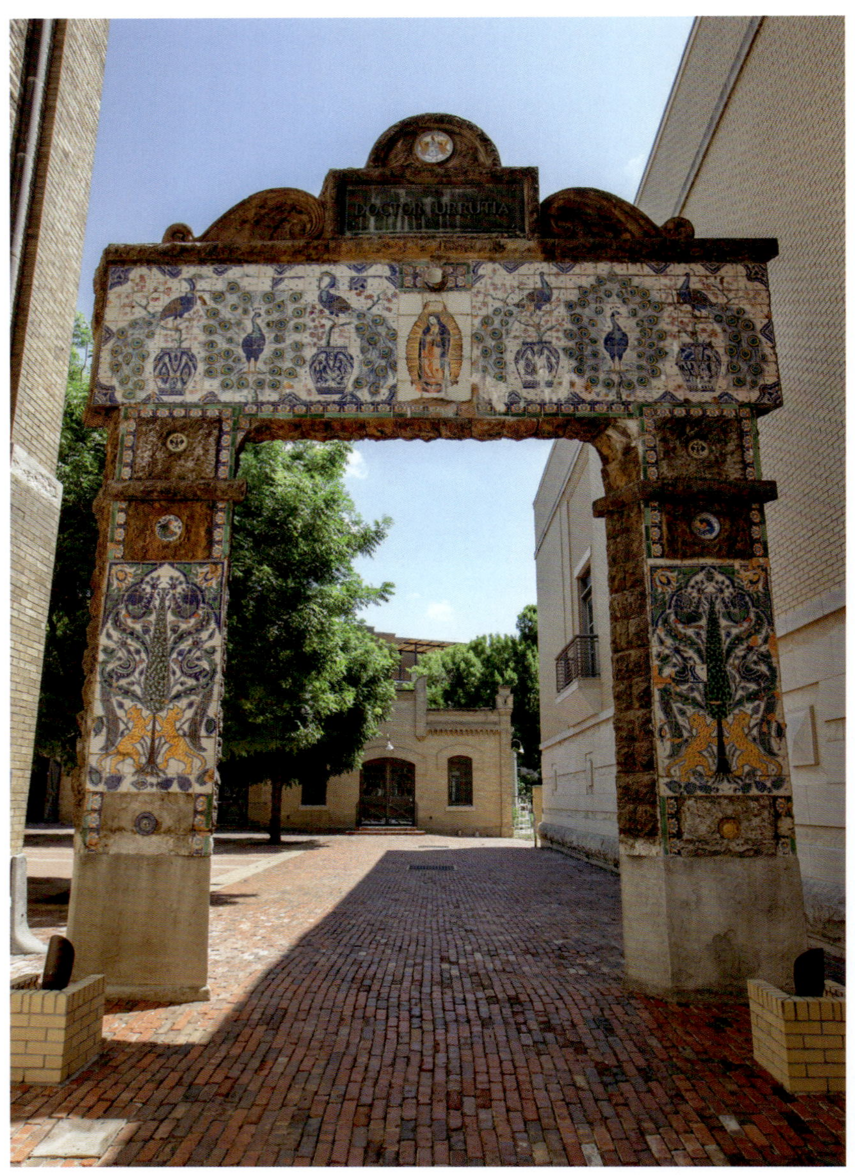

FIG. 8.12 Gate from Broadway entrance to the Urrutia estate (Miraflores), ca. 1918. San Antonio Museum of Art, San Antonio, Texas. Glazed and cut ceramic tiles.

script. Islamic traditions informed Roger's rooms just as they informed the aesthetics that Dr. Urrutia thought worthy of using to welcome visitors into his villa. Perhaps his peacocks could indicate that his guests were at the gates of a version of paradise, and they should hope not to be expelled.

Pieces like the caracal incense burner are joyful and challenging. They speak to the tremendous talents of the artists and artisans of the twelfth century, to their innovative work, and to the rich artistic traditions from which they were borrowing. This is not a story of art being hated and mistrusted. It is evidence of a deep appreciation and admiration of art in figural and nonfigural forms. These viewers, patrons, and artists were highlighting and enjoying the malleable and mysterious aspects of art, bringing the caracal to "life" by drawing the viewer in, by getting the viewer to engage with the object in a sensory way, through reading, looking, smelling. And memory too. It is hard to forget the smile of the cat. The grinning caracal makes me think about Alice and the Cheshire Cat, who appears, sitting in a tree, grinning from ear to ear. Alice is flummoxed by the appearance of the cat: "'I wish you wouldn't keep appearing and vanishing so suddenly: you make one quite giddy.' 'All right,' said the Cat; and this time it vanished quite slowly, beginning with the end of the tail, and ending with the grin, which remained some time after the rest of it had gone. 'Well! I've often seen a cat without a grin,' thought Alice; 'but a grin without a cat! It's the most curious thing I ever saw in my life!'" I know that the comparison is very far afield—a twelfth-century Islamic object and a novel written in 1865 London. Yet the caracal would have been meant to provoke a similar sense of wonder, that illusion of a cat which disappears, through a veil of smoke, with that wild and unforgettable smile etched into the memory of the viewer.

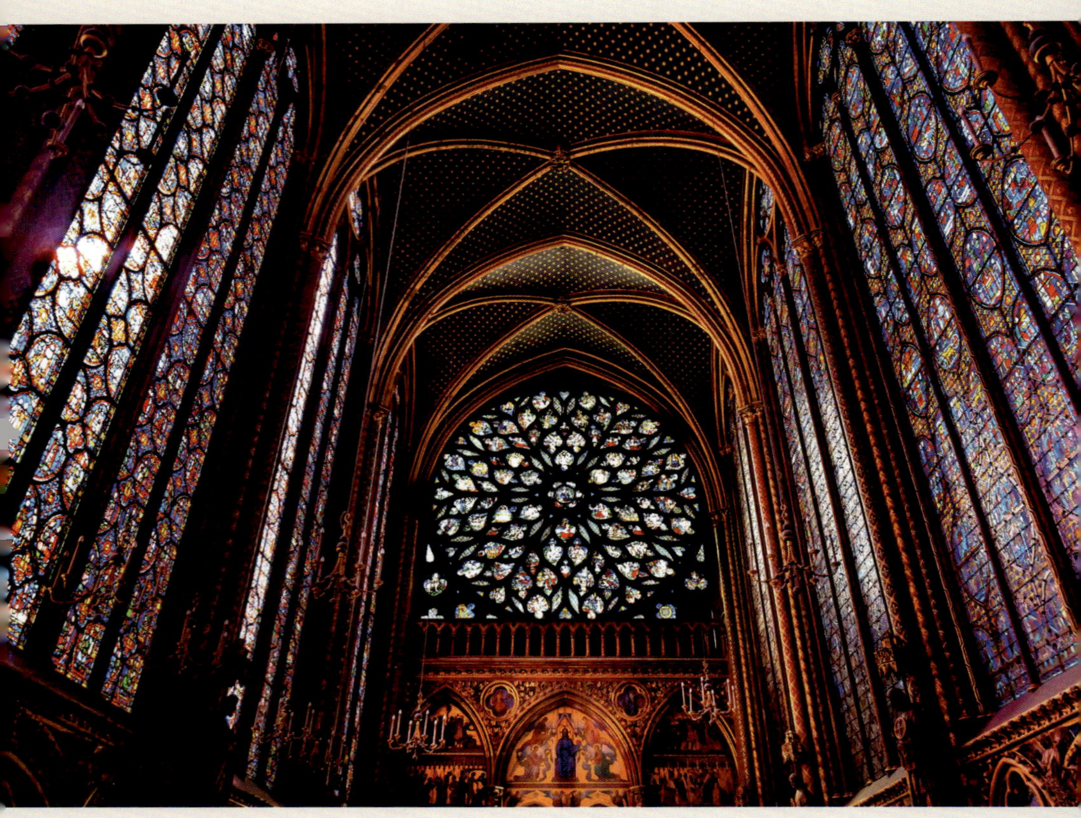

FIG. 9.1 Interior view of Sainte-Chapelle, 1239–1248. Paris, France.

Sainte-Chapelle

1239–48

GOTHIC ART

Sainte-Chapelle sits on the Île de la Cité, an island in the heart of Paris that accommodates Notre Dame and La Conciergerie, the former royal palace and prison of Paris (Fig. 9.1). It is an extraordinary example of Gothic architecture and stained glass. The building of Sainte-Chapelle started in 1239, in honor of a collection of relics that had been recently acquired by the King of France, Louis IX, later known as Saint Louis. However, as would be expected of any good Byzantinist, I am going to start the story of Sainte-Chapelle and its special relics in Byzantium, in Constantinople, the site of the derailed Fourth Crusade. The intention of this particular crusade, as with the first three, was to reclaim territories of the Holy Land that were under the control of Muslim rulers. The return to the Holy Land was the main goal for Pope Innocent III, who succeeded to the papal throne in 1198. By 1202 he had rallied sufficient support for the campaign—twelve thousand soldiers set out from Venice in order to save the Holy Land, complete with fifty war galleys and a warning from the pope that they were not to attack Christian states. But instead of making it to Cairo, the crusading armies, disregarding a letter of excommunication from the pope, attacked the city of Constantinople.

On April 12, 1204, the crusaders managed to overcome the thick city walls—scaling them from the sea and even burrowing through holes exposed after days of hurling large projectiles. By the following day, the crusaders had entered and overturned the great Christian capital—destroying the Library of

Constantinople and innumerable church treasuries. A work by Domenico Tintoretto in the Ducal Palace of Venice captures the drama of the siege of the city. It is clear from the painting that the conquest was seen in rather positive terms, at least from the perspective of the Venetians, who came away from the battles with tremendous treasures, many of which sit just outside the Ducal Palace—the four bronze horses (the quadriga) on the roof of San Marco, a porphyry statue of the tetrarchs from the palace in Constantinople, and precious Byzantine artifacts reframed as part of a large altar called the Pala d'Oro.

The original guardians of these treasures, the Greeks, were bemoaning the cruel disfigurement of their city and waiting haplessly in exile for a chance to return to their capital, which remained under the control of the Latins until 1261. The return of the Greeks to a crippled version of their once great power will be essential to the story of the Chora Church. However, even though Pope Innocent condemned the "perdition and works of darkness" committed by the Latins, the art produced in Venice explains the siege as though the attack were divinely sanctioned, as if the treasures of Constantinople had found their rightful place among the splendors of Venice.

Treasures also made their way to Paris. King Louis IX acquired, from the Latin emperor of Constantinople, Baldwin II, a slew of relics including objects connected to Christ's Crucifixion, Christ's swaddling clothes, a flask of the Virgin's milk, Moses's rod, the top of John the Baptist's head, and, most importantly, Christ's Crown of Thorns and a fragment of the True Cross. The compilation of these relics is recorded in a print from 1790 that, strangely enough, helped Indiana Jones during the Last Crusade. (A still shows Indie's father looking at the precise image of the Sainte-Chapelle relics). According to the seventeenth-century historian Le Nain de Tillemont, the cost of the relics was 140,000 livres, a sixth of one year's revenue, which, when your coffers are the entire treasury of France, is truly extravagant. The chapel itself was no small endeavor. Louis spared no expense on the materials. It was supposed to act as a massive reliquary for the relics, after all. Yet for all its splendor, it cost only a third of what was spent on the relics.

This extravagant expenditure is really quite stunning when one realizes that the objects themselves are inherently valueless. Pieces of stone and bone. But these physical remains of holy people and holy events were understood to be far more than what they seemed to be. These holy objects had a direct line to the saints in heaven. This curious disconnect necessitated explanation. Important church figures were eloquent on this form of devotion from as early as the beginning of the fourth century, which shows how deep this tradition is in the Christian Church. St. Augustine and St. Jerome wrote passionately about the importance of showing devotion to the bodies of the martyrs, and John Chrysostom explained how to properly engage with relics: "Stay beside the tomb of the martyr; there pour out fountains of tears. Have a contrite mind; raise a blessing from the tomb. Take him as an advocate in your prayers and immerse yourself perpetually in the stories of his struggles. Embrace the coffin, nail yourself to the chest. Not just the martyrs' bones, but even their tombs and chests burn with a great deal of blessing."

The other important way of explaining what these relics meant was through art. The external container or reliquary could express the extreme spiritual beauty of seemingly base materials. For example, a thirteenth-century arm reliquary from France housed at the Metropolitan Museum of Art holds the relics of Saint Fiacre. The shape of the reliquary mimics the gesture of the benediction, the moment in the Christian service when the priest asks for divine blessing for the congregation. One might assume that the relic originally came from the arm of the saint. However, this was not necessarily the case. Many X-rays of reliquaries from this period show that they contain remains unrelated to the body part they represent and sometimes contain a large assortment of different relics. The shape of the reliquary was not meant to reflect the relic in a mimetic way. It was not about where the relic was from or what his arm might have looked like when the saint was alive. The reliquary was a means of explaining what the relic could do. In this case, the reliquary illustrated that the relic it contained was a means of attaining the benediction or a blessing from the saint. And that was visualized in liturgical ceremonies in which the priests were known to actually bless the faithful while holding these objects and using them to touch the faithful.

In addition to these so-called speaking reliquaries, another popular form of protecting the sacred remains of the saintly bodies was a type of casket called a Limoges reliquary, named after the city in southwestern France. About seven

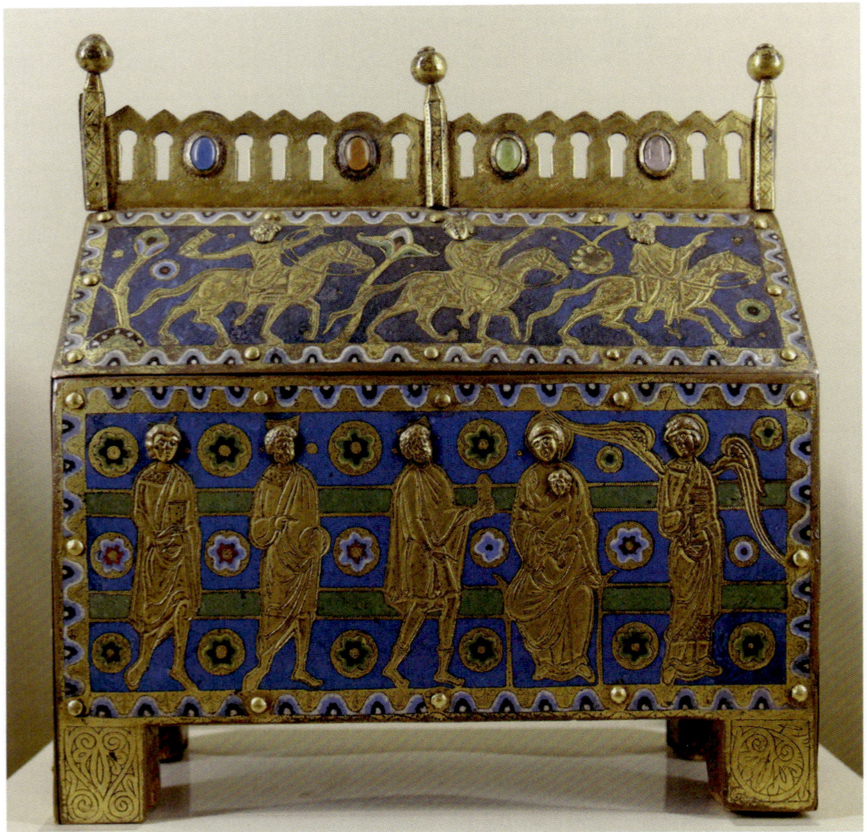

FIG. 9.2 Reliquary showing journey of the Three Wise Men (top) and the Adoration of Christ (reliquary body), ca. 1200. Limoges, France. Musée de Cluny, Paris, France. Engraved, chased, enameled, and gilt champlevé copper, 20.7 × 19.7 cm.

hundred are known to survive today. Workshops in this region of Haute-Vienne produced a tremendous number of these house- or church-shaped boxes. The tops of these objects have a pitched roof shape and often decorative ridges that suggest the finials of a building. In the illustrated example on the top register, three Magi travel on horseback to see the Christ Child (Fig. 9.2).

Below they follow the direction of the horizontal bands of green toward the seated Virgin Mary, whose newborn holds his right hand in the same gesture of benediction represented by the arm reliquary. Wavy white and blue clouds frame the figures both in their journey and at their destination, suggesting a dreamlike quality to the narrative, and also alluding to the special connection with the saints in heaven. This is an event that happened on earth, but it is also an event that is eternal, a story that must be ever present in the mind of the faithful specifically as a reminder to be always seeking Christ. Spinning wheels of mysterious and abstract stars or flowers pepper the background, again alluding to an otherworldly realm that appears in the same space as an event that took place in the world. The Magi also are of this earth and not, just like the objects contained herein. The Magi have at least one foot pinned to the earth, and yet they seem to hover at the same time, whereas the Virgin's feet do not even touch the ground. Thus the art explains that the objects inside the casket are providing a direct connection with the souls of saintly individuals, who just might promote your prayers to Christ, who might lift you spiritually, intellectually from the earth into a loftier realm.

Limoges caskets have a distinctive look which is the result of the technique with which they were made, champlevé enamel. The artist would gouge out depressions in the copper or bronze plaques and then fill them with powdered enamel, essentially powdered glass. After firing the enamel in a kiln, the surface would take on a jewel-like sheen and airlike ethereality. Additional bits of colored glass were added to the decorative finial. Here too the materials expressed the possibilities of the relics contained inside. Bits of unimportant, valueless materials—pieces of glass—could be manipulated (through a skilled hand and the application of fire) into something that looked like precious jewels. Through faith and understanding, pieces of bones were also the glorified bodies of the saints enthroned in heaven. Similarly, tiny shards of unrelated, unconnected fragments could be collected, through this act of enameling, into a cohesive whole that could represent a sky, a star, or a body. The same idea governs the fragments in the casket. Though disconnected through death, these scattered bodily remains would find completeness and unity with their original owner at the end of days. Soul and body would unite at the Second Coming. The artistic melding of those shards of glass which could create the image of a body was a beautiful metaphor for precisely what would happen when Christ returned to earth.

The Sainte-Chapelle is essentially a massive reliquary for the relics that Louis amassed. Here, too, glass plays a powerful role in presenting and explaining the relics. But whereas the enamel technique on the Limoges casket absorbs light, the glass at Sainte-Chapelle is translucent. It is a dazzling experience. These sheets of glass sparkle and glimmer in infinite ways: they paint the floors with variegated tones (predominantly blues and reds) and establish walls of colors that seem to dissolve before your very eyes.* The effect is, as Henry Adams writes about Chartres Cathedral, "a delirium of color and light." The transformation of vitreous substances into this resplendent shell of multihued light is further enhanced by the shifts in the outside world. Changes in weather, shifts in the seasons, moving clouds, the time of day—these could all redirect and redefine what was happening in this religious space. This special glass was thus facilitating a reflection of the presence of God in the form of Nature. Thus the artistic encasement for the relics (the glass) was a means of expressing the close relationship to God that the relics could make possible.

The capacities of glass were articulated by Abbot Suger (1081–1151) in his treatise *De Administratione*, written between 1144 and 1148. The text was a description and explanation of the construction of the church of Saint-Denis, of which he was the patron, a cathedral situated just outside of Paris. Lightness and brightness was something that Suger privileged a great deal. In the inscription that he composed for the consecration of the church in 1144, he wrote: "The church shines with its middle part brightened. For bright is that which brightly coupled with the bright, And bright is the noble edifice which is pervaded by the new light; Which stands enlarged in our time, I, who was Suger, being the leader while it was being accomplished." That brightness and light was not only about the beauty of the church but about facilitating contemplation of the divine. Suger explained this aspect of the glass as anagogical, coming from the Greek word *anagoge*, meaning climb or ascent. The idea was that the glass could help your thoughts move upward toward heaven. "Thus," Suger wrote, "when—out of my delight in the beauty of the house of God—the loveliness of the many-colored

* The effect of these brilliant lights and colors is made evident in this panorama: http://projects. mcah.columbia.edu/mapping-repository/Pano-tours/Sainte-Chapelle/tour.html.

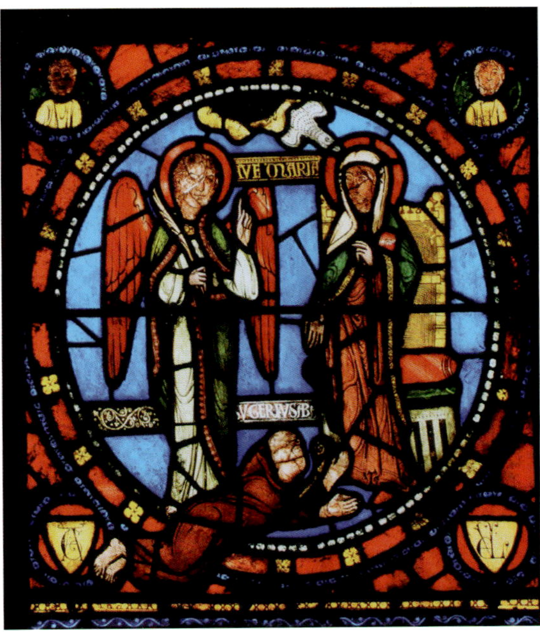

FIG. 9.3 The Annunciation with the portrait of Abbot Suger praying to the Virgin, twelfth century. Infancy window, Church of Saint-Denis, Paris, France. Stained and painted glass.

gems has called me away from external cares, and worthy meditation has induced me to reflect, transferring that which is material to that which is immaterial, on the diversity of the sacred virtues: then it seems to me that I see myself dwelling, as it were, in some strange region of the universe which neither exists entirely in the slime of the earth nor entirely in the purity of Heaven; and that, by the grace of God, I can be transported from this inferior to that higher world in an anagogical manner."

In stained glass Suger illustrated himself experiencing this sensation of transcending from the slime of the earth toward the sublime space of Heaven (Fig. 9.3). Still with his knees situated within the world of the living, the world of heraldic signs and ruddy, earth tones, Suger shows that his spiritual thoughtfulness allows him to touch the Virgin and to witness the Annunciation. The window indicates that Suger's humility is part of what allows him to transcend the inferior world—he is wearing a simple, brown, hooded monastic robe; he is tonsured; he is kneeling in reverential prayer; and he is barefoot. However, the fact that Suger puts himself in the window mirrors the more assertive and, perhaps, one might suggest, imperious tone of his writings.

The ability to expand the presence of glass within the space of the church was dependent on advances in architectural technologies. These architectural advances, and the aesthetic of the glass, are traditionally credited to Abbot Suger. Of course, Suger did not invent the Gothic architectural style, nor did he develop colored glass. Although no colored glass remains from the fifth century, textual sources describing its presence in early churches of that period are plentiful. Still, Suger usually gets a great deal of credit because he is the first to philosophize and write about the aesthetic of this new "French" style (*Opus Francigenum*), what we call the Gothic. He actually wrote three different treatises about his building project, which was to take a Romanesque medieval abbey church and give more space and, significantly, more height. To create greater height, Suger's masons employed three major features that would come to characterize the Gothic period—pointed arches, ribbed vaults, and external flying buttresses.

Pointed arches are capable of bearing a heavier load than the rounded arch characteristic of the Romanesque period. Romanesque architecture features thick walls, small windows, and rather low ceilings—all of which were due in part to the limitations of the rounded arch. With the rounded shape, the thrust of the weight presses downward and outward on the columns or walls below. This means that the higher the rounded arch goes, the more weight is pressing down and out. The only solution is to build thicker and thicker walls to counterbalance the weight so that the walls or columns do not collapse. And basically windows are not feasible. As the arch gets higher, the structure becomes more unstable, but the pointed arch alleviates this pressure. The shape aligns with the line of the thrust, which allows for higher arches and a reduced risk of that sideways thrust.*

Rib-vaults facilitated the pointed arch by concentrating the weight of stone at particular points so that it could be absorbed by piers and buttresses. Barrel vaulting, a continuous semicircular shape, defined Romanesque buildings. The ribs added a sense of great drama to the ceilings of the Gothic buildings—as

---

* The interactive project "Physics of Stone Arches" found on the NOVA website explains the physics of these arch shapes: www.pbs.org/wgbh/nova/physics/arch-physics.html.

though the walls of stone were suspended, like delicate, unfolding webs. Ultimately, the Gothic architects were able to build higher and higher, create even more and more ethereal spaces, with external buttresses that could absorb the lateral thrust of arches and vaults. By dissipating the force exerted by the arches onto those external structures, the walls could get higher and thinner without compromising the integrity of the monument.

Well, that isn't entirely true. A cathedral in Beauvais, France, pushed the new architectural technologies too far. Work on this particular monument, more formally known as the Cathedral of Saint Peter, started in 1225. The plan for this particular church was for it to have the highest vaults in all of Europe, 160 feet in height. Work on Beauvais continued until 1284, when the vaulting of the choir collapsed. A contemporary historian recounted: "On Friday November 29 at eight o'clock in the evening the great vaults of the choir fell, several exterior pillars were broken, the great windows were smashed…and divine service ceased for forty years." Today the cathedral is held together by tie-rods, essentially a girdle that surrounds the building.

Overambition aside, this style was massively popular and pervasive. The term "Gothic" was actually intended in a pejorative light. It was first recorded by the famous sixteenth-century Renaissance writer Giorgio Vasari. Admiring the classically inspired work of artists in his day (Brunelleschi, Michelangelo), Vasari dismissed the architecture of previous centuries as *maniera barbara* (the barbaric manner) or *maniera de'Gotti* (the Gothic manner) referring to the Goths, one of the largest groups of traveling hordes or so-called barbarians. But the popularity of this style was undeniable. Between 1150 and 1350, eighty cathedrals and five hundred large churches were built in the Gothic style. And that was just in France alone.

Thus when Louis was selecting the aesthetic of his private chapel, he naturally chose the Gothic, as it was the most au courant. The aim of Sainte-Chapelle was, as in the case of Beauvais, to dissolve the walls with windows. But because this was a private chapel there was no need to worry about extreme heights, and long naves were not a concern. Nor did the Sainte-Chapelle have an ambulatory with radiating chapels, a space that was essential for Abbot Suger. This was a space that would allow visitors to walk around the altar area and venerate the relics in the smaller chapels without interrupting the Mass. According to Suger this was necessary because the original building, with its narrow spaces, distracted from the services in a serious way. As he tells it, "On special days such as the feast of the blessed Denis the narrowness of the place forced women to run to the altar on the heads of men as on a pavement with great anguish and confusion." Sainte-Chapelle needed no such walking space because it was reserved for a much smaller audience, and it was not a space where any mayhem would have been tolerated.

Thus, although Louis was using the style of the grand cathedrals, his Sainte-Chapelle had a different set of inspirations and motivations. It was supposed to be the most refined version of the Gothic style possible. His building has pointed arches, ribbed vaults, and buttresses. But they are made of the most expensive materials. And they were to be as delicate and refined as possible. The buttresses are thin and unobtrusive, the lancet windows (the name for the shape of the tall, narrow panes of glass with pointed arches) were as attenuated as possible, and the walls were supposed to appear to disappear. No stone was to be left exposed. The rib vaults were completely painted in reds and blues.

One architectural model or inspiration for Sainte-Chapelle was the Heavenly Jerusalem, with its extraordinary accumulation of gemlike colors, as described in the penultimate chapter of Revelation. In this book, an angel takes John the narrator to the top of a mountain and shows him the holy city of Jerusalem descending out of heaven, delivered by God. As the narrator recounts, "The material of the wall was jasper; and the city was pure gold, like clear glass. The foundation stones of the city wall were adorned with every kind of precious stone." He then goes on to enumerate the many stones—jasper, sapphire, agate, emerald, onyx, carnelian, topaz, amethyst, pearl. The passage about the Heavenly Jerusalem also relates in a more metaphorical way to the experience one has in the space of Sainte-Chapelle. The effect of the walls is that of swirling jewels. Just like the relics—where base materials are really invaluable—things become the opposite of what they appear to be or are supposed to be. Glittering glass represents and seems to become the weighty, solid gold of the Heavenly Jerusalem. As the colored light from the windows hits the floor of the church, it appears to paint the ground you are walking on, shifting with the vagaries of the light from outside. Walls, traditionally about solidity and protection, are sheets of variegated glass.

The Book of Revelation was also part of the fabric of the church in a literal way. The rose window on the west wall (another characteristic of Gothic buildings) represents the Apocalypse. The central medallion shows the Man with the Sword, understood to be God, surrounded by the seven candlesticks. The cities of heaven emerge in petal-shaped lozenges, as does a kneeling John, who appears on the lower left, clothed in red. Episodes from the prophetic book compose the rest of the window, which looks like it is bursting outward from the center—like an explosion, like flames flashing and jabbing with centrifugal force. There is a sense of composed chaos or disorderly order, which mirrors the episodes in the text of Revelation as they are both shocking and yet seem to follow a particular order and sequence of events leading to the appearance of the Heavenly Jerusalem.

The implicit subject of the entire reliquary is kingship and the authority of Louis himself. Louis was specifically interested in appropriating the tradition of private palace chapels that had accompanied the most powerful kingdoms. For example, in Constantinople there was a special audience chamber in the imperial palace. The Norman king Roger II had constructed the Cappella Palatina in Palermo, Sicily, in 1130 with extensive and splendid mosaics, also made from glass. A final architectural model was that of Charlemagne's palace chapel at Aachen, which, like Sainte-Chapelle, was of two levels. The upper church was dedicated to Christ and had private access from the palace. The lower chapel was accessible to officials and courtiers and pilgrims.

The glass of Sainte-Chapelle was used to express the notion that Louis's authority had a historical precedent. Of the sixteen windows of the upper chapel, five show stories from Christ's life, nine come from the Old Testament, and one shows the translation of Christ's Crown of Thorns from Constantinople to Paris (Fig. 9.4). (The final window is the rose window.) The emphasis on Old Testament stories is unusual. They are given far more space and focus than in other monuments of the period.

What unifies the stories selected from the Old Testament is the great emphasis on kingship. Old Testament leaders are those who were most often invoked in coronation liturgies and in *The Mirror of Princes*, an influential contemporary text that instructed kings how to behave while in power through historical accounts of good and bad leaders. In this context—where Louis's role as king was

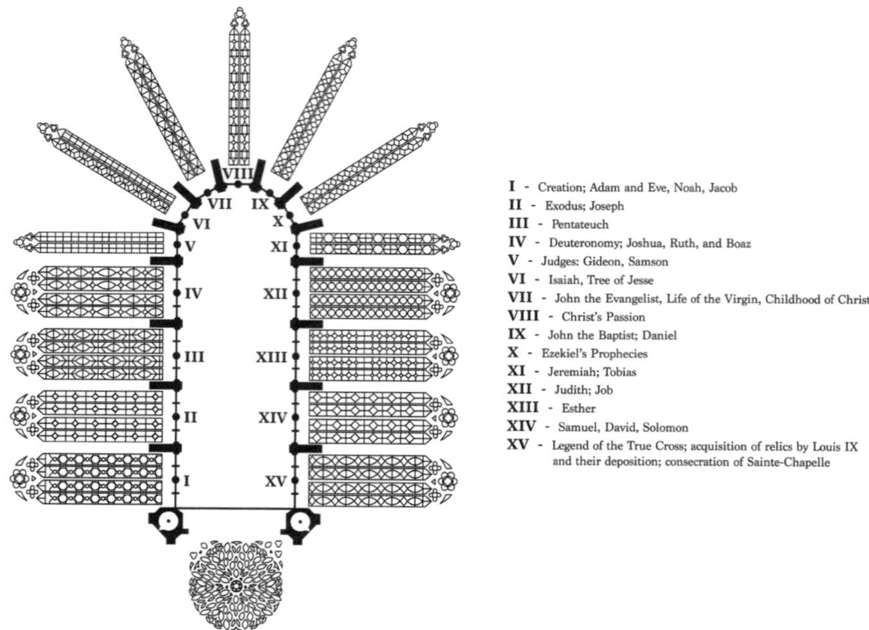

FIG. 9.4 Organization of the windows at Sainte-Chapelle.

so honored—it is clear how perfectly the attainment of the crown of thorns was as a symbol to commemorate Louis's royal sovereignty. Louis's reign is often understood to be the apogee of the French medieval cult of kingship. But this is something that was carefully curated. These things don't happen by accident. Louis worked hard to formulate an ideology that would produce this precise effect, one that would establish the Capetians (as Louis's dynasty was called) as having the God-given right to rule.

One of the lancet windows tells the story of Judith (Fig. 9.5). This might seem like a strange story to select when the emphasis is on kingship. She is not a king, obviously. In fact, she is not even royalty. She is a simple, albeit beautiful, widow. But the story of Judith expresses the abuse of military power and the responsibilities that the king has to protect his people. As the apocryphal Book of Judith recounts, she takes it upon herself to help her countrymen overcome the cruel

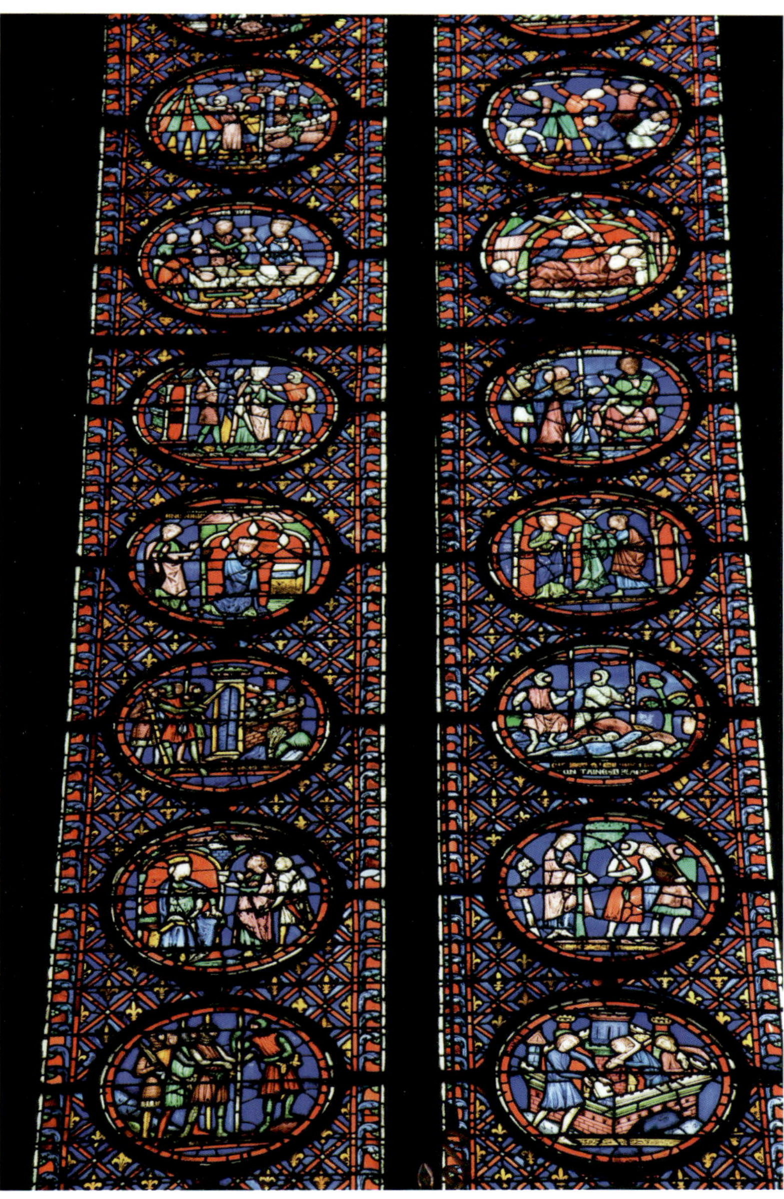

FIG. 9.5 Lancet window showing scenes of Judith at Sainte-Chapelle.

general Holofernes, who is in the employ of the evil Nebuchadnezzar, king of Babylon and the Assyrians. After chastising her townspeople for not fighting and not trusting that God will protect them, she removes her widow's weeds, anoints herself with ointment, and puts on a tiara and her loveliest attire so as to "entice the eyes of all men who might see her." In this guise, Judith visits Holofernes. After ensuring that he is well in his cups, she takes Holofernes's sword, takes hold of his hair, and cuts off his head, which she puts in her knapsack. She returns from "battle" to the city of Bethulia, where she is heralded as the greatest of heroines or, as the text says, "blessed by the Most High God above all women on earth."

But, one might ask, is (or was) it possible to read these windows—are we, more likely, seeing "through a glass darkly"? The height, the blinding color, the rather obscure references—these might seem too bewildering. The twentieth-century art historian Bernard Berenson, known for his work on Renaissance art, described the effect of glass as one of unappealing confusion: "Their pattern is not easy to decipher, so much is melted into color; and when deciphered how inferior it is in appeal!"

But it is possible to tell this story with the windows. And this is, of course, what the windows were meant to do—tell stories. Our story principally begins with Holofernes's army starting their journey and passing over the Euphrates River on horseback (Fig. 9.6). In the second register they attack and destroy the cornfields and vineyards outside of Damascus, some fifty miles from Judith's town, Bethulia (Fig. 9.7). The next window shows people of the cities along the seacoast coming to meet Holofernes, foolishly, with garlands and dances and tambourines, just before he demolishes their shrines and cuts down their sacred groves and demands that they all worship Nebuchadnezzar. The next panel shows Holofernes slaughtering a man who is holding a large key in what was intended as a gesture of welcome and offering. More murder and killing happen in the next medallion, where the massacre mirrors the treatment of the vineyards below. The next scene shows Holofernes's army cutting down the sacred groves of conquered cities. And then we are introduced to Judith, finally, praying for deliverance from the massacring army in front of a red altar with hanging lamps. The next band describes three moments in the story of Achior, a prophet who warns Holofernes not to persecute the Israelites and is punished for that suggestion.

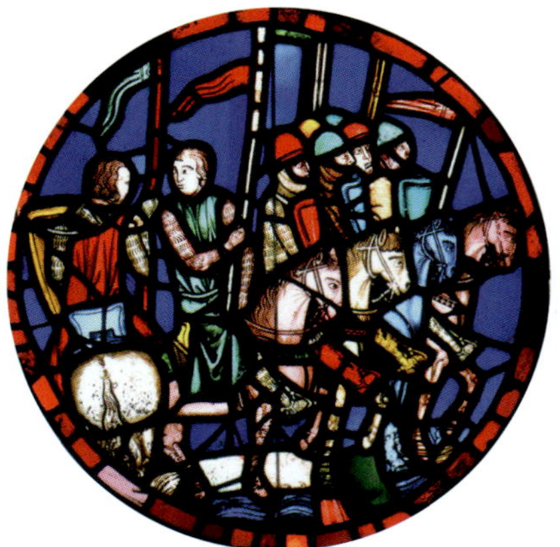

FIG. 9.6 Rondel showing Holofernes's army crossing the Euphrates River. From the Judith window, Sainte-Chapelle, 1246–1248. Philadelphia Museum of Art, Pennsylvania. Stained and painted glass, diameter 59.3 cm.

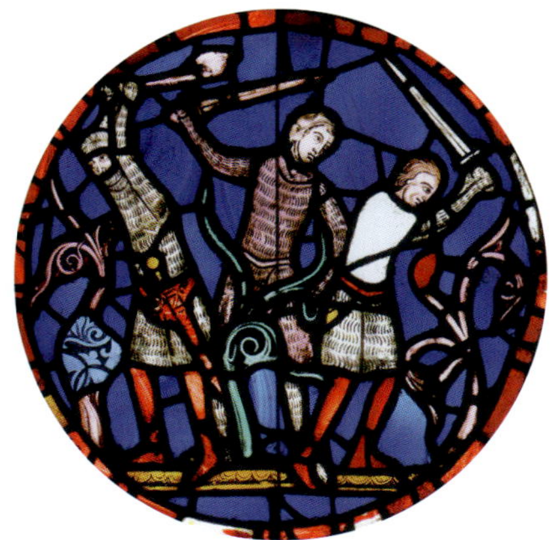

FIG. 9.7 Rondel showing the vineyards outside Damascus being devastated by Holofernes's army. From the Judith window, Sainte-Chapelle, 1246–1248. Philadelphia Museum of Art, Pennsylvania. Stained and painted glass, diameter 60 cm.

First he is tied to a tree, then the Israelites cut him loose. He then flees and finds safety in Bethulia where he speaks to the governor, Uzziah. The next medallion shows Holofernes's men at the main fountain of the city—threatening to destroy their only water source.

This is the last straw for Judith. She marches straight to the ancients and authorities of the town to chastise them for their fear-based weakness. We then see her praying again and, in the next medallion, getting ready in her boudoir for the trip to Holofernes, where she "washed her body…plaited the hair of her head…and adorned herself with all her ornaments." Judith gives her maid provisions. She is seized by the soldiers of Holofernes, then she appears before Holofernes, and then takes another bath in the next register above. After a feast with her enemy, we witness his death, in the bedchambers, while he sleeps off his drink. (Fig. 9.8)

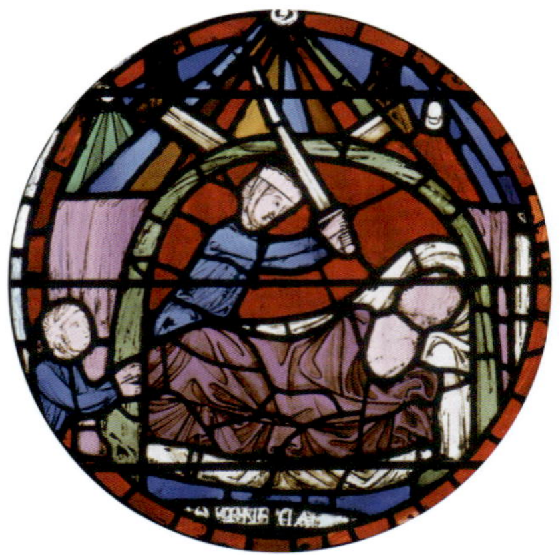

FIG. 9.8 Rondel showing Judith beheading Holofernes. Judith window, Sainte-Chapelle, 1246-1248. Stained and painted glass, diameter 60 cm.

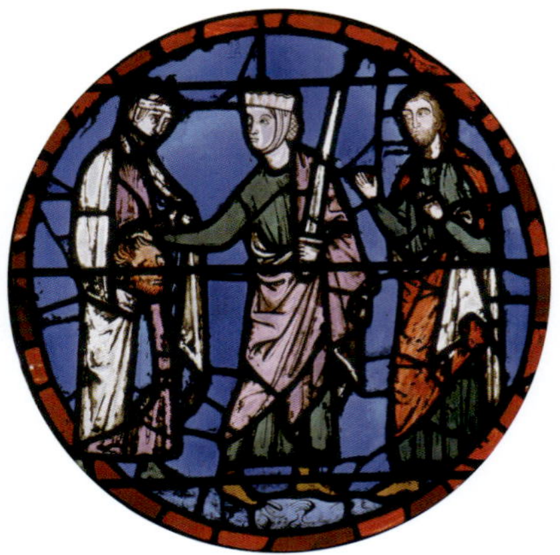

FIG. 9.9 Rondel showing Judith holding the head of Holofernes. Judith window, Sainte-Chapelle, 1246–1248. Stained and painted glass, diameter 60 cm.

Judith then appears showing the head of the dead man, which is then displayed on the ramparts as the Israelites attack the Assyrian camps (Fig. 9.9). The Israelites chase the Assyrians and return to Bethulia with their spoils. In the final register of medallions, Judith speaks to the high priest and consecrates the spoils from the Assyrian camps to God. The final medallion is dedicated to her death and shows the Israelites mourning their heroine.

There are some noticeable holes in this window. During the Reign of Terror that characterized the worst aspects of the French Revolution, religious institutions and symbols of royal power were attacked and widely destroyed. Sainte-Chapelle represented both—religious and royal. With hammers, revolutionary gangs attacked the monument, leaving it essentially in shambles. Architectural and sculptural figures were destroyed, and so were the precious relics when most of the reliquaries were burnt down for their valuable metals. (The relics that were not ruined were shipped in 1806 to Notre Dame, where they remain today.) The only record that remains of the grand assortment of relics is the eighteenth-century print that I mentioned earlier.

The glass suffered tremendously. Only two-thirds of the original glass remains in Sainte-Chapelle. A large number of the glass panels were collected by visiting Americans. For example, in the 1820s a Philadelphian named William Poyntell purchased three medallions and gave them to the Philadelphia Museum of Art. The idea of someone buying a piece of Gothic glass that had been bashed out of the window some thirty years before is stunning. Maybe it was not lying on the ground all that time. Maybe it was sitting in someone's house. Maybe it was still hanging in the wall. I can't imagine.

The whole thing is bizarre. Not to mention the fact that restoration of Sainte-Chapelle started soon after the end of the Napoleonic wars, in 1836. One of the first voices in favor of restoring the windows was Victor Hugo who, as we know, loved the Gothic, placing his hunchbacked hero in the tower of Notre Dame. As the scholar Meredith Cohen has pointed out, the restoration continued through the 1870s, more than three times as long as it took to build the structure in the thirteenth century. So the idea that Poyntell bought the glass just before the restoration campaign is confusing and puts into question what these nineteenth-century restorers were doing. In other words, the definition of "restoration" might be a bit more elastic than we are used to. Little was documented. Much was retouched. The windows were restored (sometimes quite creatively), the panels within the bays were reordered, and the narratives were completed with modern panels of, as Alyce Jordan says, "dubious iconographic accuracy." In other words, there is no real idea what the glass in this monument looked like originally, and the panels might be as much a visual document of the nineteenth-century restoration as they are about medieval artistry.

In addition to saying that the patterns of the windows were hard to decipher, Berenson also said that the quality of the individual medallions was inferior. However, the individual scenes hold their own. The scene in which Holofernes's soldiers pass over the Euphrates is lively and dramatic and engaging (Fig. 9.6). The exchange between the men at the left of the composition, who are somewhat bracketed from the right by means of their extended staffs, conveys the urgency of the moment while simultaneously expressing a sense of intimacy and pathos. The two men turn to discuss their plan of attack, twisting toward each other while balancing on their moving horses, horses that are determined to canter, insistent on the destruction of the Israelites. The way that we are given a view of the man on the left, who leans toward the right while his horse veers toward the left, the fact that we see the back of his shield, and the delicate curls of his hair as his chain-mail hood has slipped over his left shoulder—it is a sensitive portrait, if one might use that word.

The figure next to him also balances precariously on his horse—right arm pulled across his chest, legs extended as a counterbalance, a slight lean backward. Compared to the figures to the right, his face is open and uncovered, exposed. The expanse of his three-quarter profile, the lift in his eyebrows, the puckered mouth—these all express concern and thoughtfulness. Thus we are given a brief glimpse into the thinking, the inner mind-set of these men, the planning, the forethought of this attack. The armed soldiers move forward with determination, following orders with a singularity of mind much reflected by the fact that they are a singular mass of figures pushing along, just like their beasts of burden. The waves of the constantly flowing Euphrates move with them, drawing them toward the right, toward battle.

The flag in the upper right illustrates the determination and forward movement of the horde of men. It holds taut with the pull of the wind. But the flags of our men to the left are bowing and flickering downward, floundering while the men discuss the situation. They don't wear their helmets. Their heads are for thinking, not attacking, although the composition—that strong diagonal from the backside of the horse on the left through the repeated heads of the horses along the right— determines their ultimate drive, along with the others, into battle.

The complex patterns of the framing devices (which are never the same from window to window), the imaginative play of colors that draw your eye in ways that might disrupt the narrative, yet that simultaneously pull you to find and follow those stories in order—these are essential to the experience of these glass walls and show just how important the comprehension of these stories was. Quite honestly, there is nothing so much fun as taking a pair of binoculars and standing in front of these windows for hours, reading the stories, trying to figure out what they are about, piecing together the great puzzle of these multihued, shimmering, disjointed shards of glass. They were talking points for priests explaining the Bible. In some churches they were backdrops for theatrical performances

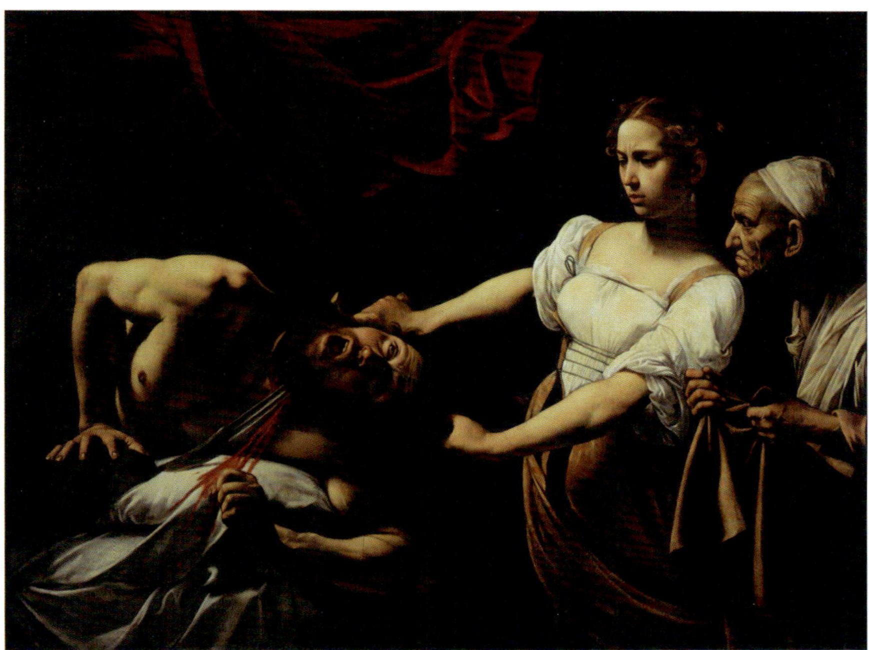

FIG. 9.10 Caravaggio, *Judith Beheading Holofernes,* ca. 1598–1599. Galleria Nazionale d'Arte Antica at the Palazzo Barberini, Rome, Italy. Oil on canvas, 145 × 195 cm.

related to the saints described in the images in the windows. They were also a way of showing local pride or membership in a particular group. Medieval guilds were known to have paid for certain windows at Chartres Cathedral. Furriers, masons, wheelwrights and tanners, vintners and shoemakers decorate the base of the lancets of those thirteenth-century windows. Men are shown constructing the very building in which their windows appeared, the spaces in which they were worshipping. Thus individuals truly read these windows for the stories they provided, identifying with figures from the Old Testament and with the figures doing the very things they did for a living.

The story of Judith is also important to the overall scheme of kingship because it provides a model for the new queens of France. Although certainly not her husband's equal, the queen was supposed to defend the Church and her subjects.

According to the scholar Alyce Jordan, a prayer in a Coronation Book asks God to imbue new queens with "authority of command, greatness of judgment, an abundance of wisdom, prudence, and understanding, a guardianship of religion and piety." These are virtues that Judith was understood to embody. Other prayers specifically called for newly crowned queens to model themselves on Judith, focusing on Judith less as the bold heroine who seduces and destroys her oppressor (which is the direction of the Caravaggio painting) and more on the fact that Judith remains chaste and virtuous (Fig. 9.10).

Two women appear in the "Relics" window nearby—Blanche of Castile and Margaret of Provence. Blanche of Castile was Louis's mother. She had assumed the role of queen-regent after the death of Louis VIII and, in 1248, would resume that role when her son went on a crusade, the seventh official attempt to recapture the Holy Land. Margaret of Provence was Louis IX's wife. She produced eleven children for Louis and even accompanied him on the crusade. Although the crusade started off well from the perspective of the French, things quickly turned sour. Louis's brother was killed, and the King himself was later captured. Essentially, Margaret took the helm of the battle—she ensured a food supply for the Christians in Damietta (which is in Egypt) and collected the silver for the King's ransom, all while giving birth to their sixth child, Jean Tristan. The audacity of Judith's quest into the enemy camp sets a model for the bold assumption of power by both Blanche and Margaret, which may have happened after the window was already up.

These windows were not just created in order to remind Blanche and Margaret and Louis about their special roles as monarchs. The images were also communicating the importance of these powerful figures to their subjects. So in addition to being a sacred space, reserved for the performance of the Mass and special feasts related to the relics, it was also a space for visitors that were not members of the royal family. In fact, a number of indulgences were offered for visitors to Sainte-Chapelle. The first papal indulgence, for example, granted on June 3, 1244, established specific dates for which pilgrims could reap rewards of mercy—forgiveness of their sins—for their effort to visit the chapel. This issuing of indulgences continued for generations. Even when people were not directly inside the chapel looking at these windows, the monument was a prominent part

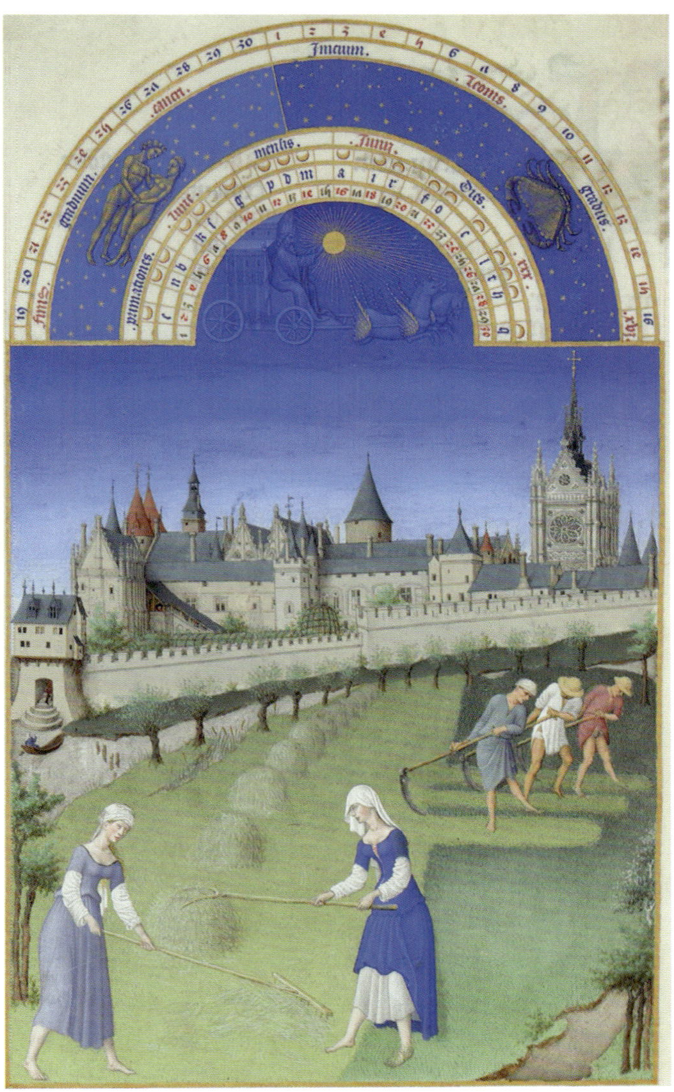

FIG. 9.11 The Limbourg Brothers, *June, Palais de la Cité and the Sainte-Chapelle. Les Très Riches Heures du Duc de Berry,* 1411–1416. Musée Condé, Chantilly, France. MS 65, f. 6v. Colors and ink on parchment, 22.5 × 13.6 cm.

of the landscape of Paris and a constant reminder of what was inside the walls. A page from the *Très Riches Heures* manuscript painted by the Limbourg Brothers around 1400 shows the elegant chapel, apocalypse rose window and all, rising above the city walls (Fig. 9.11).

Just as the light in Sainte-Chapelle reflects and refracts in innumerable directions, scattering its colors throughout the space of the church, painting its walls, ceilings, floors with its stories; just as we can read the lancets in different directions and just might be reading it in directions never anticipated by its medieval authors—this particular monument draws us through history in sometimes non-linear, anachronistic ways. It can tell the story of Byzantium and its ignoble fall to the Crusaders. It can tell the history of relics and their devotion. It can explain the development and evolution of Gothic architecture. It can describe the king, Louis—how he operated and how he wanted his rule to be understood. We can understand the medieval mind through the Old Testament scenes they selected. We can consider how powerfully the eighteenth-century revolutionaries saw these images, equating the heads of kings in the glass with the heads they were similarly devoted to cutting off throughout the Reign of Terror. We can analyze the nineteenth century's possibly nationalistic motivations in their restorations. And we can learn, as modern-day viewers, by reading the glass and reminding ourselves about Judith and Holofernes.

From Byzantium to today, this monument is a majestic portal to historical events and beliefs. A forty-year campaign to restore the glass in honor of the eight hundredth anniversary, 2014, of the birth of Louis was recently completed. This means that we can now visit and see all of the glass, which, for forty years, was under scaffolding. For this restoration, technicians dismantled all the glass into 1,113 small panels and then cleaned them with the help of laser lighting. By adding a new, molded glass surface to the original, these restorers have found a means of isolating the glass from pollutants outside and from the condensation formed by the visitors' breath (the same problem that humans were causing in the caves at Altamira). One cannot put a price on a monument of this sort. But the expenditure of $27 million on this restoration is worth mentioning. And because of this labor, this forty-year endeavor, we can see how the Sainte-Chapelle is a cohesive lens by which we can study many fragments of time.

Glass windows allow us to take a broad look at many aspects of the past and present through their images. The medieval windows at Chartres Cathedral illustrate a common interest for many of us with images showing how vintners made wine. Great modern glass has a similarly wide range of reference. The windows at St. John the Divine in New York City show scenes from our remote past (such as the medieval Battle of Tours), our less remote past (Valley Forge) and recent history (World War II, along the bottom register). We are reminded of people we know, who use computers, watch baseball, work in broadcasting, produce art—even those who study the Hagia Sophia (Figs. 9.12 and 9.13).

There are some very special windows in San Antonio in the William A. Fraser Memorial Chapel, a nondenominational space that was built in 1929 by the Woodmen of the World. This association was an important fraternal society that served many philanthropic efforts in communities across the country. The chapel was dedicated by the Woodmen to the men who had fought and died in World War I, and it was used as a space for patients in the Woodmen War Memorial Hospital, which, although now destroyed, originally sat nearby. The chapel was meant as a contemplative space for the patients of the hospital, and the stained glass windows, created by the famous artist Louis Comfort Tiffany (1848–1993), create a perfect ambience of thoughtfulness, peace, and calm. Above the focal point of the chapel (where an altar would be placed in a religious chapel), a thickly wooded forest, with tall spruces and noble pines, frames a waterfall made of those quintessential Tiffany blues. As the light enters the space of the chapel, rising in the morning and ebbing in the afternoon, the colors in the glass partitions shift and change and glimmer, as though one is walking through a forest, enjoying the splendors of nature, the very activity for which the patients of the hospital might have yearned. These windows link us to those who fought in World War I, to a hospital that treated patients through the early half of the twentieth century, and to the accomplishments of the newly established artist Tiffany. These more modern windows, like those of Sainte-Chapelle, provide a glass lens through which to experience a great sweep of time.

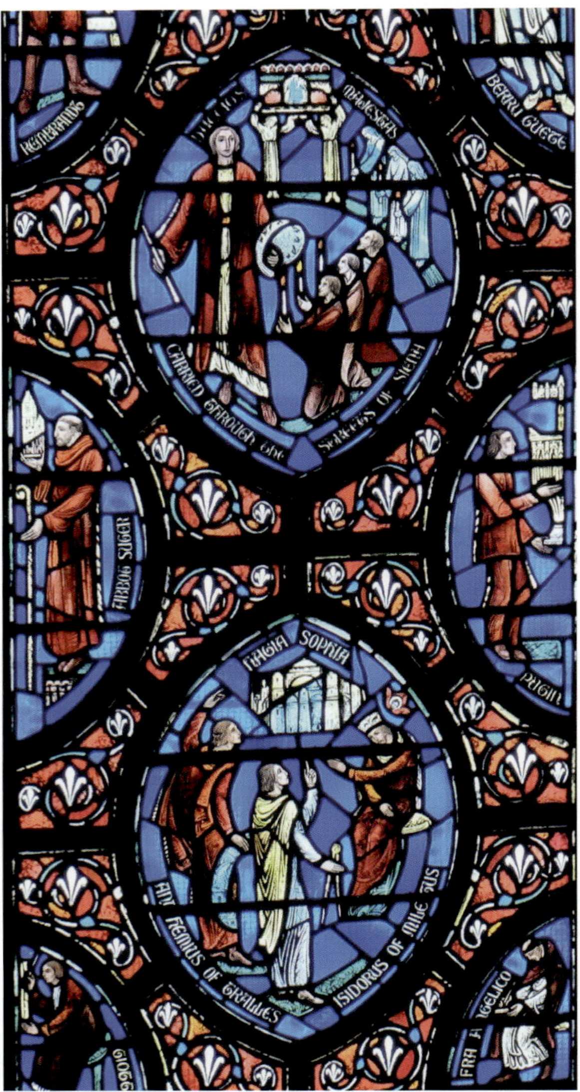

FIG. 9.12 Duccio di Buoninsegna (above) and Justinian meeting with the architects of Hagia Sophia, which appears in the distance (below), 1920–1950. Saint John the Divine, New York City, New York. Stained and painted glass.

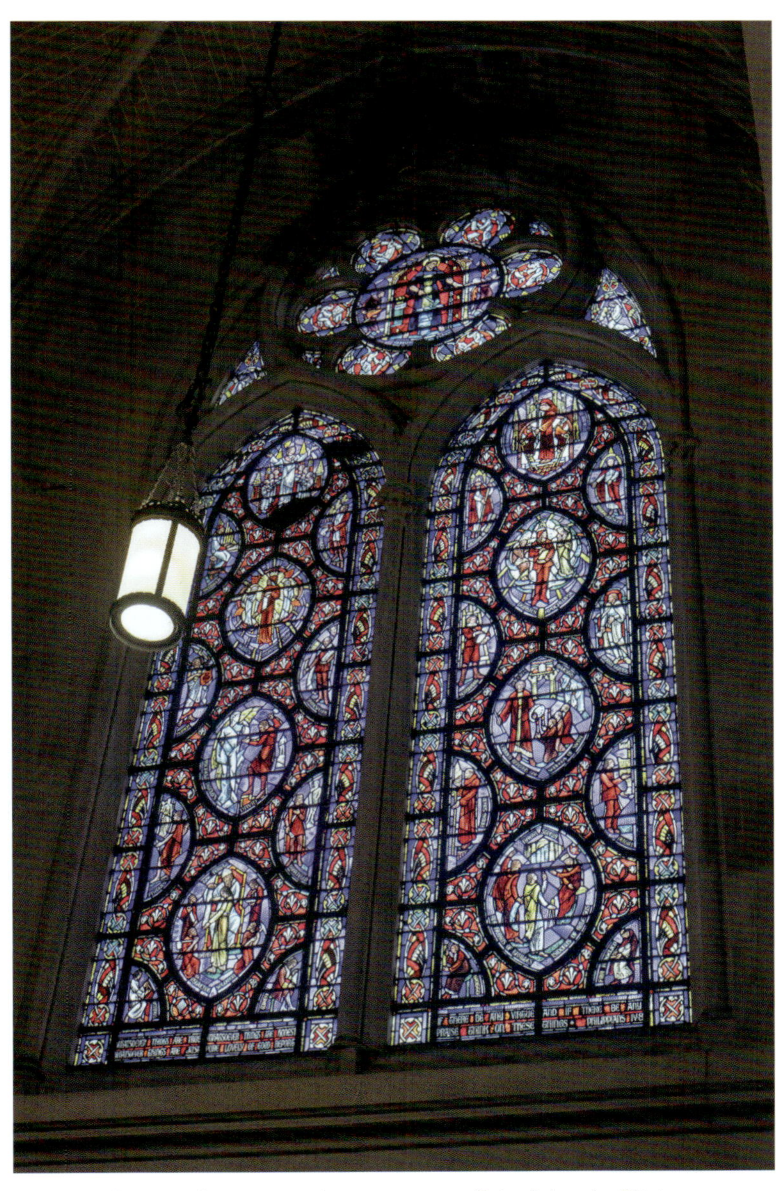

FIG. 9.13 Poets and artists window, 1920–1950. Saint John the Divine, New York City, New York. Stained and painted glass.

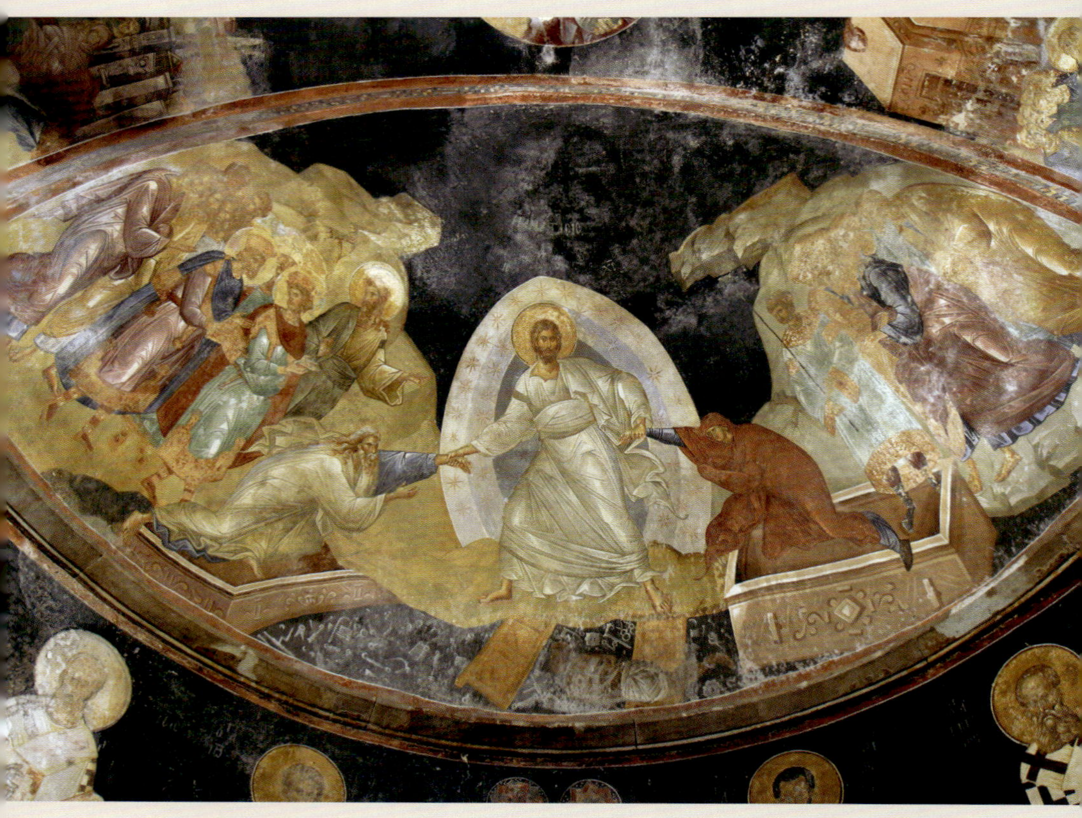

FIG. 10.1 The Anastasis, apse of the funerary chapel (*parekklesion*) in the Chora Church (now Kariye Müzesi), ca. 1315–1321. Istanbul, Turkey. Fresco.

The Chora Church

CA. 1315–21

LATE BYZANTINE ART

In the last chapter I discussed the massive reliquary of painted and stained glass that Louis IX built to house his relics, treasures that he acquired from the Latin emperor of Constantinople, Baldwin. This sale happened after the brutal and misplaced campaign of the Latins, when they took their energies meant for the crusade in the Holy Land and instead used them to attack their Christian brethren in Constantinople. This Latin rule of the East lasted from 1204 to 1261, and the ignominy of their entry into the city also characterized their rule. Winning a battle is one thing. Running an entire empire is another, and the Latins quickly found themselves with little skill in the latter.

We saw the sale of the relics in the framework of the glorious Sainte-Chapelle. Take the same account from the opposite perspective and it is easy to see that the Latins were desperate (Baldwin was essentially looking for cash, cap in hand) and the Greek heritage was being severely disrespected. The end of this Latin rule happened on August 15, 1261, when Emperor Michael VIII Palaiologos entered into the city of Constantinople, preceded by an ancient icon of the Virgin held high. This historical background sets the scene for the church called the Chora, which was originally built in the fourth century but later reconfigured and decorated in an astounding way between 1315 and 1321.* The Chora was originally part

---

* Columbia University's Miriam & Ira D. Wallach Art Gallery hosts a website about the history of the Chora Church that includes panoramas of the monument's interior: www.columbia.edu/cu/wallach/exhibitions/Byzantium/html/building_history.html.

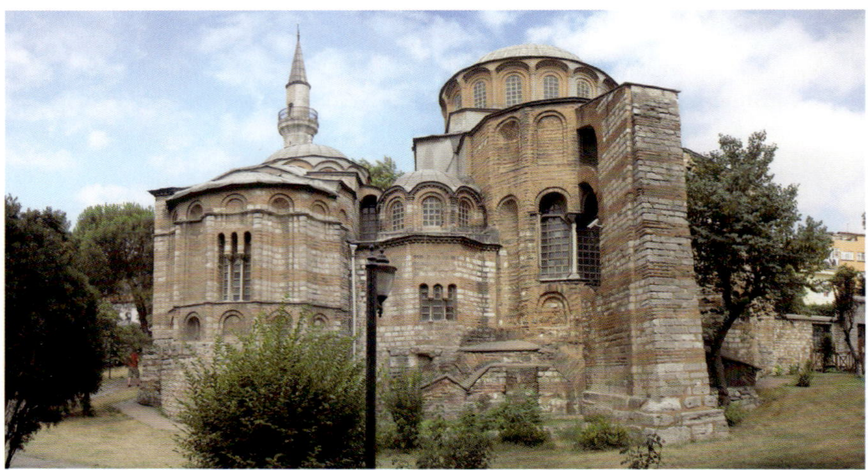

FIG. 10.2 Exterior of the Chora Church.

of a larger monastic complex, although only the church exists today (Fig. 10.2). We know that about 130 years after the completion of the Chora came the final conquest of Constantinople by the Ottoman Turks in 1453. The Chora speaks not to that later moment, but to the period of glorious return—by the Palaiologans, by the Byzantines, and by the Greek Orthodox traditions. And it is in this light that we can turn to our main image—with terms such as return, rebirth, recovery, restoration (Fig. 10.1).

Resurrection. Or, in the Greek language and tradition, *Anastasis*, which literally translates to "making to stand," "rise up," or "raising up." The Greek tradition renders the Resurrection of Christ through the traditional descent into Hell before his own physical rising. Christ is like a starburst of light. So powerful, so masterful, he descends into Hell protected by a splendid oval mandorla made of rings of ever-whitening bands of light, studded with coruscating golden stars, which were originally painted with actual gold, with gold leaf. And just as they burst outward in eight sharp points, Christ bursts into this darkened underworld with similarly radiating force. He pulls, grabs, twists, and lunges with bodily authority. His body is emphatic—broad, sloping shoulders; long, commanding arms; a thick, solid waist emphasized by a cummerbund-like shape around his middle; legs that sprawl and pull and ground his eminent and imminent form.

We cannot see the true outlines of his body, but the heavy white garments—those thickly outlined bunches and folds and creases—tell us what we need to know. He is all body, all power. Strong gray lines form triangular shapes, splaying outward from Christ's right leg and ending at the base of Christ's left calf. At this point those strong diagonal lines seem to be blocked by a band of white along the bottom of the garment, which has the effect of heightening the sense of Christ's pull, as if he is working against a constricting force, illustrated by this band of white. But at the bottom, the explosion of fluttering triangles and frenetic shapes shows the extraordinary speed and power with which Christ is moving. Even those garments that do not rest on his body are animated in a dynamic way. The part of Christ's togalike garment that hangs off his left arm cascades with strong, jagged, irregular zags and zigs, shapes that look much like the base of his garment. That swath of weighty cloth finishes with a delicate finial, a light spiral with a slight dot at the end, like a tuft of smoke from a candle that extinguishes as he burns through Hell, this deep, dark abyss where Christ shines his eternal light. This is the hideous holding tank in which Christ finds the Righteous—the forefathers and prophets who lived before Christ's birth. And in this moment, during the Anastasis, Christ saves these figures, lifting them out of their tombs and holding them in Paradise until the Second Coming when all will be judged.

Adam and Eve are at the forefront of this campaign. Although weighty in body, akin to the shape and form of Christ, they almost fly out of their tombs because the power of Christ's pull is so intense. They are helplessly but hopefully at his mercy. Their hands hang limply in his powerful grasp. It is as though they are still dead or cadaver-like, still weak from waiting all of those centuries in the thick sarcophagi from which they ascend. And yet the effects of Christ's majestic touch are immediate. Adam and Eve's sleeves seem to have turned sky blue, contrasting with the rest of their garments—white in the case of Adam and red in the case of Eve—and perhaps suggesting that they are soon to be in that Paradise in the blue beyond, that they will soon enter into Christ's sphere, into his vortex of spiky stars, which spiral around a center of that same shade of blue.

Christ's strong, extended pull continues through the prolonged arms of Adam and Eve, drawing through their bodies, expressed by the strong diagonal lines in their draperies, all the way to their hanging, dragging feet—Adam discalced and Eve wearing heavy black shoes. Christ's feet, also shoeless but more massive and pillowy than Adam's, also are extended visually through the two large rectangular forms at the base of the composition. There are two possibilities for these shapes. They might be the tops of the sarcophagi from which Adam and Eve emerge, that have blasted off and fallen to the side at Christ's arrival. They might also be the doors of Hell that Christ destroys upon his entry. These are the doors that Satan commands Hades, his lord of the underworld, to lock tight with brass and bars and locks of iron. All of those foolhardy locks—white keyholes; white broken chains; white, inefficient little tools—litter the lower band of deep-black underworld. Here Satan or possibly Hades appears captive, on his face, hands and feet ignominiously bound in white shapes similar to those keys. And he wears wrappings that look like a rolled-up white ball. It almost looks like Christ has used his large left foot to kick Satan like a ball and that he has rolled down that ladderlike sarcophagus lid or door and landed on his face. Ironically enough, the figure whose job was to tie up Christ by preventing his entry into the underworld is himself tied up and bound until the Second Coming.

That abyss, that murky and ill-defined space, contrasts with the more solid ground upon which Christ stands. And yet even that beige and stony landscape is bizarrely mysterious and ill defined. It supports Christ's feet, but it sits behind Eve's tomb while spilling over the top of Adam's. It continues up and around the body of the apse, terminating in two rocky outcrops that embrace Christ and the mandorla and evoke the arm positions of Adam and Eve which appear below. Christ really is like those sharp, golden stars that we started with—all the extremities of his body continue with centrifugal power through other arms, bodies, tomb tops or doors, a bleak and rugged terrain. These peripheral features act as extensions and manifestations of Christ and enhance the sense of his control and authority. And in contrast with Satan's unfortunate prison, strewn with those innumerable broken locks and keys, above is pure darkness with a few white strokes of paint. Two simple labels hover somewhat tentatively in the abyss: a name—Christ's monogram—and one phrase that encapsulates the entire scene, Holy Anastasis.

Texts and words have a tenuous and delicate relationship with this particular scene because the Anastasis does not actually appear in the Bible. There is an allusion to a holding tank for souls in 1st Peter 3:18–20: "For Christ also died for sins once for all, the just for the unjust, so that He might bring us to God, having been put to death in the flesh, but made alive in the spirit; in which also He went and made proclamation to the spirits now in prison, who once were disobedient." There is also the Apostles' Creed, written between 710 and 714, which states that Christ "descended into Hell," quoting a phrase that appears in Ephesians 4:9: "Now this expression, 'He ascended,' what does it mean except that He also had descended into the lower parts of the earth?"

But these shorter phrases do not explain the entire scene. A full account of the story appears in a text known as the Gospel of Nicodemus, originally dated to the fourth century but recently redated to 600 and now understood as a compilation of homilies and liturgical texts from the earlier centuries. The Gospel of Nicodemus describes the Anastasis events: "And, behold, suddenly Hades trembled, and the gates of death and the bolts were shattered, and the iron bars were broken and fell to the ground, and everything was laid open. And Satan remained in the midst, and stood confounded and downcast, bound with fetters on his feet. And, behold, the Lord Jesus Christ, coming in the brightness of light from on high, compassionate, great, and lowly…saying: 'Through all ages thou hast done many evils; thou hast not in any wise rested. Today I deliver thee to everlasting fire.'" We can see many aspects of Nicodemus's writing in the image—the shattered bolts, the broken bars, Christ appearing in brightness of light from on high. Thus the text can explain some aspects of the painting, but not all. The painting brings so much to the conversation that the text does not—the standing figures waiting, the power with which Adam and Eve are pulled from their tombs, the unsettling quality of the mysterious ground in relationship to the murky abyss.

You might recall how at Sant Climent, Christ's text starts strong and clear—"I am the light of the world"—but then the letters descend into mysterious hooks and scribbles (Fig. 7.1). These painted pages show words and images working together, revealing each other's limitations while simultaneously expressing the glory and mystery of Christ. The story of the Anastasis is a compilation of many texts from various sources, and the image is a reflection, a version, of some of those stories. There is no one-to-one correlation between written word and painted image. The two are part of a collective and synthetic attempt to express the awesomeness of the moment.

There are many connections between Sant Climent and the Anastasis. And this is a great opportunity to do a traditional art-historical compare and contrast, the bane of most art history exams. There are a number of technical, formal, and compositional similarities. Both monuments are frescoes that appear above the altar, in the apse of the church. The emphasis on Christ as the light of the world is evident in the text at Sant Climent and similarly in the scintillating gold stars and bright, white paint at the Chora. Stylized draperies of both Christ figures indicate movement and energy and power. Lastly, both show Christ, terrific and triumphant, in the center of a majestic, banded mandorla, separating him from human bystanders and articulating his divinity.

However, the mandorla also reveals a number of important distinctions that speak to the different moments that are being represented. Christ breaks through that protective shield in both paintings. But the ways in which those figures challenge that frame emphasize different aspects of Christ. In Sant Climent, Christ's feet, halo, and right hand break through the ovular form. The Christ at Sant Climent is about the Second Coming and the impending Last Judgment, so the emphasis is on Christ's gesturing right hand, his hand of judgment. This is it. The last moment. Christ is on a floating, embellished throne like a judge in court or like an emperor making major decisions. At Sant Climent we are meant to fear and regret the misdemeanors of our past and wonder at the mysteries of a world filled with flying beasts and multi-eyed seraphim.

At the Chora, the mandorla disappears behind the rocky ground so that Christ is both protected *and* standing firmly on the ground. This scene is related to Second Coming, but as a preview of that moment, as proof of what Christ can and will do for the righteous. Thus the break in the mandorla at the Chora allows a connection between Christ's extended leg, the gate of Hell, and that pathetic, overturned Satan so as to emphasize his victory over Hell. He is able to transcend those infernal doors and return to earth. In this sense, with this focus on his power and victory, we might liken him to another object that we have discussed here, the Nike of Samothrace (Fig. 4.1).

Nike, which as we recall literally means "victory," moves with the same forward thrust as Christ—right leg lunging forward while the left supports the pose from behind. The two figures both twist with determination. Nike seems to be responding to the wind and sea-spray through which she is "pulled" by the marble boat below. Her torso twists as she finds her equilibrium, and she uses her left leg as a ballast or counterbalance. Christ steers his metaphorical ship of righteousness by leaning into his weighty task, drawing balance from his firmly planted feet as he wrenches those wretches out. Nike's entire body of painted white marble was on display for all to see. She was placed above the centrally located amphitheater, high on the mountainside, lording triumphantly above all visitors to Samothrace. This Lord, Christ, is also placed on high where believers can look upward to see his pure white form with its emphatic emphasis on the grand entirety of his body.

The connection with Nike is important for two reasons. First, it introduces the notion that there are pagan antecedents for this particular image. The famous scholar André Grabar explained that the visualization of Christ trampling Satan was likely modeled after allegorical representations of victorious Roman emperors destroying their enemies, many of which are found on coins. Pagan mythology was another form of inspiration. One mythological figure traversing the boundary between the living and the dead is Orpheus, who enters the underworld to reclaim his beloved Eurydice. In the pagan tale Orpheus fails to return with his beloved. (Unless you are watching Glück's version, a beautiful opera, but not really in keeping with the tragedy of Ovid's poem.) This is an important distinction. Orpheus fails. Christ does not.

The second aspect of the connection with Nike that is relevant to the Anastasis is that they are both Greek. Nike is emblematic of the Hellenistic period and comes from an island off the coast of Greece. The Anastasis is from the Late Byzantine period and appeared in a church in Constantinople, the center of the Greek Orthodox world. This particular configuration of victory might have been seen as having ties to a specifically Hellenistic world, which was paramount at a time when making distinctions from the West was a priority. When the Byzantine historian Niketas Choniates wrote about the presence of the Latins in 1205, he made it clear how Easterners felt about the Westerners: "Between us and the Latins is set the widest gulf. We are poles apart. We have not a single thought in common."

Accounts asserting differences between the East and the West are rife during this period. And the Anastasis image seems to fit into that divide. The Greek Orthodox Church has the Anastasis scene. The Western Roman Catholic Church had different images for the Resurrection. Generally Christ appears stepping or rising out of his tomb with great authority and holding aloft a banner of triumph—a white flag with a red cross symbolizing his triumph over death. Christ appears in a similar position, emerging from the tomb while the soldiers sleep unawares, in many different media and in all shapes and sizes: embroidery, painted panel, illuminated manuscript, large-scale frescoed walls, and diminutive enameled panels. The configuration or emphasis is different in East and West. In the Western tradition Christ is the focus. The soldiers only appear in the foreground as a contrast. Christ is more alive than the soldiers, even though they are alive. His vigilance and vigor despite his manifold suffering makes their inability to stay awake all the more absurd and perverse and spiteful. Thus the attention is on the return of the living Christ. The Anastasis, by contrast, is about the resurrection of Christ *and* the righteous. Christ, Adam, and mankind—all are being lifted, all are leaving Hell. This emphasis on the experience of Christ's Resurrection by all mankind is critical in the Greek Orthodox Church.

Yet we should not only look at these divergent Resurrection scenes for signs of difference. One interesting thing to note is that the first Anastasis image appears in Rome, in the eighth century. It doesn't have a long life in Rome. There are no instances of the Anastasis in the West after the middle of the ninth century. But this shows a dialogic relationship between the East and West that spans centuries. Additionally, images of the Resurrection are, by their nature, meant to inspire confidence in Christ's ability to raise us up. Thus, they might look different, but the message of the salvation of mankind is the same.

At the Chora we see mankind in hopeful anticipation. The witnesses here are not somnambulant soldiers but eager and alert figures from the Old Testament. On Christ's right there is a group led by John the Baptist, who appears in rather somber garments—a loose-sleeved tunic of brownish yellow and an overgarment of a dull brownish green. In accordance with traditional representations, the

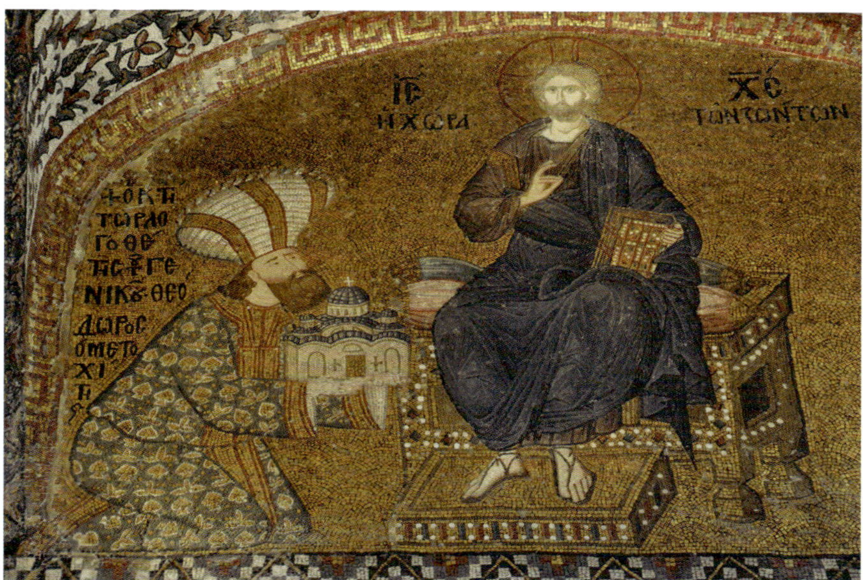

FIG. 10.3 Theodore Metochites presents the Chora Church to Christ ca. 1315–1321. Inner narthex, lunette above doorway into the naos, Chora Church. Mosaic.

Prodromos or the Forerunner, as John is known in the Greek Orthodox Church, appears as an ascetic. His features are weathered, his eyes look weary, and his hair is disheveled and unruly. John makes a gesture of benediction, with his ring finger and middle finger touching his thumb. Behind John are a series of kings, including Solomon and David, who appear just behind him. They wear royal boots of red and gold and pillbox-shaped crowns.

Behind the group of kings (six in total) are more figures that look forward to their ability to leave Hell. These are six anonymous figures holding out their hands in supplication toward Christ. Their gestures are reflected by those figures on Christ's left, led by a youthful Abel who appears with his shepherd's crook. It might seem odd that he hovers so weightlessly in the tomb of Eve, but it is actually quite tender to think that he is standing with his mother, as though forgiving her for her misdemeanors. Behind Abel stand six men that represent

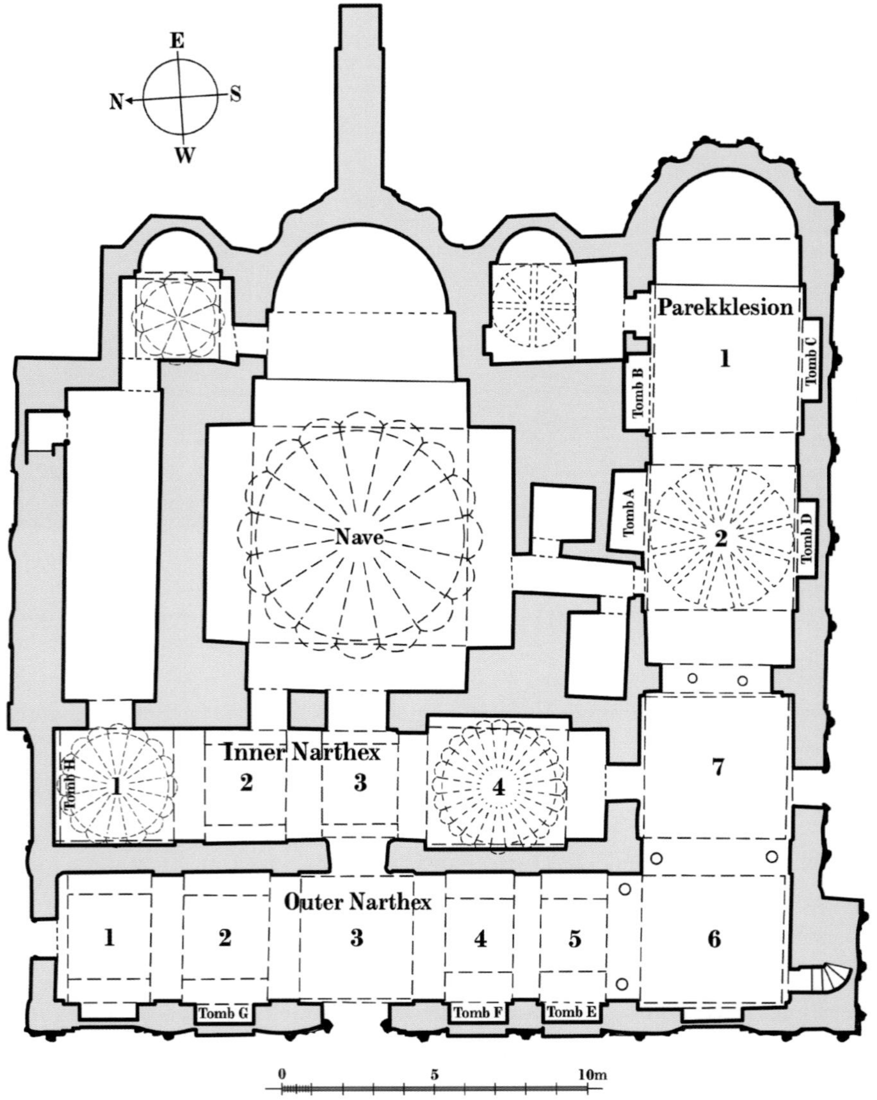

FIG. 10.4 Ground plan of the Chora Church.

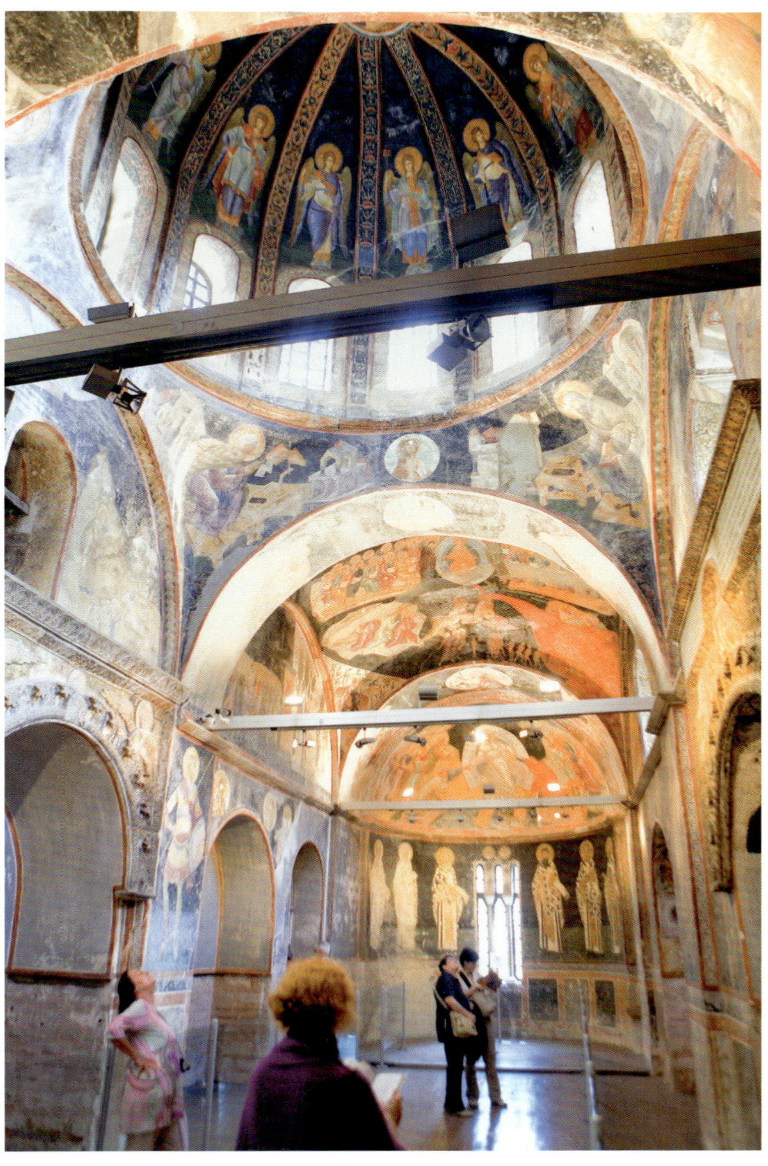

FIG. 10.5 View down the nave of the funerary chapel toward the apse, Chora Church.

the prophets and forefathers. Abel is a curious pendant to John. But Abel was understood by early church fathers as being holy and virtuous, and Saint Augustine listed Abel as the first saint at the head of a list of saints that culminates with John the Baptist.

Thus this is an image of a general resurrection, but this Anastasis has a specificity to it as well. Along the walls of the *parekklesion*, the word for chapel in Greek, are a series of *arcosolia*, arched recesses that were commonly used as spaces for sarcophagi or tombs. That powerful gesture, the way Christ leans, creates a special diagonal that continues through the arm, body, and leg of Adam, all of which is further emphasized by the shape of the sarcophagus from which Adam seems to fly. If you were to continue that line out of the composition and into the space of the church you would come to the tomb of a specific individual—Theodore Metochites (ca. 1270–1332).

Metochites's tomb doesn't look like much. It is missing a great deal—its original frescoes and what must have been a beautifully carved marble sarcophagus. During Turkish times the back of the *arcosolium* was knocked through, and all of those personalized funerary elements were lost. It is important to express the fact that Metochites selected the best space in the *parekklesion* for his tomb, with the greatest concentration of light from the windows above and the most direct "access" to Christ's painted, outstretched arm.

But Metochites's truest monument in life and death was the entire Chora Church. He did not pay just for this *arcosolium*. He paid for it all. And he depicts himself showing Christ that incredible gift as a minimodel of the church, backed by an inscription that asserts: "The Founder, the Logothete of the Genikon, Theodore Metochites" (Fig. 10.3). Whereas the placement of the tomb in the funerary chapel implies Metochites' hope that Christ will extend an arm of forgiveness, salvation, and resurrection in his direction, here we have Metochites extending his arm upward toward Christ, on the same kind of diagonal, with the hope of facilitating an exchange that will put Metochites in good stead at the end of time. The placement of this particular mosaic appears in the second entry vestibule or narthex leading into the main church or naos (Fig. 10.4). The first narthex is called the exonarthex, and the second interior narthex is called the esonarthex. This mosaic appeared right above the doorway into the naos. (Our *parekklesion* is on the south side, so on the right of the ground plan.) Surrounding this portrait of Metochites, embellishing the walls of both narthexes and much of the naos, were images and mosaics telling the story of the life of Christ and the Virgin.

I hate to miss a single piece of this monument, but I am going to be judicious and only discuss a few of the mosaics and frescoes. So this is a personalized tour of these scenes, but I hope it shows how much more there is to see in this monument. I love the scene of the Virgin learning how to walk (her first seven steps recorded in the Protoevangelium of James 6:1) and how she seems to still be learning that skill as she moves with trepidation toward the high priest in the domed vault. I think the image where she meets Joseph and his rod flowers on her behalf, the apocryphal telling of how Joseph was selected as her husband, is a little unsettling, especially when we consider how young she looks and how old Joseph is. I think the Massacre of the Innocents is too brutal. I much prefer seeing the scenes of healing the paralytic, the leper, and the man with the withered arm.

In entering the *parekklesion*, we leave behind a world of mosaics and swirling golden backgrounds and enter a space completely done in fresco, in more somber hues of paint (Fig. 10.5). Metochites and his artists thus signaled the transition between the main body of the church and the funereal, more private chapel space through the different media, techniques, and color schemes. The *parekklesion* has many images in addition to the Anastasis scene—in fact, it is covered in frescoes. In the lunette at the west end of the north wall are scenes from the story of Jacob (Fig. 10.6). He wrestles the angel, seeing, in a shocking and brutal manner, God face-to-face. Jacob tries to get his arms around the angel, bracing himself with his left leg; but the angel, with those massive outstretched wings, encompasses, literally surrounds, his opponent.

This surprising encounter with God is balanced with another, the moment when Moses sees God face-to-face in the guise of the Burning Bush. Flowing along the archway that connects these two revelatory episodes from the Old Testament is a representation of Jacob's Ladder. Jacob lies on the ground, dreaming of the ladder that rises to heaven and accommodates angels that ascend and descend as described in Genesis 28:11–13. The ladder was understood to be a prefiguration of the Virgin because she is a conduit from earth to heaven. The

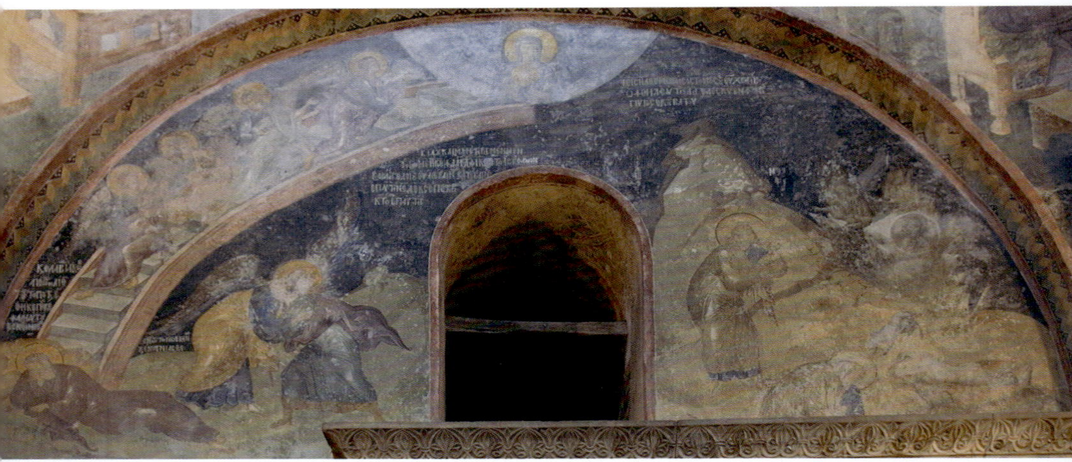

FIG. 10.6 Jacob asleep and wrestling the angel (left side) and the Lord appearing to Moses in the burning bush (right side), lunette at west end of north wall, ca. 1315–1321. Funerary chapel, Chora Church. Fresco.

Burning Bush was also interpreted as a type of the Virgin because, just as the bush burned but was not consumed, so too did Mary conceive and yet remain a spotless Virgin. The image of the Ark of the Covenant, carried by four priests on their shoulders, which appears on the south wall, was also meant to refer to the Virgin since she and the ark were both containers for God.

Devotion to the Virgin is paramount. She appears at the top of Jacob's ladder and even, oddly enough, *in* the Burning Bush. In both cases she appears holding the Christ Child against her chest. She appears in a similar pose in the exonarthex on the western wall over the main entrance. Here Christ appears in the center of her torso in an ovular, egglike shape, floating, less as a baby and more as an independent icon. The iconography is an emphatic symbol of the Incarnation and recalls the prophecy of Isaiah 7:14, repeated in Matthew 1:23, that Christ would be conceived in the womb of the Virgin. Surrounding this mosaic, throughout the narthexes are stories in which the Virgin is constantly a central figure, and her Dormition or Koimesis appears prominently in the naos, just above the entrance door, which would have been the last thing the visitor saw while exiting the church. The Koimesis is the understanding that the Virgin falls into an eternal sleep or deathless death. Her soul, here represented as a small child in swaddling clothes, is held by Christ. It is a lovely reversal of the many scenes in which Christ, as a young baby, is held up by his mother. As in the Anastasis, Christ becomes the ultimate protector, recipient, and agent of souls.

Now when we return to the portrait of Metochites, we have a new sense of precisely what he is offering—a monument of swirling colors and shimmering mosaics, stories that glorify and praise Christ's life. It is interesting to think back to the image of Abbot Suger at Saint-Denis and how he appeared in his portrait praying penitently, hovering between the "slime of the earth" and the "purity of Heaven" represented in the scene of the Annunciation (Fig. 9.3). Suger placed himself in the colored glass that was supposed to be instrumental in leading his thoughts from this world to the other world. Here, too, Metochites is made up of the same stones that illuminate the walls of these sacred hallways, that tell the stories of the life of Christ. His furrowed brow illustrates the intensity of this gesture, his hope for salvation (Fig. 10.3).

He, like Suger, is not all about humility. Metochites appears right before the entry to the main church of the Chora. It is impossible to miss the point, to forget who has brought about this splendor. At least Suger appears discalced in a dark-brown monk's robe. Metochites' dress speaks a language of money, power, and worldliness. His is an extraordinary robe—a bluish green covered in fabulous ornamental leaf forms and bordered with gold. And his hat is nonpareil. Known as a *skiadion* (literally, sunshade), the hat balloons outward from the crown of Metochites' head to form a beautiful bulb, probably made of silk, with golden stripes outlined in a red that matches the red on his robe. The same red appears in the halo of Christ, which has the traditional cross shape embedded in it. And the red appears in the cross on the gospel book and embellishes his throne.

The connections are not just coloristic, however. They are physical too. Metochites' left hand actually touches the throne of Christ, as does his model of the Chora. Oddly, the pillows on Christ's throne that are closest to Metochites seem to disappear into the background—the golden tips of the pink and blue pillows (which we can see clearly on the right portion of the throne) dematerialize into the swirling patterns of golden cubes that make the background of the lunette-shaped mosaic.

Metochites' extravagant wealth, his ability to pay for the decoration of the Chora, came from his role as the Grand Logothete of the treasury, as mentioned in the inscription. In this capacity he had control of the private purse, that of the emperor Andronicus II Palaiologos, the eldest surviving son of Michael VIII Palaiologos, the same figure who entered the city of Constantinople so triumphantly. Andronicus II handpicked Metochites as his prime minister in 1290 when Metochites was just thirty-five. Metochites rose to higher and higher positions in the court, and by 1321 he was one of the richest and most powerful men of Constantinople. He used his power and wealth to support the arts and to promote the Byzantine Empire. (Yet he negotiated one so-called successful alliance that I think we can all agree is distasteful—the marriage between the Serbian King Stephan Milutin and Andronicus II's daughter Simonis. Milutin was forty-five. Simonis was five. Some scholars think that the mosaic of the Virgin meeting Joseph drew some inspiration from life, in an unsettling way.)

The refurbishment of the Chora was a means of Metochites asserting the successes of the court, a way of indicating that the Latin conquest was a small blip and had done little to affect the untouchable Byzantine Empire. One mode of asserting this sense of power was by making subtle references and affiliations to Hagia Sophia, the extraordinary domed cathedral built by the Emperor Justinian that had served as the seat of the Patriarch of Constantinople since its construction in 537, with, of course, a break between 1204 and 1261 because of the Latins, when it was converted into a Roman Catholic cathedral. We can see that the architectural features of the Chora and the Hagia Sophia have certain visual similarities—those undulating scallop shapes, the high drum ringed with windows and situated under a prominent dome, although the top of the dome at Hagia Sophia is 182 feet high and the Chora's is about 56 feet high (Fig. 10.2). Metochites also borrowed images from inside Hagia Sophia. Consider the similarities between our portrait of Metochites and the imperial door from inside Hagia Sophia, dated to the late ninth or early tenth century. The unnamed emperor (scholars cannot agree on whether it is Leo VI or his son Constantine VII Porphyrogenitus) relates to Christ in a way that Metochites is most obviously

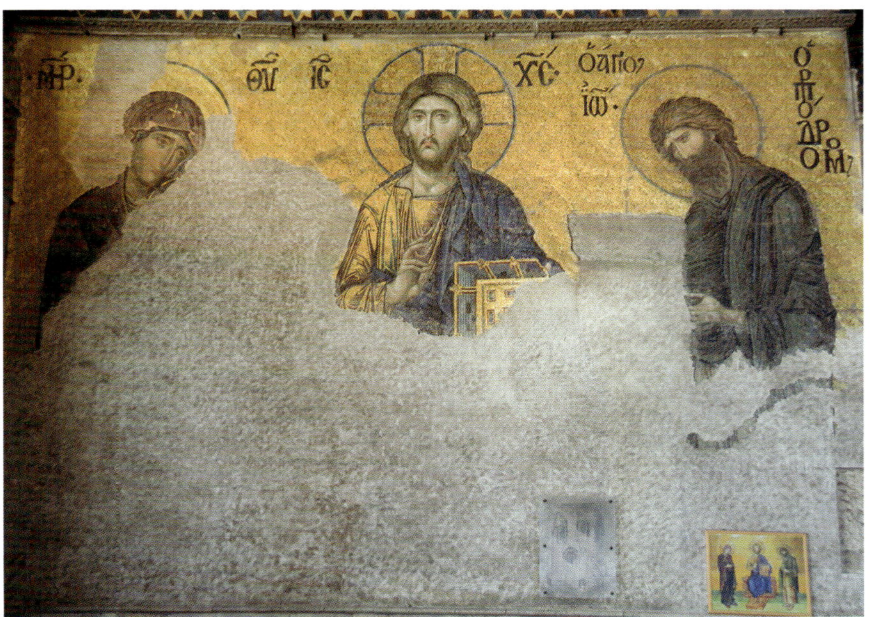

FIG. 10.7 Deësis scene, Christ with Mary and John the Baptist, ca. 1261. South gallery of Hagia Sophia. Istanbul, Turkey. Mosaic, 395 × 60.7 cm.

emulating. Both images were placed over the main entry into the body of the church.

A more complicated example is of Metochites appropriating the iconography of a mosaic that appears in the south gallery of Hagia Sophia and has been dated to 1261, where the Virgin and John the Baptist lean toward Christ in an act of Deësis or supplication(Fig. 10.7). As the scholar Robert Nelson has shown, the scene also appears at the Chora, on almost the exact same scale as the image at Hagia Sophia (Fig. 10.8). Metochites was clearly trying to emulate the scale of the Hagia Sophia mosaic. But since the Chora is not as large as Hagia Sophia, he had to drop the part of the composition that included John. In other words, the size of the mosaic, the tie to Hagia Sophia, was more important than the presence of John the Baptist. A final connection between Hagia Sophia and the Chora was physical. Robert Ousterhout discovered that the two monuments, which are

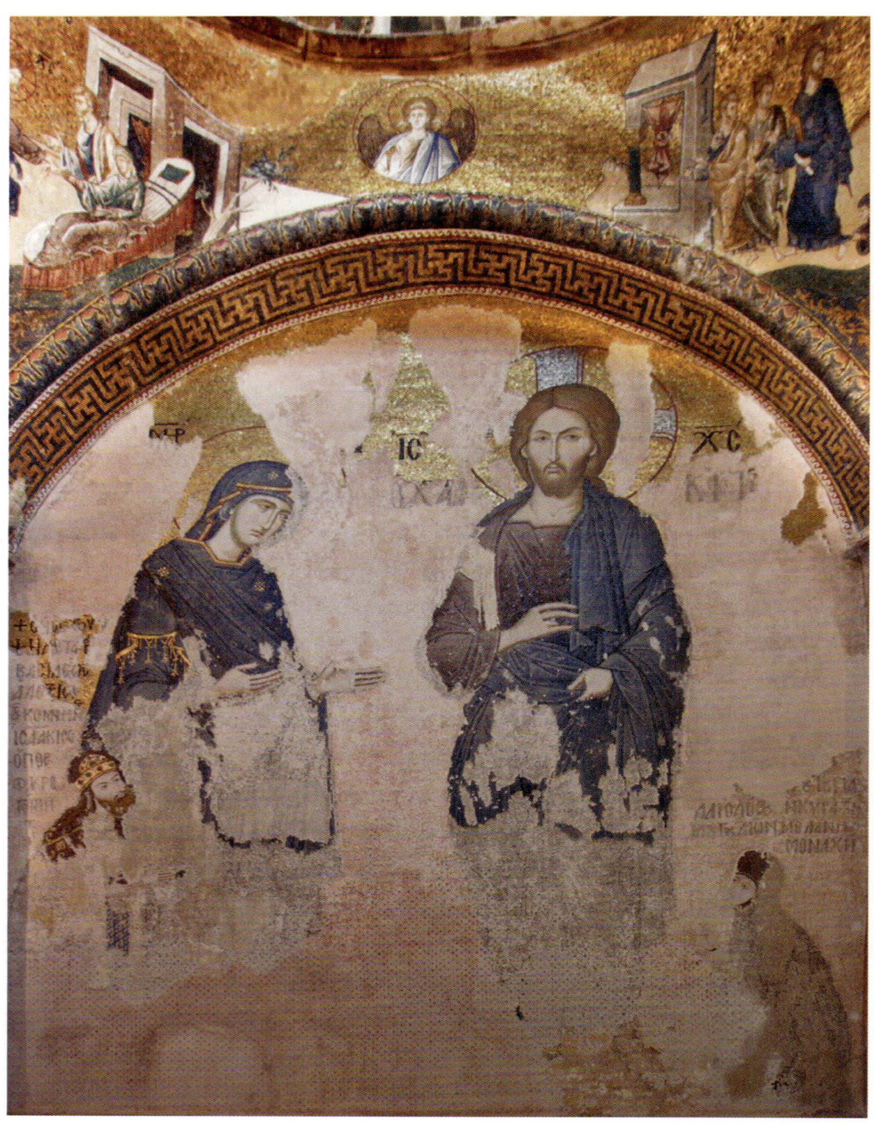

FIG. 10.8 Deësis scene, Christ with Mary and two benefactors of the monastery, ca. 1315–1321. Fourth bay of inner narthex, to right of door into the naos, Chora Church. Mosaic.

separated by three and a half miles, were originally connected by a pathway. It is not a short walk, but it was evidently common to walk from one to the other. The Chora was, at the time of its original construction, out in the countryside—far from the center of town and outside of the city walls. By Metochites' time, the city had grown and the Chora was inside the walls. This is one of the explanations for the name of the church, *chora* meaning land or country.

But Metochites was not just wealthy and powerful; he was also extremely clever. He loved writing and words and wordplay. The word *chora*, for instance, means more than just country. It has a number of mystical meanings as well. The word appears five times at the Chora. For instance, it appears in a lunette with Christ where the inscription says that Christ is "Chora of the living." Christ encompasses us. He lifts those souls out of their tombs in the Anastasis and becomes their new home, their new *chora*. The Virgin too has the same epithet with a slightly different meaning. She is the Mother of God, and as such she is the Chora or dwelling place for the uncontainable (who is God). Metochites takes the name associated with the monastery and makes it into a beautiful poetic expression of the sacredness of the space of the church, suggesting the ways in which Christ and the Virgin contain us, while we stand in this contained space. Through his writing, Metochites gives us a literary gift to go along with the church itself.

Metochites wrote throughout his life, but in his later years a more sour strain emerges. Metochites was born as the son of the archdeacon George Metochites, who was a supporter of a union between the Roman Catholic and Greek Orthodox churches under the reign of Michael VIII Palaiologos—the same emperor that reconquered Constantinople. When Michael VIII died in 1282, support for his policies (and by extension George's) dissipated, and George was sent into exile for forty-five years. This is where Metochites was discovered by Emperor Andronikos, in exile with his disgraced parents in Asia Minor. The same exile characterized the end of Metochites' life. In 1328 a civil war broke out between Andronikos II and his own grandson Andronikos III, just seven years after the completion of the Chora. Andronikos III overthrew his grandfather and put Metochites in prison on Thrace, where he stayed until 1330.

Two years of exile might not seem like a long time, but for Metochites they

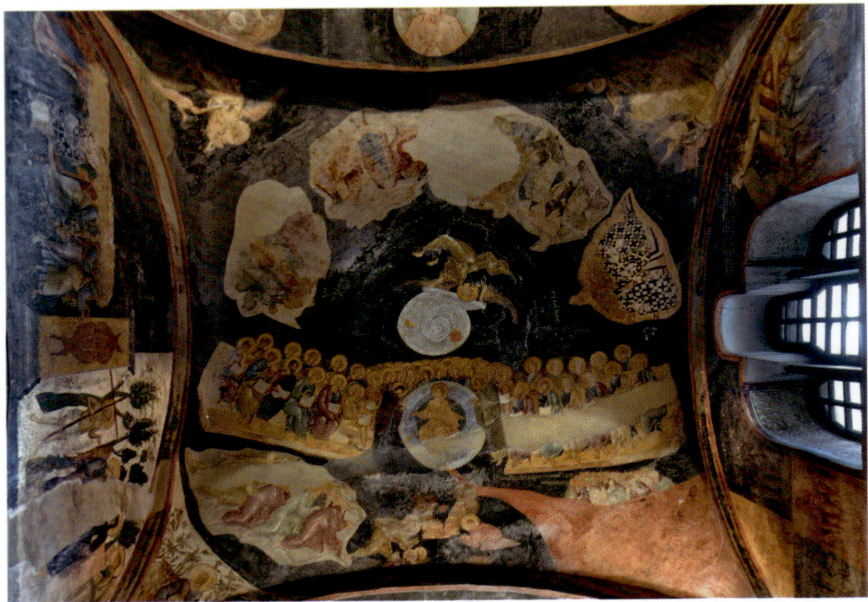

FIG. 10.9 Last Judgment with Christ seated on a rainbow, ca. 1315–1321. Ceiling of the eastern bay of the funerary chapel, Chora Church. Fresco.

were ruinous. He was treated harshly. Even worse than the conditions of his imprisonment was his overbearing worry. He was concerned about the well-being of his sons (although I do not know why since many of them were involved in the plot to overthrow him), and he worried about the state of his beloved Chora: "On account of this monastery was my heart most sorely smitten with grief, lest it should perish when the populace rose up wreaking senseless havoc in its uncontrolled frenzy." He wrote letter after letter about the importance of the preservation of the library. After two years Metochites returned to Constantinople and his beloved Chora. But staring out the window of the Chora to see the ruins where his luxurious mansion once stood was heartbreaking in a new way. In his writings from his time at the Chora, he describes the splendors of the mansion as though you are following him through his never-ending halls, trying to catch up as he guides you through his mazelike (or byzantine) gardens, past all of his fountains and vineyards and grazing beasts. The word in Greek for describing works of art is *ekphrasis*, meaning *ek* (out) and *phrasis* (speak). The goal was to "bring the subject matter vividly before the eyes," according to a primer used in Greek schools of the Roman Empire. No one does *ekphrasis* like Metochites. These writings evoke an incomparable sense of pathos and loss.

There is something very poetic about the trajectory of Metochites's life. It has waves of instability—from exile as a youth, to extreme wealth and power, and back to exile again. But Metochites does return. He comes back to his beloved monument and dies two years later amid his (mercifully) untouched books. There are some ways that we might make a connection between the story of Metochites and the Anastasis. When we started our own *ekphrasis* of the Anastasis image, we used words associated with return—rebirth, recovery, restoration. The scene also shows us many evidences of instability—ill-defined landscapes, an unknowable sense of time, no immediate certainty about the outcome.

But in the vaults just above the apse a Last Judgment scene does play out (Fig. 10.9). The damned are punished in a fiery stream and a lake of fire, and the blessed are rewarded. Above the judging Christ is an angel holding a scroll of heaven which is rolled up at the end of time, according to Revelation 6:14: "And the heaven departed as a scroll when it is rolled together." The sun, moon, and familiar stars, which remind us of Christ's mandorla, decorate the scroll's shell-like form. These moments of Second Coming and the Last Judgment contextualize the Anastasis scene, providing a visual framework for its complete meaning. Eternal law and cosmic order are ultimately established. Christ's rebirth, Christ's restitution of the righteous, Christ's return—these notions color the walls at the Chora and, in a strange way, the life of its patron.

The Anastasis still speaks its powerful language of salvation in contemporary Greek Orthodox communities. The Anastasis icon is used specifically for *Pascha*, the word used for Easter in the Greek Orthodox Church. Saint Sophia, the Greek Orthodox Church on North Saint Mary's Street in San Antonio, has a striking modern icon of the Anastasis (Fig. 10.10). It resides behind the iconostasis or altar screen. But on Pascha, at Saint Sophia, as at all Greek Orthodox churches, the image makes a special appearance outside the iconostasis and has a significant role in the liturgical service. It is quite clear that the Saint Sophia

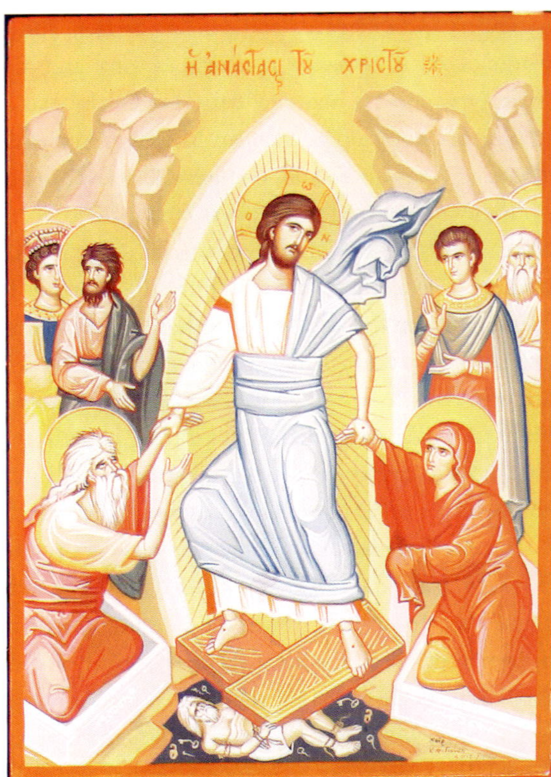

FIG. 10.10 Anastasis icon, Saint Sophia Church, San Antonio, Texas, early twentieth century. Reportedly painted by the Joasaph Brotherhood at the Karyai Monastery, Mount Athos, Greece. Pigment on wood.

Anastasis took much inspiration from the Chora Anastasis. Christ's placement, his bright garments, the way he reaches with both hands toward Adam and Eve, the craggy rocks that reach around the scene like arms, the way that John the Baptist turns to King David—it is a clear copy or, better put, a direct response to and emulation of the Constantinopolitan fresco.

Pascha is the special occasion documented in a video that was produced by the Getty Museum.* It shows the holy men at Saint Catherine's Monastery in Sinai,

* "Holy Image, Hallowed Ground," J. Paul Getty Museum, Los Angeles, CA. Director Lyn Goldfarb. 2006. vimeo.com/9708525.

Egypt, carrying icons, crosses, jeweled holy gospels, and liturgical garments through the streets of the monastic complex before entering the main church. The narrator of this documentary, Father Justin, appears in the procession and in the library where he is currently, passionately, like Metochites, saving the books. Using high-resolution digitization techniques, he is recording and preserving the monastery's some 3,300 priceless manuscripts, many of which date to as early as the fourth century. There are many remarkable aspects to Father Justin's spiritual journey to Saint Catherine's, not least of which is the start of the journey. Father Justin grew up in El Paso, Texas, and trained to be a Greek Orthodox monk in both Austin and in San Antonio. The Anastasis image allows us to consider a sweep of places and times—Hellenistic Greece, early Medieval Rome, Romanesque Spain, Gothic France, fourteenth-century Constantinople—and it allows us an opportunity to know an image and a tradition that is very much alive today, not only in Sinai but in America too.

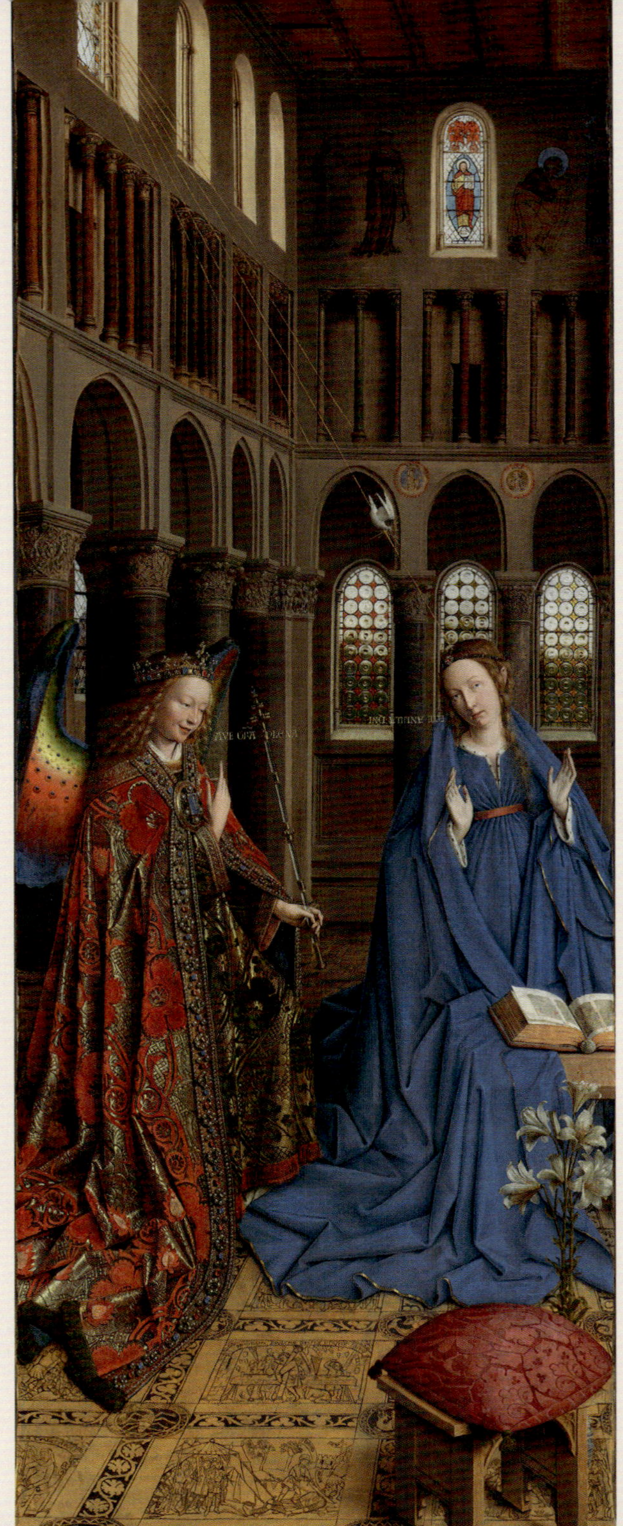

FIG. 11.1 Jan van Eyck, *The Annunciation*, ca. 1434–1436. National Gallery of Art, Washington, DC. Oil on canvas transferred from panel, 90.2 × 34.1 cm.

Jan van Eyck, *The Annunciation*

CA. 1434–36

NORTHERN RENAISSANCE ART

It is a story we are familiar with, that of the Annunciation, when the Archangel Gabriel visits the Virgin Mary, shocking her both with his presence and with the news that she will be conceiving Jesus, the Son of God. As described in Luke, Gabriel appears and introduces his presence with the words "Hail, full of Grace!" It is this very phrase that appears in the painting by Jan van Eyck (ca. 1390–1441) in Latin, as delicate, hovering, golden letters (Fig. 11.1). The salutation travels at a slight incline from Gabriel toward the Virgin Mary. It is a wonderful and exciting moment, a message from God.

But in the biblical passage Mary is troubled. Gabriel senses her anxiety and explains that she must not be concerned, that everything will be routine—she will conceive in her womb, she will bring forth a son, he will have a proper name (Jesus), and he will rule a kingdom that will have no end. This angelic logic does not fully translate. He misses a step, as she is quick to point out: "How shall this be, seeing I know not a man?"

So the angel tries again, with three different answers. He first explains that the Holy Ghost will come upon her and "overshadow" her. Perhaps seeing that his first line of argumentation is a bit esoteric, his next step is to be more concrete. He reminds her that her cousin Elizabeth is having a child, even though everyone thought that she was barren. Finally, he settles on a statement that has no possible retort, the incontrovertible assertion that "with God nothing shall be impossible."

Convinced, Mary replies, "Behold the handmaid of the Lord," the very words in the painting, which appear in thin golden script upside-down and in retrograde, moving from right to left. Whereas Gabriel's words move toward the Virgin, following the direction of his half-lidded eyes, the Virgin's words are to be read in the celestial heavens, by God. Her upturned eyes and lithely arched eyebrows encourage the path of her words. Van Eyck paints the first and last words uttered in the biblical passage. Those two brief sentences encompass the beginning and the end of the episode from Luke. And that might have been enough for one painting. But Van Eyck turns this moment into an exposition about the Christian Church, its history, its faith, and even its culture. The walls, the floors, the glass, the clothing—the entire infrastructure of the piece embraces and develops the meaning of the Annunciation, Mary's moment, as the crux of Christianity, of the transition from the Old Testament to the New.

Not only does Mary receive the word of God from the messenger Gabriel, she is struck by a singular beam of gold, a ray of light. Cascading along this beam is a bright-white dove, a representative of the Holy Spirit, around whose head is a sunburst of those golden rays. The steep angle at which the heavenly bird sits creates a sense of speed, as do the sharp ends of his wings.

Gabriel's promise that the Holy Spirit will overshadow her is being fulfilled right before our eyes. And he knows it too. His elegantly elongated index finger points directly toward his introductory words, but specifically toward the word *Ave*, which is, as we have noted, the word meaning hail from *aveo* but also the ablative singular of *avis*, meaning bird. Gabriel is an arch archangel—rosy cheeks and rosy lips, charming dimples, little glinting teeth exposed by his gleeful grin. He has a literal twinkle in his eye. Twinkling, shimmering, glimmering jewels and brocades surround the angel and appear vibrantly in his massive, variegated wings, a deluge of saturated colors, punctuated with the eyes of peacock feathers. The shared feathery wings create a link between Gabriel and the quickly descending dove.

But the dove has more in common with the Virgin. The golden ray upon which the dove swiftly travels reappears in the delicate golden outline of her weighty blue robe—on the edges of her robe and her hem. The purity of her blanched skin is closer in hue to the wings of the white bird than Gabriel's blushing cheeks.

Her upturned white palms almost replicate the position (and size) of the bird's white body. The V-shape created in his pulled-back wings reappears throughout the dress and pose of the Virgin. There is a deep V at her décolletage that is accentuated by the white ermine fur, and which is repeated by the many folds created by the cinching action of her thin red belt. Two thick folds from her outer garment also create a much deeper V, one that draws attention to the womb of the Virgin, the exact space that will hold the future Son of God as conceived by the Holy Spirit, that rapidly approaching dove.

The progress from cascading dove to the radiating lilies is also a visual treatise about the fact that the Virgin is pristine in her purity while simultaneously the quintessential mother. The Holy Spirit enters the space of the church through a window in the upper register which is called the clerestory. The significance of the light (and the dove) bursting through the window had a weighty theological meaning.

Writers like Thomas Aquinas, a thirteenth-century theologian, explained the purity of the Virgin in terms of light and glass. Aquinas wrote that, just as light passes through a glass without harming it and actually adds to its illuminating power, so too did Jesus pass through the womb of Mary without affecting it. Lilies were understood to represent the Virgin's unassailable purity by many early medieval scholars. The Venerable Bede, writing in the early eighth century, described the dazzling white flower as a perfect metaphor for the chaste flesh of the Virgin. The writer also likened the special birth of Christ to the flowering of the lily: "And pleasingly, in the lily the whiteness first reveals itself little by little on the outside, and then there appears the lovely golden color that was concealed within." According to Bede, the golden anthers (the parts of the stamen with pollen) were meant to represent the splendor of Christ's "divine brightness." It is almost as though Van Eyck has read Bede. Two attenuated white buds are about to open, perhaps referencing the pure womb of the Virgin that encases the unborn baby. Around them, bursting petals reveal little golden anthers, perhaps to represent the glorious Christ Child. Van Eyck adds golden highlights on the petals that are not unlike the outline of the Virgin's cloak. Van Eyck also gives the extended stigma a clear tripartite arrangement, an emphatic illustration of the Trinity and a true depiction of the so-called Madonna Lily.

The crisp white pages of the open book—like the unfurled, crepey white petals and her open palms—also contribute to the sense of Mary as chaste virgin and mother. In the biblical passage, Luke does not state that the Virgin has been interrupted while reading. Yet in early modern Europe this was a common means of representing Mary at the time of the Annunciation. This device allowed artists to heighten the drama of the angel's arrival, breaking the woman's quiet and thoughtful moment of repose with his splendid appearance. But the meaning of the book goes a bit deeper. Although we cannot say precisely what she is reading, it was, by tradition, a passage of the scriptures, which was a clear means of indicating her pious devotion. In fact, many scholars have suggested that Mary is probably reading one of the most important prophesies of the Old Testament, that from Isaiah: "Behold a virgin shall conceive and bear a son, and shall call his name Emmanuel." Thus Mary is not just a random woman. She is smart, educated, and devoted. Because of her knowledge of the law of God, because of her piety, she is worthy of bearing the Son of God.

Before Gabriel appears she is quietly reading the words of the Old Testament. The letters are simply dark splotches on a page. A few blue and red letters introduce passages that we cannot read. But in responding to Gabriel she is giving life to those words. The Old Testament events were read as symbolic foreshadowings of the life of Christ. Here she internalizes the dark words of the Old Testament text, and voices words of the New Testament, words that look like spun gold. Christ was also called Logos or the Word. Thus we are watching Mary give life to Christ as the Word as well as Christ as Man.

The sense of continuity from the Old Testament to the New Testament, the sense that the Annunciation is a fulfillment of prophesies from the past, appears throughout the Van Eyck painting, hovering in the corners, on the walls, on the floor. It is hard not to let these seemingly peripheral details grab your attention, and I have to admit that my reading of the painting is somewhat centrifugal. Still, all of these tiny stories—all of the miniature, minute, somewhat hidden details—ultimately reflect back on the Annunciation. Old Testament figures and stories appear as prefigurations of the New, most specifically of events in Christ's life. This cross-testament reading, wherein the Old Testament prefigured events in the New, is called typology. We saw this kind of allegorical reading at play in San Vitale, where stories like the Sacrifice of Isaac and figures like Abel and Melchizedek were understood as representative of Christ's life and piety.

Van Eyck also makes typological connections, although he chooses different Old Testament stories and explains the connections between the two testaments in different ways. In the moment of the Annunciation, Mary and Gabriel are a riot of color and finery and jewels. Below, in the floor, Old Testament stories are painted to look like *niello*, a black mixture of copper, silver, and lead that was used as an inlay on an engraved metal (Fig. 11.2). The use of *niello* appears in many objects from the medieval period. However, the pieces are usually small—like spoons and small pendants. Jan van Eyck is probably taking liberties, as I know of no actual floor decorated in this manner, nor would it seem possible to actualize. The point in paint, however, is that these stories are different from the moment happening above. These stories are foundational. They are the literal basis upon which the Annunciation rests. They are told in a medium that is not without cost, in a technique that takes time and skill. Yet they are sketchy. They are outlines. They are not fully realized. They lack the color that explodes above, in the exchange between the Virgin and the Angel, although there is a visual connection between the yellowish color of the floor and the golden rays above.

The more lustrous, more opulent material, gold, is reserved for the story above, specifically for the spoken word and the beams of light. This gold was added during one of the final stages of the painting. The letters from Gabriel's mouth sit on top of his luminous crystal scepter. The rays of heaven are even more emphatically golden because they were actually made with gold. To produce these rays, Van Eyck incised lines right though the finished paint layers and then followed those lines with a rounded and raised oil-based yellow glue. When the glue dried he applied gold so that the bursts of light rest on top of the surface. The golden light beams illuminate the space and activate the story, flowing from left to right, the same way that we read most naturally. The floor panels recede into the background. And like those faint, sketchy memories of the past, they become progressively more difficult to read, both because they are moving into the distance and because of those splendid jewel-tone garments that cover them, relegating these scenes to the historical, foundational past.

Van Eyck establishes a clear chain of command, a clear progression from Old

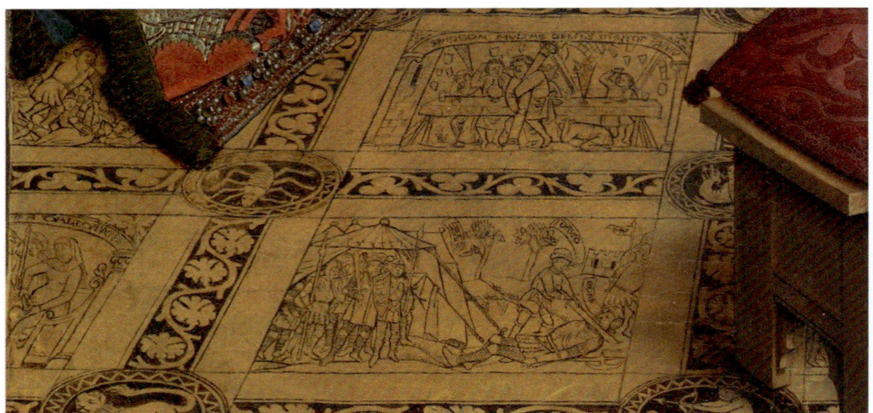

FIG. 11.2 Detail of floor in *The Annunciation* showing Samson slaying the Philistines (upper left), Samson in the temple (upper right), Delilah cutting Samson's hair (lower left), and David slaying Goliath (lower right).

to New, but he does not throw away the stories and heroes of the Old Testament altogether. Like a carefully written sermon, the artist crafts a sensitive telling of the men and women that embodied and enacted the miracles that were to be given their fullest meaning in the New Testament. David and Samson are two of the figures that Van Eyck privileges for their feats of strength and piety, and as early types, or antetypes, of Christ. The lower panel in the floor shows David after having felled the great giant Goliath with a measly stone, which seems to stay lodged in the aggressor's forehead. Youthful David, in a short skirt and jaunty hat, looks down upon the giant with a mixture of consternation and fear, while stepping forward to cut off Goliath's head. Goliath's once-powerful army scampers hurriedly off to the right. Saul's troops are only slightly less cowardly, waiting just at the opening of their imperial tent as though to see if they will be needed on the battlefield, hoping that the answer is negative.

The contrast between Saul and David is clear. Saul waits from the sidelines covered in protective armor, backed by his troops, with his sword held aloft in wary anticipation. David is swift and active. He wears a simple tunic with knee-high socks, relying entirely on a spiritual armor, on God's protection.

David's role as an anticipatory Christ was a well-established theme by the time Van Eyck took up his paintbrush. Saint Augustine, for example, understood the battle as a clear metaphor for Christ's battle with Satan. The five stones with which David armed himself were the Pentateuch. The one stone that actually hit Goliath, Augustine explains, was, or became, the New Testament.

Samson was also seen as a type of Christ, although the connection might seem a bit more obscure. Early Church Fathers acknowledged the connection to be tenuous. But as the sixth-century theologian Caesarius of Arles explained, "Samson worked as a strong man and suffered as a weak one.... In the one person I understand both qualities: I see the strength of the Son of God and the weakness of the Son of Man.... Inasmuch as Samson performed virtues and miracles, he prefigured Christ, the head of the church." Van Eyck selected the scene of Samson in the temple because it highlighted connections with the Passion of Christ. In the center of this panel Samson wraps his arms around a column and snaps it in two, causing the ceiling to crumble in a pile of bricks. This is the moment in Judges when Samson is at his lowest point; his eyes have been gouged out, he is in fetters, and his strength-producing locks of hair have been cut—although no one seems to notice that his hair has grown back (Judges 16:22). Brought out to "make sport" for a group of drunken Philistines, about three thousand or so, Samson calls upon God for one last surge of might. Samson grabs the two pillars upon which the house rests and kills everyone, including himself. An inscription that runs across a long rounded arch explains this moment: "Samson slaughtered many people at a banquet."

Unlike the biblical passage that describes two columns, this Samson breaks through one. This deviation from the text helps Van Eyck make the connection with Christ. The single pillar has more in common with the vertical bar of the cross upon which Christ is crucified. The pillar also suggests the column against which Christ is whipped by Pilate's men, before he is given the crown of thorns. The mocking of Samson is thus visually aligned with the mocking of Christ. The long banquet table also looks like this might be a perversion of the Last Supper imagery. The wrong kind of king is presiding in the floor panel, but Samson changes all of that. Buildings must be destroyed and sacrifices must be made to make way for the new order, the New Testament.

Van Eyck also provides evidence of Samson's strength before the episode in the temple. Surrounded ever so carefully by the deep-green fringe of Gabriel's robe, Samson slays the Philistines, trampling over the confused mass of slaughtered bodies. Arms and legs are placed at angles that create a pinwheel-like effect. Combined with Samson's diagonal position, his weighty lunging body, this tiny vignette, no more than an inch tall, suggests speed and confusion—it is a bloody rampage. Samson is active against the Philistines throughout the Book of Judges. But I suspect that this is the moment, in chapter 15, when he takes the fresh jawbone of an ass and slays a thousand men. Thus the shape that peeks out from under the angelic robe and hovers above Samson's head is not an inscription but the jawbone, which is about to overcome the knight's sword in one scythelike swoop. Samson, like Christ, overcomes sin. The configuration is particularly tantalizing because it looks very much like the Harrowing of Hell, the moment when Christ descends into Limbo after the Crucifixion and brings salvation to the souls of the dead—the same scene that appears in the Greek Orthodox tradition and in the Chora Church as the Anastasis. (Fig. 10.1)

This scene was popular in fifteenth-century northern Europe. Martin Schongauer's *Harrowing of Hell*, now in the Musee d'Unterlinden in Colmar, shows Christ in a pose that looks similar to that of Samson (Fig. 11.3). Of course Christ is saving souls, and Samson is doing nothing of the sort. But Samson conquers sin symbolically. Both Samson and Christ step atop evidence of sin—devils and monsters, in the case of the *Harrowing of Hell*, and wicked traitors in the Samson story. Both men carry weapons of their victory—a massive jawbone or a long standard topped with a cross.

The connection between Samson and Christ by means of the Harrowing of Hell is also made explicit in a woodblock print from the early fifteenth century in the *Biblia Pauperum*, a version of which is at the Bodleian Library (Arch. G c. 14).* In the center of a fictive architectural frame, Christ appears leaning at a diagonal to pull Adam and the other penitent sinners from the gaping mouth of Hell. Hell has a rather lionlike face, with a wild and erratic mane and a nose suggestive of a lion, not unlike the lion in the scene to the right, where Samson

* See folio 28r of the Biblia Pauperum at https://digital.bodleian.ox.ac.uk.

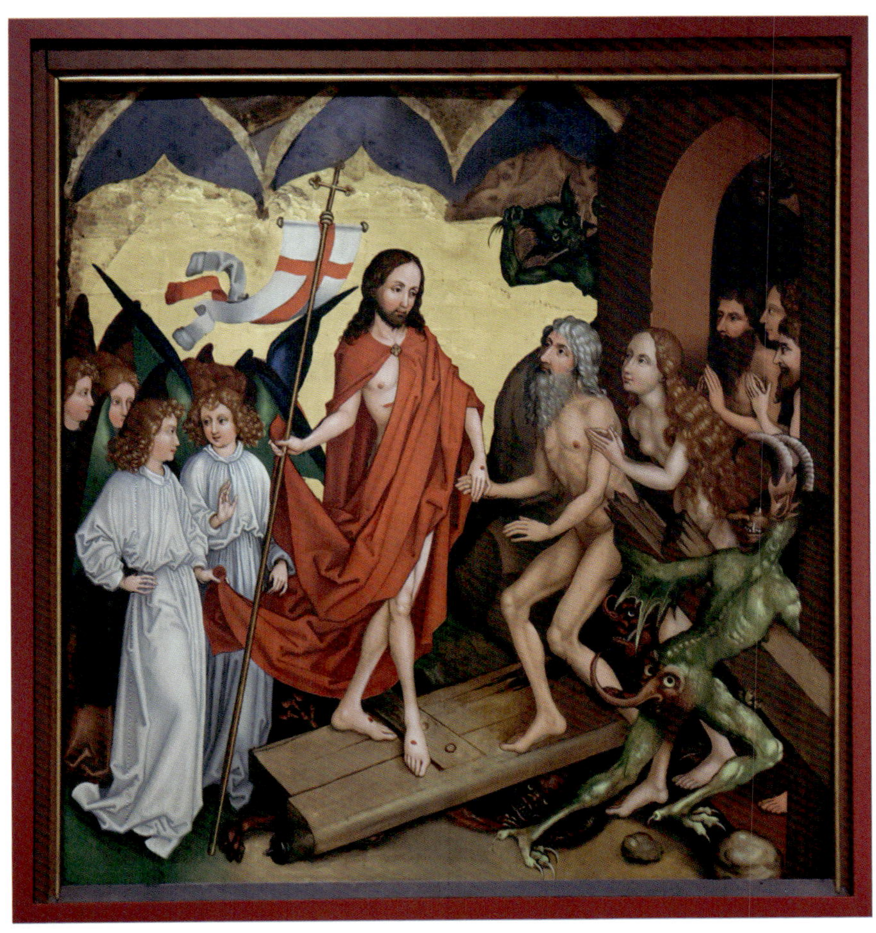

FIG. 11.3 Martin Schongauer, *Harrowing of Hell*, 1475. Detail from an altarpiece originally in the Dominican Church in Colmar. Musée d'Unterlinden, Colmar, France. Oil on wood, 116 × 116 cm.

battles a lion, as told in Judges 14:6. Samson's struggle is emphatically focused on the opening of the lion's mouth, although in the biblical passage he simply rips the lion to shreds. But by showing Samson prying the jaws of the lion open, there is a clear connection with Christ. Samson opens the lion's mouth as Christ opens the mouth of Hell. There is a sense that Samson's actions are a prologue to Christ's; he is part of the story, part of the experience of salvation. In fact, his thickly bearded face seems a great deal like that of Adam's below—it is in the same position and has the same shape. Just to the left of the Harrowing of Hell is a depiction of David slaying Goliath with his massive sword, the same scene that appears in the nearby panel on the floor of the Van Eyck *Annunciation*.

The source of Samson's undoing appears in the far left corner of the floor panel in the painting. Here we are given a glimpse into the moment when Delilah finally figures out what makes her lover so strong, those seven locks of hair. The truncated inscription indicates her femininity: "Delilah his woman" (*Dalida uxore sua*). Sitting in an armchair, she uses thick shears to cut off the waving strands, the curly wisps of hair. The notion that the Virgin was capable of reversing the sins of female figures in the Old Testament was common among medieval theologians. Thus we have a tie between Delilah and the Virgin that is typological—the Virgin corrects Delilah's sin. (There is a formal connection too since both women turn their heads at a similar angle.) The Virgin was most frequently connected with Eve, another Old Testament flawed femme fatale.

The third-century theologian St. Irenaeus explained the connection as follows: "The knot of Eve's disobedience was loosened by Mary's obedience. The bonds fastened by the virgin Eve through disbelief were united by the virgin Mary through faith." St. Jerome wrote, "Death through Eve, Life through Mary." Thus those words of Gabriel's have yet another reading—Hail, bird, and, in retrograde, Eva. Infused throughout the painting are the memories of Eve's sins, whispers of her transgression and betrayal, all of which are inverted, restored, and overcome by Ave Maria, by her birthing of the Redeemer.

Another female figure appears in a faint, whisperlike painting on the back wall of the church. A banderole over her head tells us that she is the daughter of Pharaoh. She is being presented with the little baby in the box. The script reads *Moses Fiscella* or "Moses in a small wicker basket." The banderole in her hand indicates that the baby is one "of the male Hebrews." It is hard to say whether the incomplete lettering of the inscriptions was intentional, as a way of explaining that these are older images from a distant past, or if Van Eyck's paint degraded over time. In either case, the impact is the same—these figures of the Old Testament are faded, distant, dark. But the daughter of Pharaoh is a clear type for the Virgin. She twists toward the servant woman in much the same manner as the Virgin—body facing to the left, head turning to her right. She also draws attention to her womb with her hand gesture, holding the end of the scroll directly over her stomach. The servant woman steps toward the princess with a sharply raised left knee, just like that of Gabriel, and the servant's right index finger also gestures upward. It is an annunciation, in a way—a woman of royal blood is presented with a child who is not the son of her husband.

The child, Moses, grows to receive God's covenant and is instrumental in transmitting it to man. This transmission appears to the right of the stained glass window. Moses, with a bright-blue halo, bows with humility toward God, who is represented as Christ, with a tripartite halo, which also glows in that same bright-blue hue. God/Christ calmly presents a long banderole that runs the length of Moses's stooped body—from foot to crown—which reads, "You shall not take the name of the Lord your God in vain," a passage from the Ten Commandments.

A stained glass figure watches over this painted exchange. Glimmering against the same bright blue, now in the shape of a mandorla or aureole, stands an image of God holding a book in his left hand and a scepter in his right. Scholars understand this figure as the God of the Old Testament, a reference to the singular god before the manifestation of the Trinity. The shift from one to three is represented in the tripartite formations below—both in the *triforium*, a shallow arcade with three panels each with three differently colored columns, and in the grander space of the gallery. Three narrow pointed arches frame three windows composed of medallions of colorless roundels of glass set amid colored glass with little flowers in red, green, and yellow.

The meanings of colors are not totally stable. But there was a tradition in which red represented the Holy Spirit, green the Epiphany, and yellow the Resurrection. It is rather tempting to read the color scheme in this way since the

Holy Spirit hovers above the red window, the Virgin (the focus of the Epiphany) is in front of the green window, and the last window represents the triumph of Christ in yellow. Scholars have interpreted the capital to the right of this last window as a scene of enmity, as two figures fighting, which you can only see on Google. However, it looks like something quite different, like it might be a scene of supplication instead of struggle. Perhaps this is the scene in which Christ tells Mary Magdalene not to touch him, *"Noli me tangere,"* an episode that occurs after the Resurrection.

This is a painting about changes and transitions, evolutions and progressions within human history. Floors, walls, windows, capitals—the entire building is a metaphor about the shift from the Old to the New Law. Images of the Old hover on the peripheral parts of the painting—on the floor, in the darkened upper registers, and outside. The progression from the rounded arches of the uppermost register to the pointed arches of the space occupied by Mary and the angel is also made symbolic of this change. Rounded arches had been a prominent architectural form during the eleventh to thirteenth centuries, the so-called Romanesque period. Attenuated, pointed arches were more popular during the later periods, the so-called Gothic period. "Romanesque" and "Gothic" are terms that were developed by nineteenth-century art historians, and as such those words would not have meant anything to Van Eyck. Yet the different shapes and forms did mean something; they were thought of as significant changes in style from something old to something new. The architecture is a clear confection. No building would start with pointed arches of the newer style and finish the uppermost regions in an older, outdated style. That is backward. But Van Eyck is painting metaphorically, not realism or actual architecture. Van Eyck's architecture reads from the old downward toward the new. The dome building barely visible outside the window alludes to the earlier belief system. The conquest of Synagoga by Ecclesia, the church, was a common medieval trope. Van Eyck's synagoga is barely in the picture. Ecclesia dominates.

In building his church, Van Eyck is also alluding to a future church, to the monument of the Heavenly Jerusalem as described in Revelation. The city that appears in the text of Revelation, coming down out of heaven from God, is orderly, perfectly measured, and glistening in precious stones—jasper, sapphire, emerald, amethyst. The list is exhaustive. The image of resplendent colors and jewels and gold might make us think of Gabriel's glorious coat and wings. Pearls adorn the gates of the city, just as pearls sparkle all along the hem of the angel's robe and adorn his elegant crown. Pearls also appear on the diadem of the Virgin, and a rather large cluster appears in the center of her book. In Revelation, after the Heavenly Jerusalem appears in the sky, a man on a throne (understood to be Christ) announces, "I am Alpha and Omega, the beginning and the end."

At the top of the page in Mary's book those two letters appear—a blue Alpha and a red Omega—and they seem to decorate the top of each page. Revelation also describes how seven angels with seven bowls full of the seven last plagues show the author the new holy city from the top of a high mountain. The number seven is crucial throughout Revelation, and so it is in the painting. There are seven open lilies. Seven rays of light burst through the window. (Down below, Delilah cuts seven locks from Samson's hair.) The single figure in the stained glass window at the top of the painting stands above the word "ASIA," a reference to the seven major early churches of Christianity, which are described as the Seven Churches of Asia in Revelation. Above are two red cherubim standing above two red wheels, angelic beings that appear in Ezekiel and again in Revelation, praising God day and night. The Virgin Mary also participates in this economy of deep symbolical references to the Heavenly Jerusalem. In Revelation, a woman arrives in the sky "clothed with the sun, with the moon under her feet, and on her head a crown of twelve stars." The apocalyptic woman wails in pain as she labors to give birth to a child that she protects from a huge dragon with seven heads and seven diadems. The passage does not say that this is the Virgin Mary. However, medieval scholars certainly identified her as such. Van Eyck also seems to make suggestive connections between the mysterious woman in the biblical passage and the Virgin. Scholars have mapped out the zodiac signs on the floor. The Virgo sign is not visible. Thus the scholars have concluded that Van Eyck placed the Virgin directly over the sign of Virgo, the Virgin. In a larger sense, the Virgin is standing over the entire zodiac, the moon and the stars, just like the woman of Revelation. The Virgin's diadem is twinkling with pearl-like stars, just as the woman in the biblical passage has a crown of stars. Finally the delicate golden outlines of the Virgin's dress, and the fact that rays of divine sunlight are coming upon her, suggest that she is soon to be completely "clothed with the sun" like the woman in Revelation.

It is unfortunate that we are only looking at a part of the entire composition, only the left wing of what would have had at least one complementary panel. It is hard to speculate about the subject matter of the missing piece or pieces, especially since Van Eyck is such a rara avis. He follows certain standard iconographical tropes, to be sure. The Virgin wears blue and reads next to a batch of lilies. But the entire configuration is absolutely unique. Nor can we look at Van Eyck's other Annunciation paintings for substantive clues. Each one approaches the story in an entirely different way. For example, the *Annunciation* in the Museo Thyssen-Bornemisza, Spain, is eerily beautiful, showing Gabriel and the Virgin as two stony statues, lifeless but lifelike (Fig. 11.4). Van Eyck places the figures in stony niches, and yet they seem to operate outside of those frames, protruding and casting shadows from a light source coming from the upper right. Most curious is the reflection they cast in the obsidian glass in the rear wall, perhaps a reference to 1 Corinthians 13:12: "For now we see in a glass darkly, but then face to face." Here they are, face-to-face, proclaiming the mystery of the approaching Holy Spirit, the marble dove that hangs in the air impossibly, unless this is a real white dove. But no. It is all paint, all delicate painterly tricks, luring us into the web of its storymaking and storytelling, only to remind us that we are looking at art.

Van Eyck is a master of these visual and linguistic tricks. In the case of the *Man in the Red Turban*, Van Eyck signs his name in Latin on the lower band of the frame: "Jan van Eyck Made Me on October 21, 1433" (Fig. 11.5). At the top he writes in Greek "As I can," which even in Greek sounds like the words for "As Eyck can." The signature is a little joke, and even the painting on the frame is so much like a carving that you start to wonder whether Van Eyck painted the frame, as in the Thyssen *Annunciation*. Many scholars have concluded that this painting is a self-portrait of Van Eyck, but it is impossible to know for certain. The man in the painting looks at us with a suspicious gaze, almost as though he is simultaneously daring us and warning us about trying to assume that we can identify him.

Ultimately we cannot. In fact, we do not know what Van Eyck looked like. We do not know where he was born. We do not know when he was born,

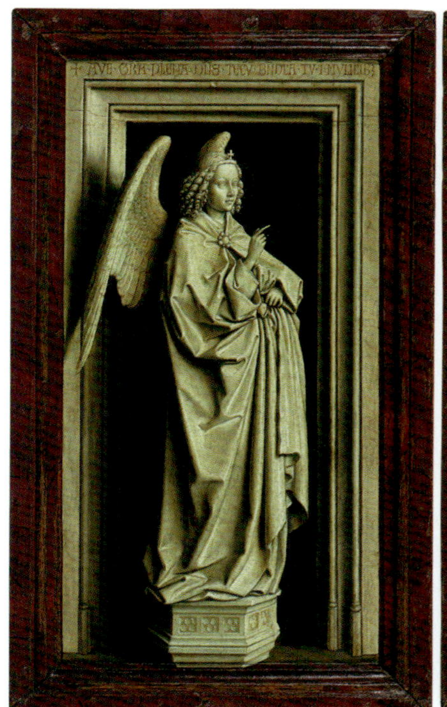
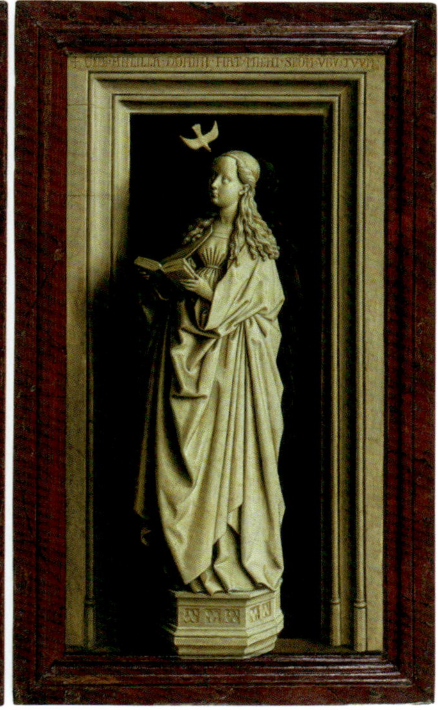

FIG. 11.4 Jan van Eyck, Annunciation, ca. 1433–1435. Museo Nacional Thyssen-Bornemisza, Madrid, Spain. Oil on panel, left wing 38.8 × 23.2 cm, right wing 39 x 23 cm.

although it was likely sometime around 1390. He first appears as a documented court painter in 1422 in Holland. By 1425 he was a superstar in the court of Philip the Good, Duke of Burgundy, not only as an artist but also as a special diplomat who was sent on "secret" missions, according to court documents. After many years of traveling he settled in Bruges, where he painted the National Gallery's *Annunciation.*

The details of Van Eyck's life are murky; documents are spotty and vague. Still, we can tell a great deal about Van Eyck's character from the painting or, rather, from information hidden under the painting. Technical investigations undertaken by the National Gallery of Art in 1994 revealed Van Eyck's incredibly

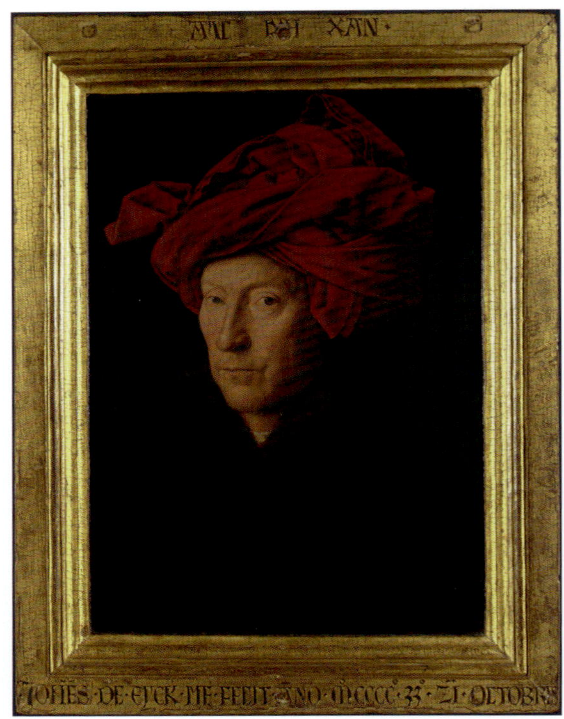

FIG. 11.5 Jan van Eyck, *Man in the Red Turban*, 1433. National Gallery, London. Oil on oak, 26 × 19 cm.

meticulous working methods. Van Eyck prepared the painting with a drawing complete with shadows and hatching, to a level of detail that is remarkable and unlike others of his time. The underdrawing also shows us that Van Eyck was never quite satisfied and was constantly tinkering to improve his painting. Originally Moses and Pharaoh's daughter were not in the painting, there were no lilies, and those spectacular floor panels were simply decorative chevrons. Thus, not only was Van Eyck extremely learned and clever, as evidenced by the rich theological and artistic references that abound in the *Annunciation*, he was also a perfectionist, constantly working to enrich and embellish the symbolic meanings in his paintings.

The underdrawing is even more valuable because the more superficial layers of the *Annunciation* have undergone a number of restorations, many of which are the stuff of nightmares. The worst "conservation" was undertaken in Russia, at the Hermitage Museum. Before the painting was in Russia, it belonged to the Chartreuse de Champmol, a once grand Carthusian monastery outside of Dijon, France. In 1819 it was purchased by the king of the Netherlands, who sold the painting in 1841 to Czar Nicholas I of Russia, the founder of the Hermitage as a museum. The painting was originally on wood. But wood expands and contracts with changes in temperature, thus causing paint to crack. The Hermitage was subject to greatly variable temperatures (and still is, I am told). In 1870 the museum decided to move the painting to canvas, which is less sensitive to changes in cold and heat. This transfer, however, was extremely dangerous, and most museum curators and conservators rejected the procedure. (I did not say it *is* dangerous because no one would ever undertake this procedure today.) The conservators at the Hermitage started by affixing paper and muslin to the front of the painting. Then they scraped and gouged the wood from the back of the painting until all that was left was a thin skin of color held together by the glue, paper, and muslin. The back of the painting was stuck onto canvas. In the final step the gluey paper was removed, often with solvents that removed important varnishes and even particles of paint. In other words, the painting would have sparkled and shimmered far more in its original state. Losses appear throughout the painting. A great deal of work was undertaken at the National Gallery in Washington, DC, to overcome the failings of this process. But it was an irreversible procedure with losses that cannot be recovered, despite extremely learned guesses as to the original state of the painting.

The transfer of the painting from Russia to America was no less dramatic. By 1930, revolution and civil war had brought the Kremlin to its knees financially. The government, desperate for money, turned to the Hermitage as a source of revenue. The curators did all they could to keep the paintings within the collection, seeing this as an act of cultural cannibalism, but it was beyond their power to do so, especially when Andrew Mellon, the famous American banker and Secretary of the Treasury, could so readily provide immediate cash to the governmental negotiators, a total of $6.5 million and $500,000 for the Van Eyck. That was during the American Great Depression, when people across the country were starving. So Mellon hid his paintings in a basement. In 1935 Mellon was placed on trial for tax evasion, at which point his secret cache was exposed.

Mellon explained the hidden paintings as part of a grand plan to build a massive public museum with free admission. In 1937 (on Mellon's birthday) Congress approved the construction of a museum on the National Mall, which was to be called the National Gallery. He never lived to see the paintings installed in their new American home, but his savvy purchases, politicking, and philanthropy all brought about the magnificent treasure house that we can visit every time we are in DC. For free.

It is interesting to consider the movement of that painting from Russia to America in 1930 because it is consistent with a much earlier trend. During the sixteenth century, Netherlandish art was extremely prominent in the New World. Augustinian and Franciscan missionaries came to the New World hoping to convert the indigenous Mexicans to Christianity, and they brought their art with them, usually in the form of prints. The style and iconography of these portable images appear on the painted walls of the colonial monuments of Mexico. One might argue that the Virgin of Guadalupe, which becomes one of the most prominent images of the Virgin Mary in Mexico, is a direct descendant of the annunciate Virgin.

The first image of the Virgin of Guadalupe, dated to 1531, is in Mexico City. But I will make my case with a more local version, that of the Virgin on the side of the Guadalupe Cultural Arts Center in San Antonio, Texas (Fig. 11.6). Created by Jesse Treviño in 2006, this forty-foot mosaic represents the Virgin as a candle, as *La Veladora*, in a blue mantle wearing a crown and in a gesture of prayer—all of which were evident in the Van Eyck *Annunciation*, although the Flemish Virgin prayed with her hands in the *orans* position. Holding the Virgin aloft is an angel who reminds us of Archangel Gabriel. Thus we have the components of the Annunciation. She stands on the crescent moon, which associates the Virgin with the woman of the Apocalypse. The massive eagle with the serpent in its beak refers most directly to the flag of Mexico, and the legend about the building of Mexico City. In medieval art, however, the serpent is a clear symbol of Satan. The serpent draws on the imagery of the Garden of Eden and the sin of mankind; the flowering nopal on the right draws on images of flowering plants that traditionally symbolized Christ's redemptive incarnation. The eagle, like the dove in the Van Eyck *Annunciation*, appears accompanied by bursts of light that draw direct lines to the Virgin. The golden tinge on the nopal

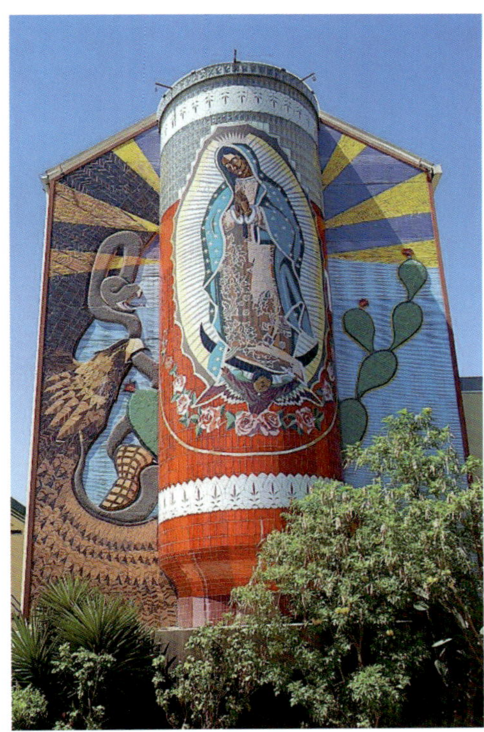

FIG. 11.6 Jesse Treviño, *La Veladora of Our Lady of Guadalupe*, 2006. San Antonio, Texas. Mosaic of glazed ceramic tiles.

plant that grows unencumbered against a bright-blue sky is drawing on the same visual tradition that produced the golden outlines of the lilies in the Van Eyck. Of course the monumental mosaic refers to contemporary practices of lighting candles with images of the Virgin Mary in religious contexts. But the resonances of the image, of the iconography, reach much further back in time.

The study of iconography, the consideration of shapes and forms and symbolic images as they change over time, allows us to see the ways in which artistic ideas move and morph from an Annunciation scene painted in fifteenth-century Flanders to paintings in sixteenth-century colonial Mexico to contemporary San Antonian mosaics—where the annunciate Virgin illuminated by the Holy Spirit now illuminates our walkways, glowing like a candle and as a candle.

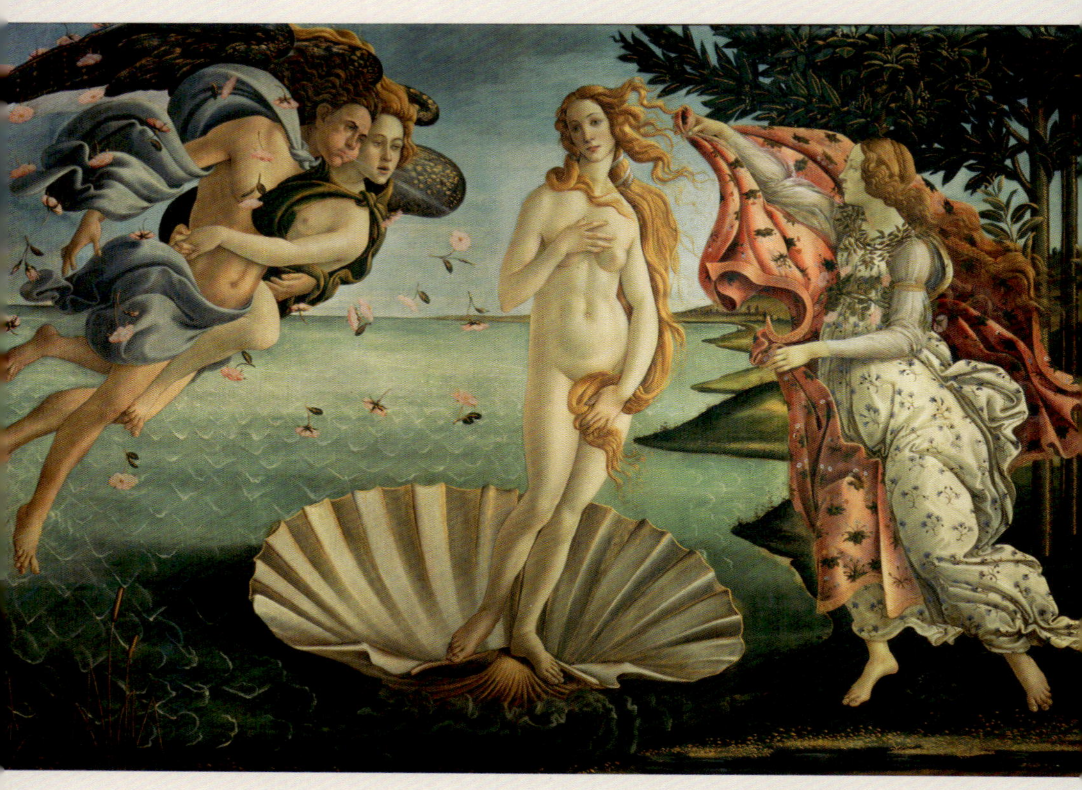

FIG. 12.1 Sandro Botticelli, *The Birth of Venus*, ca. 1483–1485. Galleria degli Uffizi, Florence, Italy. Tempera and gold on canvas, 172.5 × 287.5 cm.

$$Botticelli, \textit{The Birth of Venus}$$

Botticelli, *The Birth of Venus*

CA. 1483–85

ITALIAN RENAISSANCE ART

"Aphrodite the fair, the chaste, will I sing, she with the golden wreath, who rules the towers of sea-girt Cyprus, whither she was conveyed by the swelling breath of Zephyrus, on the waves of the turbulent sea, in soft, flocculent foam; and the Horae, with golden diadems, received her with joy, and dressed her in divine garments, and set upon her head her beautiful golden chaplet, and hung in her tresses flowers wrought in metal and costly gold. Her graceful neck and her radiant, snowy bosom they hung with chains of gold." These are lines from an ancient Greek poem in a compilation known as the Homeric hymns, a series of poems inspired by the stories of the pagan gods and inspirational to the fifteenth-century Florentine artist Sandro Botticelli (1445–1510) in his painting entitled *The Birth of Venus* (Fig. 12.1).* Venus stands weightlessly, almost as though she is floating like that aforementioned foam, balancing precariously in an upturned seashell. Her tilt to the right responds to the strands of white air coming from Zephyrus's puffed-up cheeks and Flora's breathy sigh. While Zephyrus works with great intensity, brow furrowed, gaze unwavering, Flora seems to have an air of insouciance, an attitude that relates to the face of Venus—serene, imperturbable, placid. That centralized, unflappable repose in Venus's tilted head belies the extraordinary movement of the intertwined Zephyrus and Flora and the elegant and sweeping prance of the goddess on the right. She is identified as a Hora,

* Botticelli, *The Birth of Venus*, Google Arts & Culture, https://artsandculture.google.com.

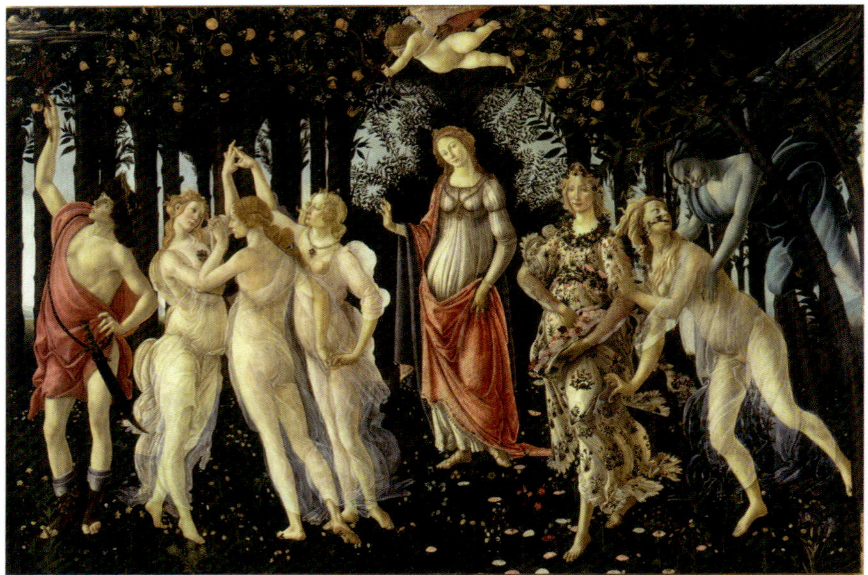

FIG. 12.2 Sandro Botticelli, *Primavera*, ca. 1480. Galleria degli Uffizi, Florence, Italy. Tempera and gold on panel, 207 × 391 cm.

one of the goddesses of the seasons also known as the Hours. Judging from the presence of the barely budding orange trees that line the coast, the young, white buds in the laurel tree that shades the goddess of the seasons, and the pink roses hovering in the air, it is most likely that we are looking at the Hora of spring.

Spring is an important subject for Botticelli and is the title of his other major mythological painting from this period, known as *Primavera*, the Italian word for spring, a painting that hangs but a few feet from *The Birth of Venus* in the Uffizi Gallery in Florence (Fig. 12.2). In addition to sharing a room in the Uffizi, the two works of art have a similar cast of characters. Again, Venus is our central figure under the darkened boughs of a mysterious copse. She appears with a few additional figures, Mercury at the far left, and the three dancing graces to our right. On the right side of the composition we have three figures that appear to be precisely those in *The Birth of Venus*—Zephyrus, Flora, and the Hora of spring. But not exactly. Rather, these are Zephyrus, Flora the goddess of flowers, and Chloris, the Greek nymph who was an earlier version of Flora. Botticelli's painting brings to life the metamorphosis of Chloris into Flora. The radical, almost violent flowers that are shown jutting from Chloris's mouth are given a controlled setting, now as decorative elements on Flora's billowing white dress, almost the same dress as the one worn by the Hora in *The Birth of Venus.*

In *The Birth of Venus,* we also witness a metamorphosis where flowers transition from being wild and fluid to tamed and civilized. The pink flowers on the left portion of our painting flutter and flip vigorously, but in the center of the painting they are fewer in number, which contributes to a sense of order and calm. The roses are more than decorative details. They enhance the narrative structure of the painting. In the placement of the roses there is an echo of the composition of the painting's protagonists. For example, two roses to the right of Zephyrus and Flora appear similarly intertwined. The uppermost rose next to Venus's right arm, another blanched, pink flower, turns its blossoms or "face" toward us, while the two cascading roses below create a triangular formation that mimics the shape of the goddess's torso. This rosy dance is brought to order in the stabilized ornamentation of the Hora's dress, and will soon be surrounding Venus when she dons the cloak, which is rosy both in ornamentation and shading. The roses have been trapped, processed, and turned into the dye that colors the rosy-hued cloak. That floral transformation illuminates the main metamorphosis, that of Venus, who is being blown into feminine form from flocculent foam.

"Flocculent foam," the Homeric hymns tells us. Flocculent is a translation of the Greek word *malakos,* which means soft. And other translations of the poem go with just that simple word. But this Greek word is more poetic than that. It is a word that appears in the *Odyssey* to describe the grassy meadows and cushiony bedding, things that make you want to touch and feel that softness. Thus the word "flocculent" is fitting because its allusion to wool enhances the sensation of seafoam, which, like unprocessed wool, is soft and loose and cloudlike.

Botticelli enhances that sense of *malakos* by painting on canvas instead of wood. This is a major contrast between *The Birth of Venus* and *Primavera,* the latter having been painted on a wooden panel. It is for this reason that scholars do not believe the paintings were intended as a pair but rather as separate commissions. Those two different material settings help explain the distinct tonalities of the paintings—darker in the *Primavera*, lighter in the *Birth of Venus*. The way the paint sits on the surface of the wooden panel allows a deeper, more saturated color scheme—reds are rich, skin is creamy, that forest is ominously murky. The more violent exchange between Zephyrus and Chloris is also better suited to these darker hues. Botticelli did something unusual in using canvas for his *Birth of Venus*. This was not a common practice because canvas absorbs pigments, giving them a muted look. In fact, if we look really closely, with the help of the high-resolution image made by the Google Cultural Institute, we can actually see the canvas through the paints. Botticelli's selection of canvas was intentional. That white linen underpinning allowed for a brighter color scheme, giving this painting a sense of airiness both in spirit and tonality—her weightlessness on that shell, the flocculent foam, the pervasive presence of the breezes and air and wind, the way that all of the figures appear to levitate above the earth, shell, sea. This buoyant ambience creates that sense of *malakos,* that softness which begs to be touched.

The paint that Botticelli used for both is called tempera, which is a combination of colored pigment and egg yolk. This may not seem all that remarkable. I certainly didn't think so until I had to try my hand at it in graduate school. It was a disaster. Egg yolk is sticky and dries really quickly. This means that you cannot move the paint once it hits the surface because it is almost already set. And this is not paint by number. These artists were not just painting with blobs of paint like we might paint a room. Artists would draw tiny, skinny, individual brushstrokes in a cross-hatching technique. Forms created by the artist are made up of an excruciating number of teeny, juxtaposed lines. The artist had to be both quick (because of the egg) and terribly precise. My time as a Renaissance artist was short. As was my temper. My tempera produced little more than a paintbrush hard as a rock, it was so sticky with egg.

Botticelli also painted with gold. By grinding the metal into a fine powder, Botticelli highlighted, in a literal way, the description in the Homeric hymn of Venus's many golden features. Botticelli used actual gold in his paint to create highlights throughout the painting—the feathery details in the divine wings of Zephyrus, the sheen in Flora's cloak, the edges of the roses that flutter in the sky, the wavering hair of Venus, the edges of her scalloped transport, the ornate hem and collar of the garment held by the Hora, and the shafts of the long, dark, green laurel leaves in the upper right-hand corner, an edgier, sharper version of the green feathers in the wings of the god. It is not unusual to see gold leaf in paint during this period. It is a rather standard feature of paintings from the early Renaissance, especially for saintly figures. However, Botticelli takes that traditional technique and uses the gold in a subtle way, in a way that adds to the ethereal, otherworldly nature of his figures. Those gilded glimpses add to that sensation of *malakos.*

Yet at the same time that we can recognize the softness of this moment, there is something precarious or brittle in the painting, something a bit harsh in the outlines. The composition, the embracing of Venus, is quite tender. So are the floating flowers and the way that they balance so harmoniously with the draperies on the right. Venus herself—her sloping shoulders, her swaying pose, her undulating hair—is also evocative of *malakos,* of alluring softness. But Botticelli's outlines are not, strictly speaking, soft. His black outlines, even when creating shading, are strict and crisp. The outline of her chin is not soft and suggestive, it is clearly delineated. The waves in the sea are repetitive and appear as formal V shapes, sitting on a glassy ocean with little intimation of depth or variation. The Hora's profile is structured and static, evocative of a carved portrait on a coin, and the choreographed placement of the trees suggests order, not nature.

Botticelli's approach to landscape really bothered Leonardo da Vinci (1452–1519), one of Botticelli's pupils. In his *Treatise on Painting,* he warns young painters that they cannot be considered worthy of praise if they cannot paint universally well:

He is not universal who does not love equally all the elements in painting, as when one who does not like landscapes holds them to be a subject for cursory and straightforward investigation—just as our Botticelli said such study was of no use because by merely throwing a sponge soaked in a variety of colors at a wall there would be left a stain in which could be seen a beautiful landscape. He was indeed right that in such a stain various inventions are to be seen. I say that a man may seek out in such a stain heads of men, various animals, battles, rocks, seas, clouds, woods and other similar things. It is like the sound of bells which can mean whatever you want it to.

But although these stains may supply inventions they do not teach you how to finish any detail. And the painter in question makes very sorry landscapes.

Leonardo implies that Botticelli is one of these people that "does not like landscapes." Botticelli's consistently meticulous brushstrokes and almost universal suffusion of light throughout the work are contrary to a sense of naturalistic atmospheric recession.

It is here that Leonardo thrives. Leonardo defines landscape specifically through soaked-sponge forms. Those soft browns, ochers, blues, and greens recede mysteriously and naturally into the distance, heightening the thoughtfulness and inexplicable air of the sitter, Mona Lisa or Madonna Lisa (Fig. 12.3). Leonardo challenges his viewer to suppose that there are possible meanings, to supply inventions. Where do those roads lead to? What does that bridge link? What body of water is that? Are those trees in the distance? Or are those shady grottos or mountains? It looks like something a thrown sponge might produce. In his writing, Leonardo both affiliates himself with Botticelli, suggesting that he has learned from the earlier master's principles, and that he subsequently superseded his master, philosophically and pictorially. Leonardo suggests that Botticelli doesn't understand that those suggestive marks are the best way of attaining a naturalistic representation of nature and getting into the psyche of the viewer. What Leonardo doesn't understand (or doesn't value) is that Botticelli is not trying to provoke the viewer into imagining rocks and clouds and woods and blurry distances. Botticelli gives the scene a delicate precision, almost as though the figures and forms in the painting are suspended in air.

This delicacy, this mannered appearance, may seem ornamental or superficial when compared with the Leonardo. These are definitely pejorative words in our daily parlance. But stripped of those connotations, there is something that is of-the-surface in the painting of Botticelli—Venus is not on the shell, she hovers above it. Her hands rest on top of her bosom, just on the surface (*super*) of her skin (*ficial* coming from *facia*, the Latin word for face). Venus's face is also modeled in a way that approximates perfection, not depth. Her face exudes delicate and perfected symmetry. The outlines of her features are precise and porcelain, in terms of tone and touch. She appears cool and distant, far too beautiful and

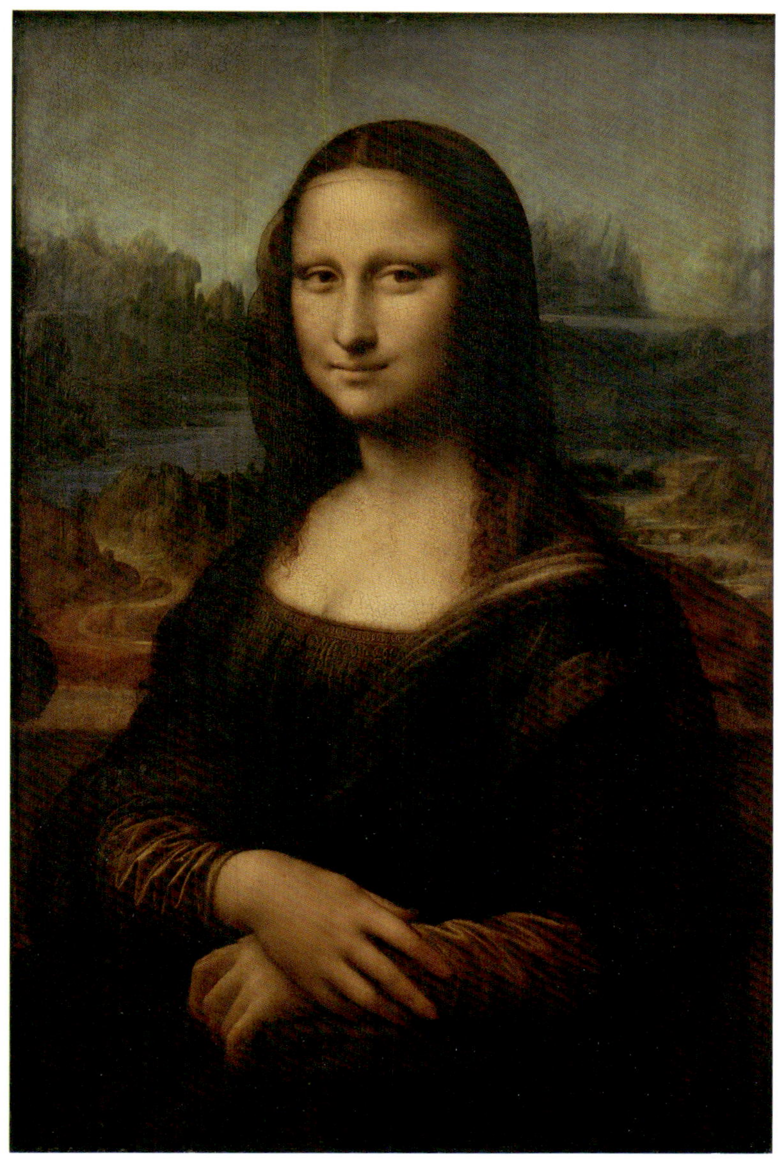

FIG. 12.3 Leonardo da Vinci, *Mona Lisa*, ca. 1503–1506. Museé du Louvre, Paris, France. Oil on poplar panel, 77 × 53 cm.

perfect to look you in the eye. And she does not. Her gaze is distracted, perhaps in thought or perhaps in the knowledge that she is on another level, that as much as we mortals stare and study we shall never attain nor understand her or her beauty. Botticelli uses a style that expresses the very exteriority of her beauty—clean, crisp, visible black outlines; thin layers of paint. It is almost as though he has laid her down, as delicately as possible, on the uppermost layer of the canvas so as to say that she is all surface.

This is quite a contrast with Leonardo's lady. Mona Lisa also avoids our gaze. Her shifting eyes also look off into the distance, out of the picture plane. Yet the two women present an interesting inversion. Venus's gaze is murky and gauzy, but the rest of her figure is ordered and specific and focused. Mona Lisa's gaze has a specific focus, looks at a single spot or individual, but the rest of her figure is murky. Leonardo seems to capture her relaxing into her left shoulder, leaning in toward the viewer in front of the painting, even as she holds her head high. Her form literally embraces, metabolizes, that chair, her dark-brown cloak melding with the shape of the wooden form. Her hands melt onto that armrest, and into each other, softly curving and enveloping each other. Much like that spongy landscape beyond, it is difficult to decipher where and how her dress falls and folds. Leonardo's use of those blurred outlines, that *sfumato* or smoky technique, heightens the sense that she is actually sitting in a chair (not hovering like a delicate goddess of the highest order), that her clothes are weighty and worldly (unlike Venus's garment, which seems to belong to the wind, not the world), and that she is pensive and contemplative and complex (unlike our goddess who is all beauty and all surface).

Clearly we have two different painters, with two different subjects, and two different styles to enhance those differences. One is not better than the other. But our appreciation of Leonardo da Vinci, our sense of his genius, is a bit stronger. I think that might be because of two things. First, I think it is the way Leonardo was so keen on representing his figures in a dimensional space, with a sense of naturalism and volume and depth. His use of linear perspective in *The Last Supper* in Milan is precise and scientific. All parallel lines converge on a singular point, the vanishing point, in this case at Christ's left temple. The result is that we intuit a sense of depth, a sense of three-dimensionality, and that we feel Christ has form and volume and weight. That vanishing point is all in relationship to the viewer's line of sight. So that's one thing. I think that we like things that are on a human scale. I am not saying that we are total narcissists. But maybe a little bit. The second thing that I think drives our great appreciation of Leonardo is that he is an innovator. We love innovators—a man who gave softness to the human form by using *sfumato* to such great effect; a man who designed tanks and machines that could fly; a man who could capture the psyche of his female sitter in a gaze that is at once inviting and disdainful. Leonardo is praised for his experimentation with tempera and oil in *The Last Supper,* even though it was a total technical disaster and that strange combination started falling off the wall almost as soon as it was painted on.

Botticelli is not an innovator, nor is he trying to be. He does not intend to make his Venus tangible, believably three-dimensional, volumetric. She is supposed to be aloof and untouchable, divine not human. Similarly, he is uninterested in a singular vanishing point. He does not use linear perspective because he isn't trying to make the scene cohere in a scientific way. This isn't science. This isn't realistic or human. This is otherworldly, spiritual, abstract, out of time, beautiful beyond human comprehension. Botticelli never left Florence except for a brief moment in Rome, where he painted a panel along the walls of the Sistine Chapel in 1481. He had little interest in the up-and-coming activities of Leonardo or the later painter of the Sistine Chapel, Michelangelo. He showed no curiosity about developments in Flemish painting, specifically their luxurious exploration of oil painting. Essentially, he was, as the scholar Daniel Arasse writes, "incontestably modern." Modern meaning Florence in the quattrocento, which is the Italian way of saying fifteenth century. He was breathing the immediate moment, not trying to go beyond that. And why not? He was living in Florence during one of the most extraordinary moments in that city's history, in the heart of the period of grand rebirth or renaissance. Florence was an amazing place of incubation because it was so rich in poets, painters, and patrons. The most important patrons were from the Medici family—the famous, untouchable, banking despots that supported the world of the arts, and specifically Botticelli. Both mythological paintings—*The Birth of Venus* and *Primavera*—were painted under the auspices of Lorenzo di Pierfrancesco de' Medici, the cousin of the better known Lorenzo de' Medici, known as the Magnificent. The Medici fostered an environment for their prized artists to thrive artistically, and not simply because the Medici paid them well and provided them with a constant source of commissions. The Medici also provided their artists with access to antiquity, to ancient texts and artifacts, which they were also collecting with intensity. Thus the artists under the Medici arm were skilled, supported, and well-read.

The discovery and newly revived appreciation (or even obsession) with the texts and art of antiquity are some of the most significant and definitive elements of this moment of rebirth. The famous art historian Erwin Panofsky argued that the best expressions of the Renaissance were those moments in which the classical forms of expression were united with classical content—a union that he found emblematized in Botticelli's works. We can see that in the close relationship between the words of the Homeric hymn and the painting. A number of ancient texts also circulating during this period described a painting by Apelles, considered to have been the greatest Greek painter. The painting no longer existed, but Botticelli had the poetic descriptions from Antipater of Sidon, Archias, and Democritus, among others. These all spoke of a Venus that Apelles had painted rising from the sea. In repainting the same scene, Botticelli was not only showing his own intelligence in having read these texts, but he was also advertising his skill. In other words, he was saying he was as great as the greatest painter of antiquity.

In addition to those textual sources that were interwoven in the painting, Botticelli was also studying statuary from antiquity. It is a stunning thing to imagine this period of early archaeology, where scholars were finding and digging out masterpieces from their own classical past. They were literally "unearthing the past," to use the title of Leonard Barkin's fabulous discussion of these rediscovered marble treasures. One such statue is the Aphrodite of Knidos (Fig 4.4). There are a tremendous number of copies of this statue, but there was a specific one that belonged to Botticelli's patron, known as the *Venus de Medici*, the same statue that astonished Nathaniel Hawthorne in his visit to the Uffizi in 1860. The similarities to Botticelli's Venus are evident—aside from looking over a different shoulder and a shorter hairstyle, the pose is almost exact. The muscles of the *Venus de Medici* are soft, her limbs are elongated, her shoulders slope at a similar angle, and her hands cover just about the same amount of her femininity. She is also white. White marble, of course. Similar to the whiteness of the flesh of the Botticelli. The flesh of Botticelli's Venus is pinkish, her lips are red, her hair is golden blond—so she is not entirely white. Yet neither was the *Venus de Medici* originally.

Mark Abbe has discussed the exciting remnants of color and paint that enlivened statuary of the Greco-Roman tradition, much of which is hard to see now. What was visible to the naked eye was quite brutally removed during the nineteenth century. When they were coming out of the ground, being discovered in the countryside and shipped to the grand villas of people like the Medici, these statues were still painted, still embellished with red painted lips and flesh tones on the skin. Many of the statues of divinities had golden hair. So did the Medici *Venus.* And this is how Botticelli saw her, how he studied her. Thus Botticelli's gold paint alludes to ancient textual sources, like the hymn, but it is also directly referencing the ancient statues that were literally emerging from the earth, like Venus, emerging from the sea. And she is so utterly sculptural, when you think about it. She looks like a marble statue in her static pose and distant gaze, a marble statue that has been painted—which is, in a sense, what she is.

Botticelli was also studying students of antiquity. In other words, he was part of a conversation with other writers, scholars, and poets about these remnants of antiquity. The famed poet Angelo Poliziano also drew upon the ancients to compose a poem about the emergent Venus. In one of his works, Poliziano describes a relief on the doors of the Palace of Venus. His is an *ekphrasis*, which, as we discussed in talking about Metochites and the Chora, is a description of a work of art that elicits reactions and emotions to a piece even when it does not actually exist. In the poem the goddess is wafted to shore by hovering and lascivious (*lascivi*) zephyrs. She appears pressing her hair with her right hand, covering with the other her sweet mound of flesh. This poem, which was a clear source of inspiration for Botticelli, says a lot about the artist and his process. He draws from Poliziano, showing her in the very pose in the poem, hair in hand. But he switches the hands. He takes the niche in Poliziano's description of Venus and makes it into a seashell. And he takes on the poet's description of Venus as "*Una donzella non con uman volto*" or the sweet, young woman with a beyond-human face. That is not an easy thing to paint. But Botticelli does that by showing Venus with a face that is remote, distant, and so perfect that it goes beyond naturalistic or human measure. Thus Botticelli is not a slave to the texts or inspirations. He uses them and studies them, but not in a prescribed way, and he is looking at a variety of inspirations—at scholarship and artistry of the past and the present.

Stylistically, Botticelli's painting has much in common with two categories of art that were quite common in earlier Florentine art. There is much that ties Botticelli's style and composition to early fifteenth-century tapestries, which were a most lavish means of coloring the walls of familial homes. In tapestries, such as those of the famed Unicorn series, figures are in the foreground, not set within a deeper landscape (Fig. 12.4). Flowers are omnipresent and highly symbolic. Both characteristics resonate with the painting by Botticelli. There is a connection in terms of technique as well, as these were actually woven with threads made of gilded wool, just as the Venus painting has strands of golden paint throughout. Finally, the purity of the centrally placed white unicorn (who also appears in a niche) provides a visual tie between the painting and the woven masterpiece.

Another category of art object that consistently placed figures in the foreground is the *cassone* (or *cassoni* in the plural), a large, rectangular box that was used to hold the trousseau of a young bride (Fig. 12.5). The front of these *cassoni* were also painted with figures close to the foreground, with little interest in naturalism in the landscapes, and no concern for a unified one-point perspective. Generally the paintings on the *cassoni* are tales of conquest, which in the context of marriage is a little unsettling. It is worth noting that both *cassoni* and tapestries are essentially furniture. They were used to decorate walls and hold personal belongings, and quite often placed in bedrooms. It is believed that the painting by Botticelli was also in a bedroom, that of Lorenzo, whose name is painted implicitly in the trees on the right—laurel trees: Laurel/Lorenzo.

Botticelli's Venus is simultaneously relevant to Christian thought and resonates with biblical personages, specifically Eve and the Virgin Mary. Scholars have seen the nudity of Venus as a suggestion of Eve before the Fall, painted in all her purity, before the necessity of donning clothes so as to cover her shame. It is hard to read the gesture of the Hora and the splendid quality of her robes in relationship to the pain and suffering associated with the expulsion of Adam

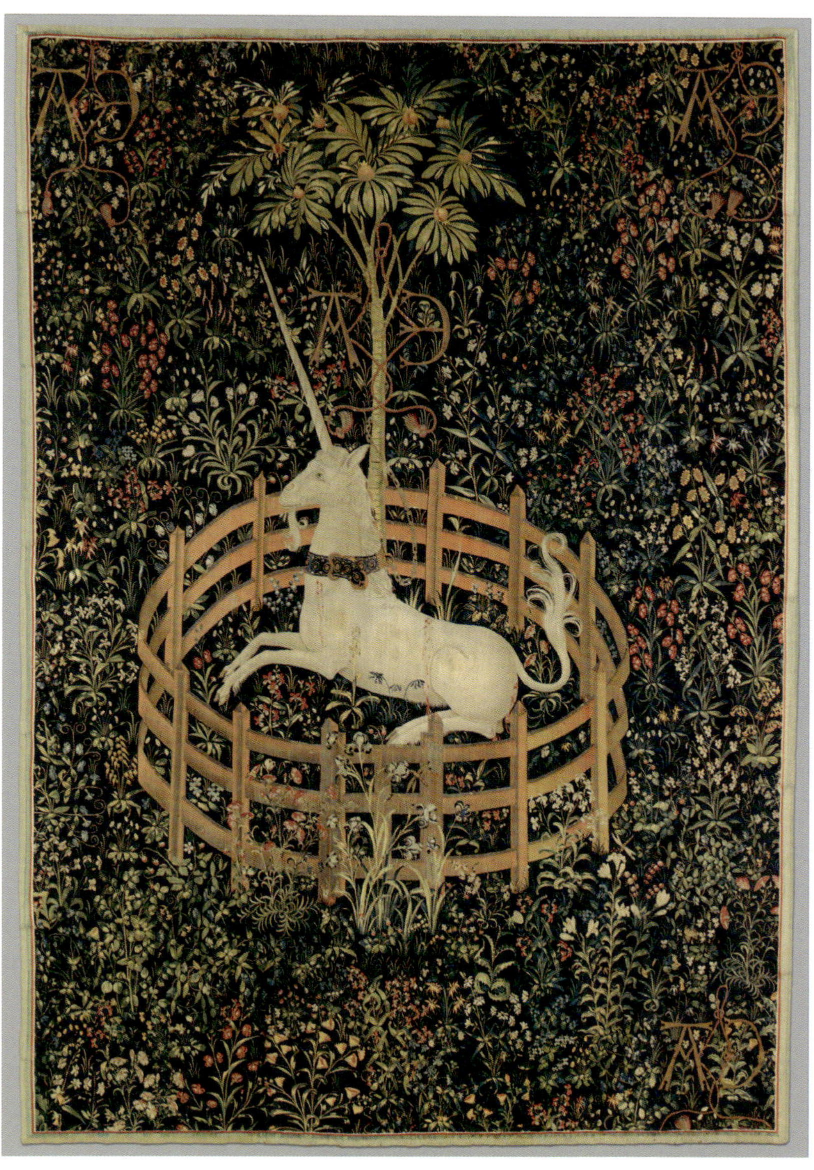

FIG. 12.4 *The Unicorn in Captivity.* From the Unicorn Tapestries, 1495–1505. Metropolitan Museum of Art, New York. Wool, silk, and metal threads. 368 × 251.5 cm.

and Eve from the Garden of Eden. Nevertheless, there are visual connections between Venus and Eve in the realm of painting, as Masaccio's woeful Eve was certainly an inspiration for Botticelli's Venus (Fig. 12.6). The differences might seem to outweigh the similarities at first glance. Masaccio's Eve throws her head back, her face contorted in woe—mouth ajar, eyes dramatically upturned but closed. Eve's hair sits flatly against her head and is mostly covered by the hands and arms of Adam, with which he conceals his face. Botticelli's Venus has hair that is thick and wild. It catches in the wind and flows along the left side of her sinuous body. She bends her head gently over her right shoulder in a way that further emphasizes the elegant shape of her figure, that S-shape curve. But different though their moods may be, the head positions of the two women are at the same angle. They also cover themselves with the same hand positions. They both bend their right arms upward so that they can cover their breasts, and with their left hands they cover the pelvic area. Admittedly Venus does a less comprehensive job than Eve with her right hand. Eve is walking, crossing her right leg over left. If Venus were to take a step forward it would be with her right leg, which hovers so weightlessly. In so doing, she would easily be in the same position as Eve, right leg over left, moving from left to right. The central crease in the torso, the slight roundness in the lower belly, the shading along the left side of the right leg—many details suggest a correspondence between the two women and the two artists responsible for making them.

Another mode of interpreting Venus is as Mary herself. One of the Virgin's most famous titles is Stella Maris, star of the sea—like Venus, another star rising from the sea. Venus's purity and modesty (her hand position, her downcast eyes) are easily connected with those same qualities belonging to the Virgin Mary. Another possible invocation of Mary in the painting is the fact that Venus is standing in a shell like a white pearl. The Virgin's purity was often described as being like a pearl by the early Church Fathers. Christ's birth was also quite often alluded to as being like the creation or birth of a pearl, which was understood to be produced when lightning flashed past a shell; in other words, it is miraculous and produced by supernatural events. What appears to be the birth of a pagan goddess is referring to the miraculous Christian birth too.

Botticelli is responding to the discoveries and excitements of the moment

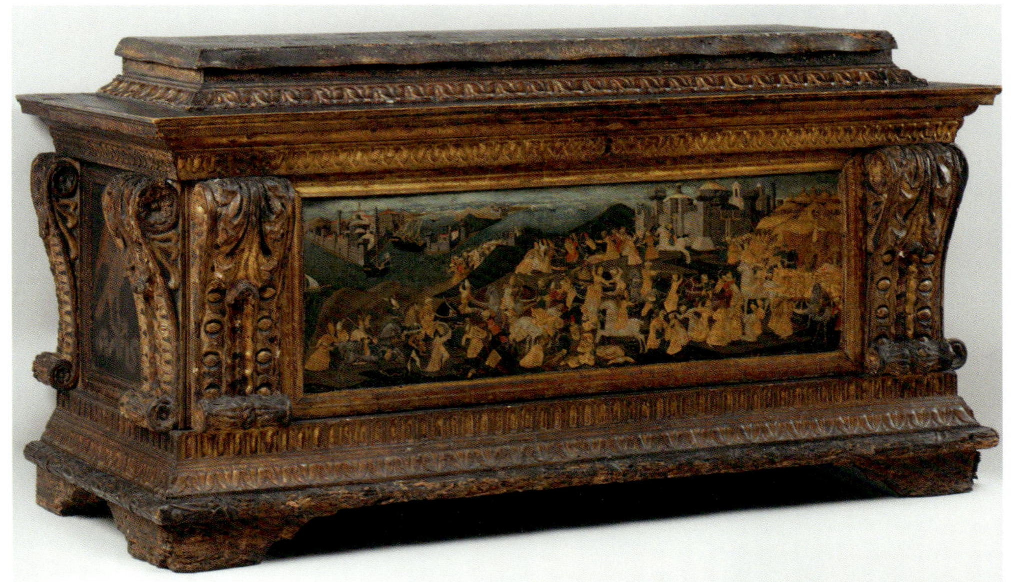

FIG. 12.5 Cassone with painted front panel depicting the Conquest of Trebizond, ca. 1461. Attributed to the workshop of Apollonio di Giovanni di Tomaso. Metropolitan Museum of Art, New York. Poplar wood, linen, polychromed and gilded gesso with panel painted in tempera and gold, 100.3 × 195.6 × 83.5 cm.

while retaining an interest in the past. He is curious about mythology without straying from Christian meanings. He is radical in his use of nudity and conservative stylistically. In a sense he is, like that emerging goddess, a transitional figure.

I think it is exciting to see all of these in-betweens—both in our painted figure and in our artist. But traditional scholarship is happier with divisions and categories. Medieval art stops. Renaissance art begins, looking away from that so-called Dark Age and solely at the classical, sublime purity of the ancient past. The fact that Botticelli dances between different aesthetics and inspirations may be one reason that earlier twentieth-century scholars felt the need to justify the Venus as a direct allusion to the Virgin. Scholars such as Ernst Gombrich, Panofsky's

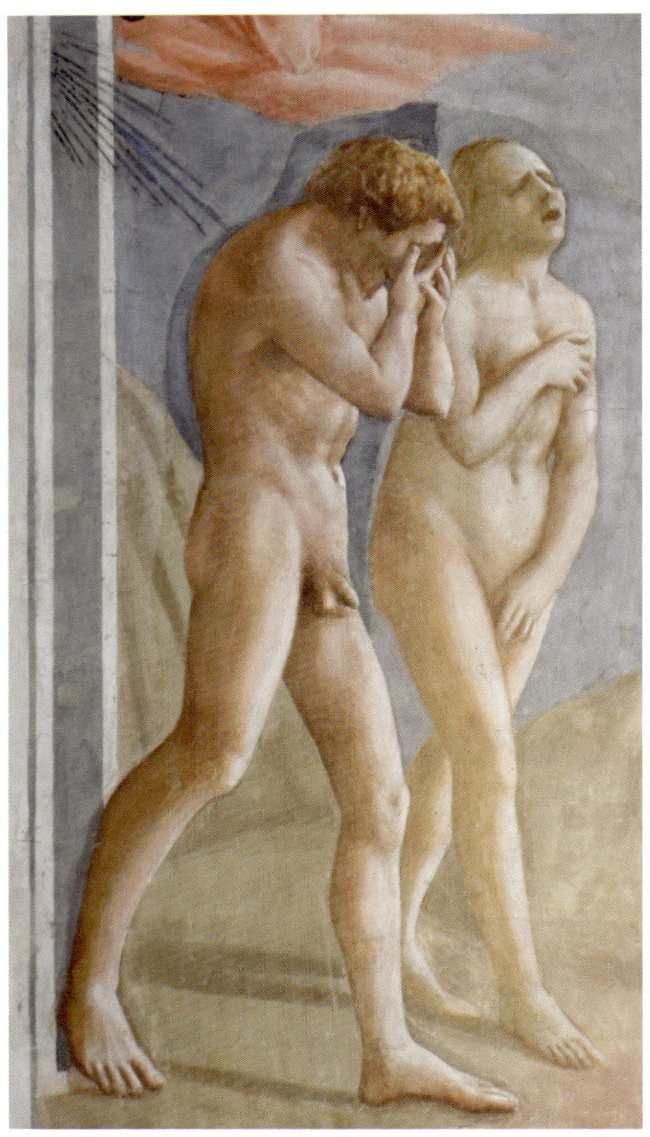

FIG. 12.6 Masaccio, *The Expulsion of Adam and Eve from Paradise*, ca. 1472. Brancacci Chapel, Santa Maria del Carmine, Florence, Italy. Fresco, 214 x 90 cm.

contemporary, proposed that there was a philosophy called Neo-Platonism that dominated in Renaissance circles. This school of thinkers promoted the idea that there was a contemplative means of ascending toward higher meaning. It is essentially what Abbot Suger proposed—material to immaterial. This interpretive tool was a means of seeing meaning beyond the surface of images, which could explain or justify problematic images. Neo-Platonism allowed a desexualized and nonthreatening way of seeing paintings that spoke to a pagan past. But we have to consider the context of this painting. This was for private viewing. It was not painted for a church. It was likely hanging in a room that functioned as a marital space. Nudity was relevant to the married couple, to their union and to the importance of birth. We also have to allow that these artists and viewers were not uncomfortable with multiple readings and meanings that perhaps were not all driving solely toward a Christian meaning, although that was certainly one possible lens for the work of art.

Actually, one of the first art-historical accounts about Botticelli is a bit confused. Writing in the mid-sixteenth century, Giorgio Vasari recorded the development of artistic talents from Giotto to Michelangelo in his book *The Lives of the Most Excellent Painters, Sculptors, and Architects*, which was first published in 1550. Vasari was a friend of Michelangelo, and he records a number of their conversations. Yet Vasari did not personally know all of the artists that he describes in his book—Giotto died in 1337; Vasari was not born until 1511. So there is a lot of narrative color to his history. It makes a great story that Giotto, while tending his flock in the countryside, drew on stones and sand and rocks, since he is supposed to be the first artist that draws from nature—in nature, on nature, from nature. Yet Giotto actually grew up in Florence and was the son of a successful blacksmith. Vasari, in telling the story of how art develops from raw nature, literally from scratch or scratches, into the glories of Michelangelo, needs a humble, simple beginning, the opposite of the Byzantine style, which he calls rubbish, clumsy, awkward, villainous, and gross. (He obviously never went to the Chora.)

Knowing the bigger agenda at hand helps us approach the writings by Vasari about Botticelli—a mere 7 pages to Michelangelo's 117, and a lackluster biography. Botticelli falls in about the middle of this progressivist narrative. Vasari certainly saw and admired the works of Botticelli, drawing upon *The Birth of Venus* for his own painting of the same name. (From that painting you would note that Vasari, although he wrote about those most excellent painters, was far from joining their rank.) But Vasari was one year old when Botticelli died, so we can assume that many of his stories are part of his grander scheme of highlighting the majesty of Michelangelo. In contrast with Michelangelo, who has the knowledge of "true moral philosophy and the gift of poetic expression," Botticelli is eccentric and distracted. When Michelangelo gets annoyed, he puts his frustrations into his art. For example, when according to Vasari a patron tells Michelangelo that the David needs a smaller nose, Michelangelo climbs up his ladder and pretends to work on it, throwing a handful of old marble dust on the floor. The patron is happy and Michelangelo climbs down, "feeling sorry for those critics who talk nonsense in the hope of appearing well informed." Botticelli, on the other hand, has a terrible and outrageous temper. In one story he gets so angry at the noises produced by a cloth-weaver living nearby that he sets up an enormous stone ("big enough to fill a wagon") such that it is set to fall and wreck the man's ceilings, floors, and looms. Botticelli is scatterbrained, can't focus on one thing at a time, gets involved in some rather questionable religious sects, and spends all of his money because he is disorganized and "haphazard," as Vasari says.

Thus Botticelli becomes an unfortunate and maligned stepping-stone in the path toward Michelangelo. But more than that, Vasari uses his anecdotes about Botticelli's sloppiness and his temper in order to dismiss the artist's style. Botticelli is eccentric and therefore so is his painting. This is a curious fallacy, but we do it all the time. The person on the movie screen is (in our minds) intricately linked to the person that walks around and goes to get coffee. Woody Allen makes a delightful comedy predicated on this false hope in *The Purple Rose of Cairo*. In the film, the handsome archaeologist Tom jumps right off the movie screen and into the arms of Cecilia, played by Mia Farrow. A letter to the Ethicist of the *New York Times* once worried that it was no longer possible to watch movies by Allen because of the director's grave personal failings. The Ethicist replied that we can still watch Woody Allen because art is bigger than one individual; art has a life of its own with layers of meaning and messages that have touches of the director, of

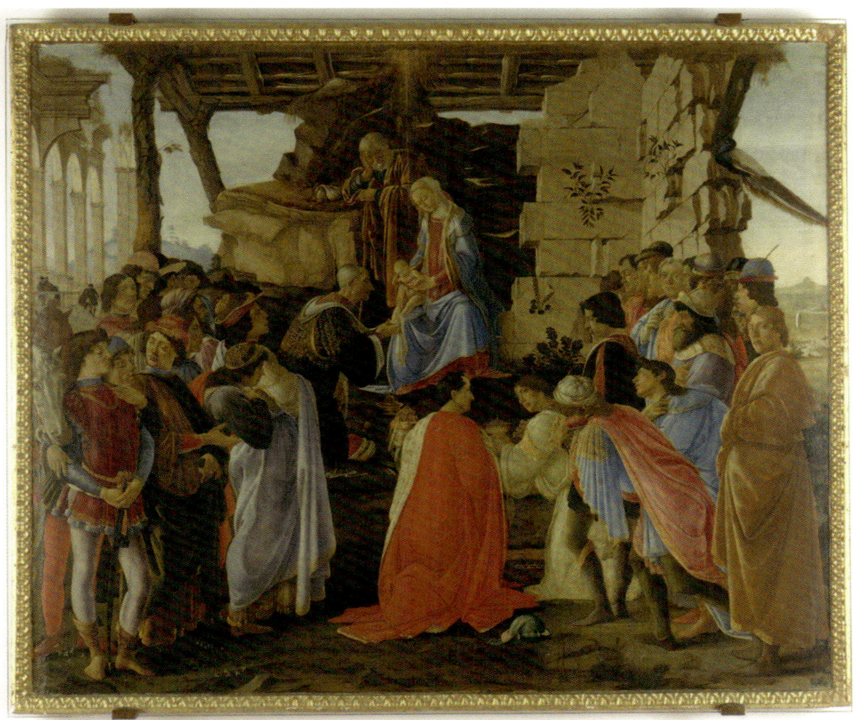

FIG. 12.7 Sandro Botticelli, *Adoration of the Magi,* ca. 1475. Galleria degli Uffizi, Florence, Italy. Tempera on panel, 111 × 134 cm.

the artist and of the actors, but within a much wider, broader, richer framework. The character we are seeing is not a person, and we do not see the artist in an unmediated way either—even when he appears to show himself in a painting. According to long tradition, the cloaked figure at the far right of Botticelli's *Adoration of the Magi* is a self-portrait of the artist (Fig. 12.7). But Botticelli the man is not the Botticelli in the painting. Even when he looks us dead in the eye, it's still Botticelli's version of Botticelli, not Botticelli.

Vasari also seems to be a little sloppy with his attribution from time to time. Art historians turn to Vasari for a great deal of information about the paintings produced during the Renaissance and have used his writings in order to understand the original location of a number of works of art that moved in later years. It is Vasari who noted the fact that the painting was in Lorenzo's house on the Via Larga. Vasari also gives *The Birth of Venus* its name. Botticelli did not. In fact, if we look closely, this is not the birth of Venus at all. The story of her birth is actually a great deal more crude. According to Hesiod's *Theogony*, written around 700 BCE, the goddess of love is born when Saturn severs his father's genitals and throws them into the sea. Out of the resultant mountain of foam Venus emerges. (The Greek name for Venus is Aphrodite, and *aphros* means foam.) At the same moment as this frothy birth, a rose bush blossoms on the land, thus establishing the traditional relationship between Venus and the rose. There are waves of foam below the seashell. We may have intimations of the mutilated body parts in the light cattails or bulrushes at the bottom of the painting. We certainly have roses. But these hints at the historical birth of Venus are secondary to the main narrative, which is really about her appearance in two senses of the word—both her beauty and her presence in the sea.

Vasari was not precise or utterly fair in his writings, but he certainly had staying power, not only in the title of the painting, but also in terms of how Botticelli was appreciated just after his death, which was very little. However, interest in Botticelli's works did reemerge in the nineteenth century, with the paintings by the Romantics and the pre-Raphaelites. These artists saw in Botticelli the hand of a melancholy dreamer, a lover of beauty and languid bodies. Women, water, flowers. Modern artists see other features of her lines and form and pose that are meaningful to more contemporary concerns—for example, Warhol uses the face of Venus to show the subtleties lost in the over-reproduction of famous faces. One of the most evocative, sublime, and, I would argue, honest odes to the painting by Botticelli is by Joaquín Sorolla (1863–1923), the Spanish artist of the late nineteenth, early twentieth century (Fig. 12.8).

The painting *After the Bath* is exemplary of Sorolla's ability to capture the glittering play of sunlight, through quick, thick brushstrokes as it dapples the young girl emerging from her swim in the ocean. Marcus Burke, senior curator at the Hispanic Society of America, has pointed out that Sorolla's bathing beauty is a clear allusion to the Venus of Botticelli. Both women emerge

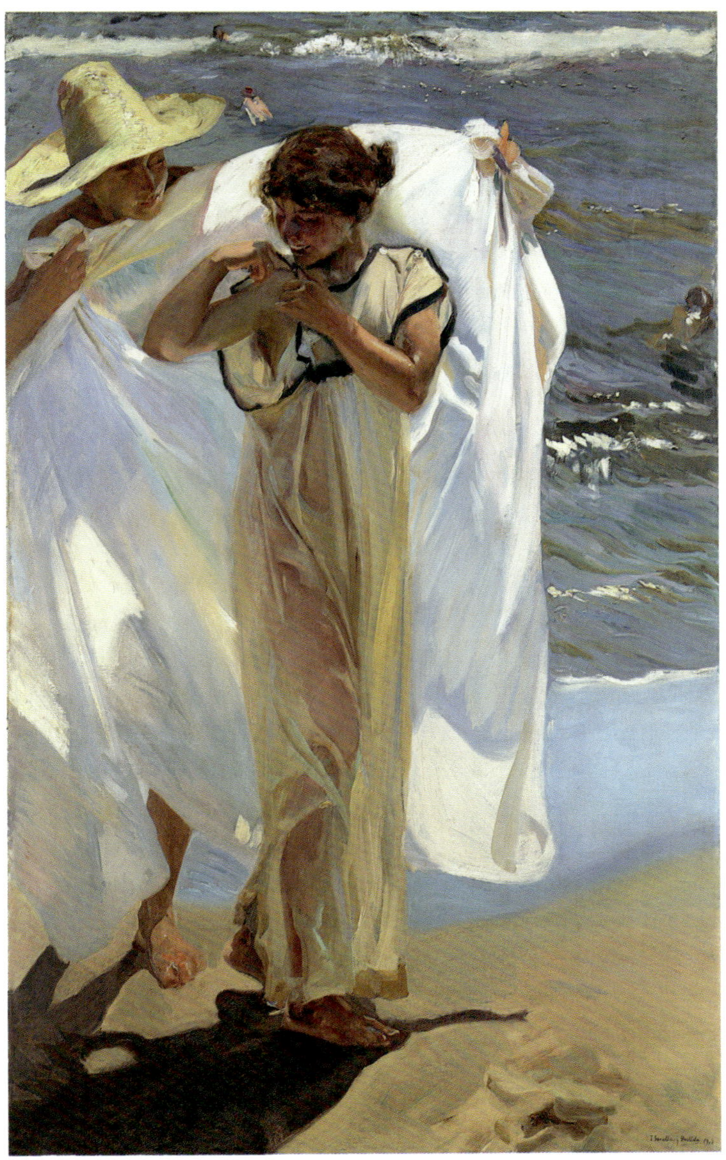

FIG. 12.8 Joaquín Sorolla y Bastida, *After the Bath*, 1908. Hispanic Society of America, New York. Oil on canvas, 176 x 111.5 cm.

from the sea, centrally placed, buoyant in their grace and ease. The boy with the broad-brimmed hat watches in a protective way from the side. He acts like Zephyrus and the Hora in one; he harnesses the wind and reaches out to offer her cover. And though this covering is less colorful than the ornamental one held by the Hora, the way Sorolla does white becomes more than just that, it has blues and purples, yellows and pinks. Both paintings are moments of transition—from water to land, from undressed to dressed—and also about art. The way the boy holds the variegated white sheet is like a backdrop, like a frame or canvas for the delightful girl whose form emerges from those thick, luscious brushstrokes of Sorolla's brush. It is majestic, this painting. Visitors to the amazing Hispanic Society have a special chance to breathe in the salty mists of Sorolla's painted sea, those hints of Botticelli's *Venus*.

Botticelli's painting speaks to and through a number of later artists and aesthetics and historical moments. But of course it did that in its day too. His painting captures the many textures of contemporary Florence—the scholars studying antiquity, the sculptures from antiquity, and the still-prevalent and relevant art from the medieval period. Botticelli was held in the highest regard in Florence, and he loved that city back. I do not think it is an accident that he embellishes his paintings with such a special focus on the flora and fauna. The meaning of Florence is just that—flowering. And this is what Botticelli brings us. It is a painting about the advent of spring, which goes hand in hand with blossoming flowers and manifestations of love.

In spring in Texas the laurel trees bloom, pollen is everywhere, pink roses slowly emerge. April is when San Antonio erupts into Fiesta, a weeklong celebration of parties and parades. The "Battle of Flowers" parade honors the fallen heroes of the Texas Revolution. Floats representing different facets of San Antonio—companies, communities, associations—are covered in bright splendid colors and, naturally, flowers. These celebrations have their earliest roots in courts and courting rituals of the Italian Renaissance. In fact, many traditions celebrated in contemporary San Antonio and Renaissance Italy are very much the same. For example, courtiers of the Renaissance would fill colorful eggs (*ovi odoriferi*) with perfume and bring them to their lovers. The cracking of the egg would create confusion and delight. San Antonians fill colorful eggs with confetti and use them during moments of fun and revelry and, like the Renaissance Italians, as expressions of spring fever. Botticelli's suspended beauty breathes directly into this moment of spring, this flirtatious time of transition, and he does so in a timeless and timely way.

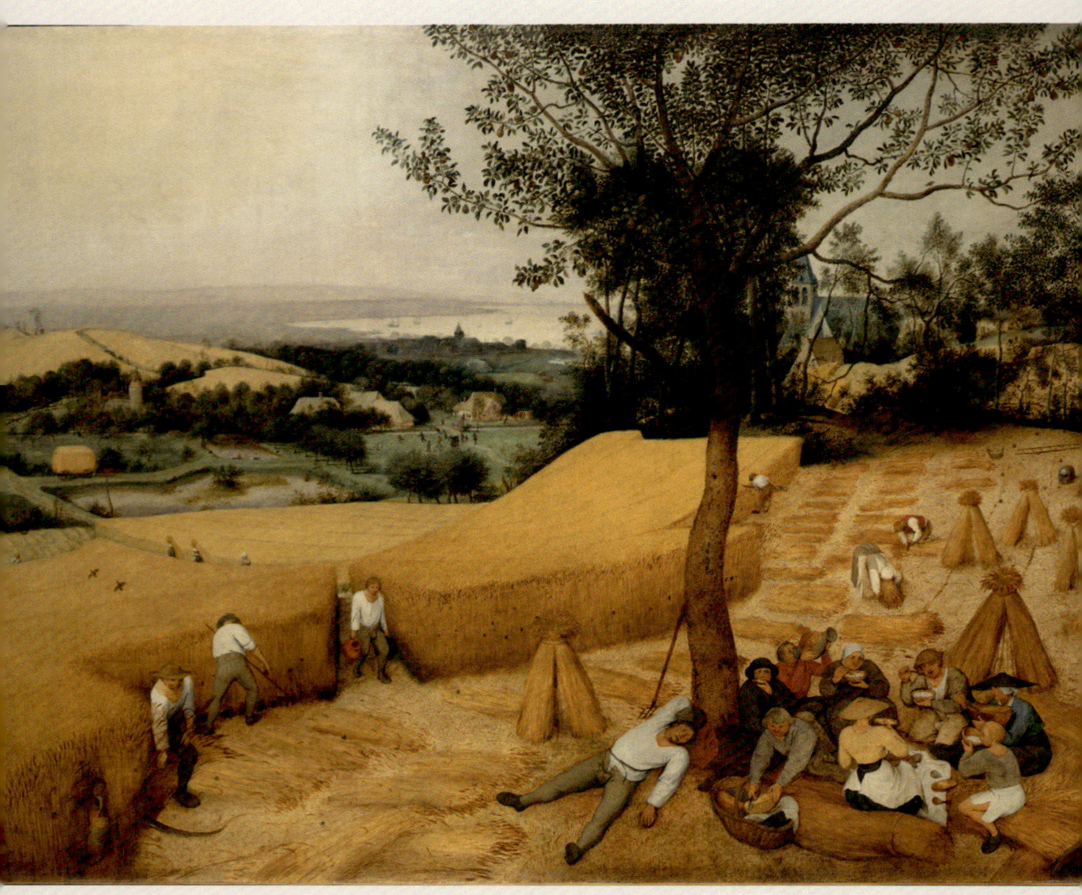

FIG. 13.1 Pieter Bruegel the Elder, *The Harvesters*, 1565. Metropolitan Museum of Art, New York. Oil on wood, 116.5 × 159.5 cm.

Bruegel the Elder, *The Harvesters*

1565

NETHERLANDISH ART

In the chapter about *The Annunciation*, by Jan van Eyck, we studied how every minute detail, every tiny corner in the painting is rich with meaning, with deep theological associations and cultural references. Actually seeing these details would have been impossible without Google Cultural Institute's astoundingly high gigapixel resolutions. When I realized that *The Harvesters*, by Pieter Bruegel the Elder (ca. 1525–1569), was part of the Google Cultural Institute, I thought that it would help only as a broad and general contrast (Fig. 13.1).* Van Eyck's painting is only about three feet tall, and some of the details we looked at were at most half an inch tall. Bruegel's painting is quite large compared to the Van Eyck *Annunciation*—it is one foot taller and four feet wider.

Jewel-like, tiny, extremely precise—these characterize Van Eyck. Remember Gabriel: blushing Archangel Gabriel with arched eyebrows, an almost indulgent half-lidded gaze, sweet and subtle dimples with a pert smile exposing twinkling white teeth. Now consider the centrally placed sleeping man in the Bruegel painting. His teeth are also exposed, what is left of them. His mouth is also ajar, but the message he brings is quite different. Golden words of God are not likely to emerge here, more likely a guttural snore. The Annunciation moment is surprising and addresses a sensitive topic, pregnancy, and a very unusual one at that. Gabriel's blush might be a reference to the surprise of his arrival and his

* Bruegel, *The Harvesters*, Google Arts & Culture, https://artsandculture.google.com.

message, this delicate conversation. Bruegel's man also has a ruddy complexion, but it is from the heat and the sun, from hours in the field. He is dead tired. His eyebrows lift into an arch but not as a means of enlivening or enlightening his face or to suggest a clever awareness. He seems to be, rather, in the middle of a deep sleep, a big breath, lost in a dream, eyes rolling back. No porcelain skin here. Bruegel's man is composed of unblended, sketchy strokes, of dark and muddy browns. Black hatch marks are readily visible and appear even in places where they might seem amiss—across his nose, along his chin. Big and broad versus tiny and delicate.

The sense of Bruegel's painting is expansive. The painting seems to grow past the frame—the hazy glow of the hay, the great gray of the infinite sky, the ever-expanding branches of the central tree. It is for this reason that I thought that the Google project image would be of little use. The effect of the painting is one of big shapes, bold forms, blobby figures that breathe (or snore) inelegantly.

Yet the painting, as it expands, also draws us in, deeper and deeper into the landscape that rolls into the distance. What seems so rough and sketchy at first blush slowly pulls us into a world of labor, land, and life that is punctuated with refined specificity, with moments and passages that make us realize that Bruegel is doing far more than painting a humorous scene of simple peasants. Nothing is simple with Bruegel. Not every last detail might have an exact symbolical or theological meaning, but Bruegel's *Harvesters* has the same depth of detail and import. What first seems to be a series of disorganized or unfocused forms, like the murky face of the man, coalesces into a grand encompassing study of man, nature, time, and beauty.

It is an epic painting. Broad brushstrokes in the sleeping man's face suit the broad and heroic landscape. Meandering pathways lead through hills and val-leys, past sweeping fields of golden wheat stalks toward distant verdant lawns peppered with dark-green groves. Yet it is a curious composition. It is not sym-metrical, and, in fact, it has moments of feeling somewhat off-kilter. Take, for example, the thick band of golden wheat that cuts across the painting. The blocky, volumetric, arrowlike form pulls us into the lower left corner and almost seems to leave us there, in a mass of weighty wheat. Angular outlines and pointing forms also communicate with complementary upturned arches. A curving scythe mirrors the U-shaped form of the landscape, which sweeps us up into a scene of distant expanses, rolling us through sprawling fields. We follow the movement of the three women walking through the field, accompanied by the two brown birds that fly nearby, into farther patches of wheat fields, in the direction of a hazy bay. That bright gray is inexhaustible. Modulated shades of gray for water and land and sky blend and fuse and melt, drawing us this time into the upper left-hand corner, into an endless, elusive, ethereal expanse.

The enigmatic and indecipherable distinction between land and sea has its direct antipode in the body of the sleeping man—a breathy distance contrasts with a breathing man who is weighty, grounded, sharply outlined. He (and his friends too) provide a stylistic and compositional counterbalance to that expansive sea scene. Still, like the endless sky, they draw us in. Drinking, eating, smiling, slurping, ignoring, staring. They are a merry band. Again we find ourselves pulled into a corner. This community draws us inward. There are no overt gestures of invitation. However, it is clear that anyone might join in, take a seat on that bushel of hay, and partake of the readily presented foodstuffs—pears, bread, milky porridge. The hat of the woman with her back toward us creates a sense of centripetal movement, outward in, like a spinning top, terminating in the tight, circular knot at the top of her hat, which is at the center of this group. If our eye follows along the bale of wheat on which she sits (which has the same shape and color as the bread she is eating), our eye moves from left to right, sends us into the right-hand corner, pulls us into a strange black hole or perhaps toward a jagged rock where the name Bruegel appears. Waves of wheat composed of streaky strokes abruptly turn into a dark, uneven frame for the pitch-black shape wherein the faintest presence of the artist resides, hidden in the corner.

In the upper right-hand corner, we enter a tangled mass of foliage and brush and the branches of pear trees. If you are using the Google Cultural Institute and you look into the darker recesses of that foliage you will see the image of a man. This fellow seems to be shaking the tree, getting the pears to fall for his friends below. It's sweet, yet you cannot help but worry. He is not in the most stable position. He is really high up. That ladder is really far below. Again we are drawn into the painting, into its stories, into its deepest corners. The central pear tree is a beautiful expression for the way that process works. It grounds the painting, but in an unusual way. It is meandering and filled with unruly branches, some of which jut off into dead stumps and dead ends, others of which continue to fluoresce outside of the picture frame. It provides a home for the snoring man and a lone partridge (yes, a partridge in a pear tree). Yet the tree is aimless, expansive, unruly, off-center, and cannot be bothered to stay within the structure of the frame.

This device of the paint pushing past the perimeter would have been remarkable in its original setting, in a room filled with other paintings of this size representing the seasons. The paintings were commissioned in 1565 by the wealthy Antwerp merchant Nicolas Jongelink for his suburban home. Six were painted. Unfortunately, only five remain. Between 1566 and 1596 something happened to one of the paintings. It might still be out there, ready to be discovered, as the protagonist of Michael Frayn's *Headlong* thinks he just might have done. If you haven't read *Headlong,* it is wonderful. You might not think that art historical research could have the makings of a true page-turner. Believe me, it does. Bruegel's paintings would seem to be ready-made for the romantic detective-story genre, not just because one is mysteriously missing but also because they are somewhat elusive in terms of their subject matter, driving much scholarly debate. The most accepted understanding of the cycle is that each panel represents two months: *Return of the Herd* is October/November; *Hunters in the Snow* is December/January; *Gloomy Day* is February/March; April/May would have been the missing painting; *Hay Harvest* is June/July; *The Harvesters* August/September.

A number of scholars believe that there may have been twelve paintings originally. This argument is based on the fact that the scene in *The Harvesters* has little in common with representations of September found in contemporary calendar cycles. Harvesting wheat, picking fruit, peasants eating and drinking—these are scenes that are commonly associated solely with August. This argument might seem too silly to bring up, a total straw man. Why would Bruegel worry about traditional modes of painting the months in these particular cycles? At the point that he was producing these panels, he was the apple of his patron's eye. It is unlikely that Jongelink, who had collected sixteen Bruegel pieces by his death, demanded certain figures and features in the series.

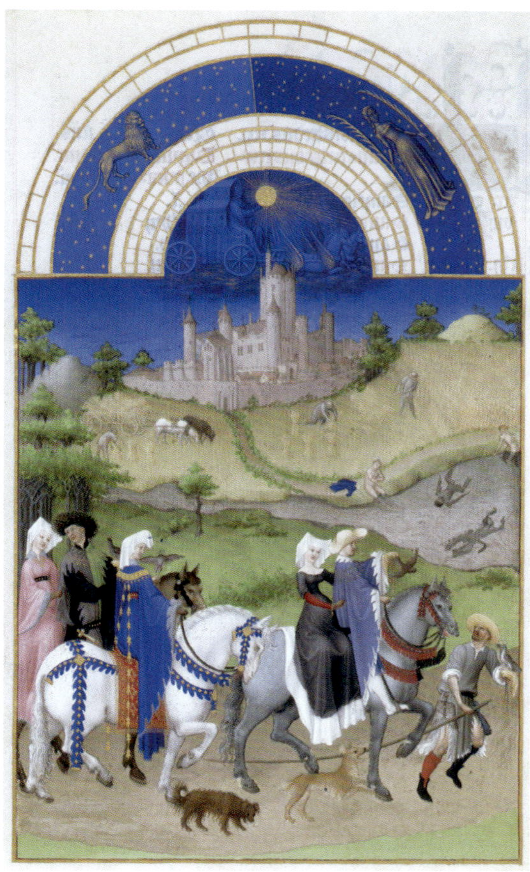

FIG. 13.2 The Limbourg Brothers, *August, Les Très Riches Heures du Duc de Berry,* 1411–1416. Musée Condé, Chantilly, France. MS 65, f. 8v. Colors and ink on parchment, 22.5 × 13.6 cm.

But it is worth noting that the illustration of calendar months was a tried and true artistic form with little deviation. Consider the masterpiece known as the *Très Riches Heures,* a book of hours intricately painted by the Limbourg Brothers for their grand patron Duc du Berry between 1412 and 1416. The Limbourg Brothers depict August with an elegant cavalcade of courtly figures who are on their way toward a hunt (Fig. 13.2). It is a scene of luxury and leisure—demure ladies with downcast eyes, tiny hips, and décolleté dresses, men with hawks poised to chase and pounce. And in the background men and women toil in the

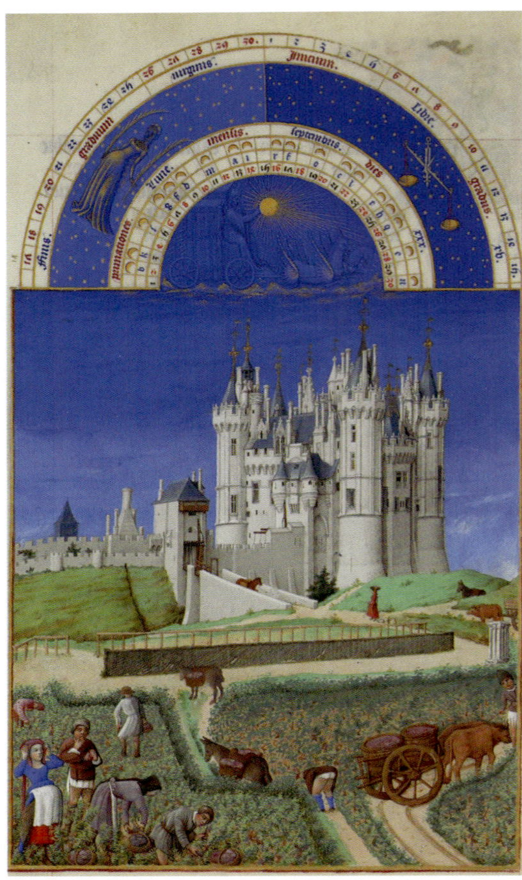

FIG. 13.3 The Limbourg Brothers, *September, Les Très Riches Heures du Duc de Berry*, 1411–1416. Musée Condé, Chantilly, France. MS 65, f. 9v. Colors and ink on parchment, 22.5 × 13.6 cm.

fields, cutting, collecting, and sorting bushels of wheat before taking a swim to cool off. Bruegel is certainly aware of the traditions associated with the months, and he embraces many of those features, even including the bathers. Following the curving pathway that draws us deeper into the painting and continuing on the path to the right, past the large cart piled with hay (called a haywain), we soon come to a rectangular watering hole where a number of pink, naked bodies are swimming and cavorting, climbing and watching, next to discarded piles of clothes. Although perhaps less grand than the chateaux belonging to the Duc du Berry, Bruegel includes a turreted, crenelated, cream-colored edifice in the background.

There is no reason to assume that Bruegel was tied to the traditional features of the months. Bruegel had no problem removing the courtly figures that were dominant in the images of August. Nor would he have been constrained from melding two months or two seasons together. He actually seems to do just that. In the Limbourg rendition of September, the castle clearly dominates the skyline, with a seemingly infinite array of icicle-like spires, towers, and turrets(Fig. 13.3). But the laborers are in the foreground, busy picking grapes from low-lying, pruned vines, sometimes none too gracefully, while carts rumble into the distance. There are also moments of repose—a man holds a bushel of grapes in his left hand and sneaks a taste with his right, while a woman takes a moment to fix her headdress before continuing again with her work.

Men and women in *The Harvesters* are also busy culling the fruits of the land—pears and wheat. As in the manuscript tradition, they stretch and strain to make the most of the crop, while carts rumble in the distance. The argument that Bruegel's paintings must be one particular month undermines Bruegel's capacity for invention, for imagination. In fact, he does not seem to be trying to replicate a specific month at all. The organic and seamless quality of the painting produces a *sense* of time. Bruegel does not include references to the zodiac, images of which appear at the top of all the Limbourg pages. Bruegel's scenes are not about keeping or recording time, they are about experiencing the *mood* of the season. Autumn. Long, heavy days; a warming yellow light that saturates and suffuses the sky and heats the land; weighty, soporific serenity.

The Flemish tradition was clearly important in the formation of Bruegel's aesthetic. Those tiny men and women in the background of the painting make us think of the Limbourg Brothers or Van Eyck and his wonderfully detailed *Annunciation*. But the figures in the foreground, the rounded bodies of the resting and working peasants, do not quite jibe with the delicate painterliness of Van Eyck and the Limbourg Brothers. There is something here that might look toward the other Renaissance, the more famous Renaissance in the south, in Italy. Traveling to Italy was de rigueur in the sixteenth century for northern European artists, who went to study the ruins of classical antiquity and the great

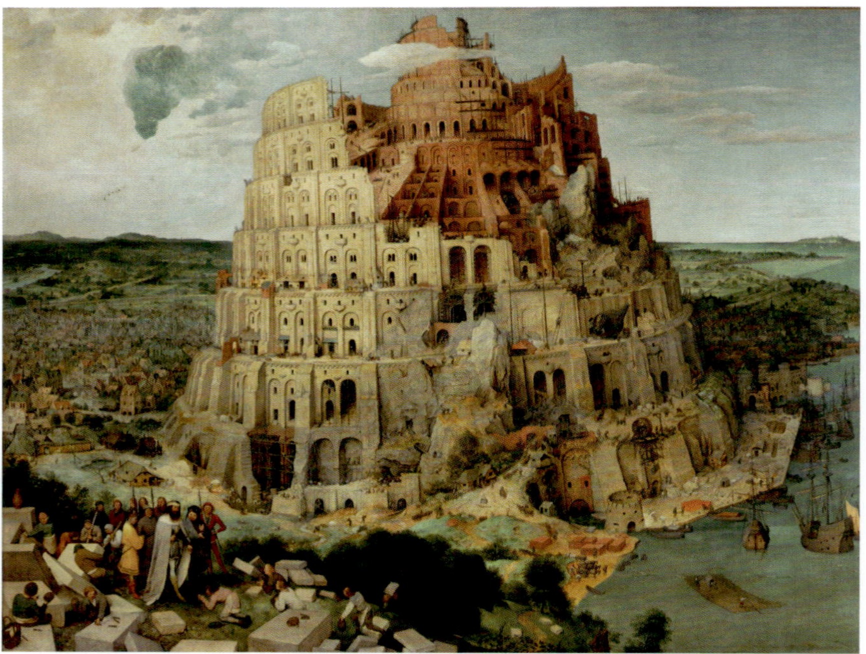

FIG. 13.4 Pieter Bruegel the Elder, *The Tower of Babel*, ca. 1563. Kunsthistorisches Museum, Vienna. Oil on wood panel, 114 × 155 cm.

Renaissance masters of Rome (Michelangelo and Raphael). Oh, good, you might think. Bruegel takes on the Colosseum or the Laocoön or the twisting sibyls of the Sistine Chapel. Not Bruegel. He made about twenty sketches on his trip, from 1553 to 1554. They are all landscapes. What's more, only two refer to Italianate monuments. One shows a cloister tucked in a valley. Another has a view of the Ripa Grande, a port in Rome that once sat on the Tiber. For the most part (and even in these two examples, one might argue), Bruegel is concerned with the land, and a detailed description of the land at that.

This is the common understanding of Bruegel—that he had no interest in Italy and basically disregarded what he saw there. Bruegel may not have been immediately interested in reproducing classical statuary or Renaissance masterpieces, but after a decade or so those experiences seem to emerge. In 1563

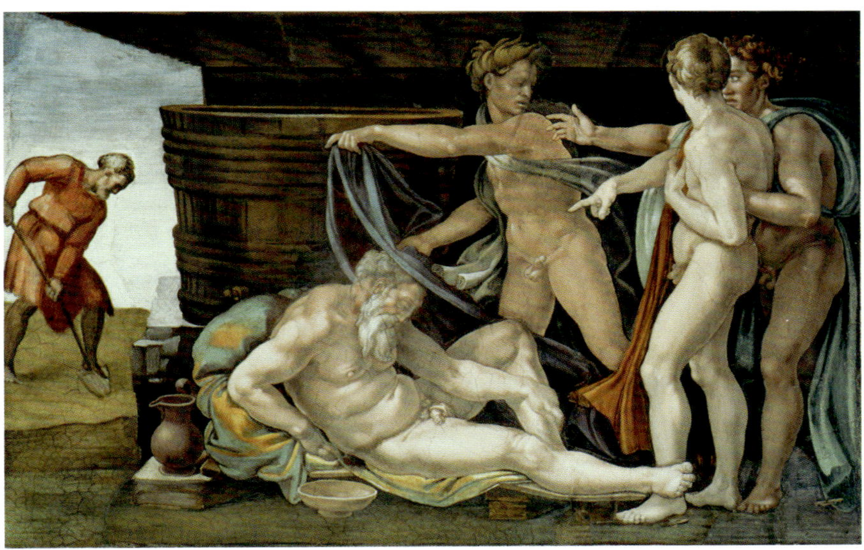

FIG. 13.5 Michelangelo, *The Drunkenness of Noah*, 1508–1512. First bay on the ceiling of the Sistine Chapel, Vatican City. Fresco.

Bruegel paints an incredible *Tower of Babel* (Fig. 13.4). Nimrod appears in the lower left-hand corner, as the instigator of the building campaign. The wicked king points down at a miserable laborer, both cruelly subjugating his people and unwittingly foreshadowing the direction, the downfall, of his huge structure. Piles of rocks in the foreground look much like the crumbling base of the tower itself. The foundations are falling apart, shifting and tumbling, while building continues apace into the clouds. Viewed from a distance, it is clear that the city is tilting quite perilously. It is also possible to see the Colosseum or the Mausoleum of Hadrian in this monument. It has the same rounded shape, the same tall bands of darkened, arcaded entryways. Even the unbuilt spaces at the top of the Tower of Babel look a lot like the losses on the exterior of the Colosseum.

Italian inspirations also reappear in *The Harvesters*, in the shapes of the men and women in the foreground. Michelangelo's painting of Noah in the Sistine Chapel provides an interesting comparison to the Bruegel painting (Fig. 13.5).

Michelangelo's painting shows the moment from Genesis when Noah, after a long day of working in the vineyards, enjoys some of the fruits of his labor and gets completely drunk. His son Ham goes right over and looks at his father's nakedness, which is bad enough. Then he calls over his brothers and tells them all about it—Dad is drunk and nude. The brothers do not look and instead cover their father with a garment. The dramatic and energetic gestures of the three sons in the Michelangelo painting are not really relevant to the painting by Bruegel. Nor is the defined and emphatic musculature of the sons of Noah. But the massive, rounded, weighty forms do relate to Bruegel, certainly more than the delicate courtly style of the earlier Flemish artists. The way Noah, drunk and tired, sinks into his makeshift bed, head hanging low, corresponds to the heaviness of the exhausted, inebriated peasant in Bruegel's painting. It is also intriguing that Noah is shown twice, working in the background and sleeping in the foreground. It is the same individual represented in almost the same pose—downturned head, pulled-back right arm, rounded back. Bruegel also puts his sleeping man in the foreground, while men that wear the same clothes and have the same sinking quality—he in sleep, they in labor—work in the distance. I would not go so far as to say that Bruegel was reviving Michelangelo in the North. But he certainly was painting in a way that was neither completely Flemish nor completely Italian, although vestiges of both are present in his paintings.

Bruegel's manner of absorbing all that he sees and then later blending those inspirations on the canvas seems to relate to the way the seventeenth-century biographer Karel van Mander described Bruegel's painting of landscapes on the Italian trip: "On [Bruegel's] travels he drew many views from life so that it is said that when he was in the Alps he swallowed all those mountains and rocks which, upon returning home, he spat out again onto canvases and panels, so faithfully was he able, in this respect and others, to follow Nature." Van Mander's point is that Bruegel is intensely accurate in his landscape paintings. But what strikes me about the Van Mander observation is the methodology behind it all, how he describes the artist absorbing or consuming all that he can and then, in a strangely visceral, instinctual way, producing his own special vision. Nothing is overcooked or overstudied. Nothing is derivative.

Bruegel's landscapes also show the artist drawing from earlier inspirations

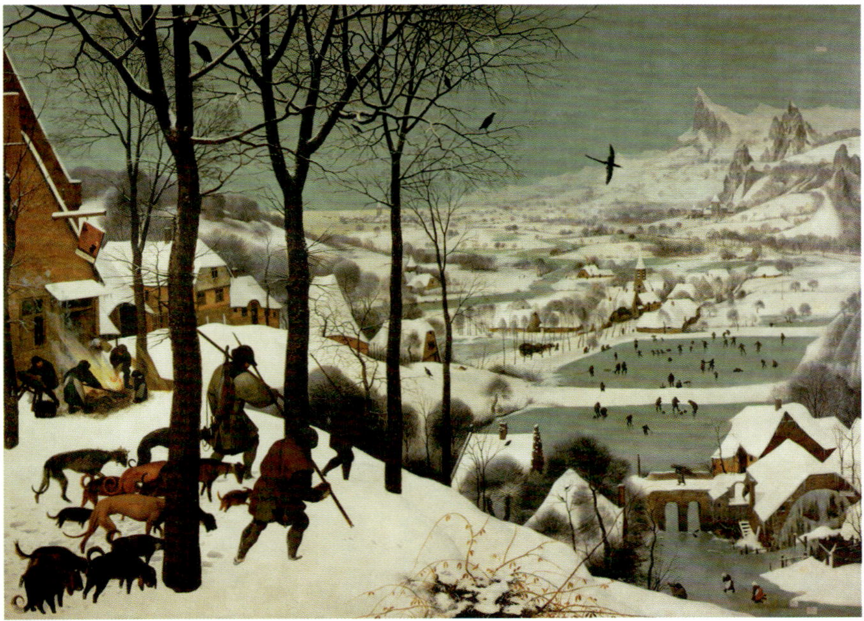

FIG. 13.6 Pieter Bruegel the Elder, *Hunters in the Snow,* 1565. Kunsthistorisches Museum, Vienna. Oil on wood panel, 118 × 161 cm.

and imbuing their observations with something unique, with something radical. In *The Harvesters*, the landscape rolls slowly into the distance; rippling, soft hills and winding roads lead toward smaller trees highlighted with flecks of bright paint such that they seem to flicker and glint in the sunlight. Deepening in depth and detail, the land, that lovely countryside, expands into a distant and high horizon. The artist draws us into that increasingly intricate world such that the landscape is almost his protagonist. It tells its own story about changes in the seasons and asserts its own natural, untamed beauty. As we explore, there are people throughout the land. However, the landscape, subject only to nature, dominates the order and activities of man, not the other way around.

Nature reigns in all the paintings contained in the series of the months. As in *The Harvesters*, Bruegel paints the winter months with sweeping diagonals that lead into deep valleys and meandering pathways.* Like the diagonal that moves along the fields of yellow wheat in *The Harvesters*, from upper right to lower left, a deep diagonal cuts from left to right in the bright-white snow in *Hunters in the Snow* (Fig. 13.6). In the winter painting, that steep drop is more precipitous, thereby indicating a slick and icy terrain, while the soft rolling quality of the land in *The Harvesters* adds to the sense of long, sleepy, weighty autumn days and nights. The hazy gray of the autumn sky in *The Harvesters* becomes a brooding blue in *Hunters in the Snow*, contrasting sharply with the bright-white snow below.

The coldness is palpable—crisp and biting. Dark, leafless trees sprinkle the broad vista like dirty fingerprints. Snow accumulates in the corners of trees, getting stuck in the bark, and lightly powders the roofs of houses and covers the bridge. Mill wheels are frozen still with ice and heavy icicles, which also weigh down the slanting roofs. Women carry heavy piles of wood, bent over with the weight, just as the women in *The Harvesters* are weighed down by bundles of wheat. The merry feasters in the lower right-hand corner of *The Harvesters* also relate to two groups of people in the wintry painting. Yet the sentiment is far more serious in the snow. The family standing around the fire is not getting drunk after a long day of work. They are trying desperately to stay warm by burning the hay that they had collected in the autumnal months. And that might not be enough because they actually seem to be about to burn their kitchen table. The second group is composed of men returning from the hunt. Sadly, not a successful hunt, from the looks of it. That one measly fox hanging on the back of the man between the trees is going to do little for their families. Below, insouciant, happy skaters, light little dark marks in the distance, play hockey, chase each other, flop.

In contrast, the hard-working men—big, rounded, weighty bodies—plod home, heads hanging low, shoulders slumped over with exhaustion from hunting, from fighting the snow, from disappointment. The dogs droop too—wet, miserable, shaggy, and hungry—mirroring their masters' inglorious return. One lone dog looks right at us, in the most nonconfrontational, melancholy way possible. It is this temperament that Lars von Trier associates with this painting in his film *Melancholia* from 2011. In the prologue to the movie, the director shows

---

* Bruegel, *Hunters in the Snow*, Google Arts & Culture, https://artsandculture.google.com.

us Bruegel's wintery painting burning slowly, like melting plastic, as a foreshadowing of his central character's decline into a despondent state of melancholia. A bride, bright and white like the snow (Kirsten Dunst), slowly reveals her hidden darker demons as the film unfolds. The painting is not about depression or melancholia. The situation for the hunters is grim and shows the reality of the challenges in winter. But those challenges are subsumed in a landscape that sprawls gloriously with little regard for man, subject to nature alone.

It is radical what Bruegel has done by turning the land into its own character, by allowing it to spread and meander and dominate. His is not the first landscape. He has artistic ancestors here, just as he did in the style of his figures. One prominent figure in the realm of landscape is Joachim Patinir (ca. 1480–1524). We can certainly see antecedents in the way Bruegel embraces the countryside imagined by his countrymen when we consider Patinir's triptych from 1518, sitting one room away from *The Harvesters* in the Metropolitan Museum of Art (Fig. 13.7). Patinir introduces us into the painting with a scene of the penitent Jerome in a higher foreground, only to soon drop us into a deeper valley that follows meandering pathways into the distance, over gently rolling hills. Rich blue mountains emerge to the left, creating a sloping diagonal that tumbles into the deep-turquoise sea peppered with small boats, a body of water that breaks over the frame and into the right wing of the triptych. High horizon lines off in the hazy distance, deep-green copses, ever-expanding vistas—this is the viewpoint and general aesthetic that Bruegel embraces, the so-called cosmic landscape.

Patinir lets nature take its own course. Bruegel does the same. The difference is that Patinir is tied to the religious theme. He seems to need to justify his wandering lens with stories and personages from the Bible. The little vignette in the valley is a scene of two men recognizing the holy hermit, one of whom appears to be some sort of Muslim "heretic," with his curved saber and yellow turban. Random animals carry deep symbolic weight. The lion refers to the account when Jerome removes a thorn from the lion's paw, one of many miracles. The peacock symbolizes the body of Christ, as the bird's flesh was understood to never decay, just like Christ's. Certainly there are episodes that are less theological, men on their way to town or returning from a hunt. But those aspects are encased in a serious Christological frame. Patinir's guidelines were structured and static, and

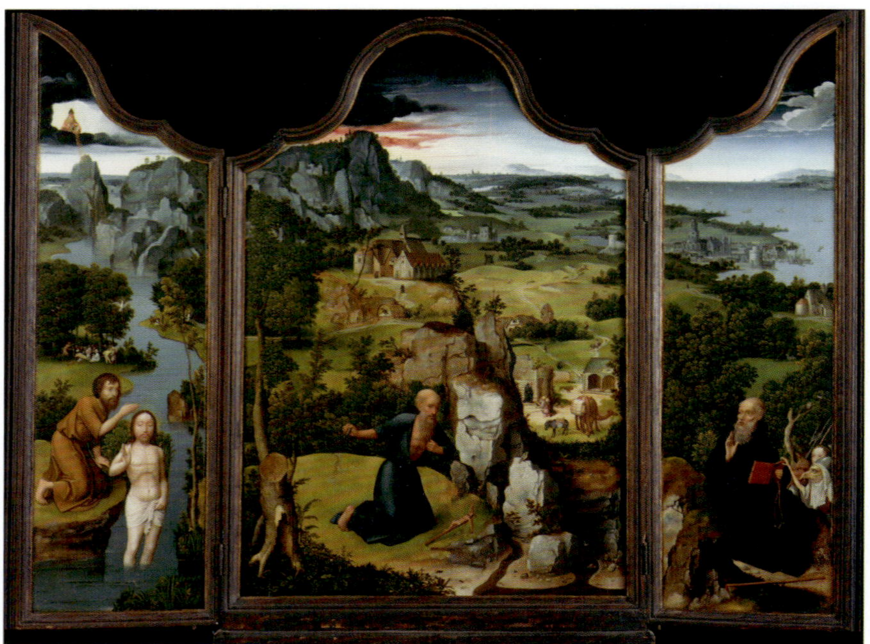

FIG. 13.7 Joachim Patinir, *The Penitence of Saint Jerome*, ca. 1512–1515. Metropolitan Museum of Art, New York. Oil on wood, 117.5 × 81.3 cm.

his landscape is a bit too. Bruegel's is rich and organic. Transitions are natural and seamless. With religion out of the picture, Bruegel is able to let the land have its own voice and breathing room, to look less structured and formal, to have that "cosmic" appearance without the validation of the church at every turn.

But the church is not gone. Bruegel may not put religion in the forefront of *The Harvesters*, but it is there, right beyond the pear tree. Admittedly, we have to ramble in a curious way to get to the church—past the vines, past the cluster of trees, through a clump of more wheat, and down into what appears to be another valley, since we cannot see the base of the church. And yes, the ringing bells probably are most interesting to the laborers as a sign of lunchtime instead of as a call to Mass. But the church is present, with a bright-blue steeple and roof that correspond to the bluish hues of the receding landscape. We could dig deeper. We could read symbolically into particulars in the painting like pears. For example, the Bible never says precisely which fruit tempted Eve. Some artists and theologians were happy to render that proverbial fruit as a pear, not an apple. In his *Confessions,* Saint Augustine steals a batch of pears. He later recounts this youthful indiscretion as an Edenic transgression. In other instances the pear is a symbol of the Incarnate Christ, of the redemption through Christ born of Mary, which is how it appears in many Renaissance paintings in Italy.

Maybe the pears in Bruegel are both. Maybe they are neither. It is hard to say with certitude. But the piece was commissioned for a private home, not for a religious setting or as an altarpiece, so I do not think we should feel the need to look for hidden evidences of piety or deep, theologically weighted symbolism, as we did with Jan van Eyck. The church is part of the daily life of these men and women in a natural way. It is always present. It does not need to be made obvious or the principal focal point of the painting.

Even when Bruegel is painting a specifically religious scene, it takes a bit of doing to find it. Take, for example, Bruegel's *Census at Bethlehem* (Fig. 13.8).* Here we have another snowy scene, as in *The Hunters in the Snow.* In fact, we might feel ourselves to be in that deeper valley that was in the distance of the *Hunters* painting, where the snowy fields and frozen lakes are filled with minivignettes—lots of children playing in the snow. There is an accumulation of people in the rundown tavern at the left. In the window a scribe records names into his ledger, and it is here that the title of the painting takes effect. Here we are seeing the census described in the Gospel of Luke: "And it came to pass in those days that a decree went out from Caesar Augustus that all the world should be registered. . . . Joseph also went up from Galilee, out of the city of Nazareth, into Judea, to the city of David, which is called Bethlehem . . . to be registered with Mary, his betrothed wife, who was with child."

Mary and Joseph *are* in this painting, although you might not see them right away. It takes our eyes a minute to register their presence with all the activity sprinkled throughout the canvas and accumulating in the lower left-hand corner. Bruegel also underplays the Madonna significantly. Van Eyck's Madonna

* Bruegel, *Census at Bethlehem,* Google Arts & Culture, https://artsandculture.google.com.

is elegant and courtly. She also seems to be larger than life, making the church seem small, barely able to contain all the excitement of the moment. Bruegel's Madonna is engulfed by the activity around her. She is sweet and modest. Her eyes are downcast, almost as though they are closed. There is little indication of her anatomical form because it is swaddled in a voluminous blue mantle. Not resplendent ultramarine blue, as in the Van Eyck, but a soft, muted blue. Her pregnant belly is only hinted at with the carefully placed, round, straw basket. Bruegel heightens the miraculous quality of the birth by showing it in a humdrum context. Something extraordinary in a landscape of the ordinary. The fact that the miraculous and momentous is tucked away means that it is incumbent upon us to look, to seek, to fight for a view.

This injunction is rendered deftly in an *Adoration of the Magi* from 1563 (Fig. 13.9). Many people come to see the baby, huddling in the snow, trying to ignore the quickening pace of the cascading flecks of snow. We too must fight. We too must look through that sheet of snow to figure out where to look and what to look for. It takes a moment to realize that we are seeing the Christ Child, over there, in the far-left corner. That little white packet on the lap of a woman who is not covered in jewels and robes in the bright-blue of lapis lazuli and surrounded by angels. Bruegel's truth, Bruegel's Christianity, is found in the crowd and in the struggle; it is found in the simplest faith, and in the miracle of God taking utterly human form, a little blobby baby.

That impulse to present religious figures without the traditional accoutrements—singing angels, flocks of saints, blasts of gold—might have to do with a historical reality that unsettled the Netherlands during the sixteenth century. In 1517 Martin Luther wrote his Ninety-five Theses, calling for reform within the Catholic Church. This moment of Reformation was contentious and very political. The Netherlands were divided into seventeen provinces and controlled with a heavy hand by the Spanish. Many of the provinces hoped to separate from the Catholic Church, not least because the Spanish were so hated. The Spanish extracted heavy taxes and passed laws with names like the Edict of Blood.

Bruegel's stripping away of the embellishments traditionally used in Catholic art might have been a response to the controversy in which his homeland was embroiled. The Spanish threat is ever-present in the paintings by Bruegel. In a more straightforward *Adoration of the Magi,* in which the Christ Child is central and easily visible although still a bit on the blobby side, a pack of men with long-bladed spears hover menacingly in the background.* A soldier wearing a peculiarly pointed helmet with odd earmuffs and an intimidatingly long, hammerlike staff watches with bewilderment. The dress of these soldiers—the long spears, the shape of this helmet—were all specific to Spain in the sixteenth century. Those same long spears appear in the background of the *Census* painting. A constant Spanish presence colors the moment, gives the painting a darker hue, and rewrites the story of the census. The biblical account has a new reference point. The oppressive tactics remain the same, but now the Roman Empire is simultaneously Spain.

That sense of anxiety, that persistent military presence, complicates the moment. All those children playing, is it just fun and games? Is this Bruegel reveling in the simplicity of children that are happy and unaware of the darker political reality? Are we supposed to read something darker in the fighting children? Or is Bruegel saying that the fighting of his contemporaries is foolish and childish? In the *Census at Bethlehem,* when we look at the little girl at the edge of the pond, standing by herself, wishing she could play with the bigger kids, knees buckled, shoulders rounded, ragged tuft of hair, two little black beads for eyes—what are we to think? Is she sad, lost, wistful, hapless? A metaphor? A joke? Are the men and women in *The Harvesters* supposed to be funny? Are we at all laughing at them? Would the wealthy merchant Jongelink have laughed? Or would he have valued their labor, their attachment with the land, their sincerity, their obliviousness to the controversial and painful state of affairs in the Netherlands?

Van Mander recounts that Bruegel would dress in peasant costume and sneak into fairs and weddings, bringing presents and pretending to be a family member so that he could observe the nature of the men and women "in eating, drinking, dancing, leaping, lovemaking and other amusements." Was Bruegel observing these peasants with respect, wishing to be a family member in truth, enjoying the deception, or with an interest in being amused himself?

A scene of bucolic enjoyment in a majestic, golden landscape turns into what

* http://www.nationalgallery.org.uk/paintings/pieter-bruegel-the-elder-the-adoration-of-the-kings

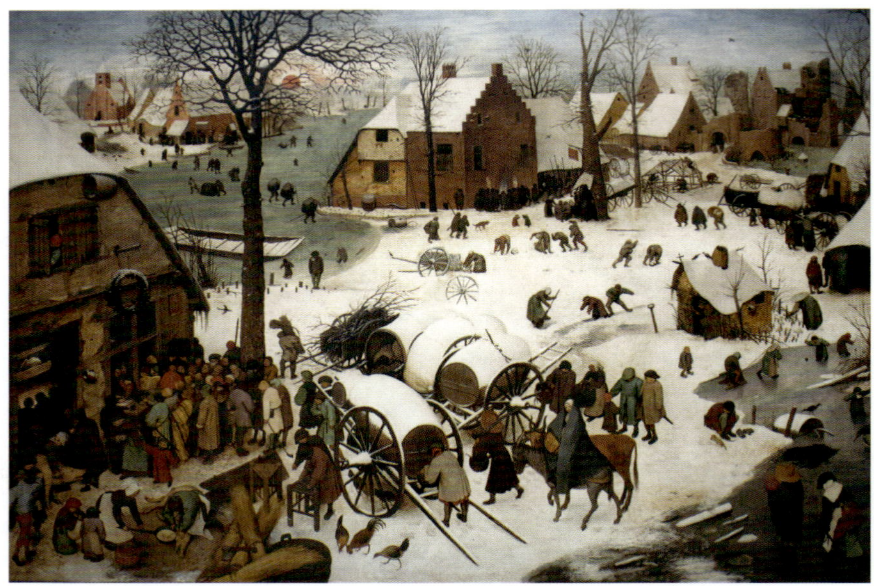

FIG. 13.8 Pieter Bruegel the Elder, *Census at Bethlehem*, 1566. Royal Museum of Fine Arts of Belgium, Brussels, Belgium. Oil on oak, 115.5 × 163.5 cm.

might become a rather slippery slope. Along the journey through *The Harvesters*, Bruegel places encoded signposts that are perhaps meant to remind us about perils and pitfalls. When we follow the women carrying the bushels, the path is clear and well marked, the journey seems straightforward and easy. Then we are presented with a cross in the road, a moment of decision making. If we take the path more traveled, to the right, toward the bathers, a large haywain interrupts our progress. That haywain might be just that, a large cart with hay. But it is suspiciously reminiscent of another pile of hay in a painting that was well known by Bruegel, the one in *The Haywain Triptych* by the bizarre and wonderful Hieronymus Bosch (ca. 1450–1516) (Fig. 13.10).

It might seem a little tenuous to tie Bosch to Bruegel based on a pile of hay. But Bosch was a major inspiration to Bruegel. One of the Magi in Bruegel's *Adoration* comes straight out of Bosch's *Adoration* painting. And many of Bruegel's

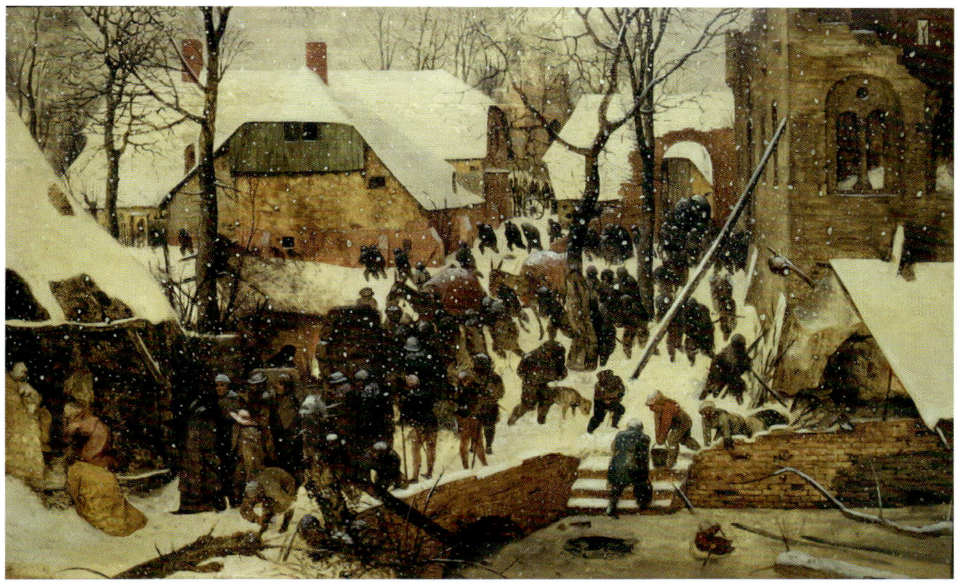

FIG. 13.9 Pieter Bruegel the Elder, *The Adoration of the Magi in the Snow*, 1563. The Oskar Reinhart Collection, Winterthur, Switzerland. Oil on oak panel, 36 × 56 cm.

early works are clearly borrowing Bosch's compositional style of scattering figures throughout the picture plane, in grim circumstances. So Bruegel's simple hay cart may be laden with Boschian antecedents. The hay in Bosch's triptych is not positive. Clearly it was, at some point, accumulated through hard work. However, at this moment it is being used solely in the most perverse ways—for flirting and lustful advances and spying. Owls are bad birds, representing evil and drunkenness. And that blue angel beast tooting his skinny trumpet is just plain ominous and creepy. Everything is complete chaos below—people are fighting and attacking one another with knives and fists. Jesus hovers above with his arms outstretched in a gesture that seems to show patience and understanding, as though he will forgive these indiscretions.

But the parade is going nowhere good. If the figures at the helm aren't indication enough, like the rat-faced man with the fish torso, the right wing of the

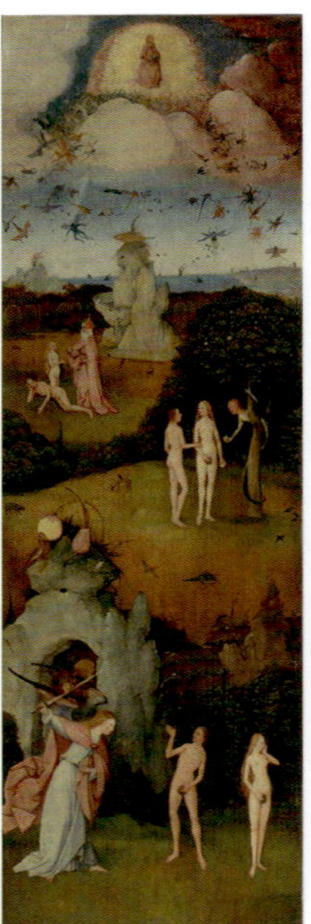
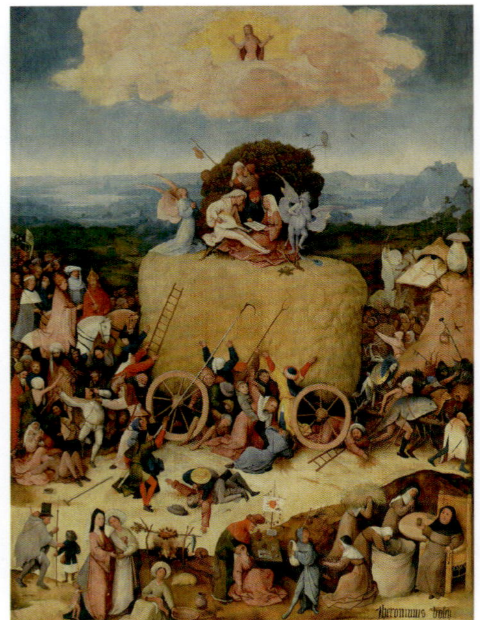
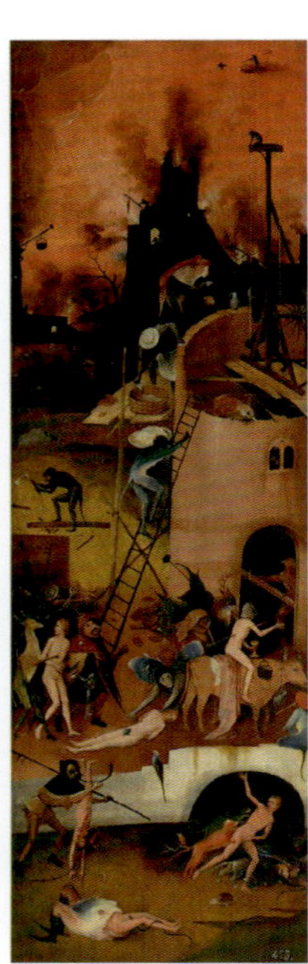

FIG. 13.10 Hieronymus Bosch, *The Haywain Triptych*, 1512–1515. Museo del Prado, Madrid, Spain. Oil on oak panel, 147.1 × 224.3 cm.

triptych is clear about the future of these baleful, lost souls—a fiery Hell populated with the most bizarre and outrageous beasts imaginable, or only imaginable by Bosch. Is the hay cart in Bruegel a sign of hard work, of success in the field, of industriousness? Or is it in any way a reminder of that abused hay cart from Bosch?

Something seemingly so simple—a landscape, a moment of repose, a representation of a season, of warmth, of play—becomes a blend of histories and traditions, anxieties and beliefs, none of which are terribly easy to discern, but all of which hover, linger, complicate. And delight. In *The Harvesters*, in the field to the right of the men in the bathing pool, just a bit farther into the small township made up of squat A-frame houses, is a group of children playing a game of "bird throwing." It is just as it sounds. A bird, a chicken, or some such fowl (an owl perhaps?) was tied to a forked branch. The goal was to throw your stick toward the bird so that you might knock off its head. This episode provides for a most delightful vignette, a glimpse into the daily life of people at play. The little boy with the red shirt and blue pants dashes toward the hapless bird, hurrying to get his stick, one of the four that has missed its mark. A boy in blue moves in the same direction, turning back to see the next attempt by the boy in the brown coat, who stands with his legs far apart and twists to the right, gaining momentum for his throw. A girl in a white wimple and long white pinafore waits her turn, and seems to get advice from two women turned in her direction. A young boy hurries to join in the fun, walking hand in hand with his father, maybe his grandfather. A man in black watches from the sidelines, hands in his pockets, hat pulled low. And a tiny girl in blue, perfectly framed by the boy in brown and the girl in the pinafore, watches with her hands held at her sides. Too young to play, watching and wondering, a speck of paint almost lost in the wider reaches of the painting, of the broader vista. We can telescope into these moments of humanity and then pull out again to see them within a tremendous landscape of broad shapes and forms.

We do not know exactly how the six paintings would have been arranged. I like to imagine that they were in a circle, paintings linking and leading to other paintings, like an all-encompassing dance to the music of time, a surround-sound vision of the year, of the changing seasons. Perhaps this is too fanciful. A six-sided room might be hard to come by. But the paintings do seem to read from one to the next, to allude to the passing of time by referencing one another.

In Texas when we complain about it being "really" cold outside, or when we hear about hideous blizzards in Boston or New York and realize how lucky we are to be eating lunch outside in February, in shorts and flip-flops, we should also remember and reflect on how miserable the heat is in the summer. Those contrasts would have been embedded in the experiences of these paintings, with the ultimate reflection being that time passes, it always does, constantly and cyclically. One season will bring the next, which is different, but related, and it is our responsibility, our labor, our use of that time and that land which keeps us alive, which keeps us going. Bruegel encourages us to embrace work and play, those difficulties that life brings and the many joys, while his paintings embrace

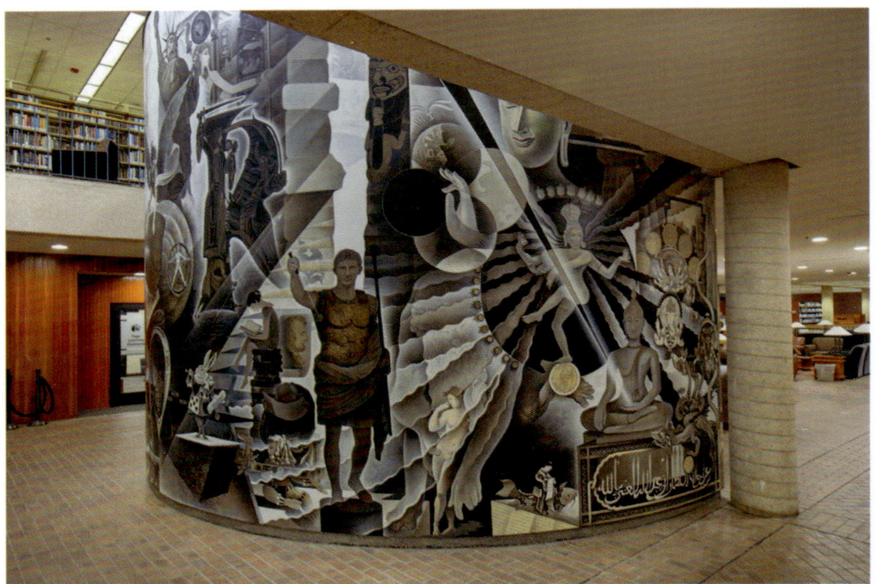

FIG. 13.11 James Sicner, *Man's Evolving Images: In Printing and Writing*, 1979–1983. View from the ground floor. Central staircase, Coates Library, Trinity University, San Antonio, Texas. Collage.

us, or may have in their original setting. Even without the paintings next to one another, they are all-consuming, mesmerizing. When you look into Bruegel you see the vestiges of Patinir, Michelangelo, Van Eyck, and Bosch lingering in his brush, in his deeper artistic consciousness, just as he does in ours.

The library of Trinity University in San Antonio has a remarkable mural called *Man's Evolving Images*, produced by James Sicner in 1983 (Fig. 13.11). The predominantly black-and-white mural wraps around the central staircase, following its curving shape as it leads from the first to the second floor. You will find Bruegel there, in another assemblage of details that creates a different ideal vision—this time of the pursuit of knowledge. One of the first images that emerges as you approach the staircase is the Augustus of Prima Porta. He raises his arm in his famous gesture as an orator, welcoming us into a montage that encompasses the great sweep of history, which comes together without rules or boundaries or chronology, in a wonderful jumble of ideas and thoughts and inspirations—an illuminated letter *R* from the twelfth-century *Moralia in Job*, the White Rabbit from *Alice in Wonderland*, the medieval Peutinger Map, the Rosetta Stone, the minaret of Samarra, an Egyptian obelisk, totems of the Pacific Northwest, and, around the side, the column of Trajan, next to a real, similarly spiral-shaped column. This fluid visual cacophony follows us as we ascend the staircase—Piazza Venezia (sitting in front of Stonehenge) is framed by Superman and Lois Lane who swoop to the right, and Laocoön who swoops to the left, unable to save his sons from the venomous sea snakes. The idea is that these black-and-white images will soon materialize in the pages of the books we will find in the stacks. The accumulation of ideas, the awareness and deepening of our sense of history and sense of earlier innovations, has the capacity to inspire us to great thoughts of our own, just as Bruegel studied and consumed consummate masterpieces before making his own. He is, of course, part of our trip up the stairs to the stacks. Just under the Laocoön, one of the classical statues Bruegel no doubt studied in Rome, are a number of reproductions of some of Bruegel's many prints. Sicner starts at the top of the sequence with *Pride*, which he repeats with two details, both of which sit behind the banister. The next print shows a scene of men on a journey, through a landscape, and then there is Bruegel's print about *Avarice*, showing money boxes and piggy banks at war. (No one is winning.) The row of prints continues with an image of *Patience* and then concludes with a scene of *Everyman*. Perhaps the modern artist, like the sixteenth-century artist, was making a call for self-awareness, for the virtue of hard work and hard study, which is a journey, which requires time and patience, but nobly overcomes pride, false knowledge. (There is no greater enemy to knowledge than a know-it-all.) Both artists encourage us to take comfort in the community of others who are doing the same—working hard, taking breaks, and embracing and consuming a landscape that must be filled with humanity and self-awareness.

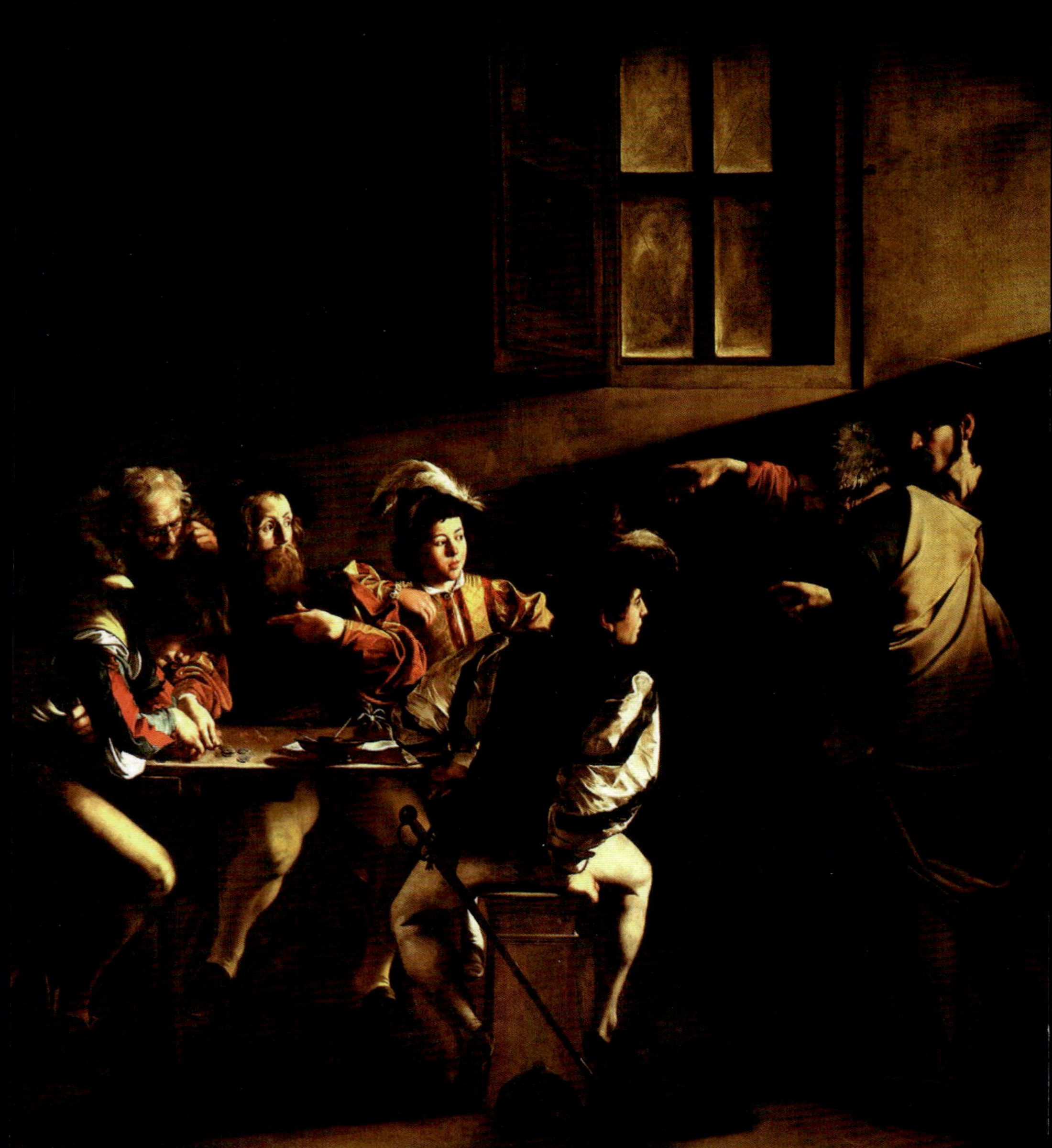

FIG. 14.1 Caravaggio, *The Calling of Saint Matthew,* 1599–1600. Contarelli Chapel, San Luigi dei Francesi, Rome. Oil on canvas, 322 × 340 cm.

ITALIAN BAROQUE ART

A door opens. A blast of light enters, raking dramatically along the back wall of a seedy room. The appearance is wholly unanticipated—both the light and the unknown visitors, one of whom has a delicate, attenuated, golden halo. Some look, some don't. The two men at the farthest end of the table huddle over their silver coins, focusing on the count, ignoring the other end of the room. The two men to the right end of the table seem perplexed. And in the middle of the melee, this ship of fools, a man, Matthew, points, stupefied, "What, who, me?" In that instant his life is changed. He has been called. Christ's gesture affects Matthew, touching without touch, calling without a sound, barely opening his mouth. Nor does Christ linger. His feet are much masked by his companion Peter's leg and the dark shadows that wait to regain their hold over the room. Yet if we look closely it appears that he has already turned to leave, feet firmly planted toward the direction of the door (Fig. 14.1).

The moment happens quickly, just as it does in the biblical account. Matthew 9:9 reads: "As Jesus went on from there, he saw a man named Matthew, sitting in the tax collector's booth. 'Follow me,' he told him, and Matthew got up and followed him." Christ's stance exudes the solidity, power, and confidence in the biblical passage. His pose is quite a contrast to those angular, jumpy, hosed legs at the left. Contrasts are key, and Michelangelo Merisi da Caravaggio (1571–1610) brings those dichotomies to the fore through his use of contrasting lights and darks. The technique is called *tenebrism*, derived from the word *tenebroso*, meaning

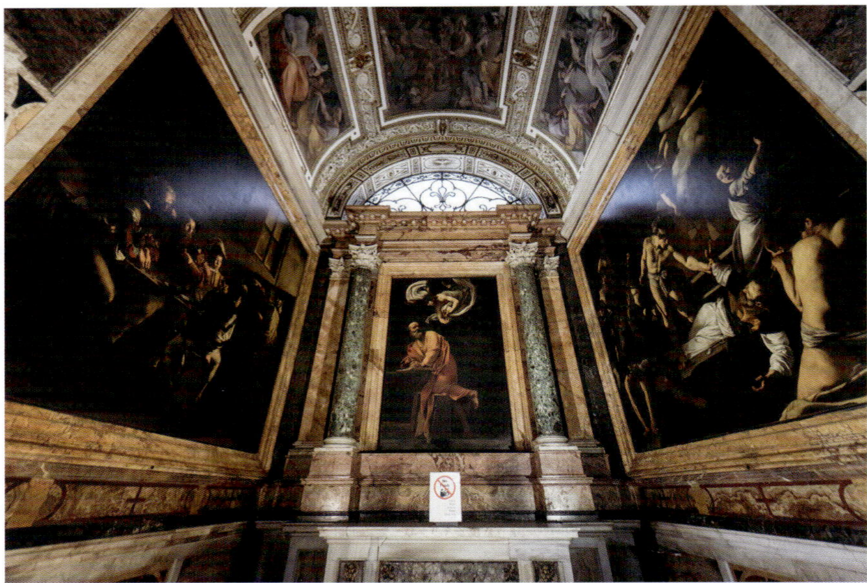

FIG. 14.2 Caravaggio, View of the Contarelli Chapel.

murky in Italian. It is essentially a wildly heightened version of *chiaroscuro*—the juxtaposition of light and dark that was so beloved by the Quattrocento painters like Leonardo da Vinci. In Caravaggio's hand, the subtlety of the *chiaroscuro* gets pushed to the farthest extremes of the spectrum, into the realm of impenetrable, violent darks and surprisingly blinding lights. But don't expect that light to come with angels or putti or beautiful gleaming virgins. Rather than pinks, gold, and ultramarine blue, we have muted maroons, mustardy yellows, muddy browns, and of course pitch-black. Rather than a sense of calm, Caravaggio's paintings make you feel uneasy, shocked, passionate, and inspired. These are the feelings that imbue and charge the Contarelli Chapel, tucked away in a corner of San Luigi dei Francesi, a Roman church situated near the Piazza Navona (Fig. 14.2). The series includes *The Calling of Saint Matthew*, *The Inspiration of Saint Matthew*, and finally the frenzied *Martyrdom*. All were in place by 1602, although *The Calling* was finished by 1600. These paintings consume the walls of the chapel and reach out into your space, grabbing your attention much like Christ's gesture grabs Matthew.

Christ's hand is a perfect example of Caravaggio's raw and worldly spirituality. It is not bright and white and gleaming. There are no rays of light exuding from it. It is shaded and darkened, heavy and pendulous, yet also weightless and suspended. The hand almost seems to hover without a body. It takes time to piece together the shape of Christ's entire form, which is broken up by Peter's bulky back. Peter also gestures in a manner that reflects Christ's hand. But there is something less confident, less all-knowing, less otherworldly about Peter's version. His pointing gesture shows frustration. It looks like Peter is remonstrating with the youth in the floppy hat or trying to teach him a lesson. Peter has to use his weight, he has to lean forward to get his point across. He is irritated. His brow is wrinkled in intensity. His shaggy gray hair is flustered, and so is he in his attempt to explain what the boy is doing wrong and what the boy should be doing instead—that is, following Christ. But the boy responds with a somewhat blank stare. Peter is not the Teacher. There is only one of those in this room. And *his* message is communicated without force, without frustration. His face is almost calm. His mouth is only slightly ajar. If he is calling Matthew it is with a silence, with a breath, with a look, with a gesture.

Gestures, glances, and garb lead us through the painting. The two young boys wear hats with floppy feathers, which mirror the curve of the hand gestures, both Christ's and Peter's. But it is clear that the boys are not comprehending the moment. The boy that Peter is trying to teach seems to be looking past Peter, perhaps toward the door. Most importantly, he doesn't look at Christ. The second, younger boy gives nothing. His stare is completely blank. It is almost as though their silly feathers—ornamental, superficial, decorative gewgaws—are a manifestation of how the boys are missing the weight of the moment. Light, fluffy feathers versus forcible fingers. The younger boy's hand gesture is the same—soft, at rest, noncommunicative, empty.

The young man's insouciance or ignorance has its counterpart in the next figure, an older man with a long beard and unkempt hair. The old man is in almost the same position as the boy. They wear the same black hat, which falls in the same lumpy way. Both faces are turned to the door at the same angle, and

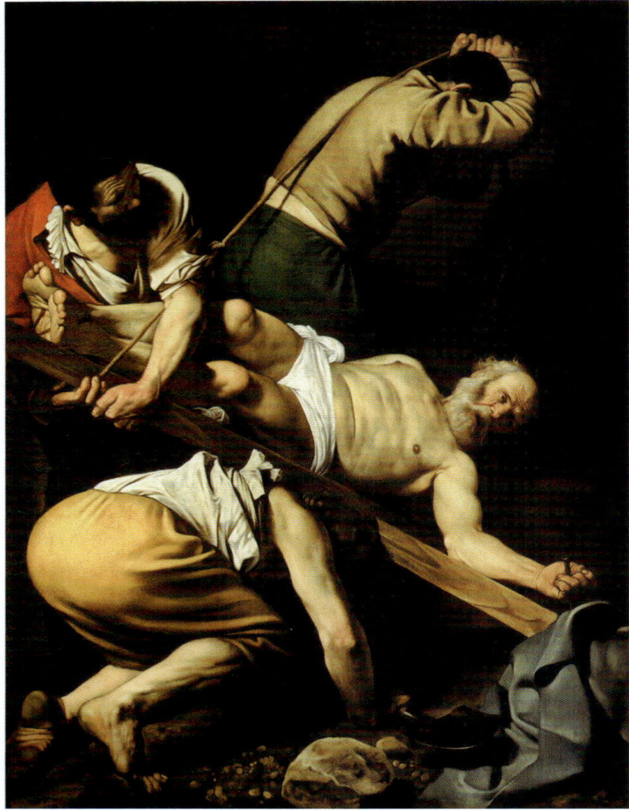

FIG. 14.3 Caravaggio, *The Crucifixion of Saint Peter*, 1601. Cerasi Chapel, Santa Maria del Popolo, Rome. Oil on canvas, 230 × 175.

both lean slightly away from the visitors at the door, with the red in the sleeves of the older man picking up the red of the boy's foppish waistcoat. But the older man is definitively more engaged. No floppy feather here. His hand does not rest impotently. It points with power, agitation, and force. His hand is arguably the epicenter of the left side of the composition, and it is a clear visual response to the prominent gestures on the right side of the painting, those of Christ and, to a lesser degree, Peter.

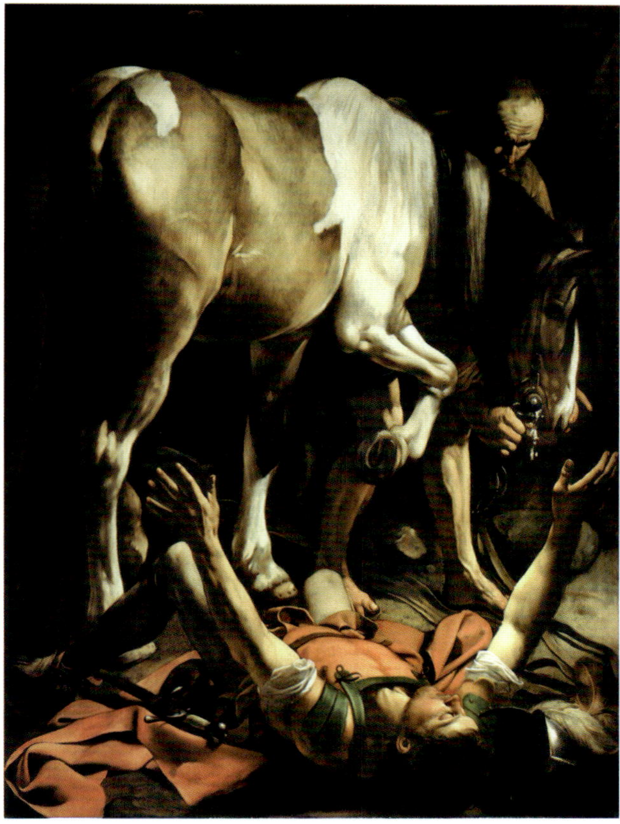

FIG. 14.4 Caravaggio, *The Conversion of Saint Paul,* 1601. Cerasi Chapel, Santa Maria del Popolo, Rome. Oil on canvas, 230 × 175.

But there is a sense of confusion too. It is not obvious that this man, this Matthew, completely understands what the man in the halo is saying to him, or that he even understands who the man with the halo is. He may be asking "Who me?" but he might also be saying "Or do you mean this other fellow?" referring to the younger man at the end of the table. In this reading we would move from the hand of Christ, follow through the pointing gesture of Matthew, and land on the younger man, who is dramatically framed by a series of tightly clenched hands. The boy at end of the table closer to Christ is ready to jump up and start a fight—overeager, agitated, his left hand readied to grab his prominent sword. The boy at the other end of the table is the opposite. He is mesmerized by the coins, caught in the midst of counting money, collecting with his right hand the silver coins that he hoards with his left. The hand that appears to be the boy's left hand, the one on the table, actually belongs to Matthew. The boy's left hand is tucked under his shoulder, grasping at a bag of money that disappears into the shadows. Misguided, myopic, and mercantile. He is also, some scholars argue, the real Matthew. This consideration has stirred up scholars for a number of years. Thomas Puttfarken recently argued for the younger man, stating that if the younger man is counting and collecting the coins, then he is the tax collector and the other men are paying their taxes.

Caravaggio makes a powerful meme out of the youth with flawed vision who gains spiritual sight through a spiritual light. Not long after the Contarelli Chapel commission, around 1601, Caravaggio painted two panels for the Cerasi Chapel, tucked away to the right side of the apse in Santa Maria del Popolo. On one side of the wall is *The Crucifixion of Saint Peter* and on the other side *The Conversion of Saint Paul* (Figs. 14.3 and 14.4). The conversion of Paul happens in chapter 9 of Acts when Paul is busy "breathing out murderous threats against the Lord's disciples." Paul travels to Damascus, and just before arriving a light from heaven suddenly flashes around him and knocks him to the ground. Paul's traveling companions are confused, because although they hear something, they can't see anything out of the ordinary. But Paul is changed. For three days he is blind and cannot eat or drink. After the third day he is no longer a persecutor of Christians but a believer.

Caravaggio accentuates Paul's change with strong diagonals and surprising features, like a large horse's rear. I know that sounds irreverent, but it's how Caravaggio tells the story. Caravaggio could have cleaned things up a bit. He might have put the horse into the background or at the very least made him a more elegant steed. But Caravaggio wants that awkwardness and unseemliness. He wants to underline the physicality of the ignoble animal, plodding and muscular and dumb. He wants to show the brutality of the moment, the pain of falling down onto one's back. And he wants to create a sense of shock. The presence of a highlighted horse's rear in a painting in a chapel is bizarre. So is the composition. It's all arms and legs—horse legs and the veined, disembodied legs of the servant. It's hard to read, difficult to understand exactly where things are and where they are going. It almost looks as if the horse is about to step on Paul. And all the roles are reversed—the beast of burden looks down on the master, as does the servant who, if we return to Acts, is presumably one of the confused men who will have to lead Paul around by the hand, just as he is currently leading the horse by the reins. The strapping young leader is reduced to the level of a helpless beast. The confident soldier who is about to use physical violence to teach Christians that they are wrong is himself being given a lesson through physical means—a fall to the ground, the inability to eat and drink for three days, the loss of sight. Of course, the sight that Paul loses, he gains in an existential, spiritual sight, which is illustrated by a dramatic use of light.

The light bursts onto the scene in the painting. Light flashes on the horse's belly, telling us from whence Paul fell. Light flashes on Paul's torso and face, highlighting the places where Paul is experiencing this conversion—his eyes and his core. The appearance of that light from an unknown source also tells us that Christ is present, albeit not bodily. It is light that Paul cannot see, and neither, for that matter, does the horse or its keeper. But Paul receives the light with extended hands. In fact, he is all about reception—body exposed, legs open. Paul is changed by the light that he cannot see. The experience literally changes the direction of his movement—the horse and keeper go one way while Paul has been spun to face the opposite direction, significantly the altar of the chapel. The light also changes the direction of his beliefs, from hating Christians to loving them. True sight only comes through obfuscated sight, both for Paul and for the viewer. We have to grapple with the darkness, the flashes of lights, the odd and confusing forms, to find the truth and the message—that Paul has been changed.

Thus the younger man being Matthew would seem to fit within the Caravaggesque oeuvre of young men or young saints, shown before taking on the mantle of Christ, who exchange blindness for sight. Of course, Matthew is not knocked on his back. But then again his "flaw" is not physical. Paul's punishment is physical because his misdemeanor is physical, because he violently persecutes Christians. Matthew's blindness is that he collects taxes, he focuses on those coins.

But the older man is also sitting at the table, participating in a collection of coins, counting the money. In fact, it looks like he is ready to get up off the bench. The young boy is mired in his money, hunched over to count the coins. He makes no sign of moving. But the older man's legs angle to the right. His muscles are taut, accentuating the fact that his knees are jutting forward. In fact, his right foot seems to be off the ground, or perhaps pushed back as though he is getting ready to propel himself forward and stand up. So who is Christ calling, exactly? Caravaggio does not give us the answer in the most direct way. There are mysteries embedded in the painting. We do not know precisely where we are or when this is happening. The dress of the men at the tables belongs to the seventeenth century, but Christ and Peter seem to be in garb appropriate to biblical times. Caravaggio throws us into a bewildering situation—the men in the painting are confused and so are we.

Caravaggio wants us to grapple with the painting, to ask questions, to look with intensity. But there is a solution to the Matthew question. As in the Paul painting, Caravaggio uses a flash of light to indicate what is happening in the narrative, in this darkened space. That strong diagonal draws our eye from the upper right of the painting to the middle of the composition, drawing a dramatic connection between the top of Christ's head and his magnetic gesture. Christ is, as we saw at Sant Climent de Taüll, the light of the world. Light hits Matthew in the face. It is a spiritual light and a literal light. Both are powerful. Both are impossible to ignore. There is only one man truly engaged in that conversation, in that message, and that man is Matthew. Matthew's story plays out in the space of a chapel, the walls of which create a veritable triptych. We cannot look at one without the others. And it is clear that, when we put them together, Matthew is consistently an older man.

The relationship between the three paintings is essential to the experience of the chapel. Caravaggio makes a number of connections between them. In *The Calling,* the shape and design of the chair upon which the youth with the sword sits is similar to the shape of the chair upon which Matthew balances precariously while writing his gospel in *The Inspiration* (Fig. 14.5). That chair hangs over a dramatic and precipitous ledge, which visually resonates with the large hole or baptismal font that Matthew leans into while facing his aggressor in

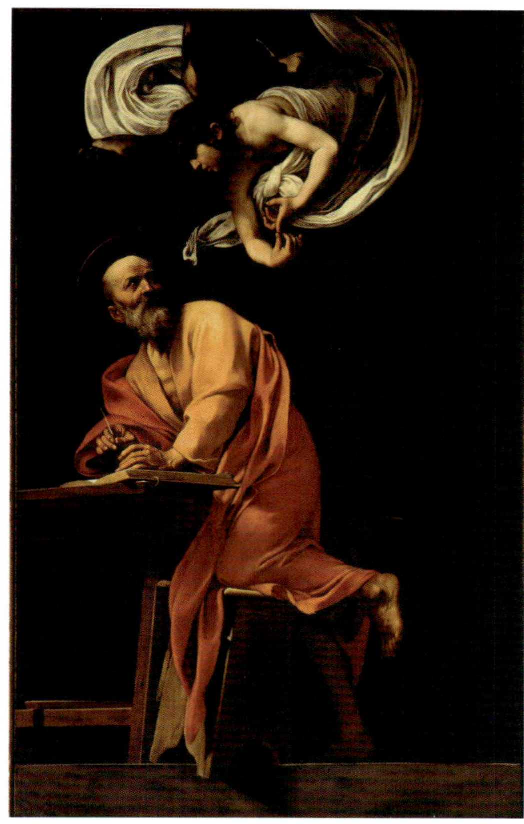

FIG. 14.5 Caravaggio, *The Inspiration of Saint Matthew,* 1602. Contarelli Chapel, San Luigi dei Francesi, Rome. Oil on canvas, 292 × 186 cm.

The Martyrdom (Fig. 14.6). The young boy with the blank stare and flopping hat at the left of *The Martyrdom* also seems to be a reappearance of the youth in *The Calling.* The altar in the background of *The Martyrdom* scene is a sacred version of the profane table in *The Calling.* Both paintings are framing a literal altar, in the chapel, in front of *The Inspiration* painting. Within *The Calling,* Caravaggio seems to make subtle hints that connect the painting to the space of the chapel. That impenetrable, blotchy window with its murky panes surrounds what is impossible to ignore, a wooden cross, alluding to the purpose of the chapel. And the way the window shutter opens might allude to the painting of *The Calling* itself since it also sits at an angle and brackets a central image, *The Inspiration.*

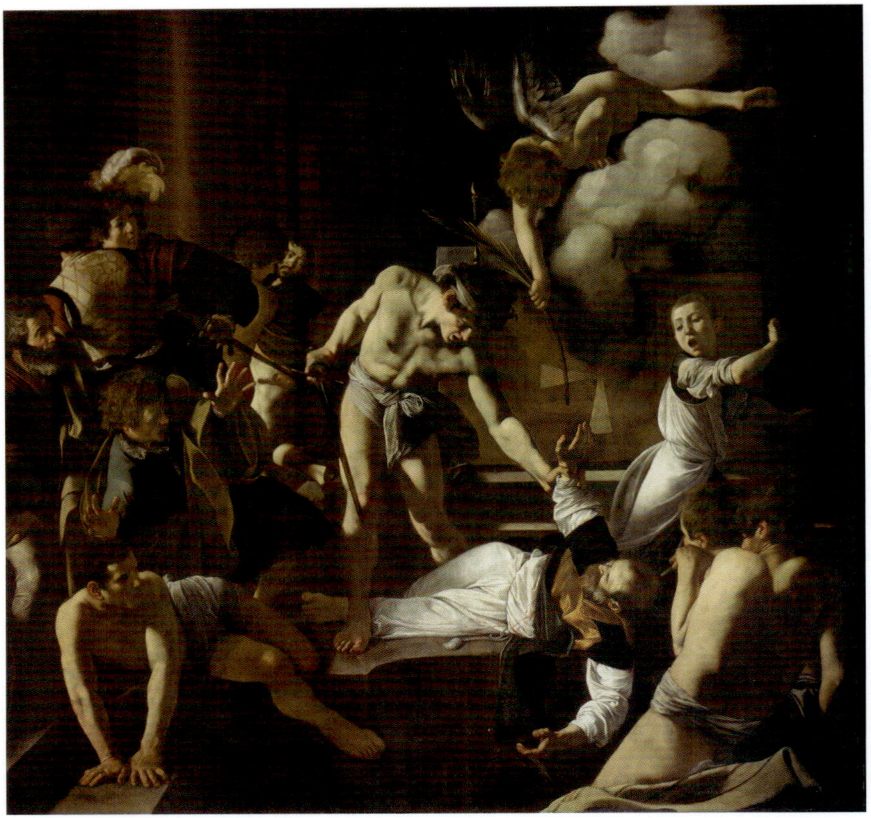

FIG. 14.6 Caravaggio, *The Martyrdom of Saint Matthew*, 1599–1600. Contarelli Chapel, San Luigi dei Francesi, Rome. Oil on canvas, 322 × 343 cm.

Thus the three paintings are directly related to each other. Yet the paintings are not connected in a sense of continuous action. Each frame stands independently. The paintings are three individual bursts, episodes, from Matthew's life. Definitive moments to be sure, but not fluid and progressive. Caravaggio does not tell stories through continuities and consistencies. He tells stories in crisp snapshots, with blasts of raw and powerful emotions, poses, and compositions.

As a contrast, consider the art being produced in Rome at this time—massive,

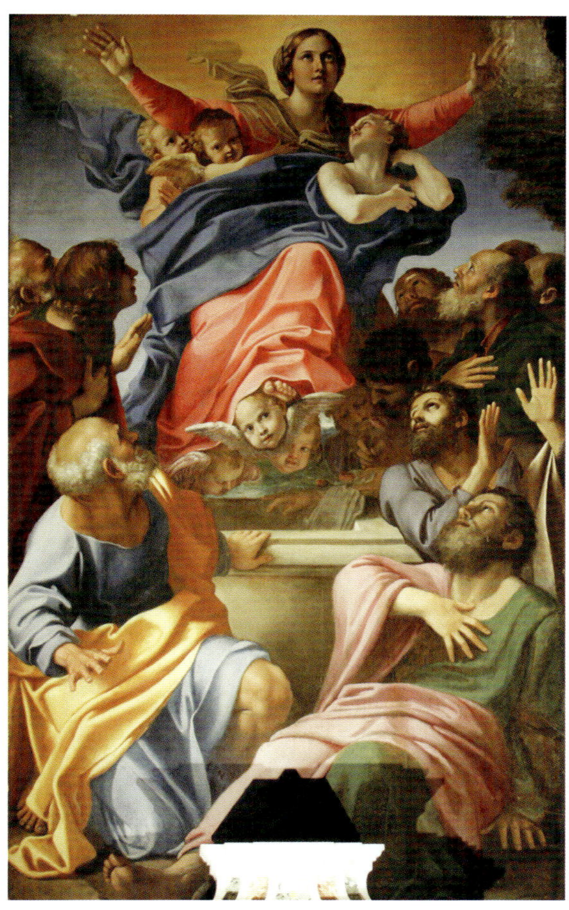

FIG. 14.7 Annibale Carracci, *Assumption of the Virgin Mary,* 1600–1601. Cerasi Chapel, Santa Maria del Popolo, Rome. Oil on wood, 245 × 155 cm.

expansive, brightly colored compositions that illustrated stories, often mythological. In the Roman palace known as Palazzo Farnese, the artists Annibale and Agostino Carracci painted the story of the marriage of Bacchus and Ariadne in a series of interconnected and plot-driven episodes. The Carracci were the men of the hour, fabulously popular and showered in commissions. Writing about Annibale, the younger of the two brothers, the biographer Giovanni Pietro Bellori gushed that the artist possessed "the most richly endowed temperament from which he developed his blessed genius, coupling two things rarely granted to one: nature and art in consummate excellence." In the *Triumph of Bacchus and Ariadne*, handsome, youthful men and women, playful putti, drunken gods—all joyously twist and turn and dance in the triumphant wedding celebration. It is optimistic, colorful, and much indebted to the ceiling of the Sistine Chapel by Michelangelo. The viewer can happily read, step-by-step, the stories leading to the mythical marriage, comfortable in the knowledge that there is a clear storyline that orients the room. The Carracci brothers also painted with a great fluidity of form. Bodies move gracefully. Colors are soft and warm. Sinuous lines lead the eye gently through the composition.

The comparison of Caravaggio and the Carracci is most striking in the Cerasi Chapel. After the triumph of the Farnese galleries, Annibale won a major commission to paint a panel for the Cerasi Chapel (Fig. 14.7). Caravaggio was selected for the two side panels, admittedly lesser spots. The contrast between the two artists could not be more obvious and, frankly, risible. Carracci shows the Virgin erupting from her tomb while the apostles, bundled in bright, technicolor robes, turn and twist in gestures of surprise. The painting is filled with heroic, muscular forms, brilliantly saccharine colors, empty gestures, ridiculous putti hiding in her robes and popping out from under her feet.

Responsible Annibale turned in his painting on time. Caravaggio did not. He struggled and fought with his compositions. His first attempt at *The Conversion of Saint Paul*, now in the Odalescalchi Balbi Collection in Rome, was rejected by the patron. This painting is a complicated composition with an angel, a dramatically reaching Christ, a violent old man without shoes, and an addled horse. Paul, in the midst of falling to the ground, covers both eyes with a desperate cry of anguish. Caravaggio's second attempt, *The Conversion* now in the chapel, was a more focused composition. And it seems to have responded to Carracci's painting. It's almost as though Caravaggio is making a jab at Carracci's work. Caravaggio takes Carracci's pristine and naïve Virgin's extended arms and upturned gaze and gives them to the sinner. The gesture that is all sweetness and light becomes a gesture of confusion, of seeking something that is invisible, and perhaps also a request for help so that he can get up. Her eyes look upward into the heavens. His eyes look upward in absolute futility. The light Paul cannot see comes out of an engulfing darkness.

A similar painterly retort seems to color Caravaggio's Peter. "Oh, how quaint," Caravaggio seems to say. "You made Peter surprised and gave him a cleverly foreshortened hand. It's darling." And then he paints Peter upside down, fore-shortened in a way that disrupts and shocks. Peter's wrinkled brow and pained expression truly capture the agony of his martyrdom. Peter even looks in the direction that his executors are pushing him toward, experiencing the fullness of his suffering. He is anticipating his own sacrifice, his own martyrdom. He looks toward the altar knowing that as he sheds his blood he will be saved by the flesh and blood of Christ. But he might also be looking at Carracci's Peter. Perhaps we might also read his face with an element of disdainful surprise. That bright burst of yellow on the crucifier's backside (a clear companion to the back of the horse) seems to be a response to the shiny yellow robe of Carracci's Saint Peter. And that extended foot of Carracci's Paul reappears too, in a much different, dirtier form. "Let me show you a foot, a real foot," Caravaggio seems to say.

There are no documents to support the idea that Caravaggio was engaging in a painterly sparring with his contemporary. It would be dangerous to suggest as much, if there were not other examples of Caravaggio being difficult, a contrar-ian, an instigator of brawls. Admittedly, many of the stories about Caravaggio come from biased biographers who seem to have had a low opinion of the artist. The same Giovanni Bellori who praised the spectacular wit and genius of Anni-bale Carracci, asserted that Caravaggio "suppressed the dignity of art" and called his compositions "inadequate," his coloring "weak" (1610). Vincenzo Carducho went further: "The coming of Caravaggio was an omen of the ruin and demise of painting, comparable to how at the end of the world the Antichrist, with false miracles and strange deeds, will lead to perdition great numbers of people, who will be moved by his works, apparently so admirable but actually deceiving, false, and transitory" (1633). Giovanni Baglione also wrote that Caravaggio had "destroyed painting." Baglione had a particular bone to pick with Caravaggio. The historian actually took the artist to court. Baglione sued Caravaggio for libel, for having besmirched the writer's reputation by circulating anonymous verses

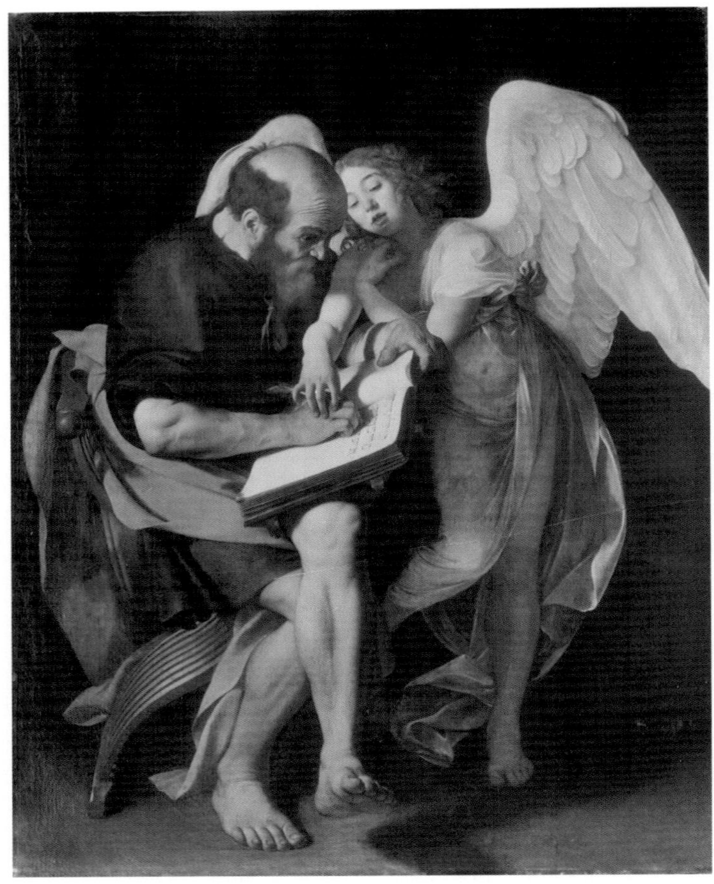

FIG. 14.8 Caravaggio, *Saint Matthew and the Angel* (destroyed), 1602.
Originally painted for the Cerasi Chapel. Oil on canvas, 295 × 195 cm.

making fun of him. Thus these writers may have been biased. But there is no
doubt that Caravaggio had few friends in the artist community.

Caravaggio also had a rocky relationship with his patrons. The rejected Saint
Paul painting was not the last time Caravaggio would be told, no, try again. His
Death of the Virgin (although praised by Peter Paul Rubens) was not accepted
by the parish for which it was painted. And the first version of Saint Matthew

writing the gospel for the Contarelli Chapel was also rejected (Fig. 14.8). We can only discuss this painting with a black-and-white image because it was destroyed in 1945, during World War II. This forever-lost painting shows an elderly Matthew writing a text, in Hebrew, with the help of the gentle touch of a beautifully mannered angel with buoyantly curly hair and a soft navel that shows through his sweeping, stylized cloak. The angel's noble, widespread wings mirror the base of Matthew's chair, known as a Savonarola chair, and his handsome and exposed left leg replicates the shape of the extended, foreshortened leg of the older man. Again, we have a foot, none too clean, penetrating our space or, more precisely, the space just above the altar, just above the place where the priest would be elevating the Host. Perhaps it was the rawness of the figure of Matthew that displeased his patrons. Perhaps Matthew was too old, too unseemly, too plebian. Baglione, already expressing his dislike of Caravaggio, reported that the painting pleased no one. Bellori later wrote, "After [Caravaggio] had finished the central picture of Saint Matthew and installed it on the altar, the priests took it down, saying that the figure with its legs crossed and its feet rudely exposed to the public had neither the decorum nor the appearance of the saint."

The scholar Helen Langdon argues that this Matthew was too unlike the Matthew in *The Calling*—heftier, less refined, less worldly. Perhaps the first painting does make him look a bit like a rube. Langdon describes his bulging eyes as indicative of his astonishment over the fact that the words appear miraculously. There is no inkwell in the room, she points out. But I think his astonishment is also about the existence of words, the fact that he is the recipient of these ideas. The painting seems to be about creation and inspiration, about that moment when, after struggling with your ideas and worrying that it won't come together, it comes, miraculously. The painting seems to show the instant when those ideas appear and how, when they do, it is a revelation, it is exciting and shocking and wonderful. Those words on the page exist where there was nothing before. I love to think that Matthew is reading the words coming from the angel and his mind and his hand and thinking, "Oh, this is good! I can do this!"

This painting is about that moment of creation, the moment of inspiration that we all grapple with, fumble for, and which Caravaggio also struggled with, especially in the creation of the paintings for the Contarelli Chapel. The commission for this chapel was his first big break. So it was massively important that he do well, and a big blow when he was told to take the central painting down and do another one. There are no documents to say precisely why the painting was rejected. But the second version, which was retained, removes the eroticism of the angel and makes Matthew less surprised, maybe more of an intellectual, more austere. That impact is still there, however. Caravaggio still captures that "aha" moment, the instant of figuring it out, grabbing a notebook and writing down your thoughts as fast as you can. There is no time to sit down. The bench hasn't settled. It might fall over that ledge. No matter. He must focus on hearing the message and writing it down, which he does with intensity. It's as though his orange cloak is on fire. He is burning with inspiration and with ideas, which are powerful and burst onto the scene, out of that darkness, here again a metaphor for not knowing, for being uncertain, for having no idea what to say or write or paint—until you do.

If *The Inspiration* is about capturing that instantaneous moment of an idea, that pure moment of insight and revelation, *The Martyrdom* is much more complicated and confused, as it was in its creation. Centrifugal figures spill away in confusion and horror and disgust while the executioner, strangely unclothed, seems to scream at the elder man. Matthew, having fallen on his left side, hangs over the ledge of the deep baptismal font. His left hand cups in a way that leads the eye in a swooping S-curve up through to his flattened right hand. At first it might seem that his right hand is in a gesture that indicates his fear, a way of telling the man with the sword to stop. But although Matthew might lock eyes with his aggressor, his hand is actually open as a gesture of willingness, of acceptance. He is holding out his hand to receive the palm leaf extended by the angel above. The angel hanging over the painted altar is a mirror for the martyr—both lie on their sides, both have one knee forward with the other drawn backward, we see the tops of heads and extended right arms, and both hover over the ledge, on the edge. Ultimately, that palm frond is more powerful than the sword. Matthew may be the only figure to recognize that. The palm is the essence, the truth, the fulcrum around which all else spins out of control.

It took Caravaggio a long time to get to this final composition. X-ray photographs show that Caravaggio started with a complex grouping of figures

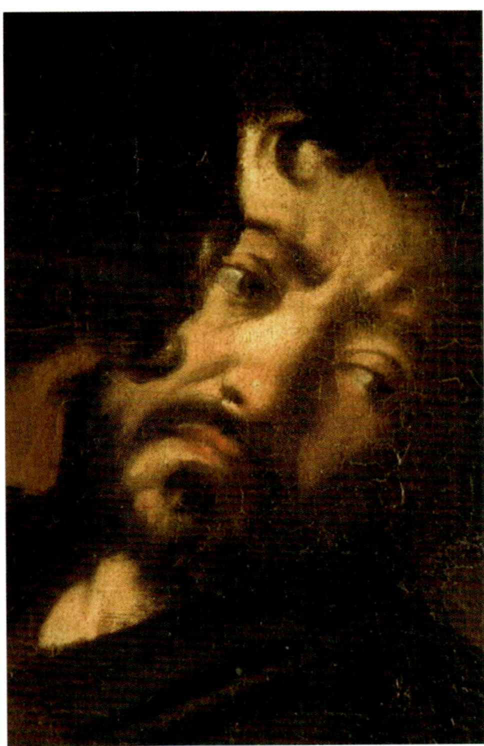

FIG. 14.9 Detail of the face of Caravaggio, from *The Martyrdom of Saint Matthew*, Cerasi Chapel.

concentrated in the foreground. The executioner stood before a standing Matthew, and to the right was an angel holding a book. It was static, hieratic, and symbolic—good versus evil. In a second version, Caravaggio turned to a composition painted by Raphael of the battle of Ostia, which has a crowd of onlookers (even including women, who are missing from all three final paintings). But that did not suit. And so he put it to the side, gave up for the moment, and turned to *The Calling of Saint Matthew*, hoping he would get the inspiration he needed to paint this martyrdom. When he came back to *The Martyrdom*, he pushed the figures toward the middle of the painting and out of the immediate foreground. Actually, he removed the foreground altogether. Instead of creating a place for stability, any ground at all, he gives us a dark, deep ditch. The altar with its untouched, ever-flickering candle, and the steps leading to its holy and sacred space, provide the only sense of physical stability in the painting. The rest is a violation of our expectations. The saint is upside down. The murderer is central and dominant, absorbing the light with a sinister beauty. No one is taking responsibility. Everyone turns and runs.

The artist, who appears in the upper left-hand corner, also flees the scene. The palimpsest of Caravaggio's different attempts, his painterly struggles, is hidden from the naked eye. But his insecurities are evident in this self-portrait (Fig. 14.9). He has pitch-black hair, weighty eyebrows, downcast mouth, piercing black eyes. He is conflicted, confused, concerned. He has one foot on the steps to the altar; the other is out the door. His left hand is turned up in shock and horror, reflecting that of the man in the foreground. He wants to escape, to avoid any implication in the violence and the brutality, but he is stuck. He can't help himself; he has to look back and see. How does that fright, his flight, relate to his deeply held religious convictions? In a strangely prescient detail he marks himself by the sword, figuratively slashing himself through with the instrument held by the man in the feathered hat. It is as if Caravaggio sees himself marked, as with the mark of Cain, foreshadowing his own violent demise, or at least indicating his own violent lifestyle—lots of taverns, lots of trouble.

Caravaggio looks back in another sense, toward the past. Caravaggio seems to have fought not only with his contemporaries and his own demons but also with the men that established the canon—Raphael, Leonardo, and of course his namesake, Michelangelo. Caravaggio was so named because of the town he came from, but his birth name was Michelangelo Merisi. Baglione tells us that Caravaggio "would speak badly of painters of the past," and Bellori asserts that the artist "not only ignored the most excellent marbles of the ancients and the paintings of Raphael, but he despised them." This isn't exactly true. We know that Caravaggio was looking at Raphael's works when considering the painting of *The Martyrdom*. Caravaggio was also clearly aware of past representations of the calling of Matthew. An interesting altarpiece by Orcagna, housed in the Uffizi, shows the scene with Christ standing outside of Matthew's tax-collecting booth and the new disciple coming right out, ready and willing to follow his new Lord. Vittore Carpaccio also illustrated the scene in 1502, highlighting

Matthew's decisiveness as he steps dramatically out of the door of his booth to meet Christ. In both earlier paintings, Christ is, as in Caravaggio's work, on the move. He looks back toward Matthew, but he is clearly moving in the opposite direction, already continuing his journey of spreading the word.

Caravaggio also most certainly knew and studied the paintings by Michelangelo of *The Conversion of Saint Paul* and *The Crucifixion of Saint Peter* housed in the Vatican. It is not a pure coincidence that he chose the same two saints and the same two moments for his paintings in the Cerasi Chapel. But it is true that Caravaggio ultimately does not pick the format of Michelangelo's Peter and Paul. He seems to borrow certain elements and highlight them in particular ways. But he makes certain that those citations retain his own mark, his signature. This is not a case of dismissal, as the early biographers assert. Yet there is certainly a sense that Caravaggio is doing his own thing. For instance, the large, expansive back of the man in the foreground of the martyrdom painting, the way he twists and contracts his muscles, is clearly derived from the sibyls in the Sistine Chapel (Fig. 16.5). Most poignant is the gesture with which we started *The Calling of Saint Matthew,* that weighty hand of Christ, a clear citation of Adam's hand in Michelangelo's majestic fresco, also in the Sistine Chapel. Howard Hibbard eloquently explains that "Christ is the new Adam," quoting 1 Corinthians 15:22: "As in Adam all men die, so in Christ all will be brought to life." Certainly the typological reading is compelling and provides an important interpretation. But it is worth noting that Caravaggio flips the hand. It faces the opposite direction. Maybe Caravaggio is actually blending the power of God's gesture with the shape of Adam's. Either way, the quotation is not exact. Is imitation the sincerest form of flattery, or is Caravaggio positing that he is the true genius? Are his borrowings out of respect, or is he saying that he has captured a truer version of inspiration, of creation, and of Christ?

The struggles of Caravaggio, of his relationship to his colleagues, his patrons, his work, himself, and his place within the canon were not relegated to the studio. Many of the things that Caravaggio is accused of in the admittedly biased accounts of Bellori or Baglione are confirmed by police records. In the words of art historian Charles Dempsey, "He was uncommonly, congenitally, and repeatedly vicious to a degree that was certainly not normal among painters. To be blunt about it, he was undeniably a thug, certainly a bully, and something of a coward." For example, there is the report that Caravaggio got so angry when an important commission to paint a fresco program in the sanctuary of Loreto was given to the artist Pomarancio instead of himself that he sent one of his *torcimanni* (a treacherous Sicilian type) to deliver a mortal insult to the older painter, marking him with a scar on his face. When his landlady Prudenzia Bruna sequestered his possessions and barred him from his rooms because he had not paid rent for four months, he responded by smashing the windows of her house with rocks. He and one of his *torcimanni* named Onorio Longhi slashed the face of one Flavio Canonico, a former guard at Castel Sant'Angelo. Caravaggio was arrested for carrying weapons on multiple occasions. And of course Caravaggio committed murder.

The story is told as follows. After grand festivities in honor of the anniversary of the coronation of the pope, on May 28, 1606, the artist bumped into a man named Ranuccio Tomassoni, with whom he had had a row a few days before. Caravaggio was with his friends, including the nefarious Onorio (ironically named). Ranuccio had his brother and two brothers-in-law. According to Baglione, the fight was started over a disagreement with a tennis match. Bellori wrote that the two men were actually hitting each other with tennis rackets. It seems that the skirmish happened near a tennis court close to the Palazzo Firenze, although the genesis of the fight may have had less to do with the score from a tennis match, as Baglione records, and more with young men looking for a fight. Young men with a proud, temperamental artist at the helm.

Either way, Ranuccio fell and Caravaggio killed the man by stabbing him in the stomach. Caravaggio, badly wounded in the head, escaped for the Alban Hills and spent the final years of his life in exile, moving from Naples to Malta (where he was thrown into jail for having caused a brawl), to Sicily, and back to Naples. All he wanted was to be back in Rome. In 1610 Caravaggio learned that he was to receive a pardon from the nephew of the pope, Cardinal Scipione Borghese. Caravaggio boarded the ship at Chiaia, Naples. The tiny ship stopped at Civitavecchia, at the mouth of the Tiber, about forty-five miles from Rome. But something happened. A mistake. Caravaggio was put in jail. According to Bellori, this was an accident; the police were supposed to arrest someone else. By the time Caravaggio had borrowed enough money to get out of jail, he was completely destitute and had to travel on foot, in the heat of the summer. But he couldn't go to Rome. He had to find the boat, which happened to be in Port'Ercole, in the opposite direction from Rome, because it was carrying a number of his precious paintings, paintings that he had labored over in Naples and which he needed to give to Scipione as a way of ensuring his pardon.

When he got to Port'Ercole, some sixty-five miles from Civitavecchia, the paintings were gone. Caravaggio's desperation must have been overwhelming. Lost, penniless, robbed of his paintings, it was in this nasty little town that Caravaggio caught a fever. He died soon after, probably in the local infirmary, although no one seems to have identified his body. And the paintings? There is no exact record of the number of paintings that Caravaggio was carrying on his misfortunate trip. Three were recovered, then two were later lost, leaving us with only a painting of Saint John the Baptist, a painting that is now in the Galleria Borghese in Rome. This painting represents quite a contrast to an earlier painting of John the Baptist from 1602, now in the Nelson-Atkins Museum of Art. In the earlier configuration the boy is youthful, sexy, confident. The latter John is sallow, malnourished, irritated, and almost looks like he is trapped, with his wrists bound.

Caravaggio is all contrasts and contradictions. An ignoble death for a masterful artist. An unmarked grave for a man whose name would be one of the most famous (or, for some, infamous) for generations to come. A man who was an ardent believer but could not control his own vicious inclinations, living as a roué, a rogue, a rebel. He painted scenes that included and valued the very people that he abused, people like the landlady whose house he attacked. He wanted to make his indelible mark but rejected the canon, while being a part of it at the same time. He wanted huge commissions, but he did not want to follow the rules established in the contracts he signed, turning in his work late and rejecting established outlines for the projects. He was all confidence and swagger, but in his paintings he is a coward who runs away from the scene of a crime, from the death of a saint. Or worse, he is a monster without a body, without a soul, his head literally hanging in shame and disgust in his self-portrait—his face is on Goliath's head in his painting *David and Goliath* (Fig. 14.10).

Things that matter aren't easy, or necessarily pretty, Caravaggio seems to say—look harder, think about what you see, think about what it might mean,

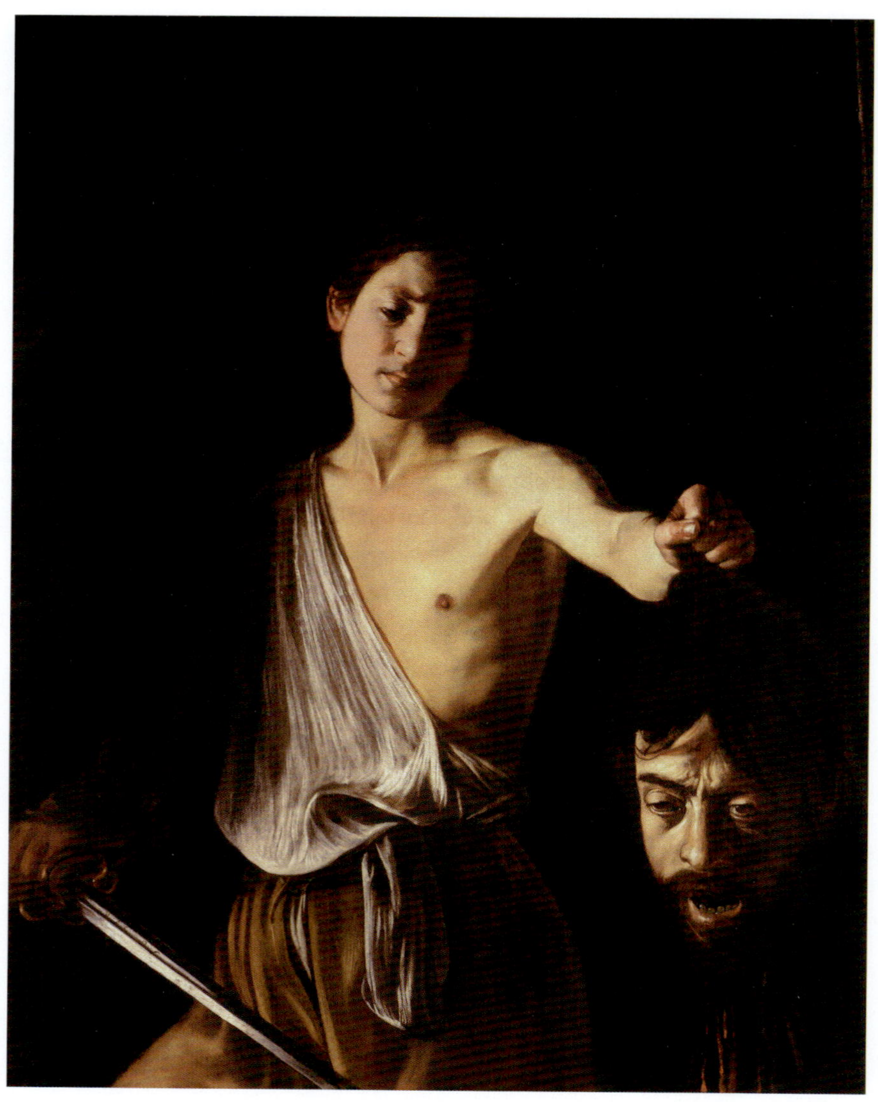

FIG. 14.10 Caravaggio, *David and Goliath*, ca. 1610. Galleria Borghese, Rome. Oil on canvas, 125 × 101 cm.

ask questions, don't jump to conclusions. Caravaggio asserts the veracity of the lives of the saints and the truth of Christ. But he does it with a grit that finds the sacred in the middle of a dark and secular world. Mysterious or mystical moments become tangible and identifiable in a way that flitting angel heads cannot convey. Those brightly colored figures are, as far as Caravaggio is concerned, just not working. So he flips them upside down and turns off the light. The sacred requires constant awareness, as complicated and tenebrous as a ray of light partially piercing the darkness.

A final contrast that defines Caravaggio is the fact that he wanted to be famous, but he was incensed about imitators. Baglione wrote, "Many young artists followed [Caravaggio's] example and painted heads from life, without studying the fundamentals of design…satisfied merely with colors; consequently they do not know how to put two figures together, nor weave together a narrative." On this point, and probably only this point, Caravaggio would have agreed. His style was his own. He did not train apprentices. He did not have a workshop, unlike Annibale Carracci, who founded one of the first art academies in Italy, the Accademia degli Incamminati, which had the sole purpose of providing a comprehensive training drawn from the styles of Raphael, Michelangelo, Titian, and Correggio. Caravaggio vociferously accused the painter Guido Reni of having stolen his "style and color" in his *Crucifixion of Saint Peter.*

But Caravaggisti do not only exist among the Old Masters. Artist Lloyd Walsh, based in San Antonio, also paints with an eye to the Baroque. His untitled painting of a white dog lying on a table directly references the *Agnus Dei* by the Baroque artist Francisco de Zurbarán, which is in the Prado and was painted in 1640. Tenebristic tendencies define Walsh's paintings. Bursts of light expose isolated forms, figures that seem to have been caught unawares and that belong to a world of the murky, ill-defined, impenetrable darkness. One of his best paintings is *The Blowfish* (2012). The animal looks as though he has been tricked and caught, not in a net but in a painting. His look is one of shock and uncertainty. Raw and realistic, fearful and frank, these bodies are trapped in an immediate moment, holding their breath with hapless suspense while suspended in time, in space, and in a starkly painted reality.

The style is eternal. The genesis is Caravaggio.

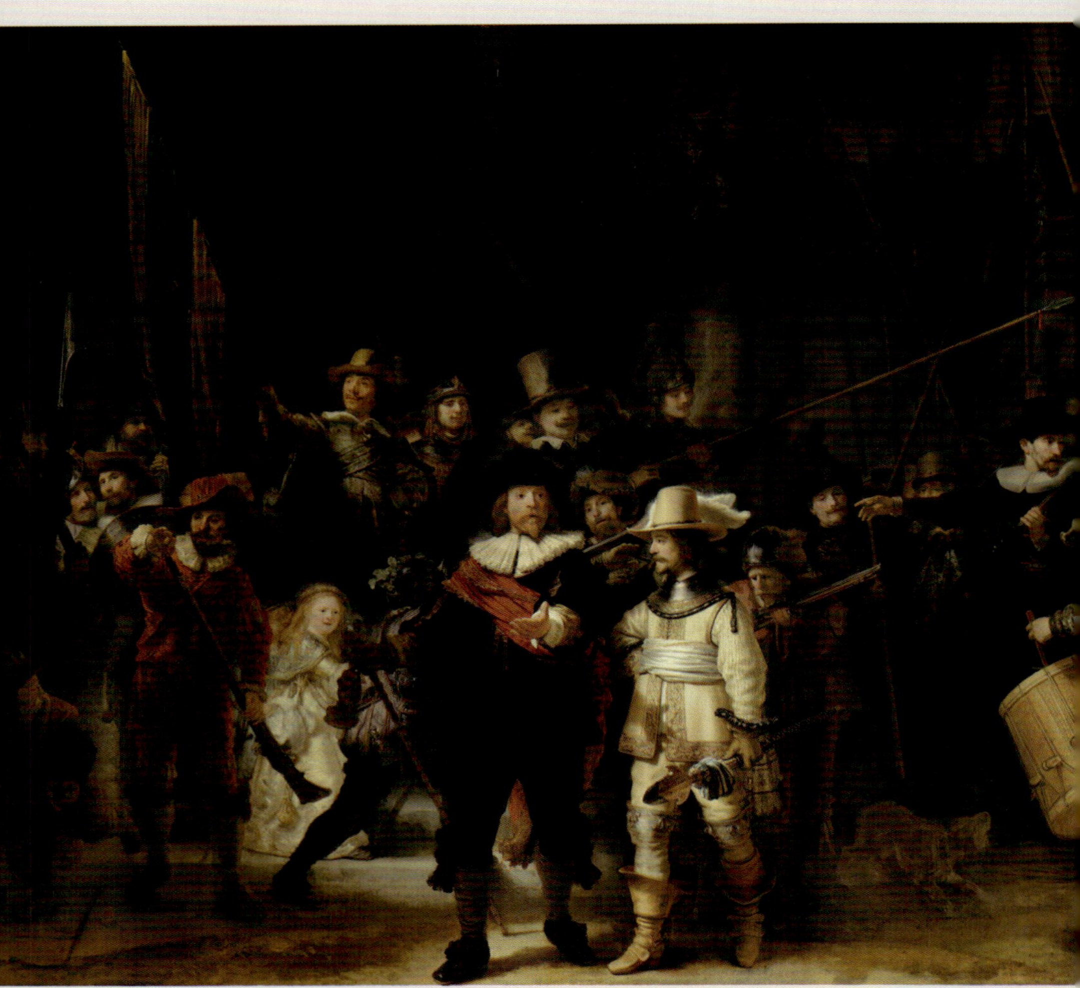

FIG. 15.1 Rembrandt van Rijn, *The Shooting Company of Frans Banning Cocq and Willem van Ruytenburch (The Night Watch)*, 1642. Rijksmuseum, Amsterdam. Oil on canvas, 363 × 437 cm (cut down from original size).

Rembrandt, *The Night Watch*

1642

DUTCH BAROQUE ART

On a quiet Sunday afternoon in September 1975, three people—a young couple and a tall man—were looking at *The Night Watch* in the Rijksmuseum of Amsterdam (Fig. 15.1). As we have all done by accident, the man went too close to the painting and was asked by the guard to take a step back, which he did. The young couple continued to the next gallery, to see a copy of the Rembrandt painting made by Gerrit Lundens. But then the man stepped forward yet again, this time with a knife. The guard grabbed the man's arm and shouted, alerting the young couple who rushed in from the room nearby. By the time they had stopped the man, the painting had been slashed in twelve long gashes, including an entire triangular piece that fell to the floor.

There was no political message as there had been in the attack on Velázquez's *Rokeby Venus* by the suffragette Mary Richardson in 1914. When a man cut Vermeer's *Love Letters* out of its frame with a potato peeler in 1971, he demanded that 200 million Belgian francs be given to refugees in East Pakistan in return for the painting.

How fragile the past is. Seventeenth-century paintings seem to be victimized regularly, and often. The attack in 1975 was not the first or last for *The Night Watch*. In 1911 it had been cut by a man wielding a shoemaker's knife. In 1990 a man sprayed acid concealed in a pump bottle onto the painting. Restorers stopped the burning of the acid before it penetrated beyond the most superficial layer, the varnish on the painting. These actions are clearly those of the unstable, but they represent a charged reaction to the painting that, in a way, we feel too. We also get drawn into its power. What is it that makes a work of art work, get at us, draw out our rawest reactions? This is a painting about men that we do not know. We can identify them, but they are long dead, their faces are relics, images from a distant past. As Hamlet says about the actor reciting lines from a play about Priam's death, "What's Hecuba to him, or he to Hecuba that he should weep for her?" And yet the words have the capacity to, as Hamlet says, "drown the stage with tears, and cleave the general ear with horrid speech, make mad the guilty and appall the free, confound the ignorant, and amaze indeed the very faculties of eyes and ears." The emotional effects that Shakespeare described and produced in 1600, Rembrandt evoked some forty years later with his *Night Watch*.

One positive result that came of the attack in 1975 was an immediate restoration and cleaning of the painting. Varnish is often added to paintings to preserve them from dust and to give them an added sheen, but they darken and yellow over time, especially when the varnishes are tinted. In one of the varnish layers the conservators found ocher pigments, and in another they found a brown substance that looked like burnt sugar and smelled sweet, perhaps because it had been mixed with honey. Honey does not belong on a painting. These layers of varnish relate to the name *Night Watch*.

The painting was never given a name by the artist. It was simply supposed to be a portrait of the men in the civic guard known as the Kloveniers. But the painting had been so sufficiently shellacked, had turned so dark and murky, that it looked like it was taking place at night. The eighteenth-century British painter Sir Joshua Reynolds was a huge fan of Rembrandt Harmenszoon van Rijn (1606–1669), learning from the earlier artist and emulating him too. Yet Reynolds wrote that he could not believe that Rembrandt had actually painted the work, despite a prominent signature by the artist, because it had such a "poor manner" about it and because it was yellowish (which is a rather ironic observation, as many of Reynolds's own works turned yellow over the centuries, making many of his gentlemen and ladies look a bit seasick). When Rembrandt's painting returned from its cleaning, it was completely different. The restoration was a revelation. The painting emerged from under the suffocating (and scented) glazes, and shed that accidental and unflattering name of *Night Watch*. The museum now labels the painting with something closer to the original purpose, as a portrait of the militiamen of Amsterdam. A fuller anglicized title is *The Shooting Company of Captain Frans Banning Cocq and Lieutenant Willem van Ruytenburch.*

Captain Banning Cocq leads the brigade with bravado, dressed in the formal black of the Dutch upper class. This was the look—almost exclusively black clothing accentuated by a crisp white collar made of layers of fine lace. It is hard to pin down the popularity of a particular style. Tastes change, and motivations for one kind of outfit over another are a bit esoteric. But it is interesting to consider a few arguments about the prominence of these starkly colored clothes. One scholar, Simon Schama, has suggested that the people of the Dutch Netherlands were overcome with an "embarrassment of riches."

Amsterdam of the seventeenth century was extremely wealthy and prominent. It was the industrial capital of the Dutch Republic, importing raw materials and exporting finished silk, leather, wool, and tobacco. It had printing presses, beautiful town squares, architectural triumphs, and a huge art market. But all that financial and material wealth did not quite jibe with the Calvinist religious principles, with a religion characterized by somber piety. The people of early seventeenth-century Amsterdam may have been avoiding ostentatious clothing so as to look as pious as they believed they were or hoped to be. Of course these materials were no less expensive than those with brighter colors. Banning Cocq's suit is made of a fine, rich, creamy velvet. Thus the dress could assert both piety and wealth in the same breath.

But there is another aspect to this reserved costume that seems to draw upon the attitudes and styles in the Spanish court. The Dutch had been recently liberated from a rather oppressive Spanish rule, having obtained political independence in 1609. The war limped along until 1648, when the Spanish armies finally retreated. As much as the Spanish presence was heartily despised, the Dutch were borrowing and emulating the dress styles of the royal family. One might think of the many portraits by Velázquez of the king of Spain, Philip IV. The Spanish king wears deep blacks and the white collar, a far cry from the overbloated regalia of the French kings. Of course, the ladies of the Spanish court appear in colorful and brilliant dresses, as we know from *Las Meninas,* but the priest, the counselor, the painter, and possibly Philip himself are all wearing the same dark garb (Fig. 16.2). The message promoted by Philip IV was that he did not need such finery to show his power because his was self-evident. Perhaps Banning Cocq's dress says something similar, that he does not need elegant clothing to show off what is already clear, which is that he is the leader of the company, at its center, in control.

Heightening the subtlety of Banning Cocq's appearance is the brilliant, scintillating dress of his lieutenant, Van Ruytenburch. Now that's an outfit. His ensemble is a bright yellowish gold. Creamy white sleeves are delicately embroidered with shimmering gilt threads, as are the edges of the silk cummerbund that wraps around his waist. The entire ensemble is filled with flourishes and decorated with finesse. His prominent hat, which is taller than that of Banning Cocq, is embellished with pearls and sparkling stones. The brim curves elegantly and sinuously. The front of the hat flips upward, a detail mirrored by the flouncy white feathers that trail behind. The rest of the outfit is similarly rich and decorative. The heavy metal collar that the lieutenant wears has a thick gold border, which is fringed with gold and turquoise threads. The same fringe (and same U-shape) appears around the base of his light-brown leather glove and at the end of his long spear composed of complex crisscrossing shapes and bright metallic balls. The gold and blues allude to the company that we are watching gather, the Kloveniers or musketeers, which had as their heraldry a golden claw on a blue field. These are the same colors that appear in the flag held in the left corner of the painting. Van Ruytenburch is thus like a walking emblem or flag for the men of the Kloveniers.

The details of his dress say much the same. On the border of his bright, A-line jacket are two rampant lions stitched in a thick golden thread, painted by Rembrandt in a heavily layered paint, a technique known as impasto. The coat of arms for Amsterdam is essentially the flag of the city—red with a black middle stripe and three white X's on the stripe—flanked by two elegant lions standing on their hind legs. Van Ruytenburch not only wears the rampant lions but seems to embody them too. He is standing to the side of Banning Cocq, who is wearing red, black, and white. Van Ruytenburch is like the rampant lion; Banning Cocq is the flag of the colors of the entire city, of Amsterdam.

There is a second figure in gold to match Van Ruytenburch or to act as the second rampant lion from the heraldic shield. This is the strange little golden girl. Somehow she is Van Ruytenburch's foil or perhaps his mirror. The shadow of Banning Cocq's hand falls diagonally across the fine jacket of the lieutenant. Banning Cocq's shadowy glove hangs just in front of the little girl. Although softer, she wears a version of the lieutenant's grand metallic collar, which hangs like a short cape from her neck. The colors are the same—silver as the base and gold for the decorative flourishes. Like Van Ruytenburch, the little girl is adorned in regalia that is meant to glorify the Kloveniers. The symbol of the musketeers, the claw of a bird of prey, appears as the large white fowl that hangs upside down by its claws from her belt. There are a number of ways in which the two—girl and lieutenant—diverge. For one, Van Ruytenburch walks toward us, or at the very least toward the lower left corner of the painting. She seems to be moving in the opposite direction. She is already standing on the first step of a stairway that leads toward the back. Her right foot appears from the bottom of her skirt, indicating that she is, possibly, going to continue up the stairs, through the mass of men.

We know who Van Ruytenburch is. But no one knows who she is, what she is doing, or what she is looking at. Her brows are furrowed; perhaps it is a look of dismay or alarm. There seems to be a sensation of mirth too. Her mouth is open in what might be the beginnings of a smile. There does seem to have been a custom in which costumed emblem carriers, often young girls or boys, would precede certain societies of rhetoric, conducting competitive recitations of theatrical writings. Perhaps Rembrandt is alluding to the theatrical aspect of the gathering. Perhaps not. I like the mystery. It is something special to imagine the nymphlike girl floating in and out of the painting, giving it a metaphorical essence even though the exact message is unclear. It is sweet that she has a friend in her unnamed mission, a little girl with her head down and dressed in light blue. Renoir said that he would discard the painting but keep the golden girl. That splash of light, that quick quixotic look, her fluttering dash through the composition, that ridiculous upside-down chicken—these features add a sense of surprise, a twinkle, a sense of the transcendent, to a painting that is otherwise about men and weighty warlike activities.

On his own, Van Ruytenburch might look elegant and refined. Next to Banning Cocq, however, he trends closer to a dandy, a little fussy, a little bit costumey. The yellow leather hose are a touch too much, and might make one think of poor, mocked Malvolio and his yellow stockings in *Twelfth Night*. The gilded blade might be gilding the lily. Ironically, the juxtaposition—black next to gold, somber next to ornamental—highlights the action and leadership of Banning Cocq. Van Ruytenburch is quite literally in Banning Cocq's shadow as the captain's extended left hand darkens the elegant jacket of his lieutenant. Van Ruytenburch turns toward his leader and in so doing shows us the side of his face. Albeit elegant in outline, there is a flatness to his visage. He is almost like a classical coin—gold, in profile, flat. These all reinforce the fact that his captain is the dynamic one, the one in command. Banning Cocq is like the artist, like the director—he makes men move.

Banning Cocq's movement, his gestures, and his open mouth, voicing a command, indicate his authority, that he is at the helm. He moves with great vigor. That bright-red sash, his one piece of "flair," wraps dramatically and diagonally across his body. It almost appears to slip down his right shoulder, unlike the carefully tucked cummerbund on Van Ruytenburch. Where it meets his scabbard, the sash is bunchy and disorderly, then it falls so that the end swings and bounces, golden tassels flipping jauntily, as he takes his purposeful step. His pose, with his right foot forward and left behind, make him look like a latter-day Augustus of Prima Porta in that contrapposto stance (Fig. 6.9). But while Augustus is confidently situated on his right foot, gesturing to a captive audience, Banning Cocq is still in midstride. His stance is more complicated. He walks toward the right but twists to look over his left shoulder, toward his lieutenant. Augustus points with authority and clarity. Banning Cocq holds out his hand in a position that is hard to parse. It could be that he is indicating the direction of the march, although it is a gentle gesture if that is the case. It might suggest cool confidence, but it is just as likely that he is midthought, expressing a conjecture, even an entreaty.

The same gesture appears in a painting from 1641 of Cornelis Claesz Anslo and his wife (Fig. 15.2). Anslo was a wealthy merchant and ship owner. But the portrait was not about his wealth or property, it was about his piety and his profession as a Mennonite preacher. Rembrandt saw this painting as an opportunity to explore the possibility of painting speech. The challenge of painting speech was something Rembrandt had first explored in *The Anatomy Lesson of Dr. Nicolaes Tulp*, about ten years earlier (Fig. 15.3). *The Anatomy Lesson* was the first major

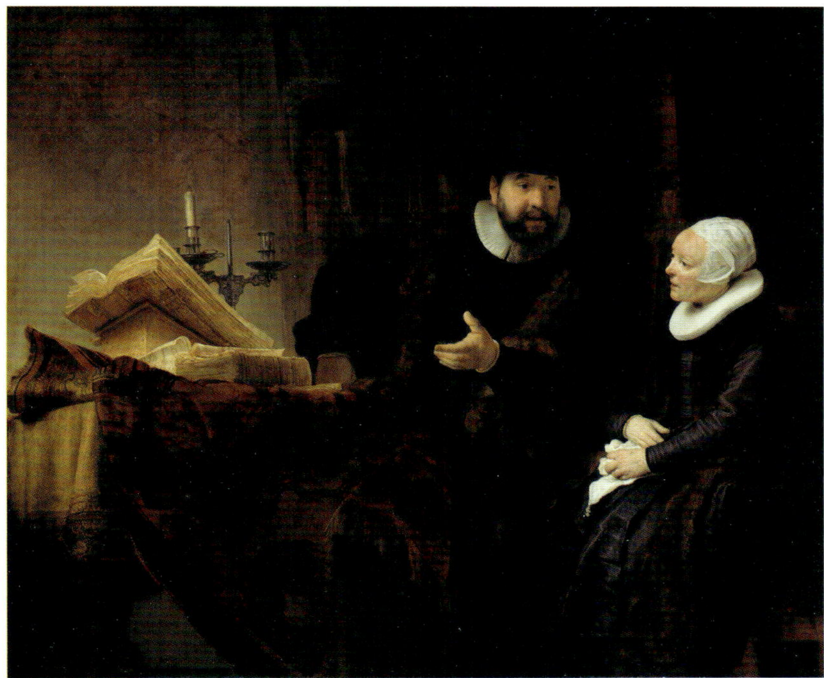

FIG. 15.2 Rembrandt van Rijn, *The Mennonite Preacher Anslo and His Wife,* 1641. Staatliche Museen, Berlin. Oil on canvas, 173.7 × 207.6 cm.

commission that the artist had received, and it was a gamble to choose such a young artist. Rembrandt proved his mettle, however, bringing life, emotion, and a psychological intensity to the room of the surgeon.

Lecturers, like Tulp, often gave public dissections of executed criminals in the guild's anatomical amphitheater. Thus there was a theatrical aspect to the subject and the scene. But other painters had made similar scenes staid and symmetrical. In *The Anatomy Lesson of Dr. Sebastian Egbertsz* by Thomas de Keyser, for example, the painting is mostly an accumulation of flat portraits, heads emerging from the darkness with perfectly ironed collars. They are dignified but totally posed. We might guess about their occupation, but there is nothing to indicate actual work, or why it might be interesting. The only figure that engages with the

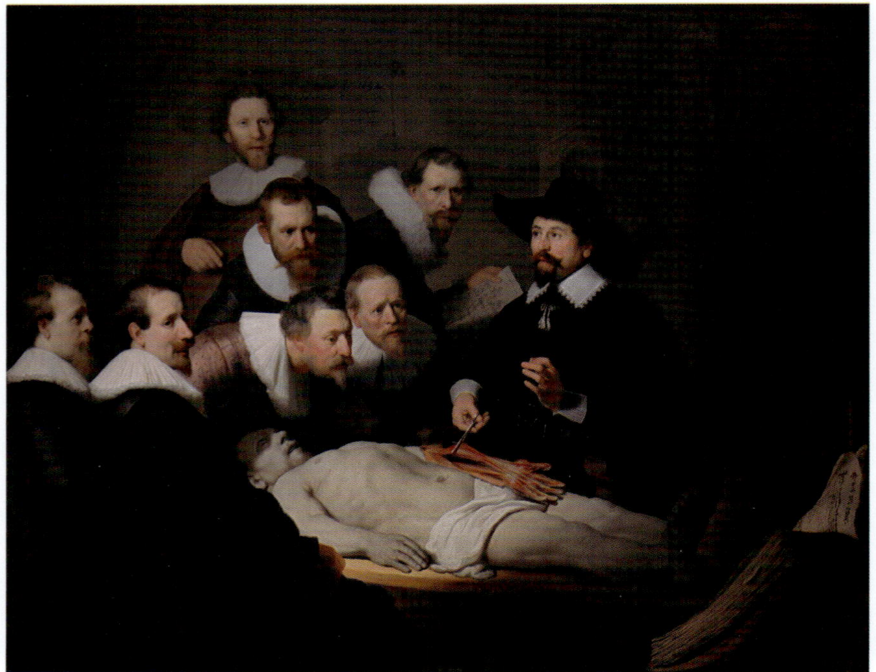

FIG. 15.3 Rembrandt van Rijn, *The Anatomy Lesson of Dr. Nicolaes Tulp,* 1632. Mauritshuis, The Hague, The Netherlands. Oil on canvas, 169.5 × 216.5 cm.

skeleton points at its vertebrae with a long pointer, as far away as he can get, with a look of suspicion or distaste. Even the cadaver is cleaned up and posed—the skeleton turns away demurely, his arms falling elegantly at his sides.

In *The Anatomy Lesson,* the corpse is sallow, limp, and white with decay. The dissected arm is raw and bloody. The men are eager to see. They pile up, looking intently, leaning awkwardly, all in the hopes of seeing the lesson better. And hearing the lesson better too. Tulp's mouth opens slightly, lecturing to his eager pupils. And he holds up his left hand, perhaps in the gesture of speaking, just as he holds the dead man's left forearm aloft with his pincers. He might be in the middle of explaining how the tendons work and gesticulating as he does. Or maybe he is enacting, with his own hand, the ways that the tendons make the hand move. Either way, diction becomes action, and Rembrandt captures that in paint. Simon Schama says the artist aimed to paint "*both* sight *and* sound," that he aspired to be able to "paint diction." When Rembrandt returned to the same challenge with Anslo and his wife, he seemed to want to make the voice stronger, more palpable, more paintable. Anslo leans toward his wife as he speaks. He also points to the texts that he reads from with his left hand, with that gesture, the Banning Cocq gesture, which seems to activate his words. We cannot see the words; they are facing Anslo. Yet he enacts them for us; his image explains the kind of message they contain—something holy, something marvelous. The words in the book are brought to life by his enthusiasm, by his breath, and by his hand.

Rembrandt also brings words to life—Anslo's words, Dr. Tulp's lesson, Banning Cocq's orders—with *his* hand. The viewer responds like the students straining to see and hear, like Anslo's wife receiving the words and marveling at them, and like Lieutenant Van Ruytenburch, getting his orders and marching to them. Rembrandt is grabbing us, making us feel the energy of the moment. Consider the progression of these three hands, all left hands—from Tulp's to Anslo's to Banning Cocq's. We can almost watch those hands reaching at us with growing intensity, trying to pull us deeper into the paintings as the drama heightens. Over the course of these three paintings, the hand seems to gesture farther into our field, the fingers expand, and the palm turns progressively upward. Left hands get special attention—there is the shadow of what was once a hand, the cadaver's; the shadow of Banning Cocq's left hand on Van Ruytenburch's dress; the empty glove that Banning Cocq holds. The left-handed glove hangs provocatively right above the name Rembrandt, his signature, the word for which is *handtekening* in Dutch.

From this extended hand the entire brigade starts to take shape, almost as though this gesture is the quintessential center of the painting, the point from which all else begins. Yet the hand is not the actual center as it was painted by Rembrandt. In 1715 the painting was cut on all four sides, most dramatically on the left and on the top. The original dimensions were recorded in a copy of the painting by Lundens, painted seven years after *The Night Watch* was completed. Restoring those edges places the central point of the composition closer to the head of a little fellow who seems to be running with long strides or taking a large step toward the upper right. All that we see of his head is the top of his helmet (called a morion). But if we follow his movements, from Banning Cocq's right shoulder to his left, we realize that the young man has shot his gun. Right next to the head of the lieutenant, no less. The feathers on Van Ruytenburch's handsome hat almost seem to be the result of the blast, which is an amusing visual joke—feathers fluttering in the explosion, or the explosion itself. Thus the naughty little fellow, shooting off his gun, getting too close to his commander, running about, is the most central point of the composition. The rest of the gang is also quite disorderly.

Yet despite all of that running around and the accidental explosions, there is a sense of order that emerges, which may have been intended as a metaphor for the Kloveniers. What had been an organized and practical association in the Middle Ages was more of a social association by the seventeenth century. These were not actually fighting men. They are not appearing on their way to battle. They never would have seen such a thing. These men were high-class dignitaries that had the money to pay for the top painter in Amsterdam to make a portrait of them. It is a parade—fun and exuberant. Men are running around, wearing their fanciest gear, and getting to hang out with their friends. Guns are booming. Music is playing. A dog is barking. Spears point in all directions. A flag flies high. It might be a bit of a mess, but out of the melee a composition takes shape; figures and forms seem to coalesce and create a series of lines and diagonals that point convincingly inward, in the direction of the central pair. It works. They might not be organized and orderly like the real professional militia, but the men come together in a convincing way, to make their march and represent the city.

The painting was commissioned in honor of a new meeting hall situated in the center of town (Fig. 15.4). The hall was the space where visiting dignitaries would be received and grand official dinners would be held. In honor of the building, the governors of Amsterdam ordered a set of group portraits of the six companies of the musketeers. On their own dime. But 120 of the 200 men paid to be included, suggesting that the price was worth it.

Instead of performing a major search campaign, the governors had the art dealer Hendrick Uylenburgh assign the paintings to artists he knew. Rembrandt

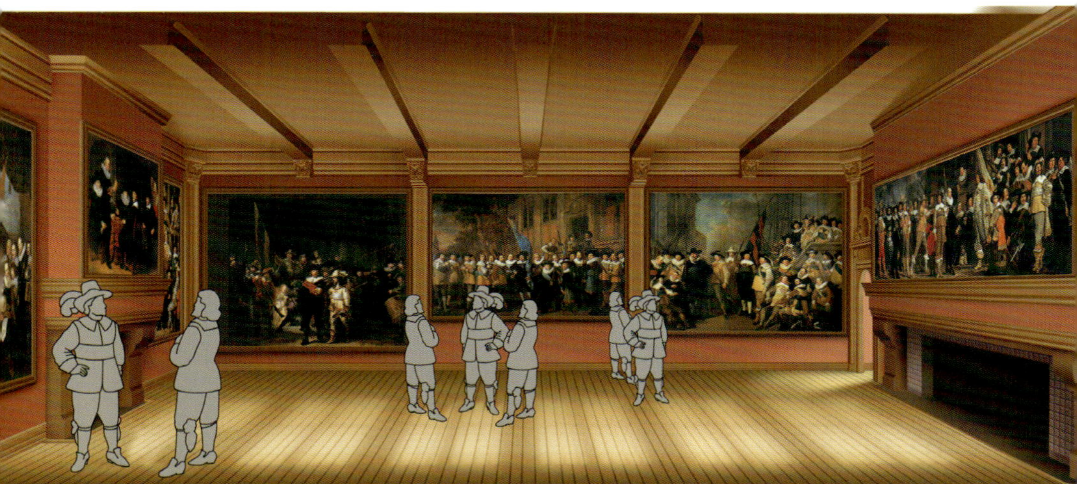

FIG. 15.4 Computer illustration of the Great Hall of the Kloveniers as it is thought to have looked in 1645.

had personal ties with Uylenburgh as he had married the art dealer's niece, Saskia. As far as connections between Rembrandt and the other painters, their common agent was one of few points of comparison. Rembrandt's painting is dramatically different. For instance, in the painting by Nicolaes Eliaszoon Pickenoy in the Rijksmuseum showing the Fourth District of Amsterdam, the men are lined up in a row, an orderliness emphasized by the rectilinear architecture in the background. The flag is central, and the captain holding the flag (with a surprisingly large head) looks as though he has been practicing his pose in the mirror for weeks before the painting. The painting by Joachim von Sandrart is similarly posed, although with less of a kick-line effect (Fig. 15.5). There is a bit more energy in the way the heads turn in various directions. But they are sitting or standing still, statically, not moving and marching. And they all seem to be focused in one way or another on that ungainly bust of their liege lady, which is cold and colorless, and pretty unattractive. Here too the architecture is strict and orderly. Classical Corinthian columns define the walls, which are topped with dignified antique statuary that stands against a clear blue sky with bright, fluffy clouds.

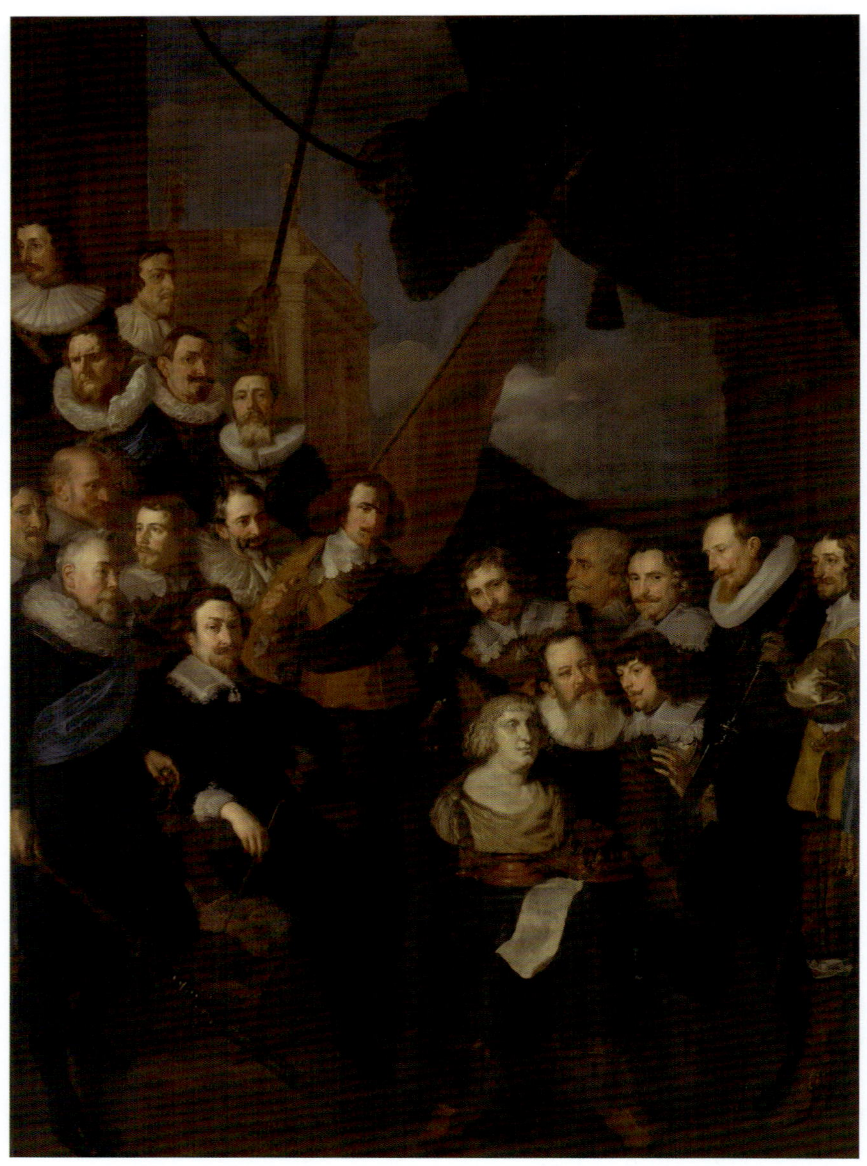

FIG. 15.5 Joachim von Sandrart, *Officers and Members of the Militia of District XIX in Amsterdam*, 1640. Rijksmuseum, Amsterdam. Oil on canvas, 343 × 258 cm.

Rembrandt's men emerge from a dark and eerie archway with massive stony walls. Here too there are antique columns, but these are of the Doric order—more austere, simple, and strict. The hanging escutcheon with its frivolous wreath and floriated finials was added after Rembrandt's death, in 1711. Its listing of the men in the company was helpful as far as documentation. However, it breaks the momentum, it undermines the power of that awesome archway, which reached deep into that unknowable cavernous space. The missing inches that were cut from the bottom of the painting also enhanced the sense of that black, gaping maw. The bright lunette of light at the bottom acts as a spotlight for the captain and his lieutenant. The brightness contrasted with the darker backdrop, emphasizing that they were coming toward us, emerging from darkness to the light, from disorder into order. In its fuller format the divergence between light and dark would have been even more evident and striking. That spectacular action and drama, the way Rembrandt stretches backward into those cavernous hallways while reaching forward into our space, distinguishes his piece from the others that were hanging on the walls.

These exact walls and archway did not exist. Rembrandt was imagining a monument, one that would articulate and emphasize the understanding that these men were the protectors of Amsterdam and its residents, even if the rendering was allegorical. The monument seems to be some sort of gateway, as if it is an entry into the city. The window with heavy bars (which can be seen better in the Lundens copy) would have been a reference to the duties of the militia, as seventeenth-century guard rooms were located to the right of the entryways. The archway is also a reference to the specifics of Amsterdam's history. In 1638 Marie de' Medici, the widow of King Henry IV of France, came to visit Amsterdam, and the city went wild. No cost was spared—water pageants were staged in the harbor, major processions celebrated her arrival, and throughout the city grand triumphal arches were built to act as places for theatrical stages. It is the bust of Marie that appears in the Von Sandrart painting, as a reference to her glorious visit. It is quite possible that Rembrandt's arch was also an allusion to Marie de' Medici's visit, although a less unattractive reminder.

Rembrandt was seemingly reaching backward in time too, toward other arches, especially one that he might have been able to see on a trip to Rome.

It was expected for young painters to travel to see the art of Italy firsthand, to sketch it and document it. But the young Rembrandt decided he would rather stay home and that he could learn everything he needed to know from the art available in his country. He explained to a writer of the time that he was in the prime of his youth and working well; a trip would just be disruptive. It is hard to imagine his disdaining a trip to Italy, especially when the Italian artists are present and fundamental in many of Rembrandt's paintings. The archway, for example, that frames the captain and his lieutenant is a compelling reference to *The School of Athens* by Raphael. The repeating arches in the Italian painting are bright, crisp, and easily legible, thus differing in an obvious way from the arches in *The Night Watch*. Yet the arcades do frame two men. Plato appears on the left, pointing upward, referencing the world of eternal ideas which formed the basis of his philosophy. Aristotle points earthward, to the world of empirical observation. The conversation (or debate) between teacher and student—Plato and Aristotle, respectively—provides the impetus for the convocation of Greek, Roman, and Arab philosophers to engage in a lively debate about meaning and truth. The twist is that the faces are contemporary. Leonardo da Vinci appears as Plato. Michelangelo's face is on the body of Heraclitus. Raphael places himself to the side, looking at us, as a witness to the fantastical convocation. Banning Cocq and his lieutenant were not great masterful philosophers or brilliant artists. However, the fundamentals of *The School of Athens* are in the painting of *The Night Watch*. Two important men appear in the center of a painting set under a deep, seemingly endless hallway. While walking forward they have a conversation and in so doing inspire many others in their labors, in their movements, actualizing a type of philosophy, one of civic pride, social justice, and peace.

Rembrandt may not have been interested in seeing the works of the Italian artists firsthand, but he seems to have been sure he wanted to be like the artists that created them. Around 1631, the year that he made it big with *The Anatomy Lesson*, he dropped the Van Rijn from his name. That same year he added a *d* to his name, perhaps to make certain that it was pronounced just so. In essence, Rembrandt was making a name for himself. Part of that self-crafting was proving his knowledge and understanding of the Italians, even if he had never actually seen their work firsthand. He even shows his familiarity with sources that men like Raphael drew upon, such as the ancient statue of the Laocoön, which provided the inspiration for the sinuous contortions of Rembrandt's *Christ on the Cross.* The painting of Baldassare Castiglione by Raphael was an inspiration for Rembrandt's *Self-Portrait* of 1640, when he was thirty-four, with the upturned beret, crisp white shirt, velvet jacket, and three-quarter pose. The noble elegance and cool confidence of Titian's *Man with a Quilted Sleeve* was another reference point.

The Italian that I see is Caravaggio. Those blinding, streaming flashes of light that highlight the action and intensify the drama are all Caravaggio. You may recall that the term for this intensified contrast of light and dark is *tenebrism,* from the word *tenebroso* or murky in Italian. Murkiness might be a necessary precursor, but it is the light that flashes violently. In *The Martyrdom of Saint Matthew* it is the light that seems to throw the viewers backward in shock, running away from the center and away from the attack (Fig. 14.6). Actually, the rounded form of the stone font where the saint lies on his side looks not unlike an inverted version of the arcade from which Banning Cocq and his men emerge. Matthew—dressed in black and white with a reddish-orange sash around his shoulders—is flanked by two men that have bright, almost golden flesh. And his open-handed gesture—reaching for the martyr's palm, perhaps offering advance forgiveness to his murderer—is very like the gesture of Banning Cocq.

The point is not that Banning Cocq is a saint or even like one. But these considerations and comparisons allow us to see the many layers, the many angles, in Rembrandt's paintings. The beautiful threads that tie Rembrandt to his predecessors are a painterly homage to his heroes. These were lessons and inspirations that Rembrandt absorbed and used to huge effect. He continued to use tenebrism explosively throughout his life, as when painting one of the most shocking and heartbreaking images of Samson (Fig. 15.6). Light from the open tent bathes the fallen hero—light that he will never see again. Blood spurts from his right eye as the soldier stabs it with his wavy-bladed knife. As he recoils in pain, grits his teeth in rage, Samson points his right toes toward his beautiful foe, Delilah, who runs with her ex-lover's golden locks in her left hand. The bright space in the middle of the composition accentuates the weapon of destruction—the shiny, metal scissors. That splash of light highlights Samson's form and his fall.

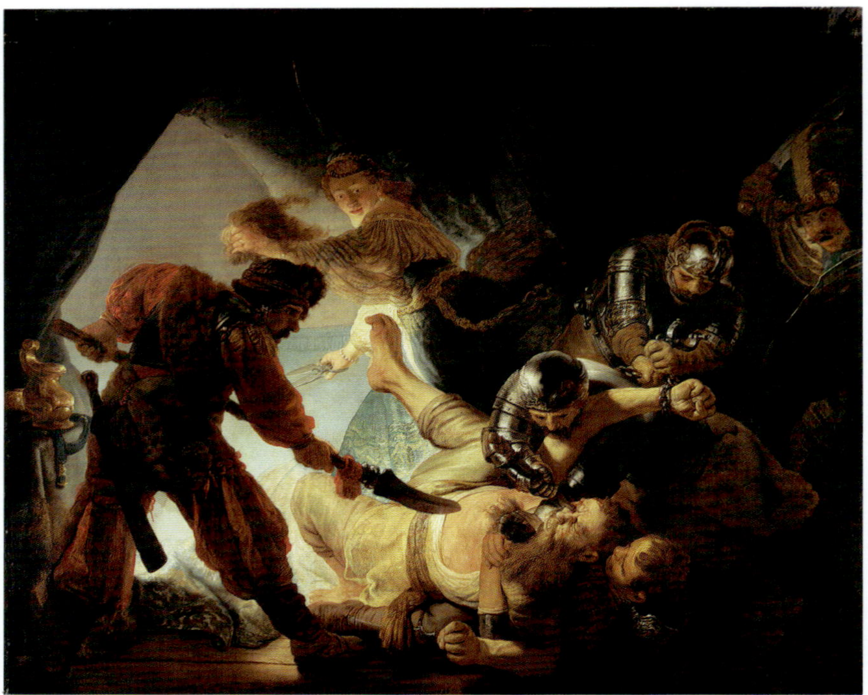

FIG. 15.6 Rembrandt van Rijn, *The Blinding of Samson*, 1636. Städel Museum, Frankfurt, Germany. Oil on canvas, 236 × 302 cm.

Darkness surrounds him, filled with nefarious and ruthless soldiers. The tenebristic contrast heightens the sense of Samson's suffering, accentuates Delilah's treason, and dramatizes the moment in a gut-wrenching way. The fallen man with his foot aloft, the guard standing diagonally, the fleeing witnesses, these all appear in *The Martyrdom of Saint Matthew* too. It is possible to see the entire composition of *The Blinding of Samson* as a quotation of Caravaggio's painting. Both men fall dramatically. Samson extends a leg, Matthew an arm. The murderer is a man posed at a diagonal—with a blade, with a sword. And all around are participants or witnesses that fill the darkness beyond.

But there is something deeper still in the connection with Caravaggio and

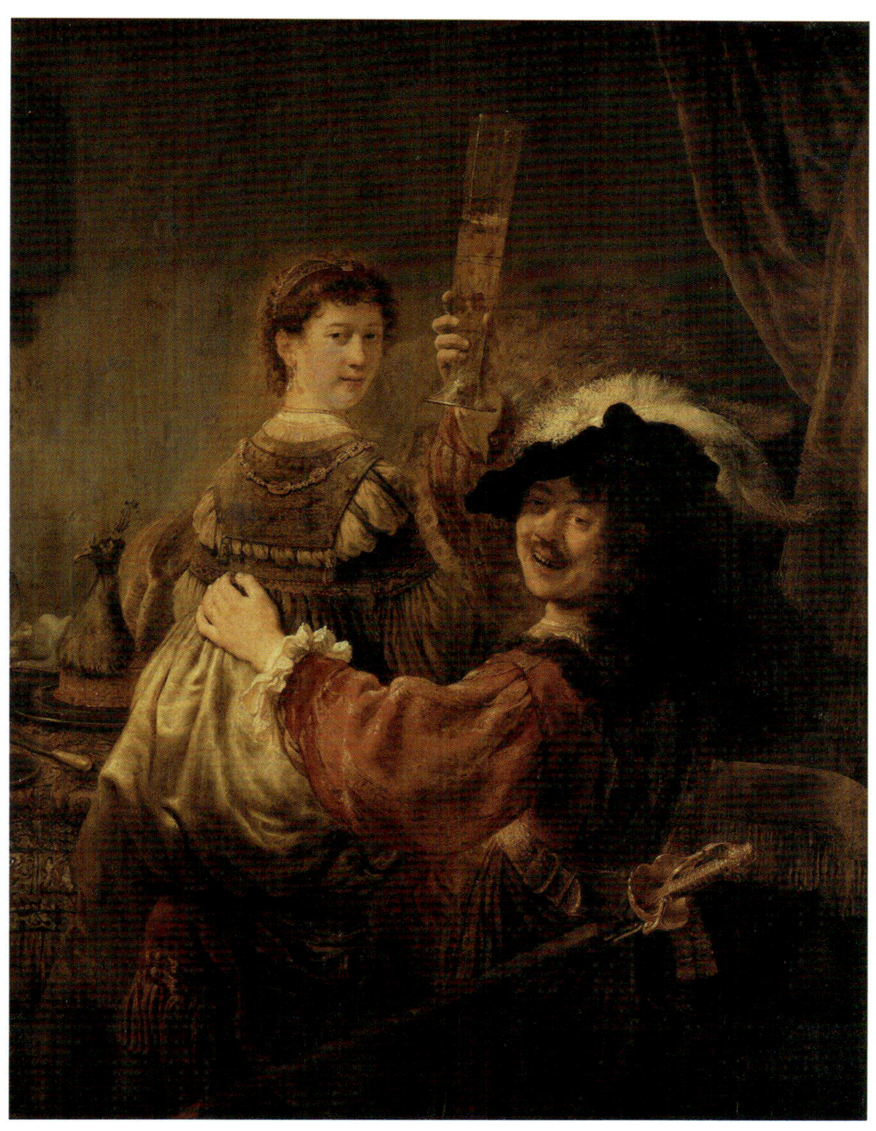

FIG. 15.7 Rembrandt van Rijn, *Rembrandt and Saskia in the Parable of the Prodigal Son,* ca. 1635. Staatliche Kunstammlungen, Dresden, Germany. Oil on canvas, 161 × 131 cm.

perhaps specifically with his painting of Matthew's martyrdom. *The Night Watch* seems to be an exploration of the artist himself: Rembrandt on Rembrandt. Caravaggio has a moment of self-reflection in his painting. We recall that in a self-portrait, the artist watches the matyrdom with a furrowed brow and a frown of fury, disgust, sadness. But he still rushes away. In fact, he couldn't be running faster. His left foot propels him forcefully forward, away from the saint, away from being implicated in the murder. Rembrandt might appear in his own work too. A little face appears to the right of the man carrying the flag. Only one eye is visible, a right eye, and a soft cap. It's not much to go on, but some scholars believe that this is the artist himself, eyeing the scene, visualizing the congregation both in person and in paint. Perhaps Rembrandt was considering his place in history, within the history of painting. Perhaps he was testing to see if he could fit in the place created by Caravaggio in his painting and in the canon. We will never know if Rembrandt pulled a Caravaggio and put himself in the shadows, shadily hanging in the background. But one consideration that might recommend this tantalizing identification is the fact that Rembrandt painted himself a lot, more than forty times, and in over half of those he wears that similarly soft and floppy artist's beret.

By 1640 Rembrandt was at the height of his career. He had captured the lion's share of Amsterdam's market in portraiture, had commissions coming in from the court in the Hague, and was married to the daughter of a wealthy mayor. In one self-portrait from 1637 he cannot contain his joy (Fig. 15.7). Saskia seems pleasantly bemused, sitting on her jolly husband's knee. He twists toward us, leaning back, extending a long-necked glass of champagne or beer. They are both decked out in fine, elaborate garments, and he wears the black beret with familiar white feathers. On the left is a huge peacock pie with an actual peacock on top, its feathers extending to the upper right of the painting, flaring out and above Rembrandt's white feathers. Peacock pie was food for the highest levels of society and was a clear symbol of utter luxury.

But is it all braggadocio and swagger? Perhaps not entirely. The setting is peculiar because it is not an elegant townhome but rather a seedy bar. The background is a blackboard where tallies would be kept in chalk of the number of drinks the patrons had bought. X-ray photographs show that there was originally

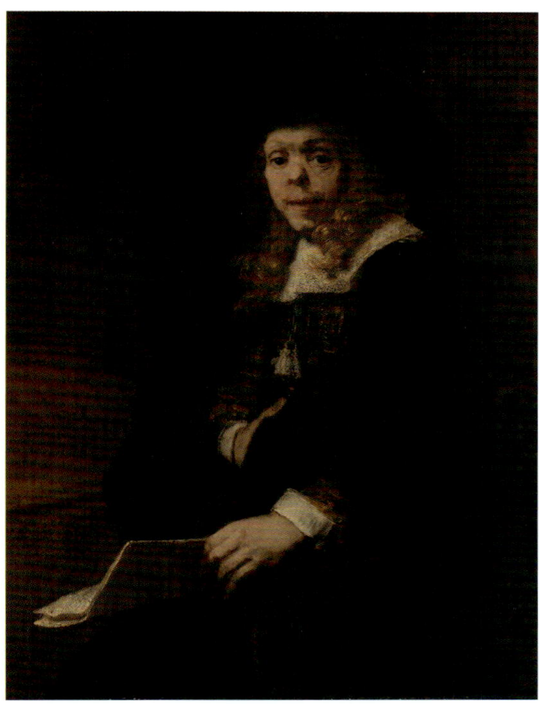

FIG. 15.8 Rembrandt van Rijn, *Portrait of Gerard de Lairesse,* 1665–1667. Metropolitan Museum of Art, New York. Oil on canvas, 112.7 × 87.6 cm.

a brothel madam behind Saskia and the artist. The setting has a good deal in common with contemporary images of the Prodigal Son from the parable in Luke 16:13. Thus viewers might have seen Saskia as a woman on a lapsed man's lap. Like Caravaggio, Rembrandt was confident and proud but also aware of his shortcomings and perhaps trying to understand them by painting them. He recognizes his flaws, even as he is enjoying them far too much to renounce them.

One of the boldest aspects of Rembrandt was the way he refused to clean things up. Gerard de Lairesse was a painter and art theorist who knew Rembrandt personally. De Lairesse wrote about how important it was for artists to mask physical disfigurement by depicting people from the most advantageous point of view. Rembrandt painted the writer with sympathy and dignity. But he does not avoid the truth, which is that the young man was suffering from congenital syphilis (Fig. 15.8). He looks much older than his twenty-five years,

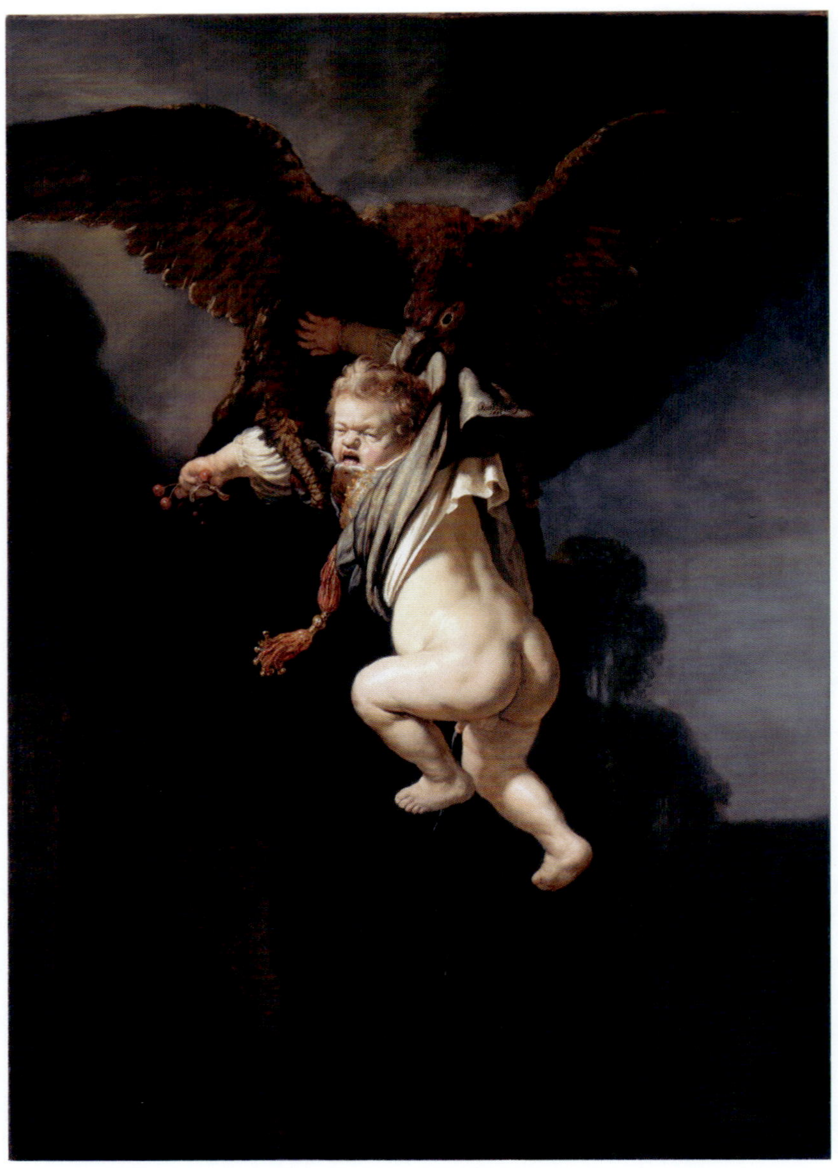

FIG. 15.9 Rembrandt van Rijn, *The Abduction of Ganymede*, 1635. Staatliche Kunstammlungen, Dresden, Germany. Oil on oak, 177 × 130 cm.

his nose is shrunken, and his features are asymmetrical. Rembrandt was trying to explain the real De Lairesse, his flaws and all. Rembrandt did not want the prettified version. He wanted to expose the reality of the man, because that was far more honest and interesting.

The degree of Rembrandt's boldness becomes clear when we consider what was happening in Antwerp, just a hundred miles away from Amsterdam, in the world of Peter Paul Rubens, where rich colors, noble nudes, and creamy textures dominated. *The Abduction of Ganymede* tells the story of a shepherd boy whose beauty caught the eye of Jupiter, the king of the gods. Jupiter transformed himself into an eagle and carried the youth up to Olympus so that he would be his cup bearer. There is no denying the erotic essence of the myth, which Rubens accentuates in his painting of the story. The boy is beautiful, with jaunty golden ringlets, perfect skin, and a majestic physique. The eagle cradles the boy gently in his right wing as he lifts him into the sky. Rubens is showing us what Jupiter saw and what Jupiter wanted. He paints to praise the perfection of a beautiful body.

Writers of the time explained the story of Ganymede as a representation of the pure soul striving toward God. Rubens appears to work with that interpretation in mind. But Rembrandt paints it for what it is, a totally unsavory story—pederasty, rape, slavery, a big bird of prey (Fig. 15.9). Gross. Rembrandt's painting basically says, it's not a nice story and I refuse to glamorize it. His Ganymede is a baby that is screaming hysterically. The dirty brown eagle bites his arm and wraps his talons around the boy's left arm. The cherries the boy holds were traditionally representative of lust and eroticism. But Rembrandt turns that symbol on its head. There is nothing sexy about this at all. The boy is so terrified that he urinates in flight. This too is a reference to paintings from the Renaissance that would show putti urinating gleefully—the *putto pisciatore*, it was called. Rembrandt is making fun of overglorifying myths and empty symbolism. In a later print called *Crying Boy* he puts a similar-looking baby where it belongs, in the arms of reality—in the arms of a mother in a house in Amsterdam.

That braggadocio or stubborn confidence started to catch up with the artist later in his life. It didn't happen immediately. *The Night Watch* was much admired. Writing in 1678, Samuel van Hoogstraten praised the way that Rembrandt combined observation from nature with a pure artistic imagination: "I feel that this

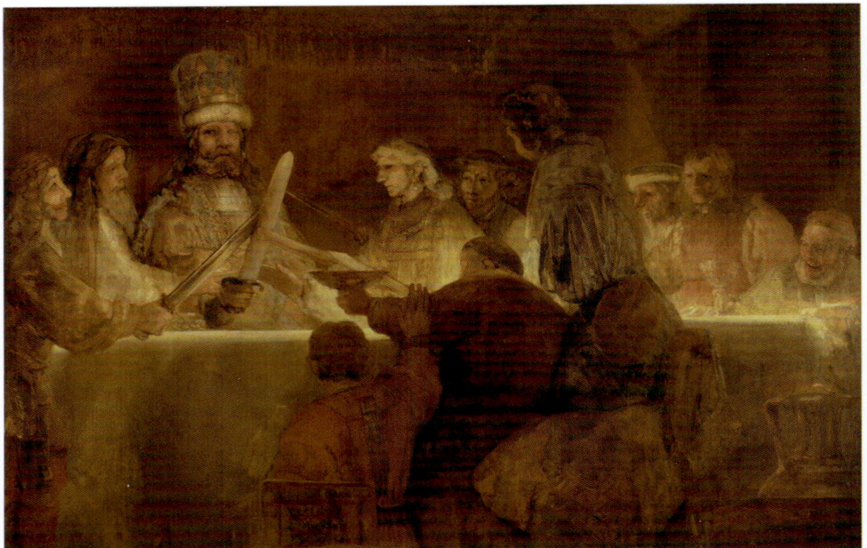

FIG. 15.10 Rembrandt van Rijn, *The Conspiracy of Claudius Civilis*, ca. 1661–1662.
Nationalmuseum, Stockholm, Sweden. Oil on canvas, 196 × 309 cm.

same work, open to criticism though it may be, will surpass all its competitors.
It is so picturesque in conception, so graceful in the placing of the figures and
so powerful that beside it, in the judgment of some, all the other paintings look
like playing cards."

Despite this praise, there was a strange shift in the reception of Rembrandt's
paintings after he completed *The Night Watch*, coupled with numerous personal
woes. Most tragically, Saskia died in 1642, the same year the painting was completed. After Saskia's death, Rembrandt had a complicated extramarital relationship that was well publicized and frowned upon. His agent Uylenburgh, Saskia's
uncle, a devout Mennonite, was probably one of those who disapproved of the
affair, as he stopped giving Rembrandt big portrait commissions. In response
Rembrandt started focusing on history paintings. He also started experimenting
with a rougher style, with a restricted color scheme and less detailed brushstrokes.
The topics were rougher too. In *The Conspiracy of the Batavians under Claudius*

Civilis, barbarians pledge an oath to revolt against the Romans (Fig. 15.10). The promise is forged with swords and drink, and overseen by the one-eyed leader Claudius Civilis. Some liked it, like the wealthy merchant Jan Six (whose portrait was also painted in Rembrandt's rougher style of paint), but not everybody did.

Criticisms about Rembrandt's paintings started to sting. His response was to bite back in the manner he knew best, with his hand. His *Satire on Art Criticism* of 1644 shows a group of men waiting to hear a judgment about a portrait lying on the ground. This judge has ass's ears, which poke through his hat. He holds a pipe for a gavel and sits on an empty barrel, a reference to the popular proverb that "hollow barrels and empty heads sound loudest." The one man that does not listen, who turns to us, reacts to the judgments of the ass-eared speaker by wiping his behind, a rather crass and clear evaluation of the art critic's expertise and evaluation. Rembrandt, during his career, had enjoyed great artistic autonomy. He painted whatever he pleased for whoever could pay. But the market proved to be fickle. He was always dependent on the judgments of those perceived asses, and it seemed that, at the end of his life, his imaginative and liberal techniques and styles came into conflict with the vagaries of taste and style. Now they wanted blended brushstrokes, bright colors, classically proportioned forms. These changes in taste, so far from his style, encroached on Rembrandt's patronage.

But Rembrandt's worst issue was that he had tremendous money problems. In 1642 Rembrandt was extremely wealthy, had a huge studio with apprentices, and owned a collection of artworks from all around the world. He was paid a terrific amount for *The Night Watch* and lived in an enviable stately home in the center of Amsterdam. But in 1650 he needed to ask for loans to pay off a debt on his lavish home. He got them, but they never seemed to cover his expenses. By 1656 Rembrandt was completely bankrupt. Even the sale of his house and its most valuable possessions, including a number of his prized paintings, could not raise all of the money required. For the last decade of his life Rembrandt lived in a small rented house in the quarter of town inhabited by painters and dealers. It was the bohemian lifestyle that he embraced so happily in the portrait with Saskia, without the fun. Now he was alone and penniless. By 1662 it was so bad that he had to sell Saskia's grave. When he died in 1669 he was buried in a rental plot.

Rembrandt kept painting toward the end of his life, even though his station had changed so dramatically. That change is palpable in the way he appears and the way he paints. In his self-portrait of 1658, Rembrandt gives the viewer a strong, steely look, again wearing his black artist's beret (Fig. 15.11). His brow is furrowed, no longer laughing and expressing a careless joie de vivre. In fact, he seems impatient and weary. He is still in costume, as he was in the painting with Saskia, here wearing a yellow tunic with a dramatic red sash, which seems to slip from its intended place at his waist. His right hand comes into our space as he holds up the ends of his voluminous costume cloak. His left hand is darker, more shadowy, gently holding or almost pawing a staff as though it were a baton of command. He is acting like a king sitting on a throne, although the fiction is readily visible, both to the artist and the spectator.

When he painted himself as the Prodigal Son twenty years before, he was living the life of that wayward man, enjoying every minute of it. But at this point in his life he was on the other end. His painting in 1666 of the Prodigal Son speaks to the other part of the story, when the son returns, hoping for forgiveness, wishing for redemption. Rembrandt is not apologizing for his *skill*, however. The scepter he holds in his left hand in the self-portrait is a maulstick, used by artists to support the hand with which they held their paintbrush. He is a king, a king of paint, a paint that he manipulates with power and force. Those brushstrokes are raw. The paint is heavy and thick. The effect is a textured, weighty tenebrism that speaks a message of unapologetic and absolute authority.

What makes a masterpiece? What inspires people to admire, adulate, adore, attack a painting? *The Night Watch* inspires intense responses and reactions. As such, it has become the icon of the museum in which it stands, the Rijksmuseum, and also of the city of Amsterdam. In a promotional video celebrating the reopening of the Rijksmuseum, which had been closed for ten long years, actors in costume astounded unsuspecting shoppers in an Amsterdam mall. The actors rushed about, re-creating the activities of the men and women of the painting, and congregating together in a spectacular (and hilarious) tableau.* The moment

---

* "Our heroes are back! // Opening commercial 'Rijksmuseum,'" www.youtube.com/watch?v= ixWdRZip2TI.

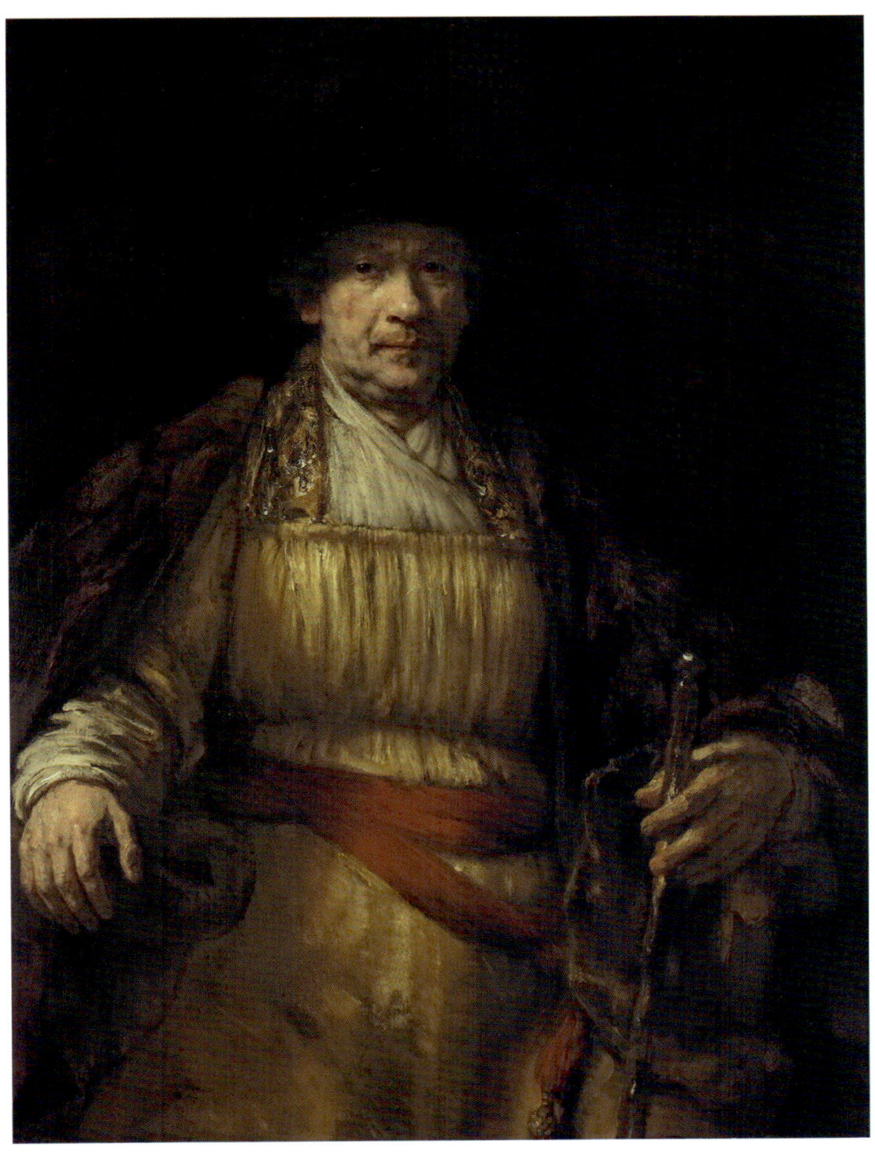

FIG. 15.11 Rembrandt van Rijn, *Self-Portrait*, 1658. Frick Collection, New York. Oil on canvas, 133.7 × 103.8 cm.

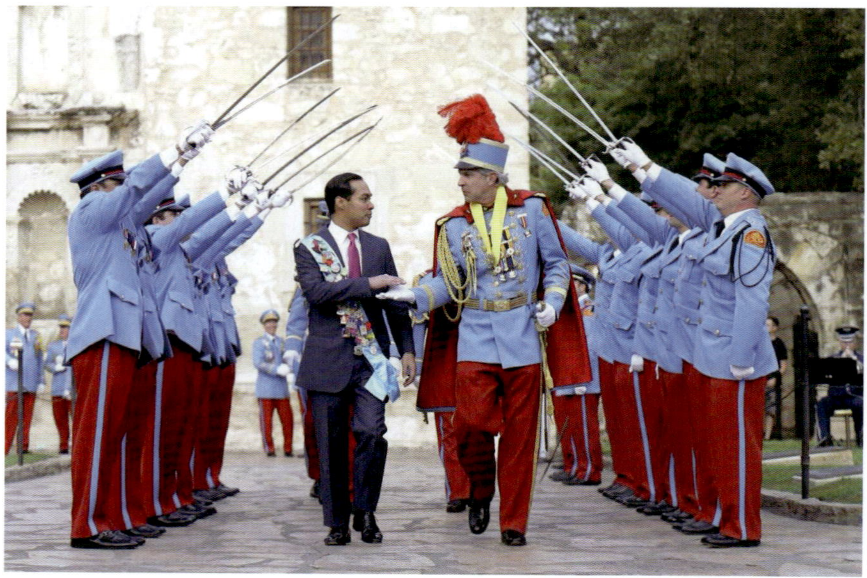

FIG. 15.12 Texas Cavaliers at the Alamo, San Antonio, Texas.

of surprise of the people in the mall is only temporary. Everyone knows this painting.

There is a deep continuity between painting and people—something that links the men of seventeenth-century Amsterdam to the people in the mall, and also the people from our own daily lives. We know lawyers like Banning Cocq and Van Ruytenburch. The man with the flag was a successful merchant, art collector, and lifelong bachelor. We know those too. The sergeant with the handsome black cap was a cloth merchant, as was the man at the left side of the painting with the elegant helmet. The man setting up his gun in the foreground, wearing red, was a grocer. We enjoy watching men dress up in fancy military regalia to protect our city, not with guns, but with their joy and enthusiasm and philanthropy—like the Texas Cavaliers of San Antonio (Fig. 15.12).

The Texas Cavaliers are a perfect example of these kinds of patriotic and peaceful protectors. This organization supports the River Parade, a main event of Fiesta during which more than forty-five floats move down the San Antonio

River. At this and other Fiesta events the cavaliers wear military regalia—bright blue coats with detailing in gold, maroon pants lined with a blue stripe, and a peaked cap like the hats worn by policemen. Like the men in Rembrandt's painting, the cavalier uniform speaks a language of protection and law enforcement. But instead of wielding weapons and protecting citizens from violence or war, the cavaliers are protecting the citizens in a humanitarian, philanthropic, cultural way—providing entertainment to the community and raising philanthropic money through those events.

This painting is about the men of the musketeers and about Rembrandt. But it is also about us. That is what makes it transcendent, in a way, and able to draw us, twenty-first-century viewers, into a painting about something that might seem rather remote. It captures the moment of people gathering together to celebrate their passion for the city. They might not be completely organized. But the painting embraces the messiness of man while celebrating his achievements and accomplishments, a message that was important to the man Rembrandt, to the artist Rembrandt, and to the works by Rembrandt that we are so passionate about today.

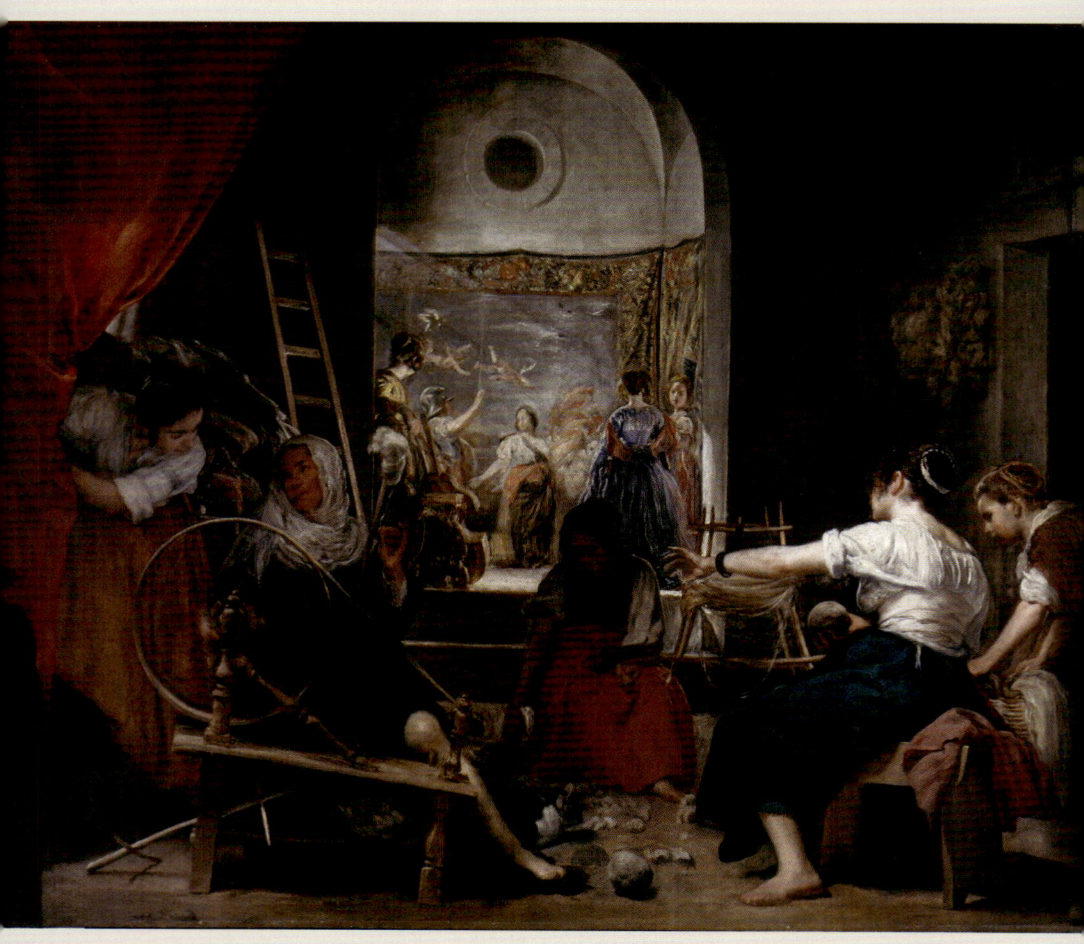

FIG. 16.1 Diego Velázquez, *Las Hilanderas*, 1655–1660. Museo del Prado, Madrid, Spain. Oil on canvas, 220 × 289 cm.

Velázquez, *Las Hilanderas*

1655–60

SPANISH BAROQUE ART

Watching a spider weave a web is something quite magical—skinny, spindlelike, pincer legs pick and place sticky strands of silk into intricate gossamer and glistening formations. Like little dancing artists, they paint their webs in the air with their peculiar medium, strange and steady streams of proteins that emerge in a constant flow from their bulbous abdomens. Those white, shimmering threads seem so delicate. Like the tulle of a dancer's costume. Like dangling swaths of lace. Like perennial, twinkling icicles.

But they are simultaneously death traps. They catch and apprehend the hapless victim of the spider. The spider works around and around, from outward in, creating frame upon frame, spinning centripetally, like a pirouetting dancer, creating a masterpiece so that it can trick and catch its prey. It catches us too. It is easy to get swept up in the movement, the creation, the beauty, and to find ourselves stuck in a compelling paradox wherein something suspended and ever so ethereal draws us in and captures or captivates us. The web looks like a work of art and works like a work of art that pulls us in toward its center.

That is also the case with *Las Hilanderas*, or *The Spinners*, another suspended, hanging work of art by the Spanish artist Diego Velázquez (1599–1660) (Fig. 16.1). The painting is tricky and hard to untangle. It was meant for an extremely educated audience, members of the Spanish court under the rule of Philip IV (1605–65). His rule was part of the Siglo de Oro, the Golden Age dated from the end of the fifteenth century to as late as 1659. During this moment the arts of every variety flourished—painting, architecture, poetry, literature, music. This was the epoch of Cervantes, Lope de Vega, El Greco, of the construction of El Escorial and Plaza Mayor. Artists traveled freely, studying and embracing new crafts, new styles from Italy and Amsterdam, England and France. Literature was also readily available, from the classical texts to the plays of Shakespeare. Velázquez worked hard to position himself so that he might breathe this air and imbibe the riches of the creative energies that engulfed the country. The painting of *The Spinners* is evidence of Velázquez's ability to embrace, absorb, and shape this tremendous cultural moment in Spain. It is a painting about his creative production. Velázquez draws (or paints) us into an extraordinary network of classical erudition and competition, all of which is framed by his singular composition.

Mimicking the spider, reading the painting from outward in, is helpful because it allows us to work our way toward the core of the piece and to quickly shed later accretions. The painting as it appears in the Prado Museum introduces us into a deep, cavernous room with a voluminous red curtain on the left and an ominous darkened doorway on the right. A huge arched ceiling in the back of the painting, composed of a somewhat strange series of groin vaults and a central oculus, creates a sense of expansiveness. But that large arcaded space is not by Velázquez. That arching ceiling was added later, at some point in the eighteenth century. The distinction between the original canvas and the added sections is not difficult to see. There is a clear line of demarcation. By removing that outer layer of paint and canvas, by returning to Velázquez's original composition, the painting takes on a greater intensity. The impact of the sunlight in the background is supposed to be focused and sharp, like a theatrical spotlight, intense and directed, not diffused throughout a large, expansive room. The ladder, with the added canvas, hovers randomly in the corner. With the artist's original dimensions the ladder hints suggestively at a space that goes beyond the frame, as does the red hanging curtain. That suggested space outside actually heightens the sense that Velázquez is giving us a specific and special view into our more confined space. This tightened lens puts the focus on the characters in the painting.

Another painting by Velázquez, *Las Meninas*, which was painted in the same late years as the painting of the spinners, provides an interesting contrast (Fig. 16.2). Here Velázquez paints himself painting the young Infanta Margarita

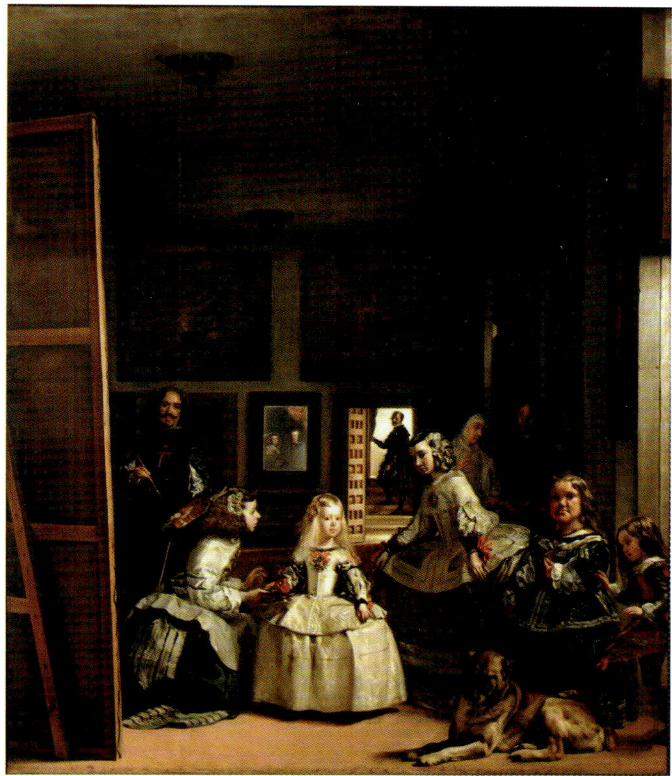

FIG. 16.2 Diego Velázquez, *Las Meninas*, 1656. Museo del Prado, Madrid, Spain. Oil on canvas, 320.5 × 281.5 cm.

Teresa surrounded by maids of honor and other members of the court. It is a painting that will weave in and out of our discussion of *Las Hilanderas*. But an immediate reaction is the expanse of that dark room, with its high, murky ceilings and dark, distant frames. In *Las Hilanderas*, the space is tight and compact. The figures shape the space, just as they give shape to the materials and garments that they are producing.

Essentially we are being shown the process of the spinners' work from start to finish. We are witnessing the transformation or metamorphosis of the fleecy glob of wool hanging on the wall on the right into the garments and clothing piled behind the woman on the left. Taking that mass of wool, the women would first card or comb the fibers such that they could be straightened and aligned. It is likely that the square tool held by the woman in the center of the painting is one of these combing cards. In the next stage, the fibers were wound on a distaff, a short forked stick. This is the stick that the veiled woman holds wedged under her left arm. She is in the act of pulling fibers from the distaff and transferring them to the spinning wheel. As she pulls, she twists the strands between her left thumb and forefinger. Although it was possible to make different thicknesses in the wool, the women in the painting have chosen to produce a rather thin thread, as evidenced by the seated woman on the right. She has the job of taking the threads produced by the wheel, keeping them from getting tangled (which she ensures by wrapping them around the wooden apparatus), and wrapping the strands into a ball.

Behind her a second woman collects the balls of yarn in a basket. These are then used to sew garments, some of the very garments that these women wear. There is a clear connection between the formation of the wrapped-up white threads and the bright-white cummerbund of the woman doing the wrapping. Her belt even has hanging threads that look just like the unfinished, dangling yarn of her workmanship. The cotton-candylike formation of wool at the top of the elder woman's distaff looks much like her white headdress—bunched up, fluffy, composed of thick, weighty, streaky fibers. Even the orbs of wool seem to relate in a special way to the representation of the women. The ballet bun worn by the woman in the green shirt looks much like the orbs of yarn, as do the elder woman's knobby knee and her head, which is also wound round with the white scarf like a skein of wool.

Velázquez makes the connection between the women and their craft essential, bodily, inextricable. These visual ties also help shape the composition. Connect the dots—ball on the floor, ball in the hand, ball in the hair—and Velázquez has created a diagonal that runs along the blue-swathed leg of the seated woman. Balancing this line are a series of diagonals on the left side of the composition. Our eye moves again from the ball on the floor, to the knob of the woman's knee, to the rapidly spinning center of the wheel. The machine itself is composed of a series of diagonals that lead from upper left to lower right, much like the burst of light that illuminates the distinct room beyond. The diagonals created in the foreground, that V-shape, lead the eye toward this separate room with that bright bolt of light.

The five working women in the foreground—weighty, hunched over, industrious—contrast curiously with the five women in this back room. These ladies are of an elevated status, a point made emphatic not only by their regal bearing and the elegance of their colorful dresses but compositionally by the two tall steps that separate the spheres, that literally elevate them. Bodies in the shadows contrast with bodies in the bright beams of light. Women in thick, monochromatic garments contrast with ladies in shimmery silken dresses. Light blues and pinks invert dark blues and seedier reds. And while the spinners labor, actually producing something, the ladies are all dressed up, in elegant costumes, playing around in funny hats or helmets, enjoying a bit of leisure time, which quite possibly is all the time.

Velázquez knew this world well. He was, after all, the court painter to the king, which is how we saw him in *Las Meninas.* In fact, he was quite committed to being more than that, to positioning himself as more than a simple artist. By all accounts he was extremely ambitious, both in the realm of painting but also in the life of the court. It would seem that he was constantly planning his next step up, his next step closer to the king.

Velázquez trained with the most famous artist in Seville, embracing all that he could, including his mentor's daughter, Juana, whom he married in 1618. In 1622 Velázquez set his sights on Madrid, hoping to capture the attention of the new king, Philip IV. The first trip to Madrid was not a success. Velázquez, undaunted, mounted a second campaign. Pulling together all of the contacts that he had in Seville, he achieved an invitation to Madrid from the Chief Officer of His Majesty's Chapel, Juan de Fonseca. After painting Fonseca's portrait, Velázquez was given a position as a court painter. Within the next five years he rose through the ranks, moving from being just one of the king's painters to the *pintor de cámara,* the first place among court painters. Of course his paintings were essential to his fame as an artist, but they were part of his rise in social status as well.

The Spanish court of the seventeenth century was a complex labyrinth of favors and favorites. One's place within the hierarchy determined certain social and financial rewards. Velázquez wanted to be at the top. Little by little he rose through highly politicized ranks, achieving a sea of increasingly prominent titles. His success culminated in 1652, when he swore the oath of office as *Aposentador Mayor de Palaccio*. In this lofty position he was put in charge of maintaining and arranging the king's quarters and overseeing the royal processions when the king traveled.

Velázquez's rise was dramatic and swift. Each promotion was a step closer into the heart of the courtly labyrinth, the favor of the king. Unfortunately for us, that rise resulted in fewer and fewer paintings. *Las Hilanderas* and *Las Meninas* were both painted in the last five years of the artist's life, so he was clearly active artistically. If he had not been traveling as the king's ambassador, however, he would have had more time for painting. He also might have lived longer. In 1660 Velázquez accompanied Philip IV to France to deliver the princess Maria Teresa to Louis XIV of France as his young bride-to-be. Quite a match. Upon their return, Velázquez contracted a virulent disease and died soon after.

In the margin of a memorandum about the artist's death, King Philip wrote: "I am crushed." The king also added a personal touch to *Las Meninas*. Velázquez painted the masterpiece before having been given the honor of knighthood. Only knights could wear the red cross of the Order of Santiago—the combination of a sword and three fleurs-de-lis at the top. Thus the red cross on Velázquez's breast was added later, after he had completed the painting. One biographer, Antonio Palomino, recounted that many believed the king himself took up the brush and painted the red cross upon Velázquez's death.

While this is perhaps too romantic, it was at the king's order, ergo, it was "by his hand" that someone did add the painted crest. This might sound like the king was putting his final claim on the artist, a means of saying that Velázquez was part of his court, a member of the order under his control. But Velázquez was truly on the quest to wear these very signs of success.

At the wedding of Maria Teresa and Louis XIV, Velázquez was dressed to the nines. Palomino marveled at the "adornment, gallantry, and finery" of the artist and described how Velázquez was dressed in the finest black suit trimmed with

Milanese silverpoint lace. Palomino also noted that the red cross of Santiago was not only embroidered on the artist's cloak but also enameled within a heavy gold chain adorned with many diamonds that hung from his neck. The artist had crafted himself to be the ultimate gentleman, the most perfect courtier. The theatricality of it all is hard to ignore. He wore the perfect costume. He crafted the persona or character of the young princess when he painted the portrait of Maria Teresa that Louis studied, illustrating her as the most perfect bride—demure, wealthy, poised, youthful. He designed the sets upon which the cast paraded—the king, his daughter, Louis XIV, the artist. He made the backdrops for the stage, decorating the pavilions with tapestries from the royal collection. In other words, he was painting the walls with tapestries.

To all appearances it is a world of the court, its theater and tapestries, that we see in the background. Yet the difference in the two worlds of the painting is not a social commentary or social contrast. It is a contrast between two kinds of pictures. One is a genre scene, and the other is about allusion and myth. Although the painting puts the spinning women in the foreground, the primary subject is in this smaller frame. In fact, the title *Las Hilanderas* is not the original name. It is another frame we can discard. In 1711 the painting was recorded as being about "women working in tapestries." This title stuck, and scholars discussed the work as a simple genre scene of women spinning. It wasn't until the twentieth century when scholars started studying the episode in the back that they realized there was something more complicated going on.

What caught their eye was the hanging tapestry. The subject matter of the tapestry in the background is not entirely discernible because it is slightly obfuscated by the bodies of the ladies. In truth, the only way to identify the scene is through art historical knowledge, through the awareness (both ours and Velázquez's) of Titian and his *Rape of Europa* painting, now housed at the Isabella Stewart Gardner Museum in Boston (Fig. 16.3). Mercifully, this was not one of the paintings stolen in the still-unsolved heist of the museum that took place in 1990. The tapestry based on the painting by Titian is clearly visible—the two putti hover above the scene (although their bows and arrows are no longer visible), Europa's pink veil flutters above her upturned face, which is similarly pink in hue, and one eye of the bull looks out with that faux innocence we see in the Titian.

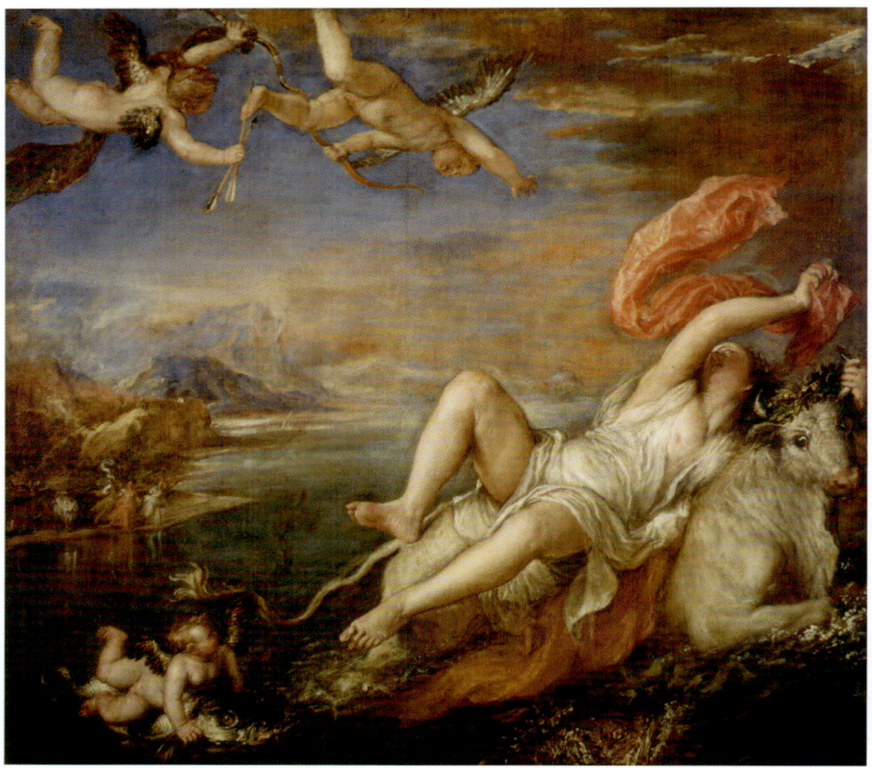

FIG. 16.3 Titian, *The Rape of Europa*, 1560–1562. Isabella Stewart Gardner Museum, Boston, Massachusetts. Oil on canvas, 178 × 205 cm.

Velázquez does cut off some of the image with the bodies of the five women, but their role in the drama of identifying the scene is important too. The helmet worn by one of the women is identifiable as the helmet of Minerva, the standard means of representing the goddess of wisdom. The lady is acting, or playacting, in costume, performing a scene involving another woman who holds her right arm out and down toward the ground. Considering the framework of this drama—the subject matter of the tapestry behind the women and the vigorous spinning in the foreground—we find ourselves watching a play or reenactment of the story of Arachne.

The story of Arachne appears in Ovid's *Metamorphoses*, in book 8. In the Ovidian tale, Minerva determines that it is time to deal with a young girl called Arachne who has been boasting that she is equal to the goddess in working with wool. Ovid describes how the nymphs would leave their haunts to watch her artistry, to marvel at her handiwork as much for the grace of her skill as for the finished product. Arachne denies any debt to Minerva and boldly announces that she will have a contest with the goddess. Minerva dresses up as a "hag with hoary locks" and hobbles onto the scene. The disguised goddess warns the young girl about being so proud, but Arachne has no interest in her advice and tells her that she is a stupid old woman. Minerva, not surprisingly, has had enough at this point and drops the disguise. Arachne blushes involuntarily but quickly regains her composure.

They start the competition. In her tapestry Minerva depicts scenes of the glorious gods upon their lofty thrones, with Jove, Neptune, and herself featured most prominently. In the corners she makes a none-too-subtle point to her competitor by showing the punishments of defiant, boastful mortals. A brother and a sister who claimed to be like Jove and Juno, turned into snow-clad mountains. Antigone of Troy, who competed with Juno and ended up a white-feathered stork. All tragic. All transformations or metamorphoses. Arachne seems to understand how this is all going to work out. Instead of bowing out gracefully, she goes down hard. In her tapestry she weaves scenes of the gods as well. But her piece records their moments of great embarrassment, of which there are many. Jove is the worst, turning into everything imaginable in order to seduce young women—a swan, a shower of gold, fire, someone's husband, and a serpent.

Most relevant to our painting, Arachne also shows Jove transformed into a white bull in order to trick and take Europa. Arachne does not win the contest, as you may have guessed. But her piece is good enough to anger Minerva, who tears up the girl's tapestry and uses a loom to beat her on the head. In despair, Arachne fastens a halter around her neck and hangs herself. The goddess then enacts the kind of punishment that she foreshadowed in her woven tapestry, in which mortals are eternally changed into objects or beasts. "You may live, you presumptuous creature," the goddess says, "but you'll hang suspended forever." The goddess sprinkles the girl with a magical juice, and Arachne is transformed into that which her name now signifies, a spider.

Like Arachne, the women in the background are representing or reenacting the stories of the gods through art, this time through playacting. The ladies stand in a stagelike space, with that raking light that now not only looks like a theatrical spotlight but just might be one. We have Minerva in her helmet. We have Arachne responding with her dramatic gesture. The ladies watching the show are perhaps dressed as the nymphs that came from far and wide to admire Arachne's skill. It is hard to say exactly which moment the actresses are depicting. Some scholars have argued that Velázquez is showing Minerva when she reveals herself to be the goddess. The pose of the actresses playing Minerva and Arachne could very well be that moment before the contest, Minerva holding up her arm to say, "It is I!" while Arachne throws her right arm out in a gesture of surprise. But the tapestry woven during the contest is already there, behind them. Thus this could also be the moment after the contest, when Minerva is getting ready to attack the poor, proud girl. Either way, this is a scene about two artists, Arachne and Minerva, acknowledging each other's skill and fighting to be the very best. Velázquez tells the story of Arachne's competition with Minerva obliquely, through a series of allusions that include the tapestry in the back, the performance, and the actions of the spinners in the foreground. And sure enough, scholars discovered that the documents from the original inventory identified the painting as being about the fable of Arachne.

All three—the tapestry, the play, the spinners—also allude to another duel, one involving Velázquez personally and professionally. Velázquez was responding to the work of an Italian painter, Titian, who had been dead for some eighty years. But the competition was even more immediate and present. Titian's masterpiece had been hanging in Philip IV's art collection, as one of his prized possessions, no less. But the king was not alone in adoring the piece. Many artists came to visit the king's collection specifically to copy paintings by Titian like the *Rape of Europa*. One such artist was Peter Paul Rubens, when he was on his second trip to Spain in 1628–29. Rubens was technically in Madrid as an ambassador, sent to negotiate peace between Spain and England, and not as an artist. Yet he still felt the need to study the Titian painting—to learn and perhaps to see if he could paint as well as the Venetian master. As such, Rubens made a close copy of the Titian painting, which he kept in his home in Antwerp. Upon Rubens's death in 1640, Philip IV spent an incredibly high price to reclaim the copy. Philip already had a *Rape of Europa* in his collection. And in fact, there is very little that distinguishes the two paintings. It is as though Philip wanted to own the entirety of the painting, its inception and its progeny. Philip was collecting a dialogue between artists. He was collecting a living art history. And he would soon get another iteration in that chain from Velázquez.

Velázquez still had to craft this lineage, he had to establish his place in the canon, just as he had to assert his place in court. He most certainly had an interest in the style of Titian, those wonderful hazy outlines, that use of glimmering color. In Ovid, Arachne does show the rape of Europa as one of the rapes in her tapestry. But Titian painted plenty of renditions of the other rapes. Thus Velázquez probably selected this particular piece of Titian's specifically because Rubens had done the copy. In fact, Velázquez had seen Rubens making the copy.

It is a stunning thing to imagine, the elder artist Rubens (who was about fifty at the time) producing his copy of the Venetian's masterpiece in front of the young, twenty-nine-year-old aspiring artist. Not only was Velázquez aiming to be an artist at that same level of fame, but he was also setting himself into a particular tradition, that of those painters who considered color to be the primary tool of painting. We consider Velázquez to be "Spanish" or "Baroque." But there was no sense of a "Spanish" school, and "baroque" was a derogatory nineteenth-century term for overwrought painting styles. Velázquez considered himself to be a colorist, part of the tradition that derived from the Venetian works by Titian and Tintoretto and was further developed by Rubens.

Velázquez clearly admired the work by these men. But there is a good deal of Arachne in Velázquez. Take the exchange between Arachne and Minerva (or Pallas Athena). The goddess warns the girl that "not all old age's effects are to be despised; experience comes with the years." Arachne angrily replies: "Leave me alone, you stupid old woman!…I'm clever enough to advise myself. Don't think your warnings have done any good. I'm set on my course."

There is something boastful about how Velázquez responds to the older painters, something terribly similar to the way that Arachne acknowledges her superior. Velázquez hides the older artist's masterpiece in the background. He seems to be saying that not only can he paint the *Rape of Europa* like Titian and like

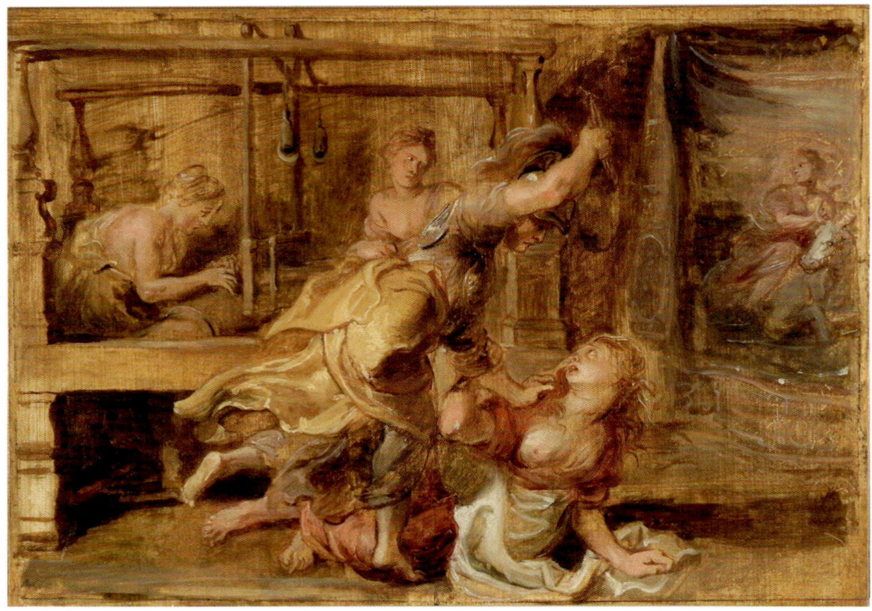

FIG. 16.4   Peter Paul Rubens, *Pallas Athena and Arachne*, 1636–1637. Virginia Museum of Fine Arts, Richmond, Virginia. Oil on wood, 26.67 × 38.1 cm.

Rubens, but that he can give it a new and perhaps more meaningful framework, that he is going to use their knowledge and attempt to surpass it. In essence, he is putting himself in a competition with his own gods—Rubens and Titian.

This is not the only time Velázquez alludes to the competition of Arachne and to his own competition with Rubens. In the mid-1630s Philip IV commissioned Rubens to make a series of more than fifty mythological paintings for his grand new hunting pavilion at El Pardo, outside of Madrid. Rubens made a number of sketches, executed a few by his own hand, and then sought out artists to complete the remainder. One of these pieces was an image of Arachne and Minerva.

The work itself no longer survives, but the preliminary sketch does. And it is strange. Rubens goes for the most sensationalistic and violent instant (Fig. 16.4). In the background of the sketch we can see poor Arachne working in fear and panic, locked in her cagelike loom, while her fingers fly as fast as they can to construct the tapestry. She reappears in the foreground being hit by Minerva, helpless, distressed, pale, and disheveled. She might be calling for mercy while she grabs Minerva's forearm for reprieve. To no avail.

The tapestry woven by the hapless girl hangs in the background. In it, Europa turns to look over her right shoulder much as Arachne does. Both are overcome and subjugated by the gods. Velázquez took this strange composition and placed it in *Las Meninas*. It hangs somewhat ingloriously on the back wall, behind the portrait of the artist. It is all ablur, dark, and almost impossible to read. The painting by Rubens (and there is a second Rubens to the right showing Apollo) hangs on the wall as a means of showing that Velázquez is indebted to the painter. He respects the older artist just as he aspires to surpass him in fame and skill.

One thing that Rubens does show that would seem to be of importance is the actual weaving. There is no weaving in the painting by Velázquez, though of course there are the spinners. And there is the final product of what their threads might create in the background, in the hanging tapestry. But the in-between—the act of weaving on looms—is missing altogether. However, if we take the connection between Velázquez and Arachne one step further, we might see Velázquez as the weaver, a weaver of paint. He makes a painting (Titian's) into a tapestry in the background. Thus perhaps the woman at the far right in the room in the back is not looking at us but at the true weaver, the artist, who would be standing in our space while he was in the act of crafting the piece, of weaving this magnificent web.

That tricky exchange of gazes suffuses *Las Meninas* too. The painting is, in one sense, a straight group portrait. But the addition of the artist himself complicates things. He looks directly at us, with a placid, confident, slightly inscrutable gaze. His weighty, dark eyebrows balance an elegant, upturned mustache. But he is not alone in looking at us. Two ghostly figures also look out at us from the framed image on the back wall, King Philip IV and his queen, Mariana of Austria. This is most likely not a painting but a mirror image of the two rulers. Might they be standing where we are, looking in at the scene of their young daughter with her courtiers? Is this why the Infanta is starting to curtsy, because her parents have just entered the room? Or is the mirror reflecting that which Velázquez is painting on the canvas, which we cannot see? Are they the same thing? The man in the doorway has been identified as José Nieto, the head of the royal tapestry works and also the individual responsible for opening and closing doors for the queen. He stands with his feet on different steps, casting a shadow toward the room, while holding a dark curtain (tapestry?) with his right. This much we know. But is he coming or going? Is he looking at us or at the king and queen?

Nieto, the monarchs, the Rubens—all are confined in thick, black frames. The women in the background of *Las Hilanderas* are also in a frame created both by the wall, a creamy-gray border, and also by the thick, floriated, variegated borders of the tapestry. Paintings within paintings. Frames within frames. Svetlana Alpers has suggested that, in *Las Meninas*, Velázquez is painting his own museum, his own gallery, in which he recalls and situates works of art according to his preference. In *The Spinners*, he goes beyond the gallery format. He also references other inspirations, other influential artists, without using frames. The girl wrapping the woven wool into the skein looks very much like the *Libyan Sybil* of Michelangelo's Sistine Chapel (Fig. 16.5). That long reaching gesture, expansive back, and twisting pose seems to come from the painting by Michelangelo. We know Velázquez was traveling in Italy and was even called back by the king for staying too long on one of his trips. In addition to the Sistine Chapel, he must have also seen the paintings by Caravaggio. The bench on the right-hand side of the painting upon which the lady in the blue skirt sits looks just like that unstable bench in the Contarelli Chapel upon which Saint Matthew is kneeling so dramatically, and also the one the dandy sits on in *The Calling of Saint Matthew*. The beam of light that bursts into that seedy tavern, mirroring Christ's powerful pointing hand, is not unlike that spotlight in the back room of *Las Hilanderas*. Perhaps in his travels Velázquez also went to Siena and saw Pinturicchio's painting of *Penelope with the Suitors* (Fig. 16.6). The story, you may recall, comes from the *Odyssey*, when Penelope is waiting for her husband's prolonged return. She promises that she will marry one of her many suitors as soon as she finishes her tapestry. She weaves by day, and completely dismantles it all at night. In the Pinturicchio painting, as in *Las Hilanderas*, there are women weaving, competitive energies (this time the men that vie for Penelope's attention), and complicated networks of frames. The view through the back window, showing Odysseus on one of his epic adventures, is like a painting on a wall, or even like a tapestry.

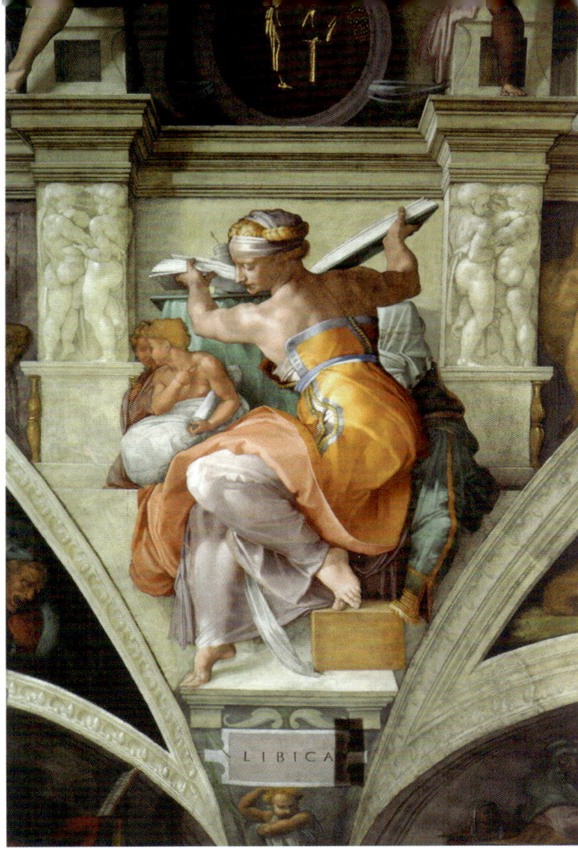

FIG. 16.5 Michelangelo, *The Libyan Sibyl*, 1508–1512. Southwestern section of the ceiling, Sistine Chapel, Vatican City. Fresco.

As with the Velázquez, we seem to be looking from an angle that places us to the left of the composition. And there is a cat playing with a ball, just as in *Las Hilanderas*.

Velázquez's quotations also include his own works of art. For example, Nieto's framed body looks much like an earlier portrait Velázquez had done of the same individual. The girl that looks out at the viewer from the scene in the background of *Las Hilanderas* might also be a quote of Nieto's pose in *Las Meninas*. They are both, after all, involved with tapestries, he professionally, she theatrically.

Velázquez also looks back to one of his earliest paintings, a scene showing a young woman working in a kitchen and being remonstrated with by the older woman on the left (Fig. 16.7). As the young and clearly upset woman works away, preparing some sort of mayonnaise to accompany those four silver, round-eyed fish, a smaller framed scene shows the story of Christ with Mary and Martha,

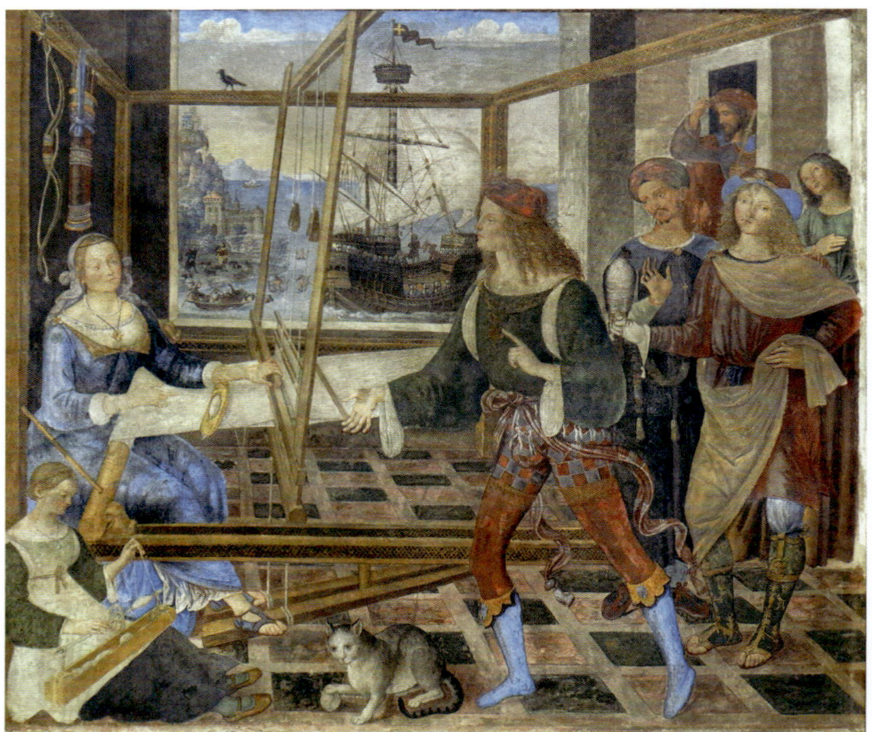

FIG. 16.6 Pinturicchio, *Penelope and the Suitors*, 1509. From the Palazzo del Magnifico, Siena. National Gallery London. Fresco, detached and mounted on canvas, 125 × 152 cm.

a biblical episode told in Luke 10:38–42. Mary sits at Christ's feet and listens to him speak. Martha, her sister, has gone to "make all the preparations that had to be made."

In this vignette Martha, standing behind Mary, returns to express her irritation that Mary is just sitting around and being useless. But Christ responds by telling Martha that Mary has indeed chosen the better option. The old woman seems to be reminding the young woman that she cannot gain fulfillment from work alone and that she should follow the *vita contemplativa* or spiritual life as well. Is the framed image a hanging painting from which the old lady draws her

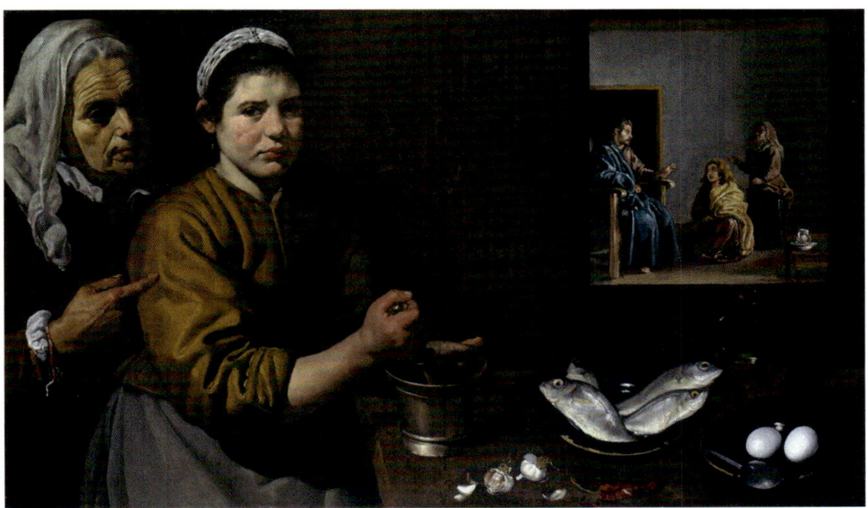

FIG. 16.7 Diego Velázquez, *Christ in the House of Martha and Mary*, ca. 1618. National Gallery, London. Oil on canvas, 60 × 103.5 cm.

moral? Is the biblical scene actually happening at this moment? Are we looking at it through a hole in the wall, or into another mirror? Is this like a thought bubble painted by Velázquez to illustrate the otherwise ephemeral thoughts of the old lady? It is not clear. But in *Las Hilanderas*, Velázquez is certainly borrowing a use of frames from his younger self.

Velázquez is also making an argument in *Las Meninas*, one that reappears in *Las Hilanderas*, and this involves the hand of the artist. Contrast the precision of his portrait, his exacting gaze, the crispness of his facial features with his imprecise right hand. His fingers are completely indistinguishable—just a pile of feathery, wispy, undelineated strokes. He is in action. He is actively painting that which we are seeing this very moment, *Las Meninas*, and a painting that we are not able to see, unless we are looking at vestiges of it through the mirror. Velázquez is showing us that we are being given a version of reality, a version of the truth. The painted version of Velázquez shows us his palette, covered in blobs of unformed paint. The painter Velázquez is doing the same, showing his process from start to finish, from the inchoate forms on the palette to the figures on the canvas.

That process leads to an incredible range of techniques. He can do forms that aren't stable, like the impressionistic sheen of the elegant garments and brocades. He can show faces that are murky and distant and part of the shadowy interior of the court. And he can paint the face of royalty, the public image of the monarchy, to precision, as in the face of the Infanta Margarita. The court biographer Palomino records a remarkable conversation between Philip IV and Velázquez about faces and portraiture: "His Majesty said to [Velázquez] that there were not lacking people who declared that his skill was limited to knowing how to paint a head; to which [Velázquez] replied: 'Sire, they favor me greatly, for I do not know that there is anyone who can paint a head.'" This anecdote is provocative, because Velázquez paints many a head. But he realizes that the truth of the head is not in realism. Every photograph that we take of ourselves looks ever so slightly different. When you meet someone that you know only from photographs, your first reaction is to consider how different they look from their image. Velázquez is working with that idea, with his feathery hand that moves and defies description, pictorial or otherwise. He is calling attention to his own hand, to his craft, to the creation of art, and the artifice of forms.

That upturned palette in *Las Meninas* takes another form in *Las Hilanderas*. The unformed blobs of paint are now unformed piles of wool that must go through many steps and processes before they produce that splendid tapestry in the back. Nothing comes from nothing, or so Lucretius writes in the first century BCE. King Lear asserts the same in Shakespeare's seventeenth-century play. Velázquez shows that that is not so. Something does come out of nothing. Velázquez shows this happening in paint. We know that the woman in the center is looking down, holding a comb in her left hand and picking something up with her right. But that hand is like Velázquez's painted hand, almost just a pile of streaky, blobby paint. As we look closer, her face also loses all form and meaning. Now it is as though we are looking at the painting of the palette in *Las Meninas*. Her face is just a mass of unformed paint.

And yet this *is* an image, this *is* a piece of Art. How remarkable it is that, at the center of the composition, in the middle of this painted web, Velázquez ensnares our eye with paint that is more paint than form, more impression than realism. This is a painting about Art—about its history and about its creation. Velázquez embraces the art of painting and slowly, cleverly shows you that what you think you see is not always what is really there. At first it looks like a simple genre scene, with women weaving. But they are simultaneously enhancing the telling of a story from Ovid, which relates to Velázquez and his relationship to other artists. A girl combing wool is just that, on the surface. But she can be so much more. She can demonstrate the rich artifice of Art.

What should this painting be named? Of course it matters how we name things. There is a large, sixteenth-century Spanish tapestry hanging in a church in San Antonio (Fig. 16.8). It was purchased and donated to the church in 1985. For a long time it was in the sanctuary, framing the minister in his pulpit. But now it is in a stairwell, which is unfortunate because it is a rather inglorious setting and because the stairwell is right next to a huge window. The beautiful dyed wools used to make tapestries are extremely sensitive to sunlight. This is especially the case with red dyes, which have all but disappeared. That is one problem. But there is another—its identification as *Joseph and His Brothers*. Joseph is the man on the throne, allegedly. But why are some of his brothers bringing him a huge box of golden rings? What is the letter being read? In the summer of 2012 I traveled to Spain with my parents. While in the town of Zamora we naturally went to see the main cathedral. Many of these Spanish cathedrals have treasuries where they house things that can be very interesting but usually are not. I often skip them. But for some reason this time I did not. I went into the treasury, up a massive, winding marble stairway. And there it was. The tapestry. Huge and glorious with the pinks and reds all intact. This moment of discovery was accompanied by a lot of fanfare, but that was only the first wave of shock. The next was discovering that the tapestry is about Hannibal, the Carthaginian military commander who lived from 247 to 180 BCE. There is a brother in the tapestry, Hannibal's brother Mago. He reads a letter that is supposed to tell the Carthaginian Senate how wonderfully Hannibal is doing in his military campaigns. The eight men of the Senate gesture wildly because they are thrilled to hear this news and probably to see the golden rings. The inscription describes the joy of the Carthaginians. But there is no Joseph. There is no Bible. Just power and gold and conquests abroad.

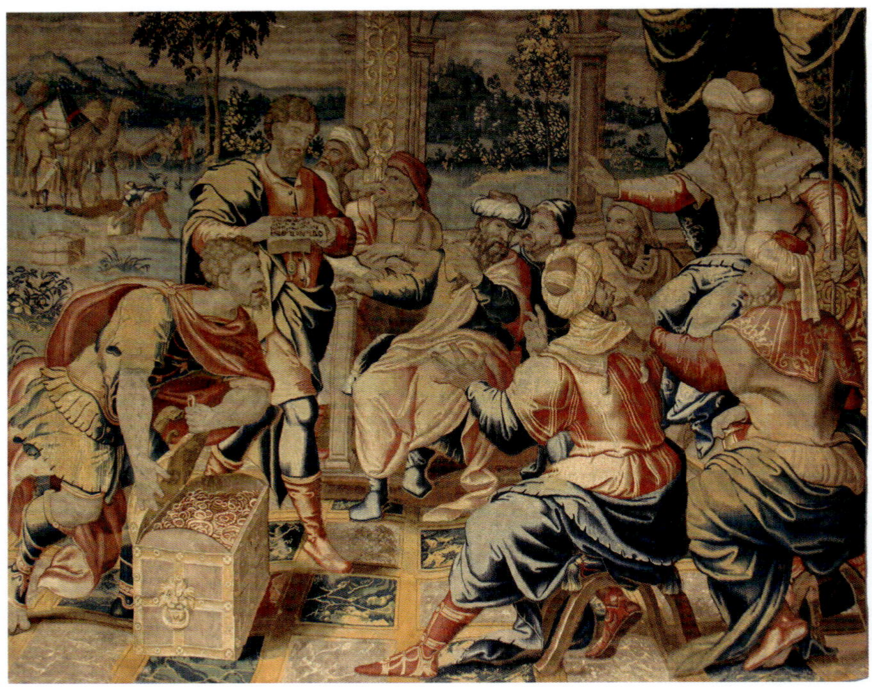

FIG. 16.8 *Mago, Hannibal's Messenger in Carthage*, ca. 1570. Design by an anonymous master of the Netherlands. Woven in Brussels, Belgium. San Antonio, Texas. Wool and silk, approx. 275 × 335 cm

Documents show that the Zamora tapestry was woven in Brussels in 1570 for the Spanish court. It has been in the cathedral since the seventeenth century. It belongs to a series that included eight similarly massive scenes, five of which survive. The entire series was probably woven a number of times, and the church has one of the surviving tapestries from another copy of the cycle. The tapestry in San Antonio is no longer surrounded by the other scenes about Hannibal and his conquests. It has also lost its border, which probably had important features still on the Zamora tapestry—the name of the weaver, the date, the Latin inscription. The Golden Age poet Baltasar Gracián (who was from Zaragoza) wrote in his book *The Oracle*: "Things do not pass for what they are but for what they seem;

few look within, and many are satisfied with appearances." Works of art can be reinterpreted, renamed, and reframed simply by mistake. Giving *Hannibal's Messenger in Carthage* the name *Joseph and His Brothers* is definitely a mistake.

The situation with *Las Hilanderas* is different. *Las Hilanderas* could have many names. But even when a name isn't wrong, it can still be inadequate. The painting *is* about spinners. But it is also about Arachne, and about acting out the story of a competition, and about painting another kind of competition. It is about a contemporary Spanish foreground that alludes to a mythological scene represented as a play and also alluded to in a tapestry. Velázquez masterfully draws us into his own spider's web, in which Arachne, art, and the artist all spiral together in a network of complex cross-references.

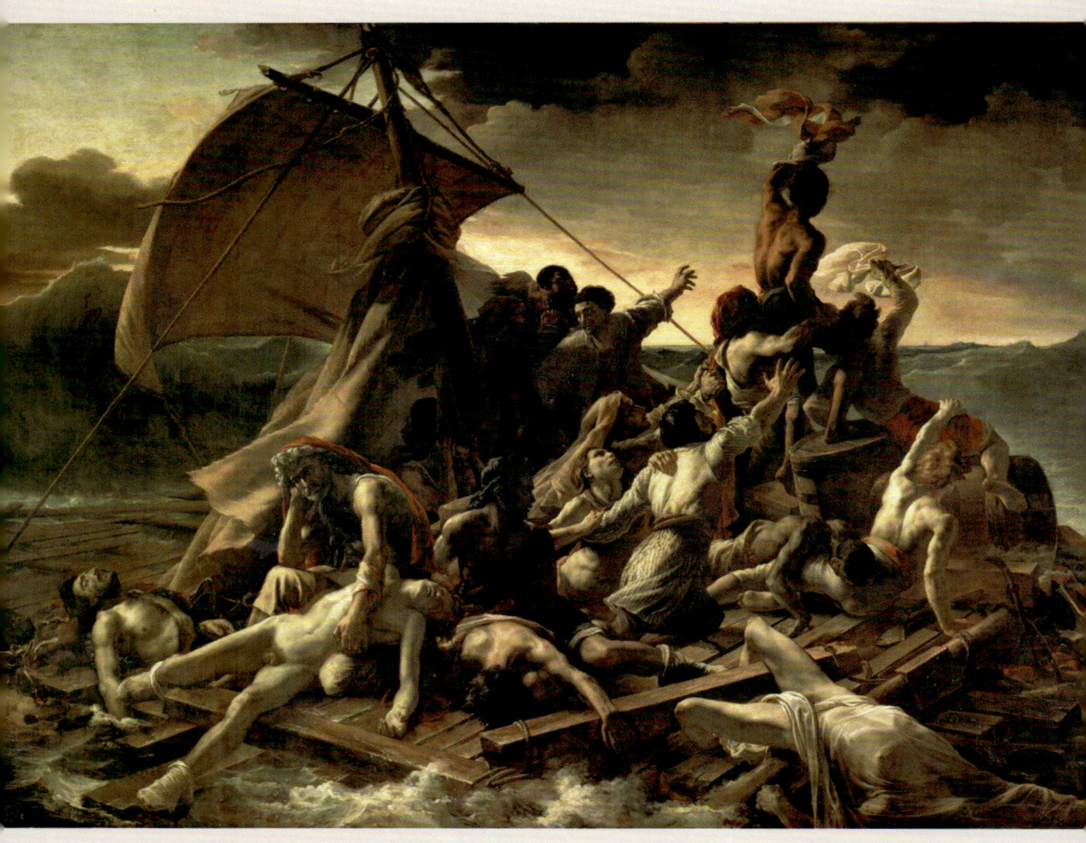

FIG. 17.1 Jean-Louis André Théodore Géricault, *The Raft of the Medusa*, 1818–1819. Musée du Louvre, Paris. Oil on canvas, 491 × 716 cm.

Géricault, *The Raft of the Medusa*

1818–19

ROMANTIC ART

On July 2, 1816, the grand French plan to colonize or "explore" Senegal hit a major roadblock. The *Medusa*, a large frigate packed with government officials, soldiers, artisans, and farmers ran aground. Along with goods to be traded with the Senegalese, a bust of King Louis XVIII, the newly restored Bourbon monarch, took the voyage, ready to radiate his image and rule over these unenlightened lands. The king's failed journey, however, was partly the result of his own faulty judgment, the selection of a woefully inexperienced captain who had only his high birth to recommend him. The inept captain followed an erratic course along the Mauretanian coast and got stuck in its treacherous reefs. The shipwreck might have been bad enough, but it was the aftermath that was the true embarrassment.

After two days of utter confusion, it became clear that the ship had to be abandoned. But the six lifeboats could only accommodate 250 of the 400 passengers on the *Medusa*. The rest—a handful of subordinate officers, a few artisans, the majority of the soldiers, and at least one woman—clambered onto a raft measuring sixty-five feet long and twenty-eight feet wide, a crude vessel composed of masts and beams lashed together with ropes. As the woeful passengers boarded the slippery beams, the raft was weighed down. One survivor, the surgeon Henri Savigny, later described how the raft "sank at least three feet, and so closely were we huddled together that it was impossible to move a single step. Fore and aft, we had the water up to our middle."

The lifeboats were supposed to pull the raft to shore, but this plan was abandoned when the officers realized that the raft was slowing down their course. The officers cut the ropes connecting their boats to the raft. It was thus left to the mercy of waves and wind, blistering sun during the daylight hours, freezing temperatures at night, and abject, gruesome hunger. On the thirteenth day a British vessel, the *Argus*, finally found the raft. Of the 115 Frenchmen who boarded the fateful vessel only 15 were still alive—covered in wounds, delirious, and forever changed. So were the people of France, and so was the young artist Théodore Géricault (1791–1824). Géricault was twenty-five at the time of the episode and twenty-eight when he finished his masterpiece, *The Raft of the Medusa* (Fig. 17.1). His rotting and ruined bodies were a reminder to Paris, to the world, about this horrible incident. But it was more than a cruel scene showing the inherent depravity of man. The painting was also about a different kind of voyage, that of France and the difficult waters it would soon navigate as it transitioned into a modern age. The painting was a powerful warning that this shift into modernity, this metaphorical trip, if done without significant social reform, could be ruinous. Rather than growing and thriving, the body politic would end up alone, adrift, and abusive—attacking itself, devouring itself, leaving nothing behind, lost to oblivion.

Géricault's painting is a total onslaught of twisted bodies, dying and dead. It is a bizarre and macabre ball of yarn—entangled yet with individual strange strands that pull in dramatic ways. There are long expansive gestures, long attenuated bodies. The line from the bottom left of the painting to the outstretched arms at the right heightens the sense of pulling. Ropes are drawn taut. Men hang onto one another, grasping and wrenching. Géricault extends the men out like distasteful taffy, exposing the fullness of their bodies and sometimes the missing parts of those bodies. He draws and then quarters them, strewing their mutilated parts along the bottom of the picture.

Reading from left to right, Géricault gives us a gruesome Morse code, a message of pure horror—dead head, dead arm and foot, dead leg, dead arm, dead head, dead arm, dead leg, dead arm, and dead head cut off by the frame. That headless cadaver on the right end is balanced with the head of the bodiless, gutless man at the far left. The splayed boy between them wears just his limp white socks, a strange detail that perverts the moment further, making his nudity, his mangled masculinity, all the more shocking and further emphasizing the fact that this man will never wear shoes, will never wear the rest of his garments. With a quarter turn he will be just like the headless man who is descending into his watery grave. These repeated triangular shapes, the A-shape of those splayed, white, morbid legs, thus creates a sense of movement, as if we were rolling to the right, flailing about on the sea.

Things are literally spiraling out of control. Water is not a source of life. It collapses upon itself, just as it threatens to consume these men. Droplets of water meet dripping lifeless hands. Faceless heads of flustered hair meet pockets of misty sea foam. If this is Nature versus Man, it is not a fair fight. Man does not stand a chance. This would seem to be the watery version of "earth to earth, ashes to ashes, dust to dust."

There is little reprieve in this painting. Even when we look to the horizon, try to look away, the horror doesn't dissipate. Those white waves along the bottom of the painting seem innocent until we remember that these men are slowly slipping into that very water. Those seemingly harmless smaller waves are harbingers of the wave that emerges like a beast, like a maw of hell, on the left side of the painting, ready to subsume and consume the figures on the boat. It is at its peak, pulled to the point where its crash is all but imminent. The lilting, fluffy clouds in the sky beautifully frame the wave. The sky is clear. What could possibly be wrong? It is another mean and disconcerting lie. That wave is ready to pounce. And even if it does not clamp its jaws directly over the boat, it will unsettle it, unbalance it, unravel more of its loose ends—those unhinged, untied beams—and more of its men, who are similarly unhinged, slipping away into death, into that water.

Those terrors of the sea seem to mock the mast and its sail. The wave and the sail have almost the same shape and position. Yet the wave has a clear path of destruction. The sail does not; it takes this ship of wrecked men in whatever direction the wind decides. There is no plan and no control. The heavy, hanging material under the sail almost looks like it has a ghoulish mouth itself. Dark blotches in the tentlike shape appear to gape at us. But these are the heads of men who look at nothing or rip at their hair in utter, despondent despair. They appear to have lost their minds, models of insanity—one man communes with a tarp, the other digs his fingers into a head that cannot comprehend what has happened.

When we look at this figure closely it is possible to see strange patches of shiny black material. This is where the artist thought to use bitumen, a paint that would have produced a dark, lustrous effect. Unfortunately, over time bitumen deteriorates and discolors, contracting and leaving a wrinkled, scaly effect. Originally the velvety quality of the special black paint would have had a richness that was inviting and sensuous. Like those dancing waves and billowing clouds, these were parts of the painting that seemed inviting but were passages of utter darkness, the most abject shadows, indications of a constant current of madness.

The two men who stare without hope, without reason, have important counterparts in two of the men that stand in the quartet to their right. These four men create a circle that seems to suggest hope and strength. The man with his back to the mast has a noble profile with a strikingly Roman, aquiline nose. He wears his proper military regalia, and although perhaps a little static, a little forced, his pose imparts solemnity and stalwartness. The man to the right looks outward toward the faintly present *Argus* with a romantic look—windswept hair, mouth held elegantly and breathlessly in suspense, high cheekbones, arched eyebrows, clasped hands. In fact, his hands are not only clasped on themselves, they are doubly clasped, by the black man who also turns toward the distant boat, hopeful and firm, and certainly a great deal less dazed than the man to the left. The loop is completed with the man turning back. His face is flashed in light, revealing a rather sallow, gray visage, a look of tremendous angst and concern. But his gesture is one of hope. He draws attention, with an expansive gesture, to the boat on the horizon. With his other arm he grabs at the first man's elbow.

The way that the men hold each other suggests a camaraderie, a companionship that is otherwise lost on the raft. In that exchange between the two men, that moment of communication, the gesturing man seems to encourage the other by saying, "I mean it. It is there. It is coming to get us. Don't give up yet." These are the only two on the boat who look each other in the eye, who appear to communicate with each other, which is fitting since they are portraits of the two men who survived the raft and wrote about the catastrophe—Henri Savigny, the ship's surgeon, is the man in the shadows with the hat, and Alexandre Corréard, the naval engineer and geographer, is the man with the expansive gesture.

By the time Géricault met the two men and had them pose for his painting, Corréard and Savigny were celebrities. They certainly were not at first, however.

It was bad enough that the men had to survive two weeks on the raft. When they were finally saved, the story was suppressed, as much as possible, by the French government. This is not all that surprising since the whole affair made the newly established Bourbon government look inept, corrupt, and nepotistic. The survivors were fined, put in jail, and dismissed from government service.

When their story did get leaked, both in France and in the foreign press, it was a bombshell. Savigny and Corréard were an instantaneous hit. They published five editions of their account between 1817 and 1821. Géricault was one of their many readers, their story grabbing his imagination in an all-consuming way.

While Géricault prepared to paint the canvas he disappeared. He hid away, completely isolating himself. He changed studios from one that was in a central, noisy part of town to a space far more isolated. He had one assistant and few visitors, generally friends that he would use as models. One model was the young artist Eugène Delacroix, who is allegedly the figure of the young man lying on his face with his left arm thrown forward. I do not doubt that Delacroix was a model for Géricault, but I imagine him more as the man with the windblown hair at the top of the composition. Perhaps this has to do with Delacroix's report that after seeing the emerging forms of the painting he ran out of the studio in a fit of astonishment: "The impression it gave me was so strong that as I left the studio I broke into a run and kept running like a fool all the way back to the rue de la Planche where I lived then."

According to the biographer Charles Clément, Géricault never left the house, ate his meals in the studio, slept next to his painting, and had a barber shave his head, quite a sacrifice for the artist, who had been known for taking great pride in his well-curled auburn hair. Painting from dawn to dusk, the artist completed the enormous canvas in approximately eight months. He collapsed in exhaustion when the task was finished, a fatigue from which he never quite recovered.

Yet painting the canvas was only the final stage in a long process during which the artist struggled to express the perfect moment, to illustrate the essence of the catastrophe. Géricault studied the writings of Corréard and Savigny in meticulous detail. He interviewed the two men and other survivors of the raft. He had the carpenter of the original *Medusa* build a scale model of the raft, which sat in his studio. And he made drawings, hundreds of drawings and sketches and paintings. Each was a step toward the process of discovering the perfect moment that would be the focus of the painting.

One of the first moments in the narrative by Corréard and Savigny was a mutiny. On the second night the soldiers on the raft attacked the officers; sixty-five men died during that fight, and as the officers were the only ones holding weapons, the only men that died were of lower status, in other words, the soldiers. Géricault took this ferocious moment as the inspiration for a number of his sketches. In the version now in Amsterdam, praying arms and a hope for deliverance at the left find a cruel balance in the presence of an unsheathed saber on the right. Strangely, a man with the saber receives an unintended blow to the brow by a man with an ax, who is actually fighting a different, nude individual. Man brutally, senselessly destroys his fellow man. The two upturned forms create a U-shape that frames a centrally placed man, a dressed officer, who holds tight to the mast and looks upward in a look of romantic despair. There is a calm, an eye in the storm, in that man at the mast.

The rest of the composition is busy, tangled, almost incoherent. The artist tried to capture a number of the details from Corréard and Savigny—their descriptions of the crowding on the raft, the officers holding to the mast, the use of barrels as a place to rest, and the seditious man who, when perceiving his plot had been discovered, "wrapped himself in a piece of drapery, which he wore folded over his breast, and, of his own accord, threw himself into the sea." The man who strangely covers himself in his own burial shroud, a large head wrapping of sorts, dives into the water in the upper right of the sketch, waving his axe in the air.

Géricault examined another episode during his process, an episode of desperation and violence on the ship—cannibalism. He tackled this part of the account only once, in a sketch composed of black chalk, ink wash, watercolor, and white gouache on a light-brown paper housed at the Louvre. The cannibal is not in the center. He appears to the left of the main mast. The crouching, eating man has a dramatically arched back that draws attention to his concave, empty stomach. The white pigment crudely defines his face, giving him a ghoulish appearance, as though he is wearing a mask. He is a faceless, nameless brute. But this is not the central focus of the sketch. The most obvious figure is the nude man standing by the mast who makes an odd gesture with his hands—pushing down on something that is not there. No one seems to note the affair, the eating. There is no blood. It's not gruesome or gory. It is just one version among many of despair and imminent death.

Géricault does not harp on the topic of cannibalism. He deals with it just like Corréard and Savigny—swiftly and with a sense of distancing. The final composition does not, in fact, show cannibalism at all. When it was first revealed, critics of the painting were confused by that fact. They expected to see more of the carnage, more of the vivid events that they had heard or read about. Of course they were too polite to write the word "cannibalism." But it was clear what they were looking for: "One vainly searches in the painting for some of the horrible episodes which will remain eternally in the memory of those who read the account of the shipwreck. One regards it with astonishment but without interest. One sees only a heap of men who seem to have left the tomb."

What these critics did not know or did not acknowledge were all the sketches, drawings, paintings that Géricault had been working through, all of which were, in essence, part of the final composition. The final painting is a sum of the artist's experiences and struggles. The figures that we see in the painting retain many of the forms and meanings that they had in the earlier sketches. Even when the bodies or body parts in the final painting do not correspond in a one-to-one manner with those earlier sketches, we can consider that they have a deep history or were worked out in some capacity in Géricault's mind at some earlier stage. The lone weapon, a bloodied axe, which hides amid the beams of the raft, reminds us of the man who wraps himself in the strange garment after causing the mutiny and jumps into the sea, as does the man with the bizarre, pinkish head covering who grabs at his fellow passenger. His pulling on the red turban of the man in front of him suggests something mutinous or at least menacing. Perhaps he is asking for help. Intentionally or not, he is certainly threatening to pull the man down.

The black man that collapses over the figure with the shock-red hair appears utterly lifeless. But the placement of his face suggests that he is somehow affixed to the other man's body. It is not a scene of cannibalism. Although it isn't cannibalism, it might have suggested cannibalism to the original audience. Similarly the gesture of the red-headed man toward the man above him is aggressive, brutal, zombielike—perhaps suggesting dead and dying men looking for their next meal.

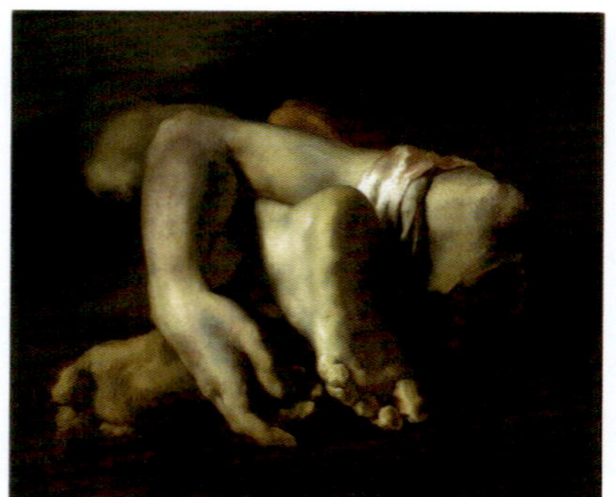

FIG. 17.2 Géricault, *Study of Feet and Hands*, 1818–1819. Musée Fabre, Montpellier, France. Oil on canvas, 52 × 64 cm.

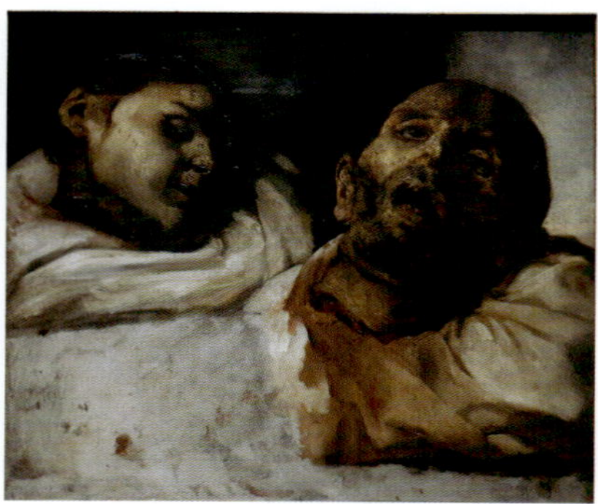

FIG. 17.3 Géricault, *Study of Severed Heads*, 1818–1819. National Museum, Stockholm, Sweden. Oil on canvas, 50 × 61 cm.

These unattached limbs have their genesis in another compilation of sketches by Géricault, composed of five drawings and nine fully developed paintings. Charles Clément, writing a few years after Géricault's death, described how the artist would visit hospitals and gather discarded human parts as models for his painting. These he would place in his studio. The severed head, legs, and feet of guillotined individuals made a stench that Clément could not bear (Fig. 17.2). But Géricault could. In fact, there is something loving in these paintings. A gruesome head—mouth ajar, speckled in spattered blood, catawampus eyes and teeth—is complemented with another that is youthful, peaceful, gentle (Fig. 17.3). The juxtaposition almost makes the horror of the first somehow sympathetic and sorrowful—gruesome and gallant. A right arm tenderly wraps around a severed left foot (Fig. 17.2). Those arms, legs, feet, heads all appear in the final painting of the raft. Sometimes they are connected to bodies that are alive, sometimes to bodies that are dead.

Once you have seen these sketches, it is impossible to disassociate the limbs of the final painting from the body parts that Géricault took out of the hospital and sat with day after malodorous day in his studio. The final composition doesn't have blood and guts or bleeding wounds, but Géricault insinuates those into the painting. Flashes of red slash through the painting; these subtle marks easily suggest the gashes, the wounds, the cuts that these men must have endured. Darcy Grigsby has pointed out that ropes spill out like tendons, as do the "intestinal, sinewy entanglements of pinkish straps" next to the man at the far left. It is as though Géricault has scooped out the man's stomach—a strangely desiccated, concave chest, like a mouth without its dentures—and plopped those knotted innards under the man's head, a gruesome pillow for his final resting place. It is possible that he is a completely severed torso left on the raft, since we cannot see his legs.

The critics were looking for something that was not there, and in so doing they were missing the most crucial feature of the painting—the boat on the horizon. What irony that the men who were supposed to be studying and observing the painting missed Géricault's emphasis on looking and seeing, the sighting of the boat. There are two triangles in the painting, an unusual composition that rejects a singular focus. The dominant triangle is at the mast, where the dignitaries stood in the actual event and in this painting. But the more important triangle in the painting is composed around the group at the right, where the man stands on the barrel waving the tattered shreds of cloth at a teensy third triangle, the distant boat of the *Argus.* The barrel has echoes of earlier sketches too. That barrel was part of the action in the sketch of the mutiny. In that sketch it supported a suffering, persecuted woman. Here Géricault gives the barrel a grander role, as the foothold upon which the black man stands. The barrel becomes the place, the pedestal, where Géricault inserts compassion and patriotism. Man supports his fellow man by providing physical stability and backup, simultaneously and significantly upending the notion of the black man as the bottom of the social hierarchy. The man to the right waves a white garment in solidarity. He ignores the man pulling on him. He focuses on the hope represented by the boat in the distance.

The sighting of the *Argus* is crucial and the true focus of the piece, the crux of its psychological and emotional intensity. But this is not a moment of pure joy. We are not sure if the *Argus* sees the raft. Salvation is not guaranteed. In fact the ship is very small, very remote. Readers of Corréard and Savigny would have known one of the most heart-wrenching moments of the narrative, the moment when the *Argus* passes by. We know that the boat finally saves the men on the raft. But the first time it sails by without seeing the men: "We did all we could to make ourselves observed; we piled up our casks, at the top of which we fixed handkerchiefs of different colors. Unfortunately, in spite of all of these signals, the brig disappeared. From the delirium of joy we passed to that of dejection and grief."

In this passage, sight is crucial. The fear of not being seen is one of the most terrifying experiences on the raft. When the boat does not see the men, the collapse from hope to despair is debilitating. It is a psychological and emotional catastrophe. This is what Géricault wants to capture or at the very least explore. Blood and cannibalism are too obvious, too sensational. Being able to paint that psychological intensity of uncertainty, that is a challenge. Are they fighting futilely to be observed? Or is this the moment when the *Argus* does return, two hours later, and finally sees the men with their rags and flags? Are they about to have their hopes, their first sign of help in two weeks, completely dashed?

In trying to re-create the episode of the raft, the artist tried to experience the horrors of the episode as fully as he could. Through his brush, pen, pencil, he was essentially reliving the story of the raft. He paints his way through the pain of the story. He also paints the viewer into the picture, or the picture into the viewer—the angst spills out of the canvas into our space. It is not a passive painting. It does not present a scene for your pleasure, for your consumption. It demands your attention. It consumes you. Géricault puts the raft at an angle, pushed up by the tumultuous sea. The men—those sinuous, life-size bodies— threaten to tumble into our space. Some actually do fall out of the picture frame, headless and lifeless. And Géricault pulls the viewer into the painting, into the story, into the psychological and physical torment experienced by these men. No one is spared. Everyone is implicated in this disaster.

In a way, the ship is an unveiled criticism of France and its government. The *Medusa* catastrophe happened just one year into the restored Bourbon monarchy. King Louis XVIII happily took the throne from which his brother Louis XVI had been forcibly removed. Politically, the country was at sea. The streets of Paris were filled with unemployed and disenfranchised veterans who had fought in the constant warring that had defined France since the beginning of the French Revolution in 1789. The social structure was essentially a caste system. It bolstered the appointment of an inexperienced, aristocratic commander for the *Medusa* and was complicit in the mistreatment of the men on the raft. Although slavery had been abolished in 1794, France was still involved in the trading of slaves. The trip to Senegal was, as Corréard and Savigny soon discovered and exposed, a clandestine continuation of that horrible enterprise.

The painting is a call to arms. Géricault seems to say that there are two choices—to continue the practices of the past (including an abusive system based on slavery and class/caste structures) or to look toward a future, toward a France where men work together and class and race are erased. Can France make the transition? That is what Géricault is asking in the painting. He may not give the clearest opinion on the matter, but there seems to be something in his final composition that says yes. In one of his oil sketches at the Louvre the *Argus* is much larger, much grander. Even though the sense is that the *Argus* is going to inevitably save the day, the moment on this raft is *less* hopeful. In the sketch the men do not strain in the same way to flag the boat; their flags are tiny.

By contrast, in the final composition the figures work and struggle and strain to see that tiny boat. So do we, for that matter. There is no guarantee that the boat is going to save the raft, but it is far better than focusing on what is happening on that grim floating tomb. The message appears to be the following: remember your mistakes, learn from them, and then fight for that beacon on the horizon, for a better future, for a better France. Géricault praises that fight, encourages that shifted focus, and he illustrates that message through the act of sighting and seeing. Critical, thoughtful viewing is crucial to Géricault's craft, to painting. Otherwise art is just fluff. And in a sense Géricault is not only asking if France will make the transition; he is also wondering if painting itself has the mettle to make the transition into this new world order, one defined by modernity and, ideally, classlessness.

Consider the Salon in which Géricault showed *The Raft of the Medusa.* The Salon of 1819 was supposed to herald the rebirth of the French Empire, now in the hands of the noble Bourbons. The east wing of the Louvre was filled to the brim with displays of cashmeres, printed wallpapers, and precision watches. The clear message was that France was once again a bastion of industry, wealth, culture, and beauty. The paintings were supposed to say the same. Most did. François-Édouard Picot's *Amor and Psyche,* also in the Salon of 1819, is elegant, alluring, and literal. It is also much indebted to Jacques-Louis David, whose

Neoclassical style was so privileged at the time. In 1819 David was in *self*-exile in Brussels. Always one for drama and flair, David was probably hoping to emulate his grand patron Napoleon, who was truly exiled on the island of Saint Helena. Because he was in "exile," David was not shown in the Salon, which led one critic to bemoan: "David, where are you now?" In spirit, however, David was there. Picot was clearly inspired by David's *Cupid and Psyche*, which was on display in a Parisian private collection and is now in Cleveland.

Géricault's painting was on the scale of a grand Davidian painting. But its subject matter was not soothing, and its style was not that crisp, porcelain technique so privileged by the Neoclassical painters. This is not to say that the men on the raft aren't grand and striking and even noble. They are powerful and muscular. Yet the figures are not smooth, with even, porcelain muscles. Here the light hits and disappears in a way that activates the muscles, mottles them, makes them seem strained and tense. There is a frenetic energy to the bodies created by this use of shading, one that expresses the wildness of their inner angst. Some features are distorted for effect, such as the man whose elongated torso writhes in the center of the painting.

Combined with the many different and dramatic diagonals, the effect is unsettling. The style and composition emphasize the fact that the men are hovering between life and death. The man in the center of the painting with the white tunic has the strong back of a grand classical statue. He twists powerfully as he reaches toward the *Argus*. But his extended hand is lit in such a way that the tendons are bizarrely heightened, making his hand appear almost skeletal.

The critics did not get it. They described the painting as *"une fricassée"*—which means that to them it was confusing and foul and illegible. This was the Salon, a place for beauty and privilege. How dare Géricault bring blood and dirt and terror into this space? But Géricault is trying to point out that the Classical idea, the pristine Academy and its insider crowd of properly trained artists, was out of touch; it was missing the more pressing issues happening beyond those walls of the Louvre. Géricault is suggesting that art can do more. He is suggesting that it is time to press in that direction, toward a new horizon, just like the men that clamber to the top of the barrel and wave at the *Argus*.

This is precisely what the old man at the back of the boat does *not* do. Known as the "Father figure," he embodies the essence of the Classical past. The earliest commentators on the painting identified this as an illustration of the Count Ugolino, described by Dante in the *Inferno*. In the poem, Ugolino's punishment is that he is trapped in the ice with the archbishop that left him to starve to death in a tower. The poet Dante discovers Ugolino gnawing on the archbishop's head. It would seem that Ugolino is avenging his aggressor, but Ugolino is also punishing himself, reenacting his hideous crime. Ugolino was left in the tower with his sons and grandsons, and the poet Dante none-too-subtly suggests that he also ate his own flesh and blood, his own sons. A painting by Henry Fuseli in the British Museum dated 1806 shows Ugolino in a pose similar to that of the Father.

Both figures are brooding and grim, with tightly curled hair and a sculptural, symmetrical face. In both, an arm dangles over the dead boy whose death he has witnessed. The encompassing body of the father figure is a visual suggestion of their terrible unity. Darcy Grigsby disdains the presence of the Father in the Géricault, claiming it is a "painfully prosaic and cobbled construction [that] disrupts the beguiling fluency and authority, the material veracity, of those other bodies." But Géricault is inserting the father and son in an intentional and purposeful way. The scene of the patriarchal bond, father and son, is also a suggestion of the patriarchal past of the painting. Dante, Fuseli, David—these are all part of the history of the painting, just like that multitude of sketches.

Géricault reveals a great respect for his predecessors. One clear form of inspiration was Michelangelo's west wall of the Sistine Chapel. Michelangelo painted the *Last Judgment* scene some twenty-five years after he painted the ceiling. The optimism engendered in the paintings on the ceiling was much lost in this later work. The later forms are heavier, overly muscular, almost frightening. Christ is powerful but also somewhat terrifying. His right hand looks like he is going to swat someone rather than provide gentle benediction, and his left hand points to the gash on his chest, an indication of his persecution and suffering. In the lower right of the composition, directly following the line of Christ's gesture, is a scene of Charon transporting the damned to Hell, another important image from Dante's *Inferno* (Fig. 17.4). Charon's ship is filled with tangled bodies that cower and slip into the sea, not unlike the men on Géricault's raft.

The other Italian artist that made an impression on the young Géricault was

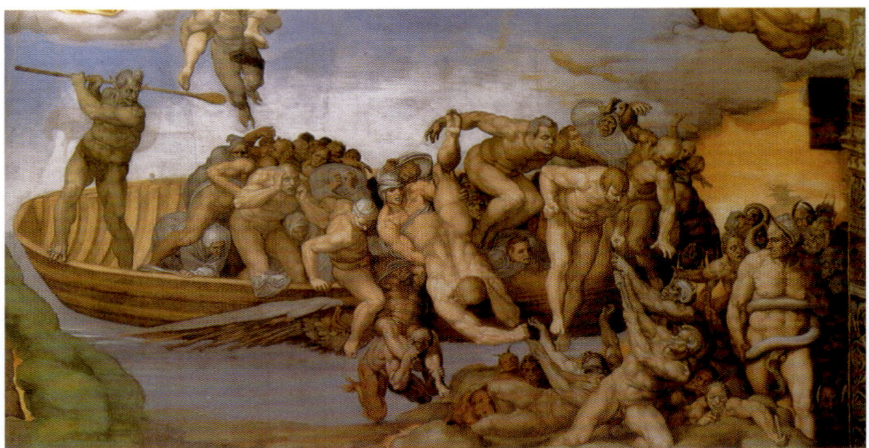

FIG. 17.4 Michelangelo, detail of *Last Judgment* showing Charon ferrying souls to the Underworld, 1536–1541. Lower right section of the western wall, Sistine Chapel. Fresco, 48 × 44 feet.

Caravaggio, with his flickering lights and somber shadows, dramatic diagonals, and somber palette. In Caravaggio's *Deposition* (see figure 3.6), Christ is lowered into a dark and bottomless tomb. Sweeping diagonals lead us from the shroud at the lower left up through entangled legs and arms to the upper right, where a woman, not unlike the men on the boat, holds her hands up to the heavens, reaching for succor and expressing all-consuming grief. Christ's body hangs in a way that is not unlike the men who slip into the sea—the feet in our space, the partially clothed bodies, the draperies that drag and hang, the heads that fall backward, mouths slightly ajar. All is pushed into our space. The darkness behind is eternal, like the sea. Géricault knew this painting well, and even made a copy of it.

Géricault absorbed and respected past traditions. He is not calling for a revolution in art. He knows far too well that revolutions just lead to brutality and Napoleon and ultimately the same monarchy that reigned before it all started. The challenge is not to throw away the past. The challenge is to redirect it toward a modern Europe and a modern art.

Géricault's life, or his life as an artist, was in many ways defined by this painting. For one thing, he did not start painting with any seriousness until he was twenty-one, when he produced *The Charging Chasseur*. Between 1812 and the wreck in 1816 he produced very little and spent much of his time in a troubled, steamy love affair with his uncle's wife. For three years he devoted his practice to capturing the message and the madness of the *Medusa*. After its grand exhibition in 1819, mixed reviews from the critics and the exhaustion of completing the masterpiece threw the artist into a state of deep depression. For two years he toured with the painting, principally in England, where it received the greatest praise and bolstered the artist's confidence—temporarily.

When he returned to France in 1821, Géricault's sole interest was in painting the mentally ill. The study of these haunted individuals, the insistent but sympathetic study of their faces, was more than a scientific interest. Géricault had a personal stake in these pictures. Failing mental health was compounded by a malignant tumor found in 1822. Visiting the artist in December 1823, Delacroix wrote that Géricault looked like a dying old man, although he was only thirty-two when he died a month later.

Immediately after his premature death, Géricault was heralded as a quasi-martyr. In *The Death of Géricault* by Ary Scheffer (1824), the artist takes on a spiritual aura, bright-white light encircling the dead man whose upturned face counterbalances that of the man in the chair, who covers his face in abject woe. Much like a canonized saint, Géricault's body was symbolically scattered and revered throughout Europe. Cast reproductions of the artist's hand and face became fixtures in artists' studios. In 1842 Charles Blanc commented that "there is no artist's studio today in which we cannot find the plaster mask of Géricault, a long mask, concave, bony, and a little smiling, whose expression is that of sweet irony and of an eternal regret."

These casts were treated like relics. Delacroix wrote about seeing the death mask and how its immortal power tempted him to kiss the face, the beard, the eyelashes. Géricault's tomb took a few years to complete because political support did not immediately mirror the artist's popular support. His painting had been critical of the current regime, after all. But when the July Monarchy took power under King Louis-Philippe, yet another flip in the government, Géricault was praised by the political regime and a monumental, unforgettable tomb was

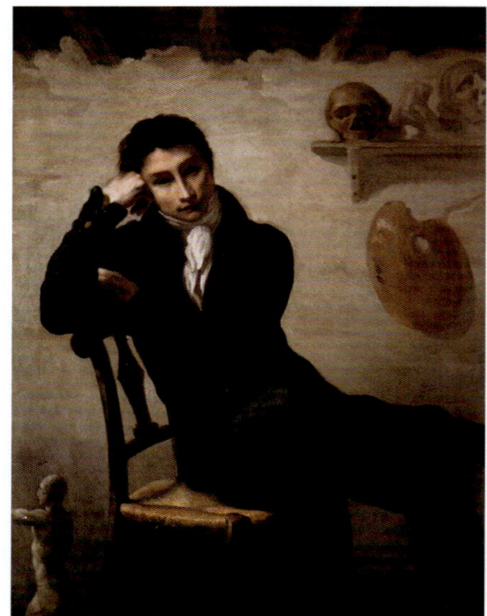

FIG. 17.5 Formerly attributed to Géricault. *Portrait of a Young Man in an Artist's Studio,* ca. 1818–1819. Musée du Louvre, Paris. Oil on canvas, 146.7 × 101.4 cm.

finally erected. His effigy shows him as the ultimate suffering genius; illness undermines his bodily power, reducing him to lie on his side. But his face and his hands are animate in an unwavering commitment to painting. Bolstered by a bronze relief of his *Raft of the Medusa,* to which his paintbrush points, the artist's genius lives on in transcendent perpetuity.

Thus Géricault posthumously became the most perfect icon of the Romantic movement, which praised the tortured individual, the suffering artist. A particular painting in the Louvre was originally thought to have been a self-portrait (Fig. 17.5). Scholars now know that it is, in fact, not Géricault or even by him. The misidentification is interesting, however, because Géricault was long associated with this type, with the melancholic, handsome man lost in reverie. The self-portrait that *is* known to have been done by his hand is quite different (Fig. 17.6). It is painted by a confident hand and shows a poised, self-assured man. He proudly displays his paintbrushes, which are produced with quick, energetic brushstrokes, easy flicks of paint. Géricault's body faces one direction and his head faces the other, as though he were caught in the midst of something,

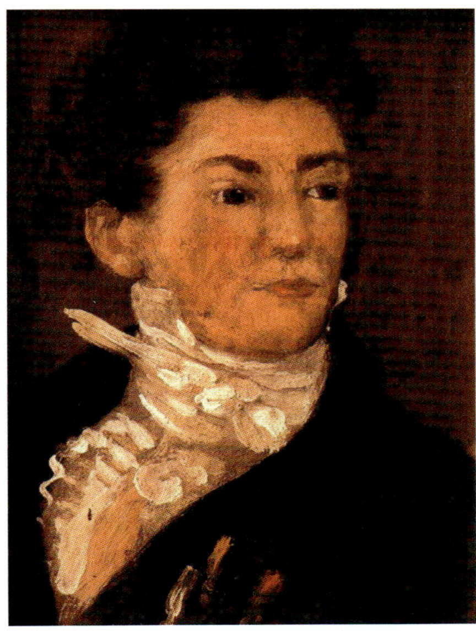

FIG. 17.6 Géricault, *Self-portrait,* ca. 1808. Private collection. Oil and paper over canvas, 21 × 14 cm.

distracted while using those very brushes. He is active, his eyes are alert and curious. This is the Géricault that jibes with the *Medusa* painting—not mopey and dreamy but aware and modern. In the misidentified painting, the artist's palette hangs on the wall, not being used, just a sign of his interests along with curious skulls and models and masks. Yet in the true self-portrait, his brushes are in his hand, being used in this very moment. Similarly, *The Raft of the Medusa* was about the pressures of modern Europe or modern man and how those concerns needed to be acknowledged and addressed, not ignored or masked.

One characteristic of the Romantic period was its obsession with horror. Mary Shelley's *Frankenstein* was first published in 1818. Monsters made by men then threaten the men who made them. How striking it is that Goya also paints his grim *Saturn Devouring His Son* in 1819 (Fig. 17.7). This gruesome painting of father eating son is not unlike Géricault's sketch of the cannibalism scene—a tubelike arm moves passively into a toothless mouth on a masklike face of horror. The story of *The Raft of the Medusa* reduced men to bestial, subhuman behavior, and Géricault's painting shows hints of that terror. These forms of horror

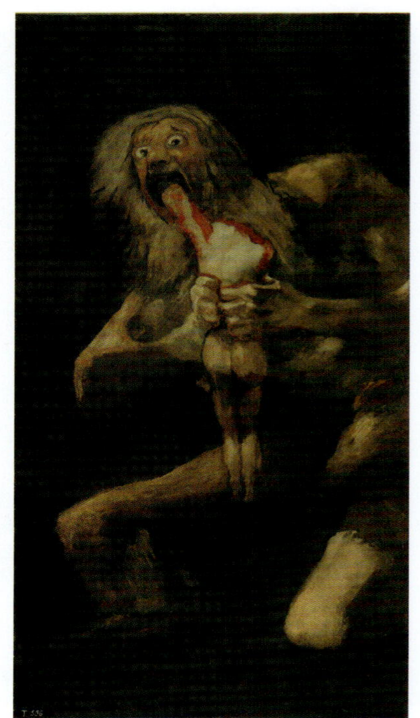

FIG. 17.7 Francisco de Goya, *Saturn Devouring One of His Sons*, ca. 1819–1821. Museo del Prado, Madrid, Spain. Oil on canvas, 143.5 × 81.4 cm.

(ungodly monsters, zombielike figures, man eating man) were on a par with the fear engendered by the shipwrecks. Doomed boats seem to have been a popular form of the horror genre—one that produced a sense of despair and fear and futility.

Delacroix painted a shipwreck not unlike Géricault's (Fig. 17.8). The scene illustrates the second canto of Lord Byron's *Don Juan*, published in 1819, wherein the men cast lots to see who is going to be eaten. Juan's dog goes first. Then his tutor. Delacroix's blues are deeper and more variegated, and the composition is focused on the central event rather than splayed in many directions, as in the painting by Géricault. Nevertheless it is clear that Delacroix was inspired by the older artist's painting. His style is certainly comparable, and Delacroix employs a similar expressiveness and drama in the gestures. He picks a story of a shipwreck and its lost lifeboat, where people go mad and eat someone in a lower social

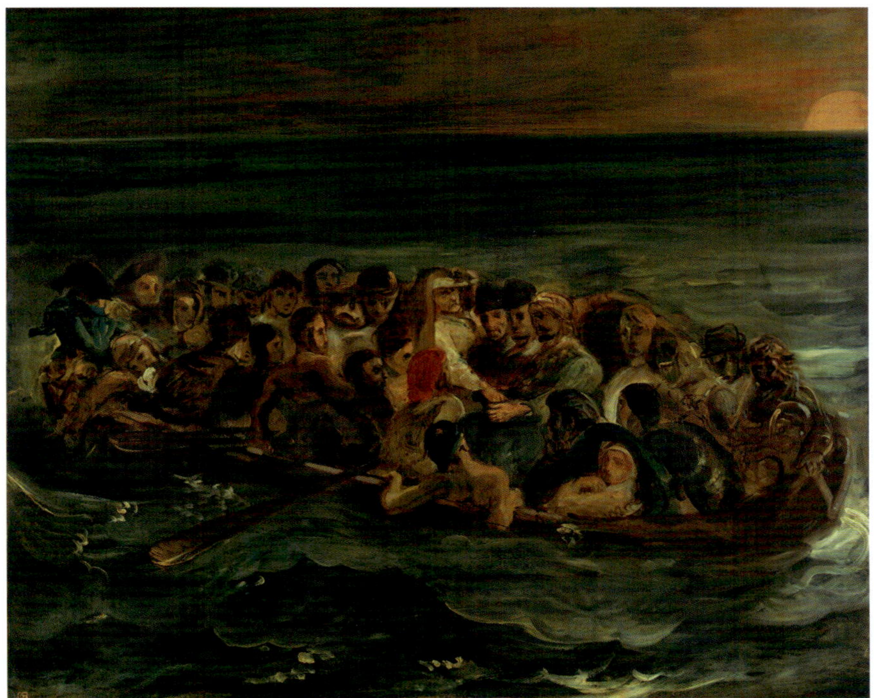

FIG. 17.8 Eugène Delacroix, *The Shipwreck of Don Juan: A Sketch*, ca. 1820–1829. Victoria and Albert Museum, London. Oil on canvas, 81.3 × 99.7 cm.

position—the tutor. He represents this moment in a way that shows the boat surrounded by the sea, slowly being engulfed by the endless expanse of water.

The story of *The Raft of the Medusa* exposes numerous states of insecurity, fragility, and precariousness—men on a raft who did not know if they would survive or be saved, a political structure that was in constant flux, an artist who was struggling with his work and himself, critics who were uncertain about the validity and value of the grand painting. The physical state of the work was also fragile. As early as 1860, a full-scale copy of the painting was produced by order of the authorities of the Louvre because the original looked so "sick" that the curators were worried it would not be preserved. This fragility proved to be

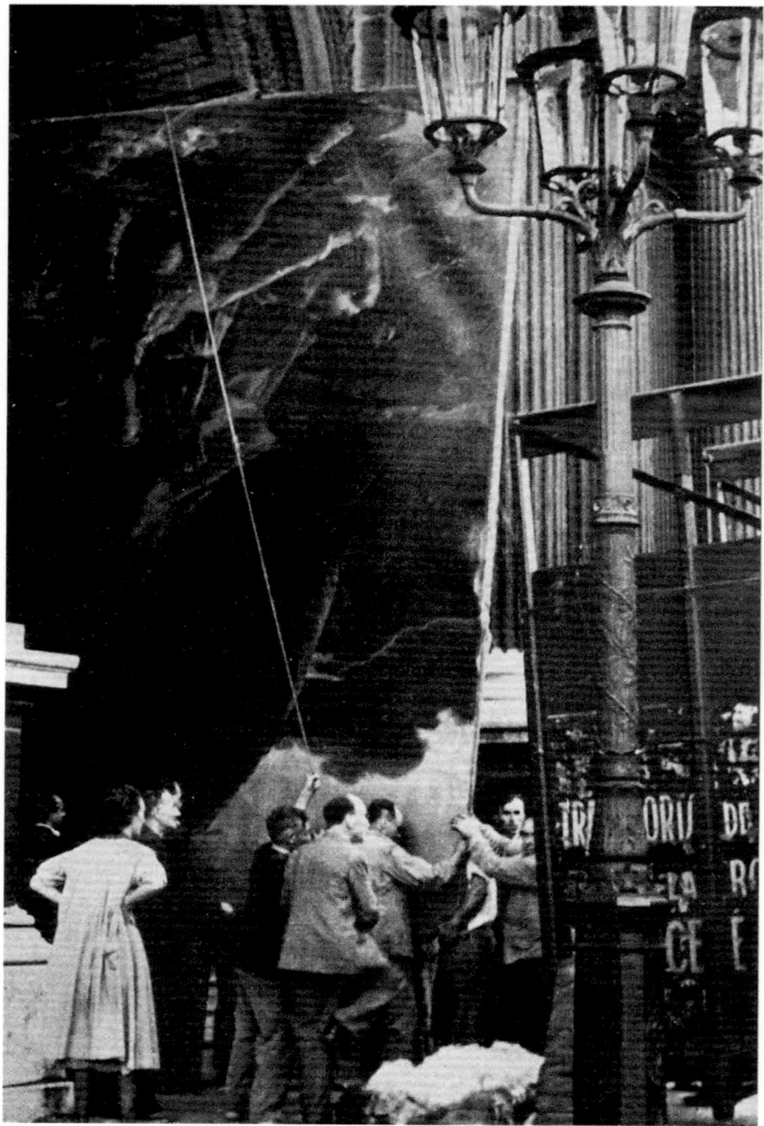

FIG. 17.9 Evacuation of *The Raft of the Medusa* from the Musée du Louvre, September 1939.

particularly problematic when the Louvre had to evacuate its paintings at the outbreak of World War II (Fig. 17.9). The paint of the *Raft* was so brittle that the work could not be rolled up, as most paintings had been. Thus the *Raft*, still unfurled, was placed on the back of a large scenery truck. Although the Parisian bridges had been carefully measured, the trolley lines had not been included in the planning, and the painting became hopelessly ensnared in crackling electrical wires. It was left in the Orangerie until the chief curator could rescue it a few weeks later, accompanied by a team of post office employees who used long insulated poles to raise the wires.

Géricault wanted to remind the world about a terrible tragedy, that man's inhumanity to man was unforgivable, that the only way to right those wrongs was to reorient, to redirect, to focus on a new France, a new future. Through art, we travel back into other worlds and return not just to our daily lives but also to the contemplation of other moments of holocaust and heroism. On June 6, 1944, the Allies made a massive communal move to right a wrong of untold horror. Through Géricault's lens, by traveling back to the tragedy of 1816 and the painting of 1819, we can frame an appreciation for the response of a later time when in one of the darkest moments in the history of man's inhumanity to man came a heroic and triumphant response worthy of Gericault's dreams.

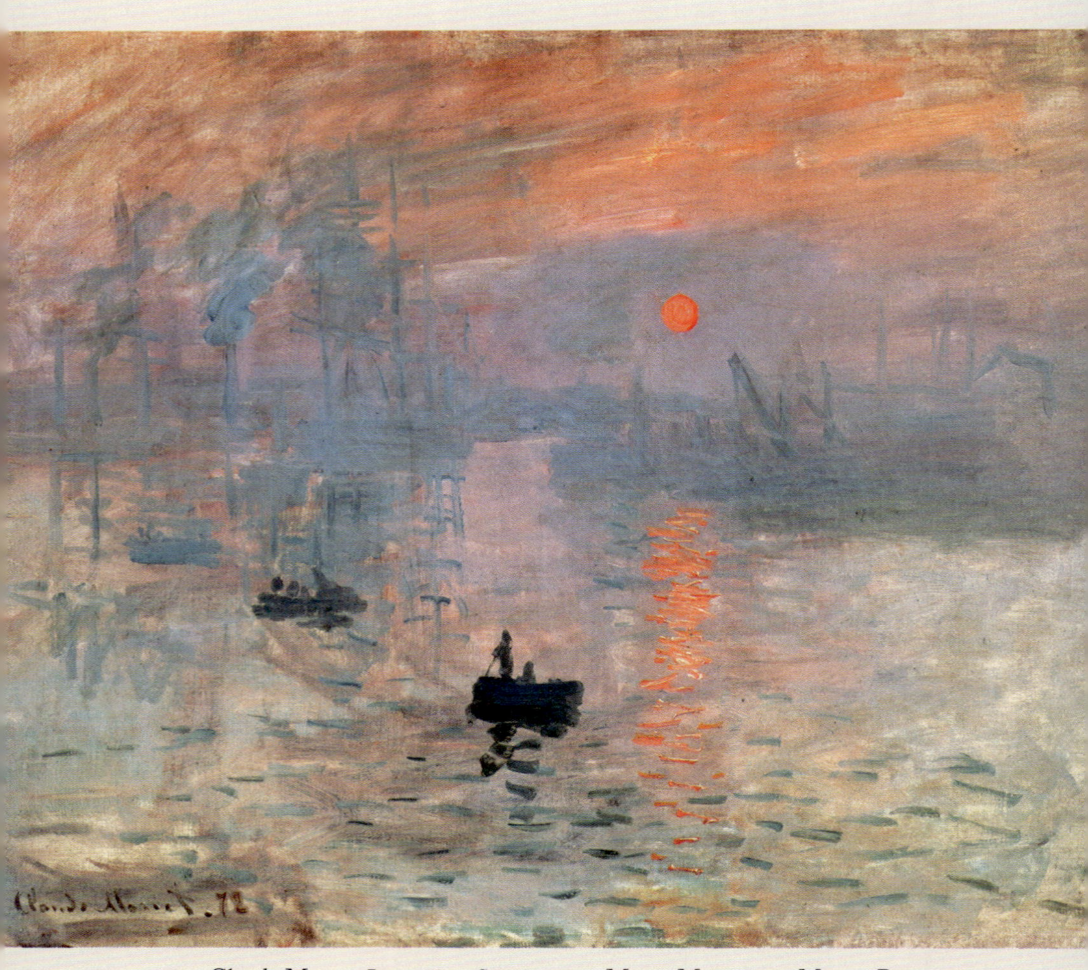

FIG. 18.1 Claude Monet, *Impression, Sunrise*, 1872. Musée Marmottan Monet, Paris. Oil on canvas, 63 x 48 cm.

Monet, *Impression, Sunrise*

1872

IMPRESSIONISM

We know these kinds of brushstrokes well (Fig. 18.1). They flicker and dart, wobble and strike. They are suggestive and instant. Thick bands of sweeping color; hazy smears and smudges; soft, suggestive lines; quick, short dashes—all accumulate to create a *sense* of a vista, a *sense* of a scene on the sea. Immediately catching our eye is a quick, round, red sun that sits amid that bright-blue tuft of sky or smoke. The sun beams energetically and dramatically in skies composed of pink, coral, orange, yellow, white, mauve. Ghostly grayish-white reflections of boats in the foreground provide a halolike sphere around the artist's slanted signature and lurk amid two small black boats and quite possibly a third one in blue. These three boat shapes lead us toward distant masts or smokestacks or maybe even machines—toward a city or modernity in some shape or other.

We do not know precisely what those forms in the distance are supposed to represent. Cut off from the rest of the painting, they almost look like trees. Devoid of their watery context, it might be hard to identify the boats as boats. But representation is not the focus of these brushstrokes. Shape is a suggestion. This is not about man or man-made forms. There is no story or moral message. Light and color, reflections and refractions—these are what the nineteenth-century artists like Claude Monet (1840–1926) were capturing with their paint and with their brushes. The result was revolutionary. Once it took hold, the work of the Impressionists, as these painters came to be called, threatened a number of

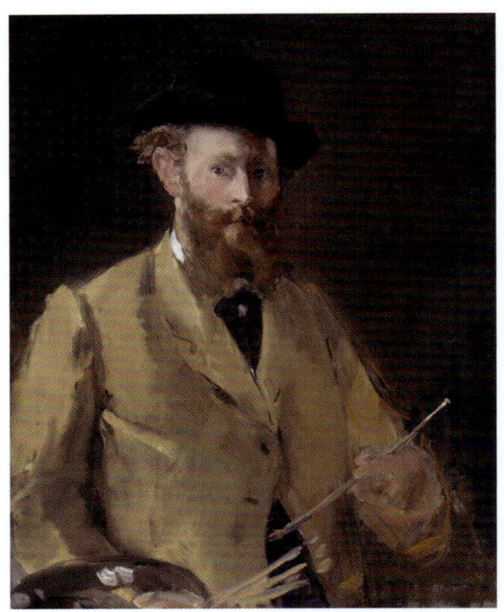

FIG. 18.2 Édouard Manet, *Self-Portrait with a Palette*, 1879. Private Collection. Oil on canvas, 83 × 67 cm.

venerable institutions like the Parisian Salon and the primacy of realism, narrative, and allegory. Monet painted so as to say that marks mean more.

But this was a long revolution. Monet was not the first to show that paint could produce a sensation of form through suggestive rather than naturalistic brushstrokes. Think back to Velázquez. In *Las Hilanderas*, Velázquez makes paint seem to disintegrate into strokes of color right before our eyes, showing us how he can make the face of a girl both discernible and not, an image and an impression (Fig. 16.1). For a group of artists in the middle of the nineteenth century, Velázquez was predicting the future; he was an early seed in an artistic movement based on impressionistic brushstrokes.

One such nineteenth-century artist was Édouard Manet (1832–1883). After a series of negative reviews, Manet found solace by making a pilgrimage to Spain to see his hero's paintings: "I am in a great hurry to see many beautiful things and to go to seek advice from the master Velázquez." In his *Self-Portrait with Palette* dated to 1878–79, Manet's brushstrokes are looser and less stable than those of Velázquez (Fig. 18.2). And yet there is suggestiveness in both painters' paint—sleeves with rough outlines and a bright sheen. The shape of the brushstrokes, the painterliness, calls attention to itself in both images. Quite clearly,

Manet modeled himself after Velázquez in his own self-fashioning, identifying with the artist as a means of identifying himself. Manet looks at the viewer with the same three-quarter gaze that Velázquez does in his painting *Las Meninas* (see figure 16.2). Manet's wrinkled brow might indicate a bit of unease or concern that Velázquez's does not. Manet's shoulders also slope a bit and seem weighed down by the mottled camel-hair jacket, while Velázquez's shoulders are thrown back with a cool sense of swagger.

Yet like his mentor, his hero, his therapist, Manet prominently displays the tools of his craft—a paintbrush in one hand (his left), a palette in the other, with about three or four paintbrushes to spare. Velázquez holds his brushes in exactly the same way—one paintbrush in one hand (his right) and a palette with extra brushes in his other. The final touch is the hands themselves, which both appear blurred in their movements, in the act of painting. Velázquez and Manet both seem to say that the hand of the artist (both painted and actual) cannot be defined by outlines and structure or, in other words, the traditional modes of painting or looking at painting. These hands reveal painting's incredible capacity to show, through sketchy, unformed blobs, a version of a subject or an object that is perhaps closer to nature, closer to truth.

Velázquez's provocative painterliness was appreciated and protected by princely patronage. Manet was fighting against a rather intense political machine, the Parisian Salon, which was held yearly in the Louvre. If you had aspirations of being a successful artist in France, you had to exhibit your works in this one salon. Collectors and patrons would only purchase pieces shown there. Trickier still was that the jury which selected pieces for the salon was composed of teachers from the French Académie des Beaux-Arts. There were other academies in Paris. Manet, for example, trained at the Académie Suisse. However, the jurists were invested in getting their own students, their protégés, into the Salon. Thus, the Salon was a small, elitist, political, and conservative institution that basically had a complete monopoly on taste in the arts. Inspiration from ancient classical and historical subjects, polished surfaces, and careful modeling—these were the favored qualities of academic art.

Just because the Salon was conservative does not mean that the most praised paintings were. Many seem downright prurient. Cabanel's *Birth of Venus* was a

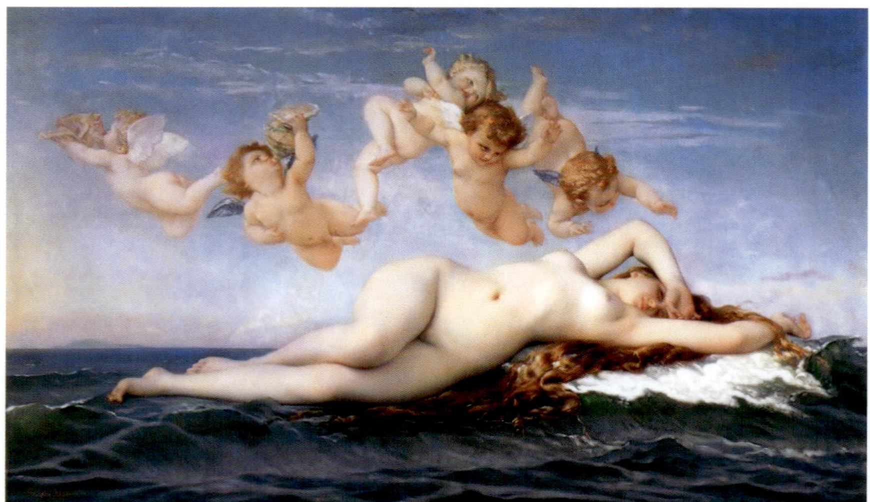

FIG. 18.3 Alexandre Cabanel, *The Birth of Venus*, 1863. Musée d'Orsay, Paris. Oil on canvas, 130 × 225 cm.

smash hit in the Salon of 1863 (Fig. 18.3). In fact, Napoleon III purchased the painting immediately for his personal collection (and probably for a rather private setting). There is nothing grippingly intellectual about this painting. Cabanel's Venus is rolling on top of the waves. She has absolutely no agency. She cannot even be bothered to lift her head or even wake up. Her half-lidded eyes look lazily toward the fussy, pink putti. One left toe stretches ever so slightly. We are looking at a beautiful nude, stretched out for our voyeuristic pleasure—undulant thighs, concave hips, shapely and perky elbows. It is really not very subtle. The Salon desired Cabanel. And it adored William-Adolphe Bouguereau. Some of Bouguereau's paintings were of classical figures and stories from antiquity. So not all paintings in the Salon were of naked ladies. However, there is a consistent theme at play—poor, lost, helpless, and extremely beautiful ladies.

Painting a nude was essential for an artist to show his capacities. Gautier, a novelist and art critic at the time, explained that "The study of human form,

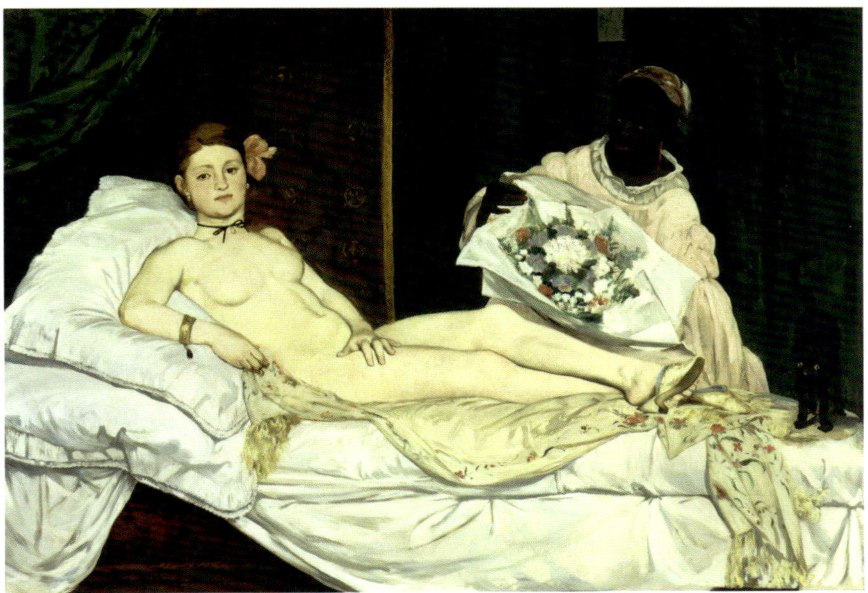

FIG. 18.4 Édouard Manet, *Olympia,* 1863. Musée d'Orsay, Paris. Oil on canvas, 130 × 190 cm.

unrestricted and free of all apparel and of all transitory fashion, is alone capable of producing complete artists. It is truth, beauty, and eternity." That was all well and good when the product was creamy, slim, and fully idealized. Cabanel and Bouguereau brought the public just that. Manet brought the *Olympia* (Fig. 18.4). Harsh light replaces soothing mist and clear, blue skies. No more pearly skin and subtle pinks here. A murky, hazy brown outlines Olympia. She is made up of blocky and dissonant forms, whereas Cabanel's nude is streamlined, seamless, and soft. His Venus couldn't be bothered. About anything. We are allowed to look and enjoy. Olympia is unsettled, pulling up her head somewhat awkwardly, covering herself with a strong and firm left hand. She should be used to intruders, or at least visitors, as she is probably a representation of a prostitute. The gift of flowers held by the woman to the right might be from a potential client. But Olympia, unlike Cabanel's Venus, is suspicious and critical of her viewer.

Olympia is a woman of the world, raw, stripped of lightness and metaphor. The viewer looks at her and she gives it right back—knowing, intense, and on guard, like the black cat that is bristling, primed for a fight.

The painting was not a triumph. Critics wrote suggesting that she take a bath, not just because she was salacious, but because she appeared to be encrusted with dirt. One critic called her "misshapen," "a sort of female gorilla, a grotesque in rubber outlined in black, an ape on a bed." These words wounded the artist. Manet was certainly not painting like Cabanel and Bouguereau, the darlings of the Salon. But he did not intend to cause a scandal or enrage the critics. He respected their thoughts, criticisms, and judgments. He wanted to get his pieces into the Salon. He wanted to be part of the traditional system.

Manet's admiration for the traditional art-historical canon is evident in the way he studied and interpreted painters of the past. Manet used the framework of a painting by Titian, the *Venus of Urbino*, as a means of expressing his modernity and the harshness of life in a bustling nineteenth-century Paris (Fig. 18.5). His painting cites the earlier Venetian piece throughout—the weighty velvet curtains, the bent right arm with the single golden bangle, those fluffy white pillows, untucked sheets on a deep-red mattress, the servants helping on the right-hand side of the composition. Certainly there are differences. The space is more closed in Manet. We do not get a sense of the wider room in which the woman reclines, as in the Titian. The cat is agitated, Titian's dog is not. Manet's outlines are brown, like the pulled-back mousy hair of Olympia. Titian's outlines glow with a golden sheen, matching the cascading and braided hair of the Venus. The gaze and musculature are also distinctive—Titian's is hazy, Manet's is taut. But those differences are even deeper signs of respect. Manet wasn't trying to change or mock Titian, as some critics claimed he was attempting to do. Manet was modernizing a Renaissance masterpiece, taking a majestic sixteenth-century image and bringing it into a nineteenth-century world.

Manet's deep admiration for the past is strikingly prominent in his portrait of Émile Zola, which richly incorporates and harmoniously blends all of Manet's inspirations (Fig. 18.6). Zola, the famous novelist, art historical critic, and champion of Manet, sits in his study with legs crossed in front of a table piled high with books and letters. Framing Zola's face are hanging frames. On the left is a

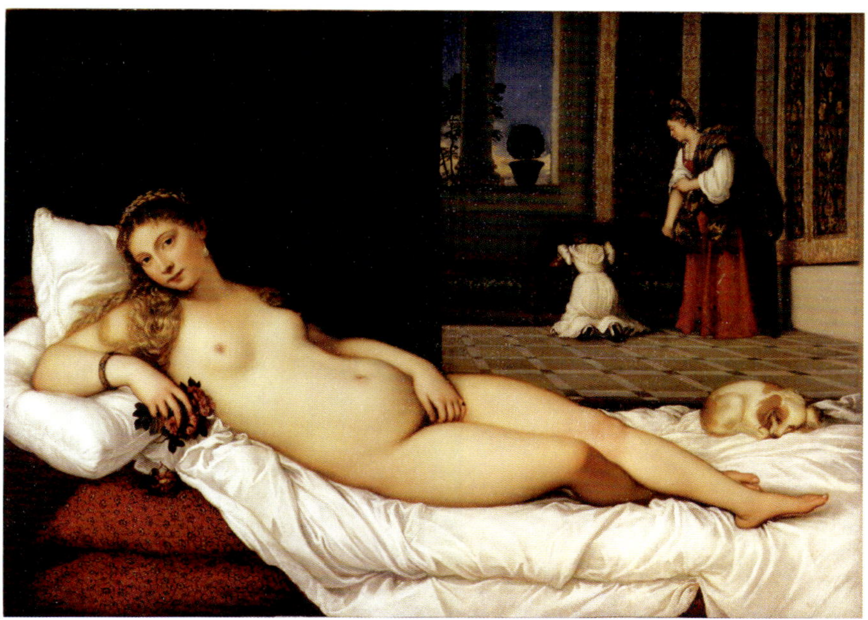

FIG. 18.5 Titian, *Venus of Urbino,* ca. 1538. Galleria degli Uffizi, Florence, Italy. Oil on canvas, 119.3 × 104 cm.

silk Japanese screen. To the right is a collage of three pieces. It includes a print of a wrestler by Utagawa Kuniaki II, the original of which hangs in Boston at the MFA. Here too we have Olympia—a smaller, grayer version of the painting— and in the background, half cut off from view, another memory of Velázquez with a truncated version of his *Los Borrachos* (The Drunks) or *The Triumph of Bacchus* (1628–29). Perhaps less triumph and more boozing. Bacchus looks like he is up to no good. He glances furtively to the side while crowning a member of an unsavory-looking group of modern peasant-men. Velázquez took a classical mythological scene and gave it a contemporary setting. He rooted out the seedier side of the story—a playboy god that can't stay sober—and developed it with darker hues and drunker dudes. Manet does the same with Olympia. He reveals the grittier modern grind within the framework of a painting by the revered artist Titian.

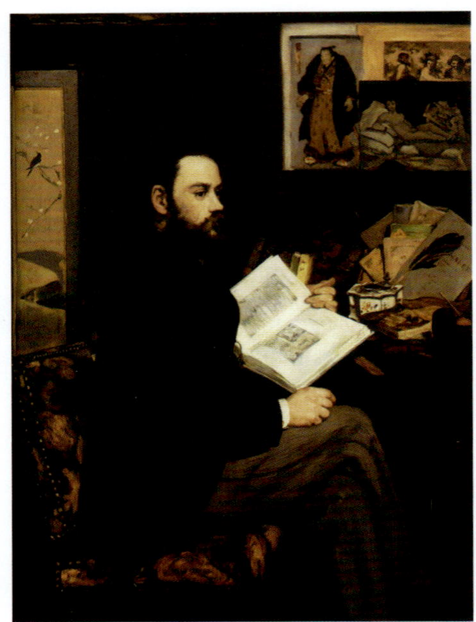

FIG. 18.6 Édouard Manet, *Émile Zola*, 1868. Musée d'Orsay, Paris. Oil on canvas, 146.5 × 114 cm.

Velázquez appears in the painting both literally and metaphorically in the way he inspired Manet's style and work, and we can go even one step further with these connections between seventeenth-century Madrid and nineteenth-century Paris. Velázquez, as we might recall, put Titian in *Las Hilanderas*. As we moved deeper into his painting and into that brightened back room, we found ourselves in front of a tapestry based on Titian's work. So Velázquez was making a modern version of Titian on the back wall. Manet's modern version of Titian (*Olympia*) also appears in the frame that hangs on the back wall. Then Manet makes his own version, his own impression, of Velázquez's *Los Borrachos*, and hangs it too in this happy collage, thus framing his hero Velázquez just as Velázquez had framed his hero Titian. Manet puts Velázquez with another hero, and that is Zola, who wrote passionately in support of Manet's work. The painting was a thank-you letter to Zola. Manet creates a halo around Zola composed of his artistic influences—Japanese screens and prints, Velázquez, Titian, and a popular text about art and color theory by Charles Blanc. There is a push and pull in

Manet's paintings between the artist's great respect for past art-historical works and his desire to represent the advances/concerns of current times, but the two were not irreconcilable. Or that was what Manet thought.

Monet was a different story. Monet was born in 1840 in Paris. After his birth, his family moved to Le Havre in Normandy, which was basically out in the provinces, far from the glitz and cosmopolitan life of Paris. Monet's father ran a grocery store, and the boy was supposed to go into the family grocery business. Instead, the young Claude started sketching and drawing, most notably caricatures and portraits for his neighbors. Next to his father's store was a frame shop, which soon became the peculiar "exhibition" setting for his paintings. These were soon spotted by a local artist, Eugène Boudin. Boudin painted seascapes that at first seemed odd to the young man because they were done outside, in the air and light, *en plein air.* Boudin had notable talent and had tried to make it in Paris. But he had little success because he only wanted to paint seascapes. So he moved back to Le Havre to work. Although Monet admitted that he thought Boudin was strange, he started spending time with the older artist, learning how to paint *en plein air,* and ultimately asserting, "Eventually my eyes were opened and I really understood nature."

In 1859 Monet moved to Paris and started training at the Académie Suisse, the same school where Manet had studied. It was in Paris that he met many like-minded artists. The spirited camaraderie that characterized Monet's group of artist-friends is captured in a painting by Frédéric Bazille from 1870 (Fig. 18.7). The painting shows the inside of the artist's studio that he shared with Auguste Renoir. Manet and Monet (wearing a hat) are in the center examining a canvas. Bazille is also studying the painting on the easel, holding a palette and standing tall and slim; however, he was actually added in later by Manet. On the left a pair of figures, Renoir and Zola, hold a separate discussion. On the right a friend of Bazille's plays the piano. Another member of the gang, Henri Fantin-Latour, also painted about these friendships in a painting called *A Studio at Les Batignolles.* In Fantin-Latour's portrait the artists appear in Manet's studio. Renoir wears a black hat and is strangely framed himself, while Manet sits and works on the central canvas. Zola looks into the distance, pensively. Monet looks at us, looks outside the picture altogether.

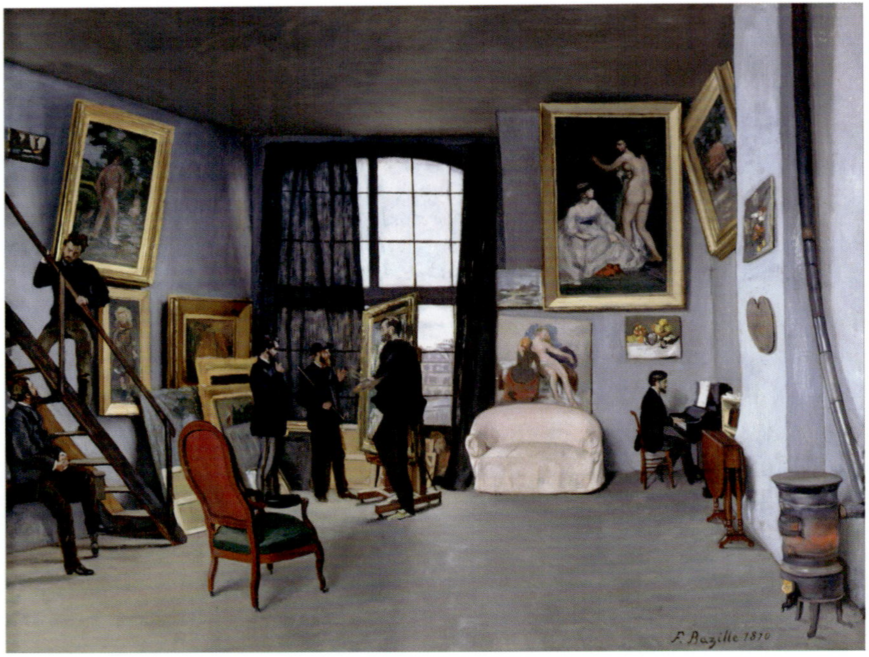

FIG. 18.7 Frédéric Bazille, *Bazille's Studio*, 1870. Musée d'Orsay, Paris. Oil on canvas, 98 × 128.5 cm.

The conversations that started in these studios continued deep into the night at local bars in the area, most famously at the Café Guerbois. There the artists philosophized about art, discussed their pieces, and painted side by side. This was actually quite unusual because they started painting side by side *outside*. This was the only way Monet would paint. He insisted on it. While Monet was painting *Women in the Garden*, Gustave Courbet (Monet's great hero) came by to visit and work with the younger artist (Fig. 18.8). During one of their work sessions, Courbet realized that Monet was not working: "Say, my young man, you are not working?" Monet responded, "As you can see, there is no sun!" Courbet suggested that he might work on the landscape. But that was not what the new wave of artists were doing. Soon, Monet's friends—Bazille, Renoir, Cézanne— followed this stricture as a sort of agenda. As Cézanne wrote: "But you know all

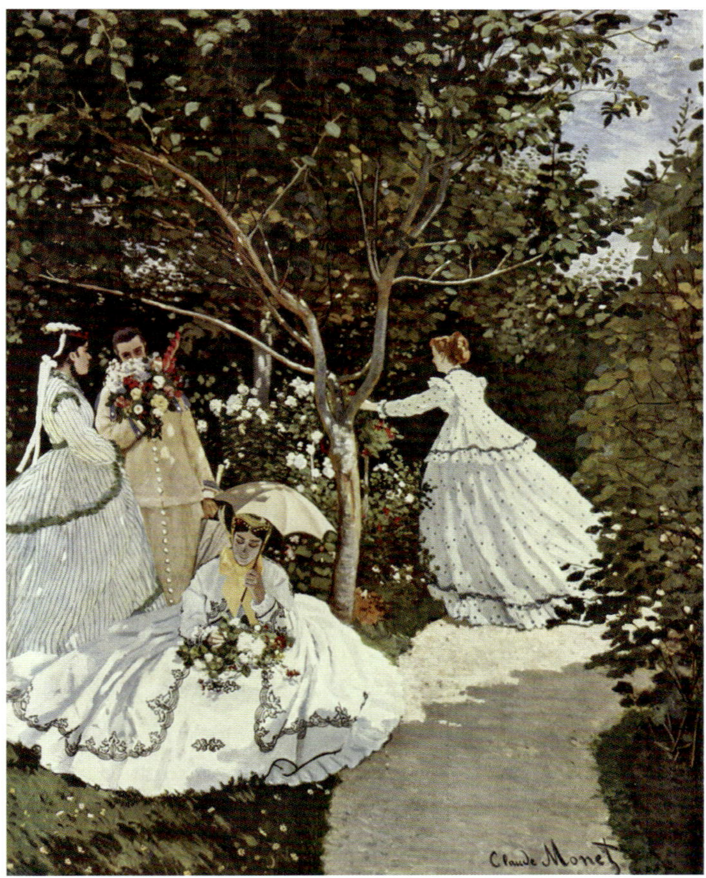

FIG. 18.8 Claude Monet, *Women in the Garden,* ca. 1866. Musée d'Orsay, Paris. Oil on canvas, 255 × 205 cm.

pictures painted inside, in the studio, will never be as good as the things done outside. When out-of-door scenes are represented, the contrasts between figures and the ground is astounding and the landscape is magnificent. I see some superb things and I shall have to make up my mind only to do things out-of-doors."

Women in the Garden exemplifies this sense of contrast. Ladies and land are ever so slightly at odds with one another, which creates a sort of eerie radiance and magnificence to the painting. The women, all of whom were modeled on Camille, Monet's girlfriend and later wife, skirt around a centrally placed tree whose limbs sprawl out beyond the borders of the painting. Olive, emerald, and muddier greens create a canopy that melds into verdant bushes and trees in the space of the garden below. Sunlight splashes throughout the piece in an undulating sea of shadows and bright bursts and waves of light. But the light does not model the forms of the ladies. We don't see volume and fullness here. The color does not slowly transition from one to the next. Outlines are stark. Color gradations are abrupt. The result is that the forms look flat. The ladies look like cutouts or paper dolls pasted against a green backdrop. In order to create this effect, Monet juxtaposes contrasting colors that are slightly dissonant. This jarring juxtaposition had a name, "simultaneous contrast." This technique was explained and lauded by Charles Blanc, the author of the book Émile Zola holds in Manet's painting. Simultaneous contrast is the effect produced when an artist places so-called complementary colors (really opposites) side by side—red with green, blue with orange, yellow with purple. Monet, who knew Blanc's theories well, gives us red next to greens, blues next to peachy oranges, and yellow next to a purple-hued shaded face. Flat shapes and brilliant, contrasting colors make the ambience the focus of the painting. The attention is on the activities and movements of air and light that surround the figures, rather than the activities and movements of the figures.

Impression, Sunrise follows a similar aesthetic, with contrasting colors and flattened forms. Reddish-orange and blue are the principal colors at odds with each other. Because of the juxtaposition, the effect is striking and almost startling, even though, taken individually, both colors are light and bright. And the forms are floating on the water in a way that is not fully integrated. Water and boat do not interact. Rather, these flat areas of color reflect a particular character of light and atmosphere. They shape our interpretation of the moment.

Contrasting colors and flat shapes were quite prominent in Japanese prints, which were popular and influential among the painters of the mid-nineteenth century. (We saw them hanging on the wall in the background of the painting of Zola by Manet.) Monet used similarly flat shapes and also studied the way that Japanese prints would use unconventional angles in order to capture a sort of "snapshot" of a scene, as often seen in images of women in gardens, who do not notice they are being watched. In his *Women in the Garden*, Monet gives us a particular view, with a slightly asymmetrical composition, in which the subjects are similarly caught unawares and do not seem to register our voyeurism.

The idea of cropped perspectives and snapshot views also draws inspiration from photography, that newly developing genre. Cameras were becoming portable and captured images quickly. As such, photos could be candid, capturing the fleeting light of landscapes and people in their day-to-day lives. The artists of this modern era drew with a photographic eye. However, instead of a flashbulb they used natural light; instead of the lens determining the frame, they painted the specific perimeters of their view; and instead of documenting reality, the artists provided a subjective, inspired, creative version of truth.

Monet was terribly proud of the painting of *Women in the Garden*. But the judges of the Salon rejected it. The brushstrokes were too broad, the palette too bright. Its rejection by the Salon was a particularly hurtful blow to the artist. The year 1866 was a rather bad year all around for Monet. He was dead broke, he was trying to hide from creditors, he had to depend on his parents financially and lived with them in the nasty port town of Le Havre, his girlfriend Camille (whom his parents hated) was pregnant, and his best work was being rejected by the snooty Salon. 1866 was rough, as was 1867. And you can add 1868, when Monet attempted suicide by trying to drown himself in the Seine. What tragic irony that he would attempt drowning when so many of his most memorable and beautiful works were set on water.

You would not know of his suffering from the work he was producing. On the seashore in Sainte-Adresse, he could let things go, let his painting take him out of the stresses around him. Monet said as much when he wrote, "I am thinking up terrific things for myself when I go to Sainte-Adresse." In *Garden at Sainte-Adresse* (1867), he offers those "terrific things" to the viewer of his painting, providing a high vantage point so that we might look down, unnoticed, at a moment of repose and quiet (Fig. 18.9). It is vibrant and airy and bright, belying the truer tumult of the artist. Monet paints away stressful fights with his father (about Camille, about being an artist) by placing him in the wicker chair in the foreground. Monet's father sits calmly, in a dreamlike state, a reverie. Other

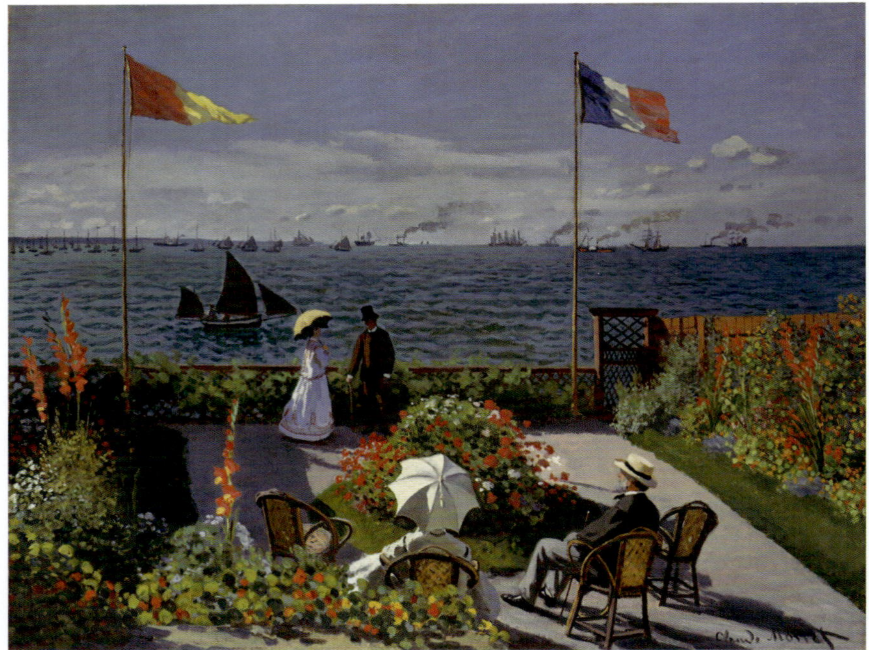

FIG. 18.9 Claude Monet, *Garden at Sainte-Adresse*, 1867. Metropolitan Museum of Art, New York. Oil on canvas, 98.1 × 129.9 cm.

family members also take their places in the garden. It is an idyllic view, one of peace and familial harmony all encompassed by a brilliant blue sea teeming with ships. Clear skies, flapping flags, gardens bursting with colors and life—this is the fiction or dream that Monet paints, that he creates with his brush, since it appeared so elusive in reality.

That insistent sense of optimism was rather prescient, it turned out, because two major encounters also shaped that dark year in Monet's life. His paintings (or more accurately the rejection of his paintings) caught the attention of Émile Zola. Zola understood that Monet was, like Manet, a much underappreciated genius, and he ran to his defense. Zola raved about *Women in the Garden*, which of course the public had never had the chance to see. Zola describes the women in summer dresses and the striking light of the sun. But most of all he praises

Monet for being bold, for doing something that produces a "strange effect": "One must love his epoch very dearly to dare such a tour de force." Zola is saying that other artists had the capacity to be brave and provocative but they played it safe, stayed within the Salon's parameters. But not Monet. He really goes for it, Zola seems to say, and that is a true contribution to civilization. In a way, Zola birthed the notion of Monet as the father of Impressionism, making the young artist into the champion, the face, of the soon-to-coalesce movement.

The other major event of 1866 was the meeting of Manet and Monet. One might expect the encounter to have happened earlier. They were two of the greatest artists of the moment. They were both struggling with the strictures of the Salon and were both painting with an eye for modern life. And their names were almost exactly the same. But Manet was annoyed by his younger (by eight years) colleague. Manet made fun of Monet for his whole *en plein air* bit: "This young man claims he paints *en plein air* as if the old masters had never dreamed of such a thing."

Yet after meeting, the two artists became great friends, painting next to each other and painting each other. Manet was completely taken with the younger man's work: "There is not another painter…who can get down a landscape as he can. And then the water! He is the Raphael of water. He knows it in its movements, in all its depths, at all its hours." Manet's own work started to change in the light of Monet's. He opened up his paintings to brighter colors, wider vistas, all the while staying true to his interest in painting modern life.

In a sprightly account of the friendship between the two artists, Willibald Sauerländer juxtaposes two paintings from this period, one by Manet of Monet and one by Monet of Manet. Manet sees Monet living his bohemian life, picking flowers in a garden where a rooster and chicken run free (Fig. 18.10). Monet's son is flopped on the ground next to Camille, who looks at us coquettishly and perhaps too with that confidence and wariness we have seen in *Olympia*. Monet paints Manet with his signature wavering brushstrokes—flowers in the tree are flickering flecks of snowy paint. But Monet puts Manet in a bit of a box (Fig. 18.11). He is in nature, sitting outside, but somehow right back in a studio setting—walls close around him; the setting is dark and so is the canvas. Monet breathed nature. He lived a renegade, bohemian life in a sincere way. Manet

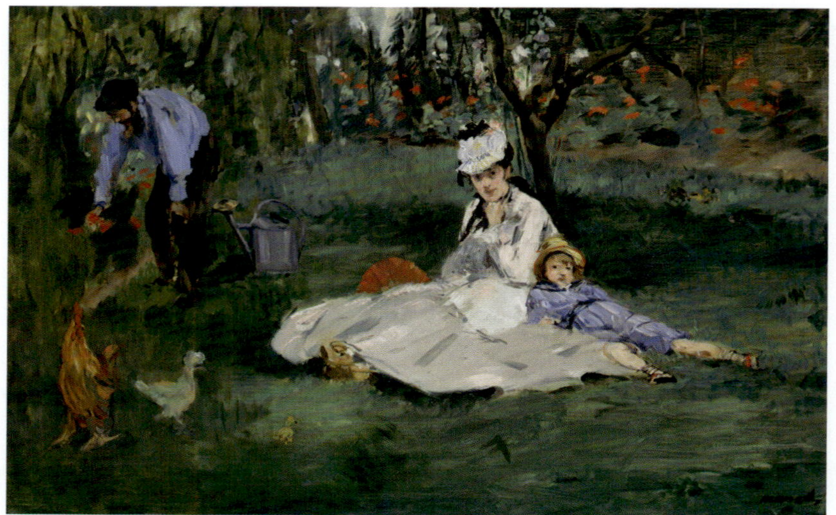

FIG. 18.10 Édouard Manet, *The Monet Family in their Garden at Argenteuil*, 1874. Metropolitan Museum of Art, New York. Oil on canvas, 61 × 99.7 cm.

could appreciate that world, but he was a true-blue Parisian. Going to the country was done to escape the city, but only temporarily, and more because that was what people did, summer at the sea. Manet was wedded to the structure of Paris, of society, even as he tried to expose its grittier, rawer, modern side. Monet didn't need that structure or validation from the system, and so he was happy to shake it up. He really had nothing to lose. And so Monet, not Manet, became the face of the Impressionist movement.

It is interesting to think about this period, about this movement and the individuals that were successful in it, in light of the Great Man Theory. This mid-nineteenth-century debate centered on two contrasting philosophies. One argued that the influential individuals of history made their mark based on personal charisma, intelligence, and wisdom, generally granted by providence. Muhammad, Shakespeare, Luther, and Napoleon were united in their divine inspiration and their extraordinary personal attributes, which they used to shape history. Nietzsche, Kierkegaard, and Hegel subscribed to this theory of the

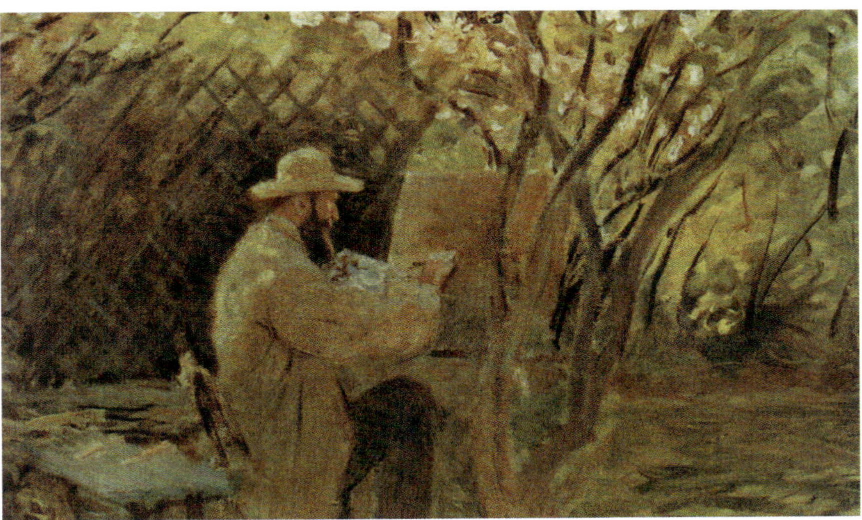

FIG. 18.11 Claude Monet, *Manet Painting in Monet's Garden in Argenteuil*, 1874. Private collection. Oil on canvas.

world. But critics argued, as Herbert Spencer did in 1896, that "the genesis of a great man depends on the long series of complex influences which has produced the race in which he appears. Before he can remake his society, his society must make him." Tolstoy insists throughout *War and Peace* on the foolishness of the idea that Napoleon's victory at Austerlitz has anything to do with Napoleon or his plans or his supposed genius. The success depends on the thousands of men that build the bridges and fight at the crossroads. History is a great wave that moves with ineluctable force, providing moments of greatness for some but not being ready for the greatness of others. Boudin, for example, might have been Monet. He painted just like Monet, *en plein air* with flickering brushstrokes. But time was not ready for him. And so he painted, he was happy, and barely anyone has ever heard of him.

Monet is the Great Man or the man for whom all the historical forces coincide. Another great artist may have been one of the forces of history that made Monet the Great Man of Impressionism. This was the tremendous Romantic

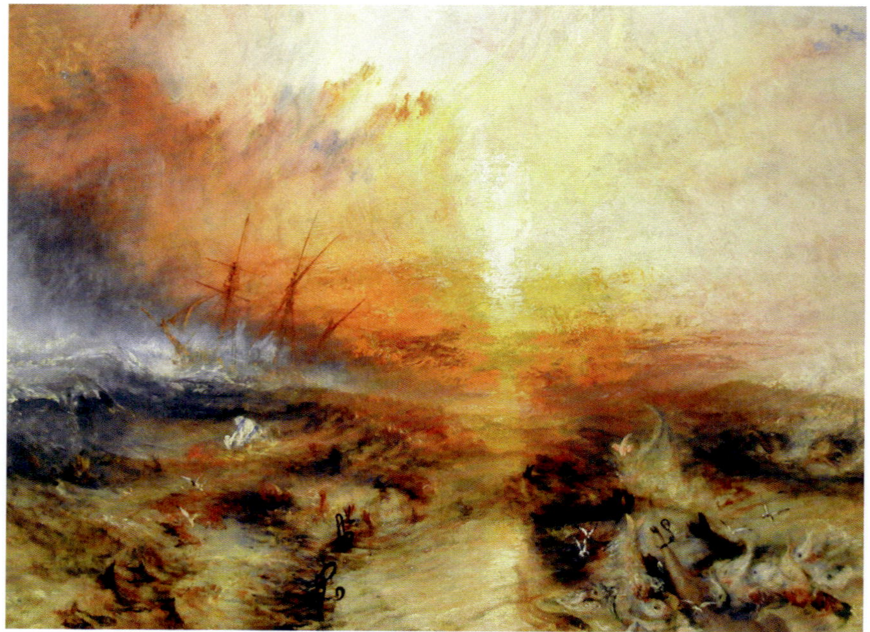

FIG. 18.12 Joseph Mallord William Turner, *Slave Ship (Slavers Throwing Overboard the Dead and Dying, Typhoon Coming On)*, 1840. Museum of Fine Arts, Boston. Oil on canvas, 90.8 × 122.6 cm.

painter J. M. W. Turner (1775–1851). Like Velázquez, Turner was working with aims and styles that were impressionistic many years before the Impressionists were on the scene. Yet when his painting *The Scarlet Sunset* (c. 1830–40) is next to *Impression, Sunrise* the stylistic connections are remarkable. Hazy, cloudy, murky paint indicates (rather than represents) water surmounted by streaming pink and red clouds. The bright-yellow sun hangs over a distant cityscape, not unlike Monet's coral sun. The beams of both suns are reflected with quick, strident strokes on the water.

A powerful sun reappears in many of Turner's paintings, such as *The Slave Ship* of 1840 (Fig. 18.12). In this painting, Turner makes a scathing social commentary about man's injustice to man. In 1781 the captain of the slave ship *Zong* ordered

133 slaves to be thrown overboard so that he could collect insurance payments. Evidence of the murdered men peppers the foreground of the painting—shackles, grasping hands, a lone leg. Scavengers and fish of prey attack the bodies of the murdered men. The ship ingloriously flees the murder scene. And as those monsters on the boat leave, sea monsters surge forward from the distance. The sky reflects the turmoil, fear, and despair of the sea. The blocks of reds and pinks and vermilions in the sky seep into the yellows and oranges of the sun. The sun is majestic, overpowering, and savage in its grandeur. In Turner, nature subsumes and often consumes its inhabitants.

Monet is not telling a story, and if he is making a social commentary, it is not overt. What is striking is the fact that the crazed, intense brushstrokes Turner uses to create that ominous, apocalyptic sky are similar to those of Monet. The brushstrokes that made Monet the representative of the Impressionist movement were already on Turner's canvases. Monet seems to have been conflicted about Turner. To one friend, Raymond Koechlin, Monet denied the influence of Turner and asserted that he had been painting his particular style long before he even knew of Turner's work. Quoted in 1918, Monet admitted to having once liked Turner but said that was no longer true: "Now I like him less—[Turner] did not lay out his color carefully enough, and he used too much of it. I have studied him well." The "anxiety of influence," to use a phrase coined by the Shakespeare scholar Harold Bloom, is rather apparent in Monet's comments. The actual influence is evident in the way that Monet constructs his painting and the way he manipulates the brush to dissolve the distinctions between sky, land, water, and man.

The historical wheels of Monet's success were set in place by the particular modern moment in which he existed—the inspirations from earlier painters like Turner, the influx of Japanese prints, the advent of photography, the new cosmopolitan landscape of nineteenth-century Paris, the vocal criticism of movements in the art world in favor of and against Monet. This was the stage upon which Monet was made a star and the so-called father of Impressionism.

Manet just could not make a break with the world of the Salon, but Monet could and did. Frustrated with the conservative snobbery of the Salon, Monet and his friends (Renoir, Pissarro, Sisley, Cézanne, Morisot, Degas) decided to establish their own salon. On April 15, 1874, the Anonymous Society of Painters, Sculptors, and Printmakers held its first exhibition as the Salon des Refusés, the exhibition of the refused or rejected. The show took place in a studio owned by the photographer known as Nadar. Hanging on the wall with 165 other paintings was Monet's *Impression, Sunrise*, number 98, which he had painted two years before.

Responses to the show were mixed, but in the case of Monet they were downright nasty. One journalist, Montifaud, wrote that "this 'impression' of a sunrise has been dealt with by the immature hand of a schoolboy who spreads pigment for the first time on whatever surface." Louis Luhraw wrote vituperatively about Monet's painting. In a long article published in *Le Charivari*, Luhraw reimagined his time seeing the painting with rancor: "Impression, I was sure of it. I was just telling myself that, since I was impressed, there had to be some impression in it…and what freedom, what ease of workmanship! Wallpaper in its embryonic state is more finished than that seascape!"

The same newspaper printed a lot of cartoons about the Impressionists, such as one where the artist shocks himself by the mess on the canvas that he has made with his massive broom-brush or a scene of the Turks using the Impressionist paintings to frighten and subjugate their enemies. Not only did Monet's painting allow critics to express their nastiest calumny; it also gave them a name for this movement that they so heartily hated. They had been looking for a name to describe this ill-defined movement. There it was, in Monet's title. Impression. Of course, that term of derision soon became a term of collective strength, of a proper movement, of an identity.

Impression, Sunrise—the scene it sets, the sun it depicts—followed Monet throughout his career, not only as a symbol of the new movement for which he was the steward but also as an idea, a composition, to which he turned again and again. We see this in *San Giorgio Maggiore at Dusk*, painted in 1908, thirty-six years after *Impression, Sunrise* (Fig. 18.13). A Venetian church on an island is quite a different subject from the port of Le Havre. But the concept, the composition at any rate, is quite similar. Again he draws the viewer into an elevated position, above the water, with monumental forms on the left and a sky suffused with brushy bands of color. The brushstrokes, however, mark a different style. In the

San Giorgio piece they are less blended, composed of more frequent dashes, like a series of unintegrated hatch marks. The colors are also more intense. Here we have deep, bright cobalt instead of baby blues and variations of rich purple tones. Then there are the yellow hay-toned blasts of paint, which almost set San Giorgio aglow. The paint is also far more tactile in the San Giorgio piece. The paint sits on the surface and creates a bumpy texture on the canvas. *Impression, Sunrise* is soft, calm, and breathy. San Giorgio is energized and almost frenetic—brushstrokes rush in one direction and then shift to go the opposite way altogether.

Rushing and darting and dashing brushstrokes are appropriate to the film career of this painting. As you might recall, this is the painting that Pierce Brosnan (himself dashing) smoothly steals from the Metropolitan Museum of Art in the film *The Thomas Crown Affair*. The painting is not in the Met, of course, nor was any portion of the filming. That aside, one might wonder why this particular painting was selected for the heist. But there is a staying power to these pieces, to these paintings, to these artists. Demand in the art market moves up and down, but with the Impressionists it just goes up. On May 5, 2015, Sotheby's in New York sold five Monet paintings for $115,378,000. One of his paintings of water lilies sold for $54,000,000. Considering the incredible staying power that the Impressionists have in the art market, in popular culture, in our psyche, it is quite surprising to consider how short-lived the movement was. *Impression, Sunrise* caused a great stir in 1874. It was controversial and radical. By the 1890s the moment was over and the painting methods employed by these men were commonplace. Monet derided the new "generation" of artists and went to live among his water lilies in Giverny.

Impressionism is everywhere. It is so popular, so pleasing. It looks great on hats and mugs and pacifiers. We are spoiled, perhaps too spoiled, by the abundance of paintings by these luminaries—both in terms of their fame and their light-filled style. The people of San Antonio have easy access to Renoir, Pissarro, Cézanne, and a tremendous Monet at the McNay Art Museum (Fig. 18.14). Many museums have these kinds of riches, so it is hard not to get inured to the triumphs of the Impressionists. After visiting the Barnes Foundation in Philadelphia I swore that if I saw another Renoir, one more pink-cheeked lady, I would throw a fit. No matter how much you love Renoir, 181 is just too many.

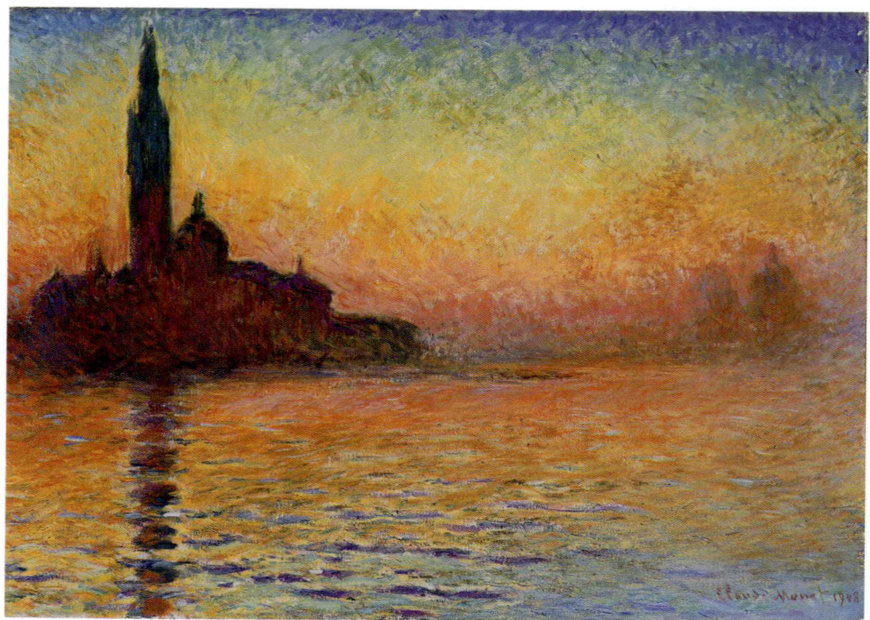

FIG. 18.13 Claude Monet, *San Giorgio Maggiore at Dusk,* 1908–1912. National Museum of Cardiff, Cardiff, Wales. Oil on canvas, 62.5 × 92.4 cm.

But we must remember that paintings by these artists were radical. They made a large ideological shift in a stodgy and snobby art world. As overwhelming as the numbers might be to some museumgoers, there is something about the mass production of these paintings that was germane to creating this shift in the art world. In the simplest terms, they had to have a body of information, a quantity of works, in order to create an identity of difference and change.

The repetitions were also part of their methodology. The Impressionist artists were trying to capture an instantaneous moment. They wanted to express the immediate instances of light and its changes. That aim demanded multiplicity because of the inherent instability in the sun and in the air. There is something about the entire enterprise that is doomed, but the point is not perfection. The point is in the chase, in the constant pursuit of that one moment which, as soon as it is articulated, is gone or changed. Monet constantly chases after a fleeting

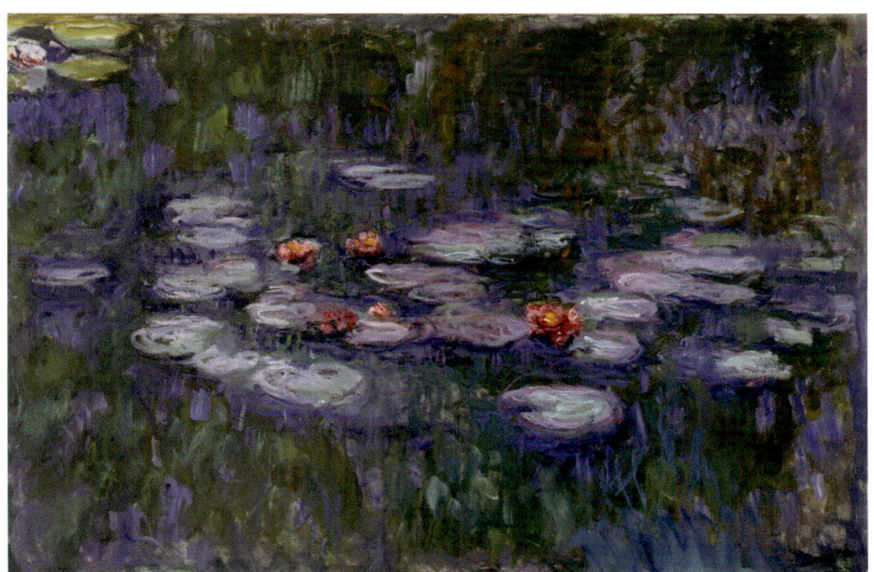

FIG. 18.14 Claude Monet, *Nympheas (Water Lilies),* 1916–1919. Collection of the Tobin Theatre Arts Fund, McNay Art Museum, San Antonio, Texas. Oil on canvas, 130 × 200 cm.

sensation, after the ineffable, which is what the lady in white appears to be doing in his painting *Women in the Garden*—chasing something we cannot see. Light is always moving, transmogrifying. Leaves flicker in unpredictable directions. Skirts billow this way and that. Perspective shifts too. *Impression, Sunrise* is all about shifting instabilities. We have one central, focal boat. But there are two others that accompany it. Or perhaps the boats are reflections or mirror images of each other.

The inspiration toward repetition makes me think of the way contemporary artists talk about their creative urges. Sometimes ideas grab hold and won't let go. This thought was articulated by the contemporary artist John Currin, who is himself haunted by the Old Masters: "You should never will a change in your work—you have to work an idea to death. I often find that the best things happen when you're near the end." How one knows that it is the end is unclear. But there is something fascinating about the idea of working on something over and over because it haunts and plagues you and must be somehow exorcized in your work. This is what I think the Impressionists were doing. Monet harbored the Haystacks series in his deepest core and just would not, could not, be done until it was done. Rouen Cathedral was the same. There are 250 paintings of water lilies, and these consumed Monet for the last thirty years of his life even when he could barely see. Some of the best-known water lily paintings are the murals at the Musée de l'Orangerie in Paris. Each of the eight panels is of a different length; the smallest is thirteen feet and the longest is forty-one. When they are lined up in a row they are not too exciting, but in their oval galleries the effect is meditative and mystical.* There you are, standing in that space, surrounded by hovering rectangles filled with scintillating splashes of water and sunlight seen through framing, bending trees. The viewpoint of these reflective repetitions adds to the mystical strangeness of the moment. Are we floating above the water? Standing knee-deep in the water? The trees are standing as expected, so how is the water everywhere? Where is the sky? Have water and sky melded?

The meditative, mysterious aspect of these pieces not only mirrors Monet's process as he sat in his own garden painting day after day, a garden that he carefully designed and curated himself, but it is also essential to the viewing experience. In October 2014 the Musée Marmottan Monet in Paris commemorated the 140th anniversary of *Impression, Sunrise*. The curator of the show had Donald Olson, an astrophysicist from Texas State University, figure out exactly where Monet was standing and what time he took brush in hand to create the masterpiece. Olson looked at meteorology records and studied the sun's position in order to determine the month, day, and time of the painting. The curator gushed about the scientist's findings: "It's something magical because all of the information is in the painting." Dates, calculations, meteorology—those are not what make a painting magical. In the documentary *Tim's Vermeer*, Tim Jenison, another Texan, tried to reduce Vermeer to a series of lenses and calculators. This strips the painting of its charisma, its aura, its magic.

Monet is "something magical" because of the way that he allows us to hover

---

* Musée de l'Orangerie, Google Arts & Culture, https://artsandculture.google.com.

above space and out of time, the way he implies water and sky and humanity, the way he creates a moment of reverie and bliss in a place of noise and stress and modern woes. His water lilies give us that sense of the magical. In the McNay painting, created between 1916 and 1919, Monet paints green lily pads as shivering, wobbly, white and purple spheres. They float like clouds among wavy strokes of purples, greens, and browns. Monet lifts us above the pond, suspending us over that variegated, restless water. He also lifts us out of reality. He gives us a hazy vision dominated by nature—shifting breezes and transient light—that allows us to consider the ineffable, that which cannot be understood by science and strict artistic principles.

A poem by Stéphane Mallarmé, although not specifically about Monet's painting, describes the transient beauty that Monet captures with his allusive and evocative brush: "Those magical, closed water lilies which / spring up suddenly, enveloping nothingness with / their hollow whiteness, formed from untouched / dreams, from a happiness that will never take place." But happiness does take place, in the poetry and in the paintings. These allow us to hold onto those moments, to transcend the banal, and to experience the forms, the impressions, of untouched dreams.

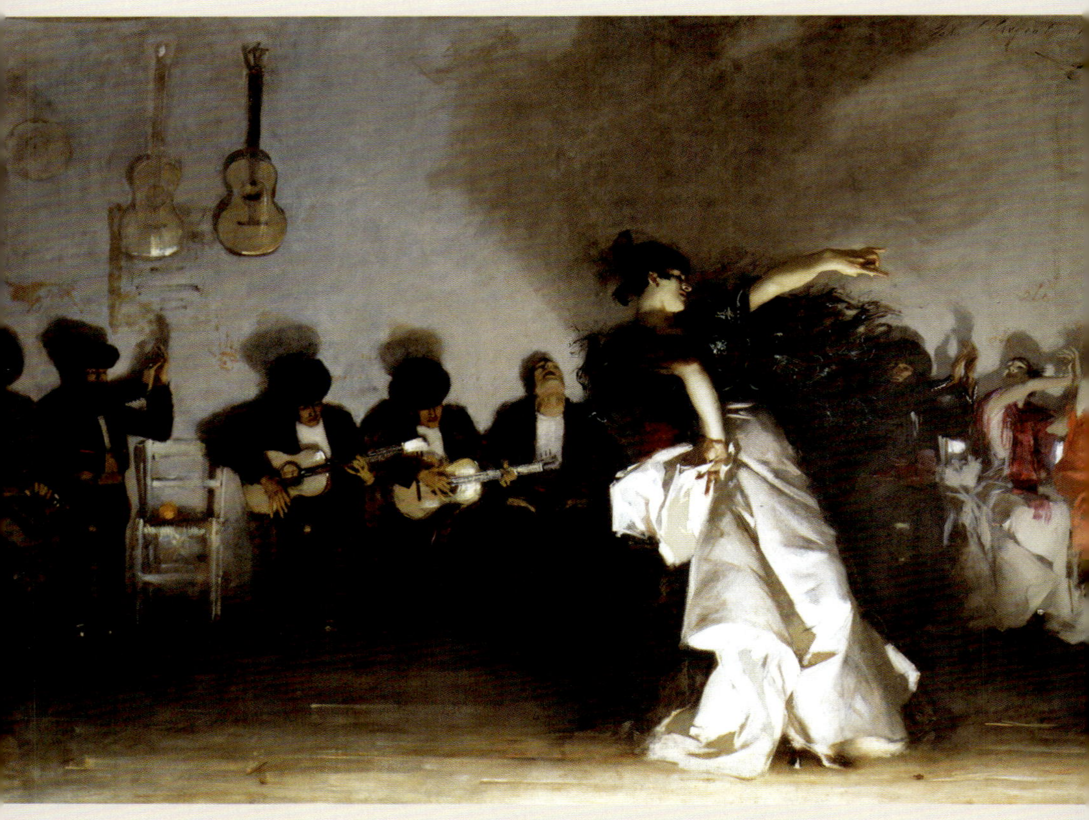

FIG. 19.1 John Singer Sargent, *El Jaleo*, 1882. Isabella Stewart Gardner Museum, Boston. Oil on canvas, 232 × 348 cm.

Sargent, *El Jaleo*

1882

AMERICAN ART

Writing in 1887, Henry James, the masterful author, described his friend John Singer Sargent's (1856–1925) early paintings, acknowledging the "slightly 'uncanny' spectacle of a talent which on the very threshold of its career has nothing more to learn." That talent is in full view in *El Jaleo* (Fig. 19.1). But when it came to *El Jaleo*, James was more cautious: "This singular work, which has found an appreciative home in Boston, has the stamp of an extraordinary energy and facility—of an actual scene….It looks like life, but it looks also, to my view, rather like a perversion of life….The merit of this production is that the air of reality is given in it with remarkable breadth and boldness; its defect it is difficult to express save by saying that it makes the spectator vaguely uneasy and even unhappy….*El Jaleo* sins, in my opinion, in the direction of ugliness." James's comments seem, at first, to condemn the painting. "Ugliness" is a word that stands out, a word that, like an ink stain, is hard to remove and obfuscates everything around it. But James is not disparaging the painting, exactly. He is not stating that Sargent's work is simply ugly. Nothing is simple in Jamesian prose. To James, the unease and the unhappiness that the painting produces veer toward something that might be aesthetically troubling or slightly askew.

But that ugliness is part of the power, of the painting's singularity, of the breadth and boldness that pulls us into the moment, the drama, and the dance. It is noisy and raw. It is a *jaleo*—a word that describes the ruckus and hubbub of the rhythmic, cacophonous, and excited noises of encouragement; the wild singing, the hand-clapping, and the foot-stamping that surround the looming, majestic, and central dancer.

She is grand and glorious, commanding the room as she twists and spirals in a dramatically diagonal, seemingly unbalanced, backward bend. The angle of her pose distracted critics. Reviewers asserted that no one could hold such a position. Cartoonists mocked the dancer by showing her about to fall or drunk. Perhaps there is something of that. What would a night in a Spanish cantina be without some of that delicious dark-red wine, a little *vino tinto*? But she is neither falling nor out of control. She is lost only in the moment, in the music, in the movement. It is difficult to know precisely which dance step she is doing. Some scholars have said it is the *zapateo*—the fast footwork and vibrating sound of heels on bare board. Only male dancers did the loud floor-beating footwork during Sargent's day, however. Women glided and spun about, moving soundlessly, while making dramatic motions and gestures with their upper body.

These kinds of movements were captured in an early film recording made in 1894 by Thomas Edison.* Within the first few seconds the dancer makes a quick and full backbend, which she subsequently counterbalances with three full forward bends, just the kinds of positions that the art critics alleged were impossible. This particular dancer, called Carmencita or the Pearl of Seville, was actually a mad sensation. Sargent painted her as such—as a bright golden pearl against a dark shell of a background (Fig. 19.2). Sargent saw her first in Paris, in 1889, and then again at a private performance at a friend's house in 1890. It was at this occasion that a Mrs. de Glen, writing in a gossipy manner, described Sargent sitting on the floor at Carmencita's feet and sliding the rose that she threw at him into his lapel.

The skirts worn by Carmencita in the glowing portrait by Sargent and in Edison's film are far shorter than those worn by the dancer in *El Jaleo*. In a second, lesser-known version of Carmencita from 1890, her dress is longer, more like that in *El Jaleo*. Yet the skirts in the second Carmencita painting respond to the shape and movements of the dancer's legs in a way that is denied the dancer in *El Jaleo*.

* Carmencita, www.loc.gov/item/00694116.

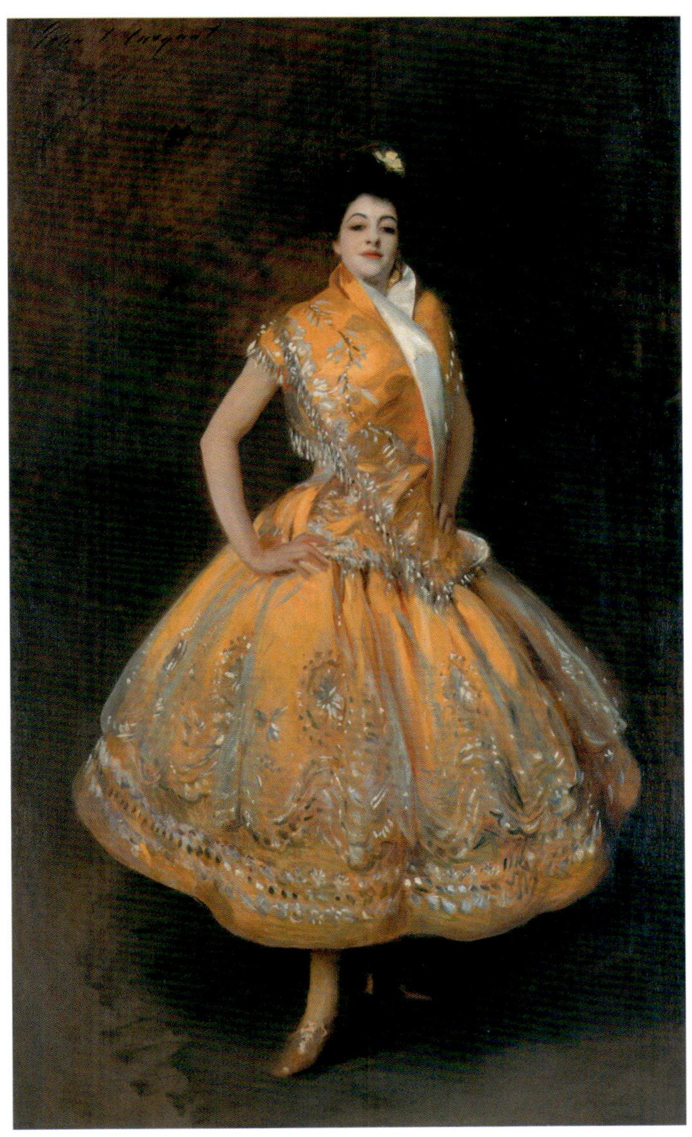

FIG. 19.2 John Singer Sargent, *La Carmencita*, 1890. Musée d'Orsay, Paris. Oil on canvas, 220 × 140 cm.

Her skirts are heavy and long. In fact, it looks as though, if she were to let them fall from her hand, they would create a long train of weighty, bunchy, starchy satin. Looping cone shapes and uneven pockets of material crease uneasily in deep, dark grooves, enhancing the weight of the fabric.

Sargent's paint placement also heightens the sense of the skirt's mass in a literal way. Impasto is a technique wherein paint is placed on the surface in thick patches. It is here, in the contours of the skirt, that Sargent placed the greatest amount of paint, at the thickest standing one-sixteenth of an inch away from the canvas. As James said, the painting "looks like life…but…also like a perversion of life." The skirt that would have entrapped Carmencita and kept her from spinning, or from "withering like a serpent," as Mrs. de Glen put it, provides Sargent with a place to explore complex shapes and shadows. He almost seems to intensify the static qualities of the skirt's fabric, making it as heavy and thick as possible, just so he can then show it in motion.

The striking dialogue between bright whites and dark shadows continues upward, illuminating the movements in the dancer's upper body. The shapes in her dress (zigzags, cones, and deep, dark creases) lead the eye upward to a dramatically inverted right hand that dexterously pinches at a swath of the dancer's voluminous dress. The twist of her right arm exposes her palm and the flashing brightness of her inner forearm. Then we are plunged back into the dark, a shadow that consumes the upper part of her arm and the majority of her neck, and splays out in the form of the black flickering fringe from her shawl. Small designs of turquoise sequins glint and sparkle, creating streams of color as she moves in the frenzied dance. She dips her head toward her left shoulder, turning slightly from us as she does. The little we see of her face, however, indicates her intensity, her great concentration. Again, light contrasts brilliantly with dark. The light from below highlights her cheek, her nostril, and the upper portion of her eye. The effect is such that our attention is drawn to her parted lips, her flaring nostril, the darkness of her eye. She is in a trance, almost masklike in her visage, almost animal in her intensity.

Brazen, like a bull, audacious in her movements, the dancer makes a striking sign with her left hand. It is most likely the end of a snap (called *pitos* in flamenco).* Yet the result is a gesture that looks like a pair of horns, like those of a bull. This is similar to a gesture that has a long history of meanings, from a sign of faith and devotion to a Sassanian king to a sign of faith and devotion to a different kind of empire at the University of Texas. If you make this gesture toward someone in Italy or Spain, you are calling that person a cuckold. Berlusconi made a particularly offensive and public version of this slight in 2002 to the Spanish foreign minister. (Josep Pique was not amused. Neither was his wife.)

But this gesture is also a way of warding off the *mal de ojo,* or evil eye, as the Spanish gypsy does to the bearded artist (who looks a bit like Sargent) in *The Evil Eye* (1859), by John Philip. He paints. She points. Perhaps the dancer in *El Jaleo* is warding off evil as she is drawn into this maelstrom, perhaps there is something demonic here. The huge shadow behind her certainly introduces a sense of the unknown and strange. It looks as though a large specter hovers over her, like the devil or a big black bull. Shadows reach up, beyond the seated viewers too, casting their movements into higher and more dramatic relief. The man to the right of the dancer holds his hands aloft, across his body, while he claps in encouragement. The shadow he casts, however, the result of the low light source, shows his hands farther apart. It is not inaccurate, but it is surprising. It intensifies the gesture, the relationship of the hands, the sense of the energy it takes to create the sounds, and the fact that this is a sort of out-of-body experience. He is in a trance, like the dancer. He claps, keeping the rhythm, but the effect is beyond the physical, in the realm of the shadows where meaning goes beyond the immediate experience. The lady in the bright orange shawl leans forward. She too makes the *pitos,* snapping her fingers. But the shadow of her enthusiastic lean toward the action reveals, it would appear, another gesture of *malocchio* or the horns. The lady in the orange shawl is encouraging her friend, the dancer, by repeating her hand gestures. The wall, or the shadows on it, participates in the painting as well, in an uncanny way.

Not only is the wall the space where movements and gestures take on new

---

* There are no castanets. Henry James said there were, but castanets are used in Spanish classical dance, not true flamenco.

and heightened expression; it is also where voices take form. Sargent seems to visualize the singing or shouts of the woman with the magenta shawl. The word *olè* appears twice in brushy red paint. One appears closer to the mouth of the woman, another hangs above her head. It is almost as though the words are leaving her mouth and rising and entering our space. Sargent shows us the shape of people making sounds. But he also shows those sounds by having the people in this present evoke voices of the past. The words on the wall are written in what is understood to be from a previous party, in previous paint. Of course, it is all by Sargent's hand, which he reminds us of in the upper-right-hand corner in his similarly elegant and slanted script.

Sargent seems to be saying he can do it all, that he can capture the past and the present, the static and the destabilized, with the mastery of his brush. It is an assertion that he makes on the left side of the composition as well. Hanging high on the wall are two guitars. The one on the left sits above a rectangular shape, the remnants of a poster long ago glued to the wall and then ripped off. It is tricky to decipher the guitar on the left because it is shimmery, so illuminated by the light shining from below that it appears to be a strange shadow of a guitar. A ghostly impression. This image is especially confusing next to the fuller, realer guitar that hangs to the right. These contrasts are an exposition of the way that light hits and moves—ephemerally, transcendentally—and a means of showing the artist's capabilities.

Sargent is, in *El Jaleo*, an Impressionist. It was not so long before Sargent that painters were challenging the closed system of the Academy, with its conservative stylistic tastes and insular selection process. Artists like Manet, Monet, Degas, and Pissarro had recently institutionalized their outsider status at the first Salon des Refusés in 1874, the year that Monet exhibited his *Impression, Sunrise* (Fig.18.1). The title, as we know, gave shape to a radical artistic movement, which emphasized the effects of light through pure, unblended colors, and where the sense of forms, rather than the strict outline, was created through spontaneous brushstrokes. Sargent, like his Impressionist brethren, did not close off forms with smooth edges. The outlines of the thick white skirt, for example, are splotchy and sketchy. The man at the dancer's back, who throws his head against the wall, perhaps in exhaustion or perhaps because he is lost in the moment, is composed of blocky patches of paint. His face is almost masklike in its simplicity. His hands are sketchy, almost inchoate forms, with shivering outlines suggesting their shape. Tremulous lines—dashes of yellow and white paint—compose floorboards that respond to the flickering lights. The strangest passage might be the blurred blotches of white that sit between the clapping man and the woman wearing magenta. Light reflecting off her white dress? Perhaps, or perhaps not. It makes little sense when it is the subject of close scrutiny. Yet from afar, it becomes part of the flash and flair, the excitement and energy of the room.

Coloristically, the two differ in many ways, but Edgar Degas (1834–1917), who happened to be Sargent's friend, was a clear inspiration. *L'Étoile* also places a dancer in the center of a stage illuminated by bright lights and composed of thick, brushy, unfinished strokes (Fig. 19.3). Here too we see her face at an angle, like the dancer in *El Jaleo*, and we sense that she is moving quickly, flowing from one step to the next, because the brushstrokes are unfixed and the outlines quiver. Sargent's lady might be a bit grittier than that of Degas—strict, weighty satin versus fluffy tulle, harsh angles versus soft landings, sharp heels versus light pink slippers. Still, both artists found inspiration in the challenge of painting movement, and they did it with similarly impressionistic styles.

Degas also explored the notion of capturing the dance, of experiencing the ephemeral art of ballet, by creating compositions that were asymmetrical and often from cropped or unusual angles. Our position is from above the stage, as though we are watching the ballerina from a seat in the mezzanine or in a box. Pulling us into the painting by pointing to our position as a spectator, Degas again heightens the sense that the viewer is experiencing something impermanent, a fragment of a moment. Sargent sketched *L'Étoile* the very year it was finished and exhibited in Paris, so he was familiar with Degas's techniques. Sargent has his performance at a less jarring angle than the Degas, with the spectator viewing the show more or less straight on. But Degas's truncated views and transient time appear in Sargent's painting. The man at the far left of the painting is incomplete, as is the leaning lady in orange whose left arm extends beyond the frame. Of course, there is also the expansive and seemingly endless shadow of the dancing woman.

In effect, *El Jaleo* was a statement, a way for Sargent to say that he was siding

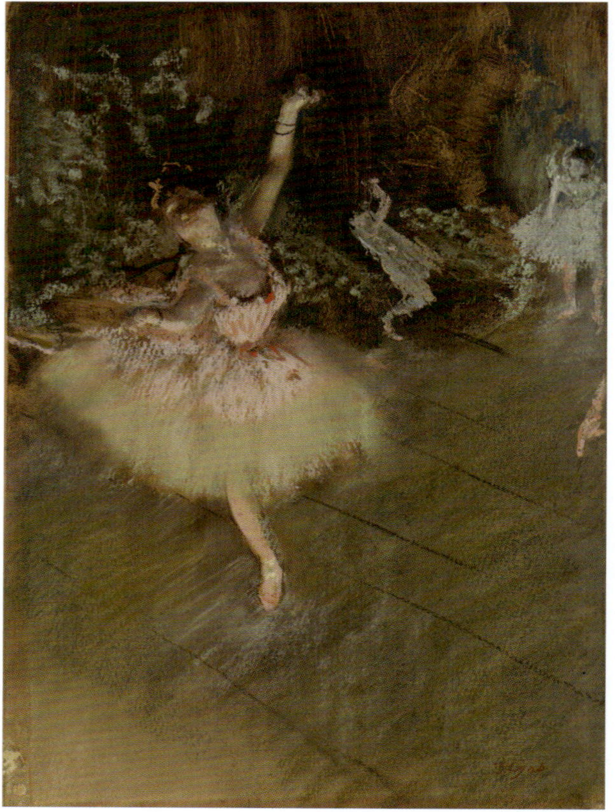

FIG. 19.3 Edgar Degas, *L'Étoile*, ca. 1876. Musée d'Orsay, Paris. Oil on canvas, 58.4 × 42 cm.

with the Impressionists, or at least that he could paint like them. It might seem too dramatic to say that there were warring factions of styles. But the art world was rather strictly divided into two camps—academic or impressionistic. A reviewer for the *Critic* wrote: "If Mr. Sargent has joined the ranks of the French impressionists, it is their gain and his loss.... He is too good a painter, too much of a gentleman and a scholar, to be found in such company." But Sargent was not like Monet, making a radical and political break with the Academy, painting outside with chickens, living the bohemian life. Nor is the painting as impressionistic as it might appear at first glance.

When Sargent sat down to produce *El Jaleo*, he did it with the speed of a proper Impressionist. Yet Sargent so readily put paint to canvas because he had spent years constructing and considering the shape of the painting. This was quite a long time coming. The first inkling of his inspiration came in 1879, when he traveled throughout Spain revisiting sites he had seen as a boy—Madrid, Valencia, Córdoba, Sevilla. Although an American, young Sargent was born in Florence and raised in Europe. Before his birth, Sargent's parents had gone to recover in Europe after the death of a young daughter. Once there Sargent's mother, Mary, absolutely refused to go back to America. According to the scholar Richard Ormond, who is also Sargent's grandnephew, when reminded of America she would "throw wobbly and fall ill." Sargent's father quit his job as an eye surgeon in Philadelphia and the family moved around, generally avoiding society and living as nomadic expatriates for the entirety of the young artist's life.

Sargent trained in Paris under the artist Carolus-Duran, who encouraged the talented young man (at the age of twenty-three) to see Spain again, although this time as an artist, not a boy. It was on these travels that Sargent started to consider, to ruminate on the theme of the dancer in the dark cantina. The first sketches depict a horizontal scene of flamenco, with a single dancer before a row of musicians. These appear on the back of torn-in-two invoices from shops in Madrid. The muses of inspiration can visit in unexpected moments. Perhaps Sargent was watching a flamenco performance, got an inspiration, and grabbed the first thing he could, old bills that were sitting in his pocket, so that he could sketch out his ideas right away. Over and over again Sargent worked on the seeds of a painting, quickly drawing faces and fingers and forms wherever and whenever he could. He worked out two oil sketches of a gypsy dancer, envisioning the kind of pose that would evolve into the lady in the center of the stage.

He played further with her position in a watercolor on paper and a larger oil painting.* In the oil painting the lady turns away so that we cannot see her face,

---

* Sargent's watercolor study for *The Spanish Dancer*, 30.16 × 20 cm, 1882, is housed at the Dallas Museum of Art: https://collections.dma.org/artwork/3095662.

in what is called a *profil perdu* (Fig. 19.4). That controversial backward lean is less emphatic, nor does her shawl flip and shimmer as it does in the final composition. Sargent was clearly onto something that he liked, however, even if the idea needed to continue cooking. Not all of his paintings and sketches are quite so directly related to the final painting of *El Jaleo*, and yet the germination, his processing of the painting, was quite arguably happening in other works as well. A quick and truncated drawing shows one woman whipping quickly from right to left.* She is caught in the middle of this move, mysteriously coy in the way she covers part of her face with her arm. The fringe of her shawl bounces and flies around in ways that resonate in the dancer in *El Jaleo*, and her hand positions are evocative of the grander painting too.

A painting from the Hispanic Society of America is another example of early and frequent considerations (obsessions) with Spain and dance and darkness (Fig. 19.5). Stars beam and blink, seemingly cascading from a pervasive, permeative black sky. One woman sways with her arms softly, coolly extended, somehow simultaneously evoking the mood of a meditative whirling dervish and the passion of a seductive entreaty. A woman mirrors her in the background, arms aloft, faint beacons of light, of more dancing and more partying, in the distance. In two preparatory sketches for the painting the women have partners. They are performing a movement called *hacienda la bisagra* (making the hinge). The men are also in the final painting, but, dressed as they are in black, they are barely visible. They merge with the blackness of the night. Their presence is a suggestion, a hint, just as the entire scene is a mysterious, momentary, and mystical impression.

The painting of *The Spanish Dancer* plays a curious part in unraveling the story of *El Jaleo*'s genesis. The painting was never exhibited, although it appears that Sargent intended the piece to be a submission for the Paris Salon. Its large size, the same height as *El Jaleo* although half its width, indicates that this was not a study but intended as a full painting. The extent to which Sargent finished the piece also indicates that it was meant to be shown. But he set it aside for reasons about which one can only speculate. And it disappeared. *The Spanish Dancer* did

---

* Sketch of a Spanish dancer, ca. 1879–80. Location unknown.

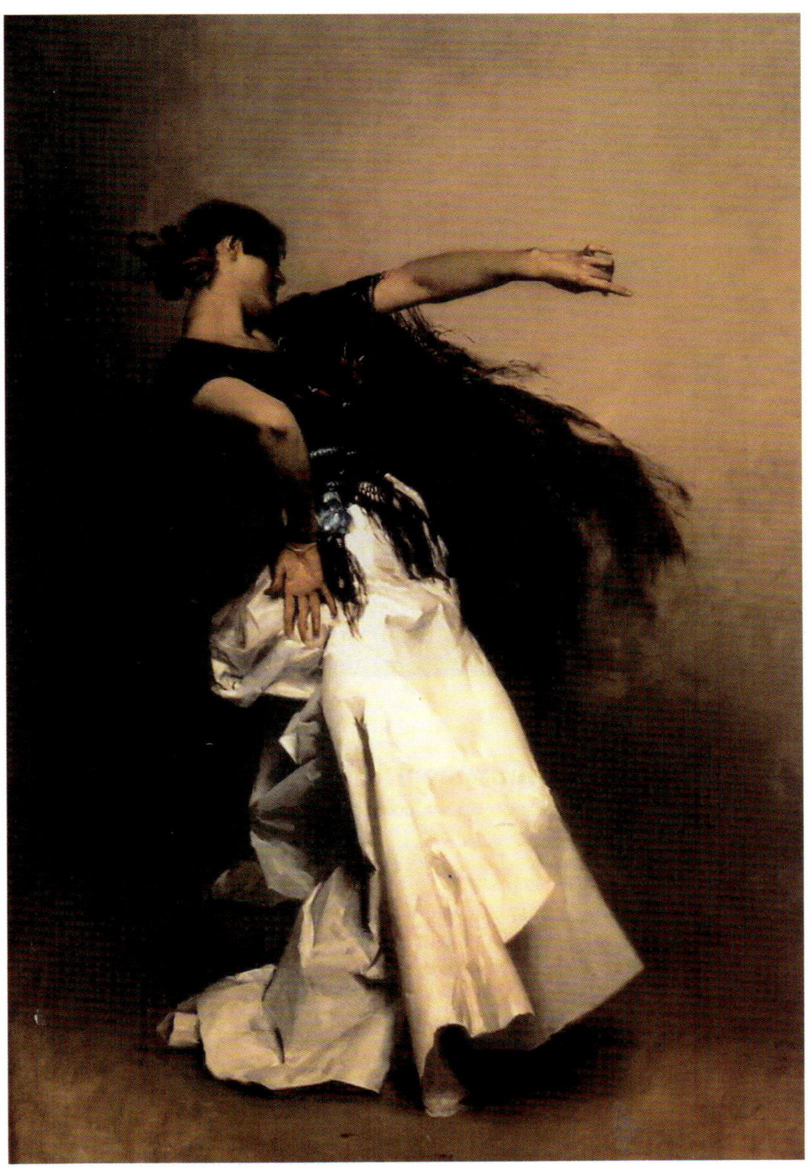

FIG. 19.4 John Singer Sargent, *The Spanish Dancer*, 1880–1881. Private collection. Oil on canvas.

FIG. 19.5 John Singer Sargent, *The Spanish Dance*, 1879–1880. Hispanic Society of America, New York. Oil on canvas, 89.2 × 84.5 cm.

not reemerge until 1897, when a man named Isaac Jean Val wrote to Sargent hoping that the artist would confirm its attribution. Sargent wrote back to say that it was indeed his work and expressed his surprise to learn of its whereabouts. He questioned how it came to be in Val's possession and asked if he might have it back. Val responded, explaining that the artist had given it as a gift to his maid, who then generously presented it to him. Sargent's surprise indicates quite clearly that he had never given the painting to the maid. Taking a page from the finders-keepers etiquette book, the painting stayed in Val's possession. None of this exchange was known until 1988, when the great grandson of the fortunate Val asked to have the painting examined by scholars from the National Gallery. That's a good day, when you go on a house call and discover an unknown painting by Sargent.

The other curious aspect of the painting is that it is not as impressionistic in style as the final painting, as *El Jaleo.* The skirt has splotchy patches of shadows, to be sure, but the lines are cleaner and crisper, the lighting softer and more suffused. Comparing the right hands of the dancer, the *El Jaleo* dancer's right hand is suggestive and becomes a bit difficult to interpret from close up. That of the woman in the once-lost painting is more legible, with clearer black outlines, distinct fingers, and a readable palm. It is more academic in nature.

Sargent could do it all. In just the span of a few months he was painting in all kinds of genres, all kinds of styles. He painted small, sweet genre scenes of women stringing onions and carrying water, of women smoking and women leaving church. He worked out the head of a mad-looking Spanish woman and painted the darling Beatrice Townsend. He sketched Venice like an Impressionist, Isabel Valle and Louise Burckhardt like an academic, and the daughters of Edward Boit with a bit of a mix. In 1882 he was also enchanted by the beauty of Madame Gautreau, who would prove to be important in his career in Paris. There is the tenderness of Mr. and Mrs. John Field and the roughness of women working in the dark on conduits of light, on rods of glass. He consumed everything he saw, and painted or sketched everything he could.

Sargent's spongy, all-consuming approach to manifold artistic influences appears in *El Jaleo.* He sprinkles clues to his passions and inspirations throughout, which, when pulled out and put together as a whole, demonstrate an altogether encyclopedic understanding of art and its rich histories. One compelling clue is the round orange that perches just above the crisscross shapes of an unraveling wicker chair. The orange is possibly a hint or relic of Manet, who painted many Spanish dancers himself. Little oranges appear at the base of Manet's painting *Reclining Young Woman in Spanish Costume* (1862–63), now in the Yale University Art Gallery. A cat plays with one orange; the other sits just below the serene yet suspicious face of the lounging lady. Her hair is pulled back, pinned against her head in a tight bun, and she wears light-pink tights. But this is not a dancer that Degas would paint. She is dressed as a Spaniard, as a Spanish man—wearing a bolero jacket and short pants. The portrait is suggestive, private, and a touch risqué. The next year Manet went further, painting a reclining lady without clothes at all. *Olympia* (Fig. 18.4).

Manet, with his women, was looking closely at the lounging ladies of the Spanish artist Francisco Goya. A *maja* is a term referring to people that dressed in traditional Spanish clothing. Yet as scholars have pointed out, the dress of Goya's *maja vestida* does not accurately portray Andalusian styles. And his nude *maja* even less so. Manuel Godoy, the minister and lover of the queen of Spain, requested two versions of the *maja* on the bed. Evidently he would show the *maja* that best suited the character of his visitors—prudish or prurient. Godoy also owned another important nude, that of the *Rokeby Venus* by Velázquez. Godoy, Goya, Manet—they were all looking at Velázquez. Goya claimed that his teachers were "nature, Rembrandt, and Velázquez." Manet felt quite the same, exclaiming, "What thrilled me most in Spain and made the whole trip worthwhile were the works of Velázquez. He's the greatest artist of all."

Sargent was looking at Velázquez too. Carolus-Duran, his teacher, encouraged Sargent with a clear message: "Velázquez, Velázquez, Velázquez. Study Velázquez without respite!" Carolus-Duran may have been Sargent's teacher. But Velázquez was, as Henry James reported, Sargent's god. Direct homages to Velázquez appear throughout Sargent's works. On his trip to Spain in 1879, Sargent made copies and sketches of many paintings by Velázquez, such as Apollo from *The Forge of Vulcan* and, most notably, *Las Meninas* (see figure 16.2). The princess Infanta Margarita and her retinue stand at attention both for the king and queen, who appear in a distant, hazy mirror, and also for Velázquez, who is presumably painting their portraits, although the canvas is turned from view.

The Daughters of Edward Darley Boit directly recalls the young ladies of *Las Meninas* (Fig. 19.6). Standing in the foyer of their Paris apartment, the four girls confront the viewer (and portraitist) with kind and calm faces, welcoming but reserved. Their crisp white pinafores strangely evoke the hoop skirts of the princess and her ladies. Sargent borrows Velázquez's masterful use of darkened

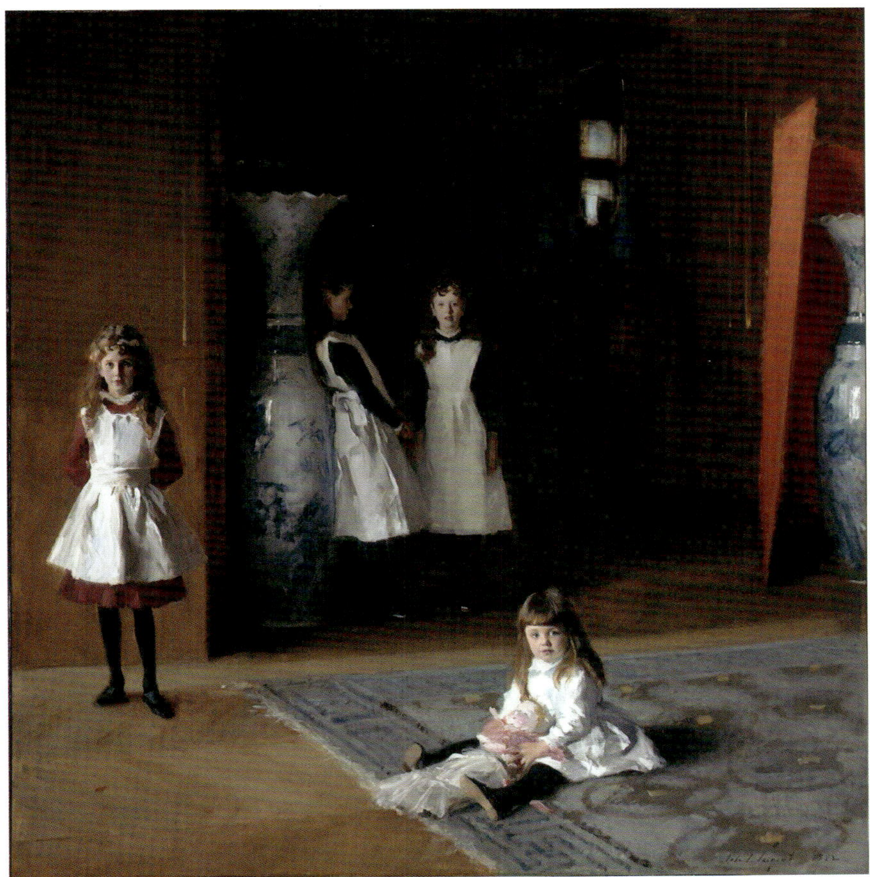

FIG. 19.6 John Singer Sargent, *The Daughters of Edward Darley Boit,* 1882. Museum of Fine Arts, Boston. Oil on canvas, 221.93 × 222.57 cm.

backgrounds splashed with light in the foreground. The later artist also looks to *Las Meninas* for shifting foci—tighter in the foreground, hazier in the background. Oblique angles of entry, distant reflective surfaces, large blank spaces (a cabinet looks like the back of the canvas)—all are reverent reminiscences of Velázquez, as are the mood and sense of timelessness. We know they will grow up. We know they will not play with dolls forever or feel quite so dwarfed by grand Japanese vases. Yet there is something timeless in the gaze of the girls, a sense of the eternal that Sargent borrowed from Velázquez's masterpiece.

Many scholars see a clearer relationship with Goya's works, most notably *El Tres de Mayo, 1808,* arguing that Sargent "turned away from Velázquez" in *El Jaleo.* The demonic frenzy of the dancer in *El Jaleo* is a far cry from the demons that lurk here, in Goya's portrait of the sufferings of the Spanish at the hands of Napoleon's brutes. Yet there are connections between the two paintings, such as the powerful use of light against a generally dark background. Brushy modulations of shape and color define Goya's men. Facial features are ghostly and distorted in both. The man throwing back his head and pushing his inverted hands down on his knees in *El Jaleo* would not be out of place in *El Tres de Mayo, 1808.*

It is not fair to say that Sargent dropped Velázquez for Goya, however. Sargent did not work like that. All of these artists, all of the works that influenced him are ever-present, albeit in varying degrees of transparency. *El Jaleo* embraces the rich palette of *Las Meninas,* which percolates with flashes of light that guide our eye through the painting. Sargent also borrows the truncated view found in *Las Meninas* and in *Las Hilanderas,* also copied by Sargent. Our view into that workshop of weaving women is not comprehensive; it is just a snippet. The woman on the left allows us to see a little more by pulling the red curtain back, and we only see a part of the young girl on the right, who collects the balls of yarn. The woman weaving her web of wool—her outstretched arm, her twisted torso, her *profil perdu,* her crisp white top, her deep lean backward—these are all borrowed by the dancer in *El Jaleo. El Jaleo* is filled with clues. Or it *is* a clue. The etymology of "clue" is a ball of yarn that unravels, guiding us on a path. The painting leads us through spinning associations back from Sargent to Manet, to Goya, to Velázquez.

Back further still. Sargent's painting is suffused with bull imagery. Hand gestures look like horns, and the dancer's movements make us think of bullfights where men or (if you like *Talk to Her,* by Pedro Almodóvar) women swirl and swivel away from their charging adversaries. But there is one more bull. Just above the man looking shiftily to his left, there is a red painted bull on the wall, which might just recall the painted bulls in a deeper Spanish past, those of the prehistoric paintings in Altamira (Fig. 1.1). In those caves deep-red bulls surround the visitor—rushing, braying, sleeping, surveying. Between the bulls there are also red handprints, not unlike the one that hovers to the right of the chair with the orange. A painted hand or a hand made by paint. The paintings of Altamira, although discovered by this point, were not yet accepted as authentic by the academic community. We may not know how Sargent felt about those debates or how much he actually knew about Altamira; but he was most certainly taken with the very kinds of images that had been found in Altamira—eerie red bulls and hovering red hands.

Sargent is more than an impressionist. He is an encyclopedia of art. For Sargent, style was, in a sense, one of the most superficial parts of the painting. In fact, we can almost see Sargent selecting the technique as a calculation. He seems to have been basing his decisions on something political, on the art market, into which he had been newly introduced. He may have determined, rightly, that the best way of making a splash on the Parisian art market was with a painting that placed him alongside the Impressionists. Perhaps he was supporting the cause. But it is just as likely that he was supporting his own cause, selecting a style that might generate excitement and get critics talking. It certainly worked. *El Jaleo*, like it or not, was a huge hit.

With those accolades and advantageous criticisms, he was bolstered to take his painting a step further by painting the greatest beauty in Parisian society, Madame Pierre Gautreau or, as we know her, Madame X (Fig. 19.7). Gautreau was the talk of the town, and of the artists too. Although she declined many artists who wanted to paint her, she agreed to let Sargent work his magic. Her haughty pose, her shockingly pale skin accentuated with hints of her favorite lavender powder, the plunging neckline—it was too much. As soon as the Salon doors were opened, visitors were exclaiming their overt aversion: "This portrait is simply offensive in its insolent ugliness and defiance of every rule of art.... The drawing is bad, the color atrocious, the artistic ideal low, the whole purpose of the picture being, not an artistic and sensational 'tour de force'...but a willful exaggeration of every one of his vicious eccentricities, simply for the purpose of being talked about and provoking argument." Sargent was mortified, although he later claimed that the portrait was "the best thing I have done." He removed the painting from the exhibition, making one concession to the critics. In its original

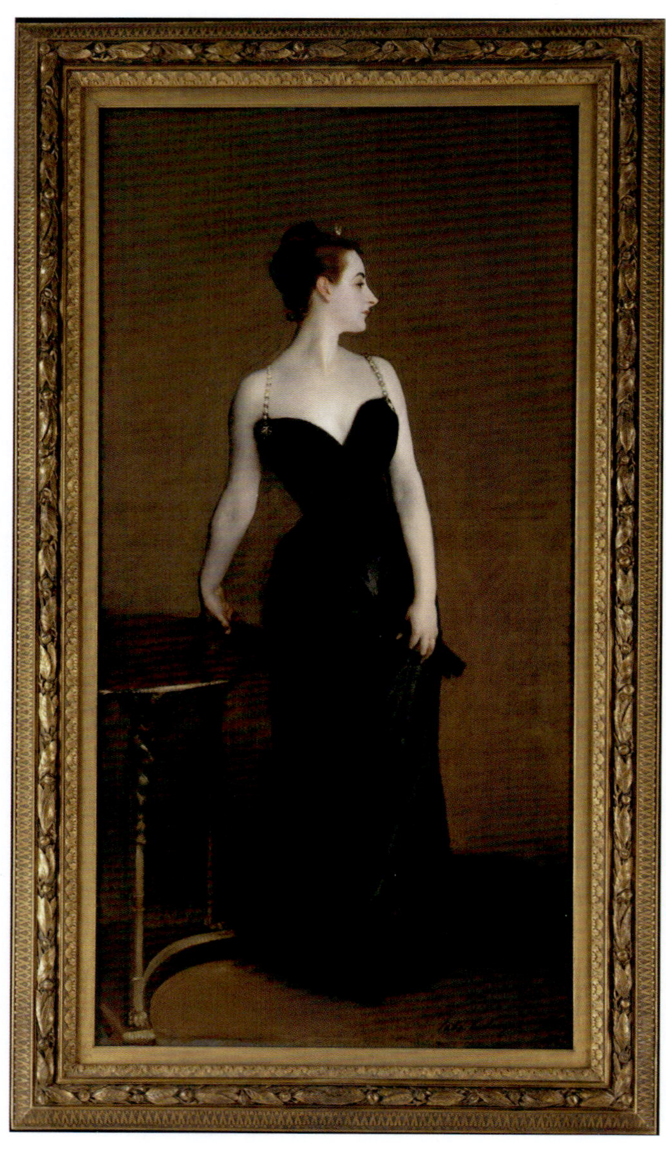

FIG. 19.7 John Singer Sargent, *Madame X (Madame Pierre Gautreau)*, 1883–1884. Metropolitan Museum of Art, New York. Oil on canvas, 208.6 × 109.9 cm.

configuration the strap was slipped down her shapely shoulder. He repainted the scandalous strap, and this is how we see it today.

This hubbub might seem rather odd. *El Jaleo* was imbued with suggestive, raw, and animal energies, but it did not cause the same outrage because it was showing a scene of exoticism, of foreigners, Spaniards. This painting was of a woman in Parisian society, where decorum reigned. But even that was not the whole problem. The issue went deeper because Madame Gautreau was an American, from Louisiana. What could be worse than an upstart, an arriviste American who married one of the most eligible men in Paris, and was beautiful, and a scene stealer? Probably nothing, so far as the hens of Parisian society were concerned. An article from 1881 indicated just how warm Parisian society was toward Americans: "I know…one determined [French] patriot who can no longer, without a lot of grumbling, say the name America.… They have painters who carry off our medals, like Mr. Sargent, beautiful women who eclipse ours, like Mme Gautreau, and horses that beat our steeds.…It is a peaceful war, but they come to hoist their victory colors over our land." Although her name was not given in the painting's title, those pearl clutchers of Paris were looking to knock her down a peg, to find fault in her. Sales dropped, and the commissions for paintings dried up. Sargent's name was sufficiently sullied, so much so that he moved to England, where he hoped he could revive the love lost in Paris.

He did not lose sight of the painting, however. He kept it with him at all times—in his studio in Paris after its removal from the Salon, and then in his new studio in London. She was a secret source of pride but also a cautionary tale about the public and patronage, about the levels of comfort of both and about how much they dictated his status and success. So Sargent set about to rebuild his popularity and acceptability. In 1884 he received his first commission in England, for a painting of three daughters from the Vickers family—Florence, Mabel, and Mildred. Seemingly smarting from the shock of Sargent's Parisian experience, English critics called it "beastly French" and voted it the worst picture of the year. No fallen strap to fix, Sargent dug a little deeper, studying the great English painters and visiting with the elderly Monet, who was working on his wonderful water lily paintings in Giverny.

What emerged from his time of reflection, two years later in 1886, was the scene of two little girls, the daughters of the artist Frederick Barnard, Dolly on the left, Polly on the right (Fig. 19.8). Captured in the gloaming and surrounded by darkening foliage, the sisters focus on their delicate task, lighting the paper lanterns. The girls are almost extensions of the flowers that surround them. The tall white lilies with petals that curl and fold are much like the white frocks with flowering, wavy collars. The yellow of the pollen in the lilies is like the yellow light glowing on their faces. Dashes of red in the flower pick up the red in their lips. Little pink roses are like little blushing cheeks. Alices in wonderland, where crepey dresses and lanterns languish in a crepuscular light.

The painting of the little girls might seem a far step from *El Jaleo*. But in a strange way, Sargent's English roses have many similarities to the Spanish dancer in the dark cantina. For one, he worked a lot on this painting. He made tons of sketches as in the case of *El Jaleo*. Although the cartoonists of the day showed Sargent aimlessly slapping paint on the canvas with a hapless Barnard daughter hunched over in the background, the artist was methodical and almost maniacal about his process. He worked from August until November (1885), posing the girls almost daily. When the roses died out he had substitutes made and fixed to the withered bushes. One can only imagine the poor little shivering, obedient girls. Second, like *El Jaleo*, the title is not directly about the girls or the flowers depicted on the canvas. Both titles are about music. *El Jaleo* is about the sounds—shouts, snaps, stamps—that create the flurry and fury onstage. *Carnation, Lily, Lily, Rose* is from a popular song called "Ye Shepherds Tell Me." Perhaps the little ladies were singing as they worked, although the song was arranged for three voices that overlap in a canon. The canon form and the lilting lyrics—*Carnation, Lily, Lily, Rose*—resonate with the shape and feel of the painting. Lily-like ladies reflect their surroundings and each other, evoking the repetitive, mirrorlike quality of the lyrics, of the title. The rhythmic cadence of the title also seems to evoke the delicate movements of the little girls in their quiet, meditative, and methodical work as they softly set the gardens aglow.

Carnation, Lily, Lily, Rose appeared about three years after the *Madame X* debacle, years that must have been stressful for the ambitious artist. But he came out a star. Commissions flooded his way for portraits, grand society paintings, which is what we might know him for best, as a matter of fact. The British

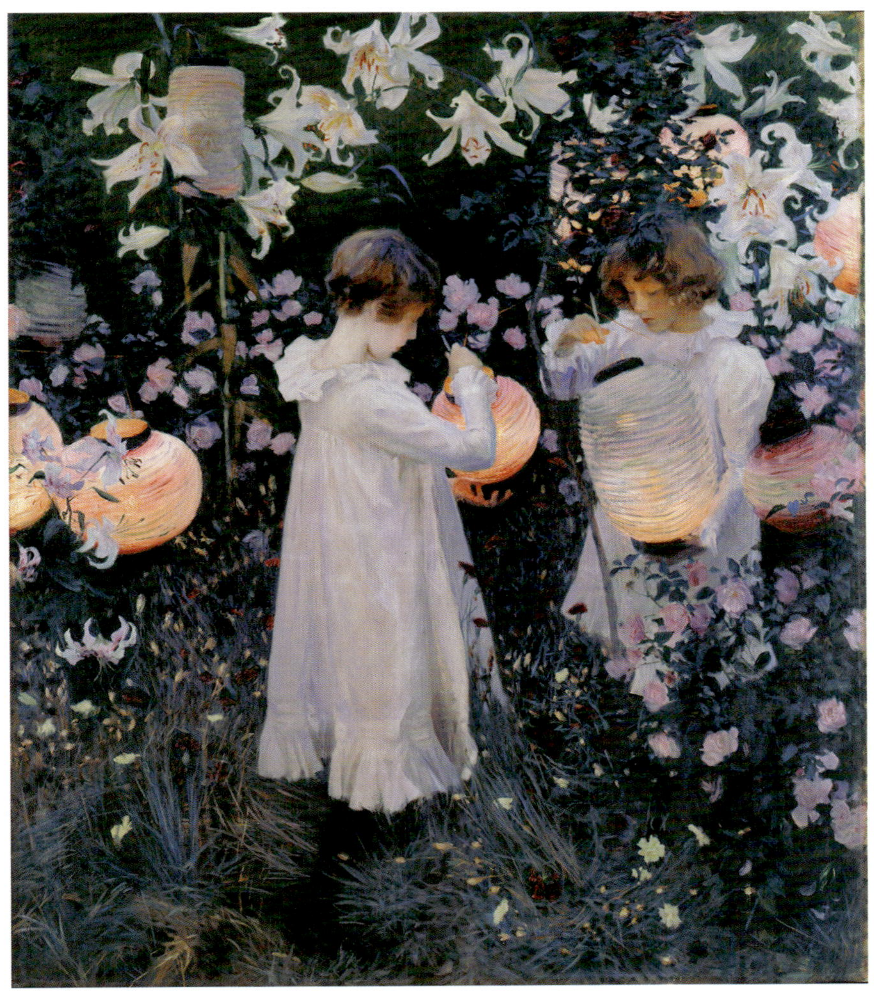

FIG. 19.8 John Singer Sargent, *Carnation, Lily, Lily, Rose*, 1885–1856. Tate Britain, London. Oil on canvas, 174 × 153.7 cm.

caricaturist Max Beerbohm captured the enthusiasm and demand for Sargent's painterly attentions. He depicts ladies of all shapes and sizes lining up with their (very small) footmen, while Sargent looks out of his window with a furrowed brow. The demand was high in London, and in America too. The San Antonio Museum of Art holds an example of Sargent's prominent American clientele, Mrs. Elliot Fitch Shepard, a rich American heiress with Vanderbilt tucked into her maiden name. Sargent's first American commission came in around 1887 from Henry Marquand, who asked Sargent to paint his wife, Elizabeth. Sargent was not entirely excited about coming to America and so he listed a price that was exorbitant, far beyond anything he thought reasonable, assuming (hoping) they would say no, thank you. Marquand accepted the price wholeheartedly. The Marquands may have brought Sargent into the American market, but it was another American, Isabella Stewart Gardner, who had the largest part in orchestrating Sargent's time in America and America's time with him.

Isabella Stewart Gardner (1840–1924) was like Madame Gautreau—famous, prominent, and powerful. Interestingly, Sargent painted her in a manner that harks to that contentious painting (Fig 19.9). The deep V of her black dress, her striking hourglass figure, and her bright-white skin all seem to refer to the source of the scandal of 1883. But Gardner was not the center of attention for her doelike beauty. It was her brassy affability and her salty charm that had the town talking. She was a constant in the gossip tabloids of the day. Newspapers sketched her walking lions that she borrowed from the zoo. She loved car races and cigarettes and wore diamonds mounted on springs such that she had shiny antennae bouncing around out of her head at all times. She invited people over for concerts, bloody boxing matches, and painting sessions, offering champagne and donuts to these lucky visitors. Sargent was part of this vibrant mix. He had always embraced the opportunity to circulate among the literati. He captured the faces of writers (Robert Louis Stevenson and Henry James), actors (Edwin Booth), composers (Fauré), and dancers (Nijinsky). And he painted Gardner.

She stands, appearing like a proper lady of society, and yet her face betrays her spunk and ardor. A shadow spills in from the right side, which makes it appear as though her head is turning, like she just cannot stand still. Her mouth is moving, her left eye darting to the side. The glowing red and gold tapestry hanging behind

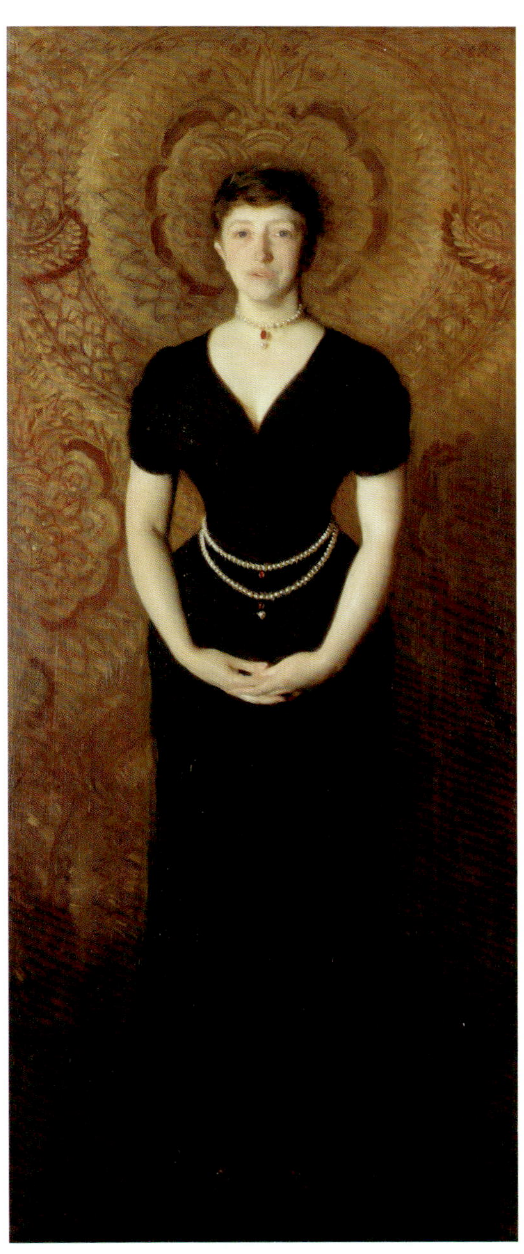

FIG. 19.9 John Singer Sargent, *Isabella Stewart Gardner,* 1888. Isabella Stewart Gardner Museum, Boston. Oil on canvas, 190 × 80 cm.

her is an evocation of her energy and warmth. The swirling acanthus leaves and billowing flower forms create a halo around her head, with the pinnacles of that gilded foliage generating a delicate pointed crown. "Like a Byzantine Madonna," Henry James wrote. As in *El Jaleo*, Sargent uses many different inspirations—both historical and personal—to express this mysterious Isabella woman. She appears as a timeless force of nature, which subtly transcends her proper pose and dress. She adored it, but her husband did not, writing to her saying, "It looks like hell, but it looks like you." He requested that she not show it publicly while he was alive. She did not exhibit the painting again. But that might have been because she loved it so much. Or maybe she wanted her husband to see it as often as possible.

Just as Isabella Gardner collected the most brilliant people, she collected many of the greatest masterpieces. One of her greatest coups was her purchase in 1896 of Titian's *The Rape of Europa* (Fig. 16.3). Writing to the famous art historian Bernard Berenson, she proclaimed: "Many came with 'grave doubts,' many came to scoff, but all wallowed at her feet." It is no wonder Sargent conceived her as a dominant, imperial, Byzantine Madonna. She collected tremendous treasures—Bellini, Botticelli, Piero della Francesca. All are housed in the spectacular Isabella Stewart Gardner Museum, a collection that is rich in masterpieces, which remains the case even without the paintings by Vermeer, Rembrandt, Degas, and Manet that were stolen in 1990. The empty frames memorialize those losses.

El Jaleo was a complicated painting for Gardner to acquire. But she wanted it, so, of course, she got it, although it took a lot of wrangling with the owner, Thomas Jefferson Coolidge. Coolidge bought the painting when it was still hanging in the Salon of 1882. After that point he never let it out of his sight. He rejected almost every inquiry about exhibiting it. In 1897 he lent it to the Museum of Fine Arts in Boston, most likely because he needed a place to put it while he moved into a new home. This was probably the moment when Gardner first set her eyes on the painting. She surely knew the unlikelihood of Coolidge parting with his prized possession. Nevertheless, in 1914 she built a place specifically for the painting in her grand mansion. It must have been quite a shock to Coolidge when he visited Gardner and she explained where his beloved painting was going to sit. Shocked or not, she got her painting and put it where it still sits today, in the so-called Spanish Cloister, a small room framed by architectural elements from medieval Spain.

A dramatic lobed frame creates a halolike effect while two marble beasts support columns and protect the sacred space. Sacred it was, as it was here that Gardner insisted her funeral would take place. For his part, Sargent seemed quite pleased with the Spanish Cloister. It was no small thing to have work hung in the same building as those other masters that he admired and emulated. He appears to have enjoyed the drama of the setting too, stating that "she had done more for it than he had." Right after you enter the museum, you turn to look down a dark, long hallway, and there she is, the dancer, bright and white in the distance. Gardner meant it to be as dramatic as possible, adding special lights along the floor at the base of the painting. These shimmer and reflect off the gilded frame she had custom-made for *El Jaleo*. The effect, the experience, is spectacular.

In many ways, Isabella Stewart Gardner was like her painting, like *El Jaleo*. The striking whiteness and elegance of the dancer's arms and profile seem to suggest that of a classical goddess. But this Aphrodite moves with the spirit of an animal, of the bulls that surround her. Gardner was a strange mix too, elegant and bold, refined and shocking. So was Sargent. He drew from so many layers of the past, so many styles and subjects and genres, that his own style is difficult to ascribe to one particular type. He was an American that barely came to America until the last chapter of his life, making him more European than American. Yet perhaps he is actually the quintessential American because he drew together so many inspirations, interests, and influences. A melting pot of paint.

Sargent was constantly absorbing new ideas and trying new things. It is no surprise that by 1907 he was exhausted with portraits of society ladies. Writing to his longtime friend Ralph Curtis, Sargent declared that he was done. "No more paughtraits," he wrote using a satirical spelling, perhaps to mimic the pronunciation of some of his elegant society ladies, the kinds standing on the Beerbohm sidewalk. "I abhor and abjure them and hope never to do another especially of the Upper Classes."

He turned his attention to public commissions, most notably the paintings in the Boston Public Library. These were a departure from his previous works because he used a strict Neoclassical style, more in line with the academic style

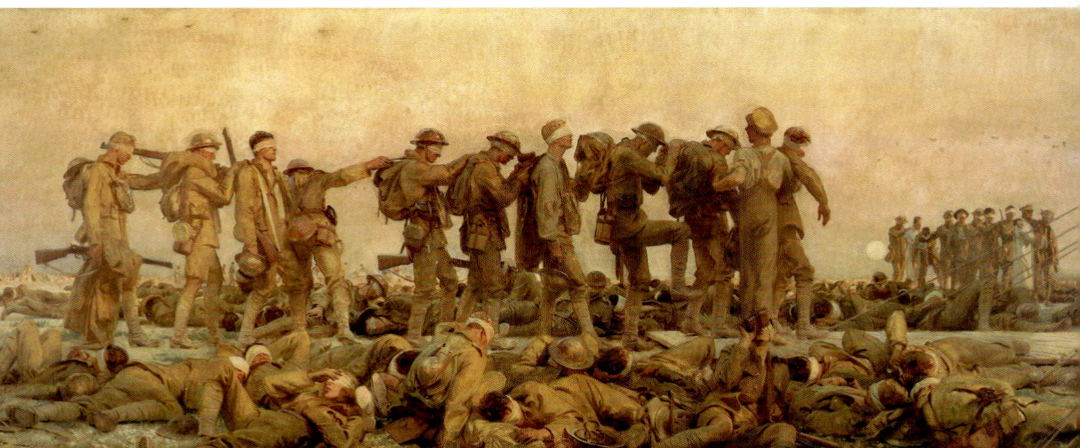

FIG. 19.10 John Singer Sargent, *Gassed*, 1919. Imperial War Museums, London. Oil on canvas, 231 × 611.1 cm.

that he had seemingly rejected with *El Jaleo*. He wanted the cycle to tell a history, so the style was to be documentarian, just as the hallowed halls the images decorated hold the textual records of truth and history. Sargent used this same realist or Neoclassical style for paintings that documented other truths, those of the pains of World War I. His painting *Gassed* depicts the grisly and pathos-inducing effects of a mustard gas attack, with wounded soldiers using each other for guidance, presumably looking for help, which is nowhere to be found (Fig. 19.10). It is a strangely joyless reversal of *El Jaleo*. Here men are bathed in the light that they cannot see, walking rhythmically along a wooden plank in an unchoreographed routine. The dancer also moves on a wooden stage, with the sounds of her friends to guide her, lost in the moment, in the dance. While her movements are desperate in an ecstatic way, the despair of the men is pained and essential.

The painting of *El Jaleo* has a darkness, but it is emphatically not about suffering. There is something dangerous and animalistic here—endless and eerie shadows, shady masklike faces, indications of loud noises, the *jaleo*, ghosts of a painterly past. Yet the laughter and delight of the women in the corner remind us that this is a festive, exuberant performance. Happy and frenzied energies invigorate the room. This complexity of mood might make one think of Carmen, the wanton cigarette girl depicted in the opera by Georges Bizet. Carmen seduces Don José, destroying his career, and runs off with the handsome toreador Escamillo, which makes Don José angry. But she does this while singing the most evocative and mesmerizing arias, music that has you just as seduced. She is really naughty and would be the villain if she weren't so awesome. I suppose you feel a bit for Don José. But mostly you just want Carmen to keep at it—to stamp and whip her way through those fools, to roll her cigarettes, to lead the smugglers through the hills. *El Jaleo* is strong and complex like Carmen. You revel in its danger, in its rawness, in its mischief. Bizet's opera was far too scandalous for bourgeois Paris when it was first performed in 1875, but it was a triumph in the United States. Like the opera, Sargent and his paintings strangely ended up just where they were best appreciated, the nation he barely knew, but the nation that his grand paintings came to define.

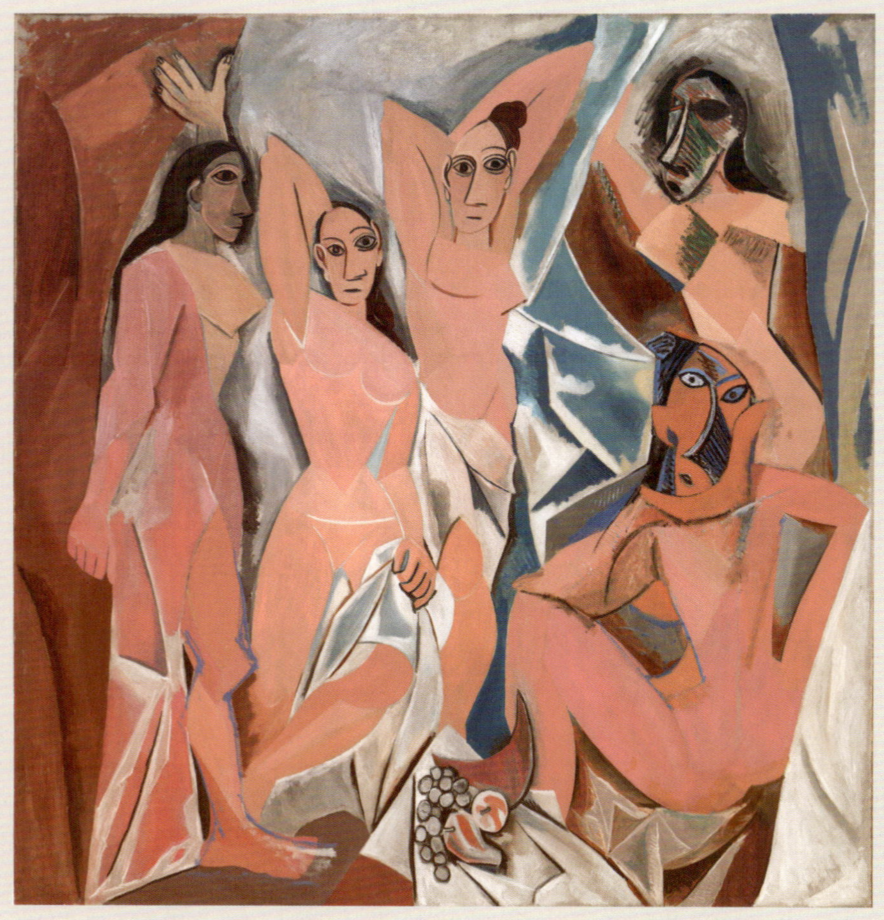

FIG. 20.1 Pablo Picasso, *Les Demoiselles d'Avignon*, 1907. Museum of Modern Art, New York City. Oil on canvas, 243.9 × 233.7 cm.

Picasso, *Les Demoiselles d'Avignon*

1907

MODERN ART

We started with the powerful and spectacular red bulls of Altamira hovering above our heads, bellowing and braying, leaping and sleeping on the ceiling of the limestone cave (Fig. 1.1). When the twentieth-century Spanish artist Pablo Picasso (1881–1973) learned of these 12,500 BCE Spanish paintings, he was shaken. "None of us is capable of painting like this," he is reported to have said. Or, more famously, "After Altamira, all is decadence."

Picasso was clearly inspired by the constellation of painted bulls. He worked through his reactions and responses to Altamira most famously in his series, *The Bull* (Figs. 20.2–20.5). Each snapshot deconstructs the beast, reducing its bovine body to more angular and abstracted geometrical shapes. He leaves us with very little, just a ghostly shell made up of simple, stark lines. Picasso produced the bull series a good forty years after *Les Demoiselles d'Avignon* (Fig. 20.1). But it is clear that his desire to unearth the most essential meaning of line and shape was already on his mind, on his canvas, as early as 1907, and it is possible that some of those desires were shaped by Altamira.

Red bulls and bright-pink ladies, forms strewn across a strange canvas without perspective, without an obvious narrative. We know generally where the figures are supposed to be. The bulls are in some unspecified field. The women are prostitutes, in a Spanish brothel, on a street called Avignon. We know that their stares, uncomfortable and frozen, are responses to the fact that someone has entered their space—a man on the hunt, whose arrival signals that a fight is about

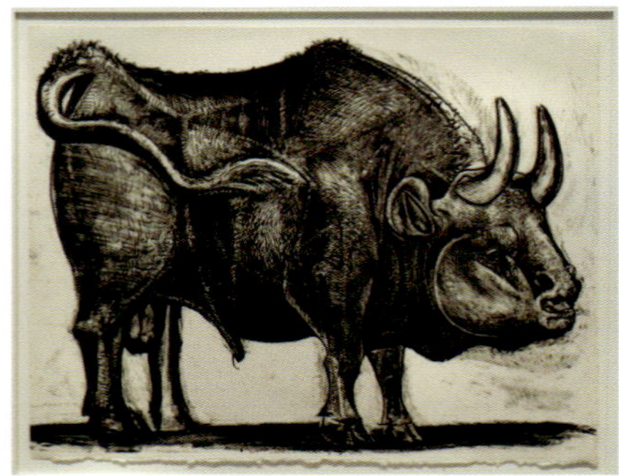

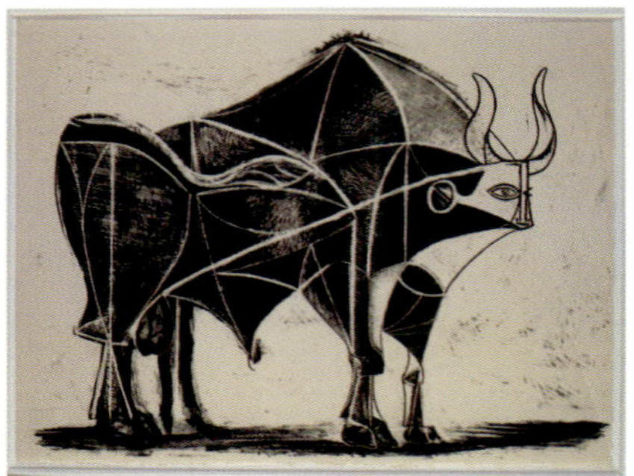

FIG. 20.2 Pablo Picasso, *The Bull*, state I, 1946. Private Collection. Lithograph. 32.6 × 44.4 cm.

FIG. 20.3 Pablo Picasso, *The Bull*, state V, 1946. Musée National Picasso, Paris. Lithograph, 32.6 × 44.4 cm.

to ensue. Some figures pause or pose. Others curl themselves into strange balls. The massive forms of the bulls surround you and engulf you in a spectacular and intimidating way. So do Picasso's ladies. Like the bulls, they hang aggressively above you, tall and tremendous obelisks that paradoxically threaten and repel even as they beckon. The tense relationship with the viewer also characterizes the interactions among the women, who are oddly disconnected from one another.

It might seem too broad, too capricious, to compare these two monuments separated by 15,000 years. But the comparison works for Picasso because he was voracious about art and its broadest history. He studied, consumed, and embraced everything from prehistoric bulls to the great masters to the work of his contemporaries. *Les Demoiselles d'Avignon* is a manifestation of his comprehensive sense of the history of art. It is almost an ode to the fact that styles and subjects change over time, and yet that beneath all of those shifts, something more stable exists: Art. Painted bulls, painted prostitutes—these are ultimately making the same point, that Art is potent, all-consuming, immutable, and eternal, even tying us back to our earliest ancestral artists.

Because there is no narrative, because the women do not interact with one another, it is not entirely clear where the painting begins or ends. One possible starting point is the woman at the far left of the composition. She is leading us

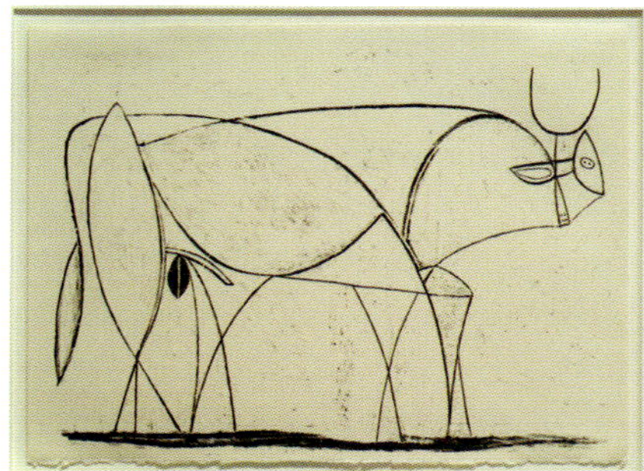

FIG. 20.4 Pablo Picasso, *The Bull,* state IX, 1946. Private Collection. Lithograph. 32.6 × 44.4 cm.

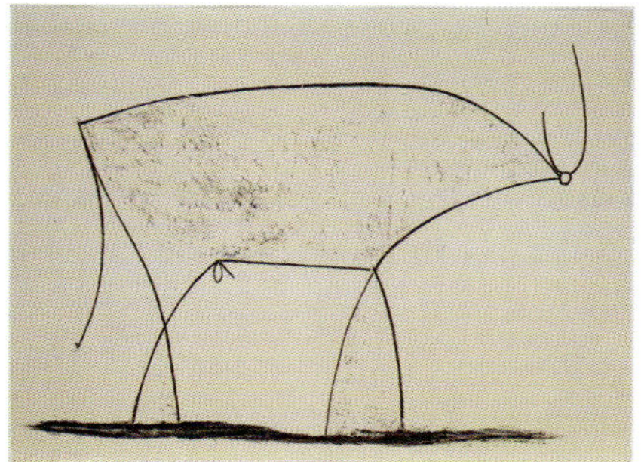

FIG. 20.5 Pablo Picasso, *The Bull,* state XI, 1946. Musée National Picasso, Paris. Lithograph, 32.7 × 44.4 cm.

into the room, holding back a heavy, sepia-colored curtain so that we too may enter, so that we may see what lies in that hidden or concealed shallow space. We can follow her progression from outside to inside, from left to right. Her role as the instigator is quite nice too because she reminds us of the art of ancient Egypt. In a way, she is like the earliest chapter in a proverbial art history textbook. Picasso is thus giving us an art history lesson in his painting, which moves from Egyptian to modern art. The strict profile of her lower body combined with a three-quarter view of the torso is a typical construction in Egyptian reliefs and wall paintings.

Picasso borrows that typical impassive facial expression—the short mouth, deep eyes, striking nose, dramatically arching eyebrows. His lady's hair drapes over her back in almost the same fluid, black, and solid form as in the Egyptian paintings. And although Picasso's Egyptian is missing a headdress, her strangely extended left arm seems to serve that very purpose. The full fingers of her splayed hand almost look like a bizarre outgrowth rather than a natural extension of her body—like a fascinator made of fingers. And it is this eerie gesture that opens the room, that allows us to see what hides behind the curtain. Her other arm participates in this sense of movement. It is straight as an arrow, heavy and blocky. It looks like a pendulum, as though it is about to start swinging from left to right, mirroring her forceful entry, drawing us also into that inner sanctum with purpose.

She has the weight and power of a grandfather clock, with her arm seemingly swinging rhythmically, marking time as we march along, an eternal and unspecified time, that same eternal time that we associate with the reliefs of Egypt. Space is particularly difficult to decipher. As the brilliant art historian Leo Steinberg wrote: "The aim is to express the recession of this upper flap [of the curtain] not through linear or aerial perspective, not by way of color or physical clues such as overlaps, but through the suasion of gesture, the supposed necessity of omitted arm between head and hand—a saccadic leap offered only to our anatomic intuition." If I may translate, Picasso does not use traditional painting techniques of perspective, so privileged in art from the Renaissance until the Impressionists. Nor does he use color to indicate depth. Rather, he is using gestures. We read the gap between the head and hand as an indication that there is a space, a depth, that exists between body and curtain. This is the way Picasso tells his story, with static forms and ritualized gestures that must be read and deciphered, like hieroglyphs, like a sentence missing words that must be filled in to make sense.

Nothing is utterly stable, of course. Those patient, static bodies from Egyptian art only provide a template, which Picasso starts to challenge even in the body of this same woman. Her right leg is stepping, but then what is that form behind the leg, that shattered mass of jagged pink shards? Is this an anticipation of Duchamp's *Nude Descending a Staircase (No. 2)*, with shapes indicating a disconnected movement, one that flows from left to right? Is it a leg, then? It does have the forms of a thigh, a hamstring, a tibia, a shin, a calf. The deconstruction of those forms might suggest fluidity, speed, or flight. Yet it is confusing because, if we just look at the top of the right leg, it looks like she has two right legs. So is this a representation of her right leg when it is or was moving? Are we meant to understand that we are toggling between movement and stasis? Or is stasis rejected altogether? Even the clearly established, confidently stepping right leg starts losing its established form as the blue outlines shake and quiver and miss their mark, cutting off parts of the leg, running past the toes.

Her body is changeable and so once was her gender. In fact, originally she was a man in a suit (Fig. 20.6). This metamorphosis took Picasso many months and

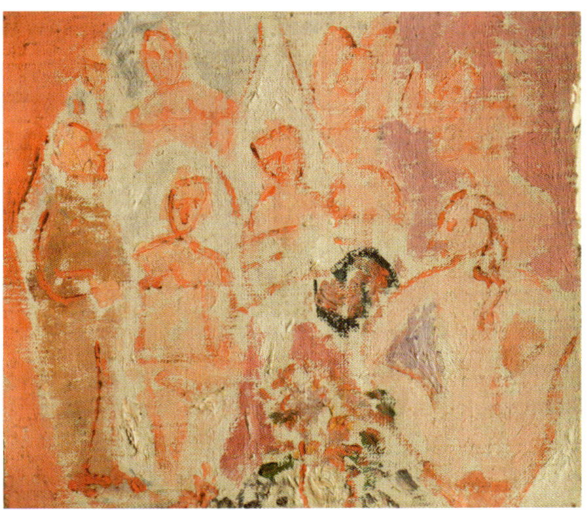

FIG. 20.6 Pablo Picasso, *Study for Les Demoiselles
D'Avignon,* 1907. Museum of Modern Art, New York.
Oil on canvas, 19.05 × 20.32 cm.

many sketchbooks.* There are hundreds of manifestations of this painting. There are rough sketches in just about every variety—in oil paint, pastel, watercolor, and lots in ink and pencil. Picasso was exploring every variety of his masterpiece from stick-figures to fleshy forms, just as he did later with the bulls. Picasso started his process of finding the perfect form of his vision sometime in the beginning of 1907. And it consumed him until the summer of that same year. He must have been swimming in sketches, daunted and frustrated by the process that had taken on a life of its own. On the cover of one of his sketchbooks Picasso wrote the words "*Je suis le cahier*" (I am the notebook). It had become its own entity, reminding Picasso of the work to be done, of the idea not yet formed. He was constantly revisiting and revising his ideas. The man at the left went through

* For an introduction to these many sketches, see "*Les Demoiselles d'Avignon:* Conserving a Modern Masterpiece," Museum of Modern Art, www.moma.org/explore/conservation/demoiselles/history _2_b.html.

many drafts before finally becoming a woman. Sometimes he carries a skull, sometimes a skull and a book. At times he has a long body and a blank face. In others he is a stocky youth with close-cropped hair, not unlike Picasso himself, as some scholars have pointed out.

The scholar Alfred Barr, writing in 1939, was the first to suggest that the man in the suit was a medical student who was meant to represent mortality and even morality. The skull was supposed to represent a *memento mori,* thus linking the activities of the women in the brothel with death, sex with danger. Even when the student figure did not carry the skull, he was a symbol of virtue and knowledge. Sometimes a second figure served as his opposite. Surrounded by food and drink and women, this figure represented vice and animal instincts, according to Barr. In the 1970s, Steinberg challenged Barr's moralizing, allegorical interpretation of the earlier sketches, pointing out that it makes little sense that Picasso (of all people) would link sex and sin. Picasso was a proud roué throughout his life. Steinberg's suggestion was that, instead, the sketches were trying to represent two responses to the undeniable and "indestructible claims of sex."

Then Picasso drops the men altogether. And when he does, he focuses on the women. By doing so, he focuses on us focusing on them. We know this is not a representation of "ladies," despite the title, which is clearly ironic. This is a brothel, but the men—both the student who transforms into a woman and the sailor that disappears—are not simply clients. They look at the women just as we look at the painting. They are spectators. Their role in the painting was to express the fact that these women are on display; they are to be seen and studied and consumed.

By removing the painted spectators, Picasso intensifies that exchange altogether. We are now in the role of those clothed men. We have lost our intermediaries, and no one is there to soften the blow. The impact is quite upsetting. The women are confrontational and angular, powerful and raw. The two central women rest their heads on their arms. But the effect is far from soft and comforting. The jagged angularity of the forms has the softness of a knife's edge, of a shard of glass. White bedsheets fall in angular, piercing folds. Fruit set out to tempt and welcome the visitor is pushed up into our faces. These strange and unnatural forms hover and threaten rather than tempt and please. The pear is bizarre and misshapen. The melon wedge is a pointed scythe. And in the background the strange blue and white forms suggest the reflections of a mirror or that we are looking at a window that has been shattered.

The confrontation is frightening. It is meant to be. When Picasso's contemporaries saw the piece, they were perplexed and appalled. The artist Henri Matisse, who was older and far more established than Picasso, called the painting an "outrage, an attempt to ridicule the modern movement" and "an audacious hoax." Georges Braque said that seeing the painting was akin to "drinking gasoline." Gertrude Stein also commented on the painting. She may not have loved the piece exactly, but then it was not a painting to be loved. It was a piece to be feared. When Stein wrote about the piece, she did so through the mouthpiece of her lover, Alice B. Toklas: "Against the wall was an enormous picture, a strange picture of light and dark colors, that is all I can say, of a group, an enormous group…all of it rather frightening. Picasso and Gertrude stood together talking. I stood back and looked. I cannot say I realized anything but I felt there was something painful and beautiful there and oppressive but imprisoned."

It is shocking. But it is not new to see women in this position, in this painted prison. Manet also introduces us to a bedchamber with an unclothed woman, Olympia, a prostitute, who tempts as she rejects (Fig. 18.4). Picasso knew this painting well. An alluring flower in her hair is balanced and counteracted by that left hand. They are similar shapes, flower and hand. One is welcoming. One is a firm no. The proffered gift, another set of flowers, presumably from a client, is opened for Olympia's pleasure. She ignores it altogether and focuses on us, just like the women in the Picasso. The formal similarities are compelling—a heavy drawn-back curtain in the upper left-hand corner, dirty red tones, crisp white untucked bedsheets, a woman entering from another curtain in the background, and, in the lower right-hand corner, spooky imbalanced eyes from a cat—a cat in a cathouse, no less.

Olympia looks a great deal like the woman just to the right of the Egyptianizing figure. Tightly drawn mouths; knowing, heavy-lidded eyes; unfurrowed brow. Both have dark-brown hair parted on the side and cascading over their left shoulders. Both hold up their heads in the same awkward angle. They are also both reclining. This is not immediately obvious. Why would it be? The woman

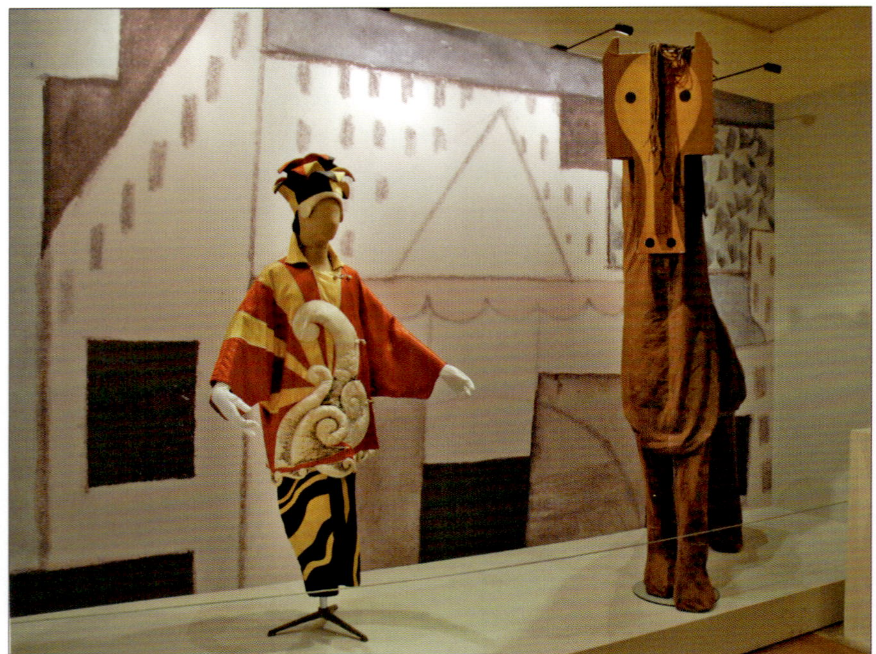

FIG. 20.7 Pablo Picasso, costumes from the ballet *Parade,* Chinese conjurer and horse, original design 1916–1917.

in the Picasso is flanked by two women that are standing—the Egyptianizing woman and the central woman. Nor does the flat background suggest that she is on her back. But we must look at her legs, which bend backward as though she is floating. This is because she is leaning back, just without the chair or bed and without the recession in space. The idea of upturning a reclining woman may not seem all that shocking, but it packs a punch. Instead of a submissive courtesan, passive and on offer, she springs up, she ricochets into our space, like that boomerang-shaped melon. She is threatening in the same way as that pile of fruit—seemingly there for our pleasure but strangely aggressive and thrown into our faces, instead of receding naturalistically and organically.

The aggression of that rewritten Manet is reflected and heightened as we move through the painting, continuing our progress from left to right. The central

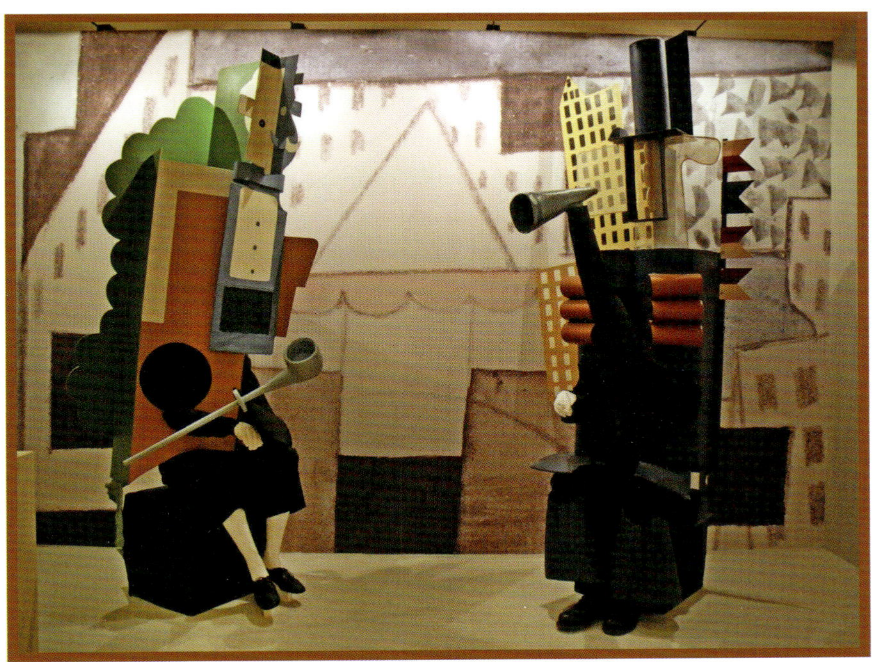

FIG. 20.8 Pablo Picasso, costumes from the ballet *Parade*, French manager (left) and American manager (right), original design 1916–1917.

woman might be a cool, breezy reference to paintings like Rubens's *Judgment of Paris* (ca. 1636). Minerva, with her arms in the sky, hopes to win the battle of the bulging beauties. Minerva is doing her best to get Paris's attention, giving him the sexy side eye. Poor thing has to work extra hard. Paris's eye seems to have already alighted elsewhere, on fair Aphrodite. Paris's next choice would probably be Juno, who is accompanied by a splendid peacock that seems ready to kiss Paris's toe. The peacock is an alluring animal. The image of a screaming green gorgon face on a shield next to Minerva is not. The centrally placed woman in the Picasso painting might have been in a soft and sexy pose, as in the Rubens. Instead, Picasso surrounds her with distortion and aggression. She also is next to a gorgonlike head. While Minerva's gorgon is secondary, Picasso's is essential and lords over the scene, watching carefully, even as one of her eyes is empty.

There are ways in which we might have read the central figure as having the confidence and power of the Nike of Samothrace, with those similarly fluttering garments affixed to her legs and her arms pulled back like the statue's beautiful wings (Fig. 4.1). Or we could have seen her in the middle of a dance, arms thrown back and hair pulled tight, in a bun, like a ballerina. But she is ultimately, as Stein described, in a painful, beautiful, and oppressive prison.

Ballet does seem to be part of the conversation. Picasso was quite enamored of ballerinas. Throughout his life he did paintings inspired by the movements of dancers, as in *La Danse*, which shows a nude dancer with her arms splayed out in a moment of strange inelegance (1925). He also designed many sets for ballets, such as *Parade* in 1917.* This one-act piece was a strange story about a group of circus artists trying to attract an audience for their show. Erik Satie wrote the music, and his collaborator Jean Cocteau added a few less traditional instruments, including a typewriter, a foghorn, milk bottles, and a pistol. Sometimes there was no music at all, as in the solo by the horse. The choreography was by Sergei Diaghilev's protégé Léonide Massine. Picasso did the designs. He did the sets, the fanciful costumes, and a massive curtain, showing the circus characters eating before their show.

During the ballet's premiere, Picasso spent a lot of time backstage where he was supposedly helping the stagehands but more likely getting close to the alluring Russian ballerina Olga Khoklova, whom he would soon marry. The creation of the piece was a tremendous combination of artistic visionaries. Public reception was not so keen, however, and the debut ended in huge scandal, lots of name-calling, and the composer Satie being thrown in jail for a brief stint.

It is interesting to consider the themes in *Demoiselles* having a three-dimensional life in *Parade*. Curtains opening and closing; a group of individuals calling for an audience, ready to be on display; women like ballerinas, moving in a space that recedes in fits and starts; angular forms that coalesce through abstracted shards to create fully formed bodies. In *Parade*, some of the dancers were to move with a beautiful angularity, mirroring the dissonant music. Some of the dancers were

---

* For a brief video with segments of *Parade*, see Europa Danse, "Picasso et la Danse," www.you tube.com/watch?v=_ChqīTyonyE.

more costume than body, like the happy horse or the managers who had to wear costumes that were over ten feet tall (Figs. 20.7 and 20.8). These, as you might imagine, were detested by the dancers. All of those years of training just to be covered up and told to stomp around. But Picasso is showing a metamorphosis, from man to mask. The managers are manipulators. The manager tells you to go to the show. He is all, in the case of the American manager, loud megaphones and massive skyscrapers (on his back). He doesn't really have a face. He is there to entreat you into paying a fee for the show, which of course you have done because you are watching the show. A dancer puts on a costume. A man puts on a mask. And before you know it, the mask takes over, and the mask is all you can see.

Masks are crucial in *Les Demoiselles d'Avignon*. Picasso went through untold notebooks trying to find the perfect positions for his painting, excising the men and pushing forward the women as he did. He was still wrestling with the painting after six months. We can see that he was looking at Manet's *Olympia*, studying it in the Louvre. And it is inevitable that he was also studying the painting placed right next to the *Olympia*, the seductive *La Grande Odalisque* by Ingres. She turns around to see her unnamed visitor, showing her sinuous back and her legs that are alluringly intertwined. *Les Demoiselles* also has a woman twisting around. She shows her triangular, angular back to the viewer, with her legs splayed in a crass squat. Her head twists around to reveal a face not of porcelain perfection and symmetry but of harsh imbalances, a broken jaw, catawampus eyes, a nose that curves vigorously like the moon-shaped melon below.

In March 1907 Picasso added a new museum to his list, the Musée d'Ethnographie du Trocadéro. There he studied the African masks, pieces brought to Paris as a result of the expanding French Empire. Fascination with the aesthetics of non-Western culture was prominent throughout artistic circles in France. Gauguin, for example, relished the untouched and erotic aspect of the French colony of Tahiti, most of which was his own fantasy. Orientalism at its worst. Picasso was inspired by the frightful qualities of these masks. When he visited the Trocadéro in 1907, he hated it, telling his friend André Malraux that it was "disgusting. A flea market. Stinking. I was alone. I wanted to get out. But I stayed." He stayed because, as he later explained, he was somehow enchanted by the pieces: "The masks weren't sculpture like other sculptures. Not at all. They were magical objects.... The [Africans] were against everything; against unknown, dangerous spirits.... I too believe that everything is unknown and hostile! Everything!... All those fetishes had the same purpose. They were weapons to help people escape the power of the spirits and become free.... *Les Demoiselles d'Avignon* must have come to me that day, not because of the forms but because it was my first exorcizing picture."

For Picasso, these talismans from an ancient tradition and an unknown, distant land were haunting and haunted. It was, according to the artist, their frenetic spiritual energies that unlocked his inspiration, helped him overcome his demons and finish the painting. Of course Picasso was also quoted as having said that to finish a picture meant killing it, ridding it of its soul. But as much as the *Demoiselles* could ever come to completion, this was it, in June 1907, when Picasso put masks on the squatting woman and the last lady entering the room. They stare at us, unblinking and grim, jagged and aggressive. These masks do not suggest seduction (which is how Gauguin would have made them). Picasso does not show the undeniably symmetrical and contemplative qualities of African masks. Nor is Picasso trying to play the ethnographer by imitating masks from a particular tribe. No, he is trying to create an aura of fear, of savagery, of a visceral spirituality that cannot be explained or contained. His masks make one think of Joseph Conrad's novella *Heart of Darkness*, written in 1899 and published in 1902. The narrator Marlow describes Kurtz, a European who trades ivory in African colonies: "He cried in a whisper at some image, at some vision,—he cried out twice, a cry that was no more than a breath—'The horror! The horror!'"

After reading the masks on the right side of the composition, those faces of aggression and shock, the other faces also look masklike. The Egyptianizing woman at the left seems to look like she is wearing a mask now. The imperturbable faces of the two central women might have just seemed simple and abstract. Yet their static asymmetry suggests that they might also be wearing a type of mask—blank stares, simple lines, unmodulated skin tones. It is a mask-face that Picasso had used before, actually, in his portrait of Gertrude Stein, the same author that had registered the fear and horror that *Demoiselles* evoked in the viewer (Fig. 20.9).

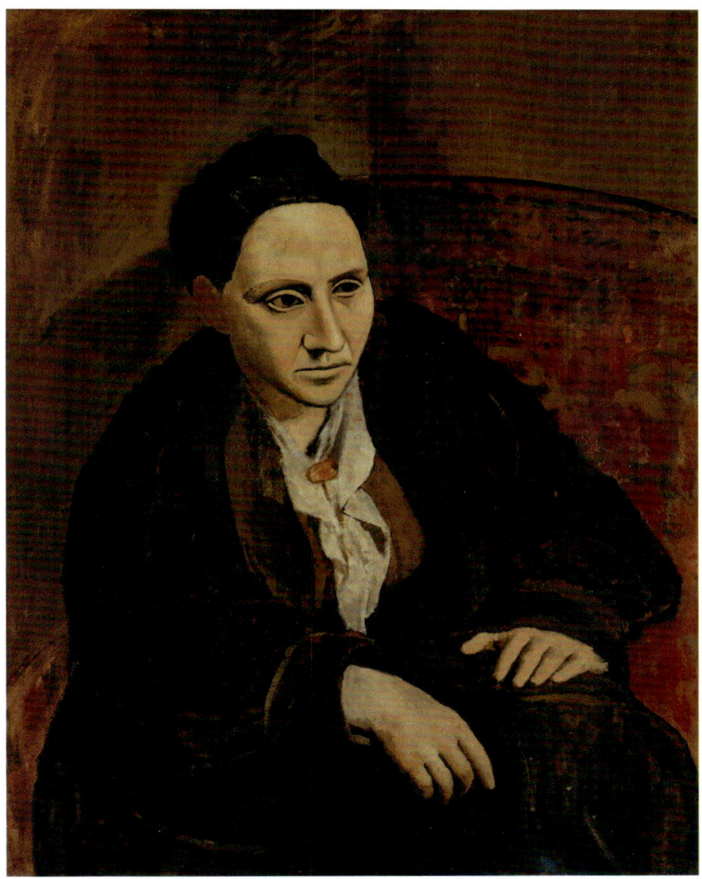

FIG. 20.9 Pablo Picasso, *Gertrude Stein*, 1906. Metropolitan Museum of Art, New York. Oil on canvas, 100 × 81.3 cm.

Stein moved to Paris in 1903 after a miserable stint in medical school at Johns Hopkins, to live with her brother Leo. A year later the siblings' elder brother, Michael, told them that their trust fund was flush, and thus they became a power couple in the collecting world. In the first year they bought paintings by Gauguin, Cézanne, and Renoir. By 1906 they had added Bonnard, Matisse, Toulouse-Lautrec, and Picasso. It was actually rather bold to pay for a Picasso because he was not terribly well known. But they did, which shows their tremendous perspicacity as collectors.

It was even bolder to have him paint a portrait, as he did for Gertrude. Picasso was not ideal as a portraitist. In her writings Stein admitted that neither she nor Picasso was particularly keen about the project. He hadn't done a portrait since he was sixteen, and she was forced to pose for the painting ninety times, until he painted out her head and exclaimed irritably, "I can't see you anymore when I look." He returned a few months later after a trip to Spain and finished her face. That was in 1906. Like his experience with *Les Demoiselles*, Picasso had to have a moment of exasperation and rage. He had to step away. He needed to cleanse his mental palette, visiting sites in his homeland, perhaps even a prehistoric cave or two. And then he could return.

But he returned with something different, a mask for a face. An image of timelessness, hinting at the distant past and a timeless future. A visitor to the Stein salon commented that she did not look like the portrait. Picasso replied, "She will." It is a knotty exchange. Portraits are supposed to look like the sitter, not the other way around. But Picasso is not interested in surfaces or appearances. Facial features are both malleable and unstable—we smile when we aren't happy, we get wrinkles even when we don't want them. Faces are false. A mask may seem false, but it reveals a larger truth. Picasso said, "Art is the lie that makes us realize the truth."

The truth about Stein is that years after the painting, years after she lived and wrote, the painting lives on, and it is associated with her. As such she does look like the painting; she came to look like the painting because Picasso painted her that way on the canvas and on our collective consciousness. Stein sits like a shaded stone, like an immovable, unforgettable monolith. Wise, knowing, and sadly alone. Years later, in 1913, Leo trashed his sister's writings, calling them "abominable." The siblings divided their beautiful collection—he took the Renoirs and she got the Picassos and the Matisses. Only once did the two siblings see each other again, in 1919. Leo simply tipped his hat to Gertrude as he drove by in his Ford. (If that story doesn't make you want to hug a sibling, I don't know what will.)

Stein's portrait and *Les Demoiselles d'Avignon* have been categorized as the earliest iterations of Cubism. Cubism is one of those art historical terms that we have to handle with care. Many of the phrases associated with artistic movements are problematic because they are later than the actual period they describe. Often they have pejorative or political roots. For example, we love Baroque art—Caravaggio, Bernini, Velázquez. But "Baroque" means "rough or imperfect pearl," in other words bizarre. Neoclassical scholars, writing some one hundred years after our beloved Baroque, gave us—and them—that name as a means of distancing themselves from what they saw as excessive and ridiculous. Gothic, Romantic—these were all later interpretations, and often derogatory ones at that.

The term Cubism was used as early as 1908 by the critic Louis Vauxcelles after seeing paintings by Georges Braque, such as *Viaduct at L'Estaque.* Cubism was not as charged as other art historical terms. In fact, it was descriptive and factual. Braque uses lots of flattened cubes to construct what is still a representational image. We see houses and an aqueduct. The blocky shapes depict space, mass, and volume that denies the flatness of the forms and the flatness of the canvas. The term "Cubism" also differs from other art historical terminology because it was not a later label. In this way, the Cubists and the Impressionists are similar. The Impressionists were named after the title of Monet's early painting of Le Havre, *Impression, Sunrise,* right when it was first exhibited. But there is a rather significant difference between the Impressionists and the Cubists. The Cubists were not trying to start a cohesive movement. These artists weren't trying to make a political point or shake up the Parisian salon or accrue recognition. There was a special room at the Salon of the Independents in Paris in 1911 for the Cubist-style paintings. But they didn't need that exposure or even acceptance. In fact, Picasso didn't even submit a painting for that exhibition. He wasn't painting for or against a salon; he was painting for himself and for the world.

He had the freedom to do just that because he had a patron for whom he also painted, Daniel-Henry Kahnweiler. Believing firmly in the purpose of the main artists associated with the movement—Braque, Gris, Léger, and, of course, Picasso—Kahnweiler guaranteed each of these artists an annual income. In exchange he had the exclusive right to buy their works and then sell them to a small circle of special clients. Kahnweiler took care of the artists, visiting them, selling their works, paying for their costs of living and materials. He recorded and catalogued their progress and held exhibitions both in Europe and abroad. Picasso is quoted as having said, "What would have become of us if Kahnweiler hadn't had a business sense?"

Of course, Kahnweiler's power was in his purse, but it was also in his ability to read the moment, to select and promote a style that would resonate with the most forward thinkers. He nurtured the artists, but he also nurtured the audience, basically telling them who and what they should be liking or buying and why. In essence it is he, not Picasso, that created Cubism. Kahnweiler decided that *Les Demoiselles d'Avignon* was the first cubist painting, even though there are actually few cubes in the painting. Picasso was a willing participant. He did not paint *Les Demoiselles* with any intention of being a Cubist artist or even the originator of the movement. Yet he does not seem to have had any problem accepting that role. His representation of Kahnweiler, his remarkable patron, is all cubes and grays and shifting perspectives. It is a portrait of Kahnweiler as an expression or representation of this artistic movement, more as an embodiment of Cubism than any kind of representation of the collector's actual features. His face, his person is consumed and defined by the very cubes that he championed so aggressively.

Picasso did not stick with Cubism for long. He did not need a style or a movement. Picasso was Picasso. He may not have balked at being called the inventor of Cubism, and why should he? Add that to the pile of accolades he had been accruing since the age of ten, when he was declared a prodigy. He was a narcissus and a chameleon. Cubism may have been used to define a set of paintings, but it would not define him.

Consider the fact that, by the time Picasso painted *Les Demoiselles*, he was only twenty-six and had already worked through two whole phases of style—a Blue Period and a Rose Period. From scenes of isolation and poverty suffused with tones of blues and grays, Picasso shifted his focus toward acrobats and harlequins. Orange and pink shades dominated, brighter hues that provided a warmer, less depressed mood, even if the figures remained alone, dreamy, aimless, lost. Before working on these particular styles, Picasso had also tried his hand at far less abstract styles. You might not name Picasso as the artist behind *The First Communion* (1896), housed in the Museu Picasso in Barcelona. He had the ability to present the most standardized, academic painting—formal brushstrokes, a

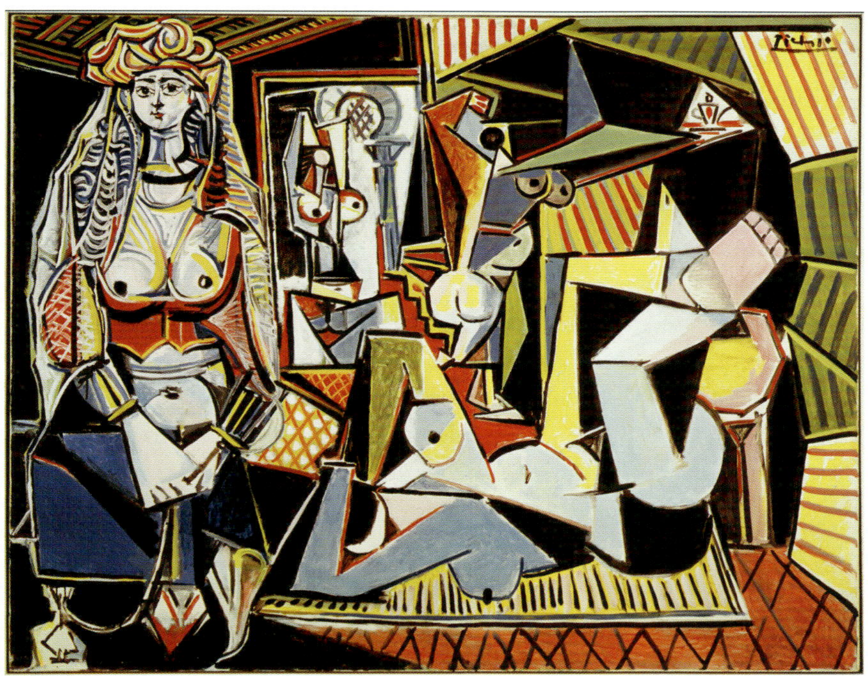

FIG. 20.10 Pablo Picasso, *The Women of Algiers*, 1955. Private collection. Oil on canvas, 114 × 146 cm.

traditional lens focused on the central figures, a sense of clear and articulated recession into space. It was painting like this that got the young Picasso admitted to the School of Fine Arts in Barcelona at the age of thirteen.

At sixteen he moved to Madrid's famous Academy of San Fernando. There he started to experiment with different styles. Academic realism shifted to symbolism and pointillism. He also started skipping class. What took the other students months to complete, Picasso could whip out in a few days. By 1900 Picasso had moved to Paris and was producing his own works with his own voice. But that voice was never particularly stable. Just consider how he shifts his brush from *The First Communion* to *Les Demoiselles* to *The Women of Algiers* (Fig. 20.10).

There is little connecting these three. It would be perverse to make a connection between Picasso's pure and penitent sister and the main woman in the painting of *The Women of Algiers*. They both wear similar headgear, a thick wreath with a cascading veil. But the woman in the later painting is obviously not a religious woman. Her altar is a splayed recumbent nude on a yellow mat with stripes. That nude appears to be repeated in a painting (or perhaps a mirror) that sits in the center of the composition, and again in what might be a sculpture. Bodies, or bits of deconstructed bodies, repeat and reflect in a room of shattered forms that seem to be toppling down around us, and around her. Like *Les Demoiselles*, the background is composed of shards and jagged, geometrical bits. Here too abstracted bodies stare at us without any sense of decorum or modesty, with their arms tucked behind their heads. But there really aren't many heads here. The faces and masks of *Les Demoiselles* are completely missing. The faces of these women are irrelevant. The scene is also more ebullient than the *Demoiselles*. The broken, tumbling, bricklike blocks are fun. Those red and blue lines are animated and vibrant. The various greens, warm reds, sunny yellows, baby blues, and bright pinks are all welcoming. Although painted in similar pinks and light blues, *Les Demoiselles* look frightened and frightening. They will serve or address us because they have little choice. This woman of Algiers seems quite confident. She seems to be even smiling a bit, welcoming you into her room. It almost looks like she could be the same woman offering herself on the yellow mat, posing for us in the painting or in the mirror, and dashing off to get us what appears to be a coffee in the distance.

The Women of Algiers was inspired by the painting of the same name by the earlier Romantic artist Eugène Delacroix. 1834 meets 1955. By comparing the two it is evident that the woman on the left is not the same person repeated in different versions. Instead, the woman on the left is accompanied by three other women. One lady (in green silk pants) sits on a yellow mat with stripes. The woman at the far right twists as she walks out of the room. And one woman sits in the sight line of a mirror that is hanging on the wall. We can also now understand Picasso's rough-and-tumble room as a series of corners and niches, rugs and curtains. He borrows and tweaks and stylizes the women, the room, and even the title right out of the Delacroix. We have seen Picasso consuming styles and artists of every variety—Manet, Ingres, Delacroix, traditional Academic style, the pointillism of Seurat, Rubens.

In 1987 the art historian John Richardson connected *Les Demoiselles* to El Greco's frenetic *The Vision of Saint John* (1608–14), a painting that Picasso was known to have seen while in Paris. Richardson called *Les Demoiselles* the "Apocalyptic Whorehouse," with "prostitutes who have the psychic energy and the redemptive power of The Fifth Seal." He even argued that Picasso placed himself in the role of Saint John, ordaining this vision of the end of the world. Whether or not you accept this argument, the fact remains that Picasso saw it all, studied it all, and painted it in some form or other on the canvas. His remarkable ability to consume and digest so many different inspirations is remarkable and shows his extraordinary gifts. In Picasso's own words (reused by Steve Jobs): "Good artists copy, great artists steal." Not surprisingly, however, this skill was less welcome among his contemporaries. His capacity for borrowing ideas unnerved many of his colleagues, who started disinviting him from their studios.

Henri Matisse (1869–1954) was one such artist. His splendid painting *Le Bonheur de Vivre* has its own relationship to the later *Demoiselles* (Fig. 20.11). Matisse's arcadia is sensual and vibrant. Joyous figures dance and lounge and play pipes. Lines are sinuous and unstable, blocks of colors randomly shift and morph, as do bodies that seamlessly blend together, like the purple lovers. Colors are fantastical, unnatural—an orange musician, green friends. And then there is a lady in yellow with her hair and arms pulled back and someone squatting nearby. Matisse saw the connection between his work and Picasso's. He was annoyed. He wrote to his daughter, saying, "I have not seen Picasso for years. I don't care to see him again…he is a bandit waiting in ambush." But that animosity changed into a deep respect and eventually friendship. By 1940 they were meeting regularly, as colleagues and as friends. In fact, *The Women of Algiers* was an homage to Matisse, painted just after the older artist's death.

It is fascinating to trace Picasso's many stylistic meanderings. *Les Demoiselles* is its own incarnation, an expression of his ability to shift from one style to the next. In fact, one of the greatest criticisms of the piece was that the style was unstable and disjointed. Kahnweiler himself explained that inconsistency, almost in an apology, by saying that the prophetic energy demanded a sacrifice of internal unity. The same was repeated by the scholar Robert Rosenblum: "The irrepressible energy behind its creation demanded a vocabulary of change and impulse

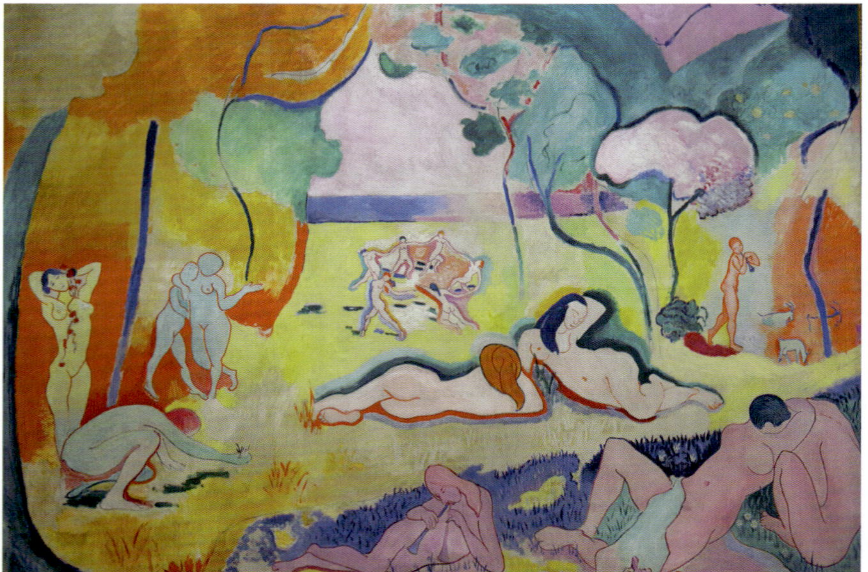

FIG. 20.11 Henri Matisse, *Le Bonheur de Vivre*, 1905–1906. Barnes Foundation, Philadelphia. Oil on canvas, 176.5 × 240.7 cm.

rather than of measured statement in a style already articulated. The breathless tempo of this pregnant historical moment virtually obligated its first masterpiece to carry within itself the very process of artistic evolution." But Picasso was almost already post-style, it would seem. In later anecdotes he expressed the fact that art is not slave to style. In one account he said: "When you draw a head you must draw like that head.... Take a tree. At the foot of the tree there is a goat, and beside the goat is a little girl tending the goat. Well, you need a different drawing for each. The goat is round, the little girl is square, and the tree is a tree. And yet people draw all three in the same way. That is false. Each should be drawn in a completely different way." The subject determines the style, he says. Unity of purpose is one thing. The idea has to be sound. Style is secondary and can be (should be) changed. In another anecdote, Picasso goes to visit his friend Max Jacob in the middle of the night. Picasso allegedly called out to his friend,

"Hey, Max, what are you doing?" Jacob replied to say, "I am searching for a style." Picasso's pithy reply? "There's no such thing."

Styles, like faces, change over time. But art is ever-present. It inspires the prehistoric painters just as it inspires Picasso. We might retrace our path through other periods of art to see more sources of Picasso's inspiration. We might even see traces of medieval art, like stained glass windows or mosaics from Ravenna (Fig. 6.1). The sixth-century mosaics are cubist in the most literal way—tiny cubes are composed to represent forms and figures in a nonnaturalistic style. A conversation between Picasso's twentieth-century cubes and those of the anonymous, sixth-century artisans is compelling and bizarrely possible. One crucial difference is that the sixth-century artists were unknown and undocumented. Picasso talks. A lot. His thoughts and reflections are relevant, of course, but they are not final. If you returned to something you had made twenty years earlier, you might be eager to explain it in ways that are slightly embellished or even dismissive or confused.

When explaining the title for *Les Demoiselles* twenty years after its making, Picasso romanticized the matter: "You know very well that its name was 'The Brothel of Avignon' in the beginning. You know why? Avignon has always been for me a very familiar name, connected to my life. I was living around the corner from Avignon Street. It is there that I bought my paper, my watercolor supplies." But this recounting is slightly askew. The painting had no name. In 1910 it was still being called a series of different titles. *The Wild Men of Paris* was one, *Study by Picasso* was another. In fact, the first time that the name *Les Demoiselles d'Avignon* was used was in an article in 1912 by Picasso's friend André Salmon. Even as late as 1916 a series of different names was affiliated with the canvas—*Le Bordel philosophique, Le Bordel d'Avignon*. Picasso is known to have used *Las Chicas de Avignon*. But in 1933 he was quoted as saying that he hated the title altogether. No matter. Picasso's voice is only one among many, and his changing perspective is completely in line with his changing art-historical styles. He lived to be ninety. He saw it all, and he painted it all. The man was his own museum. I think that is what he meant when he said, "Give me a museum and I'll fill it." Or was he just being pompous and bragging about how prolific he was? Hard to say.

You and I might not be painters. We might not be able to write poetry or do a pirouette, play a scale on the piano or sing Puccini. But we are so lucky that there are people who do. Their gifts and charisma and talents feed us, even if those artists can barely feed themselves. Art is our humanity and our salvation. To "get it" we have to be critical. We need to look with intensity. We have to be aware of those historical strands of inspiration. We need to know Altamira, Ravenna, Rubens, Manet, and Matisse to know Picasso and to understand all that comes after him. We have to revisit great works of art and bring them into our daily and dusty existence. As Picasso said, "The purpose of art is washing the dust of daily life off our souls."

IMAGE CREDITS

FRONTISPIECE Edgar Degas, *Woman Viewed from Behind (Visit to a Museum)*. Collection of Mr. and Mrs. Paul Mellon. Courtesy National Gallery of Art, Washington.

FIG. 1.1 Bison (detail) in the reproduction of the Altamira caves. Photo: Album / Art Resource, New York.

FIG. 1.2 Bison painting in Altamira caves. Photo by Sergi Reboredo / Alamy Stock Photo.

FIG. 1.3 Replica of Upper Paleolithic Altamira cave paintings. Photo: National Geographic Creative / Alamy Stock Photo.

FIG. 1.4 Altamira cave map. Drawing by Sarah Cooper, based on sketch from *The Cave of Altamira*, by Matilde Múzquiz Pérez-Seoane, Federico Bernaldo de Quirós, Pedro A. Saura Ramos, et al. (Harry N. Abrams, 1999).

FIG. 1.5 Hands from Altamira Replica painting from Altamira. Photo: World History Archive/Alamy Stock photo.

FIG. 1.6 Hand paintings from Seminole Canyon. Photo by Zereshk. CC-BY-SA. 3.0.

FIG. 1.7 Buckhorn Saloon and Museum, San Antonio. Photo by Jeshua Mauldin.

FIG. 2.1 Lion leaping at the king's chariot. Stone panel from the North-West Palace of Ashurnasirpal II. Copyright © Trustees of the British Museum / Art Resource, New York.

FIG. 2.2 Stone panel from the North-West Palace showing Ashurnasirpal II as a warrior in a chariot. Copyright © Trustees of the British Museum / Art Resource, New York.

FIG. 2.3 Narmer Palette. Photo by Nicolas Perrault III. PD-US.

FIG. 2.4 British Museum Room 10, lion hunting. Photo by Matt Neale. CC Attribution 2.0 Generic.

FIG. 2.5 Sculpted reliefs depicting Ashurbanipal hunting lions, gypsum hall relief for the North Palace of Nineveh. Photo by Carole Raddato. CC-BY-SA 2.0 Generic.

FIG. 2.6 King Ashurnasirpal shown in a dual reception at the Sacred Tree. Photo: World History Archive/AlamyStock photo.

FIG. 2.7 Lamassu. Metropolitan Museum of Art, Gift of John D. Rockefeller Jr. CCO 1.0.

FIG. 2.8 Ivory plaque of lioness devouring boy. Copyright © Trustees of the British Museum / Art Resource, New York.

FIG. 3.1 Euphronios krater front. Photo: Scala / Ministero per i Beni e le Attività Culturali / Art Resource, New York.

FIG. 3.2 Greece Athens National Archaeological Museum. Anavysos Kouros. Photo: Realy Easy Star/Alamy Stock Photo.

FIG. 3.3 Terracotta krater. Metropolitan Museum of Art, Gift of John D. Rockefeller Jr. CCO 1.0.

FIG. 3.4 Inside of the Greek Tomb of the Diver. Photo: Museo Pics, Paul Williams / Alamy Stock Photo.

FIG. 3.5 Euphronios krater back. Photo: Scala / Ministero per i Beni e le Attività Culturali / Art Resource, New York.

FIG. 3.6 Black figure amphora with Ajax and Achilles playing a game. Photo: Scala / Art Resource, New York.

FIG. 3.7 Caravaggio, *The Deposition*. Photo: Scala / Art Resource, New York.

FIG. 4.1 Nike of Samothrace. Photo by Marie-Lan Nguyen. PD-US.

FIG. 4.2 Nike of Samothrace in boat. Photo by Sailko. CC-BY-SA 2.5.

FIG. 4.3 Peplos Kore. Photo by Marsyase. CC-BY-SA 2.5

FIG. 4.4 Aphrodite of Knidos. Photo: Heritage Image Partnership Ltd/Alamy Stock Photo.

FIG. 4.5 Reconstructions of the Peplos Kore. Photo by Marsyase. CC-BY-SA 2.5.

FIG. 4.6 Augustus of Prima Porta. Image copyright © Ashmolean Museum, University of Oxford.

FIG. 4.7 Replica of Nike of Samothrace, San Antonio, Texas. Photo by author.

FIG. 5.1 Imperial room, Boscotrecase. Metropolitan Museum of Art, Rogers Fund, 1920. CCO 1.0.

FIG. 5.2 Boscotrecase ground plan. Drawing by Philip Rush, based on a drawing from The Augustan Villa at Boscotrecase P.H. Blanckenhagen and Christine Alexander. (Mainz au Rhein Pvon Zabern 1990) p. 4, fig. 1.

FIG. 5.3 Wall at Boscotrecase (detail). Metropolitan Museum of Art, Rogers Fund, 1920. CCO 1.0.

FIG. 5.4   Rothko Chapel. Copyright © 1998 Kate Rothko Prizel and Christopher Rothko / Artists Rights Society (ARS), New York. Photo by Nicolas Sapieha / Art Resource, New York.

FIG. 5.5   Cubiculum, Villa of P. Fannius Synistor at Boscoreale. Metropolitan Museum of Art, Rogers Fund, 1903. CCO 1.0.

FIG. 5.6   Marriage of Bacchus and Ariadne. Pompeiian wall painting. Photo: Scala / Art Resource, New York.

FIG. 5.7   Egyptian motifs, villa at Boscotrecase (detail). Metropolitan Museum of Art, Rogers Fund, 1920. CCO 1.0.

FIG. 5.8   Swans, villa at Boscotrecase (detail). Metropolitan Museum of Art, Rogers Fund, 1920. CCO 1.0.

FIG. 5.9   Perseus and Andromeda, Mythological Room, villa at Boscotrecase. Metropolitan Museum of Art, Rogers Fund, 1920. CCO 1.0.

FIG. 5.10   Polyphemus and Galatea, Mythological Room, villa at Boscotrecase. Metropolitan Museum of Art, Rogers Fund, 1920. CCO 1.0.

FIG. 5.11   Psyche, San Antonio Museum of Art. Photo by author.

FIG. 6.1   San Vitale apse with mosaic of Christ enthroned surrounded by angels, Saint Vitalis, and Bishop Ecclesius. Photo: Cameraphoto Arte, Venice / Art Resource, New York.

FIG. 6.2   Mosaic of Justinian I, San Vitale, Ravenna, 2016. Photo copyright © José Luiz Bernardes Ribeiro. CC-BY-SA 4.0.

FIG. 6.3   Theodora mosaic, San Vitale basilica. Photo by Petar Milošević. CC-BY-SA 4.0.

FIG. 6.4   Lamb of God mosaic, San Vitale basilica. Photo by Petar Milošević. CCO-BY-SA 4.0.

FIG. 6.5   San Vitale basilica, exterior. Photo by Chigot. CC-BY-SA 4.0.

FIG. 6.6   San Vitale ground plan. INTERFOTO / Alamy Stock Photo.

FIG. 6.7   San Vitale basilica, interior. Photo by Alfredo Dagli Orti / Art Resource, New York.

FIG. 6.8   San Vitale, marble revetment. Gianni Caredda. CC-BY-SA4.

FIG. 6.9   Augustus of Prima Porta. Photo by Till Niermann. CCO.

FIG. 6.10   Nave of Sant'Apollinare Nuovo. Photo: Architecture2000 / Alamy Stock Photo.

FIG. 6.11   Sant'Apollinare Nuovo basilica, Ravenna. Photo by Robert Harding / Alamy Stock Photo.

FIG. 6.12 Juan O'Gorman, *Confluence of Civilizations in the Americas*, Hemisfair Plaza, San Antonio. Photo by Christian Besson, Universidad Nacional Autónoma de México Collection.

FIG. 7.1 Apse of Sant Climent in Taüll. Photo: Album / Art Resource, New York.

FIG. 7.2 Sant Climent before restoration. Photo: Website of the Museu Nacional d'Art de Catalunya, Barcelona, museunacional.cat. CC-BY-NC-SA 3.0.0.

FIG. 7.3 Removing the frescoes. Photo: Website of the Museu Nacional d'Art de Catalunya, Barcelona, museunacional.cat. CC-BY-NC-SA 3.0.0.

FIG. 7.4 Apse of Sant Climent in Taüll (detail). Photo: Album / Art Resource, New York.

FIG. 7.5 Projection of frescoes, Sant Climent, Vall de Bof, Taüll. Photo: imageBROKER / Alamy Stock Photo.

FIG. 7.6 Tympanum of Saint Lazarus. Photo by Daniel Gaudry. CC-BY-SA-3.0.

FIG. 7.7 Detail of *The Last Judgment Tympanum at Autun Cathedral*. Photo: NJphoto / Alamy Stock Photo.

FIG. 7.8 Hand of God, Sant Climent (detail). Photo: Album / Art Resource, New York.

FIG. 7.9 Apocalyptic lamb, Sant Climent (detail). Photo: Heritage Image Partnership Ltd. / Alamy Stock Photo.

FIG. 7.10 Lazarus, Sant Climent, wall painting (detail). Photo: Album / Art Resource, New York.

FIG. 7.11 Byzantine mosaic of Christ Pantocrator, monastery church dome, Daphni. Photo: HIP / Art Resource, New York.

FIG. 7.12 Tom Lea, *Stampede* (mural). Used with permission of the Tom Lea Institute.

FIG. 8.1 Ja`far ibn Muhammad ibn `Ali, incense burner of Amir Saif al-Dunya wa'l-Din ibn Muhammad al-Mawardi. Metropolitan Museum of Art, Rogers Fund, 1951. CC0 1.0.

FIG. 8.2 Mosaic in Madaba, Jordan. Photo by Oscar Espinosa / Alamy Stock Photo.

FIG. 8.3 Badi` al-Zaman ibn `Abd al-Latif, *The Elephant Clock*. Metropolitan Museum of Art, Bequest of Cora Timken Burnett, 1956. CC0 1.0.

FIG. 8.4 Jameh mosque south iwan. Photo: Daroj Bajurin/Alamy Stock Photo.

FIG. 8.5 *Mihrab* (Prayer Niche). Metropolitan Museum of Art, Harris Brisbane Dick Fund, 1939. CC0 1.0.

FIG. 8.6 Detail of Brobinsky Bucket. Photo © Genevra Kornbluth.

FIG. 8.7 Bowl with Arabic inscription. Metropolitan Museum of Art, Rogers Fund, 1965. CC0 1.0.

Fig. 8.8 Dome of the Rock, interior. Photo by Erich Lessing / Art Resource, New York.

Fig. 8.9 Umayyad Mosque of Damascus, south entrance. Photo: Album / Art Resource, New York.

Fig. 8.10 Birth of the Prophet Mohammad. Photo courtesy of Edinburgh University Main Library, Special Collections.

Fig. 8.11 Pisa Griffin. Photo: Scala / Art Resource, New York.

Fig. 8.12   Urrutia Gate, San Antonio Museum of Art. Photo by Jeshua Mauldin.

Fig. 9.1 Stained glass cathedral ceiling, Sainte-Chapelle. Photo by William Perry / Alamy Stock Photo.

Fig. 9.2 Wise men, reliquary. Photo copyright © Marie-Lan Nguyen. cc-by 2.5.

Fig. 9.3 Vitrail de la Basilique Saint-Denis (chapelle de la Vierge). Photo by Vassill. cc0.

Fig. 9.4 Organization of windows, Sainte-Chapelle. Drawing by Sarah Cooper.

Fig. 9.5 Interior of Sainte-Chapelle, medieval stained glass panels (detail). Photo by Peter Barritt / Alamy Stock Photo.

Fig. 9.6 Rondel showing Holofernes's army crossing the Euphrates River. Used with permission from the Philadelphia Museum of Art. Purchased with funds contributed by Mrs. Clement Biddle Wood in memory of her husband.

Fig. 9.7 Rondel showing orchards outside Damascus devastated by Holofernes's army. Used with permission from the Philadelphia Museum of Art. Purchased with funds contributed by Mrs. Clement Biddle Wood in memory of her husband.

Fig. 9.8 Judith slaying Holofernes. Photo: Centre des Monuments Nationaux, Paris. © Bernard Acloque.

Fig. 9.9 Judith with the head of Holofernes. Photo: Centre des Monuments Nationaux, Paris. © Bernard Acloque.

Fig. 9.10   Caravaggio, *Judith Beheading Holofernes*. Photo: Scala / Art Resource, New York.

Fig. 9.11   Limbourg Brothers, *Très Riches Heures du Duc de Berry*. Photo by R.M.N. / R.-G. Ojéda. cc0-us.

Fig. 9.12 Duccio and Hagia Sophia window, St. John the Divine, New York City. Photo by Mark Menjivar.

Fig. 9.13 Poets and artists windows, St. John the Divine, New York City. Photo by Mark Menjivar.

Fig. 10.1 Anastasis fresco, Chora Church, Istanbul. Photo by Till Niermann. cc-by-sa-3.0.

FIG. 10.2 Chora Church, exterior. Photo by Gryffindor. CC0.

FIG. 10.3 Theodore Metochites presents his church to Christ, mosaic, Chora Church. Photo by Gryffindor. CC-BY-SA-4.0 International.

FIG. 10.4 Chora Church ground plan. Image by Alexander van Millingen. CC0-US.

FIG. 10.5 Byzantine paintings, Kariye Mosque and Museum (Chora Church). Photo by Lucas Vallecillos / Alamy Stock Photo.

FIG. 10.6 Fresco of dream of Jacob and Moses taking the first ten laws, Chora monastery. Photo: Images and Stories / Alamy Stock Photo.

FIG. 10.7 Virgin Mary, Christ, and John the Baptist Aya Sofya, mosaic, Istanbul, Turkey. Photo by David Pearson / Alamy Stock Photo.

FIG. 10.8 *Deësis*, Jesus, and Mary, mosaic, Chora monastery. Photo by Ayhan Altun / Alamy Stock Photo.

FIG. 10.9 Last Judgement, Church of the Holy Savior (Chora Church). Photo by Ayhan Altun / Alamy Stock Photo.

FIG. 10.10 Anastasis Icon, Saint Sophia Greek Orthodox Church, San Antonio, Texas. Photo: Author.

FIG. 11.1 Jan van Eyck, *The Annunciation*. Google Art Project. CC0-US.

FIG. 11.2 Jan van Eyck, *The Annunciation* (detail). Google Art Project. CC0-US.

FIG. 11.3 Martin Schongauer, *Descent into Hell*, altarpiece from the Dominican Church in Colmar, Unterlinden Museum, Alsace, France. Photo: Azoor Photo/Alamy Stock Photo.

FIG. 11.4 Jan van Eyck, *Annunciation* diptych. Photo: Museo Nacional Thyssen-Bornemisza / Scala / Art Resource, New York.

FIG. 11.5 Jan van Eyck, *Man in the Red Turban*. Copyright © National Gallery, London / Art Resource, New York.

FIG. 11.6 Jesse Treviño, *La Veladora of Our Lady of Guadalupe*, 2006. San Antonio, Texas. Photo: Jeshua Mauldin.

FIG. 12.1 Sandro Botticelli, *Birth of Venus*. Photo: Scala / Art Resource, New York.

FIG. 12.2 Sandro Botticelli, *Primavera*. Photo: Scala / Art Resource, New York.

FIG. 12.3 Leonardo da Vinci, *Mona Lisa*. CC0-US.

FIG. 12.4 Unicorn in captivity. Metropolitan Museum of Art, Gift of John D. Rockefeller Jr., 1937. CC0 1.0.

FIG. 12.5 Marco del Buono Giamberti and Apollonio di Giovanni di Tomaso, Cassone with painted panel depicting the conquest of Trebizond. Attributed to Marco del

Buono Giamberti and Apollonio di Giovanni di Tomaso. Metropolitan Museum of Art, John Stewart Kennedy Fund, 1914. CCO 1.0.

FIG. 12.6 Masaccio, *Expulsion from the Garden of Eden*. Photo by Marie-Lan Nguyen. CCO.

FIG. 12.7 Sandro Botticelli, *Adoration of the Magi*. CCO-US.

FIG. 12.8 Joaquín Sorolla y Bastida, *After the Bath*. Used with permission of the Hispanic Society of America, New York.

FIG. 13.1 Pieter Bruegel the Elder, *The Harvesters*. Metropolitan Museum of Art, Rogers Fund, 1919. CCO 1.0.

FIG. 13.2 Limbourg Brothers, *Très Riches Heures du Duc de Berry, August.* Photo by R.M.N. / R.-G. Ojéda. CCO-US.

FIG. 13.3 Limbourg Brothers, *Très Riches Heures du Duc de Berry, September.* Photo by R.M.N. / R.-G. Ojéda. CCO-US.

FIG. 13.4 Pieter Bruegel the Elder, *The Tower of Babel*. Google Art Project. CCO-US.

FIG. 13.5 Michelangelo, *The Drunkenness of Noah*, ceiling frescos after restoration, Sistine Chapel. Photo by Erich Lessing / Art Resource, New York.

FIG. 13.6 Pieter Bruegel the Elder, *Hunters in the Snow*. Google Art Project. CCO-US.

FIG. 13.7 Joachim Patinir, *Penitence of Saint Jerome*. Metropolitan Museum of Art, Fletcher Fund, 1936. CCO 1.0.

FIG. 13.8 Census at Bethlehem, 1566 Pieter Bruegel the Elder, Musées royaux des Beaux-Arts de Belgique, Royal Museums of Fine Arts, Rue du Musée, Brussels, Belgium. Photo: dpa picture alliance / Alamy Stock Photo.

FIG. 13.9 Adoration of the Magi, Pieter Bruegel. Azoor Photo/Alamy Stock Photo.

FIG. 13.10 Hieronymus Bosch, *The Haywain Triptych*. Museo Nacional del Prado, Madrid. Public Domain.

FIG. 13.11 James Sicner, *Man's Evolving Images: Printing and Writing*, 1983, front view. Trinity University Library, San Antonio, Texas. Photo by Jeshua Mauldin.

FIG. 14.1 Caravaggio, *The Calling of Saint Matthew*. Contarelli Chapel, Church of San Luigi dei Francesi, Rome. Public Domain. CC-PD-MARK.

FIG. 14.2 Caravaggio, Contarelli Chapel, San Luigi dei Francesi, Rome. Photo by Adam Eastland / Alamy Stock Photo.

FIG. 14.3 Caravaggio, *The Crucifixion of Saint Peter*. Santa Maria del Popolo, Rome. Public Domain. CC-PD-MARK.

FIG. 14.4 Caravaggio, *The Conversion on the Way to Damascus*. Photo: CC-PD-MARK.

FIG. 14.5 Caravaggio, *The Inspiration of Saint Matthew*. Photo: CC-PD-MARK.

FIG. 14.6   Caravaggio, *The Martyrdom of Saint Matthew*. Photo: CC-PD-MARK.

FIG. 14.7   Annibale Carracci, *Assumption of the Virgin Mary*. Photo: José Luiz. CC BY-SA 4.0

FIG. 14.8   Caravaggio, *Saint Matthew and the Angel*. Photo: BPK Bildagentur / Gemäldegalerie, Staatliche Museen, Berlin / Art Resource, New York.

FIG. 14.9   Caravaggio, *The Martyrdom of Saint Matthew* (detail). CC-PD-MARK.

FIG. 14.10   Caravaggio, *David and Goliath*. CC-PD-MARK.

FIG. 15.1   Rembrandt, *The Night Watch*. Google Art Project. CC-PD-MARK.

FIG. 15.2   Rembrandt, *The Mennonite Preacher Anslo in Conversation with His Wife*. Gemäldegalerie, Berlin. Public Domain.

FIG. 15.3   Rembrandt, *The Anatomy Lesson of Dr. Nicolaes Tulp*. Mauritshuis, The Hague. Public Domain. CC-PD-MARK.

FIG. 15.4   Computer illustration of the Great Hall of the Kloveniers as it is thought to have looked in 1645 (figure 299). Image by Bytes & Brushes, the Netherlands. Drawing by Jorien Doorn from *The Rembrandt Book*, by Gary Schwartz (Harry N. Abrams, 2007).

FIG. 15.5   Joachim von Sandrart, *Officers and Members of the Militia of District XIX in Amsterdam*. Rijksmuseum, Amsterdam. CC0. CC-PD-MARK.

FIG. 15.6   Rembrandt, *The Blinding of Samson*. Google Art Project. CC0-US.

FIG. 15.7   Rembrandt, *Rembrandt and Saskia in the Parable of the Prodigal Son*. Google Art Project. CC0-US.

FIG. 15.8   Rembrandt, *Gerard de Lairesse*. Metropolitan Museum of Art, Robert Lehman Collection, 1975. CC0 1.0.

FIG. 15.9   Rembrandt, *The Abduction of Ganymede*. Google Art Project. CC0-US.

FIG. 15.10   Rembrandt, *The Conspiracy of the Batavians under Claudius Civilis*. Nationalmuseum, Stockholm, Sweden. Google Art Project. CC0-US.

FIG. 15.11   Rembrandt, *Self-Portrait*. Copyright © Frick Collection, New York.

FIG. 15.12   Cavaliers at the Alamo, *San Antonio Express-News*, 2013.

FIG. 16.1   Diego Velázquez, *Las Hilanderas*. Museo del Prado, Madrid. PD-US.

FIG. 16.2   Diego Velázquez, *Las Meninas*. Museo del Prado in Google Earth. PD-US.

FIG. 16.3   Titian, *The Rape of Europa*. Google Art Project. CC0-US.

FIG. 16.4   Peter Paul Rubens, *Pallas and Arachne*. Copyright © Virginia Museum of Fine Arts Richmond, Adolph D. and Wilkins C. Williams Fund. Photo by Travis Fullerton.

FIG. 16.5   Michelangelo, *Libyan Sibyl*, Sistine Chapel. PD-US. CC-PD-MARK. PD-ART.

FIG. 16.6 *Penelope with the Suitors* by Pinturicchio (1454–1513), an Italian painter of the Renaissance. Dated 16th century. Photo: World History Archive / Alamy Stock Photo.

FIG. 16.7 Diego Velázquez, *Christ in the House of Martha and Mary.* National Gallery, Washington, DC, Bequeathed by Sir William H. Gregory, 1892. PD-US. CC-PDF-MARK.

FIG. 16.8 Tapestry of Hannibal's Messenger in Carthage, sixteenth century. San Antonio, Texas. Photo by Author.

FIG. 17.1 Théodore Géricault, *The Raft of the Medusa.* Photo by Erich Lessing / Art Resource, New York.

FIG. 17.2 Théodore Géricault, *Study of Hands and Feet.* Web Gallery of Art. Public Domain.

FIG. 17.3 Théodore Géricault, *The Severed Heads.* Photo: Prisma Archivo / Alamy Stock Photo.

FIG. 17.4 Michelangelo, *Last Judgment,* Charon's boat (detail), Sistine Chapel. De Vecchi, *Cappella Sistina,* 1999. PD-US.

FIG. 17.5 *Portrait of a Young Man in an Artist's Studio,* c. 1818–19. Formerly attributed to Géricault. Musée du Louvre, Paris. Web Gallery of Art.

FIG. 17.6 Théodore Géricault, Self-portrait. Historic Images / Alamy Stock Photo.

FIG. 17.7 Francisco de Goya, *Saturn Devouring His Son.* Museo del Prado. Public Domain. CC-PDF-MARK.

FIG. 17.8 Eugène Delacroix, *The Shipwreck of Don Juan: A Sketch.* Victoria and Albert Museum, London, Bequeathed by Constantine Alexander Ionides. Photo: V&A Images, London / Art Resource, New York

FIG. 17.9 Evacuation of Géricault, @ Service des bibliotheques, des archives et de la documentation generale des Musée de France.

FIG. 18.1 Claude Monet, *Impression, Sunrise.* Photo by Erich Lessing / Art Resource, New York.

FIG. 18.2 Édouard Manet, *Self-Portrait with a Palette,* 1879. Photo: The Yorck Project (2002), 10.000 Meisterwerke der Malerei (DVD-ROM), distributed by DIRECTMEDIA Publishing GmbH. PD-US.

FIG. 18.3 Alexandre Cabanel, *The Birth of Venus.* 1863. Oil on canvas. Musée d'Orsay, Paris. Photo: PAINTING/Alamy Stock Photo.

FIG. 18.4 Édouard Manet, *Olympia.* Musée d'Orsay, Paris, Google Art Project. PD-US.

FIG. 18.5 Titian, *Venus of Urbino.* Uffizi Gallery, Florence, Google Art Project. PD-US.

FIG. 18.6   Édouard Manet, *Émile Zola*. Musée d'Orsay, Paris. PD-US.

FIG. 18.7   Frédéric Bazille, *Bazille's Studio*. Musée d'Orsay, Paris, Google Art Project. PD-US.

FIG. 18.8   Claude Monet, *Women in the Garden*. Photo: Yorck Project (2002) 10.000 Meisterwerke der Malerei (DVD-ROM), distributed by DIRECTMEDIA Publishing GmbH. PD-US.

FIG. 18.9   Claude Monet, *Garden at Sainte-Adresse*. Metropolitan Museum of Art, Purchase, special contributions and fund given or bequeathed by Friends of the Museum, 1976.

FIG. 18.10   Édouard Manet, *The Monet Family in Their Garden at Argenteuil*. Metropolitan Museum of Art, Bequest of Joan Whitney Payson, 1975. CC0 1.0.

FIG. 18.11   Claude Monet, *Manet Painting in Monet's Garden in Argenteuil*. Private Collection. PD-US.

FIG. 18.12   J. M. W. Turner, *The Slave Ship*. Photo: Artepics / Alamy Stock Photo.

FIG. 18.13   Claude Monet, *San Giorgio Maggiore at Dusk*, 1908–1912. CC-PD.

FIG. 18.14   Claude Monet, *Nympheas (Water Lilies)*. Collection of the Tobin Theatre Arts Fund, courtesy of the McNay Art Museum, San Antonio.

FIG. 19.1   John Singer Sargent, *El Jaleo*. Photo: Isabella Stewart Gardner Museum. HIP/ Art Resource NY.

FIG. 19.2   John Singer Sargent, *La Carmencita*. CC-PD-Mark.

FIG. 19.3   Edgar Degas, *L'Étoile*. Musée d'Orsay, Paris. PD-US.

FIG. 19.4   John Singer Sargent, *The Spanish Dancer*. Copyright © ARC. Courtesy of the Art Renewal Center (artrenewal.org).

FIG. 19.5   John Singer Sargent, *The Spanish Dance*. Courtesy of the Hispanic Society of America, New York.

FIG. 19.6   John Singer Sargent, *The Daughters of Edward Darley Boit*. Photo: Art Collection 3 / Alamy Stock Photo.

FIG. 19.7   John Singer Sargent, *Madame X*. Metropolitan Museum of Art, Arthur Hoppock Hearn Fund, 1916. CC0 1.0.

FIG. 19.8   John Singer Sargent, *Carnation, Lily, Lily, Rose*. Tate, London, 2011. Google Art Project. PD-US.

FIG. 19.9   John Singer Sargent, *Isabella Stewart Gardner*. Photo: Art Collection 3 / Alamy Stock Photo.

FIG. 19.10   John Singer Sargent, *Gassed*. Courtesy of Imperial War Museums, London. Photo: Lebrecht Music and Arts Photo Library / Alamy Stock Photo.

FIG. 20.1 Pablo Picasso, *Les Demoiselles d'Avignon*. Copyright © Estate of Pablo Picasso / Artists Rights Society (ARS), New York. Digital image copyright © Museum of Modern Art / Licensed by Scala / Art Resource, New York.

FIG. 20.2 Pablo Picasso, *The Bull,* first state (1945). Copyright © Artists Rights Society (ARS), New York. Photo: Cameraphoto Arte, Venice / Art Resource, New York.

FIG. 20.3 Pablo Picasso, *The Bull,* fifth state (December 1945). Engraving 32.6. Copyright © Artists Rights Society (ARS), New York. Photo by R. G. Ojéda. Copyright © RMN-Grand Palais / Art Resource, New York.

FIG. 20.4 Pablo Picasso, *The Bull*, ninth state (1945). Copyright © Artists Rights Society (ARS), New York. Photo: Cameraphoto Arte, Venice / Art Resource, New York.

FIG. 20.5 Pablo Picasso, *The Bull,* eleventh state. Copyright © Artists Rights Society (ARS), New York. Photo by R. G. Ojéda. Copyright © RMN-Grand Palais / Art Resource, New York.

FIG. 20.6 Pablo Picasso, Study for *Les Demoiselles d'Avignon*. Acquired through the Lillie P. Bliss Bequest. Copyright © Artists Rights Society (ARS), New York. Digital image copyright © Museum of Modern Art / Licensed by Scala / Art Resource, New York.

FIG. 20.7 Costumes from the ballet *Parade*. Photo by Jean-Pierre Dalbéra. CC-BY-2.0.

FIG. 20.8 Costumes from the ballet *Parade*. Photo by Jean-Pierre Dalbéra. CC-BY-2.0.

FIG. 20.9 Pablo Picasso, *Gertrude Stein*. Bequest of Gertrude Stein, 1946. Copyright © Artists Rights Society (ARS), New York. Image copyright © Metropolitan Museum of Art.

FIG. 20.10 Pablo Picasso, *The Women of Algiers, Version O*. Copyright © Artists Rights Society (ARS), New York. Photo: Scala / Art Resource, New York.

FIG. 20.11 Henri Matisse, *Le Bonheur de Vivre* (detail). Barnes Foundation, Philadelphia Museum of Art. Photo: ZUMA Press, Inc. / Alamy Stock Photo.

SUGGESTED READING

Altamira

Agnew, Neville, and Janet Bridgland. *Of the Past, for the Future: Integrating Archaeology and Conservation*. Los Angeles: Getty Conservation Institute, 2006.

Bahn, Paul G. *The Cambridge Illustrated History of Prehistoric Art*. Cambridge: Cambridge University Press, 1998.

Berghaus, Günter, ed. *New Perspectives on Prehistoric Art*. London: Praeger, 2004.

Freeman, Leslie G. *Altamira Revisited and Other Essays on Early Art*. Chicago: Institute for Prehistoric Investigations, 1987.

Gamble, Clive. *Origins and Revolutions: Human Identity in Earliest Prehistory*. New York: Cambridge University Press, 2007.

Guthrie, R. Dale. *The Nature of Paleolithic Art*. Chicago: University of Chicago Press, 2005.

Lasheras, José Antonio. "The Cave of Altamira, 22,000 Years of History." Museum of Altamira, www.rockartscandinavia.com/images/articles/altamiraa9.pdf.

Lawson, Andrew J. *Painted Caves: Paleolithic Rock Art in Western Europe*. Oxford: Oxford University Press, 2012.

Saura Ramos, Pedro A. *Altamira*. Ed. Antonio Beltrán. New York: Abrams. 1999.

Stokstad, Marilyn, and Michael W. Cothren. *Art History, Vol. 1. 6th* Edition. Pearson, 2017.

White, Randall. *Prehistoric Art: The Symbolic Journey of Mankind*. New York: Abrams, 2003.

Wilford, John Noble. "With Science, New Portrait of the Cave Artist." *New York Times*. June 15, 2012.

Ashurnasirpal II Killing Lions

Aruz, Joan, Sarah B. Graff, and Yelena Rakic. *Assyria to Iberia at the Dawn of the Classical Age*. New York: Metropolitan Museum of Art, 2014.

Bogdanos, Matthew. *Thieves of Baghdad: One Marine's Passion to Recover the World's Greatest Stolen Treasures*. New York: Bloomsbury, 2005.

Burtis, John E., et al. *New Light on Nimrud: Proceedings of the Nimrud Conference, March 11–13, 2002*. London: British Institute for the Study of Iraq, in Association with the British Museum, 2008.

Cheng, Jack, and Marian H. Feldman, eds. *Ancient Near Eastern Art in Context: Studies in Honor of Irene J. Winter by Her Students*. Leiden: Brill, 2007.

Cohen, Ada, and Steven E. Kangas, eds. *Assyrian Reliefs from the Palace of Ashurnasirpal II: A Cultural Biography*. Hanover, NH: University Press of New England, 2010.

Crawford, Vaughn E., Prudence O. Harper, and Holly Pittman. *Assyrian Reliefs and Ivories in the Metropolitan Museum of Art: Palace Reliefs of Ashurnasirpal II and Ivory Carvings from Nimrud*. New York: Metropolitan Museum of Art, 1980.

Harper, Prudence O., and Holly Pittman, eds. *Essays on Near Eastern Art and Archaeology*. New York: Metropolitan Museum of Art, 1983.

Kuhrt, Amélie. *The Ancient Near East, c. 3000–330 BC*. London: Routledge, 1995.

Meuszyński, Janusz. *Die Rekonstruktion der Reliefdarstellungen und ihrer Anordnung im Nordwestpalast von Kalhu*. 2 vols. Mainz am Rhein: P.v. Zabern, 1981–92.

Russell, John Malcolm. *From Nineveh to New York: The Strange Story of the Assyrian Reliefs in the Metropolitan Museum and the Hidden Masterpiece at Canford Manor*. New Haven: Yale University Press, 1997.

———. "The Program of the Palace of Ashurnasirpal II at Nimrud: Issues in the Research and Presentation of Assyrian Art." *American Journal of Archaeology* 102, no. 4 (1998): 644–715.

———. *The Writing on the Wall: Studies in the Architectural Context of Late Assyrian Palace Inscriptions*. Winona Lake, Ind.: Eisenbrauns, 1999.

Winter, Irene J. *On Art in the Ancient Near East*. 2 vols. Leiden: Brill, 2010.

The Euphronios Krater

Homer. *The Iliad*. Trans. Robert Fagles. New York: Viking, 1990.

Hoving, Thomas. *Making the Mummies Dance: Inside the Metropolitan Museum of Art*. New York: Simon & Schuster, 1993.

Kimmelman, Michael. "Stolen Beauty: A Greek Urn's Underworld." *New York Times*. July 7, 2009.

Lissarrague, François. *Greek Vases: The Athenians and Their Images*. Trans. Kim Allen. New York: Riverside, 2001.

Mertens, Joan R. *How to Read Greek Vases*. New York: Metropolitan Museum of Art, 2010.

Neer, Richard T. *Style and Politics in Athenian Vase-Painting: The Craft of Democracy, ca. 530–460*. Cambridge: Cambridge University Press, 2002.

Oakley, John H. *The Greek Vase: Art of the Storyteller*. Los Angeles: Getty Publications, 2013.

Robertson, Martin. *The Art of Vase-Painting in Classical Athens*. Cambridge: University of
    Cambridge, 1992.
Schefold, Karl, and Luca Giuliani. *Gods and Heroes in Late Archaic Greek Art*. Cambridge:
    University of Cambridge, 1992.
Shapiro, H. A. *Myth into Art: Poet and Painter in Classical Greece*. London: Routledge,
    1994.
Steiner, Ann. *Reading Greek Vases*. Cambridge: Cambridge University Press, 2007.
Woodford, Susan. *Images of Myths in Classical Antiquity*. Cambridge: Cambridge Univer-
    sity Press, 2003.

Nike of Samothrace

Barringer, Judith M. *The Art and Archaeology of Ancient Greece*. Cambridge: Cambridge
    University Press, 2015.
Brinkmann, Vinzenz, and Raimund Wünsche. *Gods in Color: Painted Sculpture of Classical
    Antiquity*. Cambridge, Mass.: Arthur M. Sackler Museum, 2007.
Bugh, Glenn R., ed. *The Cambridge Companion to the Hellenistic World*. Cambridge:
    Cambridge University Press, 2006.
Goldhill, Simon, and Robin Osborne, eds. *Art and Text in Ancient Greek Culture*. Cam-
    bridge: Cambridge University Press, 1994.
Haskell, Francis, and Nicholas Penny. *Taste and the Antique: The Lure of Classical Sculpture,
    1500–1900*. New Haven: Yale University Press, 1981.
Havelock, Christine Mitchell. *The Aphrodite of Knidos and Her Successors: A Historical
    Review of the Female Nude in Greek Art*. Ann Arbor: University of Michigan Press,
    1995.
Jenkins, Ian. *Greek Architecture and Its Sculpture*. Cambridge, Mass.: Harvard University
    Press, 2006.
Kousser, Rachel Meredith. *Hellenistic and Roman Ideal Sculpture: The Allure of the Classical*.
    Cambridge: Cambridge University Press, 2008.
Mach, Edmund von. *Greek Sculpture*. London: Parkstone, 2006.
Mark, Ira S. "The Victory of Samothrace." In *Regional Schools in Hellenistic Sculpture*, ed.
    Olga Palagia and William Coulson, 157–65. Oxford: Oxbow Books, 1998.
Neer, Richard T. *The Emergence of the Classical Style in Greek Sculpture*. Chicago: University
    of Chicago Press, 2010.
Palagia, Olga. *Greek Sculpture: Function, Materials, and Techniques in the Archaic and
    Classical Periods*. New York: Cambridge University Press, 2006.
Pollitt, Jerry Jordan. *Art and Experience in Classical Greece*. Cambridge: Cambridge
    University Press, 1972.

The Rape of Europa. Directed by Richard Berge, Bonni Cohen, and Nicole Newnham. Actual Films, 2006.

Schefold, Karl. *The Art of Classical Greece*. New York: Crown, 1996.

Smith, Tyler Jo, and Dimitris Plantzos, eds. *A Companion to Greek Art*. New York: Wiley-Blackwell, 2012.

Spivey, Nigel Jonathan. *Greek Sculpture*. Cambridge: Cambridge University Press, 2013.

Steiner, Deborah Tarn. *Images in Mind*. Princeton: Princeton University Press, 2001.

Winckelmann, Johann Joachim. *History of the Art of Antiquity*. Los Angeles: Getty Research Institute, 2006.

Villa at Boscotrecase

Anderson, Maxwell L. "Pompeian Frescoes in the Metropolitan Museum of Art." *Metropolitan Museum of Art Bulletin*, 45, no. 3 (1987–88): 17–36.

———. "The Portrait Medallions of the Imperial Villa at Boscotrecase." *American Journal of Archaeology* 91, no. 1 (1987): 127–35.

Blanckenhagen, Peter H. von, and Christine Alexander. *The Augustan Villa at Boscotrecase*. Mainz am Rhein: P. von Zabern, 1990.

Elsner, Jaś. *Roman Eyes: Visuality and Subjectivity in Art and Text*. Princeton: Princeton University Press, 2007.

Gardner Coates, Victoria C., and John L. Seydl, eds. *Antiquity Recovered: The Legacy of Pompeii and Herculaneum*. Los Angeles: J. Paul Getty Museum, 2007.

Knauer, Elfriede R. "Roman Wall Painting from Boscotrecase: Three Studies in the Relationship between Writing and Painting." *Metropolitan Museum Journal* 28 (1993): 13–46.

Leach, Eleanor Winsor. *The Social Life of Painting in Ancient Rome and on the Bay of Naples*. Cambridge: Cambridge University Press, 2004.

Ling, Roger. *Roman Painting*. Cambridge: Cambridge University Press, 1991.

Mazzoleni, Donatella. *Domus: Wall Painting in the Roman House*. Los Angeles: J. Paul Getty Museum, 2004.

Panetta, Marisa Ranieri, ed. *Pompeii: The History, Life, and Art of the Buried City*. Trans. Catherine Bolton. Vercelli, Italy: White Star, 2004.

Pappalardo, Umberto. *The Splendor of Roman Wall Painting*. Los Angeles: J. Paul Getty Museum, 2009.

Philostratus the Elder. *Imagines*. Trans. Arthur Fairbanks. Cambridge, Mass.: Harvard University Press, 1931.

Powers, Jessica. "Beyond Painting in Pompeii's Houses: Wall Ornaments and Their Patrons." In *Pompeii: Art, Industry, and Infrastructure*, ed. Eric Poehler, Miko Flohr, and Kevin Cole, 10–32. Oxford: Oxbow Books, 2011.

San Vitale

Alberti, Livia. "Restoring the Mosaics of San Vitale." *Global Dispatches*, January 12, 2012, www.theglobaldispatches.com/articles/restoring-the-mosaics-of-san-vitale.

Andreescu-Treadgold, Irina, and Warren Treadgold. "Procopius and the Imperial Panels of San Vitale." *Art Bulletin* 79, no. 4 (1997): 708–23.

Barber, Charles. "The Imperial Panels at San Vitale: A Reconsideration." *BMGS* 14 (1990): 19–42.

Bassett, Sarah E. "Style and Meaning in the Imperial Panels at San Vitale." *Artibus et Historiae* 29, no. 57 (2008): 49–57.

Cooke, Catherine Nixon. *Juan O'Gorman: A Confluence of Civilizations.* Trinity University Press, 2016.

Deliyannis, Deborah Mauskopf. *Ravenna in Late Antiquity.* Cambridge: Cambridge University Press, 2010.

Elsner, Jaś. *Art and the Roman Viewer.* Cambridge: Cambridge University Press, 1995.

Kitzinger, Ernst. *Byzantine Art in the Making: Main Lines of Stylistic Development in Mediterranean Art, 3rd–7th Century.* Cambridge, Mass.: Harvard University Press, 1977.

MacCormack, Sabine G. *Art and Ceremony in Late Antiquity.* Berkeley: University of California Press, 1981.

Mathews, Thomas F. *The Early Churches of Constantinople: Architecture and Liturgy.* University Park: Pennsylvania State University Press, 1971.

Procopius. *The Secret History.* Trans. Richard Atwater. Chicago: P. Covici, 1927.

Schibille, Nadine. *Hagia Sophia and the Byzantine Aesthetic Experience.* Surrey, England: Ashgate, 2014.

Simson, Otto Georg von. *Sacred Fortress: Byzantine Art and Statecraft in Ravenna.* Chicago: University of Chicago Press, 1948.

Verhoeven, Mariëtte. *The Early Christian Monuments of Ravenna: Transformations and Memory.* Turnhout, Belgium: Brepols, 2011.

Sant Climent de Taüll

Ainaud de Lasarte, Juan. *Catalan Painting.* Vol. 1. New York: Rizzoli, 1990–92.

Bednorz, Achim. *Romanesque Architecture, Sculpture, Painting.* Ed. Rolf Toman. Ullman and Könemann, 2011.

Camille, Michael. "Seeing and Reading: Some Visual Implications of Medieval Literacy and Illiteracy." *Art History* 8 (1985): 26–49.

Castiñeras, Manuel, and Jordi Camps. *Romanesque Art in the MNAC Collections.* Museu Nacional d'Art de Catalunya, 2008.

Demus, Otto, and Max Hirmer. *Romanesque Mural Paining.* New York: Abrams, 1970.

Dodds, Jerrilynn, et al. *The Art of Medieval Spain, AD 500 –1200.* New York: Metropolitan Museum of Art, 1993.

Dodwell, Christopher R. *The Pictorial Arts of the West, 800–1200.* New Haven: Yale University Press, 1993.

Emmerson, Richard K., and Bernard McGinn, eds. *The Apocalypse in the Middle Ages.* Ithaca, NY: Cornell University Press, 1992.

Goering, Joseph. *The Virgin and the Grail: Origins of a Legend.* New Haven: Yale University Press, 2005.

Guardia, Milagros, et al. *La descoberta de la pintura mural romànica catalane.* Madrid: Electa, 1993.

Kuhn, Charles L. *Romanesque Mural Painting of Catalonia.* Cambridge, Mass.: Harvard University Press, 1930.

Mann, Janice. *Romanesque Architecture and Its Sculptural Decoration in Christian Spain.* Toronto: University of Toronto Press, 2009.

Parisi, Philip. *The Texas Post Office Murals: Art for the People.* College Station: Texas A&M University Press, 2004.

Post, Chandler Rathfon. *A History of Spanish Painting.* Vol. 1. Cambridge, Mass.: Harvard University Press, 1930.

Sureda, Joan. *La pintura romànica a catalunya.* Madrid: Alianza Editorial, 1981.

Incense Burner of Amir Saif al-Dunya wa'l-Din ibn Muhammad al-Mawardi

Baer, Eva. *Metalwork in Medieval Islamic Art.* Albany: State University of New York Press, 1983.

Bowersock, Glen. *Mosaics as History: The Near East from Late Antiquity to Islam.* Cambridge, Mass.: Belknap Press, 2006.

Ekhtiar, Maryam. *Masterpieces from the Department of Islamic Art in the Metropolitan Museum of Art.* New York: Metropolitan Museum of Art, 2001.

Ettinhausen, Richard, Oleg Grabar, and Marilyn Jenkins-Madina. *Islamic Art and Architecture, 650–1250.* New Haven: Yale University Press, 2001.

Evans, Helen, ed. *Byzantium: Faith and Power, 1261–1557.* New York: Metropolitan Museum of Art, 2004.

———. *Byzantium and Islam: Age of Transition, 7th–9th Centuries.* New York: Metropolitan Museum of Art, 2012.

Flood, Barry Finbar. "Between Cult and Culture: Bamiyan, Islamic Iconoclasm, and the Museum." *Art Bulletin* 84, no. 4 (2002): 641–59.

Irwin, Robert. *Islamic Art in Context.* New York: Abrams, 1997.

Khalili, Nasser D. "A Recently Acquired Incense Burner in the Khalili Collection." In

Muqarnas: An Annual on the Visual Culture of the Islamic World, Essays in Honor of J. M. Rogers, 21:215–18. Leiden: Brill, 2004.

Pitrovskiĭ, Mikahĭl Broisovich. *Earthly Beauty, Heavenly Art: The Art of Islam*. Amsterdam: Lund Humphries, 1999.

WEB RESOURCES

"Caracal Explosive Jump," www.youtube.com/watch?v=4dCXK6KhkTw.

Sainte-Chapelle

Aubert, Marcel, et al. *Les vitraux de Notre-Dame et de la Sainte-Chapelle de Paris. Corpus Vitrearum Medii Aevi. France.* Volume 1. Paris: Caisse nationale des monuments historiques, 1959.

Branner, Robert. "The Painted Medallions in the Sainte-Chapelle in Paris." *Transactions of the American Philosophical Society* 58 (1968): 5–41.

———. *St. Louis and the Court Style in Gothic Architecture*. London: Zwemmer, 1965.

Camille, Michael. *Gothic Art: Glorious Visions*. New York: Abrams, 1996.

Caviness, Madeline H. "Three Medallions of Stained Glass from the Sainte Chapelle of Paris." *Philadelphia Museum of Art Bulletin* 62, no. 294 (1967): 245–59.

Cohen, Meredith. *The Sainte-Chapelle and the Construction of Sacral Monarchy: Royal Architecture in Thirteenth-Century Paris*. New York: Cambridge University Press, 2015.

Grodecki, Louis. *Gothic Stained Glass, 1200–1300*. Trans. Barbara Drake Boehm. Ithaca, N.Y.: Cornell University Press, 1985.

Jordan, Alyce. *Visualizing Kingship in the Windows of Sainte-Chapelle*. Turnhout, Belgium: Brepols, 2002.

Kemp, Wolfgang. *The Narratives of Gothic Stained Glass*. Trans. Caroline Dobson Saltzwedel. New York: Cambridge University Press, 1997.

Papanicolaou, Linda Morey. "Stained Glass from the Cathedral of Tours: The Impact of Sainte-Chapelle in the 1240s." *Metropolitan Museum Journal* 15 (1981): 53–66.

Recht, Roland. *Believing and Seeing: The Art of Gothic Cathedrals*. Chicago: University of Chicago Press, 2008.

Sadler, D. "The King as Subject, the King as Author: Art and Politics of Louis IX." In *European Monarchy: Its Evolution and Practice from Roman Antiquity to Modern Times*, ed. H. Duchhardt, R. A. Jackson, and D. Sturdy, 53–68. Stuttgart: Steiner, 1992.

Suger, Abbot of Saint-Denis. *Abbot Suger on the Abbey Church of Saint-Denis and Its Art Treasures*. 2nd ed. Ed. Erwin Panofsky. Princeton: Princeton University Press, 1979.

Weiss, Daniel H. *Art and Crusade in the Age of Saint Louis*. New York: Cambridge University Press, 1998.

The Chora Church

Demus, Otto. "The Style of the Kariye Djami and Its Place in the Development of Palaeologan Art." In *The Kariye Djami*, ed. Paul Atkins Underwood, 4:107–60. New York: Pantheon Books, 1966–75.

Evans, Helen C., ed. *Byzantium: Faith and Power, 1261–1557*. New York: Metropolitan Museum of Art, 2004.

Grabar, André. *Christian Iconography: A Study of Its Origins*. Princeton: Princeton University Press, 1968.

Holger, Klein A., and Robert G. Ousterhout. *Restoring Byzantium: The Kariye Camii in Istanbul and the Byzantine Institute Restoration*. New York: Columbia University Press, 2004.

Kartsonis, Anna. *Anastasis: The Making of an Image*. Princeton: Princeton University Press, 1986.

Mango, Cyril A. *The Art of the Byzantine Empire, 213–1453: Sources and Documents*. Toronto: University of Toronto Press, 1986.

Nelson, Robert S. "The Chora and the Great Church: Intervisuality in Fourteenth-Century Constantinople." *BMGS* 23 (1999): 67–101.

Ousterhout, Robert G. *The Architecture of the Kariye Camii in Istanbul*. Washington, DC: Dumbarton Oaks Research Library and Collection, 1987.

———. *The Art of the Kariye Camii*. London: Scala Publishers in Association with Archaeology and Art Publications, 2002.

———. "Temporal Structuring in the Chora Parekklesion." *Gesta* 34, no. 1 (1995): 63–76.

Ševcenko, Ihor. "Theodore Metochites, the Chora, and the Intellectual Trends of His Time." In *The Kariye Djami*, ed. Paul Atkins Underwood, 4:19–55. New York: Pantheon Books, 1966–75.

Underwood, Paul Atkins, ed. *The Kariye Djami*. 4 vols. New York: Pantheon Books, 1966–75.

Jan van Eyck, *The Annunciation*

Borchert, Till-Holger. *Jan van Eyck*. London: Taschen, 2008.

———, ed. *The Age of Van Eyck: The Mediterranean World and Early Netherlandish Painting, 1430–1530*. London: Thames & Hudson, 2002.

Foister, Susan, Sue Jones, and Delphine Cool, eds. *Investigating Jan van Eyck*. Turnhout, Belgium: Brepols, 2002.

Gifford, Melanie E. "Van Eyck's Washington 'Annunciation': Technical Evidence for Iconographic Development." *Art Bulletin* 81, no. 1 (1999): 108–16.

Harbison, Craig. *Jan van Eyck: The Play of Realism*. London: Reaktion, 2012.

Kemperdick, Stephan, and Friso Lammertse. *The Road to Van Eyck*. Rotterdam: Museum
   Boijmans van Beuningen, 2012.

Lyman, Thomas W. "Architectural Portraiture and Jan van Eyck's Washington 'Annunciation.'" *Gesta* 20, no. 1 (1981): 263–71.

Panofsky, Erwin. *Early Netherlandish Painting: Its Origins and Character*. New York:
   Harper and Row, 1971.

Purtle, Carol J. *The Marian Paintings of Jan van Eyck*. Princeton: Princeton University
   Press, 1982.

———. "Van Eyck's Washington 'Annunciation': Narrative Time and Metaphoric
   Tradition." *Art Bulletin* 81, no. 1 (1999): 117–25.

Stangel, Andrew Laurie. "The Cartographic Symbolism in Jan van Eyck's 'Annunciation'
   in the National Gallery, Washington D.C." *Comiatus* 4, no. 1 (1973): 41–48.

Ward, John. "Hidden Symbolism in Jan van Eyck's Annunciations." *Art Bulletin* 57, no. 2
   (June 1975): 196–208.

Botticelli, *The Birth of Venus*

Barkan, Leonard. *Unearthing the Past: Archaeology and Aesthetics in the Making of Renaissance Culture*. New Haven: Yale University Press, 2001.

Barolsky, Paul. "As in Ovid, So in Renaissance Art." *Renaissance Quarterly* 51, no. 12 (1998):
   451–74.

———. "Botticelli's Golden Goddess." *Source: Notes in the History of Art* 32, no. 2 (2013):
   2–5.

Gombrich, Ernst H. "Botticelli's Mythologies: A Study in the Neo-Platonic Symbolism
   of His Circle." In *Symbolic Images: Studies in the Art of the Renaissance*. London:
   Phaidon Press, 1972.

Lightbown, R. W. *Sandro Botticelli: Life and Work*. New York: Abbeville Press, 1989.

O'Malley, Michelle. *Painting under Pressure: Fame, Reputation, and Demand in Renaissance
   Florence*. New Haven: Yale University Press, 2013.

Ovid. *Metamorphoses: A New Verse Translation*. Trans. David Raeburn. London: Penguin
   Classics, 2004.

Panofsky, Erwin. *Renaissance and Renascences in Western Art*. New York: Harper & Row,
   1972.

Randolph, Adrian W. B. *Engaging Symbols: Gender, Politics, and Public Art in
   Fifteenth-Century Florence*. New Haven: Yale University Press, 2002.

Vasari, Giorgio. *Lives of the Artists*. Trans. George Bull. Vol. 1. London: Penguin Books,
   1965.

Zöllner, Frank. *Sandro Botticelli*. Munich: Prestel, 2009.

Zorach, Rebecca. "Love, Truth, Orthodoxy, Reticence: or, What Edgar Wind Didn't See in Botticelli's Primavera." *Critical Inquiry* 34, no. 1 (2007): 190–224.

Bruegel the Elder, *The Harvesters*

Ainsworth, Maryan W., and Keith Christiansen, eds. *From Van Eyck to Bruegel: Early Netherlandish Painting in the Metropolitan Museum of Art.* New York: Metropolitan Museum of Art, 1998.

Gibson, Walter S. *Pleasant Place: The Rustic Landscape from Bruegel to Ruisdael.* Berkeley: University of California Press, 2000.

Goldsmith, Jane ten Brink. "Pieter Bruegel the Elder and the Matter of Italy." *Sixteenth Century Journal* 23, no. 2 (1992): 205–32.

Roberts-Jones, Philippe, and Françoise Roberts-Jones. *Pieter Bruegel.* New York: Abrams, 2002.

Sellink, Manfred. *Bruegel: The Complete Paintings, Drawings, and Prints.* New York: Abrams, 2007.

Silver, Larry. *Pieter Bruegel.* New York: Abbeville Press, 2011.

Snow, Edward A. *Inside Bruegel: The Play of Images in Children's Games.* New York: North Point Press, 1997.

Sullivan, Margaret A. *Bruegel's Peasants: Art and Audience in the Northern Renaissance.* Cambridge: Cambridge University Press, 1994.

Caravaggio, *The Calling of Saint Matthew*

Dempsey, Charles. "Caravaggio and the Two Naturalistic Styles: Specular vs. Macular." In *Caravaggio: Realism, Rebellion, Reception,* ed. Genevieve Warwick, 91–100. Newark: University of Delaware Press, 2006.

Ebert-Schifferer, Sybille. *Caravaggio: The Artist and His Work.* Los Angeles: Getty Publications, 2012.

Fried, Michael. *The Moment of Caravaggio.* Princeton: Princeton University Press, 2010.

Hibbard, Howard. *Caravaggio.* New York: Harper & Row, 1983.

Langdon, Helen. *Caravaggio: A Life.* New York: Farrar, Straus, and Giroux, 1999.

Mormando, Franco, ed. *Saints and Sinners: Caravaggio and the Baroque Image.* Chestnut Hill, Mass.: McMullen Museum of Art, 1999.

Pericolo, Lorenzo. *Caravaggio and Pictorial Narrative: Dislocating the* Istoria *in Early Modern Painting.* London: Harvey Miller, 2001.

Puglisi, Catherine. *Caravaggio.* London: Phaidon, 1998.

Puttfarken, Thomas. "Caravaggio's 'Story of St Matthew': A Challenge to the Conventions of Painting." *Art History* 21, no. 2 (1998): 163–81.

Spike, John T. *Caravaggio*. 2nd. rev. ed. New York: Abbeville Press, 2010.

Varriano, John. *Caravaggio: The Art of Realism*. University Park: Pennsylvania State University Press, 2006.

Warwick, Genevieve, ed. *Caravaggio: Realism, Rebellion, Reception*. Newark: University of Delaware Press, 2006.

Whitfield, Clovis. *Caravaggio's Eye*. London: Paul Holberton, 2011.

Rembrandt, *The Night Watch*

Bomford, David, et al. *Rembrandt*. London: National Gallery, 2006.

Carroll, Margaret D. "Accidents Will Happen: The Case of *The Nightwatch*." In *Rethinking Rembrandt*, ed. Alan Chong and Michael Zell, 91–105. Zwolle: Waanders Publishers, 2002.

Havercamp-Begemann, Egbert. *Rembrandt, The Nightwatch*. Princeton: Princeton University Press, 1982.

Kuiper, L., and W. Hesterman. "Restauratieverslag van Rembrandts *Nachtwacht* / Report on the Restoration of Rembrandt's *Night Watch*." *Bulletin van het Rijksmuseum* 24, nos. 1/2 (1976): 14–51.

Schama, Simon. *Rembrandt's Eyes*. New York: Knopf, 1999.

Schwartz, Gary. *The Rembrandt Book*. New York: Abrams, 2006.

Van Theil, P. J. J. "Beschadiging en herstel van Rembrandts *Nachtwacht* / The Damaging and Restoration of Rembrandt's *Night Watch*." *Bulletin van het Rijksmuseum* 24, nos. 1/2 (1976): 4–13.

Von Heel, Dudok. "Frans Banninck Cocq's Troop in Rembrandt's 'Night Watch': The Identification of the Guardsmen." *Rijksmuseum Bulletin* 57, no. 1 (2009): 42–87.

Westermann, Mariët. *Rembrandt*. London: Phaidon, 2000.

WEB RESOURCES

"Our heroes are back! // Opening commercial 'Rijksmuseum,'" www.youtube.com/watch?v=ixWdRZip2TI.

Rembrandt's Room, https://arthistoriesroom.wordpress.com.

Velázquez, *Las Hilanderas*

Alpers, Svetlana. *The Vexations of Art: Velázquez and Others*. New Haven: Yale University Press, 2005.

Brown, Jonathan. *Velázquez: Painter and Courtier*. New Haven: Yale University Press, 1986.

———. *Velázquez: The Technique of a Genius*. New Haven: Yale University Press, 1998.

Elliot, J. H. *Spain, Europe and the Wider World, 1500–1800*. New Haven: Yale University Press, 2009.

Ovid. *The Metamorphoses: A New Verse Translation*. Trans. David Raeburn. London: Penguin Classics, 2004.

Portús Pérez, Javier. *Velázquez's Fables: Mythology and Sacred History in the Golden Age*. Madrid: Museo Nacional del Prado, 2007.

Géricault, *The Raft of the Medusa*

Athanassoglou-Kallmyer, Nina M. *Théodore Géricault*. London: Phaidon, 2010.

Berger, Klaus. *Géricault and His Work*. New York: Hacker Art Books, 1978.

Eitner, Lorenz E. *Géricault*. Los Angeles: Los Angeles County Museum of Art, 1971.

———. *Géricault: His Life and Work*. London: Orbis, 1983.

———. *Géricault's Raft of the Medusa*. London: Phaidon, 1972.

Grigsby, Darcy Grimaldo. *Extremities: Painting Empire in Postrevolutionary France*. New Haven: Yale University Press, 2002.

Guilbaut, Serge. *Théodore Géricault: The Alien Body, Tradition in Chaos*. Vancouver: Moris and Helen Belkin Art Gallery, 1997.

Monet, *Impression, Sunrise*

Frascina, Francis, Nigel Blake, Briony Fer, et al. *Modernity and Modernism: French Painting in the Nineteenth Century*. New Haven: Yale University Press, 1993.

House, John. *Impressionism: Paint and Politics*. New Haven: Yale University Press, 2004.

Mathieu, Marianne, Dominique Lobstein, and Aurélie Gavoille. *Monet's Impression, Sunrise: The Biography of a Painting*. Paris: Hazan, 2014.

Sauerländer, Willibald. *Manet Paints Monet: A Summer in Argenteuil*. Trans. David B. Dollenmayer. Los Angeles: Getty Research Institute, 2014.

Thompson, Belinda. *Impressionism: Origins, Practice, Reception*. London: Thames and Hudson, 2000.

Tinterow, Gary, and Henri Loyrette. *Origins of Impressionism*. New York: Metropolitan Museum of Art Press, 1994.

Sargent, *El Jaleo*

Chong, Alan, Richard Lingner, and Carl Zahn, eds. *Eye of the Beholder: Masterpieces from the Isabella Stewart Gardner Museum*. Boston: Beacon Press, 2003.

Herdrich, Stephanie, et al. *American Drawings and Watercolors in the Metropolitan Museum of Art: John Singer Sargent*. Vol. 3. New York: Metropolitan Museum of Art, 2000.

Hills, Patricia, ed. *John Singer Sargent*. New York: Abrams / Whitney Museum of American Art, 1986.

Hirshler, Erica E. *Sargent's Daughters: The Biography of a Painting*. Boston: Museum of Fine Arts Boston, 2009.

James, Henry. *The Painter's Eye: Notes and Essays on the Pictorial Arts*. Ed. John L. Sweeney. Madison: University of Wisconsin Press, 1989.

Kilmurray, Elaine, and Richard Ormond, eds. *John Singer Sargent*. Princeton: Princeton University Press, 1998.

Ormond, Richard, and Elaine Kilmurray. *Figures and Landscapes, 1874–1882*. Vol. 4 of *John Singer Sargent: Complete Paintings*. New Haven: Yale University Press, 2006.

Ormond, Richard, et al. *Sargent: Portraits of Artists and Friends*. Washington, DC: National Portrait Gallery, 2015.

Volk, Mary Crawford, ed. *John Singer Sargent's* El Jaleo. Washington, DC, National Gallery of Art, March 1–August 2, 1992; Boston, Isabella Stewart Gardner Museum, September 10–November 22, 1992. Washington, DC: National Gallery of Art, 1992.

WEB RESOURCES

Carmencita, www.loc.gov/item/00694116.

John Singer Sargent, *Courtyard, Tetuan, Morocco*, www.jssgallery.org/index.htm.

Picasso, *Les Demoiselles d'Avignon*

Brown, Jonathan, ed. *Picasso and the Spanish Tradition*. New Haven: Yale University Press, 1996.

Cowling, Elizabeth. *Picasso: Style and Meaning*. New York: Phaidon, 2002.

Cowling, Elizabeth, Neil Cox, Sionetta Fraquelli, et al. *Picasso: Challenging the Past*. London: National Gallery, 2009.

Karmel, Pepe. *Picasso and the Invention of Cubism*. New Haven: Yale University Press, 2003.

Léal, Brigitte, Christine Piot, and Marie-Laure Bernadac. *The Ultimate Picasso*. New York: Abrams, 2003.

Richardson, John. "Picasso's Apocalyptic Whorehouse." *New York Review of Books* 7, no. 23 (1987).

Rosenblum, Robert. *Cubism and Twentieth Century Art*. New York: Abrams, 1961.

Rubin, William, Hélène Seckel, and Judith Cousins. *Les Demoiselles d'Avignon*. Studies in Modern Art, no. 3. New York: Museum of Modern Art, 1994.

Seckel, Hélène. *Les Demoiselles d'Avignon*. 2 vols. Paris: Musée Picasso, 1988.

Staller, Natasha. *A Sum of Destructions: Picasso's Cultures and the Creation of Cubism*. New Haven: Yale University Press, 2001.

Steinberg, Leo. "The Philosophical Brothel." *October* 44 (1988): 7–74.

INDEX

Entries in **bold** indicate images.